To Jennifer
Through the eyes of our young do we see most clearly.

Classroom Assessment for Teachers

Jo D. Gallagher
Florida International University

Merrill,
an imprint of Prentice Hall
Upper Saddle River, New Jersey ▪ Columbus, Ohio

Library of Congress Cataloging-in-Publication Data
Gallagher, Jo D.
Classroom measurement for teachers / by Jo D. Gallagher.
p. cm.
Includes bibliographical references and index.
ISBN 0-13-748104-7
1. Educational tests and measurements. 2. Examinations. 3. Examinations—Design and construction. 4. Examinations—Interpretation. I. Title.
LB3051.G26 1998
371.26—dc21 97-6240
CIP

Cover photo: ©1993 Tom McCarthy Photos, Unicorn Stock Photos
Editor: Kevin M. Davis
Developmental Editor: Linda Ashe Montgomery, Gianna Marsalla
Production Editor: Mary M. Irvin
Design Coordinator: Karrie M. Converse
Text Designer: Rebecca M. Bobb
Cover Designer: Russ Maselli
Production Manager: Pamela D. Bennett
Director of Marketing: Kevin Flanagan
Advertising/Marketing Coordinator: Julie Shough
Marketing Manager: Susan Stanton

This book was set in Garamond by Carlisle Communications, Inc., and was printed and bound by R. R. Donnelley & Sons. The cover was printed by Phoenix Color Corp.

Printed in the United States of America

10 9 8 7 6 5 4 3 2

ISBN: 0-13-748104-7

Prentice-Hall International (UK) Limited, *London*
Prentice-Hall of Australia Pty. Limited, *Sydney*
Prentice-Hall of Canada, Inc., *Toronto*
Prentice-Hall Hispanoamericana, S. A., *Mexico*
Prentice-Hall of India Private Limited, *New Delhi*
Prentice-Hall of Japan, Inc., *Tokyo*
Simon & Schuster Asia Pte. Ltd., *Singapore*
Editora Prentice-Hall do Brasil, Ltda., *Rio de Janeiro*

Preface

The Aim of this Book

Perhaps the one area teachers will admit to knowing little about when they go into teaching for the first time is evaluating the learning of their students. Most of their training has concentrated on subject matter and instructional strategies for teaching it. Although these are certainly important parts of the teacher-training curriculum, they are not all of it. Proper assessment of student learning is critical, as well. Further, although many texts have been written in the area of educational measurement, the transfer of measurement theory and research into the practice of everyday classroom assessment by teachers has been slow and fragmented, at best.

This book differs from the vast majority of educational assessment texts in that it does not stress the computation of validity and reliability coefficients after assessments have been administered. This is an artificial exercise for most classroom assessments. Rather, emphasis in this text is placed on building quality into assessments, and on successfully matching important learning outcomes with the items and tasks used to measure them. Readers are also shown in this text how to examine item and task scores after administering assessments, so that they can gain information to help them improve both their teaching and their assessment design skills.

This book is directed at three segments of the K-12 teacher audience: pre-service teachers-in-training, veterans who have not had a course in student assessment, and veterans who wish to update their assessment skills. It is designed to bridge the gap between research and practice, and to give teachers at all levels of experience some practical procedures and guidelines for assessing student learning that they can easily follow in their own busy classrooms.

Standards and Educational Assessment

This text is also designed to help teachers understand, integrate, and skillfully apply the standards governing educational assessment. These standards, called The Standards for Teacher Competence in the Educational Assessment of Students[1], were compiled in 1990 by a joint committee of representatives from three national educational organizations: the American Federation of Teachers (AFT), the National Council on Measurement in Education (NCME), and the National Educational Association (NEA). These guidelines for practice are as relevant in today's classrooms

[1]Joint Committee: American Federation of Teachers, National Council on Measurement in Education, and National Education Association, (1990). The Standards for Teacher Competence in the Educational Assessment of Students. *Educational Measurement: Issues and Practice, 9*(4), pp. 29–32. Reprinted with permission.

as when they were first created; as a result, this text is designed around them. The seven standards are first introduced and listed in Chapter 1; the first page of each subsequent chapter lists the specific standards to which that chapter refers. All of the standards, along with related subtasks, are summarized in a chart in Appendix A. This more complete listing can easily serve as a list of specific objectives for a course or workshop on classroom assessment, with the standards as course-level outcomes.

The Organization of this Text

The Chapters

The first chapter introduces the nature of assessment in schools today, relates requirements for teachers regarding assessment (the Standards), and identifies relevant legal issues. It also gives the reader strategies for using the rest of the text successfully. Chapter 2 acquaints the reader with the many assessment options teachers have to choose from, and the ways in which they are commonly classified. This overview sets the stage for in-depth discussions of each of the major types of assessments teachers develop and use, and of important concepts such as criterion- and norm-referenced assessment. Chapter 3 describes the various opportunities before, during, and after instruction that teachers have to assess learning, and addresses the importance of balancing time for instruction with time for assessment. The basic concepts of quality for assessments—validity and reliability—are also discussed.

Chapters 4 through 9 give readers specific tools and information to help them construct written tests, performance tasks, student product specifications, and portfolios based on the important outcomes of instruction. Chapter 4 discusses the three-way link between learning outcomes or objectives, assessment, and instruction. Enough depth is provided here so that readers will be able to successfully construct outcomes on which to base their assessments in the cognitive domain. (The affective and psychomotor domains, along with examples of outcomes in these domains, are presented in Appendices B and C, respectively, for interested readers.) Chapter 5 provides general guidelines for making and selecting paper-and-pencil tests—the non-item-related issues that teachers must deal with. Chapters 6 and 7 present specific guidelines for the use and construction of the major types of items used on paper-and-pencil classroom tests. In Chapter 8, readers are introduced to the assessment and observation of student performances and products used to capture learning that cannot be easily measured with written assessments. Chapter 9 discusses the use of portfolios in the classroom to document student achievement qualitatively, to foster thoughtful self-reflection, and to assess student learning.

Chapters 10 through 12 focus on using the results of assessments. Chapter 10 presents practical techniques for using assessment data to enhance both the assessments themselves and instruction. Chapter 11 describes the ways numerical assessment results are used to describe student performance. Chapter 12 presents a variety of approaches to grading and reporting assessment results to interested audiences. In Chapter 13, ethical and unethical practices for preparing students to do their best on both classroom and standardized tests are discussed, as are ethical and unethical practices of teachers who administer these assessments. Chapter 14 takes a hands-on approach to helping readers interpret the results of standardized assessments—a skill needed for communicating results to parents, and for using the results to improve instruction.

Readers may use Figure 1.2 to help them find chapters relevant to their immediate needs. This book can be used in sequence as a text in an introductory course on educational assessment, in sections for an in-service workshop on one or more topics in assessment, or as a reference by the teacher in the field.

The Spiral Approach

Some topics are discussed early in the book at one level, and are returned to later in more depth. With this recursive spiral approach, earlier topics provide a foundation for later ones. The approach does not leave important topics alone for a long period of time. Coming back to a topic at a deeper level helps recall prior learning and reinforces that much of what is learned at the time will be needed for later learning. For example, the concept of the normal curve is discussed in three separate chapters:

- Chapter 2, as it relates to defining the concept of norm-referenced assessment
- Chapter 11, as it relates to how to interpret scores in describing group and individual performance
- Chapter 12, as it relates to grading methods.

Special Features

Key Concepts

Major topic areas are listed at the very beginning of each chapter in the order they are discussed. These chapter-specific tables of contents cue readers as to what important concepts they will encounter in their reading. The key concepts are not formal objectives, but they give readers a sense of the knowledge to be gained from the chapter at a glance.

Before You Begin Reading

An important topic area that is related to the chapter content is presented at the beginning of each chapter in the form of a question. No answer to these questions is necessarily right or wrong, but both sides of the issue are presented, in order to set the stage for discussion and spark the reader's interest in the subject matter. Readers are asked what they think at the beginning of the chapter so they can ponder as they read and critically develop their own opinions. An instructor using this text may lead a brief discussion or take an opinion poll at the start of a class session after learners have read the chapter. As an alternative, the instructor may wish to introduce the

"Before You Begin Reading" question at the end of a class session to set the stage for reading yet to be done. The instructor may also have learners articulate and give support for their own positions based on what they have read and observed in schools either in their own practice or in their field observations.

Easy-Reference Checklists

Throughout the text, readers will encounter Easy-Reference Checklists, lists of practical, step-by-step guidelines for choosing and developing all types of classroom assessments. These checklists highlight essential points covered in the chapter, and help teachers choose or develop the best and most appropriate assessment possible. The checklists can be used by novice and veteran teachers alike in the classroom when developing new tests, revising old ones, or evaluating and adapting published tests. Readers may even want to use these checklists to test themselves on the development, use, and evaluation of assessments as they finish each chapter.

Sample Portfolio

Authentic assessment may best be taught by example. Included in Chapter 9, *Using Portfolios in the Classroom,* is a portfolio case study written by a classroom teacher who directed the development of portfolios for an interage class of fourth and fifth graders. Based on the chapter guidelines for portfolio assessment, this case study describes the decisions a teacher makes to successfully focus the efforts of portfolio use and to manage this assessment process. Included are examples of student work and rubrics for grading it.

Try These

This textbook also features a section at the end of every chapter encouraging readers to review the chapter content by testing their recall and their ability to apply their learning to example questions and scenarios. These questions and exercises engage readers at all levels of the cognitive domain, from the knowledge and comprehension levels, to the application level, through the analysis, synthesis, and evaluation levels. So that readers may gauge their own learning, sample answers are provided as models and possible responses. Instructors using this book may want to assign these questions as homework and allow time in class to discuss varying responses. Readers may also want to include their answers to select questions and exercises in a teaching portfolio they are developing.

Linking Learning and Practice

The more access learners have to actual tests, assignments, performance task descriptions, and other assessment-related documents, the more relevance topics will have. A good textbook is certainly the backbone of an effective course on classroom assessment, but it cannot present everything relevant to the reader's local circumstances. Instructors can customize the content of this book using this list of activities and strategies:

- Supplement discussions about national standardized assessments with those that are used in your state and your local district.
- Arrange for pre-service teachers to observe and periodically interview a competent veteran teacher to contextualize what they are learning here.
- Have inservice teachers bring in their own tests and performance tasks to collaboratively discuss and improve.
- Bring in a district assessment expert or a teacher who has participated in some aspect of district-wide assessment to discuss these topics with readers.
- Encourage and assist in-service teachers to reflect on their own practice to enhance their assessment strategies.
- Have several pre-service or in-service teachers at one grade level construct a grade-wide assessment and grading system that conforms to district criteria and criteria of good practice.

Acknowledgements

My sincere appreciation to Lorraine Gay, Betty Hubschman, Catherine Solli, Luanne Philipp, Maria Elliott, Ron Felton, Sally Pell, Paul Rendulic, and Jerry Grandiero. To Lorraine Gay especially, who helped me start this journey and continued to offer her encouragement and valued guidance through rough times and smooth, I give my most heartfelt thanks. Thank you, also, to the reviewers, for their insights and comments: Joan S. Bissell, University of California-Irvine; Susan M. Brookhart, Duquesne University; Bonnie Cramond, University of Georgia; Thomas E. Curtis, State University of New York at Albany; Lee Doebler, University of Montevallo; Joseph L. Fearing, Texas Women's University; Louise Jernigan, Eastern Michigan University; Robert M. Jones, University of Houston-Clear Lake; Bruce G. Rogers, University of Northern Iowa; and Robert W. Lissitz, University of Maryland.

A host of practicing teachers offered suggestions, tried out exercises, loaned their personal materials, and gave me the language to reach their peers. Thank you Robyn Lane, Susan Gladstein, Ken Glazer, Lilia DiBello, Zeida Fernandez, Martha Mederos, Madelyn Sierra and those who were my students.

A special thanks to Anna and Kelsey Young and Matt Irvin, whose help with student handwriting saved the day.

Thanks to Jennifer Gallagher, who shared her artistry, the contents of her book bag, and her candid thoughts regularly as the manuscript was developed. To Paul Gallagher who gave me a prod whether I needed one or not (usually I did) and stayed with me throughout the process, thanks.

My deepest gratitude to my editors, Kevin Davis, Linda Montgomery, and Gianna Marsalla and to Lynn Metzger, editorial assistant. Their excellent skills were matched by their supportiveness and caring.

Brief Contents

Contents

Chapter Ten

Improving Classroom Assessment 325

Chapter Eleven

Describing Group and Individual Assessment Performance 355

Chapter Twelve

Creating and Using Grading and Reporting Systems 391

CHAPTER 1

Introduction to Assessment

Key Concepts:

- Definitions of assessment terms.
- The nature of assessment in schools today.
- Workplace and community demands and their impact on assessment.
- Standards for Teacher Competence in the Educational Assessment of Students.
- Legal issues regarding classroom assessment: privacy, student classification, students with disabilities, and discharge of teachers.
- How to use this book.

Before You Begin Reading, Consider This

Is it appropriate to test some students in a class under one set of conditions and others under another set of conditions? For example, some students may be allowed to dictate their essay response onto audiotape, while others must write them on paper with a pen. Is that fair?

YES As long as one set of conditions does not give unfair advantage to a group, why not? A disabled student, for example, may not be able to write with a pen. He or she should not be penalized for the disability.

NO You should not compare the results because the tests were not the same. What if a person is not disabled but is accustomed to composing on a computer? Neither the tape recorder nor the pen and paper provide the best circumstances. It would be prohibitive to cater to every need, so uniform conditions should prevail unless you wish also to limit the comparability of results to those who were tested under the same conditions.

Defining Assessment Terms

Assessment, evaluation, measurement, test: All four terms have to do with the systematic process of collecting data and analyzing those data to make decisions.[1] To the casual observer these four terms may all mean the same thing, but there are some important differences among them, especially to teachers who engage in these processes in their classrooms. To jumble matters further, these terms have, in some cases, taken on new meanings or connotations and have fallen out of favor (as has the term *testing*) or have been expanded and have become more popular (as has the term *assessment*). Moreover, some experts give more narrow definitions of these terms while others define them more broadly. Rather than debate the pros and cons of various definitions of these words and further refine the art of academic hair-splitting, I will present what they have come to mean generically to teachers and how they will be used in this book. This is not to say that their definitions will not further evolve; they will. Definitions, by their nature, continue to evolve. For now, however, we need some working definitions we can use to discuss these matters coherently.

Evaluation is the process of judging worth or value on some basis; thus the term e-VALU-ation. Urban commuters may, for example, evaluate several alternate routes home from work to select the one that avoids the traffic back-up just broadcast

[1]For examples, see *Educational Evaluation and Measurement: Competencies for Analysis and Application* (2nd ed.) by L. R. Gay, 1985, Upper Saddle River, NJ: Merrill/Prentice Hall, and *Assessment* (5th ed.) by J. Salvia and J. E. Ysseldyke, 1991, Boston: Houghton Mifflin.

over the radio. A school district may evaluate alternative approaches to teaching reading to determine which one(s) work best with the students it serves. Teachers evaluate how well or to what extent their students are achieving instructional outcomes. Teachers also evaluate students at the end of the year to determine whether they are suitably prepared for the work expected at the next grade level. Good evaluation requires data gathering for informed decision making. That data-gathering process may be called measurement, if only quantitative data are used, or assessment, which may include both qualitative and quantitative data from a variety of sources and contexts.

Measurement is the process of quantifying the degree to which someone or something possesses a given characteristic, quality, or feature. Thus the term MEASURE-ment. The purpose of measurement is to produce quantitative data, such as test scores, numerical ratings on assigned projects, height, weight, visual acuity, and number of sit-ups completed in one minute. The numerical data generated in the measurement process are typically used in the evaluation of something: student achievement, for example.

Until recently, the word *assessment* was usually reserved by teachers for a group of services performed by the school psychologist or other specialized personnel—namely, to identify the nature and cause of learning problems students were having or to identify the appropriate placement of students suspected of needing exceptional education services (like gifted students or individuals with learning disabilities). The term has now moved beyond its psycho-educational roots and into the classroom. *Assessment* as a process in the classroom is also a purposeful collection of data—both qualitative and quantitative. Hence, it is a broader term than *measurement*. For teachers, the purpose of assessment is usually to make decisions about students either as a group or individually. For example, teachers diagnose difficulties, verify learning after instruction, identify prerequisite learning, and determine where to start in a learning sequence based on what students already know. In the classroom, assessment considers students' performances on tasks in a variety of settings and contexts.[2] Assessment also may be intrusive or not; in other words, students may know that they are being assessed, or it may be seamless with instruction, perhaps perceived by the students as nothing more than a chance to practice what they have learned. Data collection in assessment is accomplished in a variety of ways: observation of behavior, presentation of tasks for students to perform mentally and to record their responses in writing, or examination of products produced by the students.

Assessment can also be thought of as a noun, as in a writing assessment. In this capacity, *assessments* are questions or tasks designed to elicit some predetermined behavior from the person(s) being tested. This type of assessment usually connotes the creation of a unique performance or product as the response exhibited by a student. The conditions under which an assessment is administered may or

---

[2] *Varieties of Performance Assessment* by F. Finch and M. Foertsch, 1993, paper presented at the annual meeting of the Michigan Educational Association (ERIC Document Service No. ED 357 032).

may not be uniform across students. Generally, the more the need to compare students to each other and the higher the stakes involved, the more the need for uniform, standardized administration and scoring conditions.

A *test* is a question or a task, or a series of such, designed to elicit some predetermined behavior from the person(s) being tested. Sound familiar? The terms *assessment* and *test* are used interchangeably in this text. For many people, however, the word *test* implies a paper-and-pencil instrument, administered under prespecified conditions that are consistent across students. Its traditional usage by teachers has implied a written series of tasks to which students responded in writing (essay or short-answer items, for example) or marked their response choices with a pen or pencil (true-false, multiple-choice, or matching items, for example). Teachers who think of the word *test* as meaning only a series of multiple-choice items printed on paper for the student to answer will probably not equate the words *test* and *assessment*. Many teachers, however, have a broader definition of the term; they see a test as posing tasks and problems to students for their responses, in order to produce data that may be analyzed and used for decision making. This sounds curiously similar to the above definition of *assessment,* and rightfully so. Teachers with a broader definition of the term *test* will see that there is not much difference between the two terms.

Assessment Needs in Schools Today

Schools today are different from when you and I attended. They are still charged with transmitting the culture and socializing children into the larger society, but schools are undergoing major reforms on a local and national level and will continue to do so as the culture and the needs of society evolve. Demands on our schools come from the workplace and from surrounding communities.

Demands from the Workplace

Future workers who are now in school will be required to be, among other things, flexible and autonomous to a degree not expected before. Workers must be willing and able to learn whatever job needs to be done, because what needs to be done changes quickly in a market-driven economy. They are likely to have more jobs in their lives than their parents did, so they must be ready for a life of learning and recombining skills. Also, as more decisions are pushed down to the level of individual contributors, companies will rely less on management to make all the decisions. Workers must, therefore, be able to think critically about information at hand and weigh the alternative courses of action, often on an individual basis. These life and job requirements demand far more complex cognitive skills than ever before from a growing proportion of the population. As a result, requirements for flexibility and autonomy place demands on school personnel to teach our children how to learn, how to access and use information, how to critically appraise what they perceive, and how to make decisions. In fact, there is a significant movement in many schools toward students creating criteria and evaluating their own learning under the guidance of their teacher.

Demands of the Community

People want their money's worth. In the past, this appeared to be a greater priority for private and parochial schools than for public schools. The communities surrounding the public schools of today, however, have come to expect that the dollars they as taxpayers invest in education provide some return on investment. The demand for return on investment carries with it a demand for keeping track of what is invested, where it is invested, and the results of that investment in terms of observable outcomes. For accountability purposes, this tracking and monitoring must be done as directly as possible. Student learning is naturally a major outcome of schooling that can, in many ways, be observed and monitored. School personnel, including administrators and teachers, are, therefore, increasingly held accountable for the learning of the students entrusted to them. Parents and the students themselves also bear part of the responsibility.

Implications for Classroom Assessment

The demands of the workplace and the communities surrounding schools have several implications for classroom assessment. First, teachers must figure out not only *what* is and is not learned, but also *how* it is and is not learned. Those areas can be assessed and then fed back into instructional decisions to further enhance learning, as well as document the learning that has taken place. As a result, teachers today are concerned about preparing their students for upcoming assessments through effective instruction, constructing quality assessments, and evaluating published assessment materials for use. Second, teachers must find ways to assess, as directly and accurately as possible, higher-level educational outcomes—far above rote memorization of facts. If they are familiar with a wide variety of assessment tools and their relative strengths and weaknesses, then teachers are more likely to make good assessment choices for the various levels of educational outcomes they encounter.

Third, teachers must use the results of assessment to inform instructional decisions and enhance instructional materials and strategies. Fourth, teachers must require students to demonstrate what they have learned in a wider variety of contexts so that they are reasonably assured that the students will be able to adjust to the requirements of the workplace. Because assessment time "costs" in instructional time, all of this must be done in an effective manner so that the investment in assessment yields maximally useful information. Fortunately, methods of assessment have evolved along with methods of teaching. The good news is that teachers today have at their disposal an array of tools and procedures to assess student achievement. The bad news is that the array may seem somewhat overwhelming to a teacher who does not know how to use or choose among them.

The Standards for Teacher Competence in the Educational Assessment of Students

Just what is it that teachers do in the educational assessment of their students? Perhaps the most ambitious attempt to answer this question from a classroom perspective was undertaken by a joint committee made up of members of three national, professional education organizations: the American Federation of Teachers (AFT), the National Education Association (NEA), and the National Council on Measurement in Education (NCME). Together they performed a task analysis and hammered out seven major sub-tasks with their attending knowledge and skill requirements. The seven major responsibilities, collectively known as the "standards," are listed in Figure 1.1. For a more complete description that includes subordinate outcomes for each standard, turn to Appendix A.

The standards in Figure 1.1 and in Appendix A itemize and communicate in behavioral terms the various activities teachers typically engage in with regard to assessment in their classrooms. If you are a veteran teacher, you will recognize most if not all of them because they are part of your job. If you are new to teaching, you now have a professionally developed list of expectations for the student evaluation portion of your job based on what teachers in the field really do. Standards 1, 2, and 3 in Figure 1.1 refer to assessment methods and the process of producing assessment results. Teachers need to be skilled in these methods so that the assessment results they produce are useful for their intended purpose. Standards 4 and 5 refer to the

The Standards for Teacher Competence in the Educational Assessment of Students

1. Choose assessment methods appropriate for instructional decisions.
2. Develop assessment methods appropriate for instructional decisions.
3. Administer, score, and interpret the results of both externally produced and teacher-produced assessment methods.
4. Use assessment results when making decisions about individual students, planning teaching, developing curriculum, and school improvement.
5. Develop valid grading procedures that use student assessments.
6. Communicate assessment results to students, parents and other lay audiences, and other educators.
7. Recognize unethical, illegal, and otherwise inappropriate assessment methods and uses of assessment information.

Figure 1.1
The seven general standards for teacher performance in the area of student assessment. *Source:* Adapted from "The Standards for Teacher Competence in the Educational Assessment of Students" by Joint Committee: American Federation of Teachers, National Council on Measurement in Education, and National Education Association, 1990, *Educational Measurement: Issues and Practice, 9*(4), pp. 29–32.

use of assessment results of various types—that teachers must know under what circumstances and how to use the results of assessments. The list in standard 4 of decisions made with the input of assessment results also underscores the importance of performing the activities listed in the first three standards adequately. Standard 6 recognizes that teachers are not the only ones to produce or use assessment results and that they must interact effectively with people who may differ with them in their sophistication with assessment results. Standard 7 acknowledges that assessment methods, even good ones, may be used inappropriately by the unskilled or unethical. Teachers can guard against this only if they know how to spot bad assessment practices.

This book is dedicated to helping teachers become skilled in developing and choosing appropriate assessment methods to inform their instructional decisions. The seven standards are major themes in this book, interwoven with related concepts and applications throughout the chapters. At the beginning of each chapter, beginning with Chapter 2, the standards that are most prominently addressed in the chapter are listed. For a complete listing by standard of the related chapters, see Appendix A. The standards are multifaceted and interconnected; thus, some standards are listed in more than one chapter, and some chapters deal with more than one standard. For example, Chapters 2 through 10 all relate in different ways to standards 1 and 2, choosing and developing assessment methods; Chapter 12 concentrates on one standard—valid grading procedures.

Legal Issues and Classroom Assessment

Entire books have been written on the legal aspects of the teaching profession.[3] Individual teachers should check their faculty handbooks or speak with their administrators for specifics on the implementation of district policies and state and federal statutes. All teachers, however, should be aware of four important areas related to assessment that state and federal laws regulate. These are the right to privacy, the classification of students, the laws pertaining to students with disabilities, and the discharge of teachers due to incompetence.

The Right to Privacy

A major piece of legislation that is still being interpreted in courts and schools around the nation decades after its enactment is the Family Educational Rights to Privacy Act (FERPA). Enacted in 1974 and effective since 1976, FERPA is also known as the Buckley Amendment, for U.S. Senator James Buckley. Buckley's purpose in drafting the act was to protect students and their parents from having their personal

[3]Examples: *Public School Law* by M. M. McCarthy and N. H. Cambron-McCabe, 1987, Boston: Allyn & Bacon; *Teachers and the Law* (3rd ed.) by L. Fischer, D. Schimmel, and C. Kelly, 1991, New York: Longman; *Special Education Law* (2nd ed.) by L. F. Rothstein, 1995, New York: Longman.

and academic records made public without their consent, a practice that was rampant at the time. States are still trying to properly interpret the act because it carries the threat of withdrawing federal funding from schools that do not comply. FERPA applies to all students in any public or private school that receives federal funds of any sort. FERPA requires that:

- Student records be kept confidential among the teacher, the student, and the student's parents or guardian.
- Written consent must be obtained from the student's parents before disclosing that student's record to a third party.
- Parents be allowed to challenge the accuracy of the information kept in their children's records.
- Students who have reached the age of 18 be accorded the same rights formerly granted to their parents.

A student's record may contain many things and is not limited to the cumulative or permanent file. Records include such things as hand-written notes, grade books, computer printouts, taped interviews or performances, film, and microfiche. What is actually kept in a student's file is open to interpretation, but whatever is in the file can be considered subject to FERPA. One of the effects of FERPA has been for teachers to write factual statements in their individual reports on students and to move away from issuing opinions with little or no substantiating data. This is not to say that teachers cannot write anything negative for a student's file, only that it must be accurate and based on facts. For teachers, FERPA applies to grade books, publicly posted tracking charts or grades, and discussing a student's personal or academic record with third parties. A student has the right to see his or her own test scores and grades for a term, for example, but not the right to see everyone else's in the grade book. The posting of test scores after exams where an individual student's score can be identified can also be considered in violation of FERPA. FERPA does not give parents the right to challenge the fairness of a grade, just the accurate recording of it.

Classifying Students

Ability tracking for class scheduling and placement is an area in which the courts have become involved. The courts view grouping students (into categories such as college prep or educable mentally retarded, for example) on a long-term basis where it is used to segregate minority children into lower tracks as a thinly disguised attempt to perpetuate discrimination.[4] Ability tracking or classifying students for purposes of targeting resources for low-achievers is, on the other hand, permissible. Grouping schemes that teachers might use to maximize instruction for all is not only

[4]Probably the most widely publicized case regarding ability tracking is *Hobson v. Hansen,* 269 F. Supp. 401, 492 (D.D.C. 1967).

desirable but supported by research. Grouping itself is not bad, but the reasons behind it and its results must be closely examined. Teachers may group the students in their classes for instructional purposes, and they may use assessment results to inform their grouping decisions. They should, however, use more than a single test score for assignment to groups. Teacher observation and an assessment of the adaptive behavior of the child, for example, could be used along with test scores to meaningfully divide a class into groups.

Laws Pertaining to Students with Disabilities

Three laws that have major impacts on students with disabilities are the Individuals with Disabilities Education Act, Section 504 of the Rehabilitation Act of 1973, and the Americans with Disabilities Act. Much of what happens in schools today regarding students with disabilities is subject to scrutiny under one or more of these laws.

The Individuals with Disabilities Education Act

The Individuals with Disabilities Education Act (IDEA), formerly known as Public Law 92–142, is a funding statute that establishes 15 categories of disabilities for which federal funds are available. Individual states apply for the funding based on the number of children in each category. IDEA guarantees identified students a free and appropriate public education in the least restrictive environment. IDEA covers only children who are educationally disabled—children who, by virtue of their disability, require some form of special education services. The 15 categories are specified in the law. Under IDEA, teachers and other district staff are required to make a good-faith effort to provide appropriate instruction and help students achieve the goals and objectives set each year in their individual educational programs (IEPs). For example, districts are accountable for putting properly trained teachers with disabled students. Teachers are, in turn, accountable for using teaching and assessment techniques appropriate for the subject matter *and* the student, taking the disability into consideration. With the right teachers using the right techniques, the IEP goals and objectives can usually be achieved.

Section 504 of the Rehabilitation Act of 1973

The services available to students with disabilities under Section 504 and IDEA are the same. Although this and other significant overlaps occur between the two laws, Section 504 is broader, covering all people with disabilities, regardless of whether they qualify for special education services. Section 504 prohibits discrimination on the basis of disability, requiring schools to make reasonable accommodations for students with disabilities to fully participate in the programs and activities provided to the students in general. Section 504 is to people with disabilities what civil rights legislation has been to minorities—a remedy for past discrimination. Under Section 504, schools are required to remove artificial barriers so that students with disabilities may demonstrate the true level of their learning as it relates to the curriculum. The schools are not required to lower standards of performance or graduation requirements.

The Americans with Disabilities Act

The Americans with Disabilities Act (ADA) is patterned after Section 504, but expands its scope in many areas. Also known as Public Law 101–336, the ADA applies to all public and private organizations with 15 or more employees. Thus, it applies to public, private, and parochial schools both as workplaces (for faculty and staff) and as places of learning (for students). Teachers who are familiar with Section 504 will note that there is nothing in the ADA regulations that did not already exist under 504 and IDEA. For example, the ADA's definition of *disabled* is virtually the same as 504's definition of *handicapped,* and the language regarding reasonable accommodation in the two laws is practically identical. Regarding the assessment of learning for all students, all three laws require good assessment sense on the part of teachers and administrators. Essentially, if the assessment format or environment prevents the student with a disability from demonstrating his or her true degree of learning, then the format, the environment, or both must be changed so that they are no longer barriers. To do otherwise may result in violation of the IDEA, Section 504, or the ADA.

These laws should cause you to think about how all of your students can fully demonstrate their true performance with regard to the intended instructional outcomes, and how you can provide alternative means to those who cannot demonstrate their learning through ordinary means. Assessment of learning as it applies to students with disabilities is discussed in various ways throughout this text, most notably in the chapters indicated in Figure 1.2.

Teacher Competency

In most states, one of the causes for which teachers may be discharged is incompetence. Teachers demonstrate their competence (or lack of it) in a number of ways, including monitoring student educational progress and grading their work. If, for example, a teacher never assesses student learning in the classroom or appears to produce grades based on nothing more than mood or whim, he or she could be found incompetent to teach.[5] Some school districts have set policy on the minimum amount of assessment necessary for basing grades. As a further comment on grades, some state courts (those in Kentucky, for example) view the lowering of grades to punish student misbehavior, such as giving zeros for work missed due to unexcused absences, as a clear misrepresentation of students' academic status. The legality of the practice is not consistent across the states, however, so teachers should make themselves aware of their state's statutes and their district's policies regarding the matter.[6]

---

[5]See, for example, *Whaley v. Hennepin Indep. School Dist.* 325 N.W.2d 128 (Minn. 1982).

[6]The effect that lowering grades for punishment has on end-of-term grades is discussed in Chapter 12.

I Need to . . .	1	2	3	4	5	6	7	8	9	10	11	12	13	14
Take a classroom assessment course	✓	✓	✓	✓	✓	✓	✓	✓	✓	✓	✓	✓	✓	✓
See the big picture first regarding classroom assessment	✓	✓	✓											
See the nuts and bolts first regarding classroom assessment					✓	✓	✓	✓	✓					
Write a test; students choose answers; outcomes are clear					✓	✓								
Write a test; students choose answers; outcomes *not* clear				✓	✓	✓								
Write a test; students to supply the answers; outcomes clear					✓		✓							
Write a test; students supply the answers; outcomes *not* clear				✓	✓		✓							
Write better test items						✓	✓			✓				
Create a performance assessment; outcomes are clear								✓						
Create a performance assessment; outcomes are *not* clear				✓				✓						
Enhance performance assessments								✓		✓				
Create a portfolio system for students									✓					
Assess portfolios									✓					
Enhance instruction										✓				✓
Enhance the assessments I now use					✓	✓	✓	✓	✓	✓				
Create a grading system												✓		
Enhance my grading system												✓		
Create checklists or rating scales								✓						
Enhance checklists or rating scales								✓		✓				
Talk to parents about their children's classroom achievement or behavior									✓			✓		
Read everything related to standardized testing											✓		✓	✓
Prepare students for standardized testing													✓	
Administer a standardized test													✓	
Talk to parents about standardized test results											✓			✓
Assess the achievement and behavior of disabled students	✓		✓	✓	✓								✓	

Figure 1.2
Assessment needs of teachers and the chapters of this book that are most relevant in meeting them.

How to Use This Book

This book is designed for three teacher audiences in grades K–12: pre-service teachers-in-training, veterans who have not had training in student assessment, and veterans who wish to update their assessment skills with newer techniques and instruments like performance scoring rubrics. The book provides instruction and practice in the basics regarding the seven standards for teacher competence in assessment. It is not intended as an exhaustive text, so you will not know everything there is to know about classroom assessment when you finish it. It does, however, attempt to make assessment tools and procedures more user-friendly. It introduces you to some of the basic principles of assessment and shows you how to use the tools so that you can implement them directly or modify them for your classroom. The goals of this text are to help you gain practical knowledge and skill that can be put to immediate use creating or improving your classroom assessment practices and to gain a good foundation for more advanced training in educational assessment.

The sequence of chapters in this text is one commonly used in courses on classroom assessment, also called educational measurement or student evaluation. It is not the only effective sequence, however. You may proceed from beginning to end without skipping around, or you may read only the chapters that are most relevant to what you want to know right now. Figure 1.2 lists some of the basic needs teachers may have in regard to assessment and the chapters that most specifically pertain to them. This book can be used in a course or workshop on assessment for teachers, but it is also a good reference to use on the job. For example, if you are writing multiple-choice items for an upcoming assessment, you might quickly review the easy-reference checklist on guidelines for writing good multiple-choice items in Chapter 6 before you start.

Summary

Defining Assessment Terms

Evaluation is the process of judging worth or value on some basis. Good evaluation requires data gathering for informed decision making. *Measurement* is the process of quantifying the degree to which someone or something possesses a given characteristic, quality, or feature. *Assessment* as a process in the classroom is a purposeful collection of data—both qualitative and quantitative. For teachers, the purpose of assessment is usually to make decisions about students either as a group or individually. Data collection in assessment is accomplished in a variety of ways: observation of behavior, presentation of tasks for students to perform mentally and record their responses in writing, or examination of products produced by the students. As a noun, *assessment* is a question or task, or series of such, designed to elicit some predetermined behavior from the person(s) being tested. *Test* is used interchangeably with *assessment*.

Assessment Needs in Schools Today

Future workers will be required to be flexible and autonomous and will need the ability to think critically about information at hand. The communities that schools serve expect that the dollars they invest in education provide some return on that investment. School personnel are, therefore, increasingly held accountable for the learning of the students entrusted to them. The demands from the workplace and the communities surrounding schools require that school personnel teach children how to learn, how to access and use information, how to critically appraise what they perceive, and how to make decisions. As a result, teachers must assess higher-level educational outcomes far above rote memorization of facts. They must also use the results of assessment to inform instructional decisions and enhance instructional materials and strategies. Further, they must require students to demonstrate what they have learned in a wider variety of contexts.

The Standards for Teacher Competence in the Educational Assessment of Students

The Standards for Teacher Competence in the Educational Assessment of Students is a professionally developed list of expectations for the student-evaluation portion of a teacher's job; they are major themes in this book. These seven major assessment responsibilities, collectively known as the "standards," are:

1. Choose assessment methods appropriate for instructional decisions.
2. Develop assessment methods appropriate for instructional decisions.
3. Administer, score, and interpret the results of both externally produced and teacher-produced assessment methods.
4. Use assessment results when making decisions about individual students, planning teaching, developing curriculum, and school improvement.
5. Develop valid grading procedures that use student assessments.
6. Communicate assessment results to students, parents and other lay audiences, and other educators.
7. Recognize unethical, illegal, and otherwise inappropriate assessment methods and uses of assessment information.

Legal Issues and Classroom Assessment

The Family Educational Rights to Privacy Act (FERPA) is a major piece of legislation that is still being interpreted in courts and schools around the nation decades after its enactment. FERPA requires that: (1) student records be kept confidential, (2) written consent from the student's parents be obtained before disclosing that student's record to a third party, (3) parents be allowed to challenge the accuracy of the information kept in their children's records, and (4) students who have reached the age of 18 be accorded the same rights as formerly granted to their parents.

The courts view ability tracking or grouping students on a long-term basis where it is used to segregate minority children into lower tracks as an attempt to perpetuate discrimination. Grouping schemes that teachers might use to maximize instruction for all is permissible by the courts and supported by research. More than a single test score for assignment to groups is necessary for good grouping decisions.

Three laws that have major impact on students with disabilities are the Individuals with Disabilities Education Act (IDEA), Section 504 of the Rehabilitation Act of 1973, and the Americans with Disabilities Act (ADA). IDEA guarantees identified students a free and appropriate public education in the least restrictive environment and requires teachers and other district staff to make a good-faith effort to provide appropriate instruction and help students achieve the goals and objectives set each year in their IEP. Section 504 prohibits discrimination on the basis of disability and requires schools to make reasonable accommodations for students with disabilities to fully demonstrate the true level of their learning as it relates to the curriculum, even those students who are temporarily disabled. The ADA is patterned after Section 504, but it expands its scope in many areas. The ADA applies to public, private, and parochial schools both as workplaces and as places of learning. All three laws require that if the assessment format or environment prevents the student with a disability from demonstrating his or her true degree of learning, then the format, the environment, or both must be changed so that they are no longer barriers.

In most states, one of the causes for which teachers may be discharged is incompetence. Teachers demonstrate their competence (or lack of it) in a number of ways, including monitoring student educational progress and grading their work.

Try These

I. Matching: Match the statement with the law that grants or requires it. Write the letter of your answer in the space provided. Laws may be used once or more than once.

	Statements	Laws
_____	1. Covers only children who qualify for special education.	a. ADA
_____	2. Gives parents the right to challenge the fairness of their child's grade.	b. FERPA
_____	3. Gives parents the right to review the contents of their child's records.	c. IDEA
_____	4. May require a reduction in graduation requirements for disabled students.	d. Sec. 504 of the Rehabilitation Act of 1973
_____	5. Prohibits discrimination on the basis of disability.	e. None of the above laws
_____	6. Prohibits the use of grouping schemes for instructional purposes.	
_____	7. Guarantees that a student's grades will not be shared with a third party without written consent from the student's parents.	
_____	8. Prevents teachers from entering negative statements into a student's records.	
_____	9. Lists the specific disabilities it covers.	
_____	10. Requires an individual educational plan (IEP) for each eligible student.	
_____	11. Requires standards of performance to be set for a class to match the functioning level of the lowest performing student in the class.	

II. On a separate sheet of paper, briefly state in your own words three implications cited in the chapter that the demands of the workplace and the community have on classroom assessment. Are there others that you can think of? List them too and discuss them with a colleague, if possible.

III. Review Appendix A before answering these. The following statements are related to The Standards for Teacher Competence in the Educational Assessment of Students. For each statement regarding a possible teacher activity, decide whether or not (**Y**es or **N**o) the language of the standards supports it, either directly or by implication. Circle the letter of your response.

1. Know which assessment approach is appropriate for making decisions about students. Y N
2. Develop classroom assessments as well as choose ready-made ones. Y N
3. Create standardized tests. Y N
4. Compute common statistics such as measures of central tendency, dispersion, and reliability. Y N
5. Administer standardized achievement tests. Y N
6. Explain a student's standardized test score to his or her parents. Y N
7. Administer specialized assessments to students to determine eligibility for certain programs (for example, special education, gifted). Y N

Answers

I. 1. c, 2. e, 3. b, 4. e, 5. a *and* d (did you get both?), 6. e, 7. b, 8. e, 9. c, 10. c, 11. e

II. Your answers should reconcile with those below and the chapter text.

a. Teachers should assess higher-level outcomes more accurately and directly.

b. Teachers should use assessment results when making decisions about what and how to teach.

c. Students must show what they know and can do in more ways (contexts) than one.

III. 1. Y (I.C), 2. Y (I and II), 3. N (III.A–F does not include creating commercially produced standardized tests), 4. N (III.E requires only conceptual understanding; computation is a bonus), 5. Y (III.C), 6. Y (III.D and VI.A–F), 7. N (not required by any of the standards).

CHAPTER 2

The Teacher's Assessment Options

Key Concepts:

- Classifying assessments in different ways.
- Recognizing the four major sources of assessments: teachers, commercial test publishers, state education departments, and textbook publishers.
- Understanding the types of behaviors teachers assess with instruments: achievement, aptitude, attitude, and interest.
- Understanding the types of referents to which assessment results are compared: pre-specified criteria and the performance of other people.
- Using criterion-referenced assessment and norm-referenced assessment appropriately and effectively.

Standards Addressed in This Chapter:

1. Choose assessment methods appropriate for instructional decisions.
2. Develop assessment methods appropriate for instructional decisions.
3. Administer, score, and interpret the results of both externally produced and teacher-produced assessment methods.
4. Use assessment results when making decisions about individual students, planning teaching, developing curriculum, and school improvement.

Before You Begin Reading, Consider This

Is there any advantage in knowing a student's general ability or aptitude—his or her scores on an intelligence test, for example?

YES With this knowledge, we can set more realistic expectations for students and plan learning activities targeted to their ability level.

NO We as teachers should take students as they come to us and remain blind to any prior labels put on them by test scores or previous teachers.

Never before have teachers had so many assessment tools available to them: observation instruments, written tests, structured performance tasks with scoring rubrics, portfolios, and standardized tests, to name a few. These tools come from many sources, assess a multitude of behaviors, and may be used in many ways. To select assessment methods appropriate for instructional decisions such as providing feedback or diagnosing group or individual learning needs, teachers need to know the range of options. The variety of assessment options available, and the categories into which they may be classified, are the topics of this chapter.

Categorizing Assessment Options

There are many ways to classify assessments based on their multiple characteristics and, as a result, one assessment tool may fall into more than one classification category. For example, one assessment may be classified as a published, paper-and-pencil, standardized, norm-referenced aptitude test, and another may be described as a teacher-made, criterion-referenced, achievement, performance-based assessment. Whew!

One way to classify assessments is according to variables related to their administration. In such a scheme, tests can be categorized as individual tests or group assessments, depending upon whether they are administered to one person at a time or to more than one person. Another way to classify tests is according to difficulty vs. time variables. In such a scheme we can differentiate among speed, power, and mastery assessments.

Speed tests have a fixed time limit and items or tasks of low difficulty. A classic example is the timed multiplication tables test where students are required to answer correctly as many simple multiplication items (such as $3 \times 2 =$) as possible in 5 minutes.

Power tests contain items or tasks that vary in difficulty, usually arranged in order of increasing difficulty. The time limit on power tests is generous; theoretically, there is no time limit, but in practice teachers do not usually give students 6 months to complete the assessment. The intent is to determine a student's "best" performance under optimum conditions, including ample time for completion. A classic example of a classroom power test is a spelling test in which the words become increasingly difficult, beginning with *duck* and *soup* and ending with *hysteria* and *neurosis*. Another example of a power test is a spatial-relations assessment where students are given increasingly more intricate shapes to place into a form board.

Mastery tests have characteristics of both speed and power tests. The items or tasks are typically of low difficulty, and the time limit is generous. Mastery tests are often used for assessing achievement of minimum essentials (like functional minimums for graduation), and power tests are used to assess greater achievement levels.

The organization of later chapters (5 through 8) reflects another type of classification scheme based on types of expected student responses. Some classroom assessments, for example, require students to respond in writing (in words, symbols, or by marking an answer sheet). Others require the student to perform a task (for example, correctly mount a prepared slide and focus a microscope for viewing) or produce a product (such as create a sculpture using found objects).

The classification scheme presented in this chapter addresses major questions teachers might have about assessment options:

- Where do assessment instruments come from? Or, put another way, who makes the tests?
- What behaviors and traits can we assess with these instruments?
- How can we interpret the results of these assessments?

Figure 2.1 summarizes the classification scheme discussed in this chapter as it relates to the three questions above.

Teachers typically decide what assessments will be needed in their classrooms to assess student progress, diagnose learning difficulties, determine prerequisite skills, or place students into learning groups, for example. The assessment in-

Who makes them? Where do they come from?	Teachers Test publishers State governments Textbook publishers
What is assessed?	Achievement Aptitude Attitude Interest
How are assessment results interpreted?	Compared to established criteria (criterion-referenced) Compared to population norms (norm-referenced)

Figure 2.1
A classification scheme for assessments teachers use based on source, content, and interpretation referent for the results.

struments they use may be produced by the teachers themselves, obtained from the resource materials published as part of a textbook series, or acquired from some other source. Many experienced teachers collect and create performance tasks and test items as they do instructional strategies and materials for use in their classrooms. Teachers also typically administer tests to their students as part of a school- or district-wide assessment program. These assessments are created by someone other than an individual teacher and are distributed on a wider basis than just one classroom.

Categorizing Assessment Options by Their Source

The term *source* in this context refers to the person or persons responsible for producing the assessment. There are four primary sources for the assessments typically used in today's classrooms: teachers, commercial test publishers, individual state departments of education, and textbook publishers.

Assessments Produced by Teachers

A *teacher-made assessment* is one made by a teacher or a group of teachers for a certain content area or set of instructional outcomes for a particular group of students. Teachers are a primary source of student assessments, and for good reason. Teacher-made tests are likely to reflect what was actually taught to a greater degree than tests aimed at a wider audience or broader range of content. Teachers are the primary source of custom-made assessments because they know the learning outcomes or objectives, the instructional plans, and their students' needs better than anyone. Teacher-made assessments may be used repeatedly or they may only be administered once. Here are some examples of teacher-made assessments:

- Ms. Spindela creates a 25-item written test that covers the four objectives for an instructional unit in genetics for her eighth-grade science class. At the end of the unit, she administers the test to determine how well her students grasped the concepts presented. She also hands the scored tests back to her students and uses the results as feedback to clear up any misconceptions students have as indicated by their answers.
- At the beginning of the school year, Mr. Deutch administers a reading test he created and has refined over time. He also has the students read orally and answer questions he has prepared. He uses the results, along with information gathered from permanent records and his own observations, to help group his students for initial reading instruction.
- Prior to the beginning of classes, the fifth-grade teachers at Martin Luther King, Jr. Elementary School create a rating scale they will all use to assess the debates their students will engage in as part of a social studies unit.

It is not likely that a national test publisher would find it financially feasible to produce, for example, a performance assessment for a single third-grade class on five specific learning outcomes from three different instructional sources. Nor is it likely that it would be worthwhile for a commercial test publisher to bother producing a test on a very narrow topic that only a few schools would buy. For example, a course on the language and customs of native Hawaiians might find an audience only in the 50th state. It is not worth the effort for a commercial company to develop tests for which the market of buyers and potential for profitability are small. Thus, schools rely on teachers who are familiar with both the content and students in their own classrooms to produce appropriate assessments of student learning.

Teacher-Made Paper-and-Pencil Tests

By far, paper-and-pencil written tests are the most popular type of teacher-made test. The term *written* is used loosely here to include both constructed responses (like essays) and the selection and marking of responses chosen from among alternatives (such as multiple-choice). On an essay test, the number of questions is limited and the responders must typically compose lengthy answers. One such example might be:

> Of the U.S. Supreme Court decisions discussed in class, choose *three* and describe what education would be like today if these rulings had been decided in favor of the other party. Use examples to support your points and no more than one side of a sheet of notebook paper (single-spaced). (5 points)

Determining the value or correctness of student-supplied answers to such questions involves some degree of subjective judgment on the part of the scorer; therefore, an essay test can also be classified as a subjective test. An objective test, in contrast, is one for which subjectivity in scoring is eliminated, at least theoretically. Anyone scoring a given objective test should come up with the same score. Examples of objective assessments are multiple-choice tests, true-false tests, matching tests, and short-answer tests.

Things get a little tricky, however, with respect to short-answer assessments. If the items require completion of a sentence by filling in one word (or phrase), and only one word is correct, there is usually no problem, as in the example, "The capital of Tennessee is ____________________." With items like "In the story, the main character was ____________________," answers such as *Jerry, the little boy,* and *Alice's brother* might all be correct if they represent the same person. Thus, in questions such as this all acceptable answers must be identified. With an item like "Define accountability," teachers must be aware of the fine line between an essay question requiring a brief response and a short-answer question requiring a multiple-word response.

Paper-and-pencil tests, as the term is used here, also include tests in which either the directions or the items are read to the students for their written response. For example, because the reading skills of first-graders vary greatly, a first-grade teacher might read the directions aloud to the class, so they all know how to respond.[1]

---

[1]The nature of paper-and-pencil tests is discussed in greater detail in Chapters 5 through 7.

Teacher-Made Performance and Product Assessments

To assess some instructional outcomes or evaluate certain areas of student learning, using paper-and-pencil tests is inappropriate. Teachers cannot determine how well a student can type a letter, for example, with a multiple-choice test. Sometimes a paper-and-pencil assessment will do, but it is not always the best method; there are instructional outcomes for which other assessment options work better. For certain assessment situations, observation is clearly the most appropriate approach. Attitudes, for example, can be assessed by asking persons to respond in writing to a number of questions. But a person may say he is a good sport and then break rules to win or walk away pouting. In such cases, more accurate information could be obtained by actually watching him compete.

Observation is used as a method of assessment when actions speak louder than words. In observation assessment, teachers gather data not by asking for information but by watching closely. The student being observed usually does not write anything as she would on a paper-and-pencil test. Instead, the student performs some action and her behavior is observed and recorded by the teacher.

The value of observation is illustrated by a study that was conducted in the Southwest on the classroom interaction between teachers and Mexican-American students.[2] Although education has progressed in the time since this study was conducted, its results are still pertinent. Many teachers claimed that Mexican-American children were difficult to teach because of their alleged lack of participation in classroom activities and their failure to ask or answer questions. Systematic observation, however, revealed that the main reason they did not answer questions, for example, was that they were not asked very many! Observation revealed that teachers tended to talk less often and less favorably to Mexican-American children and to ask them fewer questions. Thus, observation not only provided more accurate information than teacher reports but also made the teachers aware that they were unintentionally part of the problem.

In addition to assessing student performance, student products may also be assessed. Book reports, dioramas, science fair projects, and artwork are all examples of tangible output that can be assessed on a number of dimensions depending on the teacher's objectives for the class. Even a student-composed answer to an essay question on a written test can be considered a product. A book report, for example, can be assessed in a number of ways, including:

- How well it summarizes the plot.
- How accurately it describes the relationship among characters.
- Whether the title, author, and main character are identified in the report.
- The student's ability to write complete sentences and/or paragraphs.
- The student's ability to use grammar, syntax, punctuation, and spelling rules appropriate for his or her grade level.

---

[2]"The Inequality of Educational Opportunity in the Southwest: An Observational Study of Ethnically Mixed Classrooms" by G. Jackson and C. Cosca, 1974, *American Educational Research Journal, 11*(13), pp. 219–229.

The teacher decides the important dimensions and criteria for success and assesses the product accordingly. As you can see above, some of the dimensions listed for a book report can be assessed more objectively than others. It is fairly straightforward, for example, to assess whether the title, author, and main character are identified in the report, but how well it summarizes the plot of the book leaves more room for interpretation.[3]

Teacher-Made Rating Scales and Checklists

Rating scales and checklists (see Figure 2.2) are instruments teachers use to help with data-gathering when assessing either a performance or a product. A rating scale is typically an instrument with a number of items related to a given variable, each item representing a continuum of categories between two extremes, usually with a number of points along the continuum highlighted in some way. Persons responding to the items place a mark to indicate their position on each item. A checklist enumerates a number of behaviors or features that constitute a procedure or product. When a procedure is involved, the steps are typically listed in the desired order. The person completing the checklist indicates whether a given behavior or feature occurred or is present.[4]

Teachers are not typically also psychometricians. Thus the assessment instruments (such as tests and observation checklists teachers produce) are not likely to be formally validated, field-tested, and revised. Larger budgets than those teachers normally have at hand are required to produce assessments that meet such rigorous requirements.[5] For these assessments we usually turn to commercial test publishers.

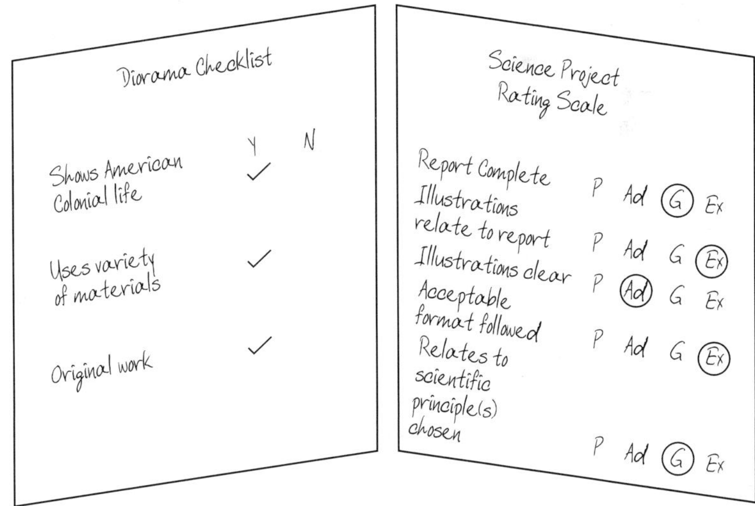

Figure 2.2
A checklist (left) and a rating scale (right). For the rating scale, P = poor, Ad = Adequate, G = good, and Ex = excellent.

[3]The nature of fair assessment of performances and products is discussed in greater detail in Chapters 8 and 9.

[4]Guidelines for constructing rating scales and checklists for assessing student performances and products are presented in Chapter 8.

[5]Requirements for all types of assessments are discussed in Chapter 3.

Assessments Produced by Commercial Test Publishers

Commercial test publishers are in the business of producing and selling assessment instruments to school districts, state departments of education, counselors, and other specialists. They are the largest producers of standardized assessments, although not all commercially produced tests are standardized. You are probably familiar with the concept. A *standardized test* is one that is:

- Developed by subject-matter and assessment specialists.
- Field-tested under uniform administration procedures.
- Revised to meet certain acceptability criteria.
- Scored and interpreted using uniform procedures and standards.

Standardization thus occurs in the administration, scoring, and interpretation of results. Standardized assessments may be performance or product tests, although the majority of them are the paper-and-pencil variety. In the past, many educators have equated standardized with multiple choice. This is no longer the case. As educational needs have changed, test publishers have responded with a variety of formats and reporting options. A review of any major test publisher's current catalog will confirm this.

Standardized tests are big business. Hundreds of thousands of standardized assessments are administered each year. Largely because of the competition among companies for various markets, considerable time and money is typically invested in the development and revision of standardized assessments. Psychometric experts and experts in the behavior to be assessed determine the content and format of the test. Fixed directions and time limits are developed so that the test can be administered in exactly the same way (as much as is humanly possible) every time it is given. Procedures are developed to ensure objectivity and uniformity of scoring. Although there are exceptions, the vast majority of standardized tests have been administered to groups referred to as *norm groups*. The performance of the norm group for a given test serves as the basis of comparison and interpretation for other groups to whom the test is administered. The scores of the norm group are called norms and are published in norms tables.

Ideally, the norm group is a large, well-defined group that is representative of the group and subgroups for whom the assessment is intended. Because most standardized tests are intended for use virtually anywhere, norms should ideally be based on a geographically representative national sample. For example, if a test is supposed to measure reading achievement and be appropriate for grades 1 to 6, then the norm group should include a number of first- through sixth-graders at various locations, and norms should be presented by grade level. The description of the norm group should include all pertinent information such as size, location, and major characteristics. The month and year of testing (March 1997, for example) should also be given, because norms for students at the end of the ninth grade, for example, would not be applicable to interpreting the scores of students just beginning the ninth grade.

Of course norm groups are not always what they should be (what an understatement!) because of factors such as inadequate sampling of the intended population. Unfortunately, it is not too unusual to find statements in standardized test manuals such as the following:

> The Picayune Algebra Test was administered to 30 ninth-grade students in Nomansland, USA; the results are presented in Table 4.

Whoopee. The performance of such a norm group would hardly qualify as national norms, even if each person came from a different state. Descriptions of norm groups for higher quality tests typically read more like this:

> The norm group was selected to duplicate the distribution according to region and size of system for students in public, private nonsectarian, and private sectarian schools throughout the country. Between February 25, 1997, and March 15, 1997, 850,000 students, representing 264 school systems in all 50 states, were tested. The breakdown of number of students by state appears in Table 7.

Norms are typically presented for different kinds of populations to permit more valid comparisons. The Stanford Achievement Test, for example, presents norms by grade level, time of testing (fall, mid-year, or spring), and test form. Another achievement test may present norms for given age groups, which do not include the scores of accelerated students or students who are mentally retarded, as well as norms for the total group, which include the scores of all students tested. Some test publishers report separate norms for special groups such as students with learning disabilities. Some large school systems have formulated norms tables for various sub-groups in the system based on the results of tests such as the Stanford Achievement Test. When available, such system norms provide a more valid basis of comparison for certain purposes, like the analysis of achievement patterns in the system over time, for example.

Norms tables typically include the distribution of raw scores as well as a number of score equivalents such as percentiles and stanines. The lowest raw scores correspond to the first percentile, the highest scores correspond to the 99th percentile, and the average raw scores correspond to the 50th percentile.[6] Thus, norms tables permit what are referred to as norm-referenced interpretations. A given student's score is compared to the scores of the norm group. If his score corresponds to the average score of the norm group, then the interpretation is that he is average with respect to the variables measured. Strictly speaking, there is no indication in norms tables of whether the score is "good," only whether it is better (or worse) than the average performance of the norm group. There may also be no interpretation that tells us exactly *what* a given student knows or can do, only whether what she knows or can do is more or less than "average."

In recent years, commercial publishers have made an effort to include teachers in the development of assessments, both for their content knowledge and their knowledge of students. In developing the ninth edition of the Stanford Achievement Test,

---

[6]This and other types of score interpretations are discussed in greater detail in Chapter 11.

for example, about 2,000 teachers from across the country were involved in setting the standards for performance. This reflects the trend of teachers' increasing involvement in creating, not just using, effective assessments of learning.

State-Produced Assessments

State departments of education are also in the assessment business, producing so many types of assessment instruments for so many various purposes so rapidly that it is not practical to list them all here. Currently, many states, for example, are producing minimum competency tests that involve assessing whether students have met state-mandated minimum standards for grade promotion or high-school graduation. In many cases these are multiple-choice, paper-and-pencil tests with certain cut-off scores for each student performance standard. In addition, certain states have chosen to assess specific content areas at selected grade levels. The Florida Writing Assessment, for example, is administered statewide to students in grades 4, 8, and 10 to assess their achievement of writing skills. Students are given a choice of topics and 45 minutes to plan and write their responses, which are then scored on a numbered scale. Thus a student's ability to write a persuasive argument, for example, can be assessed at three different points in his K–12 career. In addition, the state's elementary, middle, and high schools can use the schoolwide results as one indicator of the effectiveness of their writing program.

As a result of one of the more recent waves of educational reform, some states have rethought and redrawn their curricula and devised different forms of assessment that are, in theory, more in line with what is now taught and how it is learned by the students. This has, in certain cases, changed the nature of the assessments themselves, shifting from a heavy reliance on multiple-choice, paper-and-pencil tests to include more performance- and product-based assessments, also known as "authentic" assessment and "alternative" assessment.[7]

Not all assessments administered under the auspices of a state department of education are created by in-state experts. Some states have published their specifications and other requirements and put them out for bid by commercial test publishing companies and, in some cases, universities. Thus the state gets a high-quality assessment that meets its needs without having to hire permanent staff to produce it.

Assessments Produced by Textbook Publishers

Textbook publishers are in the business of making and selling textbooks and other instructional materials to schools and school districts. In recent years they have increased the scope of their products to include not only the student text and teacher manual but also reproducible masters for assessment. This allegedly takes the "worry" out of test construction, leaving the teacher free to do what she or he does best—teach. The teacher must still ensure that the provided items and tasks align well with his or her instructional outcomes and the content of what was taught.

---

[7]More about authentic and alternative assessment in Chapters 8 and 9.

The format of these textbook-published tests, along with item length and complexity, vary depending on the age of the students and the test content. Level K (fourth grade) of the Houghton Mifflin Reading series[8], for example, contains guidance for teachers for both informal assessment by observation and no fewer than five options for formal assessment, including the test booklets, manuals, and answer keys. Also included in this assessment package is a placement test and a more extensive reading inventory. Publishers of these comprehensive instructional packages have tried to anticipate various assessment opportunities and provide teachers with the related resources for use, as the teachers see fit, in their classrooms.

In many cases, multiple forms of textbook publisher assessment instruments and comparable tasks are available. Many teachers use the second form of a test and alternate performance tasks either for make-up purposes or to discourage cheating in the classroom. For example, if a child is absent the day a unit test is given, she can take a make-up test that covers the same unit content but does not have the same items on it as the test originally given to the class.

To the extent that a teacher uses only a single textbook, teaches only to those instructional outcomes included in the text, and does not supplement with outcomes and materials from other sources, the tests that accompany the textbook series may be adequate for assessment. Textbook publishers attempt to make their products useful and attractive to both teachers and students, aiming at a national market. Yet, they cannot be all things to all people. The students, teachers, and curricula in Orange County (Anaheim), California, for example, are similar in some ways to those in Ross County (Chillicothe), Ohio, but are v-e-r-y different in other ways. A "one-size-fits-all" textbook will, therefore, include a lot of content common to the curricula of both districts but also leave out other content that is more relevant locally to one or both districts. Similarly, the assessments included with a textbook series, even if they faithfully reflect the content of the text, will rarely cover all the concepts, principles, and skills deemed important by the individual classroom teacher. Teachers must rely on their best judgment in deciding if and how ancillary materials, including these published tests, should be used in the classroom.

Categorizing Assessment Options by the Behaviors and Traits Assessed

A teacher creates or selects an assessment to gather data about a student's various behaviors and traits, called *constructs* by measurement folk. In this section, we'll discuss the assessment of students' achievement, aptitude, attitudes, and interests.

[8] *Houghton Mifflin Reading* by Houghton Mifflin, 1989, Boston: Author.

Student Achievement

Achievement tests assess the present status of individuals with respect to proficiency in given areas of knowledge or skill. Given this broad definition, it is no wonder that the overwhelming majority of assessment done in schools is in the area of student achievement. It is also not surprising that all four of the major sources of assessment instruments referred to in the previous section of this chapter produce achievement tests. For the most part, however, achievement tests are either teacher-made or produced by commercial test publishers, so they are discussed within that context here. The overall category of achievement assessment instruments includes individual tests and batteries, as well as diagnostic tests. Each is discussed in turn.

Assessing Student Achievement Using Individual Tests and Batteries

Standardized achievement tests are available for many individual curriculum areas and also in the form of comprehensive batteries that measure achievement in several different areas. A *battery* is a series of tests (called subtests), each of which samples a different content area, like reading, mathematics, listening, and social science. All the subtests are normed on the same group so that comparisons of individual strengths and weaknesses can be made. A student usually receives both a score on each subtest taken and an overall score on the battery as a whole. A brief perusal of any volume in the *Mental Measurements Yearbook* series will give you an idea of the variety of achievement tests and batteries available to teachers.[9] The California Achievement Test (CAT) Basic Skills Battery, for example, is a commonly used battery that measures achievement in reading, spelling, language, mathematics, and study skills. You may be familiar with the CAT or other members of the achievement species—the Comprehensive Test of Basic Skills (CTBS), the Iowa Test of Basic Skills (ITBS), the Metropolitan Achievement Test (MAT), or the Stanford Achievement Test (abbreviated Stanford, to differentiate it from the Scholastic Assessment Test, which uses SAT as a registered trademark).

When assessment of achievement in a number of areas is needed, it is better to administer a battery than a number of individual tests. Besides being more convenient and efficient in terms of time and money, a battery allows comparisons that are not possible or are risky when a number of individual tests are given. Because all subtests of the battery were normed on the same group, one can compare a student's relative achievement in the various areas tested and identify areas in which he performs better than others (although, objectively, the student may not excel in any area). We might, for example, determine that Esmeralda's best subject is arithmetic, even though she may be somewhat below average in arithmetic achievement. Depending upon such factors as the number of achievement areas included, batteries can take from one hour to several days to administer.

---

[9] *The Twelfth Mental Measurements Yearbook* by J. C. Conoley and J. C. Impara, 1995, Lincoln, NE: Buros Institute of Mental Measurements of the University of Nebraska—Lincoln. This latest in a series that began in 1933 is also available on CD-ROM.

Differences Between Standardized and Teacher-Made Assessments. In addition to the characteristics already described as differentiating between standardized and teacher-made assessments, there is another major difference that applies to achievement tests. Standardized achievement tests, whether they are paper-and-pencil or performance-based, are designed to measure what most teachers cover—that is, content common to many classes of a certain kind (Algebra I or fourth-grade language arts, for example). The specialists who develop such tests analyze texts and other instructional materials used throughout the country and derive the instructional outcomes or the subject matter to be sampled by the test. The tests are carefully developed to include assessment of outcomes and content common to many school systems. For example, the ninth edition of the Stanford Achievement Test Series (Stanford 9) claims alignment with the National Assessment of Educational Progress for its reading subtests and with the Curriculum and Evaluation Standards for School Mathematics from the National Council of Teachers of Mathematics for its mathematics subtests.

There is no way a commercially produced, standardized test could include items to assess everything that any teacher might include in instruction. Thus, there will be certain facts, concepts, principles, and skills on a standardized high-school biology test, for example, that some students have never encountered, and there will be other facts, concepts, principles, and skills they have learned that will not be assessed. A teacher-made test, on the other hand, is designed to assess a particular set of instructional outcomes—precisely those intended by the teacher. Such an assessment, if based on actual texts and materials involved in instruction, more accurately reflects achievement of what was actually taught in that classroom.

Choosing Between Standardized and Teacher-Made Assessments. There are a number of purposes for which a standardized achievement test is more appropriate than a teacher-made assessment. First of all, it is important to know how well Henrietta is doing compared to other students of a similar age or grade level. Henrietta may be doing well in Ms. Chalk's class, but Ms. Chalk's class may contain only remedial students, or Ms. Chalk may be an "easy" teacher. For guidance purposes, for instance, it would be helpful to know that Henrietta is actually performing way below the national norm, or average score. Moreover, the overall performance of a group of students says something about the effectiveness of instruction. If many students (not just Henrietta) do poorly on a standardized test, the reasons should be investigated (assuming that the students are similar on relevant variables to those in the norm group). Any number of factors could be involved, such as relevancy of the curriculum (it might be woefully outdated) or the effectiveness of instruction itself.

Here is an interesting question for debate: Should teachers be held accountable for the performance of their students on standardized tests? Actually, the answer is yes and no. Teachers cannot be held accountable to the degree that students in their classes differ from the norm group or to the degree that what was actually taught differs from what the standardized test assesses. On the other hand, there should be some overlap between a given teacher's objectives and most teachers' objectives. If you took a standardized test on facts, concepts, and principles of educational assessment after finishing this book and did terribly, you would be upset. If I told you not to worry because this book does not cover any of the topics that other assessment books do, you would want to know why. The point is, there is considerable room for individual variation beyond a common core; all elementary students, for example, should be taught how to multiply two two-digit numbers.

Standardized tests are also preferable to teacher-made assessments when large-scale comparisons are to be made between performance at two different points in time. A principal, a superintendent, and a director of a curriculum evaluation project, for example, may all be interested in comparing September results with May results for the same test. Also, because such results are normally part of a student's file, teachers can use them as one source of information when planning instruction. Finally, standardized tests are usually more appropriate when the achievement of a large population is being assessed. By the nature of the way in which they are designed, standardized tests are more likely to assess what most of the students have learned across classrooms and schools.

Assessing Students' Learning Difficulties Using Diagnostic Tests

A *diagnostic test* is a type of achievement assessment that yields multiple scores for each area of achievement diagnosed; these scores facilitate identification of specific areas of deficiency or learning difficulty. Diagnostic tests may be standardized, teacher-made, or part of a textbook series and are administered after a given unit of instruction. Total scores are of very little value since the purpose is to identify precisely what a particular student can and cannot do. Indirectly, of course, diagnostic tests can also identify problems with instruction.

Advantages and Disadvantages of Standardized and Teacher-Made Diagnostic Tests. Standardized and teacher-made diagnostic tests each have their own advantages and disadvantages. Commercially produced standardized diagnostic tests are developed in cooperation with experts in the area of learning difficulties and are based on research findings concerning common sources of learning difficulty. These tests include assessment of essential skills in a given area; for those skills that are assessed, a number of different types of items are included so that areas of difficulty can be precisely pinpointed. Because a standardized diagnostic test is developed by a cadre of experts, it provides most teachers with much more valid results than they could obtain themselves using more informal techniques. Teacher-made diagnostic assessments, on the other hand, are usually cheaper to produce, use, and score.

Diagnostic tests are administered mainly to identify individual strengths and weaknesses and to identify students in need of remediation. Items in a diagnostic test represent skills that virtually all students should have achieved at a given point in their education. The nature of the appropriate remediation depends, of course, on the reasons for the identified deficiencies. Scholastic aptitude test scores are frequently used in conjunction with diagnostic test results to determine the nature of the problem. It may be that a student is performing as well as could be expected, given her assessed aptitude, and the decision might be made to either provide the student with supplementary instruction or to place her in a special class. On the other hand, the student might have above-average ability, as indicated on the aptitude test, and be underachieving for personal reasons, in which case counseling might be recommended.

Using Achievement Battery Subtests to Screen Learning Difficulties. Subtests of achievement batteries can be used for diagnostic purposes as a preliminary screening device, although they are not primarily developed for that purpose. Despite only providing one score per subtest, performance on individual test items can be analyzed. The advantage of using battery subtests for diagnostic purposes is that they can be group-administered by teachers at the beginning of the year (saving considerable time), whereas more comprehensive diagnostic tests must be individually administered. The disadvantage is that battery subtests are not designed for the purpose of diagnosis, are typically shorter, and do not provide the depth of analysis possible with a true diagnostic test. If the screening test indicates a possible problem, it may be followed up with an individually administered diagnostic test.

Because of the time and skill involved in administering, scoring, and interpreting diagnostic tests, as well as the fact that they are intended to identify specific deficiencies, it is neither desirable nor necessary to administer diagnostic tests to all students. They should be used as any other tool, as needed, for students apparently having learning problems. One frequently used diagnostic instrument is the Stanford Diagnostic Reading Test (SDRT), which has different levels for different grades and is appropriate for use in all grades. It is designed to identify specific difficulties and to facilitate the flexible grouping of students according to their identified deficiencies. The SDRT assesses four general skill areas: phonetic analysis, vocabulary, comprehension, and scanning. This test has received generally favorable critical reviews and appears to be a fairly valid and reliable instrument.

Using Standardized Diagnostic Tests. Standardized diagnostic assessments are appropriate for determining the exact nature of the problem when a student is having serious difficulty. Such determinations are usually accomplished with tests designed to allow the student to demonstrate certain mistakes or misconceptions. The incorrect answers or inappropriate performance given by the student can then be analyzed to pinpoint the problem. Diagnosis should, however, be an on-going process. In addition to administering a number of informal diagnostic instruments, teachers should constantly be alert for signs of physical problems or learning difficulty. For example, informal screening devices can be useful in detecting visual or hearing problems that may be the reason for a student's low achievement. It is rather difficult to read, for example, when the words are fuzzy or drawkcab. Further, for the same reasons that teacher-made achievement tests are more valid indicators of achievement of what was actually taught, teacher-made diagnostic instruments may be more effective in identifying deficiencies following instruction. For example, an informal reading diagnostic test, created by the teacher or selected by the teacher from the ancillary materials accompanying a textbook series, can clarify which instructional outcomes were not fully achieved. This information is especially important in hierarchical subjects such as mathematics where the learning of new skills is very much dependent on the achievement of previous skills. Teachers should always be alert for early signs of difficulty; the earlier a problem can be detected, the easier it is to correct and the less cumulative damage is done.

Student Aptitude

Aptitude tests are measures of potential used to predict how well someone is likely to perform in a future situation. Tests of general aptitude are variously referred to as scholastic aptitude tests, intelligence tests, IQ (intelligence quotient) tests, and tests of general mental ability. Because intelligence tests and even the word *intelligence* have developed a bad reputation in recent years, the terms *scholastic aptitude* and *school ability* have become more popular. The intents of all aptitude assessments, however, are basically the same. Aptitude tests are also available to predict a student's likely level of performance following some specific future instruction or training. Aptitude tests are available in the form of individual tests in specific areas, like algebra, and in the form of batteries that assess aptitude in several related areas. Although virtually all aptitude tests are commercially produced, standardized, and administered as part of a school assessment program, the results are useful to teachers, counselors, and administrators.

There is a difference of opinion among educators concerning whether teachers should have knowledge of students' general aptitude. Some feel that such knowledge is apt to bias a teacher and result in stereotyping students. Others feel that such information can (1) help the teacher to set more realistic expectations for students, (2) assist the teacher in planning instructional outcomes and activities appropriate to students' abilities, and (3) facilitate the identification of underachievers. Although both points of view have merit, it would seem that, all in all, the benefits to be derived from having such knowledge outweigh the potential problems. Counselors, of course, use such information to better understand individual students and to provide better guidance concerning, for example, career aspirations. Administrative decisions are also facilitated by knowledge of the general aptitude levels of students. Such data may be useful, for example, in the decision to place a child in a special class for the gifted or a special class for the educable mentally retarded. It must be reemphasized, however, that serious decisions such as those noted above should be based on many different kinds of data, not just on the results of a single assessment.

Assessing Students' General Aptitude

Defining General Aptitude. A variety of tests fall into the category of general aptitude, representing a variety of different definitions of general aptitude (or scholastic aptitude, or intelligence, or IQ, or what have you). Although the basic purpose of all such assessments is to predict future academic performance, there is disagreement as to the factors that are being measured and are serving as the predictors in these tests. The term *general aptitude* is defined to include variables such as abstract reasoning, problem solving, and verbal fluency. *General aptitude tests* typically ask the individual to perform a variety of verbal and non-verbal tasks that measure the individual's ability to apply knowledge and solve problems. Such tests generally yield three scores—an overall or total score, a verbal score that usually includes quantitative ability, and a non-verbal or performance score—representing, for example, total ability, verbal ability, and non-verbal ability.

General aptitude tests are intended to be measures of innate ability or potential, but they actually appear to measure current ability; some evidence suggests that scores are to some degree affected by an individual's past and present environment. Because they seem to do a reasonable job of predicting future academic success, however, and are in that sense measures of "potential," they are very useful to educators. Some educators and psychologists support the position that the ability, or potential, to do well in school is but one of many types of intelligence. Proponents of this position believe that abilities such as creativity, mechanical reasoning, and even bodily kinesthetic expression represent types of intelligence that are just as legitimate and valuable as verbal and quantitative intelligence. This point of view is certainly worthy of serious consideration.[10]

Advantages and Disadvantages of Group and Individual General Aptitude Tests. General aptitude tests may be group tests or individually administered assessments. Each type has its relative advantages and disadvantages. Group tests are more convenient to administer, they save considerable time, and they provide an estimate of academic potential that is adequate for many purposes. Batteries comprised of a number of tests suitable for different grade and age levels are also available. Because tests in a battery are similarly structured, they permit both the study of intellectual growth over time and comparisons among different levels. A well-established and widely used group-administered battery is the Cognitive Abilities Test (CogAT). The CogAT has several levels and can be administered to students in grades K–12. The multi-level edition (grades 3 through 12) includes subtests on verbal classification, sentence completion, verbal analogies, quantitative relations, number series, equation building, figure classification, figure analogies, and figure analysis. The results include separate verbal, quantitative, and non-verbal scores. Overall, the test is considered to be a respectable measure of educational potential.

Another frequently administered group assessment is the Otis-Lennon School Ability Test (OLSAT), which has seven levels and is designed for school-age children in grades K–12. The OLSAT measures verbal comprehension, verbal reasoning, pictorial reasoning, figural reasoning, and quantitative reasoning, yielding three scores—verbal, non-verbal, and total (called School Ability Index)—and is also considered to be a respectable measure of educational potential. Both the CogAT and the OLSAT are normed on the same group as their achievement counterparts (the ITBS and the

---

[10]Howard Gardner is one of these educators. See, for example, *Frames of Mind* by H. Gardner, 1983, New York: Basic Books. For a quick overview of the seven intelligences he proposes, see "Multiple Intelligences Go to School: Educational Implications of the Theory of Multiple Intelligences" by H. Gardner and T. Hatch, 1989, *Educational Researcher, 18* (8) pp. 4–9.

Stanford, respectively), thus permitting comparison of overall ability with current achievement of groups. For example, given the estimated ability of his students as a class (as measured with the CogAT), a teacher can compare this with their current achievement level as a class (as measured with the ITBS). These comparisons should not, however, be made on individual students due to the imprecision of assessment in general and to the disadvantages of group testing, discussed below.

A serious disadvantage of group tests is that, for the most part, they require a great deal of reading. Thus, students with poor reading ability are at an automatic disadvantage and may receive scores that reflect, for example, an ability level lower than their true level. Steps have been taken in recent years to lessen the reliance on reading, however, as evidenced in the subtest titles of the CogAT and OLSAT discussed above. Individual tests, on the other hand, require much less reading. Another advantage of individual assessments is that they are administered one on one, and so the examiner is aware of factors such as illness or anxiety that might adversely affect the student's ability to respond. The main disadvantage of individual tests is that they are considerably more difficult, costly, and lengthy to administer and score; specially trained personnel are required to administer them and to score them. In many school systems, a group test of general aptitude is used as a preliminary screen—taking considerably less time and administration expertise than an individually administered test. If a student's group test results warrant, she may then be assessed with an individual instrument. If there is any reason to question the validity of group tests for a particular group, very young children for example, an individual test should be used.

Two of the most well known individually administered intelligence tests for school-age children are the Stanford-Binet Intelligence Scale and the Wechsler Intelligence Scale for Children–III (WISC–III). The Stanford-Binet uses a multistage adaptive format—"fifteen separate ability tests [that] are provided for assessing examinees from below average two-year-olds to superior adults"[11]—so that an examinee takes the battery suited to his or her ability level without having to take all 15 subtests. The WISC–III, on the other hand, is part of a series of scales available to measure the intelligence of people from the age of 2 years, 11 months to adulthood:

- Wechsler Preschool and Primary Scale of Intelligence–Revised (WPPSI–R)—ages 2 years, 11 months to 7 years, 3 months.
- WISC–III—ages 5 to 15.
- Wechsler Adult Intelligence Scale–Revised (WAIS–R)—older adolescents and adults.

As an example, the WISC–III is a scholastic aptitude test that includes verbal tests covering information, similarities, arithmetic, vocabulary, and comprehension and performance tests such as picture completion, coding, picture arrangement, block design, and object assembly. The Stanford-Binet yields scores in each of four cogni-

[11]*Pathways to Success: 1992 Riverside Catalog* (p. 17) by the Riverside Publishing Company, 1992, Chicago: Author.

tive areas—verbal reasoning, quantitative reasoning, abstract/visual reasoning, and short-term memory—and a composite score called a Standard Age Score. The Wechsler scales yield a number of subscores: the WISC–III, for example, yields three—Full Scale IQ, Verbal IQ, and Performance IQ.

Assessing Students' Aptitude in Specific Areas

As the term is generally used, *specific aptitude assessments* attempt to predict the level of performance that can be expected of an individual following future instruction or training in a specific area or areas. Aptitude tests are available for a wide variety of academic and non-academic areas such as mathematics and mechanical reasoning. As with tests of general aptitude, they are used by teachers, counselors, and administrators and for the same reasons. Teachers also use them as a basis for flexible grouping—in math classes, for example. Although most aptitude tests are standardized, paper-and-pencil tests, some are performance tests. The latter are especially appropriate when the students taking the test have a language difficulty—students who are recent immigrants for example—or when the nature of the aptitude assessed, such as spatial relations or manual dexterity, is non-verbal.

Aptitude assessments are available for a number of specific areas such as algebra, music, and mechanical ability. The Minnesota Spatial Relations Test (MSRT), for example, uses blocks and a form board to assess an individual's "speed and accuracy in the discrimination of three-dimensional geometric shapes."[12] Used with individuals age 16 and over, the MSRT yields two scores—time and errors—useful in predicting success in occupations requiring visual-spatial perception and manipulation. Multi-aptitude batteries, which measure aptitudes in several related areas, are available for the assessment of both academic and non-academic aptitudes. Multi-aptitude batteries include a number of subtests normed on the same group. This permits comparisons across subtest scores in order to determine a student's relative strengths and weaknesses. The Differential Aptitude Tests (DAT), for example, include tests on space relations, mechanical reasoning, and perceptual speed and accuracy, among others, and are designed to predict success in various job areas. Adults and students in grades 7 through 12 are the target population for the DAT.

Assessing Student Readiness

Readiness or prognostic assessments are sometimes classified as aptitude tests and sometimes categorized as achievement tests. Aptitude does seem to be a more appropriate categorization, however, because a *readiness test* is administered prior to instruction or training in a specific area to determine whether and to what degree a student is ready for, or will profit from, instruction. Due to increased interest in the basic skills, reading readiness tests have been given more emphasis than other types. Reading readiness tests typically include assessment of variables

---

[12]"Review of Minnesota Spatial Relations Test, Revised Edition" by A. R. Jensen, in *The Ninth Mental Measurements Yearbook* (p. 1014) by J. V. Mitchell, Jr. (Ed.), 1985, Lincoln, NE: Buros Institute of Mental Measurements of the University of Nebraska—Lincoln.

such as auditory discrimination, visual discrimination, and motor ability. The results of such an assessment are used to identify students who, for example, are not ready for formal reading instruction due to physical immaturity. This information can be applied in working with individual students and gives direction for flexible grouping within the classroom. Readiness batteries have also been developed to assess readiness in a number of areas. The Metropolitan Readiness Test (MRT), for example, is designed to assess the degree to which students starting school (ages 4 to 7) have developed the skills and abilities that contribute to readiness for first-grade instruction. Teachers record their individual students' answers on a form for the following skill areas tested with Level 1 of the MRT: beginning consonants, quantitative concepts, reasoning, sound-letter correspondence, story comprehension, and visual discrimination. Scores are derived for each skill area, and students are given a pre-reading composite score as well. One of the most widely used school readiness batteries, the MRT, is considered to be a good test of its type.[13]

Student Attitudes

Attitude assessments, sometimes called *attitude scales,* attempt to determine what an individual believes, perceives, or feels. Attitudes toward self, others, and a variety of activities, institutions, and situations can be indirectly assessed through self-report instruments. Because students' attitudes are related to their achievement and because one of the basic goals of public education is the promotion of certain attitudes believed to be desirable in a democratic society, assessment of attitudes is a major concern in the public schools. School staff at all levels are involved in assessing attitudes and providing activities conducive to the formation of desirable attitudes. At the classroom level, outcomes related to attitudes and assessment of their achievement may be less formal, but teachers still consider them important. It would be very surprising, for example, to find any teachers who would say that they don't care whether students hate their class. Teachers are more likely to assess attitudes with informal instruments and observation than with standardized attitude assessments.

The most commonly used type of attitude scale is that developed by Rensis Likert. A Likert scale asks an individual to respond to a series of statements by indicating whether he strongly agrees (SA), agrees (A), is undecided (U), disagrees (D), or strongly disagrees (SD) with each statement.[14] Each response is associated with a point value, and an individual's score is determined by summing the point values for each statement. For example, the following point values might be assigned to re-

---

[13]School psychologists and counselors are another informative source regarding assessment instruments in education. For a detailed description of a number of achievement, diagnostic, aptitude, readiness, and other types of tests found in schools, see *Using Standardized Tests in Education* (4th ed.), by W. A. Mehrens and I. J. Lehmann, 1987, White Plains, NY: Longman.

[14]"A Technique for the Measurement of Attitudes" by R. A. Likert, 1932, *Archives of Psychology,* No. 140.

sponses to positive statements: SA = 5, A = 4, U = 3, D = 2, SD = 1. For negative statements, the point values would be reversed (SA = 1, A = 2, and so on). An example of a positive statement on an attitude scale might be:

Short people are entitled to the same job opportunities as tall people.	SA	A	U	D	SD

A high point value on a positively stated item would indicate a positive attitude, and a high total score would be indicative of a positive attitude.

Assessments of "attitude toward self" are referred to as *measures of self-concept.* One frequently used self-concept assessment instrument is the Piers-Harris Children's Self Concept Scale (How I Feel About Myself). The Piers-Harris scale is intended for use with children in grades 4 through 12 and can be administered either individually or in a group. It is considered to be a reasonably good measure of self-concept.

Student Interest

Interest can be assessed in the classroom in the same ways that attitude and other behaviors can, formally or through the use of informal, teacher-made instruments like checklists, rating scales, and essay questions and through observation. Knowing students' interests can be of value to teachers in promoting motivation, constructing examples, and making learning activities more relevant to students. At the school level, an ideal assessment program includes a standardized interest inventory. The results of such tests are of interest to all school staff, especially counselors. A standardized *interest inventory* asks an individual to indicate personal likes and dislikes, such as the kinds of activities in which she prefers to engage. Responses are generally compared to known interest patterns. The most widely used type of standardized interest measure is the vocational interest inventory. Such inventories typically ask the respondent to indicate preferences with respect to leisure activities such as hobbies. The respondent's pattern of interest is compared to the patterns of interest typical of successful persons in various occupational fields. The individual can then be counseled as to the fields in which she is likely to be happy and successful.

Two frequently used vocational interest inventories are the Strong-Campbell Interest Inventory (SCII) and the Kuder Occupational Interest Survey (KOIS). The SCII measures interest in a number of professional and business fields. It presents numerous activities, and the respondent indicates whether he likes, dislikes, or has no opinion regarding each activity. These responses are then compared to those of persons in various professional and business occupations. The KOIS measures interest in broad occupational areas such as mechanical, scientific, persuasive, and social science. Each item lists three activities, and respondents indicate the activity in which they would most like to engage and the activity in which they would least like to engage.

Categorizing Assessment Options by How the Results Are Interpreted

Using Referents to Give Results Meaning

Assessment results, regardless of the source or type, need a referent to give them meaning. In educational assessment, a *referent* is a set of ideas or concepts that provides context for the results. A test score, for example, in and of itself means nothing. Referents help people to understand the assessment results and to make them meaningful. Two types of referents are usually needed to provide adequate context for interpreting assessment results: the skill or knowledge content area in which the student was assessed (*content referent*), and to whom or what the results are compared (*comparison referent*). If, for example, I tell you that Hermie got 18 correct, what does that tell you about Hermie's performance? Without a referent, absolutely nothing. Now if I tell you that a score of 17 was required for a mastery classification for certain instructional outcomes in second-grade mathematics, you don't know anything about the performance of the rest of the class, but you do know that Hermie attained mastery in math. If, instead, I tell you that the average score on the test was 15, at least you know that he did better than average in math.

The above "ifs" actually illustrate the two basic comparison referents for interpreting assessment results: criterion-referenced and norm-referenced (see Figure 2.3). When the comparison referent is one or more pre-specified criteria, we use the term *criterion-referenced assessment* (CRA) or refer to a criterion-referenced test (CRT); when the referent is the performance of a comparison group, we use the term *norm-referenced assessment* (NRA) or refer to a norm-referenced test (NRT). In a criterion-referenced approach, the results for each student are compared to predetermined, fixed criteria. In a norm-referenced approach, the results of each student are compared to the results of others who took the same test. The kind of interpretations we ultimately wish to make affects both the development and analysis of assessment instruments, although the results of criterion-referenced tests are sometimes used to make norm-referenced interpretations, and the results of norm-referenced tests are sometimes used to make criterion-referenced interpretations.

Criterion-Referenced Assessment

Any assessment that interprets and reports each student's score, not in comparison to another student's score, but in terms of predetermined criteria, is *criterion-referenced*. In criterion-referenced assessment, one student's score has nothing to do with any other student's score; the score is instead reported in terms of a set of fixed constructs, dimensions, or categories under which the performance is judged. Thus, when criterion-referenced standards are used, all students taking the test may do "well," achieving most or all the instructional outcomes, or all may do "poorly."

Interpretation Approach	Comparison Referent	Hermie's Score	Comparison Score	Interpretation
CR	Objectives assessed by the test	18	Mastery = 17	Hermie attained mastery
NR	Performance of other students	18	Average = 15	Hermie did better than average

Figure 2.3
A comparison of criterion-referenced and norm-referenced approaches to the interpretation of Hermie's score.

Defining Criterion-Referenced

Not all assessment experts concur that *criterion-referenced* is the best term for this method of score interpretation based on predetermined, fixed criteria of performance. There is disagreement over both the proper nature of the criteria and over the best way to describe them. Thus, you will see the terms *domain-referenced* and *objectives-referenced,* defined below, used in various contexts.

As originally defined by Glaser in 1963, criterion-referenced assessments are those that "depend upon an absolute standard of quality," as contrasted with norm-referenced assessments that "depend upon a relative standard."[15] He later expanded on his original definition by defining a criterion-referenced test as "one that is deliberately constructed to yield measurement that is directly interpretable in terms of specified performance standards."[16] According to this definition, criterion-referenced assessment is essentially the same as what is referred to as *domain-referenced* measurement, and in fact, a criterion-referenced test is used to compare a person's performance with a well-defined behavior domain. A well-defined behavior domain, according to Popham, refers to a class of learner behaviors (such as the ability to multiply correctly any pair of single-digit numbers) rather than a specific behavior (such as can multiply correctly 5 × 7).[17]

Objectives-referenced assessment (ORA) is assessment in which specific items or performance tasks are keyed to specific instructional outcomes. Whether objectives-referenced assessment is essentially the same as criterion-referenced assessment (CRA) depends on the nature of the outcomes. If the outcomes upon which the items and tasks are based are expressed in terms of clearly defined classes of behavior,

---

[15]"Instructional Technology and the Measurement of Learning Outcomes" by R. Glaser, 1963, *American Psychologist, 18,* p. 519.

[16]"Measurement in Learning and Instruction" by R. Glaser and A. J. Nitko, in *Educational Measurement* (p. 653) by R. L. Thorndike (Ed.), 1971, Washington, DC: American Council on Education.

[17]*Educational Evaluation* (3rd ed.) by W. J. Popham, 1993, Upper Saddle River, NJ: Prentice Hall.

then ORA = CRA. But such is not always the case. In all too many instances, instructional outcomes are overly specific, of the "can multiply 5 × 7" variety. In reality, most assessments that are called criterion-referenced are objectives-referenced. Whether such assessments are truly criterion-referenced depends on the wording of the outcomes.

What difference does it make if an assessment is labeled a criterion-referenced assessment or an objectives-referenced assessment? Well, it does not matter what we call an assessment, but it does matter how it was developed. The difference is in the interpretation of results. If a test contains items based on objectives of the "can multiply 5 × 7" variety, then the results are very limited in generalizability in terms of what the student has actually achieved. On the other hand, if a test contains items that represent a class of behaviors (like "can multiply any pair of one-digit numbers"), the results are generalizable to the whole class of behaviors. This second type of test is clearly preferable. Although many feel strongly that *domain-referenced* is the most accurate way to describe such assessments, and although technically speaking some assessments do not meet the definition, because of common usage I will henceforth use the term *criterion-referenced* to include all situations in which the results are interpreted relative to predetermined, fixed criteria of performance.

Clarifying the Relationship of Criterion-Referenced Assessments to Mastery and Non-Mastery Tests

A common misconception is the belief that all criterion-referenced tests are, by definition, mastery tests. This misconception is a result of confusion concerning the meaning of the term *criterion,* as in criterion-referenced test. Many have interpreted it to mean some required, minimum level of performance or cut-off score, as in pass = 75%. However, Glaser's original intent was for *criterion* to refer to a domain of behaviors assessing an outcome, not to a number. Actually, a criterion-referenced test may or may not have a cut-off score. A criterion-referenced test with a cut-off score is a *mastery test;* if a student has achieved a given cut-off score, say 8 out of 10 correct, we say that the student has attained or demonstrated mastery. Thus, all mastery tests are criterion-referenced tests, but not all criterion-referenced tests are mastery tests (see Figure 2.4). Most criterion-referenced tests are, in fact, not mastery tests. The majority of mastery tests are administered at the elementary-school level.

Of course, setting a minimum cut-off score is a tricky business. If it is set too low, you run the risk of classifying some individuals as "masters" when in reality they are not (called *false positives*). If it is set too high, you are in danger of classifying some students as "non-masters" when in reality they are (called *false negatives*). For classroom assessment, the level of achievement equated with mastery usually depends on the source of the test. District-produced or textbook publisher–provided tests typically indicate the number correct that represents mastery. For teacher-developed tests, the decision is made by the teacher, based on professional judgment. If some students do not achieve mastery, the teacher must decide whether further instruction and practice are in order or the cut-off score is

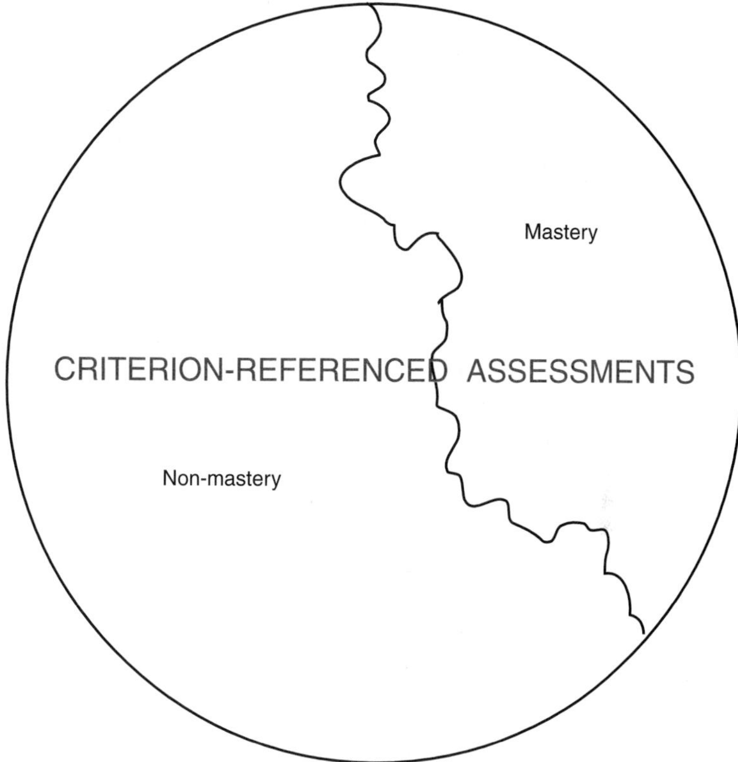

Figure 2.4
Mastery and non-mastery tests as subsets of criterion-referenced tests. Most criterion-referenced tests are non-mastery; most mastery tests are administered at the elementary-school level.

unrealistically high. Although this is not always an easy question, factors such as knowledge of student characteristics, the outcomes being assessed, and a little experience usually combine to produce a reasonably sound decision. For a high-priority instructional outcome such as "Given a paragraph, identifies the main idea," additional efforts will typically be made to bring as many students as possible to a mastery level.

As noted, most criterion-referenced tests are not mastery tests, nor should they be. Mastery tests are appropriate for basic, essential skills, skills for which it is both important and feasible for most students to demonstrate achievement. For a non-mastery, criterion-referenced test, there is no cut-off score and scores may vary greatly, representing a wide range of achievement or degree of mastery. For the outcome "Differentiates between valid and invalid conclusions," for example, you may not expect most students to "master" the skill. For a related test, however, the decision would still have to be made concerning whether "enough" students did "well enough." If only half the class could correctly classify at least 7 of 10 conclusions, you would probably devote additional instructional time to the outcome. If, on the other hand, most students did reasonably well, you would probably "move on."

Thus, a major difference between mastery and non-mastery criterion-referenced tests is your expectations concerning level of achievement and the proportion of students who achieve that level. For a mastery test, the focus is on the individual; you want every student to achieve at a high level. For a non-mastery test, the focus is on the group; you want at least a majority of the students to do reasonably well. Of course, what constitutes "reasonably well" is a matter for teacher judgment.

Applying Criterion-Referenced Assessment to Instructional Situations

Although the basic concept of criterion-referenced standards was not new at the time, interest in and use of criterion-referenced tests grew steadily following Glaser's 1963 article. The growth in use of criterion-referenced tests understandably paralleled the increased interest in objectives. The popularity of criterion-referenced tests was also fostered as a result of rising criticism of the use of norm-referenced assessments, especially standardized ones, for making judgments about students.

Unhappiness with norm-referenced assessments is still a strong force in education today, but enthusiasm for criterion-referenced assessment is not universal either, and teachers are still searching for "perfect" assessment tools. Critics generally seem to feel that in criterion-referenced assessment too much attention is placed on lower-level outcomes at the expense of higher-level outcomes. Their concern relates to misuse of criterion-referenced assessment rather than to the usefulness of criterion-referenced assessment itself, though. There are clearly situations in which undue emphasis is placed on the mastery of certain "basic" skills. These situations, however, do not invalidate the soundness of the concept of criterion-referencing, and the majority opinion is that criterion-referenced assessment is quite useful and more appropriate than norm-referenced assessment in a number of situations. In the field of medical education, for example, criterion-referenced assessment is widely accepted and applied; it matters little if a doctor was "above average" in surgery, as long as she can correctly remove a ruptured appendix.

Similarly, criterion-referenced assessment is appropriate for most, if not all, instructional situations. The use of learning outcomes and criterion-referenced assessment gives direction to instruction and allows us to assess how we are doing—that is, to determine to what degree students are achieving intended outcomes. Because criterion-referenced assessment permits pinpointing of areas of difficulty with respect to specific outcomes, corresponding instructional strategies and materials can be readily identified and modified. For certain instructional systems (like mastery or individualized), criterion-referenced assessment is an excellent approach as a result of its focused attention on what each individual student can or cannot do relative to the criteria for success.

Norm-Referenced Assessment

Any assessment, standardized or not, that reports and interprets each student's score in terms of its relative position to other scores on the same assessment is *norm-referenced.* If your total IQ score based on the Wechsler Adult Intelligence Scale–Revised is 100, for example, the interpretation is that your assessed intelligence is average—average *compared to* scores of people in the norm group. The raw scores resulting from administration of a standardized norm-referenced assessment are typically converted to some other index indicating relative position. One such equivalent probably familiar to you is a percentile. A given percentile indicates the percentage of the scores that were lower than the percentile's corresponding score. For example, a raw score of 42 on an achievement test might be equivalent to the 54th percentile, which would mean that 54 percent of the raw scores were lower than 42. Thus, if you scored at the 95th percentile, your score was higher than 95% of the scores. If your score was "average," what do you think your percentile would be? Right! The 50th percentile. Of course, none of these figures says anything about your absolute achievement. There is no indication of what you know and can do, or do not know and cannot do. The only interpretations are in terms of your achievement compared to the achievements of others.

Norm-Referenced Assessment and the Normal Curve Concept

Norm-referenced standards are based on the assumption that assessed traits involve normal curve properties. The normal curve and its characteristics will be discussed in greater detail in Chapter 11, but the basic concept can be explained here. The idea is that a trait, let us say math aptitude, exists in different amounts in different students. Some students have a lot of it, some have a little of it, and most have some amount called an "average" amount. Now, if you gave a math aptitude test to lots and lots of students and plotted their scores, you would get a normal curve, sometimes referred to as a bell curve because of its shape (see Figure 2.5). Most of the scores (the highest frequency) are average, fewer scores are above or below average, and very few are far above or far below average. If a trait forms a *normal curve,*

Figure 2.5
A normal curve.

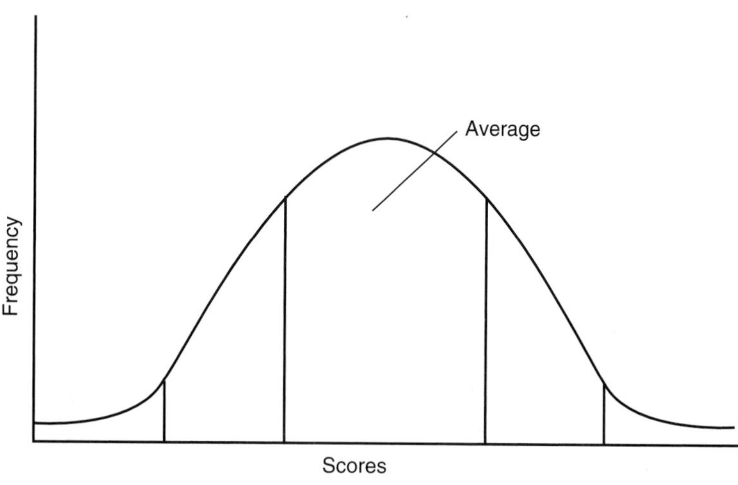

then the percentages in each section, or division, are constant. The average group always contains approximately 65% of the scores (68.26 to be exact); the above average group and below average group each contain approximately 15% of the scores; and the far above and far below groups each contain approximately 2.5% of the scores. Some of you may be familiar with "grading on the curve." In its extreme form, the above percentages are sometimes applied to scores to determine grades. Thus the top 2% to 3% of the scores become As, the next 15% Bs, the next 65% Cs, and so forth.

Norm-Referenced Assessment and Score Variability

With a few exceptions, standardized tests are norm-referenced. Norm groups are selected with the intention of having a representative group with a wide spread of scores regarding the trait being measured. As mentioned previously, results are subject to misinterpretation to the degree that students taking a test are different from those in the norm group. When standardized tests are designed and developed, the intent is to include items that will produce a wide spread of scores and discriminate among test takers; that is, items of average difficulty. If, for example, a tryout of a new test reveals a number of items that almost everyone gets correct (or incorrect), they will probably be eliminated. Thus, there is typically much more score variability than is usual for a classroom test; teachers rarely discard items and performance tasks just because most students got the items correct or performed the tasks well. This variability permits appropriate application of a number of score-analysis techniques. As you will see in Chapter 3, for example, all classical approaches to computing test reliability require score variability: the more, the better.

The results of standardized tests are frequently used for classification or selection purposes, and a good spread of scores facilitates decision making. To use an example that may be painfully familiar to you, scores on the Scholastic Assessment Test (SAT) and the Graduate Record Exam (GRE) are each frequently used as a criterion for admission to undergraduate and graduate school, respectively. Everyone who wants to cannot go to a specific college or graduate school because there is not enough room and there are not enough resources. Scores on the SAT and GRE have been shown to be related to some degree to performance in post-secondary school. Most of us agree that using SAT and GRE scores as data for selection purposes is better than having students draw straws or participate in a lottery (probably!). Therefore, a high score increases the probability of admission and a low score decreases the probability of admission. If these tests did not permit discrimination among people—that is, if scores were very homogeneous—they could not be used for selection purposes. Similarly, the results of standardized assessments are used for purposes such as grouping according to aptitude, determining who will receive scholarships, and counseling students about career decisions. These uses of the results are possible only because the tests do a good job of ordering students on a wide continuum of performance.

Applying Norm-Referenced Assessment to Instructional Situations

As discussed earlier, there is opposition to the use of norm-referenced assessments, especially standardized ones, for making judgments about students. However, although they definitely should not be used exclusively, they do serve several useful purposes in addition to those described above. Students are indeed different. They do possess different traits to varying degrees. It is helpful to both the student and society to know where a student's relative strengths and weaknesses lie. Furthermore, the real world is norm-referenced, and students should learn to adjust to that fact. Employers, for example, do not say, "If you do X amount of work, or just do your best, you will get a nice raise." Rather, those who do the best work, relative to others, are more likely to get the best raises (at least theoretically!).

So how does norm-referenced score interpretation relate to mastery systems? In such a system the intent is that nearly everyone achieves mastery; they just take different amounts of time to get there. The mastery concept is a good one for certain "essentials." But even in such a system there is score variability. If a mastery score is 16 out of 20, then some students will score 20, some 19, some 18, some 17, and some 16, and the amount of time taken to achieve mastery will vary tremendously. The variability is typically not reflected in grading procedures, although it could be. Grades could be assigned on a norm-referenced basis to reflect, for example, time or attempts required to achieve mastery, but this is not usually done.

Further, knowing the performance of students in a given class, even if all students are achieving all objectives, does not tell us how well those students are doing compared to the rest of the world (figuratively speaking!). This information is valuable feedback for teachers and other school personnel, and it is information that individual students and their parents have a right to know. Thus, although the results of a norm-referenced test (a standardized achievement battery, for example) do not tell us nearly as much about actual level of performance as a criterion-referenced classroom assessment, they do provide information regarding relative performance, which is of value to individuals for personal reasons and for decision making.

Comparing Criterion-Referenced Assessment and Norm-Referenced Assessment

The basic difference between criterion-referenced assessment and norm-referenced assessment is in the interpretation of results; criterion-referenced assessment uses pre-specified levels of performance as its comparison referent, and norm-referenced assessment uses the scores of others as its comparison referent. On a criterion-referenced test, one's performance is judged on its own merits, not in relation to the performance of others. Because the purpose of criterion-referenced assessment is to determine a level of proficiency with respect to knowledge or skill, variability is irrelevant or even undesirable; considerable variability typically indicates a number of persons who are not achieving the intended objectives. On the other hand, because the results of norm-referenced tests are used to differentiate among students, score

Difference Variable	CRA	NRA
Score interpretation comparison referents	Pre-specified, fixed categories, levels, dimensions of performance	Scores of others who also took the test
Score variability	Irrelevant or undesirable	Desirable
Item/task difficulty	Outcomes dependent	Average is desirable
Size of group tested	Smaller	Larger

Figure 2.6
Summary of the differences between criterion-referenced assessment and norm-referenced assessment.

variability is important. Relatedly, criterion-referenced tests contain items and tasks of whatever difficulty level is necessary to assess achievement of the intended outcomes. Norm-referenced tests contain mostly items and tasks that discriminate—that is, ones that are neither too easy nor too difficult. Also, usually criterion-referenced assessment is concerned with the performance of smaller groups, such as a class, and in the case of mastery learning it is concerned with the performance of individual students. Norm-referenced assessment, on the other hand, usually involves assessing the performance of large groups of students. These differences are summarized in Figure 2.6. Each is useful when administered in appropriate situations.

Interestingly, criterion-referenced and norm-referenced assessments look alike. You could probably not tell by looking at a test whether it was a criterion-referenced test or a norm-referenced test. The differences are in the purposes for which each is constructed and in the interpretation of results. Neither one is preferred in all cases. Which is more appropriate depends upon the situation and the decisions to be made. Criterion-referenced assessment is typically more appropriate for student assessment for instructional purposes conducted by the teacher because it focuses on exactly what was taught. The results are also useful for on-going revision of instructional procedures. Norm-referenced assessment is more appropriate for assessing the performance of larger groups such as that involved in school-level assessment. The results of norm-referenced tests are useful for student-guidance purposes and for classification or grouping decisions.

Summary

Categorizing Assessment Options

To select assessment methods appropriate for instructional decisions such as providing feedback or diagnosing group or individual learning needs, teachers need to

know the range of options. There are many ways to classify assessments based on their characteristics. One way to classify assessments is according to variables related to administration: group or individual tests. Another way is to classify tests according to difficulty-vs.-time variables. A *speed test* is one in which the time limit is fixed and the test items or performance tasks are of low difficulty. A *power test* is one where the items or tasks vary in difficulty and are usually arranged in order of increasing difficulty from very easy to very difficult, and the time limit is generous. A *mastery test* is one in which the items or tasks are of low difficulty and the time limit is generous. Another classification scheme is based on type of expected student response: written responses or products or performances. Assessments can also be classified according to who produces them, what is assessed, and how the results are interpreted.

Categorizing Assessment Options by Their Source

There are four sources for the assessments typically used in today's classrooms: teachers, commercial test publishers, individual state departments of education, and textbook publishers. A *teacher-made assessment* is made by a teacher or a group of teachers for a certain content area or set of instructional outcomes for a particular group of students. Teacher-made tests are likely to reflect what was actually taught to a greater degree than assessments from other sources. Paper-and-pencil written tests are the most popular type of teacher-made test. Teachers also observe student performance and evaluate student products because, for many instructional outcomes and areas of learning, use of paper-and-pencil tests is an inappropriate way of assessing students. Rating scales and checklists are useful instruments to help with data gathering when assessing either a performance or a product.

Commercial test publishers are in the business of producing and selling assessment instruments to school districts, state departments of education, counselors, and other specialists and are the largest producers of standardized assessments. A *standardized test* is: (1) developed by subject matter and assessment specialists, (2) field-tested under uniform administration procedures, (3) revised to meet certain acceptability criteria, and (4) scored and interpreted using uniform procedures and standards. Standardized assessments may be performance or product tests, although the majority of them are the paper-and-pencil variety. Psychometric experts and experts in the behavior to be assessed determine the content and format of standardized tests. The vast majority of standardized tests have been administered to groups referred to as *norm groups,* the performance of which for a given test serves as the basis of comparison and interpretation for other groups to whom the test is administered. Norms are usually presented for different kinds of populations to permit more valid comparisons. Norms tables typically include the distribution of raw scores as well as a number of score equivalents such as percentiles and stanines. In recent years, commercial publishers have made an effort to include teachers in the development of standardized assessments, both for their content knowledge and their knowledge of students.

State departments of education are also in the business of making and administering assessments. Not all assessments administered under the auspices of a state department of education are created by in-state experts; they may be put out for bid. As a result of one of the more recent waves of educational reform, some states have shifted from a heavy reliance on multiple-choice, paper-and-pencil tests to include more performance- and product-based assessments.

In recent years textbook publishers have increased the scope of their products to include not only the student text and teacher manual but also reproducible masters for assessment. In many cases, multiple forms of textbook-publisher assessment instruments and comparable tasks are available. There is no guarantee that multiple forms of tests that accompany school textbooks are, indeed, equivalent. To the extent that a teacher uses only a single textbook, teaches only to those instructional outcomes included in the text, and does not supplement with outcomes and materials from other sources, the tests that accompany the textbook series may be adequate for assessment.

Categorizing Assessment Options by the Behaviors and Traits Assessed

Achievement tests assess the present status of individuals' proficiency in given areas of knowledge or skill. The overall category of achievement assessment instruments includes individual tests and batteries, as well as diagnostic tests. Standardized achievement tests are available for many individual curriculum areas such as reading and math, and they also come in the form of comprehensive batteries that measure achievement in several different areas. A *battery* is a series of tests sampling different content areas, each of which is normed on the same group to allow comparisons of individual strengths and weaknesses. When assessment of achievement in a number of areas is needed, it is better to administer a battery than a number of individual tests. Standardized achievement tests, whether they are paper-and-pencil or performance-based, are designed to measure what most teachers cover—that is, content common to many classes of a certain kind. There is no way a commercially produced, standardized test could include items to assess everything that any teacher might include in instruction. There are a number of purposes for which a standardized achievement test is more appropriate than one that is teacher made: when comparing students to others of a similar age or grade level, for guidance purposes, when evaluating the effectiveness of instruction overall, and when large-scale comparisons are to be made between performance at two different points in time.

A *diagnostic test* is a type of achievement assessment that yields multiple scores for each area of achievement diagnosed; these scores facilitate identification of specific areas of deficiency or learning difficulty. Diagnostic tests are administered mainly to identify individual strengths and weaknesses and to identify students in need of remediation. subtests of achievement batteries can be used for diagnosis as a preliminary screening device, although they are not developed for that purpose. Because of the time and skill involved in administering, scoring, and interpreting diagnostic tests, as well as the fact that they are intended to identify specific deficiencies, it is neither desirable nor necessary to administer them to all students. Diagnosis should be an on-going process. In addition to administering a number of informal diagnostic instruments, teachers should constantly be on the alert for signs of physical problems or learning difficulty.

Aptitude tests, both general and specific, are measures of potential used to predict how well someone is likely to perform in a future situation. Tests of general aptitude are variously referred to as scholastic aptitude tests, school ability tests, intelligence tests, IQ tests, and assessments of general mental ability. Educators disagree over whether teachers should have knowledge of students' general aptitude. *General aptitude tests* typically ask the individual to perform a variety of verbal and non-verbal tasks that measure the individual's ability to apply knowledge and solve problems. General aptitude tests may be group tests or individually administered assessments. As the term is generally used, *specific aptitude assessments* attempt to predict the level of performance that can be expected of an individual following future instruction or training in a specific area or areas. A *readiness test* is administered prior to instruction or training in a specific area to determine whether and to what degree a student is ready for, or will profit from, instruction. Due to increased interest in basic skills, reading readiness tests have been given more emphasis than other types.

Attitude assessments, or attitude scales, attempt to determine what an individual believes, perceives, or feels. Because students' attitudes are related to their achievement and because one of the basic goals of public education is the promotion of certain attitudes believed to be desirable in a democratic society, assessment of attitudes is a major concern in the public schools. The most commonly used type of attitude scale was developed by Rensis Likert and asks an individual to respond to a series of statements by indicating whether he strongly agrees (SA), agrees (A), is undecided (U), disagrees (D), or strongly disagrees (SD) with each statement. Assessments of "attitude toward self" are referred to as *measures of self-concept.*

Interest can be assessed in the classroom in the same ways that attitude and other behaviors can—formally or through the use of informal, teacher-made instruments (checklists and rating scales) and observation. The most widely used type of standardized interest measure is the vocational *interest inventory,* which typically asks the respondent to indicate preferences with respect to leisure activities such as hobbies. Counselors compare the respondent's pattern of interest to the patterns of interest typical of successful people in various occupational fields.

Categorizing Assessment Options by How the Results Are Interpreted

Assessment results, regardless of the source or type, need *referents* to give them meaning. In educational assessment, content referents and comparison referents provide context for interpreting results. Two common types of comparison referents are criteria and other people. A *criterion-referenced* approach interprets a student's performance or score as compared to predetermined, fixed criteria. A *norm-referenced* approach interprets a student's performance or score as compared to the results of others who took the same test.

There is disagreement over both the proper nature of criteria as well as over the best way to describe them. The term *domain-referenced* is used to describe the interpretation of assessment results that are compared to a well-defined behavior domain; the term *objectives-referenced* is used to describe the interpretation of results compared to specific instructional objectives. A criterion-referenced test with a cut-off score is a mastery test; thus, all mastery tests are criterion-referenced tests, but not all criterion-referenced tests are mastery tests. Most criterion-referenced tests are not mastery tests. A major difference between mastery and non-mastery criterion-referenced tests is the teacher's expectations concerning levels of achievement and the proportion of students who achieve that level. Critics of criterion-referenced assessments feel that too much attention is placed on lower-level outcomes at the expense of higher-level outcomes. For most instructional situations, criterion-referenced assessment seems to be more appropriate than norm-referenced assessment.

Norm-referenced interpretations are based on the assumption that assessed traits involve *normal curve* properties: some students have a lot of the trait, some have a little of it, and most have some amount called an "average" amount. The results of the assessment are subject to misinterpretation to the degree that students taking a test are different from those in the norm group. The results of standardized tests are frequently used for classification or selection purposes, and a good spread of scores facilitates decision making. Among educators there is opposition to the use of norm-referenced assessments, especially standardized ones, for making judgments about students.

A criterion-referenced test contains items of whatever difficulty level is necessary to measure achievement of the intended outcomes. A norm-referenced test contains mostly items that discriminate—that is, items that are neither too easy nor too difficult. A criterion-referenced assessment is concerned with the performance of smaller groups, such as a class; in the case of mastery learning it is concerned with the performance of individual students. Norm-referenced assessment, in contrast, usually involves assessing the performance of large groups of students.

Try These

I. For each assessment question below, determine the appropriate assessment method and instrument by filling in the accompanying table. Each column represents a decision to be made about the type of test that is appropriate. An example is done for you.

Example: How many of my students (fourth grade) are able to decode words on the fourth-grade word list?

1. Can my students benefit from reading instruction?
2. What careers might be a good fit with what Andy likes to do?
3. Can Darnelle throw a softball from home plate to second base accurately four out of five times?
4. What do our students think about the after-school activities currently offered?
5. How does our school compare to the rest of the country in science instruction?

6. Does Emily know her state capitals?
7. Is Josh likely to do well in a classroom for gifted students?
8. Can my second-period students use a microscope properly and safely?
9. How many students achieved the objectives of Unit 8 of the social studies book?
10. Does Nadine have a low self-concept?
11. Why is Nat having difficulty reducing improper fractions?
12. Did Shelby master the intended outcomes?
13. Do my students have the prerequisite knowledge required by the instructional unit I am about to teach?
14. How many simple shapes can Enrique place correctly into the form board in 3 minutes?
15. Is Angel still having trouble writing a coherent paragraph?

Item	**Speed** **Power** **Mastery**	**Group** **Indiv.**	**Paper and** **Pencil** **Perform** **Product**	**Teacher** **Test Publisher** **State** **Text Publisher**	**Achievement** **Aptitude** **Attitude** **Interest**	**CR** **NR**
Ex	*P*	*Indiv.*	*Perform*	*Teacher*	*Achievement*	*CR*
1						
2						
3						
4						
5						
6						
7						
8						
9						
10						
11						
12						
13						
14						
15						

II. For each of the following statements, indicate whether it is true for:
Criterion-referenced assessments only (C)
Norm-referenced assessments only (N)
Both (B)

_____ 1. Can be used to assess achievement.

_____ 2. Used to determine a student's level of achievement in comparison to a fixed standard.

_____ 3. Reports level of achievement in relative terms.
_____ 4. Can be used to assess mastery of a set of instructional outcomes.
_____ 5. Is used to compare one student's performance to that of other students who took the same test.
_____ 6. Can be used to put students into flexible learning groups.
_____ 7. Reports a student's performance in absolute terms.
_____ 8. Requires score variability.
_____ 9. Attempts to spread students out across a continuum of performance.
_____ 10. At times has been called domain-referenced and objectives-referenced.
_____ 11. Provides a basis for interpretation of scores.
_____ 12. Provides important information concerning students.

Answers

I.

Item	Speed Power Mastery	Group Indiv.	Paper and Pencil Perform Product	Teacher Test Publisher State Text Publisher	Achievement Aptitude Attitude Interest	CR NR
1	P	G	P&P	Test Pub	Aptitude	NR
2	P	G/I	P&P	Test Pub	Interest	NR
3	M	I	Perform	Teacher	Achievement	CR
4	P	G	P&P	Teacher	Attitude	CR
5	P	G	all	Test Pub	Achievement	NR
6	P	G/I	P&P	Teacher	Achievement	CR
7	P	I	Perform	Test Pub	Aptitude	NR
8	P	I	Perform	Teacher	Achievement	CR
9	P	G	P&P	Text Pub	Achievement	CR
10	P	G/I	P&P	Test Pub	Attitude	NR
11	P	I	P&P	Test Pub	Achievement	CR
12	M	G/I	all	Teacher	Achievement	CR
13	P	G	P&P	Teach/Text Pub	Achievement	CR
14	S	I	Perform	Test Pub	Achievement	CR/NR
15	P	G/I	Product	Teacher/Text Pub	Achievement	CR

II. 1. B, 2. C, 3. N, 4. C, 5. N, 6. B, 7. C, 8. N, 9. N, 10. C, 11. B, 12. B

CHAPTER 3

Assessment in the Classroom

Key Concepts:

- The on-going and cyclical nature of assessment activities before, during, and after instruction.
- The validity of the interpretations of assessment results: types of evidence, how each is established, and when each type is important.
- The concept of correlation and how it is used in determining the quality of an assessment.
- The reliability of the interpretations of assessment results: types of estimates, how each is established, and when each type is important.
- The concepts of true score and assessment error.
- The interpretation of correlation, validity, and reliability coefficients.
- The concept of standard error of measurement, its relationship to true score, and the derivation of confidence intervals and bands.

Standards Addressed in This Chapter:

1. Choose assessment methods appropriate for instructional decisions.
2. Develop assessment methods appropriate for instructional decisions.
3. Recognize unethical, illegal, and otherwise inappropriate assessment methods and uses of assessment information.

Before You Begin Reading, Consider This

What if a teacher carefully examined the tests supplied with the textbook series he was using and found them to parallel the text well, but not assess learning for all of the important skills and knowledge he had included in a unit he intends to teach? Should he stick to using the publisher's tests?

YES The publisher's tests probably cover enough important material to assess whether students grasped at least most of the ideas and concepts taught. The quality of the items is also probably better than what the teacher could put together in the little time he may have for such things.

NO The publisher's tests should be thrown out in favor of an assessment constructed by the teacher. Otherwise, important knowledge and skills will not be assessed and the teacher will have no indication of whether his students acquired them.

The On-Going Nature of Assessment

Teachers are constantly making evaluative decisions about their students. Good decisions require good information; thus, the assessment of students and their learning is a continuous process. Teachers gather information about their individual students and classes in many ways, some formal, some informal. They watch. They listen. They administer tests. They evaluate projects. They ask questions. They pose problems for solution. They interview students, either as a group or individually. Figure 3.1 contains a sample of these decisions teachers make, posed as questions.

Teachers should plan assessments before any teaching begins, and they should continue to use assessments throughout the instructional process to guide their actions and decisions. That's right: assessment is conducted at the beginning, in the middle, and at the end of instruction, if there is an end. The schematic in Figure 3.2 illustrates that there is typically a series of temporary "ends" in a continuous cycle. For example, you start your teaching effort with a set of instructional outcomes. Then you design and implement instructional strategies to facilitate their achievement. Then you assess achievement—a temporary end in the instructional cycle. Based on the results, you review (and, perhaps, revise) your instructional outcomes and strategies and proceed. Thus, the process is cyclic, with feedback from one cycle guiding the next. Teachers should not just assess outcomes; every stage of the process should be subject to assessment, beginning with the outcomes.

The Phases of Assessment

Any instructional endeavor involves a whole host of decisions that must be made, including decisions about outcomes, strategies, and assessment. Each phase of evaluation involves different kinds of decisions. These various decisions can be

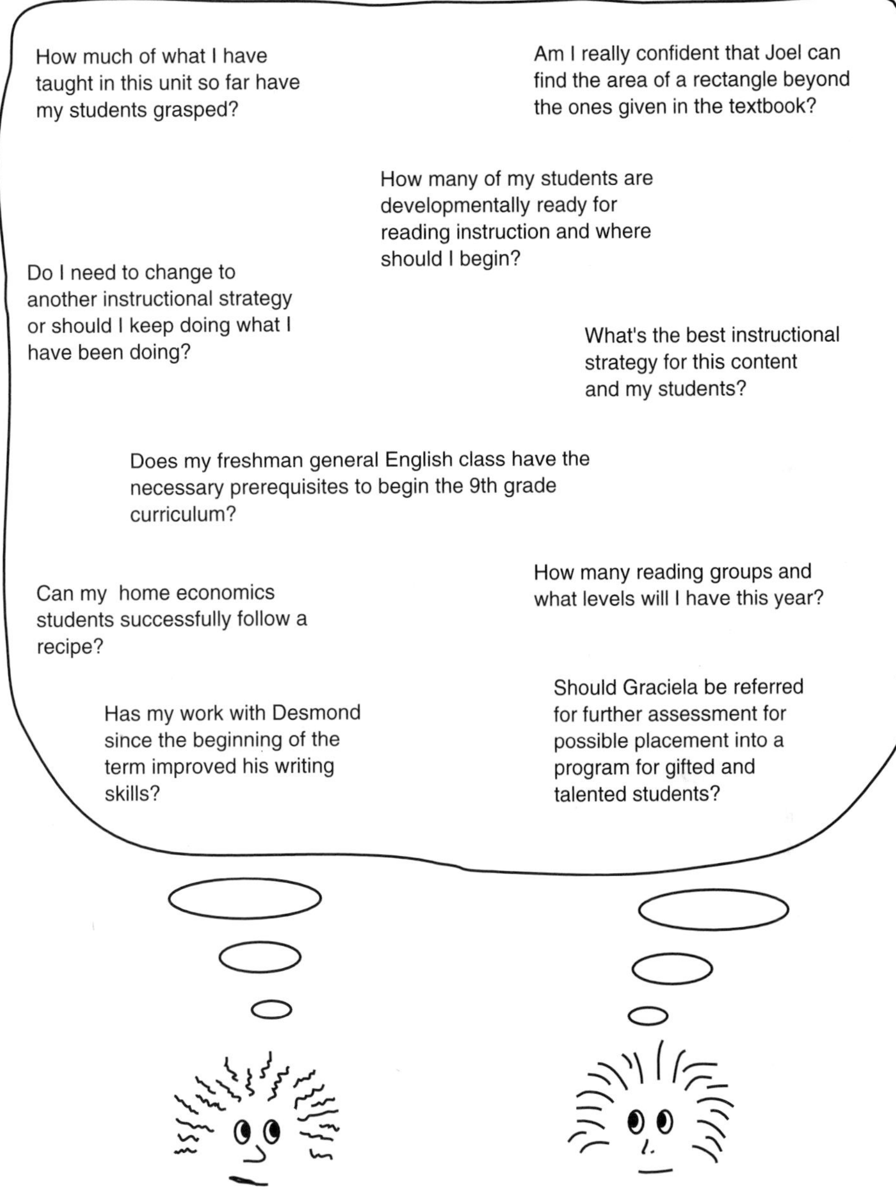

Figure 3.1
A few of the many decisions teachers make that require assessment data.

classified by stages of the instructional process: before, during, and after instruction (see Figure 3.2). The planning phase before instruction deals with "What will we do?" questions; the process phase during instruction asks "How are we doing?"; and the after-instruction phase is concerned with "How have we done?" A

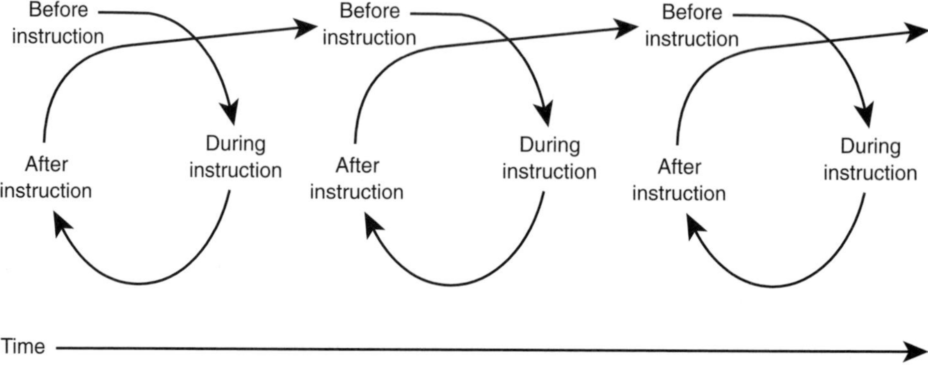

Figure 3.2
The cyclic nature of assessment and decision making in the instructional and student evaluation processes over time.

discussion of the events in each of the three phases of student evaluation follows. Keep in mind that the process of decision making is basically the same, regardless of what is being evaluated.

Assessment Issues to Consider Before Instruction

This initial phase of evaluating student learning takes place prior to actual teaching and involves making decisions about what course of action will be taken toward what ends. The activities in the planning phase include: the analysis of the learning environment and the students' characteristics, the specification of goals and instructional outcomes, the selection and/or development of assessment instruments, the delineation of teaching strategies and activities for attainment of the outcomes, and the preparation of a lesson plan or time schedule. Although the delineation of teaching strategies and activities and the preparation of lesson plans are important, they are typically covered in separate college-level courses and so are not explained here.

Analyzing the Situation. Prior to teaching, it is important to analyze the instructional situation as it presently exists to establish the limitations of your teaching effort. This step includes activities such as finding out background information on students (like their reading levels) and determining the existing constraints that limit what and how you can teach. This will probably first involve examining the cumulative records of your students in order to establish a frame of reference based on their abilities and histories. This information may be enhanced if portfolios of each student's work are available. Constraints and resources need to be carefully reviewed to make reasonable decisions concerning the feasibility of varying courses of action. You do not want to plan for something you cannot afford or cannot obtain. A math teacher, for example, cannot plan to use pocket calculators if the school cannot afford them; a football coach cannot plan Saturday morning practice sessions if the school is closed on weekends; a history teacher cannot plan to use videocassettes in instruction on the Civil War if video equipment and tapes are not available or obtainable within the given budget.

Analysis of the instructional situation would not be complete without identifying the students in your class with disabilities and the accommodation requirements of those students with regard to assessment. The advice of Richard Fischer applies to most such situations—the best way to get information about students' disabilities and instructional and assessment needs is to ask the students (and their parents) up front, because such knowledge is crucial to establishing workable accommodations.[1] Specific strategies for accommodating students with disabilities will be discussed later in this text.[2]

After a complete analysis of the learning environment and the proposed instructional event, more realistic goals and outcomes can be formulated.

Specifying Desired Outcomes. Goals are general statements of purpose typically phrased so that they are not directly observable; each goal is then translated into one or more specific outcomes or objectives, which are observable. *Instructional outcomes* are specific statements supplying information about what is to be accomplished and how well and are expressed in terms of student behaviors that can be observed or otherwise sensed. The desire "to improve arithmetic achievement level" is a goal, whereas the statement "All students will be able to add correctly any three two-digit numbers" is an outcome.

Outcomes serve as the "guiding light" for students and teachers. They tell students exactly what is expected of them, thus allowing them to focus their efforts appropriately. They give direction to all instruction and to subsequent assessment. Because instructional outcomes form the foundation of all subsequent evaluation activities, it is critical that they themselves be evaluated in terms of relevance, assessability, substance, and technical accuracy.[3]

Specifying Prerequisites. In most cases, specification of a given set of instructional outcomes is based on the assumption that students have acquired certain skills and knowledge beforehand. If the assumption is incorrect, then the outcomes are not appropriate. These assumed behaviors are referred to as prerequisites or entry behaviors. Systematic instruction and evaluation require that these prerequisites be specified and assessed. Assessment of entry behaviors is especially important at the beginning of the school year or at the beginning of any new unit of instruction when you do not have firsthand knowledge concerning the present capabilities of your students. Knowing what students were allegedly taught last year is not good enough. Even if they really did learn everything they were supposed to, there is no guarantee that they retained it. Substantial research evidence indicates there is considerable

---

[1]"The Americans with Disabilities Act: Implications for Measurement" by R. J. Fischer, 1994, *Educational Measurement: Issues and Practice, 13* (3), 17–26, 37.

[2]See especially the section "Assessing Students with Disabilities" in Chapter 13.

[3]Chapter 4 deals with creating and using instructional outcomes effectively.

forgetting over periods of time such as summer vacation. There is not enough research evidence yet to draw any conclusions about the effects of "four-by-four" scheduling[4] on student retention of material, but an 18-week semester is longer than any summer vacation.

To arrive at prerequisites, ask yourself the following question: What must my students know or be able to do prior to instruction so that they may benefit from instruction and achieve my outcomes? You can teach division, for example, from September to June, but students will never learn how to divide if they do not know how to add, subtract, and multiply. If you find through observation or formal assessment that a number of students do not possess one or more specified prerequisite capabilities, then your outcomes must be revised; more than likely, new ones will be added that must be achieved before instruction on the original set begins. Whether students possess the necessary prerequisites is generally determined by administering a test of entry behaviors.

Selecting and Developing Assessment Instruments. More often than not, determining the degree of student achievement of outcomes requires the administration of one or more assessment instruments.[5] Instrument development is not a task that should be taken lightly. It may not take much to develop a test or checklist, but it does take considerable time, effort, and skill to develop a "good" one! Developing good instruments takes skill in assessment. The mere fact that thousands of assessments are developed each year by thousands of people with little skill does not alter that premise. True, a teacher must, of necessity, develop a myriad of instruments during a school year, each suited to her particular needs and outcomes. But the value of the results of such instruments is questionable at best when they are developed by people who lack the proper preparation. It is more than a little unnerving to think of all those decisions about all those students being made on the basis of results from all those poor assessments. By studying the contents of this book, you are taking an important step in developing your own assessment skills.

At a very minimum, posttests of desired behavior are required. After some appropriate period of time has elapsed or following a unit of instruction, achievement of the objectives must be assessed. Thus, normally such a test will include no more or no less than the outcomes dictate. Also, administering a pretest of the same material prior to instruction is almost always a good idea. Unless you are very sure that students have no knowledge or skill related to your intended outcomes, it is a good idea to assess what they may already know, both as a group and as individuals. It gives you a baseline with which to compare posttest results and an indication of where to concentrate your teaching efforts. You may find, for example, that most of your students have already achieved a given outcome.

---

[4]Four-by-four scheduling concentrates instruction in a given semester on fewer subjects, but for a longer period of instructional time each day. In one variation, high school students take four courses per semester for a total of eight courses for the year. There are 5 to 15 minutes between classes, each of which is 90 minutes long. Thus a student will earn a full credit in science, for example, by completing Biology I in the first half of 10th grade.

[5]Teachers' assessment options are reviewed in Chapter 2.

Also, as previously indicated, assessment of entry behaviors is recommended. Such a test must measure any skill or knowledge that is prerequisite to understanding forthcoming instruction and that cannot be safely assumed to be possessed by students. These assessments of entry behaviors differ from pretests because they assess skills and knowledge that students should have acquired prior to the intended instruction. A pretest, in contrast, covers the outcomes you intend to teach. Future instructional activities will depend upon how many students do or do not possess the necessary prerequisites and upon what they already know about the subject. All needed instruments should be identified prior to teaching, but they are not necessarily all available at that time, especially if one or more must be developed. Posttests, for example, may be developed during the teaching phase.

Assessment Issues to Consider During Instruction

During the instructional process, teachers make decisions based upon the events that occur around them. In individualized instruction programs, the results of initial assessments are used to make decisions concerning optimal placement of each student; different students start at different points in the curriculum depending upon their entering level of proficiency. Following initial assessment, the teacher executes planned instructional strategies and activities in the predetermined sequence. Data collected during this phase provide feedback concerning whether execution is taking place as planned and whether the strategies and activities are effective. In other words, teachers might ask themselves the following questions: Are we "on track"? Am I doing what I said I was going to do? If I am, is it working? If it is not, what can I do about it? What should I do differently from now on? The basic purposes of this phase are to determine whether the teaching effort is being executed as intended, to determine the degree of student achievement, and to identify ways in which improvements can be made. If several teaching strategies are being used simultaneously, then at various points decisions will be made as to which ones are working and which are not. A teacher might conclude, for example, that less time should be spent on teacher-generated board examples, an activity that fails to hold students' attention for very long, and more time should be spent on small-group problem solving, an activity that students seem to enjoy and profit from.

Very few efforts work out exactly as planned. There is nothing wrong with making changes in midstream if the end result will be improved. If you observe your students and see, for example, that your instructional strategy is not working, it is your responsibility to make some revisions in method or material. After all, the goal is student learning, not a perfectly executed lesson plan. The whole purpose of student evaluation during this phase is to guide future activities for the sake of improvement. Further, the same data that provide feedback to you also provide feedback to the students. Each student can evaluate his own progress in various areas and make decisions as to how, and how much, energy will be expended in each area. Feedback, such as a high quiz score, also provides students with reinforcement for learning.

Assessment Issues to Consider Following Instruction

This phase involves making decisions at the end of instruction or, more likely, at the end of one unit or cycle of instruction. Decisions made during this phase are typically based on the results of formal assessments (of achievement, attitude, and behavior, for example). The major purpose of this phase is to collect data in order to make decisions concerning the overall effectiveness of instruction. During this phase, teachers determine to what degree the intended instructional outcomes were achieved, what to do next, and what the implications are for future cycles of instruction.

The results of the post-instructional phase of student evaluation are used in at least three major ways. First, they provide feedback and direction to all teachers and students who were involved; thus, each cycle of an activity benefits from analysis of the outcomes of the previous cycle. Second, post-instructional assessments provide feedback to outside decision makers such as parents and principals. Third, depending upon the type of assessment involved, different groups can utilize the results. Knowledge of student performance, for example, is useful information for guidance and counseling personnel.

Results of assessments following instruction need to be interpreted with care. Failure to achieve instructional outcomes, for example, is not necessarily fatal; degree of achievement needs to be considered. If 95% of your students achieved a set of outcomes, for example, you could consider your teaching a job well done. It is pretty safe to say that all students are not likely to achieve all outcomes, unless they are very low-level outcomes. Although more will be said on this subject later in the text, for now it is enough to say that for any given grade level and subject, there are outcomes that should be achieved by virtually all students and other outcomes for which this expectation is unreasonable.[6]

Determining Quality in Assessment

The results of any assessment, to be useful, should be both valid and reliable. These characteristics are the fundamental concepts of quality in assessment. Other qualities of tests, such as ease of administration or cost, pale in comparison to the importance of assessment validity and reliability; therefore this discussion will focus on them.

Understanding Validity in Interpreting Assessment Results

Validity is the most important concern for any assessment. *Validity* is the degree to which an instrument measures what it is supposed to measure and, consequently, permits appropriate interpretation of scores. When we refer to the validity of an

[6]See Chapter 4 for more on this aspect of instructional outcomes.

assessment, we are usually discussing whether we can use the results as intended. Consider the following situations:

> Based on his students' assessment results, a teacher concludes that most of them have mastered the intended instructional outcomes.
>
> Based on the results of a standardized personality inventory, a counselor refers a student for further psychological testing.

In each case, the quality of the decision is a function of the validity of the assessment involved—that is, the validity of the interpretation made based on the scores. Have you ever taken a test that you thought was unfair? Most people have. At least once in our lives we have received a score we thought did not accurately reflect our level of achievement. If you think back, you probably thought the test was unfair for one or more of the following reasons:

- It wasn't what you expected; it included topics you thought weren't included and hence didn't study.
- The directions or task descriptions were unclear.
- The items were poorly worded, confusing, or ambiguous (or all three!).
- The items or performance tasks were too difficult.
- You didn't have enough time.

These factors, and others like them, are all related to validity. If an assessment is valid, it will include only appropriate, well-constructed tasks, and it will have clear directions and a reasonable time limit.

A common misconception is that an assessment *is* or *is not* valid, period. An assessment is not intrinsically valid; it is *valid for a particular purpose and for a particular group*. The question is not whether an assessment is "valid or invalid" but, rather, if it is "valid for what and for whom." A measuring cup is a valid instrument for measuring liquid volume. It is invalid for measuring the height of a table. Similarly, a test of biology achievement is not very likely to be a valid personality test. It would be obvious to almost anyone looking at a test of biology achievement that the test did not measure any aspect of personality. Determining whether the test was a valid assessment of biology facts and principles is a more difficult task. Likewise, a test that is a valid assessment of vocabulary for high-school students is certainly not a valid assessment for second-graders. Again, this would undoubtedly be self-evident to anyone examining a high-school-level vocabulary test. Whether the test was valid for both ninth-graders and seniors, if either, would not be so obvious.

It is the "valid for whom" concern that is at the heart of the test-bias issue. To the degree that a test is not appropriate for any reason for a given group, to that degree it is invalid for that group. If an assessment is biased, so are the results, and false conclusions are likely to be drawn concerning the status of individuals or groups with respect to the variable assessed. Although bias may result from improper test administration, scoring, or interpretation, the major source of bias is in the assessment itself. For a paper-and-pencil test, for example, the reading level may be too high, or the items may contain unfamiliar vocabulary. When a standardized assessment is developed, every effort is made to include items that are equally "fair" to all students. Certain terms and expressions, however, are bound to be more familiar to certain groups than to others. Some tests include analogy items, for example. If unfamiliar terms are used, some individuals may miss an item not because they don't understand the concept, but because they don't understand the terms. A student living in South Florida or Hawaii might very well miss the following item:

Ignition key is to motor as kindling is to ________________.

because of unfamiliarity with the term *kindling*. (The answer is *fire*.) Therefore, assessment designers attempt to balance items so that, for example, some items will be more familiar to northerners and others will be more familiar to southerners.

Validity is a matter of degree, not a characteristic that is present or absent. This is as true for observation instruments such as rating scales and checklists as it is for objective assessments such as multiple-choice tests. An assessment may have low validity, satisfactory validity, or unusually high validity for a particular purpose and for a particular group. Thus, if we speak of an assessment as being a valid measure of something, we are implying that it has at least a satisfactory degree of validity for the purpose and group we have in mind.

Further, validity is a somewhat temporal quality. An assessment that once had adequate validity will not necessarily have it in the future. As demographics and the curriculum change, for example, so must related assessments of achievement.

Distinguishing Among Types of Validity Evidence

Assessments are designed for a variety of purposes, and scores are used to make a number of different kinds of inferences. Depending on how the results will be used—that is, upon the interpretations being made—required evidence of validity varies. There are several major types of evidence of validity: content, construct, concurrent, and predictive. Because of the kind of evidence required for concurrent and predictive purposes, they are collectively referred to as criterion-related. Figure 3.3 summarizes the following discussion regarding the types of validity evidence, how each is established, when the type is important, and major factors affecting the quality of the evidence.

Content Evidence of Validity. *Content evidence of validity* establishes the degree to which a test measures an intended content area or given set of instructional outcomes and is of prime importance for achievement assessments. Content evidence includes both item/task congruence and appropriate sampling. *Item/task congruence* is concerned with whether the test items or performance tasks represent assessment in the intended content area, and *sampling* is concerned with how well the assessment samples the total content area. A performance test designed to assess biology lab skills might have good task congruence because all the tasks do indeed deal with biology, but it might have poor sampling validity if all the tasks deal only with safety procedures.

Type of Validity Evidence	Description	How Evidence Is Established	Important When . . .	Major Factors Affecting the Evidence
Content	Degree to which an assessment measures a given body of content or set of outcomes	Content area experts judge the match between items or tasks and the intended content area or set of outcomes	Assessing achievement of instructional outcomes; assessing knowledge and skills	Clarity of instructional outcomes; definition of content area; expertise of judges; ability of test maker to create appropriate tasks for content and students; number of items/tasks per sub-area or outcome
Construct	Degree to which an assessment measures a hypothetical, unobservable trait	Research studies over time	Assessing constructs: achievement, anxiety, creativity, intelligence, self-esteem, etc.	Strength of theory underlying construct; how well construct is articulated in behavior; ability of test maker to create appropriate tasks to elicit behavior
Criterion-Related: Concurrent	Degree to which results of one assessment are interchangeable with those of another or with some other criterion	Obtain for the same group at approximately the same time scores on the new assessment and the criterion measure; correlate the two sets of scores	Attempting to substitute one assessment for another established, valid method of assessment	Ability of test maker to create an assessment that is desirable (i.e., cheaper, faster, easier to administer) without sacrificing quality; current state of the assessment art
Criterion-Related: Predictive	Degree to which results of an assessment can be used to predict future performance	Identify criterion; administer the predictor assessment to a group; wait until criterion variable occurs for the same group; obtain an assessment of the criterion; correlate the two sets of scores	Predicting future situations: college and special program admissions; selection; readiness testing; aptitude testing	Length of time between predictor and criterion variables

Figure 3.3
Summary of types of validity evidence.

A test with good content evidence of validity adequately samples the appropriate content area in both breadth and depth. This is important because we cannot possibly assess each and every aspect of a certain content area using all the alternative assessment strategies available; the required assessment would be enormously long. And yet we do wish to make inferences about performance in the entire content area based on performance on the items and tasks included in the assessment. Such inferences are possible only if the test items and performance tasks adequately sample the domain of possible items and tasks. This sampling is, of course, easier for well-defined areas such as spelling or math than for fuzzier content areas such as social studies.[7]

For teachers, the content area to be sampled is usually very specifically defined in terms of instructional outcomes. Your job is to ensure, to the best of your ability, that achievement of all intended outcomes is assessed and that a sufficient number of items and/or tasks is included for each. This is a critical issue in performance and product assessment, where the sample of tasks is typically very small. Although what is sufficient varies from outcome to outcome, rarely is one item or performance task enough. If your instructional outcome were "Identifies major characteristics of the planets," for example, sampling validity would require that your test include a number of items relating to different kinds of characteristics, such as the largest planet, the planet closest to the sun, and the planet with water on it. On the other hand, it would not be necessary to have an item for every possible characteristic studied.

Whether the content evidence available is enough to deem an assessment valid is determined qualitatively by expert judgment. There is no formula for computing it, and there is no way to express it quantitatively. For standardized, norm-referenced tests, usually experts in the area covered by the test are asked to assess its content evidence. These experts carefully review both the process used in developing the test, as well as the test itself, and make a judgment concerning how well items or performance tasks, both individually and collectively, represent the intended content area. This judgment is based on whether all sub-areas have been included and in the correct proportions. Content experts compare what ought to be included in the test (given its intended purpose, the content area it purports to cover, and the level of student to be tested) and what is actually included.

For criterion-referenced assessments in general, and especially for classroom tests, the process of determining validity using content evidence is facilitated because the description of students' intended behaviors is more detailed. For classroom assessments, you, the teacher, assume the role of expert. Your charge is to insure that the tasks and items on the assessments you use are congruent with the instructional outcomes they are designed to assess. Actually, it is pretty difficult to construct a criterion-referenced classroom assessment that does not have at least adequate content evidence of validity. If the instructional outcomes are reasonably specific and the

---

[7]For an investigation into the validity of performance assessments that illustrates the issues teachers struggle with regarding task and sampling validity, see "Performance Assessments: Political Rhetoric and Measurement Reality" by R. J. Shavelsen, G. P. Baxter, and J. Pine, 1992, *Educational Researcher, 21*(4), 22–27.

items or performance tasks actually measure the outcomes, some degree of validity is practically automatic. Of course, the more carefully the assessment is designed and constructed, the higher the validity. Most of this text is dedicated to preparing you to do just that—design and construct valid and reliable assessments.

Construct Evidence of Validity. *Construct evidence of validity* is the degree to which a test assesses an intended hypothetical construct. Recall from Chapter 2 that a construct is an unobservable trait, such as intelligence, which explains behavior—actually, a cluster of behaviors. You cannot see a construct, you can only observe its effect. In fact, constructs were "invented" to explain behavior. We cannot prove they exist; we cannot perform brain surgery on people and see their intelligence. Constructs, however, do an amazingly good job of explaining certain differences between individuals. For example, some students learn faster than others, learn more, and retain what they have learned longer. To explain these differences, a theory of intelligence was developed and it was hypothesized that there is something called intelligence, which is related to learning and which everyone possesses to a greater or lesser degree. Assessments were developed to measure how much intelligence a person has. As it happens, students who score high on intelligence tests indicating that they have a "lot" of it tend to do better in school and other learning environments. Because most assessment in education involves constructs,[8] all measures of achievement, aptitude, and personality require construct evidence of validity.

Decisions based totally or partially on the assessment of constructs are valid only to the extent that the measure of the construct involved is valid. For example, the selection criteria for a program for gifted students might include a specified minimum score on an intelligence test (116, for example), a specified minimum score on a test of creativity, a specified minimum grade-point average for the previous academic year, teacher recommendations based on observation and interaction with the student, and parental consent. If recent, appropriate scores were not available, tests of intelligence and creativity would need to be administered to likely candidates (perhaps those students who met the grade-point-average requirement and whose teacher recommended them). The validity of the resulting selection decisions would be a direct function of the validity of the intelligence test and creativity test administered. If the intelligence test did not really measure intelligence or the creativity test did not really measure creativity, decisions based on test results would probably be wrong in many cases.

Validating an assessment of a construct is by no means an easy task. Basically, it involves testing hypotheses deduced from a theory concerning the construct. Generally, a number of independent studies are required to establish the credibility of an assessment of a construct.

Criterion-Related Evidence of Validity. *Criterion-related evidence of validity* is the degree to which the scores on an assessment are related to the scores on another, already established test (called a criterion) or to some other appropriate

---

[8]Achievement, attitude, anxiety, creativity, curiosity, readiness, and self-esteem are all constructs, to name a few.

criterion, such as a score rendered by a review panel. Criterion-related evidence of validity can be classified as concurrent or predictive. If scores for both the assessment and the criterion are collected at the same time, educators refer to concurrent evidence of validity. A teacher would be interested in concurrent evidence of a measure's validity if, for example, she wanted to know how a new assessment of weather principles works compared to the one she presently uses. On the other hand, if criterion scores are not collected at the same time as scores on an assessment but will become available at some time in the future, a teacher would be interested in predictive evidence of validity. If, for example, a teacher wanted to know how well a reading readiness test predicted reading achievement in third grade (the criterion), he would be interested in the predictive evidence of the readiness test's validity. The degree of relationship between scores of the assessment of interest and the criterion is usually expressed as a correlation coefficient. Concurrent and predictive evidence of validity will be discussed in greater detail in this chapter after the following introduction to the concept of correlation.

Correlation in Criterion-Related Evidence of Validity. In everyday English, if things or events are correlated, it means they go together, they are associated with each other in some way—they are "co-related." Correlation basically means the same thing in assessment. If two variables or measures (like two sets of assessment scores) are *correlated,* it means that scores within a certain range on one measure are associated with scores within a certain range on the other measure. For example, there is a relationship between intelligence and academic achievement; people who score high on intelligence tests tend to have higher grade-point averages, and people who score low on intelligence tests tend to have lower grade-point averages. As a concept, correlation is important to the understanding of both the criterion-related evidence of validity and the reliability of assessments. In this section, correlation is discussed as it relates to concurrent and predictive evidence of validity. In a later section, its relation to reliability is discussed.

Degree of relationship between the two sets of scores is expressed as a correlation coefficient, r, a decimal number between .00 and +1.00 or −1.00 (see Figures 3.4 and 3.5). Using the scores from the two measures of interest, a correlation coefficient is computed, and this coefficient indicates the degree and type of relationship between the two sets of scores. If the relationship is strong, it may be used to make predictions. For example, if we know there is a strong relationship between scores on an algebra aptitude assessment and subsequent achievement in algebra, we can use aptitude assessment scores to predict a level of achievement in algebra.

If two measures are strongly related, a correlation coefficient near +1.00 or −1.00 will be obtained; if two measures are not related, a coefficient near .00 will be obtained. If two measures are positively (+) related, this means that a person with a high score on one measure is likely to have a high score on the other measure, and a person with a low score on one measure is likely to have a low score on the other measure. The closer the coefficient is to +1.00, the stronger the relationship (see Figure 3.4).

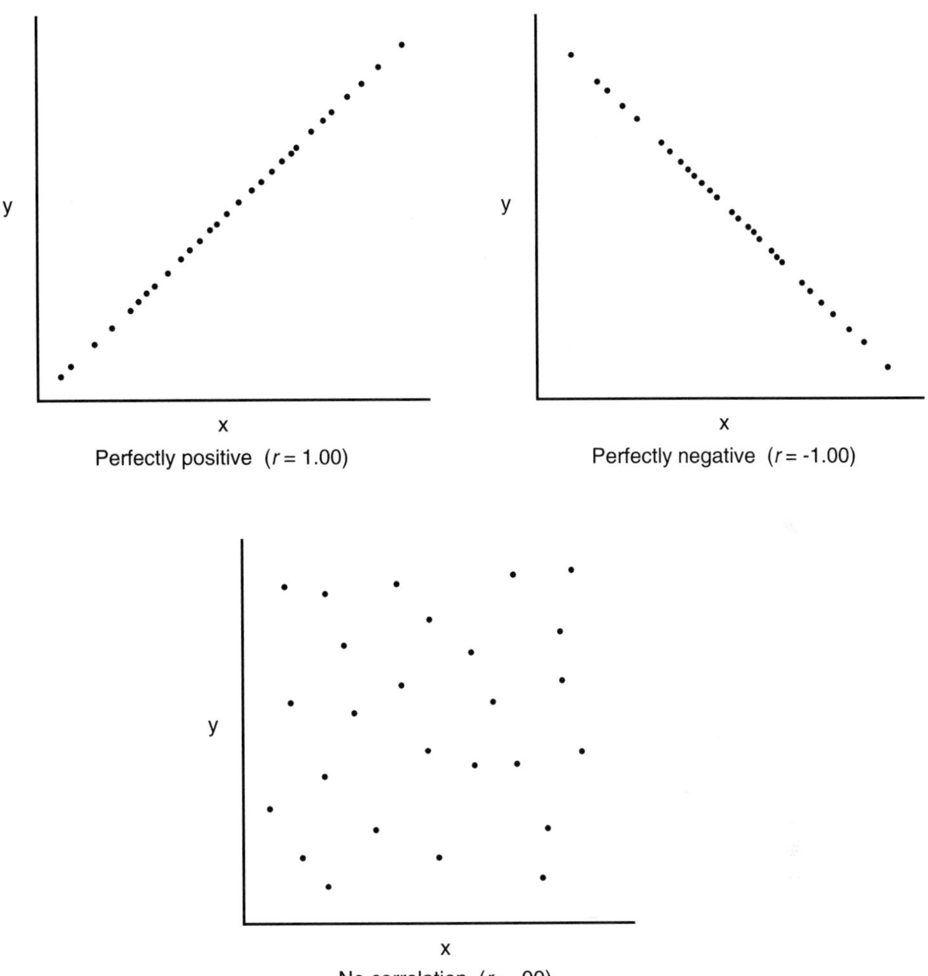

Figure 3.4
Scatterplots on an X and Y axis for a perfectly positive correlation, a perfectly negative correlation, and no correlation. Note the angle of the data points in the positive vs. the negative correlation and that no such line is implied by the data points when there is no relationship.

If you correlated the following pairs of measures for students in your class, in each case you would likely get a relatively high positive correlation coefficient:

midterm grades . . . . final grades
science project scores . . . . science test scores
reading comprehension test scores . . . . . vocabulary scores

If, on the other hand, the scores on the two measures are negatively (−) or inversely related, this means that a person with a high score on one measure is likely to have a low score on the other measure, and a person with a low score on one is likely to have a high score on the other; increase in score on one measure is associated with a decrease in score on the other (and vice versa). The closer the coefficient is to −1.00, the stronger the relationship (see Figure 3.4). Thus, a −1.00 is just as strong as a +1.00; they simply indicate different kinds of relationships. If you correlated the following pairs of measures for students in your class, in each case you would likely get a relatively high negative coefficient:

days absent . . . . .grade-point average

hours per week spent watching TV . . . . . .homework completion rate

attention span . . . . .number of instances of misbehavior

If a coefficient is near .00, the scores on the two measures are not related. This means that a person's score on one measure is no indication of what that person's score is on the other measure (see Figure 3.5). If you correlated the following pairs of measures for the students in your class, you would likely get a coefficient near .00:

math computation test scores . . . . . .distance of student's commute from home to school

time to run the 100-yard dash . . . . . .number of siblings

intelligence test scores . . . . .head circumference

Figure 3.6 presents three scores for each of 10 fifth-grade students: science test scores, science project scores, and weight. As the table illustrates, science test scores are positively related to science project scores and not related to weight. The students with progressively higher test scores have progressively higher project scores. These scores are plotted in Figure 3.7. As you can see, when there is no relationship the data points are all over the graph and form no pattern. The positive relationship, however, approximates a straight line; if the relationship were perfect ($r = +1.00$), all the data points would be on the same line, which would be at a 45° angle (/) as in Figure 3.4. An example of a negative, or inverse, relationship is given for comparison purposes only because negative coefficients are rare in assessment score

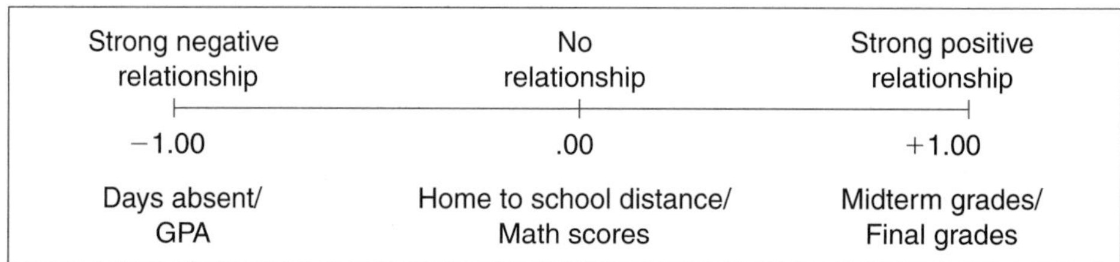

Figure 3.5
The continuum of correlation coefficients and indicated relationships for three example pairs of measures.

	High Positive Relationship (r = .90)		No Relationship (r = .03)	
Student	**Science Test Scores**	**Science Project Scores**	**Science Test Scores**	**Weight**
1. Bart	60	62	60	102
2. Boopsie	65	68	65	96
3. Dom	70	74	70	84
4. Rosie	75	64	75	72
5. Bucky	75	78	75	108
6. Milbert	80	82	80	80
7. Robby	80	84	80	88
8. Suzi	85	94	85	76
9. Joshua	90	88	90	92
10. Jessie	95	96	95	112

Figure 3.6
Sets of assessment scores illustrating a high positive relationship and no relationship.

analyses and usually represent an undesirable result, as in the case of a negative correlation between grade-point average and rate of absence from school.

Interpretation of a correlation coefficient depends upon how it is to be used. How large the coefficient needs to be in order for the assessment scores to be useful depends upon the purpose for which it was computed. Within the discussion of concurrent and predictive evidence, guidelines for interpreting validity coefficients will be presented. Although you will not be calculating correlation coefficients in this text, you should at least be aware that such coefficients are usually computed using a mathematical formula that produces a coefficient referred to as a Pearson product moment correlation or, more commonly, a Pearson *r*. Calculating correlation coefficients requires assessment results to be expressed quantitatively, not qualitatively.

Concurrent Evidence of Validity. *Concurrent evidence of validity* is a type of criterion-related evidence of validity; it measures the degree to which the scores from an assessment are related to the scores on another, already established assessment administered at the same time or to some other valid criterion available at the same time. Although a correlation coefficient for concurrent evidence of validity is rarely computed for teacher-made assessments, it is often reported for standardized tests. Often, a test is developed that claims to do the same job as some other tests, more easily or faster. If this is shown to be the case, then the concurrent evidence of the new test is established, and in most cases the new test will be utilized instead of the

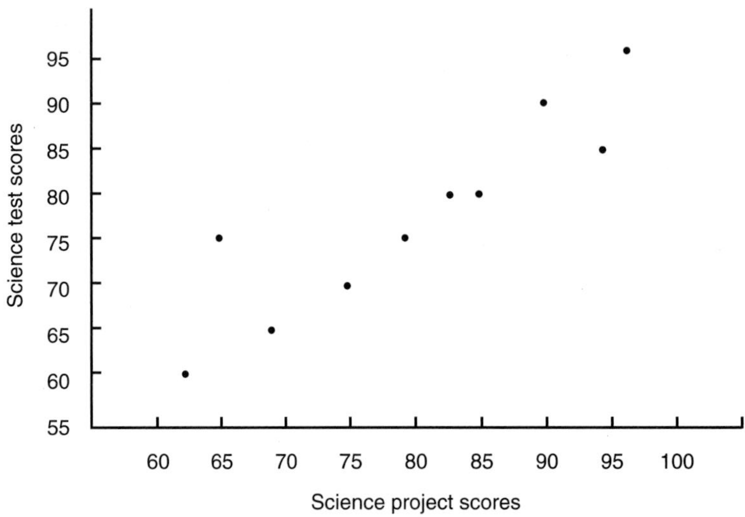

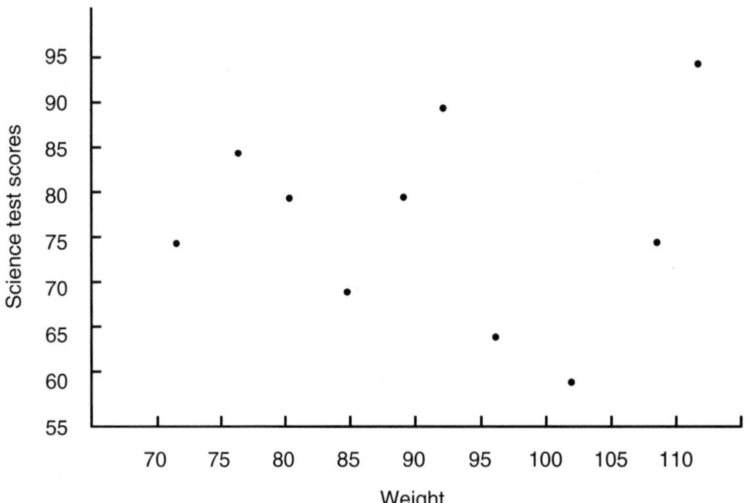

Figure 3.7
Plotted data points for scores presented in Figure 3.6 illustrating a high positive relationship (r = .90) for science test and project scores and no relationship (r = .03) for science test scores and weight.

other, more cumbersome tests. A paper-and-pencil test that does the same job as a performance test, or a short test that assesses the same behaviors as a longer test, will certainly be preferred in many situations.

Concurrent evidence of validity is determined by computing the correlation between scores on the new test and scores on some other established, valid test or criterion (like grade-point average). In other words, scores for the new assessment and the already established assessment are obtained for the same group at approximately the same time, and the scores are then correlated. The resulting decimal number, or validity coefficient *(r)*, indicates the validity of the new assessment. If the coefficient is high, the new assessment has a good amount of concurrent evidence of validity.

Any time you wish to substitute one assessment for another that allegedly measures the same thing, concurrent evidence of validity is important. Suppose, for example, that Professor Ima Jeenyus developed a group test of intelligence for children (let's call it the JTIC) which took only 15 minutes to administer. If scores on this test did indeed correlate highly (say .85) with those same students' scores on the hour-long, individually administered Wechsler Intelligence Scale for Children–Revised (WISC–R), then Professor Jeenyus' test would definitely be preferable in many situations. On the other hand, if the correlation was low (say .28), this would indicate that the new assessment was not measuring the same things as the WISC–R. The JTIC would, therefore, have low concurrent evidence, and it would not be considered a valid substitute.

Of course, even if the concurrent evidence coefficient were satisfactory, whether we would actually use the JTIC over the WISC–R would depend upon the seriousness of the decision to be made based on the results. If, for example, the scores were going to be used to help determine whether a student should be placed in a special educational environment, the WISC–R would definitely be the better choice. Intelligence is a construct, and, as noted earlier, a number of independent studies is generally required to establish the credibility of a test of a construct. The WISC–R has been studied extensively and is an example of a well-validated instrument. Validity evidence for Professor Jeenyus' test, on the other hand, may be limited and based mainly on its ability to produce score interpretations that approximate those resulting from the use of the WISC–R. If, however, an intelligence test were to be given for strictly demographic descriptive purposes to help develop a profile of the abilities of students in a particular school as a whole, for example, Professor Jeenyus' test would be quite suitable. Its concurrent evidence coefficient of .85 (.80 is considered acceptable) indicates that resulting interpretations of scores would be fairly accurate. For decisions about individual students, we want the best, most accurate, most valid assessment possible. For decisions about groups of students, teachers are willing to sacrifice a bit of validity for an assessment instrument that can be more easily administered to the group.

Predictive Evidence of Validity. *Predictive evidence of validity* is a type of criterion-related evidence that shows the degree to which an assessment can foretell how well an individual or group will do in a future situation. An algebra aptitude test with high predictive evidence will fairly accurately predict which students will do well in algebra and which students will not. Predictive evidence is extremely important for tests used to classify or select individuals. Two such tests are the Scholastic Assessment Test (SAT) and the Graduate Record Examination (GRE), which are used to select students for admission to undergraduate school and graduate school, respectively. Many colleges require a certain minimum score for admission (1000, for example) in the belief that students who achieve that score have a higher probability of succeeding than students who do not. This belief is based on predictive data resulting from a number of studies.

Although they may be calculated for standardized tests such as those mentioned above, predictive evidence coefficients are rarely, if ever, computed for teacher-made assessments. As a teacher, however, you may be involved in decisions concerning special placements for students. These decisions are likely to be based at least in part on scores from one or more standardized tests. The decision to remove a child from the normal educational environment and to place her in a special class, for example, is a serious one. In such situations it is imperative that the decision be based on the results of valid measures, including measures with a high amount of predictive evidence.

The predictive usefulness of a given instrument varies with a number of factors like the curriculum involved, textbooks used, and geographic location. The Mindboggling Biochemistry Aptitude Test, for example, may predict achievement better in courses using the *Brainscrambling Biochemistry I* text than in courses using other texts. Thus, if a test is to be used for prediction, it is important to compare the description of the manner in which it was validated with the situation in which it is to be used.

No assessment, of course, is perfectly predictive. Therefore, predictions based on the scores of any test will be imperfect. However, predictions based on a valid predictor assessment will be more accurate than predictions based on hunches or subjective speculation. Further, predictions based on data from a combination of several assessments will be more accurate than predictions based on the scores of any one test. Therefore, when important classification or selection decisions are to be made, they should be based on data from more than one indicator. For example, we can use students' high-school grade-point average to predict their college grade-point average at the end of the freshman year. We can also use their scholastic aptitude score or rank in graduating class to predict college grade-point average. A prediction based on all three variables, however, will be more accurate than a prediction based on any one or two of them.

The predictive evidence of the validity of an assessment is established by determining the relationship between scores on the test and some measure of success in the situation of interest. The test used to predict success is referred to as the *predictor,* and the behavior it predicts is referred to as the *criterion.* In establishing the predictive evidence of a test, the first step is to identify and carefully define the criterion. The criterion selected must be a valid measure of the behavior to be predicted. For example, if we wished to establish the usefulness of an aviation science aptitude test as a predictor, final examination scores at the completion of a course in aviation science might be considered a valid criterion, but number of days absent during the course probably would not. As another example, if we were interested in establishing evidence for the utility of a high-school-level writing assessment in predicting success in college, grade-point average at the end of the first year would probably be considered a valid criterion for determining success, but number of extracurricular activities in which the student participated probably would not.

Once the criterion has been identified and defined, the procedure for determining predictive evidence of validity is as follows:

1. Administer the assessment (the predictor variable).
2. Wait until the behavior to be predicted (the criterion variable) occurs.
3. Obtain measures of the criterion.
4. Correlate the two sets of scores.

Using the example of establishing the validity of a high-school-level writing assessment for predicting success in college, the steps would be as follows:

1. Administer the writing assessment to high-school students.
2. Wait until the end of the freshman year of college for the same students.
3. Obtain freshman-year grade-point average for each student.
4. Correlate the writing assessment scores with the grade-point averages.

The resulting number, or validity coefficient, indicates the validity of the assessment results; if the validity coefficient is high, the assessment is valid to use as a predictor. For example, suppose we wished to determine the predictive usefulness of a reading readiness assessment. First we would administer the assessment to a large group of students beginning school. Then we would wait for a period of time and administer a reading achievement test to the same students, perhaps at the end of first grade. The correlation between the two sets of scores would determine the prediction capability of the readiness test; if the resulting correlation coefficient was high (say .75), the test would have acceptable predictive evidence. The students who scored high on the reading readiness assessment would tend to score higher on the reading achievement test. From an instructional standpoint, if you administered a reading readiness assessment with a high degree of predictive evidence, then you could be relatively assured that if your class, as a group, scored high, they were, indeed, ready for reading instruction.

How high the validity coefficient needs to be in order to be useful depends mainly upon how the assessment results are going to be used and the seriousness of the decisions to be made. Coefficients in the .60s and .70s are usually considered *adequate* for group prediction purposes. Thus, if assessment scores were going to be used to make special placement decisions about individual students, you would not be satisfied with a predictive coefficient of .72. If, on the other hand, assessment scores were going to be used to evaluate a group of students' overall level of readiness for instruction in a subject, .72 would be acceptable.

To some degree, what is acceptable also depends on what is available. If, for example, only one test of creative writing aptitude were available and its predictive coefficient were .54, we might administer it and interpret the scores as being very general indicators of likely success in creative writing endeavors. A coefficient much below .50, however, is generally not useful for any type of prediction because it does not indicate a strong enough relationship to permit reliable predictions. A combination of several assessments in this range, however, may yield a reasonably satisfactory prediction.

Of course, when decisions about individual students are to be made, we are especially concerned with the consistency of indicators. We have more confidence in our score interpretations if they are consistent with other information we have, like teacher observations and parental input.

You may have noticed (if you had a high score on the SAT or GRE) that the procedures for determining concurrent evidence and predictive evidence are very similar. The major difference is when the criterion measure is administered. In establishing concurrent evidence, the criterion is administered at the same time as the predictor or within a relatively short period of time. In contrast, in establishing predictive evidence, one usually has to wait for a much longer period of time to pass before criterion data can be collected.

Understanding Reliability in Interpreting Assessment Results

In everyday English, reliability means dependability or trustworthiness; a reliable friend is one you can count on. The term means essentially the same thing with respect to assessment. Basically, *reliability* is the degree to which a test consistently assesses whatever it assesses. The more reliable an assessment, the more confidence we can have that the scores obtained from the administration of the assessment are essentially the same scores that would be obtained if it were readministered to the same group. Reliability indicates the degree to which errors of assessment have been controlled; to the degree that such errors are eliminated, scores will be consistent or reliable. When we refer to the reliability of an assessment or test, we are actually discussing the reliability of the scores and the related interpretations and decisions. When we speak of reliability, we are usually referring to the score consistency of a group. When we discuss score consistency, we may be concerned with the score consistency of the group or the accuracy of individual scores.

An unreliable assessment is essentially useless. If an assessment were unreliable, then scores for a given group would be expected to be quite different every time it is administered. If a scholastic aptitude test were unreliable, a student scoring 120 today might score 140 tomorrow and 95 the day after tomorrow. If the test were highly reliable and if the student's score were 110, then we would not expect that score to fluctuate too greatly from testing to testing. A score of 105 may not be unusual, but a score of 145 would be very unlikely. As with validity, any good assessment must be reliable. This applies to all types of paper-and-pencil tests, as well as observation instruments and criterion-referenced and norm-referenced assessments. The reliability of a performance rating form, for example, is just as important as the reliability of a multiple-choice achievement test. Anyone using the same rating form to rate the same behavior should come up with essentially the same rating.

The Relationship Between Reliability and Validity

Any type of assessment involves some kind of error. There are many factors affecting a score besides the degree to which a person possesses the trait being assessed. Some sources of error are related to temporary and permanent characteristics of the people taking the test. A person's scholastic aptitude score, for example, may be in error due to illness at the time the test was taken. Other sources of error are related to characteristics of the test itself or to the way in which it is administered, scored, or interpreted. A student's achievement score, for example, may be in error due to a large number of inappropriate items—items that assess something other than what was taught. Errors of measurement may be random or systematic. Random errors affect reliability whereas systematic or constant errors affect validity.

If an achievement test were too difficult for a certain group of students, all scores would be systematically lowered and the test would have low validity for that group (remember one of the key questions to use when assessing validity: "valid for whom?"). The same test, however, might yield consistent, or reliable, scores. In other words, the scores might be systematically lowered in the same way every time. A student whose "true" achievement score was 80 and who scored 60 on the test would prove the test's invalidity. (The concept of true score is discussed in the next section.) But if she scored 60 every time she took the test, the test would be deemed reliable. This case illustrates an interesting relationship between validity and reliability: A valid test is always reliable, but a reliable test is not necessarily valid. If a test is measuring what it is supposed to be measuring, it will do so every time and be reliable, but a reliable test can consistently measure the wrong thing and be invalid! Suppose a test that purported to assess social studies concepts really assessed social studies facts. It would not be a valid assessment of concepts but it could certainly assess the facts very consistently. Consequently, if you have limited resources and want to improve the quality of your assessments, your wisest investment would be to increase their validity from both content and construct perspectives. The guidelines offered in subsequent chapters will help you do this.

Reliability and True Score

Because of the many sources of assessment error that are beyond the test developer's control, random errors of assessment can never be completely eliminated, though every effort should be made to minimize them. To the extent that random errors are minimal, a test will be reliable. Classical test theory is based on the assumption that each person's score on a test really represents the result of a combination of two factors—the person's "true" score and errors of assessment:

$$X = T \pm E$$

where: X = score obtained on the test

T = true score

E = errors of assessment score

Classical test theory also assumes that the errors of assessment are random: that some students' scores are affected positively (their obtained score is higher than their true score) and some negatively (their obtained score is lower than their true score), and that overall the positive and negative errors average out and equal zero.

Thus, a person's *true score* is the score that, theoretically, a person would obtain if there were no errors of assessment and the test were totally reliable.

Another way of thinking about true score relates to the idea that any given test is but one of many possible tests that could have been constructed to assess the same behaviors. Any achievement test, for example, contains one set of items or tasks, or both, selected from a very large pool of those possible. If we could construct all possible tests (or even a very large number of them!), administer them all to an individual, and score each test, the person's average score would theoretically be his true score for that test. This assumes of course that all the tests would be identical in every way (that they would all have the same number of items, for example) and that taking one test would not affect performance on any other test (there would be no advantages gained from practice). Thus, the score a student obtains for any given assessment really represents an estimate of the individual's status with respect to the variable being assessed, an estimate affected by many factors.

All this talk about error might lead you to believe that assessment in education is pretty sloppy and imprecise to say the least. Actually, it's not as bad as it may sound. Many assessments measure intended traits quite accurately. In fact, as Nunnally has pointed out, measurement in other areas of science often involves as much, if not more, random error.[9] To use his example, the measurement of blood pressure, a physiological trait, is far less reliable than most psychological measures. Any number of "conditions of the moment" may temporarily affect blood pressure: joy, anger, fear, anxiety, and whether the person's body is at rest during testing, to name a few. Consequently, a person's blood pressure reading, like an individual's score on an assessment, is also the result of a combination of "true" blood pressure and error.

Reliability and Test Length

A general principle of assessment is that, usually, longer tests are more reliable. Relatedly, an excellent way to increase reliability is to increase the length of a test. This does not mean putting the test on longer sheets of paper(!). Other factors being equal, adding items and tasks to a test that are as good as the items or tasks already included increases the reliability of the resulting scores, because adding items to written tests and tasks to performance assessments improves the sampling of the intended behavior domain and improves the representativeness of the items and tasks. The more items/tasks we have, the better we can sample the behaviors we are assessing, be they achievement outcomes, attitudes, or skills. Improved sampling results in higher validity too (you knew that) and reduces chance factors such as the effects of guessing, bluffing, and finessing; thus, we get a better estimate of true score—what the students really know and can do.

Suppose you studied day and night and all weekend for an important exam while your friend, Animal, partied. Suppose also that when the exam was given out it consisted of one multiple-choice item. Would you think it was a fair test? Of course not. Further, you would be really ticked off if you missed the item and your friend, Animal, guessed and got it correct. Having two items would help a teensy bit, three

[9] *Psychometric Theory* (2nd ed.) by J. C. Nunnally, 1978, New York: McGraw-Hill.

items a bit more, and so forth. The point is, there should be enough items or tasks so that people like you can demonstrate that they really know the material and the Animals can show that they don't.

Of course, tests can be too long. You wouldn't be thrilled with a 200-item exam either. When a test is too long, unwanted factors such as fatigue, writer's cramp, crossed eyes, and stiff neck may occur. In most cases, especially with respect to classroom assessments, a balance must be struck so that the assessment is long enough, but not too long. For certain situations, such as when important decisions are going to be based on assessment results, very long assessments are necessary. The college admissions test you probably took[10] was not exactly a shorty. In general, however, lengthening an assessment to improve reliability does have reasonable limits. An increase in test length is not accompanied by an equal increase in reliability. If you double the length of a test, for example, you do not double the reliability. This makes sense because the theoretical maximum for reliability coefficients is 1.00. If a test has a reliability coefficient of .70 to begin with, no matter how many items or performance tasks you add, the reliability is never going to be 1.01! In fact, the higher the reliability to begin with, the less is to be gained by increasing the length of the assessment.

When Reliability Estimates Are Unreliable

Teachers do not typically compute correlation coefficients to estimate the reliability of their classroom tests. One reason such calculation is not encouraged in this text is the fact that reliability formulas do not "work" well when the range of scores is restricted and there is not a wide spread of scores. Such is the case for many classroom tests, especially mastery tests, on which score variability is expected to be low and most students are expected to do well and demonstrate achievement of the intended instructional outcomes. When reliability estimates are computed for the results of such assessments, the coefficients tend to be low and misleading in terms of the actual "goodness" of the tests. The scores below and the related discussion should give you the general idea why this is so. Examine the scores carefully for any relationship among them. What do you see?

Final Exam Score	Aptitude Score
95	100
91	100
89	100
86	100
84	100
84	100
83	100
80	100
77	100
75	100

[10]Remember the SAT or the ACT?

If you correlated those two sets of scores, what would you guess the correlation coefficient, r, would be? Well, how much relationship does there seem to be between the scores? There is no relationship, so $r = .00$. This rather extreme example illustrates the concept: All things being equal, the lower the variability of the scores, the lower the correlation coefficient.

Distinguishing Among Types of Reliability Estimates

By now you've learned that scores can be reliable, or consistent, in several different ways. Relatedly, there are various approaches to estimating reliability. Reliability estimates are usually, but not always, calculated using correlation techniques. When correlation techniques are used, the part of the correlation continuum involved (see Figure 3.5) is the positive half, between .00 and +1.00.

As with validity coefficients, teachers do not typically calculate reliability estimates for classroom assessments, although reliability is just as important for classroom tests as for others. And because you may be involved in selecting or interpreting the results of standardized tests being used to make decisions about students as well, you should be familiar with the basic concepts, approaches, and types of reliability estimates discussed in this chapter and summarized in Figure 3.8.

Scorer/Rater Reliability. An assessment is unreliable to the degree that scores are a result of factors other than true performance, like errors of assessment. Scoring and rating are sources of errors of assessment. The more subjectivity there is in the scoring, the more opportunity there is for error factors (such as scorer bias) to distort true scores. By definition, an objective test (such as a multiple-choice assessment) is one for which subjectivity in scoring is, at least theoretically, eliminated. If the correct answer is option C, various scorers will have no trouble agreeing that a student did or did not choose C. No matter who or what scores an objective assessment, the score should be the same.

Free-response items, such as short-answer items and essay items, however, are very likely to involve subjectivity, as are instruments such as rating scales used in the assessment of student performance and products.[11] In formal assessments (like statewide tests), scoring reliability is usually estimated by correlating the scores assigned to the same students by one of the following methods:

1. One scorer on two different occasions—called intrascorer/intrarater reliability, or
2. Two or more independent scorers on the same occasion—called interscorer/interrater reliability.

Scorer/rater reliability may also be expressed simply as percent agreement. If, on a 10-item checklist, for example, you and I agree on 8 of the 10 items whether Geraldo

[11]For a discussion of the difficulties in providing high-quality data about student performance using subjective ratings of portfolios, for example, see "The Vermont Portfolio Assessment Program: Findings and Implications" by D. M. Koretz, B. Stecher, S. Klein, and D. McCaffrey, 1994, *Educational Measurement: Issues and Practice, 13*(3), 5–16.

Type of Reliability Estimate	Description	How Reliability Is Established	Important When . . .	Comments
Intrascorer/ Intrarater	Degree to which 1 judge assigns same rating(s) to a performance or product on 2 different occasions	Same judge rates, then re-rates performance or product of a group; correlate the 2 sets of scores or compute percent agreement	Scoring is subjective; 1 judge of performance; consistency of judgment over time is important	Requires re-rating at least a portion of the performances or products; percent agreement easiest to compute
Interscorer/ Interrater	Degree to which ≥2 judges assign same ratings to a performance or product	2 or more judges rate performance or product of a group; correlate the 2 sets of scores or compute percent agreement	Scoring is subjective; >1 judge of performance; consistency of judgment across judges is important	Requires at least 2 judges; percent agreement easiest to compute
Test-Retest	Degree to which scores are consistent over time	Give *same* test to the *same* group at 2 different times; correlate the 2 sets of scores	Test is used as a predictor; used as aptitude test; assessing anyone or anything (important for all assessments)	Requires waiting period; time interval between testings, maturational rate of group tested are important factors
Equivalent Forms	Degree to which scores are consistent from form to form	Give 2 forms of a test to the *same* group at the *same* time (or within a short time interval); correlate the 2 sets of scores	"Teaching to the test" must be avoided; using 1 form for pretest and 1 for posttest; using 1 form for make-up test; cheating must be discouraged	Requires 2 forms; forms may each be very short and better if combined
Stability & Equivalence	Degree to which scores on 2 different forms are consistent over time	2 forms of a test are administered to same group at 2 different times and the 2 sets of scores are correlated	Both stability and equivalence are paramount (rare)	Most conservative reliability estimate
Internal Consistency: Split-half	Degree to which items on 2 halves of a single test are consistent with each other	Divide test into 2 comparable halves; compute each test taker's score for each half; correlate the 2 sets of scores	Only 1 form of test is available; only 1 administration is possible	Watch out for differential difficulty of items/tasks on the 2 halves; coefficient must be corrected with Spearman-Brown formula
Internal Consistency: Kuder-Richardson formulas	Degree to which all the items (or tasks) on a test relate to all other items (or tasks) and to the total test	Score each item (or task) dichotomously and enter each item score into proper formula	Only 1 form of test is available; only 1 administration is possible; making sure all items measure same thing; items are scored dichotomously	KR-20 is best, but tedious to compute by hand; KR-21 is easily computed, but tends to be high; KR-21′ is easily computed and a good estimate of KR-20; all require dichotomously scored items/tasks
Internal Consistency: Cronbach's alpha (α)	Degree to which all the items (or tasks) on a test relate to all other items (or tasks) and to the total test	Assign points to each item (or task) and enter each item score into formula	Only 1 form of test is available; only 1 administration is possible; making sure all items measure same thing; items are scored on multi-point scale	Best for non-dichotomously scored items; tedious to compute by hand

Figure 3.8
Summary of types of reliability estimates.

met the performance standard or criterion, our percent agreement would be 80%. If we wanted to do this for a class of students, we could average our percent agreement across students by adding the individual percentages, dividing the sum by the number of students we both rated, then multiplying the answer by 100. We then would have an indication, expressed as a percentage, of how consistent we were as scorers.

As a teacher, you should make every effort to make the scoring of your assessments as objective as possible, eliminating most sources of assessment error. Later in the text, you will be given strategies for increasing the scoring objectivity of subjective assessments such as essay tests and performance observations.[12] When scoring subjective assessments, you can informally determine how objective your scoring is by rescoring a random sample of test papers or tasks. If you have an essay item worth 20 points, for example, first score the item for all students, putting your score on the back of the paper. Then randomly pull out five papers, rescore the item, and compare the number of points you assigned to each student on the two occasions to estimate your intrascorer reliability. The number of agreements, divided by five in this case, then multiplied by 100 is your percent agreement. The point assignments obviously should not be very different for the scoring to be reliable!

Test-Retest Method. A *test-retest* reliability coefficient estimates the degree to which assessment scores are consistent over time. It indicates score variation that occurs from testing session to testing session as a result of errors of assessment. In determining test-retest reliability, we are interested in evidence that the score a person obtains on an assessment at some moment in time is the same score, or close to the same score, that the person would get if the assessment were administered some other time. Although important for all assessments, this type of reliability is especially important for tests used as predictors, like aptitude tests. Such a test would not be very helpful if it indicated a different aptitude level each time it was given to the same student or group of students.

To estimate test-retest reliability, the *same* test is administered to the *same* group at two different times, and the two sets of scores are correlated. If the resulting coefficient, referred to as the *coefficient of stability,* is high, the test has good test-retest reliability. A major problem with this type of reliability is the difficulty of knowing how much time should elapse between the two testing sessions. If the interval is too short, the chances of students remembering responses made on the test the first time are increased, and the estimate of reliability tends to be artificially high. If the interval is too long, students' ability to do well on the test may increase due to intervening learning or maturation, and the estimate of reliability tends to be artificially low.

Thus, when test-retest information is given concerning a test, you should also look at the time interval between testings as well as the actual coefficient. Although it is difficult to say precisely what, in general, the ideal time interval should be (especially because it depends somewhat on the kind of test involved and the developmental rate of the group tested), less than a week will usually be too short.

---

[12]See Chapters 7, 8, and 9 for more information on this subject.

Equivalent-Forms Method. Equivalent forms of a test, also referred to as alternate forms, are two tests that are identical in every way except for the actual items or tasks included. The two forms assess the same variable, have the same number of items or tasks, the same structure, the same difficulty level, and the same directions for administration, scoring, and interpretation. In fact, if the same group takes both tests, the average score as well as the degree of score variability should be essentially the same on both. Only the specific items or tasks are not the same, although they do measure the same trait or instructional outcomes. In essence, test-givers are selecting, or sampling, different items and tasks from the same behavior domain. They are interested in whether scores depend upon the particular set of items and tasks selected or whether performance on one set is generalizable to other sets.

An *equivalent-forms* reliability coefficient estimates the degree to which scores are consistent from form to form. When alternate forms are available, it is important to know the equivalent-forms coefficient to be reassured that a student's score will not be greatly affected by which form is administered. Sometimes two forms of an assessment are administered to the same group, one as a pretest and the other as a posttest. It is crucial, if the effects of the intervening activities are to be appropriately assessed, that the two tests be assessing essentially the same things. In addition, using equivalent forms eliminates any inadvertent "teaching to the test."

The procedure for determining equivalent-forms reliability is very similar to that for determining test-retest reliability: the two forms of the test are both administered to the *same* group at the *same* time (or within a relatively short time interval), and the two sets of scores are correlated. If the resulting coefficient, referred to as the *coefficient of equivalence,* is high, the test has good equivalent-forms reliability. If you wanted to determine the equivalence of two forms of a unit test that were provided with a textbook, you would do the following after appropriate instruction on the unit:

1. Administer Form A of the test, followed by Form B to half of your students.
2. At the same session, administer Form B, followed by Form A to the other half of your students.
3. Correlate the scores (the number of items answered correctly) on Form A with those on Form B for all students who took both forms.

Stability and Equivalence Method. If the two forms of the test are administered at two different times (the best of all possible worlds for estimating reliability!), the resulting coefficient is referred to as the *coefficient of stability and equivalence.* In essence, this approach represents a combination of test-retest and equivalent-forms reliability and thus assesses stability of scores over time as well as the generalizability of the sets of items. Because more sources of assessment error are possible with the combination of methods than with either method alone, the resulting coefficient is likely to be somewhat lower. As a result, the coefficient of stability and equivalence represents a conservative estimate of reliability.

Even though test-retest, equivalent forms, and both methods together are considered to be very good estimates of reliability, it is not always feasible to administer two different forms of the same test, or even the same test twice. Imagine telling your students that they had to take two unit tests or two final examinations! Imagine someone telling you to take the SAT or the ACT twice! Fortunately, other methods of estimating reliability require administering a test only once and are appropriate for many assessments.

Internal Consistency Methods. Internal consistency methods involve only one administration of an assessment and are used most appropriately when the items or tasks are basically homogeneous and assess essentially the same behavior, such as spelling ability. The basic idea is that if a test has internal consistency, achievement rates for individual items or tasks should be highly correlated. Because only one administration of a test is required, certain sources of assessment error are eliminated, such as differences in testing conditions, which can occur in establishing test-retest estimates, for example. The most widely used approaches for estimating internal consistency are the split-half method and the Kuder-Richardson methods.

The Split-Half Method. The *split-half* method involves dividing a test into two comparable halves or subtests, computing each test taker's score for each half, and correlating the two resulting sets of scores; if the coefficient is high, the test has good split-half reliability. Although there are a number of ways to divide a test in half (randomly, for example), in reality, the odd item-even item strategy is most often used. This approach works out rather well regardless of how a test is organized. Suppose, for example, a test is a 20-item power test and the items get progressively more difficult. Items 1, 3, 5, 7, 9, 11, 13, 15, 17, and 19 as a group should be approximately as difficult as items 2, 4, 6, 8, 10, 12, 14, 16, 18, and 20. Items 1 and 2 will be easy, 3 and 4 will be more difficult, and so forth.

Because longer tests tend to be more reliable, and because split-half estimates actually represent the reliability of a test only half as long as the actual test, a correction formula is used called the Spearman-Brown prophecy formula. Thus, reported test information (such as information reported for standardized achievement tests) typically includes "corrected" split-half coefficients. One problem with the correction formula is that it tends to over-correct or give a higher estimate of reliability than would be obtained using other methods.

Kuder-Richardson Methods. *Kuder-Richardson* methods estimate the internal consistency reliability, not through correlating test scores, but by determining how well all the items (or tasks) on a test relate to all other items (or tasks) and to the total test. There are several Kuder-Richardson formulas, commonly referred to as KR-20, KR-21, and KR-21′ (pronounced KR-21 prime). Application of a KR formula results in an estimate of reliability that is essentially equivalent to the average of the split-half reliabilities computed for all possible halves. The KR-20 formula is the most accurate and is a highly regarded method of assessing reliability. Computers have eliminated the mathematical labor involved in calculation, and it is probably the most reported type of reliability estimate for standardized assessments. The KR-21 is an easy-to-apply approach that provides an estimate of the KR-20 reliability coefficient.

Because the KR-21 estimate is generally very conservative (low), the KR-21′ formula was developed to get a closer approximation of the KR-20 value while retaining the ease of hand-calculator computation.

Cronbach's Alpha Method. All of the Kuder-Richardson formulas require that each item or task be scored dichotomously, as correct or incorrect, or as 1 or 0. If items are scored such that different answers are worth different numbers of points, including 0, 1, 2, or 3 (as they might be if a rating scale was used to observe performance or score an essay answer, for example), then *Cronbach's alpha* (α), also referred to as coefficient alpha, can be used. Test publishers typically report Cronbach's α as an estimate of internal consistency reliability for their assessments that are scored non-dichotomously.

Figure 3.9 summarizes the number of administration sessions and forms required for the eight reliability estimating methods just discussed. Keep in mind when reviewing assessment information that although the size of the reliability coefficient is of prime importance, the method used to calculate it should also be considered.

Interpreting Reliability Estimates

If an assessment were perfectly reliable, all reliability estimates of the scores would be 1.00. This would mean that a student's actual score perfectly reflected her true

Number of administration sessions	Number of forms: 1	Number of forms: 2
1	Split-Half KR-20 KR-21 KR-21′ Cronbach's alpha (α)	Equivalent Forms
2	Test-Retest	Stability and Equivalence

Figure 3.9
The number of administration sessions and forms required for eight reliability estimating methods.

score and status with respect to the variable or trait being assessed. No test is, however, perfectly reliable; scores are invariably affected by errors of assessment resulting from a variety of causes. But some tests do a better job than others, and the real question is "What degree of reliability is considered acceptable?"

Classroom Assessments. As mentioned earlier, traditional reliability formulas do not work well for many classroom assessments, mainly because of the restricted range of scores that reduces the coefficient. Reliabilities in the .50s are not uncommon for classroom assessments. For mastery tests, coefficients near zero may be obtained (if, in fact, all or most students have mastered the intended outcomes). Of course, for nonmastery tests such as chemistry exams, reliability coefficients may be quite good. The point is that although high coefficients indicate high reliability, low coefficients do not necessarily indicate low reliability. You may be wondering why teachers ever apply a basically inappropriate technique for measuring reliability in the first place. The reason is that, presently, no approach to the calculation of the reliability of criterion-referenced test scores is generally accepted as being both appropriate *and* practical for teacher use, although much work has been done in this area and some promising efforts are under way. In the meantime, teachers can currently reach a level of confidence in the reliability of their classroom assessments by taking an alternate approach, one that uses the results of item analysis, a process to be discussed in Chapter 10.[13]

Standardized Tests. What constitutes an acceptable level of reliability is to some degree determined by the type of assessment, although a coefficient over .90 would be quite acceptable for any assessment. Many standardized achievement and aptitude assessments that report such high reliabilities are available, and it is therefore not necessary to settle for less. For individual areas of achievement (like biology) and certain specific aptitudes (such as mechanical aptitude), coefficients in the .80s are both common and acceptable. Personality measures do not typically report extremely high reliabilities (although some do), and therefore one would be very satisfied with reliability in the .80s (a reliability estimate of .84, for example) and would most likely accept a reliability coefficient in the .70s. Attitude scale reliabilities, for example, usually fall in the .60s to .80s range, with most being in the .70s.

If a test is composed of several subtests, then the reliability of each subtest, not just the reliability of the total test, must be determined. Because reliability is a function of test length, the reliability of a given subtest is typically lower than the total test reliability. Examination of subtest reliability is especially important if only one or more of the subtests are going to be administered rather than the total test. Be a smart consumer when it comes to examining test information: If a test manual states that "the total test reliability is .90 and all subtest reliabilities are satisfactory," you should immediately become suspicious. If subtest reliabilities are "satisfactory," the publisher will certainly want to tell you just how satisfactory they are. Most of the well-established tests do report subtest reliability coefficients.

---

[13]"Item Analysis of Criterion-Referenced Tests" by L. R. Gay and J. D. Gallagher, 1995, *Florida Journal of Educational Research, 35*(1), 54–62.

Standard Error of Measurement

When we discuss score consistency, we may be concerned with the reliability of a group's scores or with the accuracy of individual scores. When we speak of reliability, we are usually referring to the score consistency of a group. When we speak of the accuracy of an individual's score (how much confidence we have in that individual's score), then we are interested in the standard error of measurement. The standard error of measurement is generally reported for standardized test results and facilitates proper interpretation.

Basically, the *standard error of measurement* (SEM) is an estimate of how often you can expect errors of a given size. High reliability is associated with a small standard error of measurement, and low reliability is associated with a large standard error of measurement. If an assessment were perfectly reliable (although one never is), a person's obtained score would be his true score. But in our imperfect world, an obtained score is an estimate of a true score. If you administered the same test over and over to the same group, the score of each individual would vary. How much variability would be present in individual scores would be a function of the test's reliability. The variability would be small for a highly reliable test (zero if the test were perfectly reliable) and large for a test with low reliability.

If we could administer the test many times we could see how much variation actually occurred. Of course, realistically we can't do this; administering the same test twice to the same group is tough enough. Fortunately, it is possible to estimate this degree of variation (the standard error of measurement) using the scores resulting from the administration of a test once to a group. The standard error of measurement allows us to express in a number how much difference there probably is between a person's obtained score and true score, the size of this difference being a function of the reliability of the assessment.

We want reliability coefficients to be large and standard errors of measurement to be small. For reliability coefficients, "large" means the closer to 1.00, the better. For standard errors of measurements, however, it is impossible to say how small is "good." This is because the standard error of measurement is expressed in the same units as the test itself, and what counts as "small" is relative to the size of the test. Thus, SEM = 5.2 would be large for a 20-item test but small for a 200-item test.

Constructing Standard Error of Measurement Confidence Intervals. Standard error of measurement estimates are frequently used to construct bands, or confidence intervals, around individual scores. If Winston, for example, gets a score of 84 on a test with a standard error of measurement of 5 (abbreviated SEM = 5), then we can add 5 and subtract 5 from 84 to form an interval:

$$84 + 5 = 89 \text{ and } 84 - 5 = 79$$

Therefore, our interval is 79–89. In other words,

$$\text{score} \pm 1 \text{ SEM} = 84 \pm 5 = 79\text{–}89.$$

Using normal curve properties—which were discussed in Chapter 2 and will be again in Chapter 11—we would say that we are pretty confident (actually, about 68% confident) that Winston's true score falls within the interval 79–89. Of course we could be wrong, but we are probably correct. Because of the 68% degree of confidence, this is also referred to as a "two-thirds confidence interval." In practice, plus or minus one standard error of measurement is commonly used. You should understand that SEM = 5 does *not* mean that a student's true score absolutely does not differ from her true score by more than 5 points, but it does mean that 68% of the time a person's observed score will be within ±5 points of her true score.

Using Standard Error of Measurement Bands. Differences in the obtained scores of different students may be due to error and not real differences in true scores. Standard error of measurement bands can be used to make such determinations. Overlapping intervals suggest that the true scores on a test are not really different whereas intervals that do not overlap suggest true score differences. Suppose we have the following scenario for three students:

	Student	*Obtained Score*
SEM = 4	Tabitha	70
	Lulu	72
	Felicia	82

We can compute score ±1 SEM for each student and we get the following:

Student	*SEM Band*
Tabitha	70 ± 4 = 66–74
Lulu	72 ± 4 = 68–76
Felicia	82 ± 4 = 78–86

Graphically, they might look like this:

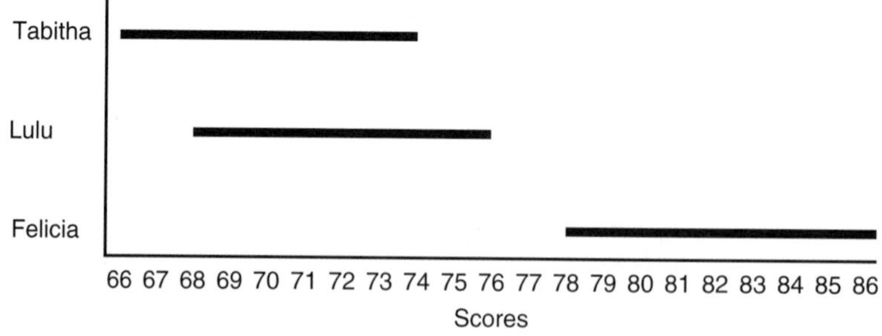

Tabitha's interval overlaps with Lulu's (they both include the score 72, for example), but neither overlaps with Felicia's. Thus we would say that Tabitha's and Lulu's true scores are essentially the same but Felicia's is really higher than theirs.

If the bands overlap a little, then other factors should be taken into consideration in making the decision about true score differences. For example, compare the scores of Felicia and Fenster:

Student	*Obtained Score*	*SEM Band*
Felicia	82	78–86
Fenster	89	85–93

Here are their standard error of measurement bands shown graphically:

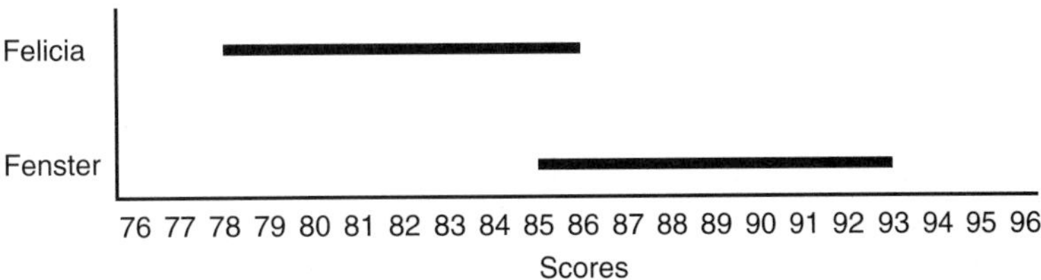

Technically, the bands do overlap (they both include 85 and 86), but not much. If you knew that Fenster is a straight-A student and Felicia is a hard-working solid B student, you might conclude that despite the slight overlap, Fenster's true score is in fact probably higher.

The concept of overlapping bands is also used to evaluate a student's performance on various subtests of a standardized test to determine for which areas a student's performance is essentially the same and in which areas the student exhibits definite strengths and weaknesses. This application of standard error of measurement bands will be discussed further in Chapter 14.

Summary

The On-Going Nature of Assessment

Assessment should be planned prior to execution of any teaching effort and should be used throughout the cycle of instruction—at the beginning, in the middle, and at the end. The beginning or planning phase includes an analysis of the situation, specification of goals and instructional outcomes including prerequisites, selection and/or development of assessment instruments, delineation of strategies and activities for attainment of the outcomes, and preparation of lesson plans. Analysis of the instructional situation also includes identifying students with disabilities and the accommodation requirements of those students with regard to assessment. During instruction, the basic purposes of assessment are to gather data to (1) determine whether the teaching is effective and if the students are learning successfully and (2) identify ways in which improvements can be made. After instruction, it is determined to what degree the intended *instructional outcomes* were achieved, what to do next, and what the implications are for future cycles of instruction.

Determining Quality in Assessment

Validity

The results of any assessment, to be useful, should be both valid and reliable. These two characteristics are the fundamental concepts of quality in assessment. *Validity* is the degree to which an assessment measures what it is supposed to measure; it is the most important concern for any assessment. Whether a decision based on the results of an assessment is a good one is a function of the validity of that assessment—that is, the interpretation made based on the scores or results. A test is not intrinsically valid or invalid; it is valid for a particular purpose and for a particular group. If an assessment is invalid, it is by definition biased. Although bias may result from improper test administration, scoring, or interpretation, the major source of bias is the test itself. Low scores do not automatically imply test bias; they do imply that the group assessed does not possess a high degree of whatever the test measures for some reason. Validity is a matter of degree, not a characteristic that is present or absent; it is also a somewhat temporal quality in that a test that once had adequate validity may no longer, and a test that currently has adequate validity will not necessarily have it in the future.

Depending on how the results will be used and the interpretations that will be made based on these results, required evidence of validity varies. *Content evidence of validity* establishes the degree to which an assessment measures an intended content area or set of instructional outcomes; it is of prime importance for achievement tests. *Item/task congruence* or *item validity* is concerned with whether the test items represent assessment in the intended content area. *Sampling validity* is concerned with how well the test samples the total content area. Whether content evidence is sufficient is determined by expert judgment. When selecting a classroom assessment, the teacher assumes the role of expert and determines whether the test will produce scores that are content valid for the situation involved.

Construct evidence of validity is the degree to which an assessment measures an intended hypothetical construct. A construct is an unobservable trait, such as intelligence or achievement, that explains behavior. Validating a test of a construct involves testing hypotheses deduced from a theory concerning the construct.

Criterion-related evidence of validity is the degree to which the scores on a test are related to the scores on another, already established test (called a criterion) or to some other appropriate criterion. If scores for both are collected at the same time, we refer to *concurrent validity*. If the criterion scores are available at some time in the future, we are interested in *predictive validity*.

The *correlation*, or degree of relationship between scores of the assessment of interest and the criterion, is usually expressed as a correlation coefficient, *r*, a decimal number between .00 and +1.00 (or −1.00). If the relationship is strong, it may be used to make predictions. If a coefficient is near .00, the scores on the two measures are not related. How large a coefficient needs to be for the assessment scores to be useful depends upon the purpose for which it was computed. The mathematical formula generally used to produce a coefficient is referred to as the Pearson product moment correlation or, more commonly, a Pearson *r.*

Concurrent evidence of validity is the degree to which the scores on a test are related to the scores on another, already established test administered at the same time or to some other valid criterion available at the same time. Coefficients related to concurrent validity evidence are rarely computed for teacher-made assessments but are often reported for standardized tests. The strength of concurrent validity evidence is determined by computing the correlation between scores for the new assessment and the already established assessment, both of which have been administered to the same group at approximately the same time.

Predictive evidence of validity is the degree to which a test can predict how well an individual or group will do in a future situation. Predictive evidence is extremely important for tests used to classify or select individuals. Coefficients related to predictive validity evidence are rarely, if ever, computed for teacher-made assessments, but they are often reported for standardized tests. The strength of predictive validity evidence of a given instrument varies with a number of factors, such as the curriculum involved, textbooks used, and geographic location. Predictions based on a combination of several test scores will invariably be more accurate than predictions based on the scores of any one test. The predictive strength of a test is determined by establishing the relationship between scores on the test and some measure of success in the situation of interest. The test used to predict success is referred to as the *predictor,* and the behavior predicted is referred to as the *criterion*. Coefficients in the .60s and .70s are usually considered *adequate* for group prediction purposes. The procedures for determining concurrent evidence and predictive evidence are very similar, with the major difference being the time interval between the predictor and the criterion measures. In establishing concurrent validity, they are both administered at (or nearly at) the same time. In establishing predictive validity, there is a much longer period between the two.

Reliability

Reliability is the degree to which a test consistently assesses whatever it assesses; it also indicates the degree to which errors of assessment have been controlled. A valid test is always reliable, but a reliable test is not necessarily valid. Classical test theory is based on the assumption that each person's score on a test (X) really represents a combination of two factors: the person's "true" score (T) and errors of assessment (E), expressed as an equation, $X = T \pm E$. A student's *true score* is the score that, theoretically, the student would obtain if there were no errors of assessment and the test were totally reliable. A general principle of assessment is that, in general, longer tests are more reliable; as a result, an excellent way to increase reliability is to increase the length of a test.

There are various approaches to estimating reliability, many of which are calculated using correlation techniques. Regardless of how reliability is computed, however, it is expressed as a decimal number between .00 and 1.00. Teachers do not typically calculate reliability estimates for classroom assessments, but coefficients are often reported for standardized tests. Reliability is equally important for classroom assessments and any other tests.

There are other situations for which reliability must be investigated, usually when the scoring of assessments involves subjectivity, such as with student performances and products. When scoring involves subjective judgment, we are concerned with intrarater reliability (one scorer on two different occasions) and/or interrater reliability (two or more scorers on the same occasion). Estimates of interrater or intrarater reliability are usually obtained using correlational techniques, but they can also be expressed simply as percent agreement. Teachers can informally determine how objective their scoring is by rescoring a random sample of test papers or tasks and comparing the two scores for the items or tasks.

A *test-retest* reliability coefficient estimates the degree to which scores are consistent over time. Although important for all assessments, this type of reliability is especially important for tests used as predictors. To estimate test-retest reliability, the *same* test is administered to the *same* group at two different times and the two sets of scores are correlated, resulting in a *coefficient of stability*. When test-retest information is given concerning an assessment, the time interval between testings and the actual coefficient are both important.

Equivalent forms of a test are two tests that are identical in every way except for the actual items or tasks included. An *equivalent-forms* reliability coefficient estimates the degree to which scores are consistent from form to form. Equivalent-forms reliability is established by determining the relationship between scores resulting from administering two different forms of the same assessment to the same group at the same time, resulting in a *coefficient of equivalence*. If the two forms of the assessment are administered at two different times, the resulting coefficient is referred to as the *coefficient of stability and equivalence*.

Internal consistency methods of establishing reliability involve only one administration of an assessment and are used most appropriately when the items or tasks are basically homogeneous and assess essentially the same behavior. *Split-half* reliability is determined by establishing the relationship between the scores on two equivalent halves of an assessment administered to a total group at one time. Regardless of how the test is organized, an odd item/even item split should produce essentially equivalent halves. Because longer tests tend to be more reliable, and because split-half reliability represents the reliability of a test only half as long as the actual test, a corrective known as the Spearman-Brown prophecy formula must be applied to the coefficient. *Kuder-Richardson* methods estimate the internal consistency reliability by determining how well all the items (or tasks) on a test relate to all other items (or tasks) and to the total test. The KR methods result in a reliability estimate that is essentially equivalent to the average of the split-half reliabilities computed for all possible halves. There are several Kuder-Richardson formulas, commonly referred to as KR-20, KR-21, and KR-21′ (KR-21 prime). All of the KR formulas require that each item or task be scored dichotomously, as correct or incorrect, 1 or 0. For assessments with items or tasks scored such that different answers are worth different numbers of points, say, 0, 1, 2, or 3, *Cronbach's alpha* (α), also referred to as coefficient alpha, can be used. Test publishers typically report KR-20 or Cronbach's alpha coefficients (depending on the scoring method) as estimates of internal consistency.

Teachers do not typically compute estimates of reliability for their tests because reliability formulas do not typically work well when the range of scores is restricted and there is not a wide spread of scores. If a teacher computes a reliability estimate and the resulting coefficient is high, the assessment test is definitely reliable. If, on the other hand, the coefficient is low, it does not necessarily mean that the test is not reliable. No test is perfectly reliable; scores are invariably affected by errors of assessment resulting from a variety of causes.

What constitutes an acceptable level of reliability is to some degree determined by the type of assessment, although a coefficient over .90 would be acceptable for any test. For standardized achievement and aptitude tests, there is generally no good reason for selecting a test for which the reliability is not at least .90. Personality measures do not typically report such high reliabilities (although certainly some do), and therefore one would be very satisfied with a reliability in the .80s and might even accept a reliability in the .70s. If a test is composed of several subtests, then the reliability of each subtest, not just the reliability of the total test, must be assessed. Because reliability is a function of test length, the reliability of a given subtest is typically lower than the total test reliability.

Due to the restriction in range, traditionally computed reliabilities in the .50s are not uncommon for classroom assessments. For mastery tests, coefficients near zero may be obtained. Presently there is no approach to the calculation of the reliability of criterion-referenced test scores generally accepted as being appropriate and practical for teacher use. Instead, evaluation of the quality of a classroom test can be based solely on the results of item analysis (see Chapter 10).

When we speak of the accuracy of an individual's score or ask how much confidence we can have in any individual's score, then we are interested in the standard error of measurement. The standard error of measurement is generally reported for standardized test results and facilitates proper interpretation. The *standard error of measurement* (SEM) is an estimate of how often you can expect errors of a given size associated with a person's test score. High reliability is associated with a small standard error of measurement, and low reliability is associated with a large standard error of measurement. It is possible to calculate the standard error of measurement using the scores resulting from a single administration of a test to a group. The size of the difference between a person's true score and obtained score is a function of the reliability of the assessment. The standard error of measurement is expressed in the same units as the test itself, and whether the standard error of measurement is considered large or small is relative to the size of the test.

Standard error of measurement estimates are frequently used to construct bands, or confidence intervals, around individual scores. We are approximately 68% confident that a person's true score falls within the interval $X \pm 1$ SEM, where "X" is the individual's obtained score. Overlapping intervals suggest that the true scores on the test are not really different, whereas intervals that do not overlap suggest true score differences.

Try These

I. Match each statement with the appropriate type of validity evidence by writing the letter corresponding to the type of evidence on the blank in front of each statement. The letters may be used more than once, and more than one letter may be appropriate for a statement.

A. Content
B. Construct
C. Concurrent
D. Predictive

_____ 1. Requires item validity and sampling validity.
_____ 2. Is of prime importance for an aptitude test.
_____ 3. Permits substitution of a shorter assessment for a longer one.
_____ 4. Is most important for an achievement test.
_____ 5. Would be of concern to a developer of an assessment of aspirations.
_____ 6. Would be of concern to a teacher creating a performance test of critical thinking.
_____ 7. Is determined by the judgment of expert reviewers.
_____ 8. Involves a time lag before the criterion is measured.
_____ 9. Is reported as a correlation coefficient.
_____ 10. Is most important for a test to determine if students have mastered the intended outcomes.

II. Match each statement with the appropriate type of reliability by writing the letter corresponding to the type of reliability on the blank in front of each statement. The letters may be used more than once, and more than one letter may be appropriate for a statement.

A. Test-retest
B. Equivalent-forms
C. Split-half
D. Kuder-Richardson methods
E. Interrater or intrarater
F. Cronbach's alpha

_____ 1. Requires a correction formula.
_____ 2. Estimates the stability of scores over time.
_____ 3. In general, the best estimate of internal consistency.
_____ 4. When corrected, tends to overestimate reliability.
_____ 5. Estimates the degree to which two tests assess the same thing.
_____ 6. Is of importance for all assessments.
_____ 7. Requires items/tasks to be scored dichotomously.
_____ 8. Is most important for observation instruments and performance assessments.
_____ 9. Involves dividing the items/tasks of one test into two sets.
_____ 10. Requires more than one form of the test.

_____ 11. Requires students to be tested twice with the same test.

_____ 12. An internal consistency estimate that works with items/tasks assigned multiple points.

III. Briefly list on a separate sheet of paper the procedure you would follow to establish the content validity evidence for a set of assessments included with a textbook series you are using.

IV. Your school district has used the Practically Perfect Reading Readiness Test for many years. The PPRRT works exceptionally well in determining whether young students have the prerequisite development and skills to begin reading instruction. Its major drawback is that it takes two sessions (1 1/2 to 2 hours) and must be administered individually rather than to a group. The selection team of which you are a member has been charged with finding a suitable substitute for the PPRRT. How would you advise the team on validity and reliability issues regarding candidate assessments? On a separate sheet of paper, list specifically:

a) What type of validity is of paramount importance?
b) What steps should be followed to establish this type of validity?
c) What type of reliability is of paramount importance?
d) What steps should be followed to estimate this type of reliability?

Answers

I. 1. A, 2. D, 3. C, 4. A, 5. B, 6. B, 7. A, 8. D, 9. C & D (bonus points if you got both!), 10. A

II. 1. C, 2. A, 3. D, 4. C, 5. B, 6. A, 7. D, 8. E, 9. C, 10. B, 11. A, 12. F

III. Your answer may be written in many ways, but should include these steps: (a) Examine test items and performance tasks to determine match between textbook outcomes and assessments. (b) Determine overall match between actual items/tasks, text outcomes, and school/district outcomes. (c) Render judgment.

IV. a) Concurrent validity.

b) Select random representative sample of students; administer both the PPRRT and the new test to the sample; correlate the scores and determine if the coefficient is high enough to permit substitution.

c) Test-retest reliability.

d) Select random representative sample of students; administer the new test twice to the group with 2 to 4 weeks between testings; correlate the scores and determine if the coefficient is high enough.

CHAPTER 4

Instructional Outcomes: The Backbone of Good Assessment

Key Concepts:

- Defining instructional outcomes.
- Understanding the advantages and disadvantages of instructional outcomes.
- Organizing instructional outcomes into taxonomies.
- Understanding levels of outcomes and outcome specificity.
- Writing instructional outcomes.
- Evaluating instructional outcomes.

Standards Addressed in This Chapter:

1. Choose assessment methods appropriate for instructional decisions.
2. Develop assessment methods appropriate for instructional decisions.

Before You Begin Reading, Consider This

Instructional outcomes or objectives have to come from somewhere or someone. Should teachers create their own outcomes to guide their instruction and assessment efforts?

YES Developing outcomes is an inherent part of the instructional and assessment process and, thus, an inherent part of the teacher's job. Teacher-developed outcomes can guide those processes better than "off-the-shelf" outcomes. And developing their own objectives forces teachers to think through the intended outcomes. Thus, the teaching strategies and form of assessment will be much more congruent with the outcomes.

NO Teachers have enough to do without having to write instructional outcomes! This is a job for experts like curriculum developers. Because instructional outcomes have been around since the 1950s, there are vast numbers of them available, and teachers can find those that are useful to their own classrooms and instructional plans. Besides, a teacher developing her or his own outcomes does not guarantee that the instruction or the assessment of achievement will be congruent with them.

Understanding Instructional Outcomes

In general, outcomes are the desired results of an effort, the results intended at the end of a series of activities. *Instructional outcomes* are specific statements of what is to be accomplished and how well, and are expressed in terms of observable, assessable student behavior. They are, in a sense, operational definitions of the learning that should be taking place in the classroom. Specification of outcomes should occur early in the assessment process, regardless of when assessment occurs in relation to instruction.

If these instructional outcomes sound like the objectives you may have learned to write as part of your teacher training in building lesson and unit plans, you are right. Instructional outcomes are useful in assessment, as well as in planning curricula. Instructional outcomes inform both your teaching and your assessment practices. Also, the interaction between your teaching and assessment informs each other, so that you can adjust either one formally (perhaps at the beginning of an academic year) or informally (in the middle of a lesson) to make all three parts of the triangle work together. In assessment, however, you do not have to come up with a second set of outcomes (one set for teaching and one set for assessment). The same set should serve both purposes, as illustrated in Figure 4.1. But as you will see in this chapter, instructional outcomes should be written with assessment in mind.

Modern educators recognize the importance of instructional outcomes in the development of effective teaching and assessment strategies, in part because of the pi-

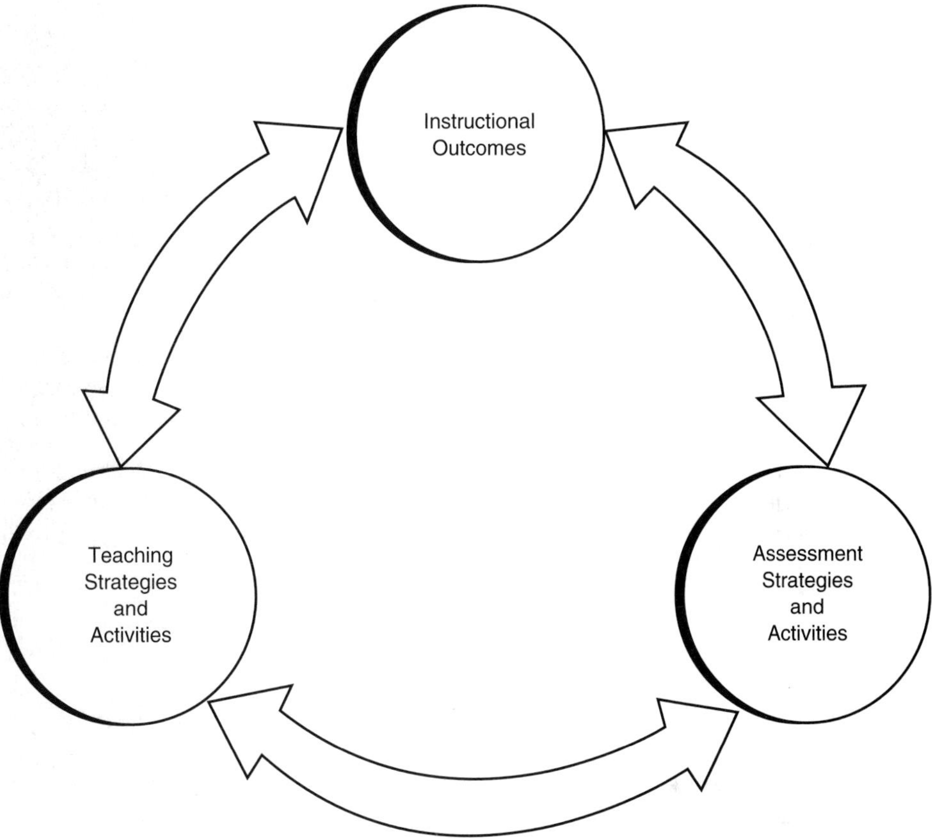

Figure 4.1
The interaction among instructional outcomes and the teaching and assessment strategies derived from them.

oneering writings of Ralph Tyler in the early 1930s.[1] The outcomes movement was further fostered by the popularity of programmed instruction in the early 1960s. Although interest in programmed instruction declined, interest in outcomes increased, due at least in part to a short but effective book by Robert Mager entitled *Preparing Instructional Objectives*.[2] The book was originally written with specific reference to programmed instruction, but the concepts it presented are obviously and easily generalizable to any type of instruction and, perhaps more importantly, to any educational activity.

---

[1]See, for example, *Constructing Achievement Tests* by R. W. Tyler, 1934, Columbus: Ohio State University.
[2]*Preparing Instructional Objectives* by R. F. Mager, 1962, Palo Alto, CA: Fearon.

Some educators are of the opinion that some of the "truly important" outcomes of instruction cannot be expressed in specific, assessable terms. Although more will be said on the subject later in the chapter, the fact that an outcome is observable and assessable does not necessarily mean that it deals with a trivial expectation. Nobody said assessment of these sometimes abstract outcomes was necessarily easy, but even elusive outcomes such as music appreciation and good citizenship can be assessed if educators can specify what they mean. As a teacher and assessor, you have to know what you mean when you say you want students to appreciate music. What exactly would a student have to do to demonstrate music appreciation? Buy classical compact discs? Listen to "Performance Today!" on public radio? If a desired outcome cannot be expressed as an assessable behavior, it is probably not because it is unassessable; it is probably because the desired outcome has not been sufficiently thought through or clearly articulated.

Instructional outcomes, objectives desired of students, are a little trickier than some other types of outcomes simply because of their indirect nature. As defined by Mager, an instructional outcome is "an intent communicated by a statement describing a proposed change in a learner—a statement of what the learner is to be like when he has successfully completed a learning experience."[3] But learning is an inferred event for the most part, not a directly observable phenomenon, and thus, teachers face a challenge when assessing it. If a pep club has an objective "to sell $500 worth of chocolate-nut caramels by November 15," determining whether the objective is achieved is a very straightforward process. Money is directly observable, and someone needs only to count the money collected. In contrast, if a teacher has an outcome to the effect that students "will be able to write complete sentences," the process of determining outcome achievement is more complex. The actual ability to write a complete sentence is not directly observable because learning takes place inside of students' heads. In fact, there are two factors involved—whether students can write complete sentences and whether they acquired this ability as a result of instruction. Thus, first it must be determined what behavior or performance will constitute sufficient evidence that the desired ability exists. In the case of writing complete sentences, an infinite number of such sentences exist; it might be decided, however, that if a student can write five complete sentences it will be inferred that she has the desired capability. Whether a capability is acquired, or learned, as a result of instruction can be determined only by observing performance at two different points in time, before and after instruction, and seeing if performance has changed; a positive change in performance implies that learning has taken place. Thus, although learning itself cannot be directly observed or assessed by teachers, changes in performance can.

In the types of assessment performed by teachers in the classroom, instructional outcomes form the basis for what will be assessed. This is true regardless of the timing of the assessment in relation to instruction. This is also true whether the teacher

---

[3]See R. F. Mager, 1962, p. 3.

selects or modifies an existing test (perhaps from a textbook series) or creates one.[4] It is important to realize that instructional outcomes form the basis for establishing the content validity of a test, and so clear, assessable outcomes are critical to good assessment of achievement. To the extent that classroom assessments and test items reflect the performance called for in the outcomes, they are content valid.[5]

How Using Instructional Outcomes Improves Teaching, Learning, and Assessment

Based on what you have read about instructional outcomes thus far, you probably have concluded that outcomes are a universally accepted component of any educational endeavor. This, unfortunately, does not happen to be the case. There are some educators (and some non-educators) opposed to outcomes on a variety of grounds: Some objections are related to the nature and purpose of outcomes themselves, and others stem from reactions to the politics involved in the outcomes-based education (OBE) movement. The following discussion is intended to point out the uses and abuses of instructional outcomes in the classroom, not to change your politics.

Supporters of outcomes assert that their main advantage is that they give direction to or guide the activities of a teaching effort. Without instructional outcomes, activities are haphazard at worst and loosely directed at best; with outcomes, activities are focused and organized. This contention has a good deal of common-sense appeal: Even persons who express negative attitudes toward outcomes use them in their everyday activities, often informally, and without the conscious awareness of doing so.

Very few rational individuals, for example, get into their cars in the morning and drive for 50 minutes with a vague destination such as "wherever I happen to be after driving south for 50 minutes" or no destination in mind at all. People tend to have very definite intended destinations: school, the office, or the local grocery store. Because of unforeseen circumstances, such as an automobile accident or a traffic jam, they may not get there or they may take longer than they expected, but they know where they are headed. Further, they probably have determined the most efficient route to take. The analogies to education are obvious and numerous. It is as irrational to teach for 50 minutes without a definite objective in mind as it is to drive for 50 minutes without a definite destination. It certainly does not seem logical to say that a teacher will teach for 50 minutes per day for 180 days and whatever the students happen to know at the end of the year will be okay.

Outcomes provide direction in a number of ways. They suggest general strategies and specific activities for their attainment and, in doing so, help teachers plan instruction. Different sets of outcomes will usually generate different strategies.

[4]You will find more on the use of instructional outcomes in the creation and selection of paper-and-pencil test items in Chapters 5, 6, and 7. The use of outcomes in the creation and selection of performance and product assessments is discussed further in Chapter 8.

[5]See Chapter 3 for an explanation of content evidence of validity.

Suppose that there are three French teachers, Mr. Addams, Ms. Bermudez, and Mr. Charles. Mr. Addams has no specific outcomes; he is simply "teaching French." Ms. Bermudez has a set of outcomes related to students being able to speak conversational French. Mr. Charles has a set of outcomes related to students being able to read and write French. Can you see how their classroom activities probably differ? Almost anything Mr. Addams does, even if he just reads a French textbook out loud every day, is appropriate and constitutes "teaching French." Ms. Bermudez, on the other hand, probably spends a lot of time speaking French, playing recorded conversations in French, and having students converse in French. Mr. Charles probably devotes a lot of time to having students translate written passages from French into English, either orally or in writing. Instructional outcomes also give direction to the students themselves. They know what is expected of them and can use their study time efficiently. Pity the students of Mr. Addams! What should they study? Should they memorize the text or practice pronunciation? Telling students precisely what you want them to know and be able to do is not "teaching to the test"; it is teaching to your own instructional expectations. If you tell students that you want them to be able to translate a simple sentence in English into French using vocabulary acquired to date, that is not the same as telling them that you want them to be able to translate the song, "I Love Paris in the Springtime," into French.

Outcomes also serve a diagnostic-prescriptive function. If you know where your students were when you started and where you want them to be following instruction, then at any point in time you can assess how much progress has been made and act accordingly. Further, regardless of when you assess their status or progress (during the instruction or at the end), your outcomes dictate to a great extent the way in which you collect status data. If an outcome deals with student achievement, an appropriate assessment of that achievement is probably called for. If, on the other hand, an outcome deals with decreased instances of disruptive behavior, observation is probably required. The existence of outcomes does not necessarily mean that the instruction will be more successful than it otherwise would have been (there are many other factors at work), but they do allow teachers and students alike to determine what has been accomplished. Without outcomes, it is questionable whether it is even possible to evaluate student learning at all. How can it be said that an effort did or did not "do the job" if "the job" was never specified?

Outcomes also serve a communication function. Teachers can communicate to students and parents not only their outcomes for instruction, but also where students are, as a group or as individuals, with respect to those outcomes. Administrators can communicate similar information to school boards and the community at large. Communication is enhanced primarily because discussion can deal with specifics, not vague generalities. A parent wishing to help his child at home with arithmetic would not benefit much from a statement to the effect that "Jules cannot do fractions." In contrast, the message that "Jules is having difficulty multiplying and dividing improper fractions" would provide more direction to home help sessions.

How to Avoid the Misuse of Instructional Outcomes

Critics of instructional outcomes believe that their use can result in rigid and conforming procedures, standards, and behavior that discourage creativity and spontaneity and fail to take into consideration individual differences. Some also question whether all important educational results can be articulated as outcomes. With respect to instruction, for example, they feel that outcomes may be suitable for only a limited number of cut-and-dry areas, such as arithmetic, and are inappropriate for all other areas. Critics also contend that teachers have a natural tendency to select outcomes that are not the most important but that are the easiest to assess, resulting in outcomes representing expectations of trivial importance. It is easier to assess a student's acquisition of facts, for example, than her ability to synthesize; consequently, chances are, given a choice, teachers will select outcomes describing what students "will know." Furthermore, those who are skeptical of instructional outcomes claim that the really important outcomes of any effort are long-term results, not short-term accomplishments; therefore, outcomes dealing with here-and-now achievement are largely irrelevant. After all, they ask, what difference does it make if a student can identify the cause of a significant event in a reading selection? What we really want is for students to be able to successfully function in society after graduation.

Very little evidence shows that the existence of outcomes actually results in greater achievement. Even those who agree with the concept of outcomes on a theoretical level suggest that, in reality, their use is impractical, because any given effort can spawn an unmanageable multiplicity of outcomes. Reading comprehension, for example, may entail close to 100 separate outcomes, such as "given a work which conveys a moral, the learner will identify the moral" or "given a significant event from a reading selection, the learner will identify its cause."[6]

There is obviously a great deal of truth in the above objections, but they represent mostly potential dangers associated with the misuse of instructional outcomes, not flaws inherent in outcomes themselves. Analysis of many criticisms of outcomes reveals that they deal at least in part with problems arising from their misapplication or from poor administration. Several of the misgivings could easily be translated into suggestions, or caveats, for writing outcomes; for example: "Avoid selecting outcomes simply because they are easy to assess." For example, many people each year are killed in automobile accidents as a result of speeding, reckless driving, and driving while drinking. Yet, we do not say, "Stop manufacturing cars!" Instead we say, "Slow down," "Drive carefully," "Wear your seat belt," and "If you drink, don't drive." The logical conclusion is not that cars in general are dangerous, but that they can be dangerous when misused. The same logic applies to the use of instructional outcomes. Although some specific responses to each objection have been discussed earlier within a different context, we'll briefly look again at each one in order to make

[6] *Structure of Reading Skills* by M. Patalino and G. Strangel, 1971, Los Angeles: Center for the Study of Education, UCLA Graduate School of Education.

clear how you can avoid misusing instructional outcomes in your own teaching and assessment.

First, outcomes are not restrictive in and of themselves. For any outcome, alternative strategies can be utilized to promote achievement. If your outcome is to get to work at 44 East Drudgery Street, there are probably any number of reasonable routes that you can take. One route may be a few miles longer but have less traffic and thus take less time. Another route may be the shortest in terms of both miles and time but requires a 50-cent toll. Based on your priorities, you will select the route best suited to you. Similarly, a teacher will utilize a strategy that is best suited to his students, given available resources. There is plenty of room for creativity in terms of putting to best use what is available. Further, the use of outcomes by no means negates the existence of individual differences. Different students, for example, may be working on different outcomes at different times; each student may take a different length of time to achieve a given outcome; and different instructional strategies may be used with different students. All students may or may not have the same outcomes; there may be a set of minimum outcomes to be achieved by all and a number of optional or enrichment outcomes. So, outcomes—although they could be restrictive if used improperly or inflexibly—are not inherently restrictive.

The issue of the "objectifiability" of all desired educational outcomes stymies some. Educators have reached a degree of consensus regarding the appropriateness of outcomes in basic skills areas such as reading and math. The lack of consensus regarding other more elusive areas, such as music appreciation, stems not from the inability of the outcomes to be assessed, but from the inability of people to specify what they really mean by music appreciation. And, if you cannot say what music appreciation means—if you cannot translate an outcome into observable behavior—how can you teach it and, more critically, how can you know whether students "have" it? But with enough thought, even the fuzziest of outcomes can be operationally defined and translated into observable, assessable behaviors.

That educators may tend to select trivial, easy-to-assess outcomes is their own fault and not an inherent fault of outcomes. All important desired outcomes can be expressed in observable, assessable terms, although the task is not always easy. With a reasonable amount of serious effort, however, it can be done. As for the alleged irrelevance of short-term outcomes, most critics and fans of the use of instructional outcomes agree that long-term outcomes are the real concern of educational efforts. But long-term outcomes do not just happen; they require a proper foundation and systematic development. When the relationship between goals and outcomes is discussed later, you will see that all outcomes are at least theoretically related to some long-term outcome or goal. For example, a basic goal of a public-school education, a desired long-term outcome for graduates, is economic self-sufficiency. This goal can be analyzed into component abilities such as literacy, preparedness for future training, and vocational skill. Each of these can be further analyzed into a greater number of abilities such as the ability to read and comprehend, the ability to write coherently, the ability to compute, the ability to make intelligent vocational choices, and so on and so on and so on. Each of these discrete, prerequisite skills and knowledge can be developed over a period of years in different courses at different times.

In isolation, any given outcome may appear to be of little consequence. But when looked at in combination with other related outcomes—present and future—their relevance is much more evident.

It is true that, anecdotal data aside, there is very little conclusive research data supporting the effectiveness of the use of instructional outcomes. This is due at least in part to the fact that related studies are typically conducted in real-world environments such as classrooms. In such situations a myriad of controllable and uncontrollable variables operates, making it very difficult to determine the effect of any one variable of interest. In any event, outcomes make sense logically because they do permit assessment of exactly what has been accomplished. Further, there are many other organizational activities, such as lesson planning, that are accepted as good practice despite the absence of evidence regarding their specific effectiveness in raising standardized test scores.

The basic assertion that any effort can spawn a multiplicity of outcomes is true, although the multiplicity is not necessarily unmanageable. When a general desired outcome such as reading comprehension, computational skill, or coherent writing is translated into a set of observable, assessable behaviors covering all aspects of the desired outcome, the result is likely to be a large number of specific outcomes. It must be emphasized, however, that the component behaviors exist regardless of whether or not they are identified. Not specifying outcomes does not decrease the number of relevant behaviors. They do not go away. To purposely not identify them because the result might be somewhat overwhelming is an "ostrichy" avoidance tactic to say the least. In fact, the reality that so many component behaviors are involved in any major outcome constitutes a good argument for identifying them. Without a list of such behaviors it is much more likely that a number of them will be overlooked, thereby decreasing the chances of achieving the general desired outcome. Thus, although it is true that a given area may spawn a large number of specific outcomes, the benefits to be derived from articulating them makes the effort worthwhile. And although keeping track of individual outcomes achievement and related clerical activities may well require more organization and time, logically it would seem easier to organize and manage day-to-day activities when they are directed toward the achievement of specific outcomes. If anything, having outcomes facilitates organization in such a system.

Overall then, dissatisfaction with the use of instructional outcomes is based more on their possible misuse than on the inherent nature of outcomes. There are poorly written outcomes dealing with important student performance and well-written outcomes dealing with trivial performance. But the existence of such outcomes does not diminish in any way the potential advantages to be derived from well-written, relevant outcomes. The important point for teachers is that, to be effective, you need to be clear on what you want the students to accomplish, what it looks like when they are doing it, and how to get students to demonstrate it in assessment situations. Using instructional outcomes can help achieve these goals. A later section of this chapter will guide you in creating and evaluating instructional outcomes for use in your own classroom.

Of course, outcomes are not always required for every activity. Just as there are times when one may take a ride for pure enjoyment, with no particular destination in mind, there is a place in education for minimally directed exploratory activities. In one sense, such activities do have an outcome, like increased awareness or self-expression, but the intent is not the achievement of any other specific, assessable skill or knowledge. However, activities like these comprise a very small percentage of the total educational enterprise. For the vast majority of educational endeavors, instructional outcomes are highly appropriate and useful.

Distinguishing Between Instructional Outcomes for Individuals and Groups

All outcomes indicate intended student behavior; there are differences, however, in terms of the nature of the intended behavior. One basic difference is that certain types of assessment, and their corresponding outcomes, are primarily concerned with the performance of individuals whereas others are primarily concerned with the performance of groups.

Student assessment is concerned mainly with individual performance. Instructional outcomes are concerned with changes in student performance or behavior that indicate learning has taken place as a result of instruction. These types of individual instructional outcomes are variously referred to as *performance outcomes, behavioral objectives, learning outcomes,* and *classroom objectives*. For a long time the word *objective* was in vogue. Recently, favor has been granted to *outcome,* which emphasizes more the result of the teaching-learning experience, rather than the process. The two terms are used interchangeably in this text and by many experts. Other terms are occasionally used (there is no scarcity of descriptive terms in the field of assessment!), but the ones above are the most common terms used.

Certain instructional outcomes are considered required, minimum essentials. They are outcomes that should be achieved by virtually all students, regardless of ability or background, and are called *mastery outcomes* or *minimum skills outcomes*. The concept is not a new one to education, but it gained prominence and widespread adoption as a result of the accountability movement in the 1980s, which maintained that there are certain skills and knowledge that are essential prerequisites to the learning of subsequent skills and knowledge. The culminating skills and knowledge are required for effective functioning in a democratic society; students are entitled to instruction that will help them achieve these. Thus, various mastery outcomes may be identified at all grade levels.

Outcomes for assessing the effectiveness of instruction express expectations intended for groups, not individuals. The groups involved are, of course, made up of your students, but the primary interest is in their performance as a whole, not as individuals. An example will help to clarify the distinction between individual and group outcomes. Suppose the area of interest is reading comprehension. Specific instructional outcomes might include the following:

- Given passages unfamiliar to the student and written at an appropriate difficulty level, the student will correctly answer related factual questions four out of five times.

- Given new passages written at an appropriate difficulty level, the student will select the main idea for each from among four choices four out of five times.
- Given new passages written at an appropriate difficulty level, the student will select the best title for each among four choices four out of five times.

As noted earlier, reading comprehension might entail in the neighborhood of 100 specific outcomes. For each student it could easily be determined at any time whether and which outcomes had been achieved.

You might be interested in the progress of the class as a whole; that is, you might want to know what percent of the class had achieved what percent of the outcomes at any given point in time. Your intent might be, for example, to have 90% of the class achieve a certain set of mastery outcomes. This type of question, however, as opposed to "How is Darryl doing?" would be of prime interest in assessing the effectiveness of the instruction, and the emphasis would be on clusters of outcomes. Group outcomes might include:

- Ninety percent of the students will successfully achieve the criterion for outcomes 1–27.
- Seventy-five percent of the students will successfully achieve the criterion for outcomes 28–92.

Classifying Instructional Outcomes Using Taxonomies

In science, a taxonomy is an orderly classification of plants and animals according to their presumed natural relationships.[7] The term has been borrowed by educators to describe a comprehensive classification scheme for instructional outcomes. These taxonomies classify all outcomes into a hierarchy of categories based on presumed complexity. Each succeeding category involves behavior believed to be more complex than the one previous, and each is considered to be prerequisite to the next; in other words, performance of outcomes at a higher level implies the ability to perform related outcomes at lower levels. The stated purpose of the taxonomies is to facilitate communication.[8] The identification, naming, and description of categories of instructional outcomes permit educators to use the same terms to describe the same behaviors in the same way. The existence of the taxonomies also focuses attention on a wide range of instructional outcomes, thus making it less likely that all the outcomes for a given effort will involve lower-level behaviors only. The taxonomies themselves are very helpful because in addition to describing behaviors in each of the categories and sub-categories, they also provide illustrative examples.

---

[7]This definition is courtesy of Webster.

[8]*Taxonomy of Educational Objectives, Handbook I: Cognitive Domain* by B. S. Bloom (Ed.), 1956, New York: David McKay.

Taxonomies of instructional outcomes have been proposed corresponding to three domains of learning—the cognitive domain, the affective domain, and the psychomotor domain. Although there is overlap, it is believed that all instructional outcomes can be classified as belonging primarily to one of the three domains. The *cognitive domain* deals with, as the name implies, cognitive processes, and the taxonomic categories range from simple recall of facts to the making of evaluative judgments. The *affective domain* involves feelings, attitudes, interests, and values, and the categories range from willingness to receive or attend to characterization by a value. The *psychomotor domain* is concerned with physical abilities, such as muscular or motor skills, manipulation, and neuromuscular coordination. Cognitive processes like critical thinking, for example, are themselves a major focus of learning. These processes are also involved in the attitudes and skills of the other domains. For this reason, the cognitive domain is the most important of the three domains of learning. A fuller description of the cognitive domain and examples of outcomes classified by taxonomic level are presented in the following sections. Descriptions and classified examples of outcomes for the affective and psychomotor domains are contained in Appendices B and C, respectively. The three taxonomies presented in this text are not the only ones ever created. They have been more widely accepted, however.

Bloom's Taxonomy of Learning Processes in the Cognitive Domain

The taxonomy of cognitive outcomes, developed by Bloom and his associates, has definitely made educators aware of the wide range of abilities involved in cognitive learning. Each of the six major categories represents a different kind of learning process. By articulating descriptions and examples of the kind of behaviors involved in each category, educators have been able to ensure that higher-level learning is considered and planned for. Since publication of the cognitive taxonomy in 1956, emphasis has shifted considerably from memorization tasks to more meaningful outcomes as well as more meaningful assessment. Below is a brief description of each of the major categories of the cognitive taxonomy of educational outcomes. The numbers to the left of the category name indicate that there are sub-levels of learning and outcomes within each category. The topic *budget deficit* has been used to illustrate how the intended behavior changes and becomes progressively more complex at each level of the taxonomy.

1.00 Knowledge. This category includes memorization behaviors, specifically the recall or recognition of previously encountered information. (For example, the ability to define the term *budget deficit* from memory.)

2.00 Comprehension. Behaviors in this category are those that show understanding, not just memorization, such as being able to explain or interpret as an indication of comprehension. (For example, the ability to explain ways in which a budget deficit affects an economy.)

3.00 Application. Application involves being able to use or apply an abstract concept in a specific situation. (For example, the ability to apply general principles of deficit spending and reduction to the current United States economy.)

4.00 Analysis. Analysis involves the ability to break down a communication into its component parts and to identify the relationships that exist between them. (For example, the ability to determine the common elements in three different plans for reducing the budget deficit in the United States.)

5.00 Synthesis. Synthesis refers to the ability to combine elements and parts to form a unique whole, in the shape of a new communication. (For example, the ability to develop an original plan for reducing the budget deficit in the United States.)

6.00 Evaluation. Evaluation is the making of judgments about the value of some communication—a piece of work, a solution, a method—for a given purpose. (For example, the ability to critique a proposed plan for reducing the budget deficit in the United States.)

Examples of Instructional Outcomes for the Cognitive Domain

The outcomes listed below in each level of the cognitive domain reflect the range in specificity and content you are likely to encounter in practice. They are included here not as examples of well- or badly constructed outcomes for assessment purposes, although some are more clear than others. You will notice, for example, that some are very specific about the behavior called for, the conditions under which the behavior is to be performed, and the criteria for acceptable performance. Others may be specific in one of these three areas but not the other two. In practice, you may find yourself rewriting fuzzy outcomes or creating new ones to give more direction to your teaching and assessment efforts.

Depending on the wording of an outcome or how it is interpreted, it may be classified differently. The author's intent is not always known. There are two examples of this in the list below. One has to do with "fact and opinion"; the other has to do with "logical fallacies in an argument." Keep in mind also that any outcomes written at the comprehension level or above require novel situations, examples, and communication for appropriate assessment. If you use the same pictures, examples, and so forth in assessment that you used in teaching the concepts originally, you are, in effect, testing the student's memorization capacity—knowledge—and nothing beyond it. Later in this chapter, you will learn more about the components of useful outcomes, especially as they relate to assessment. Outcomes in the cognitive domain that are classified at the knowledge level are also referred to as *lower-level outcomes.* Those classified at the comprehension level or beyond (through evaluation) are alternatively referred to as *higher-level outcomes.*

Knowledge

Given definitions of various landforms, match each with the appropriate term four out of five times.

Given the growth stages of a housefly in scrambled order, student puts them in correct chronological order.

Select the correct verb form for a given sentence.

Know the difference between fact and opinion. (See the analysis section for an outcome that is similar but at a higher level.)

Put in proper procedural order the steps in troubleshooting electronic failures in video cassette recorders.

Comprehension

Translate given novel Spanish sentences into English.

Explain in everyday language how the pressure of the water flowing through a Venturi tube is affected by the shape of the tube.

Given novel, commonly found, three-dimensional objects, classify them as spheres, cubes, cylinders, or pyramids.

Given data not seen before, draw appropriate conclusions from them.

Given novel data in graphic form (bar chart or histogram), predict the continuation of indicated trends.

Interpret pictures and drawings (assuming the ones given in the test situation are novel to the student).

Determine the meaning of a sentence that contains negative words.

Interpret the information in a given student's cumulative folder.

Infer main ideas from titles, chapter headings, etc.

Application

Make change for $1.00 for singular and multiple purchases of less than $1.00.

Solve everyday arithmetic problems involving addition and/or subtraction.

Using the rules of pronunciation, pronounce correctly given unfamiliar words.

Analysis

Distinguish factual statements from statements of opinion in a given communication. (See the knowledge section for an outcome that is similar but at a lower level.)

Detect logical fallacies in an argument. (See the evaluation section for an outcome that is similar but at a higher level.)

Given an advertisement or commercial not experienced before, the student will state, in writing, the propaganda tactic used.

Synthesis

Compose a sonata of at least 7 minutes' duration.

Perform an original skit that communicates the effect humans have on the planet.

Generate a plan to implement a solution to a given human problem that states who will perform what actions, due dates for those actions to be completed, and plans for foreseeable contingencies.

Plan a unit of instruction for a given teaching situation at the elementary level.

Formulate a personal philosophy of education.

Evaluation

Given a plan for the economic development of Zaire, evaluate its usefulness for Kenya.

Indicate the logical fallacies in an argument. (See the analysis section for an outcome that is similar but at a lower level.)

Critique a given screenplay according to the principles of screenplay writing.

Judge a work of art according to the principles of composition and aesthetics.

Considering Factors Affecting the Design of Instructional Outcomes

The above examples illustrate the broad range of instructional outcomes teachers can articulate and make use of in their classrooms. But as we have seen, many factors affect the quality and usefulness of instructional outcomes used for teaching and assessment. The next section will address some of these considerations.

Distinguishing Among Levels of Instructional Outcomes

Instructional outcomes can be written at varying levels of specificity. At one end of the continuum we have very broad statements of long-term outcomes; these are typically referred to as goals, long-term goals, or *general instructional outcomes.* At the other end of the spectrum we have very precise statements of more immediate outcomes, each representing only one behavior or result; these are usually referred to as *specific instructional outcomes.* In the dictionary-definition sense, virtually no difference exists between a goal and an outcome; a goal is defined as "a thing for which effort is made," and an outcome is defined as a "result or consequence."[9] Traditionally in educational assessment, however, the terms have been used to make the distinctions initially described. And, of course, a variety of intermediate levels of specificity exist as well. We may, for example, speak of course outcomes, terminal outcomes, or milestone outcomes; in each case we are indicating a level of specificity somewhere between a broad goal and a specific outcome. Figure 4.2 provides a summary of the terminology associated with the levels of specificity of outcomes and illustrative examples.

[9] *The World Book Dictionary* by C. L. Barnhart and R. K. Barnhart (Eds.), 1987, Chicago: World Book.

Level of Specificity	Definition	Related Terms	Example
Goals	Broad statements of long-term outcomes	General objectives	Students will become economically self-sufficient
General instructional outcomes	More precise statements of shorter-term outcomes	Second-level outcomes Unit objectives Intermediate objectives Course objectives Terminal outcomes Cumulative outcomes Milestone outcomes	Balance a checkbook
Specific instructional outcomes	Precise statements of immediate outcomes	Instructional objectives Behavioral outcomes	Students can add amounts of money including dollars and cents ($X.XX) not totaling more than $999.99 without a calculator

Figure 4.2
A summary of terminology associated with levels of outcome specificity.

Setting Goals

Goals are global statements of long-term outcomes, and their achievement is not assessed directly. Although educational goals do represent the important outcomes of the educational system, the system cannot be held directly accountable for their achievement. Rather, as noted previously, achievement of shorter-term outcomes believed to be prerequisite to broader, long-term outcomes are assessed. Thus, goals do not deal with definite skills, but related specific outcomes do. The notion of "economic self-sufficiency" as a goal, for example, entails any number of basic skills and vocational skills.

There is a reasonable degree of consensus concerning the overall purpose of education and what the goals of the educational system should be. The purpose of education is to provide individuals with experiences resulting in their acquisition of the knowledge, skills, and attitudes allowing them to meet their individual needs as well as the needs of society. Of course many of these needs tend to overlap; it is to the benefit of society and the individual if the individual is economically self-sufficient. True, there is no way in our present society to know in advance with certainty what students will "need" in the future; it is possible, however, to make very reasonable projections. Further, although in earlier times it was literally possible to teach all known knowledge, this is clearly no longer even remotely feasible. Therefore, education today emphasizes computer skills, search and information-retrieval skills, and critical thinking skills, whereby students learn how to locate desired information and critically appraise it for their use.

Goals, such as those in America 2000, tend to be established at the national level, adopted at the state level, and ultimately put into practice at the classroom level. Interestingly, the Seven Cardinal Principles of Secondary Education, put forth by a commission of the National Education Association, represents goals that are as appropriate today as they apparently were in 1918 when they were written. These principles are concerned with the individual's health, role as a family member, basic skills (referred to as "fundamental processes"), vocational skills, citizenship, use of leisure time, and moral behavior. The words change and emphases shift, but the basic goals of education remain the same. Any specific outcome should relate to one of those goals. Music appreciation outcomes, for example, would relate to worthy use of leisure time.

Establishing General Instructional Outcomes

Prior to their delineation into specific outcomes, goals are frequently first translated into what are typically referred to as *general instructional outcomes*. In practice, outcomes at this level are also referred to as goals since they do represent relatively global outcomes. Outcomes at this level are more precise than goals but not as detailed as specific outcomes. They are, in various situations, referred to as cumulative outcomes, intermediate outcomes, terminal outcomes, milestone outcomes, course outcomes, and tasks. Such outcomes are usually assessable and typically represent more complex behaviors expected as a result of achievement of a number of prerequisite specific outcomes. An end-of-course outcome for a typing course, for example, might be that students will be able to type a dictated, one-page letter in proper form, in a given number of minutes, with no more than a specified number of errors. Such an outcome would clearly be cumulative in nature, requiring prior achievement of any number of specific outcomes. Here is another such outcome: Students will be able to write a book report, including title and author, a summary of the plot, and a description of the main character(s). Actually, this encompasses a cluster of outcomes from all three domains and two subject areas—reading and writing. Included in the cluster could be any or all of the following:

Summarizes in his or her own words the main story line of a book of fiction.

Checks books of fiction out of the library to read on her or his own time.

Writes in proper cursive style compositions of more than one page.

Reads books written at the student's corresponding grade level or above.

Edits and revises drafts of his or her own writing into final form.

Uses common editorial marks to improve written drafts.

Completes homework assignments.

Distinguishes between the main character and supplemental characters in a written work.

The above list certainly does not exhaust all the possible specific outcomes that could be included in the overall task of writing a book report. Depending on the grade level of the student and the teacher's intent, the emphasis for assessment of the completed report might change as well.

Recall from Chapter 3 that educational efforts usually do not have one end but a series of temporary ends in a continuous cycle. Thus, general instructional outcomes specify outcomes intended at the end of a given cycle: a unit, a course, or a time span. To use a non-education example, public agencies such as Big Brothers/Big Sisters might very well set objectives on a yearly basis, and one of its objectives might be "to increase the number of Big Brothers in Chicago by 10% (from 400 to 440) during the 6-month period beginning September 1." This objective follows naturally from the agency's major goal and, in turn, would entail any number of specific objectives to be achieved during the 6-month period. Clearly, there may well be cycles within cycles, and therefore general instructional outcomes represent varying degrees of specificity and comprehensiveness. Thus, for example, you may see units within courses and unit outcomes leading to course outcomes. Further, there are lesson outcomes that lead to unit outcomes.

Establishing Specific Instructional Outcomes

Specific instructional outcomes deal with the most discrete intended outcomes. They are the assessable outcomes upon which day-to-day activities like instruction are based. Thousands and thousands of specific instructional outcomes have been written for virtually any curriculum area you can think of. Many professional organizations, especially those concerned with specific curriculum areas (like the National Council of Teachers of Mathematics), have published lists of such outcomes. A number of state departments of education and local education agencies have initiated outcomes-development efforts. Teachers themselves have generated an incredible number of outcomes too. Some have collaborated with their students to develop outcomes that were meaningful and relevant. Of course, if you obtained available sets of outcomes in a given area (such as 10th-grade biology) from a number of different sources, the outcomes in the various sets would not be exactly the same. Although there is a great deal of similarity in the outcomes of different collections, they do vary by level of specificity, depth and breadth of content area represented, and degree of communicability (or how well they articulate the specific behavior intended).

Educators disagree whether instructional outcomes should be selected or developed by users. Proponents of selection argue that outcomes development should be left to the experts and that sufficient outcomes are already available to meet most educator needs. Supporters of user development believe that the process of determining outcomes has value in and of itself and that outcomes are more meaningful when time is taken to think through and specify intended outcomes as opposed to merely picking them from somebody else's list. Although both positions have merit, it would seem that the average educator has better things to do with her time than to reinvent the wheel. Teachers do, however, need goals for each lesson. If suitable outcomes are already available, or if there are outcomes that would be suitable with slight modification, there does not seem to be much point in starting from scratch. Of course there may be times when appropriate outcomes are simply not available. In that case, the teachers must develop them. If a teacher prefers to develop his own outcomes and is willing to take the time necessary to do an effective job, there are certainly benefits to be realized.

Determining the Appropriate Degree of Outcome Specificity

So far we have looked at three general levels of specificity for writing instructional outcomes, each level representing a progressively finer degree of specificity with respect to the intended performance. Specific instructional outcomes represent the most discrete intended outcomes. Yet, you may ask, "How specific is specific?" To effectively communicate the intended performance, how detailed does the outcome need to be, and how exact does the description of intended performance need to be? An outcome can be so vague that it is ambiguous or so detailed that it is trivial and impractical. Compare the following two outcomes:

A. Use a calculator.

B. Given a hand-held calculator that performs the operations of addition, subtraction, multiplication, and division and given the oral command to find the product of two one-digit numbers, the student will turn on the calculator, push the button corresponding to the first digit, push the multiplication button, push the button corresponding to the second digit, push the equal-sign button, read the response on the display portion of the calculator, and record the response in writing on a separate sheet of paper.

Which outcome do you think is written at an effective level of specificity? A? B? All of the above? None of the above? If you picked "none of the above," you are beginning to get the idea. Outcome A is clearly too fuzzy to be of much use. The person who wrote it probably knows what performance is intended but the intent is not clearly communicated to anyone else. If you cannot tell what is intended, it is impossible to know when it has been achieved. The outcome "use a calculator" could mean any number of things, including outcome B. The intent of outcome B, on the other hand, is pretty clear, and almost anyone would be able to determine whether a student had achieved outcome B. But is all that detail really necessary? Probably not. If all outcomes related to using a calculator were spelled out in such gory detail, it would take many moons and sheets of paper. Further, the first given ("given a hand-held calculator that performs the operations of addition, subtraction, multiplication, and division") would be repeated in every one. Not only would that be very boring, it would also not be necessary. If it were a necessary given, it could be stated one time, prior to the list of outcomes. As it is, it is not necessary because virtually all calculators perform those operations. Other obvious redundancies in the outcome make it unnecessarily lengthy and clumsy.

Clearly some reasonable middle ground between A and B exists. A sensible, guiding principle, which was proposed by Robert Gagné in the mid-1960s, suggests that each outcome should represent a distinct task, a task being defined as "the smallest component of performance which has a distinct and independent purpose."[10] Applying this guideline, outcome A is too broad because it involves more than one task, and outcome B is too detailed because it involves activities extraneous to the basic purpose. An appropriate outcome might read "performs multiplication problems involving two one-digit numbers." The phrase "uses the calculator to" at the beginning of the outcome would probably not be necessary since this outcome would be one of a set, all dealing with use of the calculator. Gagné's suggestion is also useful because it eliminates outcomes with no obvious purpose, outcomes that prompt the feeling "Why does anyone want to do that?"

It seems as if as many guidelines for developing outcomes exist as there are experts developing them. Many of these guidelines are so prescriptive and result in such overly detailed outcomes that they do more harm than good. Instead of being helpful guides for writing outcomes, they make a relatively simple process appear to be terribly complicated. The overkill scares some people, who then shy away from outcomes altogether. Those who defend their "44 components of a good outcome," for example, believe that it is avoiding the issue to say that outcomes do not have to be super-specific, that it is the time and trouble that are objectionable, not the process. Au contraire! The more simply worded outcome is clearly more functional. Think of someone giving you directions to a restaurant to meet for dinner. Now, which set of directions below do you think would be more helpful and less confusing?

A. From your house go to Fourth and Main, turn right, drive two blocks, and the restaurant is the first building on the right.

B. From your house (401 Elm) go past 403 Elm, the blue house with white shutters; go past 405 Elm, the brick house with the white picket fence; go past 407 Elm . . . etc., etc., etc.

If you followed the directions in option B, you'd probably miss dinner and still be on the road at breakfast time!

Tailoring Instructional Outcomes for Students with Disabilities and Exceptionalities

"How specific is specific?" also depends on the students for whom the outcomes are intended. For students in the general population, the discussion above is probably sufficient. Increasingly, however, students with disabilities are being "mainstreamed," or taught in regular classrooms. The classroom teacher may work with other resource persons—school psychologists, special education teachers, counselors—to create an appropriate learning environment for students with some spe-

---

[10]"Educational Objectives and Human Performance" by R. M. Gagné, in *Learning and the Educational Process* (p. 12) by J. D. Krumboltz (Ed.), 1965, Chicago: Rand McNally.

cial needs that also fosters interaction with students who don't have disabilities. In some cases, the outcomes developed for students with disabilities and exceptionalities may look somewhat different than those for the rest of the class. Depending on the particular instructional challenge, teachers may need to revise the outcomes that they typically use, perhaps breaking them down further into part-skills or knowledge for students with disabilities. The concept of *enabling outcomes* has been applied to deal with such situations. To use the calculator example, "performs multiplication problems involving two one-digit numbers," might be fine for most students. For a student functioning with a disability, a teacher might break the task down further into enabling outcomes; for example, "demonstrates the ability to use each button appropriately" or "correctly records calculator displays (answers) on a separate sheet of paper."

Teachers may also need to design individualized instructional outcomes for particular students. For example, a student who is gifted but withdrawn may be the only one in her class of accelerated students to work toward the objective of taking a leadership role in one or more small-group instructional activities. This objective may be written as part of her individual educational plan. Or, a teacher may want to work with a student who has a mental disability to increase on-task behavior and decrease out-of-seat behavior. Specific outcomes for an intervention program for the student would be written that pertained to that student only. These outcomes could easily span all three domains of learning.

Because the range of disabilities and exceptionalities in school-aged children is so vast, it is impossible here to prescribe precisely what you should do. But all teachers should recognize that outcomes that are appropriately specific for students in the general population may not be appropriate for teaching and assessment with students labeled "exceptional" for certain reasons. As you encounter and gain experience with students with disabilities and exceptionalities and work with resource personnel, you can refine your outcomes to meet specific student needs.

Designing and Evaluating Instructional Outcomes

Selection or development of instructional outcomes is really the most important aspect of any educational endeavor, be it group instruction, execution of a special program, or construction of an individualized educational plan for a student. The outcomes give direction to every remaining activity. Fuzzy outcomes tend to lead to fuzzy efforts; trivial outcomes tend to lead to a waste of time and money. If a teacher had the outcome "to increase vocabulary," for example, and if students learned one or two new words during the school year, the teacher could accurately state that the outcome had been achieved. Thus, prior to execution of the effort, general intended outcomes must be translated into specific, assessable, meaningful outcomes. It is not enough to have a general idea of what you want to teach; you must determine precisely what you want to achieve and, more precisely, what you want your students to achieve and when.

Designing Effective Instructional Outcomes

Whether you develop outcomes or select them, the same basic criteria of quality should be applied in evaluating each outcome. First, as previously discussed, the appropriateness of the level of specificity must be evaluated. Is it too vague? Too detailed? Is it appropriate for the students for whom it is intended? Is it functional? Does it convey a distinct purpose? In assessing the quality of an outcome, you should also examine the outcome's communicability. An instructional outcome should communicate the intended results clearly and should facilitate its own assessment. In other words, all qualified persons should assess the outcome in basically the same way, and all should agree that it had or had not been achieved. A well-written outcome to a great extent dictates the method of assessment and tells you how you will know if it is achieved. Consider the following outcomes:

A. Given a reprint of a report of a scientific experiment, the student will identify the hypothesis and corresponding conclusion.

B. The student will recite from memory any poem at least 100 words in length of his or her choice.

Both of these outcomes suggest how achievement of the outcomes will be determined, and any qualified person would probably be able to determine whether either had been achieved. True, the word *identify* in outcome A is a little fuzzy in that there are several ways in which this could be done; the student could underline the hypothesis and conclusion, or tell someone what they were, or write them on a sheet of paper, and so forth. But the point is that it really does not make any difference. The intent of the outcome is that students be able to recognize hypotheses and related conclusions; there are a number of equally acceptable ways in which this ability can be demonstrated. Outcome B clearly specifies that the student will *recite;* thus, *writing* a poem from memory would not be acceptable. In this case the method of showing knowledge of a poem is important. The emphasis in the outcome is on recitation, not only on the knowledge of a poem.

Many people falsely believe that an outcome calling for a paper-and-pencil response is somehow inferior to one calling for an actual performance. Within this framework, an instructional outcome assessed with a multiple-choice test item, for example, is not as "important" or as "good" as one that requires a student to do something—adjust a microscope, for example. This belief is based on the false assumption that paper-and-pencil tests assess only lower-level learning such as recall of facts, whereas actual performance entails higher-level learning such as application or problem-solving. Many higher-level outcomes can be assessed with some form of written test—yes, even with a multiple-choice test. Conversely, a performance can represent a very trivial outcome. For example, which represents the more important outcome, the ability to identify a complete sentence or the ability to draw a straight line with a ruler? Creating appropriate assessments to measure both higher-level and lower-level outcomes will be discussed further in subsequent chapters. For now, though, keep such questions in mind.

Various experts have proposed different ways of constructing outcomes, specifying different types and numbers of components that should be present.[11] Most of them are variations on the approach taken by Mager. As Mager's approach is fairly generic across disciplines, it is used here to demonstrate how to construct outcomes that are useful for both instructional planning and assessment based on three fundamental components: behavior, conditions, and criterion. Briefly, the behavior component addresses the performed evidence of learning, the conditions are the given contexts in which assessments take place, and the criterion defines how well the task must be performed.

The Behavior Component

The *behavior component* describes what observable, assessable performance will constitute satisfactory evidence that the desired learning has occurred. This is also the most easily recognizable and consistently present of the three components; virtually all instructional outcomes written with student performance in mind contain a statement about the behavior, although they may not contain either of the other components. Note that the behavior should be stated in terms of the learner, not the teacher or the content area. Alas, occasionally one encounters alleged outcomes such as the following:

A. Explain to students how to plant a bean seed.

B. Supreme court decisions affecting education, 1950–1993.

Neither A nor B indicates what the result of instruction will be; therefore, they are not instructional outcomes. A says what the teacher will do, not the student; B simply states an area to be covered. Theoretically, both of these "outcomes" could be achieved without anybody learning anything!

As all of the previous examples in this chapter have illustrated, an outcome should state the intended performance task using an action verb that represents an observable outcome. Thus, an outcome that states that "students will learn French" is inadequate. We must determine what a student must do to indicate that French has been learned; one outcome might be that "students will translate French passages into English." Thus, vague verbs such as *understand, know,* and *appreciate* are to be avoided, whereas specific action verbs such as *translate, compute, select, identify, list,* and *solve* are appropriate. Remember that if an outcome is well written, then all qualified persons will assess it in essentially the same way and agree on whether it has been achieved. Whether all teachers would agree on how to assess "knows fractions" is doubtful.

As the previous examples of effective instructional outcomes have also illustrated, each outcome should entail achievement of one and only one behavior; otherwise, assessment of achievement will be confounded. A student may achieve

[11]See, for example, *The Conditions of Learning and Theory of Instruction* by R. F. Gagné, 1985, Ft. Worth, TX: Holt, Rinehart & Winston.

one part of an outcome but not another. The outcome "knows fractions" is not well written for a variety of reasons, one of which is that it involves any number of undefined behaviors. The outcome "reduces fractions to lowest terms," in contrast, deals with one capability. Similarly, "gives a patient a checkup" involves many skills, whereas "takes a pulse" involves one. Outcomes like "gives a patient a checkup" are fine as intermediate outcomes, but are not adequate as specific outcomes. On the other side of the coin we have outcomes appearing trivial because they deal with one instance or one application of a behavior, not the behavior itself. Thus "takes the pulse of a 22-year-old woman" and "reduces the fraction 25/60 to lowest terms" are too specific.

One final word on the behavior component (okay, more than one!). In most outcomes, the statement of the intended outcome is preceded by a phrase indicating who will perform the action, for example, "The student will identify the main character in a short story." Usually this is not necessary because the person who is to exhibit the behavior is obvious. Although it is repetitious and boring, it really does not hurt anything, and it does make for complete sentences. Some people feel more comfortable with outcomes such as, "The student will correctly identify the main idea of a paragraph" than with "correctly identifies the main idea of a paragraph." Either way, it is no big deal.

The Conditions Component

The *conditions component* of an outcome lists the "givens," the context in which the behavior will be exhibited. Conditions usually specify necessary materials, tools, allowable resources, or imposed restrictions, and the word *given* is not necessarily used, although it often is. Thus we might say at the beginning of an instructional outcome, "Given a map of the United States, the student will . . ." or "Without the aid of a dictionary . . ." or we might add the phrase ". . . using any standard reference materials" at the end of an outcome. Conditions are too often inserted when they are obvious. If students are to construct geometric figures, like circles, it is not necessary to say, ". . . given a piece of paper and a pencil," although it may be necessary to specify ". . . given a compass."

Of course, there are instances in which the presence or absence of a condition changes the whole meaning of an outcome. It certainly makes a difference whether a scout is supposed to be able to start a fire with or without matches! Similarly, if students are supposed to be able to apply a certain statistical technique (such as standard deviation) to a given set of numbers, it makes a big difference whether or not the outcome says "Given the formula . . ." Conditions can become especially important when considering how to assess learning. There is no law that says every outcome has to have a condition, however. Thus, conditions should be stated only if they clarify the intent of the outcome. If conditions are fairly obvious or if there are several equally acceptable conditions (for example, "given a piece of paper and a pencil" and "given a chalkboard and chalk"), do not take the time, energy, or space to include them. If, for a group of outcomes, all of the conditions are the same, they need to be stated only once rather than repeated for each outcome.

The Criterion Component

When stated, the *criterion component* of an outcome is the part that tells us how well the behavior must be performed. It is the standard against which actual performance is compared and is alternatively called just that—the "standard." If the criterion is obvious or if the expectation of perfect accuracy is implicit, as for "Identify three natural sources of vitamin E," it is generally not stated. A quantitative criterion may be expressed in terms such as percentage or proportion of correct answers, percentage of increase or decrease, time to completion, or distance. If the criterion is complex or dependent upon the group involved (the criterion for a written book report, for example), it may be stated separately. No law says that instructional outcomes must be stated in one sentence with tortured syntax. The basic purpose is to establish how well or how often a performance must be exhibited in order to constitute sufficient evidence that the outcome has been achieved. Thus a classroom teacher may have an outcome for a student to "decrease out-of-seat behavior *by 25% within a 2-week period*." It is fairly easy to determine to what degree this outcome has been achieved.

Some instructional outcomes are a little trickier, however. For example, suppose the outcome is that students be able to formulate the past tense form of any regular verb. The question when assessing students' learning is: How many times and for how many verbs does the student have to do it correctly before you are reasonably convinced that she can do it for all such verbs? One test item for one verb certainly would not be sufficient. Fifty items for 50 different verbs probably would be very convincing but also very time-consuming. Thus, given that it is a relatively simple skill, you might be satisfied if, given five verbs not previously used in instruction, the student stated the past tense form for all of them. For certain outcomes the criterion must take into consideration the human error factor. For example, even players who definitely have the ability to serve a tennis ball into the proper service court miss more than occasionally. Thus a high-school physical-education teacher might be satisfied if a student could correctly serve six balls out of 10 attempts. Similarly, on a set of arithmetic problems you might settle for eight-out-of-10 accuracy. The stringency of the criterion really depends on the nature of the outcome and is sometimes refined on the basis of analysis of the items (after testing) associated with the outcome, a topic discussed in Chapter 10.

A difference does exist between a quantitative criterion for an individual student and one for a group or class of students. Most teachers would like for all students to reach criterion on each and every outcome, but this is not usually feasible within the context of the typical classroom. With the exception of mastery systems, even if all the students have not achieved all of the outcomes, there comes a time when the teacher must move on. There are several strategies that can be applied, but the one probably most often used in practice is simply to assess the level of achievement, whatever it may be, without formally comparing it to any predetermined standard and to make an existential decision. Thus, if the class as a whole does "reasonably well" on a test of microcomputer operating systems, further explanation in that area is unnecessary. If a sizable number of students do poorly, more instruction may follow, perhaps using a different instructional strategy. Another approach is to set a criterion for group achievement as well as for individual achievement. For example, a teacher may be satisfied with the overall performance of the class—enough to move on—if at least 80% of the students reach criterion on the outcomes assessed.

As you have probably gathered, there is no scientific formula for setting a criterion of achievement; a great deal of judgment is involved. Further, unless you are involved in some type of individualized instruction, outcomes are not generally assessed one at a time. One test or assessment session may include items representing 10 or more outcomes, thereby complicating the task of determining outcome achievement. Although outcomes guide the instructional process, they should not bog it down. For certain kinds of outcomes, criteria of performance may not be quantitative at all. A qualitative criterion is especially likely when complex behaviors are involved. A qualitative criterion may list necessary elements or required features of the student's product or performance. In addition, a qualitative criterion may also specify quantitatively what percentage of these elements or features must be present for the student to "reach criterion." If the outcome is that the student be able to develop a weekly budget based on a given amount of money, for example, the criterion portion might specify certain items (like food) that must be included for the budget to be acceptable. Judging the persuasiveness of a student-written letter is a qualitative endeavor as well. Also, in many training programs partial performance is not acceptable. In a small-appliance repair class, for example, the criterion might be that a previously broken electric toothbrush operate properly without shocking its user.

Evaluating Instructional Outcomes

The use of outcomes in the planning, execution, and assessment of an effort is probably one of the best things that ever happened to education. True, a lot of lousy outcomes are floating around. But in most cases, even less-than-adequate outcomes are better than no outcomes at all. Outcomes give direction to selection of teaching strategies and the design of appropriate assessments and serve as standards by which we judge the progress of students. The basic concept is that intended outcomes should be stated in advance of instruction and assessment and in language that communicates. In a well-intentioned effort to standardize the writing of outcomes, however, a number of sets of overly prescriptive guidelines have been disseminated by a variety of individuals and groups. Regardless of the source or number of outcomes, however, the following reasonably short set of guidelines can be used for evaluating them:

1. The intended outcome should be specified in objective, observable terms: Cite only one *behavior* per outcome, and avoid specifying an instance of a behavior rather than the behavior itself.
2. Any *conditions* affecting performance that are not obvious or that significantly alter the intent of the outcome should be specified.
3. The *criterion* of acceptable performance should be specified if necessary.

As you apply these guidelines to the instructional outcomes in your area—either ones you have written or obtained from a curriculum guide, syllabus, or other source—you will gain a sense of how to critically appraise outcomes for use in your instruction and classroom assessment. The Try These section at the end of this chapter will get you started, and the following checklist will help you identify good instructional outcomes.

✓ *Easy Reference Checklist*

Guidelines for Good Instructional Outcomes

- ❑ Outcome expressed in objective, assessable terms.
- ❑ One behavior per outcome.
- ❑ Outcome specifies a behavior, not an instance of a behavior.
- ❑ Outcome specifies conditions that affect performance.
- ❑ Outcome specifies conditions that significantly alter the intent of the outcome.
- ❑ Outcome specifies criterion of acceptable performance if not obvious.

Summary

Understanding Instructional Outcomes

Instructional outcomes are specific statements of what is to be accomplished and how well and are expressed in terms of observable, assessable student behavior. An instructional outcome is an intentional result communicated by a statement describing a proposed change in a learner. Teachers must determine what behavior or performance will constitute sufficient evidence that the desired capability exists. Whether a capability is learned as a result of instruction can be determined only by observing performance at two different points in time (before and after instruction) and seeing whether performance has changed. Learning itself cannot be directly observed or measured by teachers in a classroom, although changes in performance can.

Advocates of the use of instructional outcomes contend that their main advantage is that they give direction to or guide the activities of an effort. Outcomes suggest general strategies and specific activities for their attainment. Instructional outcomes give direction to students as well as to teachers. Outcomes also serve a diagnostic-prescriptive function; at any point in time you can assess where your students are and how much progress they have made, and you can then act accordingly. Outcomes dictate to a great extent the way in which you collect assessment data. The existence of outcomes does not necessarily mean that instruction will be more successful than it otherwise would have been, but they do allow determination of what has been accomplished. Outcomes serve a communication function as well; teachers can communicate to students and parents what is being done and why.

The criticisms of instructional outcomes are not always criticisms of outcomes themselves; instead, they are criticisms that arise from their misuse. Critics believe that the use of outcomes produces rigid, conforming procedures and standards and behavior that discourages creativity and spontaneity. They also contend that outcomes fail to take into consideration individual differences. But outcomes are not restrictive in and of themselves; any outcome alternative strategies can be used to promote achievement. Further, the use of outcomes by no means negates the existence of individual differences; different students, for example, may be working on different outcomes at different times. Critics also question whether all important educational results can be articulated as outcomes, and they claim teachers have a natural tendency to select outcomes that are easy to measure, not necessarily important. All important desired outcomes can be expressed in observable, assessable terms, however. The lack of consensus on the appropriateness of outcomes in areas other than basic skills stems not from the inability of the outcomes to be assessed, but from the inability of educators to specify what they really mean. Really important outcomes, critics continue, are long-term results, not short-term accomplishments, and therefore outcomes dealing with here-and-now achievement are largely irrelevant. But all outcomes are, at least theoretically, related to some long-term outcome or goal. There is very little non-anecdotal evidence that the existence of outcomes actually results in greater achievement, but outcomes make sense logically, and even if they do not directly result in greater achievement, they do permit assessment of exactly what has been accomplished. Critics also allege outcomes are impractical because any given effort can spawn an unmanageable multiplicity of outcomes. But component behaviors for an outcome exist whether or not they are identified; without a list of such behaviors it is much more likely that a number of them will be overlooked, thereby decreasing the chances of achieving the general desired outcome. Overall then, opposition to outcomes is based more on their possible misuse than on outcomes themselves. Of course, education has a place for minimally directed exploratory activities; such activities, however, comprise a very small percentage of the total educational enterprise.

Outcomes look basically the same regardless of the type of assessment; all outcomes indicate intended results. One basic difference is that certain types of assessment and their corresponding outcomes are primarily concerned with the performance of individuals, whereas others are primarily concerned with the performance of groups.

Individual instructional outcomes are variously referred to as *performance outcomes, behavioral objectives, learning outcomes,* and *classroom objectives.* The term *objective* has been replaced by many educators with *outcome,* which emphasizes the result of the learning experience, rather than the process of learning. Certain instructional outcomes should be achieved by virtually all students, regardless of ability or background; these are referred to as *mastery outcomes* or *minimum skills outcomes.*

A group instructional outcome might be to have 90% of a class achieve a certain set of mastery outcomes; this type of outcome, however, as opposed to "How is Darryl doing?" would be of prime interest in assessing the effectiveness of the instruction, and the emphasis would be on clusters of outcomes.

Classifying Instructional Outcomes Using Taxonomies

Taxonomies classify all instructional outcomes into three behavior domains and a hierarchy of categories based on presumed complexity. Each succeeding category in a domain involves behavior believed to be more complex than the previous one, and each is considered to be prerequisite to the next. The purpose of the taxonomies is to facilitate communication, but they also focus attention on a wide range of behavioral outcomes, thus making it less likely that all the outcomes for a given effort will involve lower-level behaviors only. All instructional outcomes can be classified as belonging primarily to one of the three domains of learning—*cognitive, affective,* and *psychomotor.*

Bloom's taxonomy of cognitive outcomes has made educators aware of the wide range of abilities involved in cognitive learning. Each of the six major categories represents a different kind of learning process. The major categories of the cognitive taxonomy of educational outcomes are as follows:

1.00 Knowledge. Memorization; recall or recognition of information.

2.00 Comprehension. Understanding; ability to explain or interpret.

3.00 Application. Ability to use or apply an abstract concept in a specific situation.

4.00 Analysis. Ability to break down a communication into its component parts and to identify the relationships that exist between them.

5.00 Synthesis. Ability to combine elements and parts to form a unique whole, a new communication.

6.00 Evaluation. Ability to make judgments about the value of some communication for a given purpose.

Knowledge-level outcomes are also referred to as *lower-level outcomes.* Those classified at the comprehension level and beyond are called *higher-level outcomes.*

Considering Factors Affecting the Design of Instructional Outcomes

At one end of the outcomes continuum we have very broad statements of long-term outcomes; these are generally referred to as goals or general instructional outcomes. At the other end of the spectrum we have very precise statements of more immediate outcomes, each representing only one behavior or result; these are generally referred to as specific instructional outcomes. There are a variety of intermediate levels of specificity.

Goals are global statements of long-term outcomes; the definition of long-term varies somewhat depending upon the effort. Goals do not deal with definite skills; related specific outcomes do. Although educational goals do represent the important outcomes of the educational system, the system cannot be held directly accountable for their achievement. Achievement of goals is not measured directly; rather, achievement of more short-term outcomes believed to be prerequisite is measured. The emphasis in classrooms today is on computer skills, search and information-retrieval skills, and critical thinking skills, whereby students learn how to locate desired information and critically appraise it for use. Goals tend to be established at the national level, adopted at the state level, and integrated into practice at the classroom level. The words change and emphases shift through time, but the basic goals of education remain the same.

In practice, *general instructional outcomes* are also referred to as goals because they do represent relatively global outcomes. General instructional outcomes are more precise than goals but not as detailed as specific outcomes. They are, in various situations, referred to as cumulative outcomes, intermediate outcomes, terminal outcomes, milestone outcomes, course outcomes, and tasks. Such outcomes are usually assessable and typically represent more complex behaviors expected as a result of achievement of a number of prerequisite specific outcomes. General instructional outcomes specify results intended at the end of a given cycle: a unit, a course, or a time span. There may well be cycles within cycles, and therefore general instructional outcomes represent varying degrees of specificity and comprehensiveness.

Specific instructional outcomes deal with the most discrete intended outcomes; they are the measurable outcomes upon which day-to-day activities such as instruction are based. Outcomes have been developed by professional organizations (especially those related to curriculum areas), state departments of education, local education agencies, and teachers. Proponents of outcome selection argue that outcome development should be left to the experts and that sufficient outcomes are already available to meet most anybody's needs. Supporters of user development believe that the process of determining outcomes has value in and of itself and that outcomes are more meaningful when time is taken to think through and specify intended outcomes as opposed to merely picking them from somebody else's list. If suitable outcomes are already available or if there are outcomes that would be suitable with slight modification, do not start from scratch.

An outcome can be so vague that it is ambiguous or so detailed that it is trivial and impractical. A sensible, guiding principle suggests that each outcome should represent a distinct task, a task being defined as "the smallest component of performance which has a distinct and independent purpose." More simply worded outcomes are clearly more functional.

The outcomes developed for students with disabilities or exceptionalities may look different than those for the rest of the class. Teachers may need to break down standard instructional outcomes into smaller *enabling outcomes* and/or design outcomes pertaining to individual students' challenges and capabilities. As teachers encounter and gain experience with students with disabilities and exceptionalities, they can refine their outcomes to meet specific student needs.

Designing and Evaluating Instructional Outcomes

The selection or development of instructional outcomes is the most important aspect of any educational endeavor. The outcomes give direction to every remaining activity: fuzzy outcomes tend to lead to fuzzy instruction and assessment, and trivial outcomes tend to lead to a waste of time and money. The appropriateness of the level of specificity of outcomes must be evaluated. An outcome should communicate the intended result well enough so that any teacher would assess it in essentially the same way and be able to tell whether it had been achieved. There is a false hierarchy in the minds of many who think that an outcome that entails a paper-and-pencil response is somehow inferior to one that calls for an actual performance. The assumption that paper-and-pencil assessments can only measure lower-level learning is false.

The *behavior component* indicates which observable, assessable performance will constitute satisfactory evidence that the desired learning has occurred. An outcome should state the intended performance using an action verb that represents an observable outcome. Avoid vague verbs; use specific action verbs. Each outcome should entail achievement of one and only one behavior, otherwise assessment of achievement becomes confounded. Some outcomes appear to be trivial because they deal with one instance or one application of a behavior, not the behavior itself. It is usually not necessary to begin an outcome with a phrase that indicates who will perform the intended outcome (for example, "The student will . . .").

The *conditions component* of an outcome addresses the given context in which the behavior will be exhibited. Conditions usually specify necessary materials, allowable resources, or imposed restrictions, and the word *given* is not necessarily used. Conditions are often inserted even when they are obvious, although sometimes the presence or absence of a condition changes the whole meaning of an outcome. Stated conditions should be included only if they clarify the intent of the outcome.

When stated, the *criterion component* of an outcome is the part that tells how well the behavior must be performed; it is the standard against which actual performance is compared. If the criterion is obvious or 100% accuracy is expected, it is generally not stated. A quantitative criterion may be expressed in terms such as percentage correct, percentage of increase or decrease, time to completion, or distance. If the criterion is complex or dependent upon the group involved, it may be stated separately. The basic purpose is to establish how well or how often a performance must be exhibited in order to constitute sufficient evidence that the outcome has been achieved. The stringency of a criterion depends on the nature of the outcome and is sometimes refined on the basis of analysis of the items associated with the outcome after assessment. Unless a student is involved in some type of individualized instruction, outcomes are not generally assessed one at a time; one assessment session or test may include items representing several outcomes. For certain kinds of outcomes, criteria of performance may not be quantitative at all. Qualitative criteria are especially likely when complex behaviors are involved.

Intended outcomes should be stated in advance of instruction and assessment in language that communicates clearly the expectations for student performance.

Guidelines for evaluating outcomes suggest that: (1) the intended outcome should be specified in objective, observable terms and encompass one behavior only; (2) any conditions affecting performance that are not obvious or that significantly alter the intent of the outcome should be specified; and (3) the criterion of acceptable performance should be specified when necessary.

Try These

I. For each of the following behaviors, write **C** on the line if it is primarily a cognitive behavior and **O** if it is primarily some other (affective or psychomotor) behavior. Also, for each behavior identified as cognitive (C), write **H** on the line if the behavior represents a higher-level outcome (comprehension through evaluation) and **K** if it represents a knowledge outcome.

_____ 1. Listens to others with respect.

_____ 2. Names (zero–nine) given numerals (0–9).

_____ 3. Constructs a diorama depicting some aspect of daily life in colonial America.

_____ 4. Obeys safety rules on the playground and in the classroom.

_____ 5. States the meaning of road signs.

_____ 6. Writes letters to editors or congresspersons regarding issues he or she feels strongly about.

_____ 7. Writes grammatically correct sentences.

_____ 8. Pays attention to a film about genetics.

_____ 9. Transforms simple declarative sentences into interrogative sentences.

_____ 10. Participates in extracurricular science-related activities.

_____ 11. Listens to classical music at least once a week.

_____ 12. Interprets novel graphs.

_____ 13. Selects titles for given paragraphs, stories, and selections.

_____ 14. Participates in team sports.

_____ 15. Defines the term *assessment* using his or her own words.

_____ 16. Balances chemical equations.

_____ 17. Buys only organic foods.

_____ 18. Prepares an income tax return.

_____ 19. Given the name of a continent or major subcontinent, points to it on a world map.

II. Determine whether each of the following specific instructional outcomes is fine the way it is written, or if it should be improved. On a separate sheet of paper rewrite those that need improvement. Remember to use the guidelines listed in this chapter and summarized in the checklist when evaluating and rewriting the outcomes.

1. Constructs a diorama depicting some aspect of daily life in colonial America.
2. Obeys safety rules.
3. Prepares an income tax return.
4. Transforms four out of five given simple declarative sentences into interrogative sentences.
5. Solves everyday arithmetic problems.
6. Participates in extracurricular science-related activities at least once during the school year.
7. Judges a work of art.
8. Participates in a spelling bee at his or her grade level.
9. Defines landforms.
10. Given novel, commonly found three-dimensional objects, classifies them as spheres, cubes, cylinders, or pyramids at least two out of three times.
11. Makes correct change.
12. Distinguishes between textures that are rough/smooth, hard/soft, and sharp/dull for given materials.

Answers

I. 1. O, 2. C, K, 3. C, H, 4. O, 5. C, K, 6. O, 7. C, H, 8. O, 9. C, H, 10. O, 11. O, 12. C, H, 13. C, H, 14. O, 15. C, H, 16. C, H, 17. O, 18. C, H, 19. C, K.

II. 1. Unless you want to get picky and specify the dimensions of the diorama or the particular aspect of daily life to be depicted, this outcome is pretty complete.

2. What safety rules? Where? How about this: "Obeys safety rules as posted in the lab while conducting science experiments"?

3. This could get very complicated unless the outcome is more specific. Try this: "Prepares a correct income tax return for a given individual. The individual's tax requirements are such that a 1099A short form is appropriate."

4. This one seems to have all the right pieces and communicates well.

5. Does *everyday* mean word problems? What operations are required? Are decimals and fractions allowed as well as whole numbers? There are a number of ways this one could be improved. Here's one: "Solves application (word) problems involving the addition or subtraction of whole numbers of less than 100."

6. Unless you are concerned with just which extracurricular science-related activities might qualify, this one appears okay.

7. Pretty vague, eh? At the least, it needs the basis on which a judgment is to be made. Try this: "Given a novel two-dimensional painting, the student judges it according to the principles of composition and aesthetics."

8. Looks good as is.
9. Define the term *landforms* or define specific landforms? If so, which landforms; all the ones there are or just the ones studied in class? Probably one of the following will work, depending on how the outcome is to be tested:
   a. Given the term for any of the landforms studied in Unit 8, the student will describe it in his or her own words.
   b. Given definitions of the various landforms studied in class, match them with the appropriate term.
   c. Describe the features of the following landforms:
      Delta
      Fall line
      Mountain
      Plain
      Plateau
10. P-r-e-t-t-y specific. Just one question: Does the outcome developer care if we use pictures of the objects or must we use the real things? If that's critical, it should be specified.
11. This one gets the "good try, needs work" stamp. Here are some alternatives:
    a. Given a one-dollar bill for a purchase total of under $1.00, the student gives back the correct change.
    b. Identifies equivalent amounts of money of $1.00 or less involving combinations of the following: one-dollar bill, half-dollar, quarter, dime, nickel, penny.
12. Is this just rote memory of materials and their characteristic texture? This one implies that students will do this on the basis of touch. Should this be done blindfolded? Should students see the materials just prior to being blindfolded? I leave this one to your imagination and good judgment.

CHAPTER 5

Creating Paper-and-Pencil Assessments for the Classroom

Key Concepts:

- Understanding the nature of written assessment.
- Considering the advantages and disadvantages of paper-and-pencil assessments.
- Using general guidelines to create and select paper-and-pencil assessments.
- Setting cut-off scores for mastery assessments.

Standards Addressed in This Chapter:

1. Choose assessment methods appropriate for instructional decisions.
2. Develop assessment methods appropriate for instructional decisions.

Before You Begin Reading, Consider This

Do written tests serve useful purposes in the classroom?

YES Written tests are a useful and economical way to assess whether students have achieved the outcomes of schooling. They provide feedback to the students on their learning and to the teachers about their instruction.

NO Written tests neither get at all the learning that takes place in the classroom, nor do they provide relevant tasks that reflect what the students ultimately need to do in real life. There are much better ways of assessing learning that reflect a truer picture of achievement.

Paper-and-pencil assessments gauge your students' accomplishment of instructional outcomes by providing them an opportunity to demonstrate this accomplishment in written response to a prompt calling forth the behavior to be demonstrated. The prompts (or, as they are also called, the items) are usually written, but not always, as in the case of an oral spelling test. The responses are also typically in writing—the students may write them out or indicate their choice from among the ones given. When taking a paper-and-pencil test, students may answer questions, evaluate statements (verbal or numerical), perform tasks, or in some other way respond in a written fashion to the stimuli presented. The response may be in words or in symbols (they may, for instance, blacken in circles that correspond to answer choices) and may be done by hand or by some other method, such as using a computer. The teacher's typical weekly quizzes, unit tests, and final examinations are all examples of paper-and-pencil tests, and they are often used as a basis for assigning grades in a particular subject. Thus, they are often the assessments upon which the judgment is made. For example, if you are an elementary teacher required to record two grades per week for spelling, you may administer a weekly spelling test (one grade) and assign spelling homework or seatwork (the second grade), both of which would "count" in some way toward the student's spelling grade for the marking period. Paper-and-pencil assessments are not only used as posttests following instruction, they can also be used as pretests and tests of entry behaviors, as well.

Considering the Advantages and Disadvantages of Paper-and-Pencil Assessments

Paper-and-pencil assessments have several features that make them a useful and versatile classroom assessment option. First, they can be used to assess learning at many levels of the cognitive domain for many types of subject matter, and they can also be used to indirectly assess affective outcomes.

Second, paper-and-pencil tests require no special equipment or set-up time. The only requirement may be some form of duplicating equipment if the test items are presented in written format and a pencil and paper or answer sheet (obviously!) for student responses. With modern duplicating methods, you can easily produce written test items for each student for a relatively low cost. As they are typically completed at the student's seat, paper-and-pencil tests also require no special lab site or place for administration.

A third advantage of paper-and-pencil assessments is that they can be administered to students individually or as a group. This flexibility allows you to administer make-up tests or equivalent forms (tests where the items on the two forms are different but both sets assess the same outcomes) easily and to assess the learning of groups of students as they complete instruction.

Fourth, many excellent paper-and-pencil tests and items have already been created, allowing you to select the best ones for your particular students and curriculum. With the advent of microcomputers, banks of items have been created in many subject areas across the grades.[1] Although some of these items may have been field-tested, you are the final judge of their usefulness for your students, your instructional outcomes, and your circumstances. Even if you do not use the previously created assessment items themselves, they are an excellent source of ideas for creating items of your own design.

A fifth advantage of paper-and-pencil assessments lies in their utility as a written record. A finished test (or answer sheet and test booklet) provides a written record of the student's performance. This written record can be shared with others—the student, his or her parents, or your principal, for example—and can be easily stored in the student's folder or added to his or her portfolio.

Sixth, the results of paper-and-pencil tests can be analyzed in several ways, providing valuable input for student remediation or reteaching, for future lesson or unit planning, and for improving instruction.[2] For example, you may learn from an analysis of student test data that, as a group, your students are somewhat shaky on a concept that will become the foundation for the next lesson. As a result, you can decide to provide extra reinforcement for that concept, perhaps even reteaching it using different methods in the next lesson, so that your students have a firm scaffold for new learning.

Paper-and-pencil tests have many things going for them, but they also have their disadvantages. Paper-and-pencil assessments, by their nature, are neither appropriate for testing most psychomotor skills (the major exception is, of course, writing), nor are they highly useful for direct assessment of affective outcomes. As an assessment option, paper-and-pencil tests also rely on words, for the most part, to communicate. Although maps, diagrams, and symbols may be used, words are highly emphasized in paper-and-pencil testing. The psychomotor skill of executing the

---

[1]For more information on test-item banks, contact your national professional subject-matter organization—the National Council of Teachers of Mathematics (NCTM), for example. Other sources include professional journals in your area or discipline.

[2]More on how to perform these useful analyses is found in Chapter 10.

breast stroke in swimming, for example, could hardly be tested with paper and pencil. With paper and pencil, you *can* assess whether a student can recognize the proper leg, arm, and head positions at various points in the stroke, but the only way to see if she can perform the stroke is to observe her in action in the water Likewise, with a paper-and-pencil test you may assess whether a student knows the contribution of opera to the worlds of music and theater, but you are not likely to know whether he has developed a deep appreciation of opera unless you observe his music-listening or opera-attendance habits. And for this assessment to be valid, it must be done over a longer period of time than you will have the student in your class.

A second disadvantage of paper-and-pencil assessments is that students who do not read well may be unduly penalized when taking a paper-and-pencil assessment. A primary student, for example, may not be able to decipher the symbols "25¢" or "$.25," but knows what a quarter-dollar looks like and knows that one of them is worth two dimes and one nickel when asked to equate them using actual change. Additionally, poor or slow readers may not finish the test or may misinterpret items or directions, thus reducing their scores. And if the responses involve a lot of writing, as in the case of an essay test, a student's poor sentence construction or indecipherable handwriting may detract from an otherwise stellar response.

Using Guidelines to Create Effective Paper-and-Pencil Assessments

Anyone who thinks test development is easy probably does not know much about what is involved. True, developing *a* test is easy, but developing a *good* test requires considerable knowledge, skill, time, and, in some cases, money. Assessment is sort of like dancing—anyone can move his feet around and call it dancing, but good dancing requires knowledge of appropriate steps and skill in executing them. In any assessment situation, any number of variables or instructional outcomes could be tested. It is usually preferable, however, to limit the number of variables or outcomes to those that are most important. This is especially true when the assessment is to be developed, rather than selected; it is better to assess just a few things but assess them well.

Each type of assessment may involve idiosyncratic development concerns and procedures. The process of developing essay tests is somewhat different from the process used for developing multiple-choice tests, for example, just as developing knowledge-level tests differs from developing tests assessing higher-level outcomes. Regardless of the assessment type, however, teachers may apply several principles of good assessment construction to help them develop effective assessments; the rest of this chapter focuses on those general guidelines. Later, Chapters 6 and 7 will concentrate on the guidelines specific to particular types of items used on paper-and-pencil assessments. The goal of these three chapters, then, is to help you to design and construct a paper-and-pencil test to assess a given set of instructional outcomes. A summary of the guidelines discussed in this chapter appears in the checklist at the end of the chapter.

Determining the Content for Paper-and-Pencil Assessments

In designing any assessment, the first thing you have to determine is what it will cover. This means determining how big a "chunk" of content will be covered. Next, you should delineate all the important aspects of that chunk. And finally, you should select the aspects of the chunk that will be included in the assessment.

The size of the chunk to be covered should represent a meaningful unit of instruction articulated as a cluster of instructional outcomes, not as an expression like "Unit 8 of the science textbook." Outcomes usually form meaningful clusters or topics, and one or more clusters can be covered in a test. These clusters may include some outcomes that are suitable for assessment with a paper-and-pencil test and other outcomes that are better assessed by examining a student performance or product.[3] As the discussion in this chapter will illustrate, many of the guidelines set forth for paper-and-pencil tests apply to performance and product assessments as well. For now, however, consider only those instructional outcomes for which assessment is most appropriately done with paper and pencil.

An assessment will normally cover instruction over a range of several days to several weeks, even months. A test covering a small chunk of instruction, say several days' worth, prevents cognitive overload on the part of the students and permits a larger, more representative sampling of the behaviors represented by the selected outcomes. When the chunk to be covered is small, teachers can include more items per outcome. Of course, certain cumulative tests like final exams require broader coverage and may represent months of instruction. A test that covers a small cluster of outcomes can assess your students' achievement in more depth than a test that must cover a large number of outcomes. Because there is never going to be enough time to assess everything (and who would want to!), your task as a teacher is to decide which outcomes are the most important to cover and to balance the amount of time spent on assessment with the amount of time spent on instruction.

Because they form the backbone of instruction and assessment, instructional outcomes should be specified before creating the test (and before designing the instruction, for that matter). Specifying the instructional outcomes, whether you created them or borrowed them from a curriculum guide, helps define the important aspects of the content to be assessed. If no specified outcomes exist, you should at least have a detailed content outline prior to instruction. For example, a content outline regarding the three branches of the U.S. government might include the heading "The Executive Branch" and subheadings such as "Eligibility Requirements" and "Constitutional Powers and Limitations." Using a content outline that includes all knowledge and skill outcomes desired of students, you can create an assessment instrument. Although each and every desired outcome may not be measured on the test, they should all at least be candidates for inclusion.

If specific instructional outcomes have been created, then your task is easy. Just select the outcomes you want to assess, and the desired performances should already be specified in them. If they are not, these behaviors will have to be identi-

---

[3]See Chapter 8 for more on assessing the performance of processes and the development of products.

fied at this point. Keep in mind that you should be concerned with more than just a student's possession of knowledge. As discussed in Chapter 4, with respect to Bloom's taxonomy, many subject areas permit assessment at several levels of cognition. With respect to "Eligibility Requirements," for example, do you want students to be able to list such requirements from memory (an assessment of knowledge-level cognition) or be able to read a description of a given person's qualifications and determine whether that person is eligible to run for president (an assessment of higher-level cognition)? Maybe both. You should also, at this point, identify and set aside the outcomes that are not appropriate for assessment with a paper-and-pencil test. These outcomes may be assessed in other ways; methods for doing so will be addressed in later chapters.

The next step in designing an assessment is to devise a scheme for sampling behaviors from those identified in the outcomes. With the exception of certain mastery tests, a test invariably represents a sample of behaviors, because assessing each and every aspect of each and every outcome is not feasible. Further, if you carefully select the outcomes you do assess, you can generalize to the total pool of outcomes with a reasonable degree of confidence. The more structured and well defined the content is, the easier it is to establish validity. For example, assume you want students to be able to identify the capital city of each of the 50 states. You could have one gigantic set of matching items or, perhaps, 50 items where students write in the name of the capital city. You can probably safely assume, however, that a student's ability to identify the capitals of a representative 10 states is highly indicative of that student's ability to do so for all 50. If Evan correctly identifies the capitals of 5 out of 10 states, he probably knows about half of the capitals. The trick is to select the 10 states to appear on the test so that they are *representative* of all 50. Does it matter? It might. Suppose, for example, you chose the following states: Connecticut, Delaware, Maine, Massachusetts, New Hampshire, New Jersey, New York, Pennsylvania, Rhode Island, and Vermont. Notice anything? Do these states have anything in common? Yes, they are all located in the northeast section of the United States. If Evan is from Boston, he may have no trouble naming all of the required capitals and yet not know the capital of any state west of the Mississippi or south of the Mason-Dixon line. The requirement that the test items constitute a representative sample of desired behavior is a way of ensuring the test's validity. Representative samples can be chosen randomly or through the method of stratification.

One way you could select the 10 states to appear on the test would be to select them randomly. *Random selection* gives each item an equal chance of being selected. The odds that all 10 states chosen would be located in the Northeast would be extremely slim. Actually, just being aware of the need for representativeness helps immensely; after having read this section, you would know to select some capital cities from all the areas of the country. You don't need to take the time to write down all the capital cities on individual scraps of paper and then pull 10 out of a hat to ensure a random sample; just keep representativeness in mind when designing assessments.

Another way to ensure that the behaviors to be assessed are representative of those that could be tested is to stratify the possibilities prior to selection. *Stratifying* is the act of categorizing all the possibilities and selecting from each category to guarantee that all the important categories are represented. In the case of the state capitals, you could categorize the pool by geographic region (dividing capitals into categories like the Northwest and the Southeast) and select at least one state from each region. In the case of a large number of knowledge outcomes to be tested, you could stratify by types of knowledge, such as the habitat, diet, and method of reproduction for a representative animal from each class: amphibian, bird, fish, mammal, and reptile.

The concern for adequate sampling and resulting validity is necessary regardless of whether the assessment results will be norm-referenced or criterion-referenced. The basic principles are also the same with or without a set of specific instructional outcomes. Adequate sampling is easier, however, when the outcomes are clearly specified and fall within a restricted range. Not only is it easier to select from the possible behaviors, but it is also feasible to select a higher percentage of them. Take spelling.[4] You might have two lists of spelling words. One list might contain 10 very important words and your goal is student mastery; the other list might contain 50 words that are of secondary importance. In both cases you might determine that a score of 90% will indicate that the outcome has been attained. You could easily include all 10 words on the first list on one test but you would probably not include all 50 words on the second list on one test; you might select 10 or 15, a sample, of them. You would probably continue instruction and assessment until a given percentage of the students achieved mastery of the first list, whereas you would probably have lower expectations for the second list.

The next step in general test design is to determine the taxonomy level of the outcomes that will be assessed on the test. If your outcomes follow the format illustrated in the instructional outcome below, this step will be easy because the taxonomic level is already identified:

> The student will draw a conclusion based on a given sequence of facts in a story told in words or in pictures. (Comprehension)

The reason for specifying the taxonomic level of the outcomes to be assessed is simple. Once you know the level of the outcome, you can better devise an appropriate test item that calls forth the same level of behavior in the student. If the outcome above instead read: "The student will draw conclusions based on given facts," then your task of designing an appropriate assessment would be far more difficult. As you have probably learned from your training or from experience, different levels of outcomes have different instructional requirements. They also have different assessment requirements.[5] The extra detail in the outcome above regarding words and pictures in a story format gives clues to what an appropriate item for this outcome would contain. Recall the example of "Eligibility Requirements" of "The Executive Branch" of the United States government and the options given for assessing knowledge-level and higher-level outcomes. Specifying the taxonomic level is also important when

---

[4]Please! (My apologies to Henny Youngman.)

[5]You will see how they are qualitatively different in Chapters 6 and 7.

the test designer is not also the item writer. In statewide assessment, for example, or when more than one person is responsible for creating test items, the test designers create very detailed test specifications to communicate to those who will create the items just exactly what is required.[6] This communication is critical when more than one person is involved in producing a test. Even for a smaller-scale, single-author classroom test, this maxim holds true: the better the planning, the better the result.

Determining the Appropriate Number of Items for Paper-and-Pencil Assessments

Ideally, the outcomes to be addressed dictate the number of items to include on the test. You should first decide how many items constitute a sufficient opportunity for a student to demonstrate achievement of an outcome. Once you have done that for each outcome, it is easy to sum the total. For example, for one outcome you may decide that five items are appropriate, and for another, eight is the right number of items. There is no law that says a test must have 10, 20, or 100 items, or any other multiple of 10, for that matter. If the sum of the needed items is 17, so be it. This is a direct approach that takes little time and eliminates a lot of computation that is required for some other methods. One way to summarize the effort represented in this section of the chapter is to create a worksheet for yourself, not your students, that lists separately the instructional outcomes that have been selected for assessment (see Figure 5.1). On this worksheet specify the taxonomy level of each outcome[7] and the optimum number of items for assessing it. You can do this in pencil, or you can use a computer for added flexibility. Once you have the major decisions made, totaling the number of items is simple. Whether you use the short form (behavior only) of the outcomes or the long form (behavior, conditions, and criterion), you can then draft the items for the test using a worksheet like the one in Figure 5.1 as a guide.

Item Sufficiency

The number of items is determined by "what it takes" to assess a student's achievement of a particular instructional outcome; to find this out, ask yourself how many opportunities you think are sufficient for a student to demonstrate skill or knowledge acquisition. *Item sufficiency* means that a correct response to an item (or items) constitutes sufficient evidence that the student has demonstrated the intended behavior and, thus, has achieved the instructional outcome. Depending on the nature of the outcome, it may not be possible to develop one such item; several items may

---

[6]As a content specialist, you may have the opportunity to write items for or otherwise participate in a large-scale assessment effort. For more information regarding detailed test specifications, see *Modern Educational Measurement: A Practitioner's Perspective* by W. J. Popham, 1990, Upper Saddle River, NJ: Prentice Hall.

[7]A code such as K, C, Ap, An, S, and E works well for the six levels of the cognitive domain: knowledge, comprehension, application, analysis, synthesis, and evaluation.

Outcomes	Taxonomy level	No. of items
1.		
2.		
3.		
4.		
5.		
6.		
7.		
8.		
9.		
10.		
	Total Items →	

Figure 5.1
An assessment planning worksheet for determining the number of assessment items for a given set of instructional outcomes. For each outcome to be assessed, the worksheet lists its taxonomy level and the optimal number of items.

be required to meet the sufficiency guideline. For knowledge of state capitals, for example, I determined that 10 items would be adequate. This is why it is important to devise a scheme for sampling from the pool of behaviors contained in the outcomes. For those behaviors included in the sample, each item on the test constitutes an opportunity for students to demonstrate achievement.

Another consideration in determining a sufficient number of items is the importance of the outcome and the instructional time you devoted to it. Not all outcomes are equally important. For example, is it more important that students understand the causes of the U.S. Civil War or that they be able to name the major battles of that war? Deciding that they need to know both leaves you with twice as many items.

Usually, one item per outcome is not sufficient, especially if the assessment is comprised of selected-response (like multiple-choice) items, is criterion-referenced, or is a mastery test. If a student correctly answers, say, three items related to the same outcome, you can have more confidence that she has truly achieved it than if she answers only one item correctly out of one on the test. A student could conceivably guess the correct answer to one item on a selected-response test. In contrast, for a short-answer test, one item may be sufficient; it is pretty tough to correctly guess the definition of nuclear fusion, for example. As a general rule, higher-level outcomes usually require more items per outcome. A definition is a definition, but a concept may have more than one application.

Assessment Length

You know from Chapter 3 that longer assessments tend to be more reliable and valid, but an assessment can be too long, causing student fatigue, for example. A classroom test that is too long for most students to finish provides a less than complete picture of their achievement. But a test should be as long as it needs to be for item sufficiency. What to do? If you judge it to be too long given the age and development of your students or the length of the class period, it is better to split it into two tests to be administered over two consecutive days than to shorten the test for the sake of convenience. Keep in mind that decisions concerning the number of items required to assess given outcomes are basically judgments, and no magic formula exists for determining the ideal number of items. As with setting the criteria of acceptable performance for instructional outcomes, these decisions about test length are tentative and subject to continual revision based on your experience with your students.

For example, suppose you are creating a test for five instructional outcomes, and you have dutifully listed those on your worksheet. Suppose also that for outcome number four you have written "3" in the column for optimum number of items. Later, as you finish writing the three items, you realize that although they assess some facets of the behavior in the outcome, other important facets are not addressed by the items you have written. As a result, you decide that one or two more items will be necessary to fully assess outcome four. You scan the worksheet to be sure that two more items will not make the test too long for your students and the allotted assessment time. You then replace the "3" with a "5" in the number of items column and write the items. The foregoing process, of course, takes longer to explain than to do.

This is all well and good, but what if, for instance, you have determined from your worksheet that you need 37 items but you do not have the class time for a 37-item test regardless of how you split it? In that case, you can either take time away from something else or take some items from the assessment. Either way, it is best to start with the optimum number of items and work from there. If you must cut items from the test, you have some options to consider. Which option you choose depends on the nature of the outcomes to be assessed, how many items are optimum for those outcomes, and how much time you can devote to test administration. You can:

- Subtract a number of items from one or more selected outcomes.
- Subtract the same number of items per outcome for all outcomes tested.
- Eliminate one or more selected outcomes and their constituent items.

The first option involves reviewing each outcome and the number of items you originally thought was optimum to assess it. Perhaps for a few outcomes, one or two fewer items would still provide enough opportunities for students to demonstrate acquisition and finish in the time available. The second option is an across-the-board decision. This may sound like an easy way out of the dilemma, but you must consider what one less item would mean for each outcome before choosing this option.

If, for instance, you have few items planned for an outcome to begin with, reducing the number of items further will provide even less an opportunity for the students to demonstrate acquisition. The third option is typically chosen when you can delay assessment of one or more outcomes to a later time or when the outcome is not as essential as you had originally thought. By eliminating an outcome, you also eliminate all the items associated with it from the assessment.

The worksheet in Figure 5.1 is a tool to help you scan your options, consider their consequences, and make an informed judgment. If you give mastery tests, you can also use the worksheet in determining the level of mastery required for each of the listed outcomes. Just indicate this with a split number in the "No. of Items" column. A "4/5" in the column, for instance, shows that five items will be on the test for the outcome and that a student demonstrates mastery of that outcome by answering at least four of the five correctly.

Constructing Well-Designed Items for Paper-and-Pencil Assessments

The guidelines for constructing well-designed items are essentially the same whether the assessment is criterion-referenced or norm-referenced, a distinction outlined in Chapter 2. Recall that you probably cannot tell one from the other by looking at them; the difference is in the intent. Many of the general guidelines offered here and in the following two chapters seem obvious, but some things are only obvious when you are aware of them (it is pretty obvious that the sun is a star, right?). As you will probably deduce from the discussion to come, one key to good item writing is plain old common sense. Many of these general guidelines for constructing good paper-and-pencil test items are also corollaries to principles for good test design, which means that if you follow these guidelines, you are likely to produce not only better items but better assessments, too.

Outcome-Item Correspondence

Items on an assessment should directly reflect the intended instructional outcome or objective. More specifically, *outcome-item correspondence* means that the behavior called for by the item should be precisely the same behavior specified in the outcome. The item should not "sort of" match the outcome. It should fully match the outcome. This principle applies whether you were handed the outcomes, you created the outcomes from scratch, or you obtained them from a curriculum guide. For example, if an outcome stated that students should be able to solve quadratic equations, then an item asking the students to define the term *quadratic equation* would not be appropriate. The only appropriate items would involve presenting students with quadratic equations to solve. If, indeed, the ability to set up quadratic equations from word problems was also important, then an additional instructional outcome (specifying that students should be able to set up quadratic equations given appropriately structured word problems) and its attending items would be necessary. Relatedly, items calling for demonstration of more than one outcome should definitely be avoided. Consider the following item:

> If you dip litmus paper into an acid solution, what happens to the litmus paper? What happens if you dip it into an alkaline solution?
>
> a. It turns red in an acid solution and blue in an alkaline solution.
>
> b. It turns blue in an acid solution and red in an alkaline solution.
>
> c. In both cases it becomes neutralized.

This item assesses two pieces of information, one relating to acid solutions; one relating to alkaline solutions. It would be better to have two items, one for each reaction. Outcome-item correspondence is closely related to the concept of item sufficiency, discussed earlier in this chapter. The assessment planning worksheet for checking item sufficiency (Figure 5.1) is a good tool for planning item construction, but you must also review the items created for a particular outcome afterward to ensure that, in combination, they correspond to the intended instructional outcome and provide sufficient opportunity for students to show what they have learned.

Item Communication

Communication is generally defined as the process by which meanings are exchanged between individuals. In reference to assessments, *item communication* means that an item should communicate clearly to the students the meaning you intend. It should present a clear task and be as free of ambiguity as possible. The way the student interprets the item should be the very way you intended it to be interpreted. The item should also communicate effectively to any competent scorer, so that any such scorer can correctly determine whether a student has responded to the item correctly. If an item directed students to write a one-page essay on ethics, it would probably not be clear either to the students or the scorers (other than the person who wrote the item) whether the students were to discuss the importance of ethics, their knowledge of what is ethical, or some other unspecified aspect of ethics. If, on the other hand, the item directed students to list and describe four ethical dilemmas typically encountered by members of the U.S. House of Representatives, there would probably be little question as to the criteria for an appropriate response.

Item Difficulty

Item difficulty refers to the proportion of students who respond correctly to an item. Item difficulty is an item characteristic that can be manipulated by you, the assessment developer. Appropriate levels of difficulty are a function of both the type of assessment and the outcomes upon which the assessment is based. Criterion-referenced mastery tests, criterion-referenced non-mastery tests, and norm-referenced tests have different item-difficulty requirements. Recall from Chapter 2 that mastery tests are designed to assess achievement of minimum essentials and are characterized by items of a uniformly low level of difficulty. Teachers should not be concerned with whether such a test may be "too easy"; in fact, they would be deliriously happy if by some chance all students achieved all of the outcomes and got perfect scores. Criterion-referenced non-mastery tests, on the other hand, normally contain items of varying degrees of difficulty. As with mastery tests, the difficulty of each item is determined by the nature of the instructional outcome being assessed. Teachers should never purposely try to make an item on a criterion-referenced assessment any more or less difficult than it needs to be to achieve outcome-item correspondence.

The issue of item difficulty gets a little trickier with norm-referenced tests because such tests are designed to result in a wide spread of scores. The best way to ensure an acceptable range of scores is to use items of average difficulty, so that half of the students are likely to answer the item correctly and half of them are likely to answer it incorrectly.[8] There are situations in which item difficulty is purposely manipulated, such as with norm-referenced standardized tests. When a norm-referenced test is based on a content outline and general outcomes, there is no problem; item difficulty can be manipulated at will. Complications arise when a norm-referenced test is based on specific objectives. Manipulating the difficulty of items in this case can disturb outcome-item correspondence.

There are right ways and wrong ways to manipulate item difficulty, and care must be taken by those who purposely manipulate the difficulty of test items. The correct way to increase (or decrease) the difficulty of an item is to increase (or decrease) the difficulty of the required responses. You may, for example, create an application item that requires a deeper understanding of the concept than you might normally expect students to demonstrate. There are a number of "wrong" ways to manipulate item difficulty: You can make a test question fuzzy and ambiguous, or use high-level vocabulary like *loquacious, sagacity,* and *suzerain* to challenge students; or you can make items less difficult by including little clues to the correct answer, for example. Consider the following multiple-choice item:

Who was the author of *David Copperfield?*

a. Yasser Arafat

b. Charles Dickens

c. O. J. Simpson

d. Snoop Doggy Dogg

Most students could probably figure out the correct answer even if they had never heard of Charles Dickens (*especially* if they had never heard of Charles Dickens!). Manipulating difficulty in these ways only serves to decrease validity. Item difficulty should be related to the competence of the students who can answer it correctly, not to extraneous variables bearing little or no relationship to the intended knowledge or skill.

Item Novelty

Item novelty is a concept that applies primarily to assessing student acquisition of higher-level outcomes. *Item novelty* refers to the practice of presenting the student with an item that was not previously used during instruction. If this condition is not met, an item intended to assess a higher-level outcome may, in fact, be only a knowledge-level item.

---

[8]More on determining and manipulating the difficulty of items in Chapter 10.

For example, suppose your objective is that students be able to analyze consumer product information provided on several products of the same type and to determine which is the most acceptable based on given criteria. Suppose also that in class, you conduct an analysis exercise with your students for three vehicles—the Luxan SC sport coupe, the Elliott 350 coupe deluxe, and the Avistar Twinkle—and the class concludes that, given their relative seating capacity, overall cost, and style, the Luxan is the best of the three for a number of reasons. Now if on a subsequent assessment you provide your students the *same information* on the *same cars* and ask the students to perform the same comparative analysis, the item would require no more than recall of information discussed in class and would be a knowledge-level item. A student only has to be conscious in class and *remember* the correct answer and reasons; he does not have to perform the analysis or the evaluation. To get an accurate assessment of student acquisition of the outcome, you must present new or novel information on three *different* products, none of which was previously discussed or used as an example in your teaching.

Writing Directions for Paper-and-Pencil Assessments

Recall that assessment error is reduced by providing clear directions to students and that item communication is an important part of writing well-designed assessments. When students know what to do, their degree of confidence is higher, their anxiety level goes down, and they ask fewer questions during assessment, which also reduces the distractions in the classroom for those trying desperately to concentrate. Directions to the students help frame the rest of the test and set the tone for what is to come. In short, they help orient the student to the test, its structure, and its content.

Clear directions for most types of paper-and-pencil assessments contain three components. First among these is communicating the basis on which the answer choices are to be made. Whether the student is supposed to select one answer from the options on the test or from the possible answers in his head is a critical distinction. Often, the basis for an answer is stated in the item itself (as in the item: "Which of the following generals fought in the battle of Gettysburg?"). Sometimes the basis for answers is the same for all the items, with this information appearing in the general directions (as in this example: "Select the best definition for each of the following 10 vocabulary words").

A second component of giving clear directions is clarifying the method in which answers are to be marked. Consider the following phrases gleaned from actual classroom assessments:

. . . circle the letter . . .

. . . underline . . .

. . . bubble in . . .

. . . mark with an "X" . . .

. . . ring the word . . .

. . . write in complete sentences . . .

. . . draw a line . . .

. . . circle your answer . . .

. . . write your answer . . .

. . . blacken the circle completely . . .

All of these tell students something about how they are to respond. Your students want to know what you are going to look for when you score their test, and you should tell them in the directions.

The third component of giving clear directions to the students is telling them the number of points available for each item. This may or may not be the same for all items, depending on the outcomes assessed and the types of items used on the test. Regardless of whether they are all the same, available points should be indicated in the directions. The exception to this would be if the number of available points on a test varied not only by item type, but also by item. In this case, it would be better to indicate within the item how many points a correct answer is worth. This can be done by putting the number of available points for the item in parentheses at the end of the item, or at the end of the stem in the case of a multiple-choice item.[9]

Communicating directions to students effectively can be done in a number of ways. If the basis for answers, how to respond, and points per item are all the same for all of the items on the test, then you only need to say so once at the beginning of the test. If the item type changes (say, from essay to multiple-choice), you may need to provide specific directions at the point of transition in the test. If this is the first assessment opportunity of the year for your students, realize that they are learning not only the content you've taught them but also *how to take your tests*. Depending on the challenges your students face or on their developmental level, you may wish to read the written directions aloud before the test begins. If all of your assessments are to be answered the same way and all of the items are always worth two points each, you may think that it is not necessary after the first few assessments to write any directions. It will not hurt, however, to include directions on assessments; some students can use an extra reminder, new students may come into your class, or other individuals outside your classroom (like parents, counselors, or other teachers) may want to examine the students' (or your!) work.

General directions are placed before any of the items and contain instructions to the students that pertain to the entire test. Specific directions, on the other hand, may vary by item type. These are placed just before the items to which they refer. If the directions change a number of times in one test, stating in the general directions that it is important for the students to read the specific directions carefully as they encounter them is wise.[10] Directions, whether general or specific, should always be prominently positioned and separated from the actual items. Putting the word DIRECTIONS in capital letters or boldface can capture the students' attention.[11] Horizontal lines are another helpful visual cue in grouping items and their attending directions (see Figure 5.2).

---

[9]See Chapters 6 and 7 for examples.

[10]Specific directions for various item types are considered in Chapters 6 and 7.

[11]I have not yet figured out how to make them flash on the page or glow like a neon sign, but I am working on it.

Test: The Three Branches of Government

Name ____________________ Date ____________________

General directions: *This test covers chapter 7 in your textbook. You may write on the test, but please write or mark your answers on the separate answer sheet. Unless stated differently in the item, each answer is worth 2 points. Good Luck.*

True-false *(directions)*

1. Easiest true-false item.
2.
3.
4.
5.
6.
7.
8. Most difficult true-false item.

Multiple-choice *(directions)*

9. Easiest multiple-choice item.
10.
11.
12.
13.
14.
15.
16. Most difficult multiple-choice item.

Short-answer *(directions)*

17. Easiest short-answer item.
18.
19.
20.
21. Most difficult short-answer item.

Essay items *(directions)*

22. Easiest essay item.
23.
24. Most difficult essay item.

Figure 5.2
Example of a paper-and-pencil assessment showing placement of directions, arrangement of item types, and use of horizontal lines as visual separators.

Organizing the Items on Paper-and-Pencil Assessments

You can arrange items on a paper-and-pencil assessment in a number of ways. An efficient arrangement should make scoring easy for you and should not present any obstacles to your students. One way to accomplish this is to arrange the items by type and, within that type, arrange the items from easiest to most difficult. Suppose, for example, you have created or selected 24 items for a test on the three branches of the United States government and that the breakdown, by type, of these 24 is as follows:

3 essay items,

8 true-false items,

5 short-answer items,

8 multiple-choice items.

For reasons you will see in Chapters 6 and 7, true-false items are generally thought to be easier than multiple-choice items, and multiple-choice items are thought to be easier than short-answer items. Short-answer items, in turn, are thought to be easier than essay items. Rearranging the grouping to reflect this, you have the following numbered items:

1–8	true-false
9–16	multiple-choice
17–21	short-answer
22–24	essay

Within each of those four groupings you should also arrange the items from easiest to most difficult, so that when you look at the whole test the items follow the pattern shown in Figure 5.2.

Grouping all like-type items together is efficient in two ways. First, it allows you to write the directions once for each group of items. This saves time as well as paper for both you and your students. Second, by putting the directions above the first item of the type, you signal the students that a change in format is coming, requiring a change in their test-taking strategy. Thus, they do not have to shift back and forth between formats as they navigate through the individual items. The directions for the entire test should come first, following just after student identification information and preceding any type-specific directions. Notice in Figure 5.2 that there are no actual items on the "test." The point of the figure is to illustrate a sample test page layout that accommodates two levels of directions and different types of items and uses visual cues to group items. For textbook space purposes, the numbers for the items are single spaced. On a real assessment, the items would have much more space separating them, as much as students would need to answer the items fully.[12]

[12]Good examples of item layout can be found in Chapters 6 and 7.

Just exactly how do you determine which items are the easiest and which ones are the most difficult? By their answers, your students determine this for you, because it is from their perspective that difficulty is judged. In theory, we place easy items at the beginning to give our students the best opportunity for early success. This bolsters their confidence to go on to the more difficult items. *You* may think, however, that a particular item is the easiest one of its type on the assessment, whereas your *students* may think otherwise. Once you have given the test you can use item-analysis data[13] to detect the easier items and rearrange the sequence for the next time you give it. If this is a first-time administration, use your best judgment, keeping your students' perspective in mind, and revise your arrangement based on item-analysis data.

In the case of a mastery test, where practically all the items are of the same relatively low difficulty level, you can usually arrange the items by type and by outcome. This is possible because, typically, all of the items that are written for a particular outcome are of the same type. When all of the items are written at the knowledge level, an alternative approach is to arrange the items according to the logical order of the material. You might, for example, arrange the items on a fifth-grade science test on amphibians in categories of habitat, diet, and method of reproduction. The most appropriate arrangement depends upon the type and content of the assessment. When designing assessments, be aware of the alternatives and consciously attempt to make the best decision for a given situation.

Considering Other Issues in Paper-and-Pencil Assessment Development

After the directions and the items have been written, all must be assembled into a legible, functional whole. There are a number of suggestions summarized in the checklist for good paper-and-pencil assessments at the end of this chapter, which, if followed, will facilitate both test-taking and scoring. First, items should be numbered consecutively, from 1 through 24 for example, and plenty of white space (at least a double line width) should be used between items.

Second, answer spaces should be of equal size and large enough to accommodate the longest response, especially on short-answer tests. Answer spaces should be placed in a vertical column in the right-hand or left-hand margin, or a separate answer sheet may be used.

Third, if an item is accompanied by any type of illustration, such as a diagram, or by a short paragraph of information, the material should be accurate and placed directly above the item, if possible, or parallel to it. Further, especially for illustrated items, it is always important to have items start and end on the same page. For example, the stem of a multiple-choice item should not fall on the bottom of one page and the answer choices on the top of the next; having to flip-flop pages back and forth is a concentration killer.

---

[13]Information on item analysis can be found in Chapter 10.

Fourth, the assessment should be typed if at all possible. Typing is not always feasible due to available resources and the nature of the test content; it takes an experienced *and willing* typist to type an algebra test or a Spanish test. The more important the test is, the more important it is that it be legible and typed.

Last, the final version of the assessment, typed or not, should be proofread carefully. Making two proofreading passes through the test, once for content and once for accuracy, is a good strategy. The first reading may reveal unclear items and inadvertent grammatical errors. A second reading allows you to concentrate on identifying errors such as misspelled words and misnumbered items. It is also a good idea to have a colleague proofread your test. As with any written work, a second pair of eyes can spot errors that you are too close to see.

Reproducing Paper-and-Pencil Assessments

When you are satisfied that the assessment is ready, you must select a method of reproduction. Options abound. Some teachers prefer mimeograph stencil or ditto master. These methods can produce good copies if the number of copies required is not too high. Photocopying usually results in high-quality copies if the machine has been well maintained. The cost of these copies has also dropped in the last few years. Other teachers print tests directly from a computer printer. This is fine, too, unless the resulting print is difficult to read or the computer printer is already in high demand. The method you use is not important as long as the resulting copies are neat and easy to read. Blurred print, light copies, and ink smudges can affect scores as much as fuzzily worded items. Finally, every student should have a copy of the test. It is wise to make a few more copies than needed; if not collated properly, for example, an assessment may be missing a page, and there is invariably a student who says, "I messed up my test. Can I have another one?"

Selecting Paper-and-Pencil Assessments

Recall that many paper-and-pencil tests and items have already been created, so teachers may not have to create assessments from scratch. For example, consider the following scenarios. In one school, Mr. Turano is provided with a complete instructional package to teach his fourth-graders language arts. This instructional package includes not only a detailed teacher's version of the students' textbook but also a resource file containing pretests, group and individual placement tests, and two equivalent forms of posttests for each chapter and unit. Thus, Mr. Turano has the options of, for example, using the Chapter 2 assessment supplied by the textbook publisher, using one from another source that covers the same content, or constructing his own assessment. In another school, Ms. Beeche and her fellow fourth-grade teachers are provided enough books for their students and one extra for themselves. This extra copy is the same student version and there are no other trappings of an instructional package. Ms. Beeche must make or find her own assessments and instructional materials beyond the basic text. Both Mr. Turano and Ms. Beeche have choices to make in how they will assess the learning of their students in language arts. Whether they select tests or test items from available resources or choose to make their own assessments, the information contained in this chapter and in Chapters 6 and 7 will help them. The design and construction guidelines can also be used as criteria for judging candidate assessments.

A word or two to overworked and weary teachers (that is, most of us): If the items on publisher-provided or other ready-made assessments follow the general and specific guidelines for well-designed assessments, then the proverbial wheel need not be reinvented. It makes no sense to martyr yourself dreaming up test items, directions, and so forth if perfectly good ones already exist and if you have permission to use them. If, on the other hand, a perfectly good assessment does not exist, you must join the assessment construction business. Validity and reliability (in that order) are your first concerns; following the guidelines will help guarantee a high degree of both.

Setting Cut-Off Scores for Paper-and-Pencil Mastery Tests

No less than 16 methods have been proposed for setting performance standards or cut-off scores for criterion-referenced mastery tests, all of them relying on the judgment of human beings.[14] Some additionally involve the use of mathematical formulas in deriving the "magic" score, above which a student is designated a master and below which the student is designated a non-master. Although there are technical procedures available to set cut-off scores for tests, these should be reserved for competency testing at the end of the year, a situation with higher stakes attached to the results. Cut-off score-setting procedures may involve several teachers and, perhaps, parents, as well as item-analysis data gathered from previous administrations of the assessment. Individual teachers just do not have the time to devote to standard setting, nor do the consequences of most classroom test results warrant it. For classroom tests, using an assessment planning worksheet like the one shown in Figure 5.1 with proportions in the "No. of Items" column (4/5 or 6/9, for example) to determine mastery by outcome is sufficient. Experts such as Lorrie Shepard have warned that "classroom teachers should not spend more time on test development (including standard setting) than they spend on teaching."[15]

As a teacher you may be involved at some time in setting cut-off scores for tests at the district or state level. This can be a tricky business. If you set standards too

---

[14]"Test Score Validity and Standard Setting Methods" by R. K. Hambleton, in *Criterion-Referenced Measurement: The State of the Art* (pp. 80–123) by R. A. Berk (Ed.), 1980, Baltimore, MD: Johns Hopkins University Press.

[15]"Setting Performance Standards" by L. A. Shepard, in *A Guide to Criterion-Referenced Test Construction* (p. 188) by R. A. Berk (Ed.), 1984, Baltimore, MD: Johns Hopkins University Press.

low, you run the risk of misclassifying some students as "masters" when in reality they are not (false positives) or of classifying some as "non-masters" when in reality they are (false negatives). Although beyond the scope of this book, a thorough review of the standard-setting procedures as well as consideration of the consequences of misclassification is in order for those who participate on standard-setting committees.[16]

✓ *Easy Reference Checklist*

Guidelines for Good Paper-and-Pencil Assessment Design (Including General Guidelines for Item Construction)

- ❑ Selected content is well defined.
- ❑ Content chunk size fits into allotted assessment time.
- ❑ Selected sample of behaviors represents the pool of intended instructional outcomes.
- ❑ Taxonomy level of the outcomes is identified.
- ❑ Assessment has sufficient number of items per outcome.
- ❑ Final number of items fits into time allotted.
- ❑ Items directly reflect intended outcomes.
- ❑ Items communicate meaning as intended.
- ❑ Items are written at appropriate level of difficulty.
- ❑ Higher-level items present novel situations.
- ❑ General directions are provided.
- ❑ General directions are clear.
- ❑ Item-specific directions are provided when needed.
- ❑ Items generally proceed from easiest to most difficult.
- ❑ Items are numbered consecutively.
- ❑ Answer spaces/sheets facilitate answering and scoring.
- ❑ Page-flipping is not necessary to answer any item.
- ❑ Test is typed.
- ❑ Test is proofread.
- ❑ All copies of test are legible and complete.

[16]The Hambleton and Shepard references would be good places to start a review of standard-setting procedures.

Summary

Paper-and-pencil assessments gauge your students' accomplishment of instructional outcomes by providing them an opportunity to demonstrate this accomplishment in written response to prompts calling forth the behavior to be demonstrated. The prompts, or items, are usually written. The responses are also typically in writing—the students may write them out or choose them from among the answers given. Paper-and-pencil assessments are often used as a basis for assigning grades in a particular subject and can be used as pretests and tests of entry behaviors and as posttests following instruction as well.

Considering the Advantages and Disadvantages of Paper-and-Pencil Assessments

Advantages of paper-and-pencil assessments include the following:

1. They can be used to assess learning at many levels of the cognitive domain for many types of subject matter and can indirectly assess affective outcomes.
2. They require no special equipment or set-up time.
3. They can be administered to students individually or as a group.
4. Many excellent paper-and-pencil tests and items have already been created.
5. They provide a written record of the student's performance.
6. Results of paper-and-pencil tests can be analyzed in several ways, providing valuable input for student remediation or reteaching, for future lesson or unit planning, and for improving instruction.

Disadvantages of paper-and-pencil assessments include the following:

1. They are not appropriate for assessing most psychomotor skills, with the exception of writing, nor are they highly useful for direct assessment of affective outcomes.
2. Students who are not very verbal or who are poor or slow readers may be unduly penalized when taking a paper-and-pencil test.

Using Guidelines to Create Effective Paper-and-Pencil Assessments

In selecting content, first determine what the assessment will cover and determine the size of the "chunk" of content. Second, delineate all the important aspects of that chunk. Third, select the aspects that will be included in the test. A test will normally cover an instruction period ranging from several days to several weeks or even months. A test that covers a small chunk of content prevents cognitive overload on the part of the students and permits a larger, more representative sampling of the behaviors reflected in the selected outcomes. More items per outcome can also be included on a test covering limited content. Your task as a teacher is to decide which are the most important outcomes to cover and to balance the amount of assessment time with the amount of instructional time.

Instructional outcomes form the backbone of instruction and assessment, and they should be specified before creating the test because they specify the important aspects of the content. The important aspects of the content to be assessed may also come from a curriculum guide. It is helpful to devise a scheme for sampling from the pool of behaviors contained in the outcomes when selecting the aspects that will be included in the assessment. The test items must constitute a representative sample of desired behaviors to be valid. To ensure that the behaviors to be assessed are representative of the behaviors that could be assessed, teachers may use *random selection* or *stratification* prior to selection. It is easier to select from the possible behaviors when the outcomes are clearly specified and fall within a restricted range.

The next step in general test design is to determine the taxonomy level of the outcomes that will be assessed on the test. Specifying the taxonomy level of the outcomes is useful for two reasons: (1) Knowing the level of the outcome, you can better devise an appropriate test item that calls forth the same level of behavior in the student, and (2) it facilitates communication between the test designer and the item writer when they are not the same person.

Ideally, the number of items included on the assessment is driven by the outcomes to be assessed: decide how many items constitute a sufficient opportunity for a student to demonstrate achievement of each outcome, then sum the total. *Item sufficiency* means that a correct response to an item (or items) constitutes sufficient evidence that the student has demonstrated the intended behavior and, thus, has achieved the instructional outcome. Usually, one item per outcome is not sufficient, especially if the test is comprised of selected-response items, is criterion-referenced, or is a mastery test. As a general rule, higher-level outcomes usually require more items per outcome.

An assessment should be as long as it needs to be, but should not be too long. A classroom test that is too long for most students to finish provides a less than complete picture of their achievement. They may not have time to complete the test, or they may experience test-fatigue, for example. No magic formula exists for determining the ideal number of items. If you must cut items from the test, consider the following options: (1) subtract a number of items from selected outcomes, (2) subtract the same number of items per outcome for all outcomes tested, or (3) eliminate one or more selected outcomes and their constituent items.

Well-designed items will conform to these guidelines:

1. *Outcome-item correspondence.* The behavior called for by the item should be precisely the same behavior specified in the outcome.
2. *Item sufficiency.* Collectively, the items should provide sufficient opportunity for students to show what they have learned.
3. *Item communication.* Items should communicate clearly to the students the meaning you intend. They should present a clear task.
4. *Item difficulty.* The difficulty of the item should reflect the difficulty or complexity of the outcome.

5. *Item novelty.* The situation presented in the item should be one that was not previously encountered during instruction. Item novelty applies primarily to assessing student acquisition of higher-level outcomes (comprehension through evaluation in Bloom's taxonomy).

Assessment error is reduced when students know what to do. Directions to the students help frame the rest of the assessment and set the tone for what is to come. They help orient the student to the assessment, its structure, and its content. Clear directions for most types of paper-and-pencil tests contain three components: (1) the basis on which the answer choices are to be made, (2) the method in which answers are to be marked, and (3) the number of points available for each item. Depending on the developmental level or disability of your students, you may wish to read the written directions aloud before the test begins. General directions are placed before any of the test items and contain instructions to the students that pertain to the entire test. Specific directions may vary by item type and are placed just before the items to which they refer. Directions, whether general or specific, should be prominently positioned and separated from the actual items.

There are a number of ways of arranging items on a paper-and-pencil assessment. An efficient arrangement is to group the items by type and within that type arrange the items from easiest to most difficult. By their answers, your students determine for you which items are the easiest and which ones are the most difficult; it is from their perspective that difficulty is judged. Once you have given an assessment you can use item-analysis data to detect the easier items and rearrange the sequence for the next time you give it. In the case of a mastery test, you can usually arrange the items by type and by outcome. When all of the items are written at the knowledge level, an alternative approach is to arrange the items according to the logical order of the material. The most appropriate arrangement depends upon the type and content of the test.

There are a number of suggestions, which, if followed, will facilitate both test taking and scoring:

1. Items should be numbered consecutively with plenty of white space between items.
2. Answer spaces should be of equal size and large enough to accommodate the longest response, especially on short-answer tests.
3. If an item is accompanied by any type of illustration, such as a diagram, or by a short paragraph of information, the material should be accurate and placed directly above the item, if possible, or parallel to it.
4. Items should start and end on the same page.
5. The test should be typed if at all possible.
6. The final version of the test, typed or not, should be proofread carefully.

Test reproduction methods for classroom tests include using mimeograph stencil machines, ditto master machines, photocopy machines, and computer printers. These methods produce different quality copies, and the costs are accordingly different.

Whatever the method, it is important that the resulting copies are neat and easy to read. Every student should have a copy of the test, and it is wise to make a few more copies than needed.

Teachers may have access to pre-written assessments, or they may have to design their own. Use the design and construction guidelines in this chapter as criteria for judging or drafting candidate tests and items.

Setting Cut-Off Scores for Paper-and-Pencil Mastery Tests

Although there are technical procedures available to set cut-off scores for mastery tests, these should be reserved for competency testing at the end of the year or other high-stakes tests. For classroom assessments, using the assessment planning worksheet with proportions in the "No. of Items" column to determine mastery by outcome is the most logical approach.

Try These

I. Prepare a design for a paper-and-pencil assessment for a chunk of content and a group of students of your choice. The content should be appropriate for assessment with paper and pencil. Use your own version of the assessment-planning worksheet (Figure 5.1) to list the specific instructional outcomes to be assessed, determine their taxonomy levels, and determine the number of items. The number of items should be enough to adequately sample the behaviors in the outcomes but not fatigue the students.

II. Obtain a paper-and-pencil test from a colleague, an inservice teacher, your instructor, your own files, or some other source. Obtain also the assessment worksheet or list of outcomes the test covers, if available. Using the guidelines presented in this chapter as criteria, critique the test. Your critique should include evidence of guidelines followed, evidence of guidelines not followed, and specific suggestions for improvement.

CHAPTER 6

Creating Selected-Response Items for Classroom Assessments

Key Concepts:

- Constructing and choosing good selected-response (multiple-choice, two-choice or true-false, and matching) items.
- Knowing when to use each of the selected-response item types.
- Scoring selected-response items.
- Relating item types to corresponding instructional outcomes in assessment.

Standards Addressed in This Chapter:

1. Choose assessment methods appropriate for instructional decisions.
2. Develop assessment methods appropriate for instructional decisions.

Before You Begin Reading, Consider This

Is it true that selected-response items can't effectively assess higher levels of the cognitive domain?

YES Although outcomes can be written to correspond to higher levels of cognition, selected-response items call for memorization of material only, a lower-order or knowledge-level behavior.

NO Selected-response items can assess both knowledge and higher levels of cognitive ability. Selected-response items are good for outcomes written at the knowledge level calling for memorization but can also be used to measure higher levels of cognitive thinking.

This chapter and Chapter 7 both deal with the types of items commonly found on paper-and-pencil classroom tests. The chapters are formatted in a similar fashion by item type for ease of understanding and comparison. This chapter format is summarized in Figure 6.1 and includes the following sections:

1. A description of the item type and its appropriate use, including advantages and disadvantages relative to other item types.
2. Guidelines for constructing good items, including negative and positive examples of items and directions to the student specific to the item type.
3. An item-evaluation checklist that summarizes the guidelines for easy reference.[1]
4. Examples of instructional outcomes and related items for the type classified by taxonomic level.
5. Information on scoring items.

Common to all *selected-response* items is that the correct answer lies in the item itself. It has been built into the item by the teacher. The task of the student is to figure out which of the answers presented in the item is the *keyed correct answer,* the one the teacher has designated as correct. Well-written items require the student to use the principle, concept, or strategy acquired to arrive at the correct answer. Poorly written items can give extraneous clues to the answer or make it easy for a student to guess the correct answer. Thus, the student avoids using the principle, concept, or strategy. Items can also be overly difficult, well beyond the complexity of the related learning outcome. The three major types of selected-response items are two-choice (like true-false), multiple-choice, and matching. Each of these will be discussed in turn.

---

[1]The checklist includes both the generic guidelines for all selected-response items and those for the particular type described.

		Description and Use	Construction Guidelines	Evaluation Checklist	Instructional Outcomes and Items	Scoring
Selected-Response (Chapter 6)	Two-Choice					
	Multiple-Choice					
	Matching					
Free-Response (Chapter 7)	Essay					
	Short-Answer					

Figure 6.1
Presentation matrix illustrating the sequence of discussion for each item type in Chapters 6 and 7.

Two-Choice Items

Understanding Two-Choice Items and Using Them Appropriately

The most well-known *two-choice* item type is true-false, in which the student decides whether a declarative statement (also known as a proposition) is wholly true or either partially or wholly false. No doubt you encountered a few of them in your own schooling. There are other two-choice item types as well, including fact-opinion, yes-no, warranted conclusion–unwarranted conclusion, and cause-effect items. The category of two-choice items includes any item that contains two answer choices, one of which is correct.

The true-false item has enjoyed a popularity in classroom testing far beyond its modest limits, probably because true-false items—at least bad ones—are easy to write. Good ones, on the other hand, take care and time to produce, because true-false items are studies in absolutes. Marking a statement true means that it is true in all contexts and under all conditions. Otherwise the statement must be marked false. For this reason, these items are typically used to assess knowledge of specific facts—sometimes, unfortunately, obscure and trivial facts. They can also be used to test definitions and meanings of terms. Here is an example from the world of computers:

A pixel is an addressable dot that can be illuminated on a CRT screen. T F

Here is an example of the yes-no variety that indirectly assesses attitude, an outcome in the affective domain:

I enjoy the time I spend in school. Yes No

Relative to the other item types, two-choice items have certain advantages. First, due to their relative brevity, more two-choice items can be squeezed into the same time period than any other item type. For the types of subject matter and instructional outcomes suitable for two-choice items, this permits a broad sampling of content and reasonably reliable tests. Recall that, all other things being equal, longer tests (those that have more items) are more reliable than shorter tests. Second, relative to completion, short-answer, and essay items, two-choice items are easy to score and objective; results are the same regardless of who scores the items using an answer key.

Two-choice items also have a few relative disadvantages. Unfortunately, many types of subject matter are not well suited to these items. Two-choice items are also notoriously open to guessing. Think about it: For every item, students have a 50% chance of getting it right regardless of how badly they are prepared. Combine this with the difficulty of writing items that do not contain any inadvertent clues to the correct answer, and the odds increase in favor of the underprepared student. Teachers have tried to compensate for some of the drawbacks of two-choice items. The *correction item* variation of the true-false item, for example, directs students to state what is true when they answer an item false by rewriting it as a true statement. This enables students to not only recognize false statements but also demonstrate knowledge of what is true regarding the subject. It also reduces the points awarded for pure, uneducated guessing. For example:

Directions: In each of the items below, one word has been underlined. If you think that the underlined word correctly completes the statement, circle the T. If you believe that the underlined word incorrectly completes the statement, circle the F and write in the blank the word or words that correctly complete the statement.

1. If you mix blue and yellow paint you get <u>purple</u>. T F ____________
2. Jamaica is part of the <u>Hawaiian</u> islands. T F ____________

The correct answers would be:

1. If you mix blue and yellow paint you get <u>purple</u>. T (F) green
2. Jamaica is part of the <u>Hawaiian</u> islands. T (F) Greater Antilles

Any time a correction item is used, the word or phrase that is to be corrected should be emphasized in some way, using underlining or italics, for example. Otherwise, students may rewrite the entire statement and it may not be the one you intended. For example, if "Hawaiian" was not underlined in the above item, a student who answered it false and rewrote it as follows would have to be given credit:

Kahoolawe is part of the Hawaiian islands.

Bad two-choice items are no help to teachers, even if they are easy to construct and score. Good two-choice items, given enough of them for a reasonably reliable test, provide teachers with a useful tool for assessment. The next section shows you how to construct good two-choice items.

Using Guidelines to Construct Well-Designed Two-Choice Items

The general guidelines for good item construction presented in Chapter 5 also apply to two-choice items. In addition, there are guidelines that apply specifically to two-choice items, which draw on common sense and aim at getting the truest picture of student performance possible. Some of these guidelines make good intuitive sense but are not yet empirically tested. The guidelines are summarized in the Easy-Reference Checklist at the end of this section, which is handy to use when writing or choosing two-choice items.

1. *Word statements positively, avoiding tricky negatives, especially when items are to be judged true or false.* Answering false to a negatively worded statement creates a double negative. For example:

The unicorn is not a real creature. T̲ F

The choice "false, is not" is confusing. Eliminating the word *not* takes care of the problem here:

The unicorn is a real creature. T F̲

If you absolutely must word a statement negatively, emphasize the negative wording with underlining or *italics*. But first, try first to word it positively.

2. *True items and false items should be about equal in length.* There is a tendency for novice item writers to put every qualification imaginable in a true statement so it is, in fact, totally true. This makes the statement interminably long and easy prey for the uninformed but test-wise student. For example:

There are 365 days in a calendar year, except leap year, which has 366 days in order to account for the fact that there are really 365 ¼ days in a year. T̲ F

Whew! If it is necessary to have a few lengthy "true" items, you should have an approximately equal number of lengthy "false" items. In other words, the length of an item should have nothing to do with its truth or falsity.

3. *True-false items should be either completely true or completely false.* There should be one defensible correct answer. If there is *any* situation for which a statement is not true, then the statement is technically false. For example:

Normal body temperature is 98.6°F. T̲ F

If your students are in the elementary grades and studying the human body in health for the first time, this might be a totally true statement and, therefore, the item no problem. If, however, your students are adults enrolled in a nursing program, they probably know of exceptions to this statement. Some individuals, for example, have a "normal" body temperature of 98°. To be totally true, the item would have to be reworded as follows:

For most people, normal body temperature is 98.6°F. T F

Watch out, however, for guideline two regarding the relative length of statements. Now consider this next example for an outcome that states, "students will demonstrate knowledge of colors of common objects":

Bananas are yellow. T F

Many primary students learning their colors could be expected to mark this one true. But some primary students trying to achieve the same objective may mark this item false if the bananas they typically see are green (underripe) or brown and black (overripe). Totally true or totally false *for whom* is the question here. As a teacher, you will be in the best position to anticipate the answers of your students, but don't be surprised if you get an "off-the-wall" answer that turns out to be totally correct from the student's experience. Can the above item be fixed? Yes; for example, by showing a picture of a yellow-colored banana next to the item and changing the wording to "The banana is yellow," you avoid the problem.

4. Specific determiners should be avoided in true-false items unless they puzzle the uninformed student. Specific determiners are words such as *always, all, never, none, every,* and *inevitable* that indicate sweeping generalizations. They also tend to indicate to the unprepared but test-wise student that an item is most likely false. Words such as *generally, usually, often,* and *sometimes* are typically associated with true items. For example:

All scorpions have eight legs. T F

Theoretically that is true. But there is bound to be at least one little scorpion somewhere with only seven legs, wounded in a fight with another scorpion, perhaps. The point is that such words should be avoided because they affect the correct response more than the content of the item. They almost challenge the student to think of a situation, however outlandish, where the statement would not be true. Specific determiners can also be used intentionally to trip up the underprepared but test-wise student. Because some "always" or "never" statements are indeed true, and some "often" or "generally" statements are indeed false, these specific determiners can be used to attract the test-wise student to an incorrect answer. In general, you should be aware of words that can give away the answer to the test-wise student, and you should also know that you can use these same words to challenge these test-wise students. Here is one way to reword this item to eliminate the specific determiner:

As members of the arachnid class, scorpions have eight legs. T F

5. The item should assess the students' grasp of an important proposition. In hot pursuit of totally true or totally false statements (guideline three) that do not violate guideline two, novice item writers sometimes create items that fit those criteria but test obscure or trivial propositions. For example:

George Washington had false teeth. T̲ F

There are many more important propositions than this one about this country's first president. Items like this take up testing time and provide little in the way of useful assessment data for making decisions about student learning. At best, trivial and obscure propositions can be used to pass the time and keep the class occupied on a rainy day or when the cassette player eats the tape in the middle of an instructional video. They should not, however, be used on tests that count. You, of course, are the judge of what is trivial and what is important based on the learning outcomes tested and the developmental level of your students.

6. *The item should be based on a single idea.* Testing two (or more) propositions in the same item may sound more efficient, but, in fact, is not. For example:

At sea level, water boils at 212°F and freezes at 0°F. T F̲

In this case, there are two propositions, one of which is true and the other false. The student who answers the item false may know that water really freezes at 32°F, or may think that water freezes at 0°F but boils at 100°F. In other words, a student may answer the item correctly for the wrong reason. You can get a much better idea of what students know by testing propositions separately, like this:

At sea level, water boils at 212°F. T̲ F

At sea level, water freezes at 0°F. T F̲

After writing an item, check for the word *and* in the statement. That *and* is a clue that you may have included more than one proposition.

Recall from Chapter 5 that good directions to students include the basis on which the answer choice is to be made. If you want students to mark false any items that contain even the slightest bit of falsity, then your directions should say so, simply and clearly. Here is an example from health science:

Directions: For items 1–3 circle the T if you think the statement is completely true. If you think the statement is partially or totally false, circle the F. Each item is worth two points.

1. The esophagus connects the stomach to the mouth. T̲ F
2. Gastric juice helps break down fats. T F̲
3. Most of the food we eat is absorbed into the bloodstream through the large intestine. T F̲

You saw an example of directions for correction items earlier in this chapter. Here are directions for a two-choice test where students are to discriminate between valid and invalid inferences based on given information:

Directions: Read the paragraph below. For items 4–6, circle the S next to the statement if you think it is supported by the information in the paragraph. Circle the U if you think the paragraph does *not* support the statement. (1 point each)

Sally has a weird cat. The cat sleeps in the bathroom sink. It won't go out without its red bandanna. It also hides socks behind the living room sofa. Some people don't know where their socks go when they vanish, but Sally always knows. At least the cat doesn't hide her library books!

4. Sally's cat eats socks. S <u>U</u>
5. Sally knows where the socks in her house go when they vanish. <u>S</u> U
6. Library books are too heavy for the cat to hide. S <u>U</u>

Note that the letters to circle are to the right of the items. Putting them all in one place makes the test easier to grade. Putting the answers on the right, in a column, makes it easier for most students to respond but may make it more difficult for lefties. Again, you are in the best position to decide how to make it easy for your students.

✓ *Easy Reference Checklist*

Guidelines for Good Two-Choice Items

- ❑ Item calls for behavior stated in outcome.
- ❑ Item difficulty reflects difficulty/complexity of outcome.
- ❑ Higher-level (comprehension through evaluation) items present novel material.
- ❑ Statements are worded positively.
- ❑ Tricky negatives are avoided.
- ❑ True items and false items are approximately equal in length.
- ❑ True-false items are completely true or completely false.
- ❑ Specific determiners are avoided *or* are used to discourage test-wiseness.
- ❑ Item assesses an important proposition.
- ❑ Item is based on a single idea.
- ❑ Directions include basis for answer choice.

Considering Related Instructional Outcomes

Two-choice items are useful for assessing achievement of instructional outcomes in the cognitive domain and those cognitive outcomes related to the affective and psychomotor domains. It is important, for example, that students know bicycle safety rules if they are to follow them at home and at school. The related outcomes from the two domains might look like this:

> Students routinely practice safe bicycle rules and habits. (Affective)
>
> Students know the bicycle safety rules. (Cognitive)

Cognitive outcomes are also important to the ultimate achievement of psychomotor outcomes. For example, a student must mentally recall the steps in executing a golf tee shot to physically accomplish the task. Related outcomes from the two domains might look like this:

> Students can execute a golf tee shot such that the ball travels at least 150 yards and stays in the fairway. Other criteria include proper stance, grip, swing, and follow-through. (Psychomotor)
>
> Students can identify the steps in making a tee shot in golf. (Cognitive)

We often assess cognitive learning as a part of achieving outcomes in the other two domains. But assessment of cognitive learning in this case should not be thought of as interchangeable with assessment in either the affective or the psychomotor domain. At best, two-choice items and their paper-and-pencil relatives can indirectly assess learning in the affective and psychomotor domains regarding the students' actual behavior. You may find out from the results of a paper-and-pencil test, for example, that a student can discriminate between true and false propositions regarding the school bicycle safety rules, but you do not know if the same student routinely obeys the rules unless you have observed the student, on more than one occasion, riding his bike on school grounds.

We cannot assess behavior from self-reported affect, but we can, at least, determine the self-reported affect such as stated attitudes and opinions with a paper-and-pencil assessment and with two-choice items (as in, I like to read in my spare time Y N). On many occasions, however, a finer discrimination than "yes" or "no" is needed. In these cases, answer choices such as "never," "sometimes," "often," and "always" are added, and the item is no longer a two-choice item.

Theoretically, two-choice items can be written to assess learning outcomes at higher levels of the cognitive domain, as the following example illustrates:

$$2x^2 + x^2 + 4 = 3x^4 + 4 \qquad \text{T} \quad \underline{\text{F}}$$

For higher-level outcomes, however, short-answer or multiple-choice items are usually preferred because they provide information concerning errors and thus are more instructionally useful. Students who choose F for the above item, for example, might do so because they know that $2x^2 + x^2 + 4$ really equals $3x^2 + 4$, or because they believe it equals $2x^4 + 4$, or because of some other reason. Because writing items that are totally true or totally false is difficult, especially at the higher levels of the cognitive domain, two-choice items are better suited for the assessment of abilities related to logical argument. For example, given information followed by a series of propositions (sentences that can be said to be true or false), students can indicate whether a stated conclusion is valid or invalid. Also, we can sometimes "collapse" a number of multiple-choice items into a series of true-false items by presenting one stem or partial proposition followed by a series of responses. For example:

In order to become part of the United States Constitution, a proposed amendment must be

1.	approved by the president.	T	<u>F</u>
2.	proposed by two-thirds of each house of Congress.	<u>T</u>	F
3.	ratified by two-thirds of the states.	T	<u>F</u>

Knowledge-Level Outcomes

Within the cognitive domain, two-choice items are useful for assessing the achievement of instructional outcomes at several levels (knowledge and application, for instance). This does not mean, however, that they are useful for all outcomes written at a particular level (every comprehension outcome, for example). Look at the following knowledge-level outcomes and see if you can identify any that are well suited for assessment with a two-choice item.

1. Given definitions of various forms of energy, the student will match them with the term that best fits the definition.
2. Given the growth stages of a housefly in scrambled order, student puts them in correct chronological order.
3. Knows the difference between fact and opinion.
4. Knows terminology associated with the human nervous system.
5. Selects the correct verb form for a given sentence.
6. Lists in writing the criteria by which the nutritive value of a meal can be judged.

Let's look at each of them. The first outcome begs for a set of matching items and so is not appropriate for a two-choice item. The second outcome calls for an item that presents either pictures or words describing the growth stages of a housefly for the student to unscramble. This could be done physically (rearranging pictures), verbally (re-ordering a list of words), or by multiple-choice (stating the growth stages in various orders, one of which is correct). It is not a good candidate, however, for a two-choice item. The third instructional outcome is a good candidate. The following are examples of items that could be written for it:

A fact is something that is known to be true.	<u>T</u>	F
An opinion is what a person thinks about something.	<u>T</u>	F
What a person thinks about something is called a fact.	T	<u>F</u>
Something that is known to be true is called an opinion.	T	<u>F</u>

Notice that this outcome specifies that the student know the difference between the two terms. It does not call for the student to identify given statements in a communication (a letter, for example) as fact or opinion, which would assess performance on the analysis level of the taxonomy. If the outcome were worded at the analysis level, it could be tested with a series of two-choice items. These items would look different from the ones listed above and could direct a student to label quoted or paraphrased statements from a novel communication as either F or O, for example.

The fourth outcome could be tested in a number of ways because it is not very specific, at least for assessment purposes. A series of true-false items related to human nervous system terminology might look like this:

A synapse is the point at which a nervous impulse passes from one neuron to another.	T (underlined)	F
The branching, tube-like extensions of the body of a nerve cell that resemble the arms of a starfish are called axons.	T	F (underlined)
The brain is considered part of the peripheral nervous system.	T	F (underlined)

Of course, multiple-choice, matching, and completion items could all also be used to test the acquisition of the fourth outcome. Additionally, the student could be given a diagram of a nerve cell and directed to label indicated parts.

In the fifth instructional outcome, *selecting* the correct form of a verb implies that the correct form is given along with others. As the number of verb choices is not specified in the objective, two-choice items are a viable option. The student might be asked to underline the correct verb form for each sentence as these items illustrate:

He [went, gone] to the store.

The boat [sunk, sank] in the storm.

Her father [make, made] the prizes for the carnival.

Instructional outcome six specifies that the student must list in writing the criteria for judging the nutritional value of a meal. Therefore, selection of answers is not appropriate; the student must recall them from memory and write them down. When outcomes are created with assessment in mind, they are often specific enough to indicate the item type best suited to the task. They give guidance to the item writer to assess achievement of outcomes at the pertinent level of the taxonomy *and* relating to what was taught. Notice that outcome six calls for the student to list criteria, not judge the nutritional value of a given meal (a behavior classified as evaluation in the taxonomy). A test item that did ask the student to make this type of judgment would clearly be inappropriate for the level of outcome as it is stated—a clear case of over-assessment.

Higher-Level Outcomes

Included in this section are some examples of higher-level instructional outcomes from the cognitive domain that can be tested for two-choice selected-response items. This is not an exhaustive list, but it is intended to show some of the range possible with two-choice items.

Outcome: The students will be able to interpret given information regarding the people, industry, and culture of a state. (Comprehension)

Item: The student is given a folder containing charts, graphs, and tabular information on California and the following directions:

Review the contents of this folder. For each of the following statements, bubble in A on your answer sheet if you think the statement is supported by the contents or B if you think the statement is not supported by the contents. You may look back in the folder after first reading.

1. California leads the nation in the production of oranges.
2. The period of 1988–94 was a slump for California industry.
3. California ranks second to New York as a port of entry for Japanese cars.
4. The population of California has dropped in the last five years.

Outcome: Make change for $1.00 for multiple purchases of less than $1.00. (Application)

Directions: For items 5 and 6, circle YES if the correct change was given. Circle NO if the change given was *not* correct. If the change was *not* correct, write the correct change on the line.

5. Paul buys a cup of yogurt for 73¢ and a fireball for 10¢ at the corner store. From his $1.00, the clerk gives him back 7¢.

   YES NO, Correct Change = 17¢

6. Vinda goes to the candy store and buys 49¢ worth of malted milk balls and a piece of bubble gum for 5¢. She hands the clerk a $1.00 bill. The clerk gives her 46¢ in change.

   YES NO, Correct Change = ____________

Outcome: Given an advertisement or commercial not experienced before by the student, the student will recognize the propaganda tactic used. (Analysis)

Item: The students are shown three 15-second commercials that were videotaped in another class whose learning objective was to create a commercial using a selected propaganda tactic. The directions on the test paper in front of them are as follows:

Directions: For each of items 7–9 you will be shown a 15-second commercial. Decide if the propaganda tactic used in each commercial is the same as the one listed below. If it is, circle YES, If not, circle NO.

7. Testimonial	<u>YES</u>	NO
8. Comparison of products	YES	<u>NO</u>
9. Product character	<u>YES</u>	NO

As you can see, higher-level outcomes can be assessed with two-choice items. The item type is useful in many instances, but when assessing higher-level outcomes, two-choice items are probably not as useful as good short-answer or multiple-choice items. You will see the versatility of the multiple-choice item in the next section.

Multiple-Choice Items

Understanding Multiple-Choice Items and Using Them Appropriately

Unless you have spent most of your life in isolation or in another country, you have probably encountered multiple-choice items. *Multiple-choice* items present a problem, task, statement, or question and a number of possible answers through which the student sorts. Unlike the two-choice item, three or more answer choices are presented to the student. The student must locate, identify, or recognize the best- or correct-answer choice in order to receive credit for the item. Components of the multiple-choice item consist of the following parts:

1. A *stem,* which is the presented task, usually in the form of a question.
2. The answer choices together, called *options,* which further separate into:
   a. The *keyed correct answer* and
   b. The wrong answers, called *distractors.*

Here is an example of a multiple-choice item from the world of computers:

What is the primary output device for microcomputers called?

<u>a</u>. Cathode ray tube.

b. Central processing unit.

c. Keyboard.

d. Random access memory.

In the above example, the stem asks a question and four options are presented, with *a* as the keyed correct answer and *b–d* as distractors. The number of options may vary, usually ranging from three to five. There are also *correct-answer* multiple-choice items and *best-answer* multiple-choice items. Arithmetic computation items are examples of the correct-answer type, as are states and their capitals. The following items illustrate:

1. 723
   ×413
   a. 1,136
   b. 31,819
   c. 288,596
   d. 298,599
2. What is the capital of Ohio?
   a. Akron
   b. Cincinnati
   c. Cleveland
   d. Columbus
   e. Toledo

In best-answer multiple-choice items used to measure problem-solving ability, for example, students may select from several possible answers, one of which is better than the others and, therefore, the keyed correct answer. What constitutes "best" is stated either in the directions or in the stem itself, as the following illustrates:

3. You own a popcorn company. Customer complaints and market research indicate that in some markets, customers frequently burn the popcorn by not shaking the pot as kernels pop. Which of the following is the best way to solve this problem according to the criteria for problem solutions discussed in class?
   a. Modify the directions on the container to emphasize pot-shaking during popping.
   b. Start a television campaign to show people how to pop corn.
   c. Remove your product from markets in which a majority of people do not know how to pop corn.

Multiple-choice items are the most widely used type of assessment item in paper-and-pencil testing, and with good reason. With them, you can measure not only knowledge but also many of the important educational outcomes beyond the knowledge level of the cognitive domain, such as understanding, ability to solve problems, recommendation of appropriate action, and prediction of events and consequences. Affective outcomes and attitudes also may be indirectly assessed with multiple-choice items through self-report, as the following example illustrates:

Directions: Circle the letter of the option that most closely reflects how you feel about the subject.

What do you think of the quality of the cafeteria food in this school?

a. Better than I usually get at home.
b. Pretty good, all things considered.
c. Okay.
d. Pretty bad.
e. So bad I get sick just thinking about it.

Multiple-choice items are also easily and objectively scored, whether answers are recorded on the test itself or on a separate answer sheet. For instructional purposes, multiple-choice items are very effective; plausible distractors (based on misconceptions or common errors) make results useful for item analysis and diagnosing learning problems. By analyzing the options your students select, you can detect factual and procedural errors and misunderstandings.[2] Multiple-choice items are also relatively unaffected by a student's response set—the tendency on the student's part to make a particular choice (answer *b*, for example) when she does not have a clue to the right answer. Finally, multiple-choice items can easily be created, revised, used, stored, and reused via microcomputer.

Relative to other item types, multiple-choice items have certain advantages. For example, multiple-choice items are less susceptible to chance error as a result of guessing than true-false and other two-choice items. The opportunity for purely guessing the keyed correct answer to a multiple-choice item is reduced to one in three with three options and is further reduced as the number of options increases. The "best answer" subspecies of multiple-choice items also avoids the need for unqualified true and false statements. It does not require that one alternative be completely correct, just more correct than the other options. With the exception of two-choice items, multiple-choice items can sample more instructional content in the same period of time than any other item type—good news if you are pressed for assessment time in the classroom. Compared to matching items, multiple-choice items avoid the necessity for homogeneity of large amounts of material. The options in a multiple-choice item function only for that one stem; they should be, of course, homogeneous for that item. The options in a multiple-choice item also contribute structure that may be missing from completion or short-answer items and thus avoid the ambiguity and vagueness that is sometimes present in these items.

The multiple-choice format also has disadvantages, some stemming from the nature of the type and others stemming from misuse of the type. First, it is difficult to create two or three plausible and attractive but wrong answers time and again, as anyone who has seriously tried will tell you. Thinking up all those distractors takes time, too. This is especially a problem at the primary level due to the students' limited vocabulary and experience in any one content area. As a result, teachers sometimes resort to writing items at the knowledge level regardless of the level of the instructional outcome the item is supposed to assess. Writing any type of item, for that matter, at higher levels of the taxonomy is—you guessed it—taxing. But constructing good multiple-choice items is possible with practice and feedback garnered by analyzing the results of your tests.

Second, students can sometimes recognize a correct or best answer among the options that they could never construct on their own. This has led some critics to say that the multiple-choice format is only useful for assessing a student's ability to rule out obviously incorrect options. Third, multiple-choice items are neither well suited

---

[2]More about this in Chapter 10.

to assessing a student's ability to express synthesized thoughts or strategies used to arrive at an answer, nor to writing out creative solutions or organizing and presenting ideas. Obviously, the type is not a good one for assessing everything—some problem-solving skills in math and science, for example, are perhaps better assessed using another strategy.

Using Guidelines to Construct Well-Designed Multiple-Choice Items

The general guidelines presented in Chapter 5 for creating effective paper-and-pencil assessments also apply to multiple-choice items. In addition, there are guidelines that apply specifically to the multiple-choice format. In a rather exhaustive analysis of 46 authoritative textbooks in the field of educational assessment, Haladyna and Downing[3] distilled 43 separate multiple-choice item-writing rules into a taxonomy with three major content categories: general, stem construction, and option development. By computing the number of times a particular rule was cited, the authors created a short list of guidelines with 32 or more citations each.

1. State clearly as much of the problem in the stem as possible, including the central idea. The stem of a multiple-choice item sets the stage and presents the task to the student. It is, therefore, very important that it be well crafted—complete and clear, yet concise and free of irrelevant material. About the only exception to this would be if the instructional outcome required students to choose among relevant and irrelevant material to solve a problem. Consider the following:

An arachnid is . . .

a. an arthropod with three pairs of legs and antennae.
b. an arthropod with three pairs of legs but no antennae.
c. an arthropod with four pairs of legs and antennae.
d. an arthropod with four pairs of legs but no antennae.

The student does not know what the task is until he reads the options. "An arachnid is . . ." is not much help. There is also too much unnecessary reading contained in the options. This is often a problem with multiple-choice items that are stated in incomplete sentences. For this reason, the following is a corollary to guideline one.

2. State the stem in a question rather than in an incomplete sentence. Although some experts maintain that both the question format and the incomplete sentence format are viable, research studies have shown that the question format is superior.[4] An incomplete stem can present a more difficult item than warranted by the objective assessed. The stem as a question provides a complete thought to the student and

---

[3]"A Taxonomy of Multiple-Choice Item-Writing Rules" by T. M. Haladyna and S. M. Downing, 1989, *Applied Measurement in Education, 2*(1), 37–50.

[4]T. M. Haladyna, 1994. Author's personal communication with the researcher.

avoids the inadvertent grammatical clues to the right answer that are sometimes associated with incomplete stems and their options. Notice how the above item improves when phrased as a question:

How many pairs of legs does an arachnid have?

a. 2

b. 3

c. 4

Or, try it this way:

What is an arthropod with four pairs of legs but no antennae called?

a. Annelid

b. Arachnid

c. Insect

d. Mollusk

Of course, referring back to the outcome the item assesses will help you decide which of several stem wordings is better. The point is that students should spend most of their time thinking about the answer, not trying to figure out the question, which leads us to the next guideline.

3. Word the stem positively; avoid negative wording. Negative wording in a multiple-choice item can confuse students and raise further their already heightened anxiety levels. It also can make the item appear more difficult than originally intended, based on the objective. Here are some examples:

Poor:

1. Which of the following countries is not in South America?
    a. Argentina
    b. Bolivia
    c. Spain
    d. Venezuela

Good try; needs work:

2. All of the following countries are located in South America *except* . . .
    a. Argentina
    b. Bolivia
    c. Spain
    d. Venezuela

Better:

3. Which of the following countries is located in Europe?
    a. Argentina
    b. Bolivia
    c. Spain
    d. Venezuela

Item one requires the student to know only that Spain is not located in South America and, so worded, probably does not reflect the instructional outcome. Can you imagine an outcome that says, "Given a list of countries, students will select those that are *not* located in South America"? I don't think so. More than likely it read something to this effect: "Students will select the appropriate continent to which a major country belongs." Some students will not get credit for the first item because they missed the *not* in the stem, looked no further than the first option, and chose *a* as their answer. The second item demonstrates a slight improvement because the negative wording is highlighted, but this item requires the same knowledge from the student as the first item. Item three requires the student to know that Spain is located in Europe and that the others are not, a definite improvement over item one. Perhaps an even better approach, in this case, would be to create a set of matching items with countries on the left and continents on the right.

4. Use logic in arranging options. If the options are words, phrases, or short sentences, alphabetize them. If they contain numbers, arrange them in numerical order, or chronological order for dates and time. This makes things simple for both you and your students. You have less to worry about regarding the placement of the keyed correct answer (see guideline nine), and your students can scan the options quickly without getting stuck. This guideline is exemplified in all the examples in this section of the chapter, even the poorly written one beginning "An arachnid is . . ." Procedural order is another perfectly useful logical arrangement of options as well. Vertical arrangement of options below the stem is also preferable to horizontal placement. If you have arranged options in numerical order, for example, and then arranged them horizontally as illustrated, you have defeated the purpose of the logic:

a. 1948   c. 1964
b. 1954   d. 1993

or:

a. 1948   b. 1954
c. 1964   d. 1993

Textbook and test publishers sometimes arrange them this way so that more items will fit on a page, thus reducing printing costs. Seeing options published this way may lead you to believe that horizontal arrangement is preferable. It is not. A sheet of paper may be saved in the process, but student search time has been extended, contributing to confusion and anxiety in the student and unreliability in appears in a multiple-choice item on a classroom test and, therefore, not a good distractor (see guideline eight). The following item illustrates another inappropriate use of "none of the above":

According to the principles of supply and demand, if there is a shortage of coffee beans, what will happen to the price of a cup of coffee? It will . . .

a. decline.

b. stay the same.

c. rise.

d. None of the above

In this item, clearly "none of the above" is not the keyed correct answer. All contingencies are covered in the first three options, so a fourth option looks rather silly and fools no one. Second, "none of the above" is also inappropriate for best-answer-type items in which the student is asked to select the *best* alternative from among several of varying degrees of correctness. Selecting "none of the above" as the best course of action in solving a problem, for example, does not indicate that the student knows what to do, just what not to do given the options listed. Third, items with "all of the above" as an option occur sometimes as alternatives to the "circle all that apply" type item mentioned in guideline six, above. Consider the following item:

Which of the following is a fossil fuel?

a. Coal

b. Natural gas

c. Oil

d. All of the above

Some students will miss the item because they will look no further than the first option (which is perfectly correct based on the wording of the stem), mark it correct, and move on to the next item. Other students will get the item right because they saw that the first two options were correct, noticed that "all of the above" was an option, and chose it. They may not have known that oil was a fossil fuel until they read the last option.

8. Use plausible and attractive distractors. Each distractor you include in a multiple-choice item has a job to do: to tempt the uninformed students. Therefore, what constitutes plausible and attractive is actually in the eyes of these students. Distractors should appear reasonable if the students either missed your instruction on the topic, didn't read the material, did not prepare for the test, or did not learn. Examine the following item:

Who painted the Mona Lisa?

a. Alexander the Great

b. da Vinci

c. Galileo

d. Napoleon

the test results. A test is not the place to be stingy v around the items. It is better to arrange the options ver ists, like this:

a. 1948

b. 1954

c. 1964

d. 1993

5. *All options for an item should be fairly consistent in le* knowledge among the students in my high school U.S. g didn't know the answer to an item on Mr. Munro's test, one. It was almost sure to be the right answer. Convers convince me that this is still true in this century. Mr. Munr correct answer directly from the textbook and quickly m go with it. This worked for him because it didn't take m students, too, because we got more right answers than although we may not have really grasped some of the c our academic progress had been generated. If you do the disregard the length of the options you create, expect you accordingly; word gets around fast. If you find yourself w choice items, try first to shorten the correct answer. If yo correct answer any shorter, lengthen the distractors a bit s so obvious.

6. *Use only one option as the keyed correct answer.* This n and unnecessary, but I include it to emphasize its importa to why the keyed correct best answer is superior to the approach this is to take the position of your students and for each of the distractors. If there is really no argument ba in the stem, the item is probably fine. Some teachers cre where the students are directed to "circle all that apply." able for two reasons. First, when closely examined, these i lection of true-false statements. As such, they are better p choice items. Second, more than one correct answer to a scoring when you have to determine how many points t one correct answer selected out of a possible three. By mind when writing or selecting items, you avoid conflicts return their test papers.

7. *Do not use "none of the above" or "all of the above" as* lieve that "none of the above" and "all of the above" are us cumstances and prescribe their use accordingly. But, for a should be avoided when constructing classroom assessme are usually used when you cannot think of that last distrac for "none of the above," which is overwhelmingly the key

To answer this question correctly you do not have to know who painted the Mona Lisa; only who of the four choices is an artist and who is not or, worse, only that three of the four are not artists. This revised item contains more useful distractors:

Who painted the Mona Lisa?

a. da Vinci

b. Rembrandt

c. Renoir

Some teachers worry over the appropriate number of options for their multiple-choice items or wonder whether it is permissible to mix four-option items with three-option items on the same test. Some experts advocate as many distractors as possible, provided they are plausible and attractive to the uninformed student. Many attractive and plausible distractors certainly reduce the possibility of a student guessing the correct answer, but they also increase the amount of reading necessary per item. Current research in the area of multiple-choice testing suggests keeping the total number of options to three: one keyed correct answer and two quality distractors.[5] This is practical advice for teachers. Fewer options reduce reading and search time—students complete an item faster with minimal increase in opportunity for pure guessing. Pure guessing on classroom tests is less likely than on standardized tests anyway. The time saved with fewer options can be used in the following ways:

1. Increase the number of high-quality items and thus the reliability of the test without increasing testing time.
2. Devote more time to instruction.

9. Place the keyed correct answer in each possible position (a, b, c, etc.) approximately the same number of times. If you follow guideline four and use logic in your arrangement of options, the position of the keyed correct answer naturally varies. After all the items have been written and you have a draft test, check to see that there is balance among the times *a, b,* and *c* are each keyed correct. The balance need not be exact (on an 18-item test *a* is correct exactly six times, as is *b* and *c*), but many novice item writers fall into the trap of over-using an option (*c,* for example) as the keyed correct answer. You would be surprised at how many students (even young ones) also know this and look for it on your tests. You can use a die to help you decide the position of the correct answer if you need to adjust the balance. These guidelines are summarized in the checklist on the following page.

Considering Related Instructional Outcomes

One of the beauties of multiple-choice items is their ability to assess achievement of instructional outcomes at many levels of the cognitive domain. As with their two-

[5]T. M. Haladyna, 1994. Author's personal communication with the researcher.

✓ *Easy Reference Checklist*

Guidelines for Good Multiple-Choice Items

- ❑ Item calls for behavior stated in outcome.
- ❑ Item difficulty reflects difficulty/complexity of outcome.
- ❑ Higher-level (comprehension–evaluation) item presents novel material.
- ❑ Problem is stated clearly.
- ❑ Problem is fully stated in stem.
- ❑ Stem is stated as a question.
- ❑ Incomplete stems are avoided.
- ❑ Stem contains central idea of item.
- ❑ Stem is worded positively.
- ❑ Negative wording is avoided in stem.
- ❑ Options appear in alpha-numerical or other logical order.
- ❑ Options are listed vertically.
- ❑ Options are consistent in length.
- ❑ Only one option is correct per item.
- ❑ "None of the above" is avoided.
- ❑ "All of the above" is avoided.
- ❑ Distractors are plausible and attractive to uninformed students.
- ❑ Three options (best) or four (maximum) are used.
- ❑ Position of keyed correct answer is balanced.
- ❑ Directions are present and stated clearly.

choice counterparts, multiple-choice items are useful for assessing cognitive outcomes related to the affective and psychomotor domains. Multiple-choice items can also be used to indirectly assess attitudes and opinions, especially when a finer discrimination than two choices is called for, as the following examples illustrate:

Directions: For each of the activities described, circle the answer that most accurately reflects how you feel about the activity.

1. I like to read in my spare time.

   Always Often Sometimes Never

2. I like to play team sports.

   Always Often Sometimes Never

Knowledge-Level Outcomes

Although multiple-choice items are useful for assessing the achievement of instructional outcomes at the knowledge level and higher, they are not appropriate for all outcomes written at a particular level. Look at the following knowledge-level outcomes and try to identify those that are suitable for assessment with multiple-choice items.

1. Given definitions of the various landforms, the student will choose the term that best fits the definition four out of five times.
2. Accurately recites from memory Lincoln's Gettysburg Address without hesitation.
3. Given a line drawing of a microcomputer (with components attached), labels the indicated parts.
4. States Mendel's laws of segregation and independent assortment in genetics.
5. Identifies stated changes in matter as chemical or physical.
6. Given the growth stages of a housefly in scrambled order, student puts them in correct chronological order.

As written, the first outcome is a good candidate for multiple-choice assessment. The following items illustrate two different approaches to assessing it:

1. Define *plateau.*
   a. A large, high plain above sea level.
   b. A dry, flat area below sea level.
   c. A narrow, steep valley formed by glaciers.
2. Which of the following terms best describes a large, high plain above sea level?
   a. Crevasse
   b. Mountain
   c. Plateau

Which is best? Well, the learning outcome states that the definition will be "given" and that the student will "choose the term that best fits the definition." In the first item the term is given and the student must choose the definition that fits it. The second item requires the student to select the term that fits the definition given; therefore, item number two is most true to the learning outcome. If knowledge of three or more landforms were to be assessed, economy of space and assessment time could be achieved with a matching set of definitions and terms. The second item also presents less to read than the first.

The second learning outcome, reciting the Gettysburg Address, is not intended for paper-and-pencil assessment at all, but for oral performance. Labeling the parts of a computer, outcome three, would probably best be assessed with short-answer type items in the form of blanks next to arrows pointing to a particular part or component in a line drawing of a microcomputer configuration. It could be turned into a series of multiple-choice items by including three or more options for each item to be labeled from which the student chooses. The following four items illustrate:

Directions: For each of the numbered parts of a typical microcomputer system, circle the letter of the option that correctly labels the part.

Learning outcome four requires students to merely state a number of rules or principles either in writing or verbally. As written, the outcome would best be assessed with a short essay item that asked the student to state Mendel's laws of genetics. A multiple-choice item would be a less-than-direct test of the student's ability to state the laws. Outcome five is representative of those that deal with knowledge of classifications and categories, which in Bloom's taxonomy is part of knowing "ways and means of dealing with specifics."[6] As the following item illustrates, whether the outcome is distinguishing changes in matter; classifying two-dimensional shapes into circles, squares, or triangles; or sorting Shakespeare's plays into comedies, tragedies, and histories, multiple-choice items are appropriate:

Which of the following is a chemical change?

a. Burning of oil.

b. Evaporation of alcohol.

c. Freezing of water.

The last learning outcome tests knowledge of a previously taught sequence. A popular way to test this with a multiple-choice item is to present various sequences as options, from which the student selects the one that best fits the task as presented in the stem:

What are the stages of growth in a housefly, in chronological order?

a. egg—larva—pupa—adult

b. egg—pupa—larva—adult

c. larva—egg—pupa—adult

d. pupa—egg—larva—adult

---

[6] *Taxonomy of Educational Objectives, Handbook I: Cognitive Domain* (p. 68) by B. S. Bloom (Ed.), 1956, New York: David McKay.

Higher-Level Outcomes

Beyond the knowledge level of the taxonomy, multiple-choice items are useful in assessing, for example, students' ability to do the following:

- Interpret pictorial or verbal information.
- Understand concepts.
- Solve problems, mathematical and otherwise.
- Recognize logical fallacies in arguments.
- Recommend appropriate action.
- Predict events and consequences.
- Apply concepts and rules.

In this section are some examples of higher-level instructional outcomes from the cognitive domain that are appropriately assessed with multiple-choice items. This is by no means an exhaustive list, but it is intended to show some of the range possible with multiple-choice items.

Outcome: Students will interpret the information contained in pie charts, histograms, and bar charts. (Elementary-level science.)

Directions: Use the following chart on energy use in the United States for items 1 and 2:

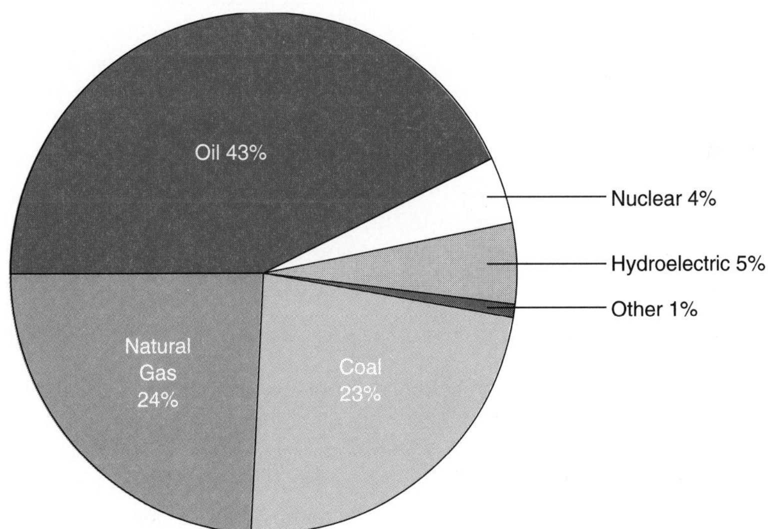

1. How much energy used is from fossil fuel?
   a. 43%
   b. 67%
   c. 90%

2. The amount of nuclear energy used is about the same as the amount of what type of energy?

   a. Coal

   b. Hydroelectric

   c. Natural gas

Outcome: Students will perform operations containing variables with exponents. (High-school-level algebra.)

Item: $2x^2 + x^2 + 4 =$

   a. $3x^4 + 4$

   b. $3x^2 + 4$

   c. $2x^4 + 4$

Multiple-choice items can be useful in math and related subjects for diagnosing difficulties students have with mastering the instructional outcomes. The distractors in the above example represent answers obtained by incorrectly performing the operations called for in the stem. If, for example, a student thought that to add variables with exponents you just added the exponents, he might choose option *c*. One item answered like this may indicate nothing more than carelessness on the part of the student, although a number of items like this answered in the same way demonstrates a pattern worth discussing with that student. And if many students select the same distractor, that is a clue to a different problem.[7] Asking your students how they came up with their answers can be a particularly enlightening experience. In this way, multiple-choice items can help you target instruction and remediation to those students and areas most in need. The distractors, then, are plausible and attractive to the student who is not yet clear on the concepts, principles, or rules covered in instruction.

As you can see from the examples below, multiple-choice items can also assess your students' acquisition of cognitive instructional outcomes far beyond the knowledge level.

Outcome: Detect logical fallacies in given arguments. (High-school-level life skills.)

Item: Some high-school students were discussing changing the grading system from A = 90–100 points, B = 80–89 points, C = 70–79 points, D = 60–69 points, F = ≤59 points to a grading system that included "+" and "−". Arguing for the change, Mario said, "A student with an 88 or 89 average shouldn't be punished for doing better than just B work by receiving a B just because he doesn't have an A average. He should get a B+. It would be a good incentive to do even better next time."

Based on the logic presented in the argument, what is left unstated by Mario?

---

[7]More about analyzing distractors to improve your assessments and your instruction in Chapter 10.

a. Students who would have received an A for a 90-point average would be punished also under the new system by receiving an A−.

b. Teachers cannot make that fine a discrimination among the work of their students.

c. The difference between a C and a C+ is not the same as between a B+ and a B.

Below, two higher-level outcomes are assessed with items that draw from the same scenario.

Outcome: Given a description of an experimental study (including problem, hypothesis, data collection method, and results), students will select conclusions based on the study. (Middle-school science.)

Outcome: Students will predict events based on given information.

Scenario: A fish farmer was raising trout for sale to fish markets. She wanted to find a way to get the trout to grow faster so she could take them to market faster. The fish farmer knew that some things happened faster at higher temperatures. She guessed that if she made the water warmer in the feeding tanks, the trout would grow faster. She tested her idea by doing an experiment and recording growth of the trout to adult length in two tanks with different constant temperatures. The data she collected showed that in 12°C water, the trout grew into adults in 26 months. In 7°C water, the trout grew into adults in 32 months.

Items:

1. What conclusion can be formed from the data collected?
   a. Trout need warmer water to breed in.
   b. Trout grow fastest when the water temperature is constant.
   c. Trout grow faster in warmer water.
   d. Trout grow faster in cooler water.
2. As a result of conducting this experiment, what is the fish farmer most likely to do?
   a. Buy more trout eggs from her supplier.
   b. Increase the size of the feeding tanks.
   c. Keep the feeding tank temperature at 7°C.
   d. Keep the feeding tank temperature at 12°C.

There are thousands of multiple-choice items at a variety of levels in the taxonomy for almost any subject matter in the curriculum. If you are in a position to select items for your use from a textbook series publisher or journal in your discipline, keep two things in mind: first, the items should draw the same behavior from your students as stated in your instructional outcomes; second, the items should be appropriate for your students in terms of reading level, sophistication, and level of discrimination needed among options. If the ready-made items do not meet these criteria, they may not be the time-saver for which you had hoped.

Matching Items

Understanding Matching Items and Using Them Appropriately

Matching items are sets of multiple-choice items for which two things are true: one, that there is a strong theme to them, rendering them homogeneous with one another; and two, that the answer choices are written once and serve as answers and distractors for all the items in the set. Sets of matching items include three component parts:

1. *Directions* to the student.
2. *Premises*—the part that poses the stimulus, problem to be solved, or first party in the relationship.
3. *Responses*—the answer choices or second party in the relationship.

One popular format for matching items includes directions to the student followed by a list of premises in a column on the left and the responses in a column on the right, as in the following illustration:

Directions: Match the country with its capital. Write the letter of your answer in the space to the left of the country. Each capital may be used once or not at all. Each item is worth 2 points.

Countries	**Capitals**
_____ 1. Brazil	a. Bogotá
_____ 2. Chile	b. Brasilia
_____ 3. Colombia	c. Buenos Aires
_____ 4. Uruguay	d. Caracas
_____ 5. Venezuela	e. La Paz
	f. Montevideo
	g. Santiago

The theme or relationship in the above matching set is, of course, countries and their capitals. In this case, the countries are the premises and the list of capitals the responses. Because each city listed is a South American capital, they all serve as distractors for the five premises. The student answering these in turn still has three plausible and attractive choices for the capital of Venezuela. Another popular format, especially in the elementary grades, is the matching set with a word bank, as in the following illustration:

Directions: Read the names of the groups of people in the box. Then read the sentences that describe the people. Write the name of the group described beside each sentence. Some words may be used more than once. (1 point each)

Arawaks	**pirates**	**slaves**	**Spaniards**	**French**

slaves 1. By 1789, about a half-million people from this group lived in Haiti.

Spaniards 2. This group ruled Hispaniola for 200 years and called their main town Santo Domingo.

pirates 3. This group took over the western part of Haiti because of its ample food supplies and ideal hiding places.

French 4. These wealthy citizens were given the best farmland in Haiti.

pirates 5. This group came to be known as buccaneers.

Arawaks 6. This group named their island Haiti, which meant "mountainous land."[8]

At first glance, these six items may look like short-answer items, but the word bank in the box above provides the responses for the premises stated in the items. The set meets the criteria for matching items. The student must write the correct word, however, not just a letter to indicate his answer. Without much trouble, you could probably rewrite this set into two side-by-side columns labeled "Descriptions" and "Groups." Sometimes answers are indicated by drawing lines between columns of premises and responses so that the student does not have to write anything. This is especially appropriate if students have not yet learned to form letters or if physical limitations prevent them from doing so.

Relative to the other item types, matching items have certain advantages. First, many subject matter areas can be assessed with matching items. The following list of column headings, although not even close to exhaustive, illustrates some of the range that is possible:

Countries, states	Capitals
Major rivers	Countries, continents
Road sign meanings	Road signs
Definitions	Terms
Pictures, names of objects	Functions of objects
Rules	Examples

[8]Abridged and adapted from Workbook for *The Western Hemisphere: America's Neighbors* of the Ginn Social Studies Series, © Copyright 1986, by Ginn and Company. Used by permission of Silver Burdett Ginn Inc.

Historic events	Dates
Major characters	Shakespeare's plays
Artists	Their works
Characteristics	Planets
Dance	Country of origin
Discoveries	Discoverer

One way to know when a matching set of items may be appropriate is if you find yourself repeating the same or similar distractors for several multiple-choice items. When this is the case, you may be able to combine these similar items into a homogeneous matching set. This leads to the second advantage of matching items. Compared to multiple-choice items, matching items save both space on the printed page and assessment time. They too are easily and objectively scored.

One of the main disadvantages to using matching items is a result of their strength as indicators of student knowledge. Because matching items use associations and relationships, teachers have typically used them to assess knowledge and not much else. Some teachers over-rely on matching exercises, promoting rote memorization of facts. There is nothing wrong with students memorizing a few facts, mind you, but not at the expense of other important learning outcomes. Another main disadvantage is that matching items, if not thoughtfully written, are given to the inclusion of unintended clues to the correct answers. This is usually due to the item writer's struggle with finding factual and related material (for the item type) that is also important to assess (for the instructional outcome). An example of this is the *im*plausible and *un*attractive response or two added to a list of responses just to make it longer than the list of premises.

Judging from many of the major textbook series and from observing teachers, matching items are very popular in classroom assessment. Unfortunately, too many bad matching sets have been created in proportion to good ones. Bad items of any type, it seems, are easier to produce than good ones. Inclusion in a textbook does not exempt a matching set of items from principles of good item writing. The matching sets you have seen so far in this text are relatively good ones. Here is an example of a really bad set of matching items.

Hot and wet	1. How the islands of East Asia were formed.
Shanghai	2. The climate of Southeast Asia.
Volcanoes	3. Narrow ledge built on a hillside for farming.
35%	4. Largest city in China.
Terrace	5. How much of the world's population lives in East Asia.

Why are these so bad? First, although there is the flimsiest of themes (East Asia), there is no real homogeneity to the premises, which, in this exercise, are wrongly placed in the right-hand column. The lack of both homogeneity and any extra responses makes the entire set easy prey for the test-wise but uninformed student. Even if you knew absolutely nothing about the area, you could probably figure out that the answer to number five has to be a number and that Shanghai is the only choice that sounds like a city and, therefore, must go with number four. The rest can be answered through process of elimination. Second, there are no directions. The student must assume or ask the teacher about the basis for matching premises and responses, in addition to asking how to record answers. Third, the column with more to read is on the right. This is contrary to our natural tendency (for readers of English) to read the first entry on the left and then search the right column for a match. For reading and searching efficiency, the columns should be switched. Fourth, there is no logical order to the responses, which adds search time. This set of premises and responses would be much better off as a series of multiple-choice items, each with its own plausible and attractive distractors. The students would be better off as well. So, how do teachers construct good matching items that are useful assessment tools? So glad you asked.

Using Guidelines to Construct Well-Designed Matching Items

As you know by now, the general guidelines for good item construction[9] apply here as well. Presented here are guidelines specific to matching items. They are helpful in reducing assessment error whether you are writing the items yourself or reviewing a reproduction master from a teacher's textbook resource file. These guidelines are summarized in the handy checklist at the end of this section.

1. Choose homogeneous premises and responses for each set of items. The degree of homogeneity in a matching exercise is directly related to the degree of discrimination required from the student. The more homogeneous the material, the finer the discrimination required in detecting the relationships between premises and responses. Consider the difference in the homogeneity of the following matching sets: historic events and their dates; and historic events of the early 20th century and their dates. The second set of items would be much more homogeneous than the first set and would require much finer discriminations among the responses. You saw in the example set on East Asia the simple discriminations necessary to get correct answers when the material is heterogeneous. Such gross discriminations may be appropriate for primary-grade students, but anyone above that level will see that set for what it is, a conglomeration of things requiring test-taking savvy rather than acquired knowledge. The responses in the East Asia example are not homogeneous enough to be effective distractors for the individual premises because the premises are not, themselves, homogeneous enough. As another example, consider the difference in the degree of discrimination necessary between matching (a) major rivers and the *continents* on which they are found, and matching (b) major rivers and the *countries* in which they are found. A finer discrimination is required, of course, to match a river with the smaller land mass of a country. As you may have guessed, the degree of homogeneity in a matching exercise depends on the level of your students and the instructional outcome to be assessed.

---

[9]See Chapter 5.

2. *Title each list of premises and responses.* This guideline helps ensure homogeneity: With these headings in mind, you are less likely to include unrelated premises or responses. The titles also give meaning to the lists. See the countries-capitals set of items that appeared earlier in this chapter for an example of this guideline.

3. *Keep the lists of premises and responses short.* Doing so helps achieve homogeneity. Keeping a short list homogeneous is much easier than tinkering with a long one. Four to seven items is optimum. Certainly, in a few (very few) cases, you might have 10 or so items, but this should be a rarity.

4. *Use logic in arranging premises and responses.* If they are words, phrases, or short sentences, put them in alphabetical order. If they are numerical, arrange them from low to high, or put them in chronological order if they are dates and times. This makes things simple for both you and your students. You don't have to worry about varying the order to avoid giveaway clues, and your students can search the lists quickly without having to "psych out" your ordering scheme.

5. *Use "imperfect" matches rather than "perfect" matches.* Perfect matches, where every response goes with one (and only one) premise, allow the students to use process of elimination rather than their acquired knowledge to answer successfully. Imperfect matches can be achieved in two ways. One way is to use unequal numbers of premises and responses. If your matching set contains five premises, for example, list seven or eight responses so that the last premise to be matched has several plausible distractors. Another way is to use responses (or at least some of them) more than once. This is illustrated in the earlier matching set about the island of Hispaniola and its population groups.

6. *Use longer phrases as premises, and shorter phrases and words as responses.* The column with more to read should be on the left, as premises, with the logically arranged list of fewer words or numbers on the right, as responses. In this way, search time is minimized. If you create a matching set for historic events and their dates, for example, list the events, in alphabetical order, on the left in a column labeled "Events" and the dates, in chronological order, on the right in a column labeled "Dates."

7. *Place all premises and responses of a matching set on the same page.* Flipping back and forth between test pages while reading premises and searching through responses is annoying to the test taker and all people in the classroom. Do not make your students waste search time and distract others. Put everything, including the directions, on one page, and allow ample space between lines and between sets.

8. *Give students clear directions to follow, and include the basis for matching and instructions for marking answers.* Clear directions are very important for students answering matching items, perhaps more so than for any other paper-and-pencil item type. When written well, the basis on which matches are to be made is suggested by the column headings, if not by the premises and responses themselves. Nevertheless, the basis for matching should be included in the directions, as should the proper way to mark answers, the points available for each item in the set (if dif-

ferent from the rest of the test), and information about how many times responses may be used. Directions should be considered part of the item set. The directions for the countries-capitals set and the group-description set regarding Hispaniola, discussed earlier in the chapter, are good examples.

✓ *Easy Reference Checklist*

Guidelines for Good Matching Items

- ❑ Set calls for behavior stated in related outcome.
- ❑ Item difficulty reflects difficulty/complexity of outcome.
- ❑ Higher-level sets (above knowledge) present novel material.
- ❑ Homogeneous premises and responses are used for each set.
- ❑ Lists of premises and responses are both titled.
- ❑ Lists are short (four to seven items).
- ❑ Verbal material appears in alphabetical order.
- ❑ Numerical material appears in numerical order.
- ❑ Dates appear in chronological order.
- ❑ Imperfect matches are used.
- ❑ Perfect matches are avoided.
- ❑ Premises are longer phrases or words, responses are shorter.
- ❑ Premises appear on left, responses on right.
- ❑ Entire set appears on one page, including directions.
- ❑ Directions include basis for making matches.
- ❑ Directions include how many times responses may be used.
- ❑ Directions include how to mark answers.

Considering Related Instructional Outcomes

Matching items are useful for assessing achievement of instructional outcomes in the cognitive domain. In order for a matching exercise to be appropriate for an instructional outcome, there must be a relationship inherent in it, such as related terminology, facts, specifics, classifications, principles, and generalizations in a given subject-matter area. These are all parts of the knowledge level of the taxonomy, by far the level most assessed with matching items. Comprehension is another level appropriate for matching items. Lists of Swahili expressions and equivalent English phrases, for example, assess part of the ability to translate from one language to another if the phrases have not been rotely memorized. Rules and novel examples of those rules may appear side by side in a matching set if the rules and examples are related to one another. This is illustrated in the following matching exercise on the central nervous system.

Which part of your central nervous system controls which function? Write the letter of your answer in the space next to the number. The answer choices may be used more than once.

Functions	**Parts**
CB 1. sees	CB = cerebrum
S 2. pulls hand off hot stove	CL = cerebellum
CB 3. identifies constellations	M = medulla
CB 4. touches or feels	S = spinal cord
M 5. keeps the heart beating	
M 6. blinks the eye	
CL 7. walks a tightrope	
M 8. sneezes	
CB 9. takes a science test	

Assume that the seventh-grade students in Ms. Gladstein's science class had been given initial instruction on the functions of the four parts of the central nervous system. Some of the premises listed in the above matching exercise may test at the knowledge level and some at the comprehension level. For example, suppose that Ms. Gladstein, in her instruction, told the students that the cerebrum controls thought and the senses, such as touch and sight. Suppose also that she told them that the medulla controls the involuntary muscles, but did not tell them specifically that heartbeats and sneezes were under its control. In the set above, then, premises 1 and 4 would be at the knowledge level, whereas premises 3, 5, 8, and 9 would be at the comprehension level.

Knowledge-Level Outcomes

Read the following knowledge-level instructional outcomes and see if you can identify which ones are suitable for assessment using a set of matching items. Remember the criteria for good matching sets include homogeneity and attractive, plausible responses.

1. Given verbal definitions of various landforms, match them with the appropriate term four out of five times.
2. Given facts about population groups in Canada, the student will recall the group they describe.
3. Given a function to be performed in WordPerfect (classroom version), the student will select the appropriate pull-down menu to initiate the function.

4. Knows terminology associated with the human digestive system.
5. For given algebraic equations, identify the given axiom, property, or definition that justifies that the expression on the left is equal to the expression on the right.

The first outcome calls for the students to "match" written descriptions with the proper term, so a matching set is very appropriate here, as the following set illustrates:

Directions: Match the landform with its description and write the letter of your answer in the space provided for each item. Some of the landforms may not be used.

Description	Landform
__B__ 1. A large, flat, almost treeless area of land at or near sea-level.	a. Mountain
__A__ 2. A natural hill very high above the earth's surface.	b. Plain
__C__ 3. A large, high, almost treeless area of flat or rolling land.	c. Plateau
	d. Ravine
	e. Volcano

Outcome two specifies recall. Technically, completion/short-answer items appear to be in order because the student must recall the population group from memory, not choose it from a cluster of possibilities. Outcome three presents an interesting situation that could be assessed by a performance test with the teacher observing each student in front of a computer with the program loaded. In a classroom situation, however, this may be difficult to do. The teacher may decide, therefore, to use a paper-and-pencil test, because observing 30 students perform at the same time is impossible. As there are nine pull-down menus across the top of the working screen in WordPerfect (version 6.0) and anywhere from 6 to 18 choices on each menu, a matching set of items for all would be cumbersome to develop and overwhelming for the student. One way of handling this is to concentrate on a few at a time. For a beginning word-processing student, for example, a teacher might concentrate on the following menus: File, Edit, Layout, and Tools. This could be reduced further by limiting the menu choices to those most important (or the most frequently used). Thus, a matching set might look like this:

Directions: Match the function with the menu in which it is found. Write your answer in the blank provided for each item. The menu headings are listed and may be used once or more than once. (2 pts. each)

Function	Menu (File / Edit / Layout / Tools)
1. Look at an entire page as it will be printed.	File
2. Use the thesaurus.	Tools
3. Exit the program.	File
4. Set the margins.	Layout
5. Check the spelling of a word.	Tools
6. Change the spacing between lines.	Layout
7. Move blocks of text around in a document.	Edit

Instructional outcome four can be assessed in a number of different ways and with different types of items due to its ambiguity. *Terminology* may be interpreted as labeling the parts of the digestive system shown in a schematic diagram. The outcome may also be interpreted to mean knowing the proper names for the parts of the digestive system based on what each part does. Thus, a matching set of items might appear as the following:

Directions: Match the characteristic or function with the part of the digestive system. Write the letter of your answer in the blank to the left of each item. The answer choices may be used once, more than once, or not at all. (1 point apiece)

Characteristic/Function	Part
F 1. Where most nutrients are absorbed.	a. Esophagus
C 2. Almost no digestion occurs here.	b. Gall bladder
E 3. Where digestion begins.	c. Large intestine
G 4. Contains gastric juice.	d. Liver
D 5. Produces bile.	e. Mouth
G 6. Contains strong muscles to churn food.	f. Small intestine
	g. Stomach

Instructional outcome five presents the teacher with a choice. If he uses the same examples as were used in the initial instruction, the students merely need to memorize what they saw on the chalkboard or did for homework. This is, of course, knowledge-level testing. If, however, the teacher composes novel examples, the students must bring what they know of the order of operations to bear on the item, identify which operation must be performed first, then identify which axiom, property, or definition the operation represents. This is a test of comprehension. An example matching set appears in the next section.

Higher-Level Outcomes

Included in this section are some examples of higher-level instructional outcomes from the cognitive domain that are appropriately assessed with matching items.

Outcome: Given triangles not seen before, students classify them by angles and sides.

Item:

Directions: Match each of the following triangles with their correct names according to their *angles and sides.* Write the *two letters* of your answer on the line indicated. The names will be used more than once. Equal sides, equal angles, and 90° angles are marked. (2 points each)

Triangles

D F 1.

A B 2.

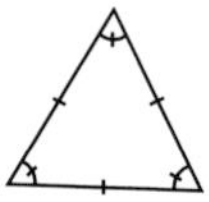

D F 3.

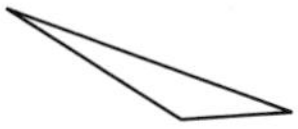

E F 4.

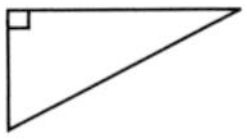

A C 5.

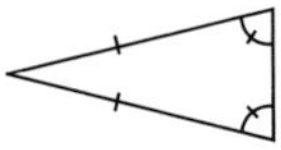

D F 6.

E F 7.

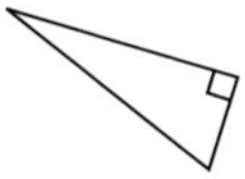

C D 8.

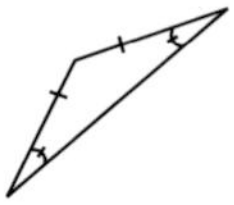

Names

a. Acute

b. Equilateral

c. Isosceles

d. Obtuse

e. Right

f. Scalene

Outcome: For given algebraic equations, identify the given axiom, property, or definition that justifies that the expression on the left is equal to the expression on the right. Note: Student does not have to solve the expression or go beyond the first step in the order of operations.

Item:

Directions: For each item, choose the axiom, property, or definition which justifies that the expression on the left side is equal to the expression on the right. Write the letter of your answer in the blank. *Do not* solve the item or go beyond the first step. Each axiom, property, and definition may be used once, more than once, or not at all.

Expressions	Axioms, Properties
B 1. $x + y = y + x$	A. Associative axiom, multiplication
B 2. $a + (b + c) = a + (c + b)$	B. Commutative axiom, addition
F 3. $3x + 4x = (3 + 4)x$	C. Commutative axiom, multiplication
F 4. $5m + 5n = 5(m + n)$	D. Definition of subtraction
F 5. $k \cdot 5 = 5k$	E. Definition of division
D 6. $2n - 5 \cdot 3 = 2n + (-5 \cdot 3)$	F. Distributive axiom
H 7. $\frac{11}{b} \cdot \frac{b}{11} = 1$	G. Multiplication identity axiom
G 8. $\frac{11}{b} \cdot 1 = \frac{11}{b}$	H. Multiplicative inverses axiom

Scoring Selected-Response Items

Scoring selected-response items takes little time and can be performed by someone who is not necessarily as content knowledgeable as you; an aide or volunteer can score tests if you are lucky enough to have one. These items can also be scored by machine. Whether tests are machine or hand scored, you must prepare an answer key. For hand scoring, you can use a copy of the test and mark the keyed correct answers in the same manner in which you directed your students. For hand or machine scoring, you can use a single sheet as a separate answer key. Using a single-hole punch, create a template to place over a student's answer sheet. Thus, with one stroke you can indicate both an incorrectly answered item and its correct answer. Just tally up the strokes for points to be subtracted from the total available. If machine scoring is used, the answer key is fed in first and tells the machine what to accept as the answers. The machine then scans each following answer sheet and scores it appropriately. Most scoring machines also produce item-analysis data (such as information on how many students answered each item correctly).

Summary

Selected-Response Items

Common to all *selected-response* items is that the correct answer lies in the item itself. The task of the student is to figure out which of the answers presented in the item is the *keyed correct answer,* the one the teacher has designated as correct or best. The three major types of selected-response items are two-choice, multiple-choice, and matching.

Two-Choice Items

The most common *two-choice* item type is true-false. Other types include fact-opinion, yes-no, warranted conclusion–unwarranted conclusion, and cause-effect. Two-choice items are typically used to assess knowledge of specific facts. They can also be used to test definitions and meanings of terms. The correction variation of the true-false item directs students, when they answer an item false, to rewrite it as a true statement. When a *correction item* is used, the word or phrase that is to be corrected should be emphasized in some way, using underlining or italics, for example.

Two-choice items have some advantages for teachers:

1. Due to their relative brevity, more of them can be squeezed into the same time period than any other test item type, permitting a broad sampling of content and longer, reasonably reliable tests.
2. Relative to completion, short-answer, and essay items, two-choice items are objective and easy to score.

Teachers should be aware of the item-type's disadvantages as well:

1. Many types of subject matter are not well suited to these items.
2. Two-choice items are notoriously open to guessing.
3. It is difficult to write items that do not contain any clues to the correct answer.

In constructing two-choice items, teachers should follow these specific construction guidelines:

1. Statements should be worded positively, without tricky negatives, especially when items are to be judged true or false.
2. True items and false items should be about equal in length.
3. True-false items should be either completely true or completely false.
4. Specific determiners should be avoided in true-false items unless they puzzle the uninformed student.
5. The item should assess the students' grasp of an important proposition.
6. The item should be based on a single idea.

Two-choice items are useful for assessing achievement of instructional outcomes in the cognitive domain and those cognitive outcomes related to outcomes in the affective and psychomotor domains. Two-choice items are also suited to the assessment of attitudes and opinions through self-report. Theoretically, two-choice items can be written to assess learning outcomes at higher levels of the cognitive domain. At the higher levels of the cognitive domain, two-choice items are better suited for the assessment of abilities related to logical argument.

Multiple-Choice Items

Multiple-choice items present a problem, task, statement, or question and a number of possible answers through which the student sorts. Components of the multiple-choice item consist of a *stem* and several *options,* which further separate into the *keyed correct answer* and the *distractors*. The number of options may vary, usually from three to five. Research has shown that three is optimum. There are *best-answer* multiple-choice items and *correct-answer* multiple-choice items. Multiple-choice items are the most widely used item type in paper-and-pencil testing. Multiple-choice items can measure not only knowledge but also understanding, ability to solve problems, capacity to recommend appropriate action, and ability to predict events and consequences. Affective outcomes and attitudes may also be assessed with multiple-choice items through self-report.

Using multiple-choice items has its advantages:

1. Multiple-choice items are easily and objectively scored, whether answers are recorded on the test itself or on a separate answer sheet.
2. For instructional purposes, plausible distractors (based on misconceptions or common errors) make results useful for item analysis and diagnosing learning problems.
3. Multiple-choice items are relatively unaffected by a student's response set.
4. Multiple-choice items are easily used, stored, and reused via microcomputer and low-cost software designed for item banking.
5. Multiple-choice items are less susceptible to chance assessment as a result of guessing than are two-choice items.
6. The best-answer subspecies does not require that one alternative be completely correct, just more correct than the other options.
7. With the exception of two-choice items, multiple-choice items can sample more instructional content in the same period of time than any other item type.
8. Compared to matching items, multiple-choice items avoid the necessity for homogeneity of large amounts of material.

Multiple-choice items also have their disadvantages:

1. It is difficult to repeatedly create two to four plausible and attractive, but wrong, answers.

2. Some critics have said that the multiple-choice format is only useful for assessing a student's ability to rule out obviously incorrect options.
3. Multiple-choice items are not well suited to assessing a student's ability to express synthesized thoughts or strategies used to arrive at an answer, nor can they measure a student's ability to write out creative solutions or organize and present ideas.

Follow these specific construction guidelines when writing multiple-choice items:

1. State clearly as much of the problem in the stem as possible, including the central idea.
2. State the stem in a question, rather than using an incomplete sentence.
3. Word the stem positively; avoid negative wording.
4. Use logic in arranging options.
5. All options for an item should be fairly consistent in length.
6. Use only one option as the keyed correct answer.
7. Do not use "none of the above" or "all of the above" as options.
8. Use plausible and attractive distractors.
9. Place the keyed correct answer in each possible position about the same number of times.

Matching Items

Matching items are sets of multiple-choice items for which two things are true: one, there is a strong theme to them, rendering them homogeneous with one another, and two, the answer choices are written once and serve as answers and distractors for all the items in the set. Components of matching items include *premises, responses,* and the *directions* to the student. One popular format for matching items includes directions to the student followed by a list of premises in a column on the left and the responses in a column on the right. Another format especially popular in the elementary grades is the matching set with a word bank. Sometimes answers are indicated by drawing lines between premises and responses so that the student does not have to write anything.

The advantages of matching items include:

1. Several subject matter areas can be assessed with them.
2. As compared to multiple-choice items, they can save both space on the printed page and assessment time.
3. They are easily and objectively scored.

Their disadvantages are:

1. They are typically used to assess knowledge and not much else.
2. Over-reliance on matching exercises tends to promote rote memorization of facts.

3. Heterogeneous premises or responses lead to the inclusion of unintended clues to the correct answers.

Good matching items can be developed using these specific construction guidelines:

1. Choose homogeneous premises and responses for each set of items.
2. Title each list of premises and responses.
3. Keep the lists of premises and responses short.
4. Use logic in arranging premises and responses.
5. Use "imperfect" matches rather than "perfect" matches.
6. Use longer phrases as premises and shorter phrases, words, and dates as responses.
7. Place all premises and responses of a matching set and the directions on the same page.
8. Give clear directions indicating the basis for matching and the proper way to mark answers.

Outcomes at the knowledge and comprehension levels for which there are inherent relationships can be assessed using matching items.

Scoring Selected-Response Items

Scoring selected-response items is objective: The results are the same regardless of who or what scores the items using an answer key. Selected-response items also facilitate machine scoring. Teachers can use a scoring template placed over a student's answers to save time.

Try These

I. Indicate which type of selected-response item would be most appropriate for assessing each of the behaviors below by writing the abbreviation in the blank. Types of items may be used more than once.

M = Matching
MC = Multiple-choice
TC = Two-choice
NSR = Not appropriately assessed with selected-response items of any type.

_____ 1. Given a weather map, forecasts the weather for a given area.
_____ 2. Given chemical compounds to be prepared, identifies the expected reaction.
_____ 3. Identifies the correct term for a given definition.
_____ 4. Solves word problems involving percents with a four-function calculator.

_____ 5. Indicates which given steps are part of the process of passing a bill in Congress.
_____ 6. Selects the correct date in history for each given important historical event.
_____ 7. Indicates the correct food group to which a number of given foods belong.
_____ 8. Supports or refutes the position, "School attendance should be voluntary."
_____ 9. Given a list of foods, indicates which are high in fat.
_____ 10. Given a list of possible requirements, indicates whether each is an eligibility requirement for people desirous of becoming candidates for the presidency of the United States.
_____ 11. Develops a plan for reducing school vandalism.
_____ 12. Identifies the inventor of a given invention.
_____ 13. Correctly edits own writing for grammar and punctuation.
_____ 14. Given a set of atmospheric conditions, identifies the associated type of weather pattern.
_____ 15. Given a list of words, identifies which are compound.

II. Read each of the following items. If you think the item violates one or more construction guidelines, state on a separate sheet of paper which of the guidelines the item violates and rewrite the item so that it is practically perfect and violates no guidelines. If it is practically perfect as it is written, state "OK as is." Intended correct answers are indicated.

Two-Choice Items

1. Granite is not a form of igneous rock. T **F**
2. Leftover hamburger is good material for a compost pile. T **F**
3. Rivers flow from north to south. **T** F
4. George Washington had a white horse. **T** F
5. When a compound is prepared, a chemical reaction always occurs. **T** F
6. The color of a star is related to its temperature and shape. T **F**
7. It never snows in Florida. T **F**
8. The president of the United States during the Watergate scandal was Richard P. Nixon. T **F**

Multiple-Choice Items

Just as you did for the two-choice items, read the following items and for each state on a separate piece of paper the guideline it violates, if any. Rewrite as necessary to produce practically perfect multiple-choice items.

1. Which of the following is a pachyderm?
   a. Zebra
   b. Elephant
   c. Turtle
   d. Gorilla

2. What is the capital of Italy?
   a. Bologna
   b. Florence
   c. Genoa
   d. Milan
   e. Naples
   f. Rome
   g. Turin
3. A quasar
   a. is a distant celestial object that emits infrared light.
   b. is a distant celestial object that emits ultraviolet light.
   c. is a nearby celestial object that emits ultraviolet light.
4. What do you get besides water when you combine Na (OH) and HCl?
   a. Bicarbonate
   b. Hydrochloric acid
   c. Salt
   d. Sodium
5. What does 5/10 equal?
   a. 1/2
   b. .50
   c. 50%
   d. All of the above
6. What should you do if you are trying to lose weight?
   a. Consume 5,000 calories daily.
   b. Eat in cafeterias.
   c. Exercise regularly, assuming you have no medical problems, you have had a checkup, and you eat no more than you normally would if you were not exercising.
7. What is the approximate distance from the earth to the sun?
   a. 93 miles
   b. 93 million miles
   c. 180 million miles
8. Which of the following is not a power of Congress?
   a. Command the armed forces.
   b. Declare war.
   c. Make tax laws.
   d. None of the above
9. A chemical combination of the atoms of two or more elements that has a definite, unchanging composition by weight and is always formed by a chemical reaction is called what?
   a. Compound
   b. Isomer
   c. Mixture

10. In 1750, what country claimed parts of what is now Canada? Mark all that apply.
    a. Britain
    b. France
    c. Germany
    d. Spain
11. What is the largest continent in the world?
    a. Asia
    b. England
    c. Mississippi River
12. Which of the following is not a part of the human digestive system?
    a. Brain
    b. Intestines
    c. Mouth
    d. Stomach

Matching Items

You know the drill by now: read the items; on a separate sheet of paper, state the violations, if any; rewrite to practical perfection.

Set One

Match the country with its continent: Write the letter of your answer in the blank in front of the country.

__D__ 1. Canada		a. Africa
__C__ 2. France		b. Asia
__C__ 3. Germany		c. Europe
__B__ 4. Japan		d. North America
__A__ 5. Kenya		e. South America
__D__ 6. Mexico		
__B__ 7. Pakistan		
__E__ 8. Paraguay		
__E__ 9. Peru		
__B__ 10. Philippines		
__A__ 11. Somalia		
__B__ 12. South Korea		
__C__ 13. Spain		
__C__ 14. Sweden		
__B__ 15. Thailand		
__A__ 16. Zaire		
__A__ 17. Zimbabwe		

Set Two

__E__ 1. Balboa		a. Discovered America.
__C__ 2. Magellan		b. Sixteenth president of the U.S.
__A__ 3. Columbus		c. Sailed around the world.
__D__ 4. Washington		d. First president of the U.S.
__F__ 5. Cortez		e. Discovered the Pacific Ocean.
__B__ 6. Lincoln		f. Conquered the Aztec empire.

Set Three

Match the rock with its type by writing the letter of your answer in the space in front of the number. The types may be used more than once.

	Rocks	Type
C	1. Clay	a. Igneous
B	2. Gneiss	b. Metamorphic
A	3. Granite	c. Sedimentary
C	4. Limestone	
C	5. Shale	

Answers

I. 1. MC, 2. MC, 3. MC or M (if a lot of them and the terms are homogeneous enough to serve as distractors for each other), 4. NSR, 5. TC, 6. M, 7. M, 8. NSR, 9. TC, 10. TC, 11. NSR, 12. M, 13. NSR, 14. MC, 15. TC.

II. The rewrites of the following items should be taken as suggestions. Your rewrites may differ somewhat but still should not violate any of the guidelines.

Two-Choice Items

1. Statement worded negatively.

   Granite is a form of igneous rock. T F

2. OK as is.
3. Not completely true or false. Just adding the word *generally* presents a specific determiner; better to rewrite it as a multiple-choice item to add structure.

   Most rivers in North America run in which direction?
   a. East to west.
   b. North to south.
   c. South to north.
   d. West to east.

4. Not an important proposition. Eliminate from the test.
5. OK as is. This is a good use of a specific determiner to discourage test-wiseness.
6. Based on more than one idea—two propositions. Also, not completely true or false. (Bonus points if you caught both violations!)

   The color of a star is related to its shape. T F
   or
   The color of a star is related to its temperature. T F

7. Inappropriate use of the specific determiner *never* and negative wording.

   It snows in Florida. T F

8. Trivia *and* tricky (should be M. for Milhous).

   The president of the United States during the Watergate scandal was Richard Nixon. T F

   or

   The president of the United States during the Watergate scandal was John Kennedy. T F

Multiple-Choice Items

1. Options are not in logical (alphabetical) order.

   Which of the following is a pachyderm?
   a. Elephant
   b. Gorilla
   c. Turtle
   d. Zebra

2. Too many options; three to four are enough, already.

   What is the capital of Italy?
   a. Bologna
   b. Florence
   c. Rome

3. The stem does not contain the central idea of the problem, and the stem is not in question form. (Bonus points for spotting both violations!)

   Which of the following is the best definition of a quasar?
   a. A distant celestial object that emits infrared light.
   b. A distant celestial object that emits ultraviolet light.
   c. A nearby celestial object that emits ultraviolet light.

   or

   What do astronomers call a distant celestial object that emits ultraviolet light?
   a. Nova
   b. Quark
   c. Quasar

4. OK as is.

5. Use of "all of the above." Turn it into a series of two-choice items.

   What does 5/10 equal? For each item mark *a* on your answer sheet if it equals 5/10. Mark *b* if it does *not* equal 5/10.
   1. 1/2
   2. .20
   3. 50%

6. Options are not consistent in length.

   What should you do if you are trying to lose weight?
   a. Consume 5,000 calories daily.
   b. Eat in cafeterias.
   c. Exercise regularly.

7. Distractor *a* is neither plausible nor attractive to the uninformed.

   What is the approximate distance from the earth to the sun?
   a. 52 million miles
   b. 93 million miles
   c. 180 million miles

8. This one has several problems. First, the stem contains negative wording. "None of the above" is also improperly used (read just the stem and option *d* if you don't believe me!). Rewrite as a series of TF items about the powers of Congress (see item 10, below) OR

   Which of the following is a power of Congress?
   a. Enforce the tax laws
   b. Interpret the tax laws
   c. Make the tax laws

9. Depending on the group assessed, the stem could be more concise and achieve clarity at the same time.

   A chemical combination of the atoms of two or more elements is called what?
   a. Compound
   b. Isomer
   c. Mixture

10. Too many correct answers. Rewrite as series of individual two-choice items.

    In 1750, which countries claimed parts of what is now Canada? Mark on your answer sheet *a* if yes or *b* if no.
    27. Britain
    28. France
    29. Germany
    30. The Netherlands
    31. Spain

11. The distractors are just not plausible.

    What is the largest continent in the world?

    a. Africa
    b. Asia
    c. Europe
    d. North America

12. The stem uses negative wording. Rewrite as a series of TF items (as in item 10, above), or

    Which of the following is a part of the human digestive system?

    a. Brain
    b. Heart
    c. Lungs
    d. Stomach

Matching Items

In Set One, the column titles are missing, there are no directions as to how many times options may be used, and the list of countries is too long. Here is one rewrite:

Directions: Match the country with its continent: Write the letter of your answer in the blank in front of the country. Continents may be used once, more than once, or not at all.

Countries	Continents
_____ 1. Canada	a. Africa
_____ 2. France	b. Asia
_____ 3. Germany	c. Europe
_____ 4. Japan	d. North America
_____ 5. Kenya	e. South America
_____ 6. Mexico	
_____ 7. Pakistan	

Set Two has six problems. Bonus points if you got them all! (1) No directions, (2) columns not titled, (3) lists not homogeneous, (4) lists not in logical order, (5) lists are switched, and (6) perfect matches were used. It could be broken into two sets of matching items, each fleshed out with a few more premises and responses: presidents and their order of presidency, and discoverers and what they discovered. For the presidents, it may be a better idea, depending on the outcome to be assessed, to present the presidents studied in alphabetical order for the student to re-list chronologically.

Set Three is OK as is.

CHAPTER 7

Creating Free-Response Items for Classroom Assessments

Key Concepts:

- Constructing and choosing good free-response (short-answer and essay) items.
- When to use and not use each of the free-response item types.
- Types of instructional outcomes typically assessed with a particular free-response item type.
- Scoring free-response items.

Standards Addressed in This Chapter:

1. Choose assessment methods appropriate for instructional decisions.
2. Develop assessment methods appropriate for instructional decisions.

Before You Begin Reading, Consider This

Is it preferable to assess higher-level learning outcomes with essay questions?

YES Life is an essay question! Essay questions present a much more realistic problem for the student to solve that just cannot be achieved with any other type of item. It is the best way to see if the student can transfer learning to the real world.

NO Hah! All essay questions test is the ability to say nothing and make the teacher think you have said something. They penalize the student who can work in the realm of application or even synthesis but may not be able to articulate thought into the written word. Articulate but otherwise dull students can score points on an essay question that other, less-articulate students cannot, even though they can demonstrate in other ways that they really know their stuff.

This chapter and Chapter 6 both deal with the types of items commonly found on paper-and-pencil classroom tests. The chapters are formatted in a similar fashion by item type for ease of understanding and comparison. This chapter format is summarized in Figure 7.1 and includes the following sections:

1. A description of the item type and its appropriate use, including advantages and disadvantages relative to other item types.
2. Guidelines for constructing good items, including negative and positive examples of items and directions to the student specific to the item type.
3. An item evaluation checklist that summarizes the guidelines[1] for easy reference.
4. Examples of instructional outcomes and related items for the type classified by taxonomic level.
5. Information on scoring free-response items.

Common to all *free-response* items, also called constructed-response items, is that the students are not forced to select an answer to an item from among those given as they do in selected-response but, rather, are "free" to construct their own responses. The teacher has built a task for the students in the item, just as in selected-response items (two-choice, multiple-choice, or matching items), but has left the answer for the students to supply. The structure and wording of the item usually let students know what length or how many words the response should be. Just as with selected-response items, well-written free-response items require students to recall facts and use principles, concepts, and strategies acquired to arrive at a correct or acceptable answer.

---

[1]The checklist includes both the generic guidelines for all free-response items and those for the particular type described.

		Description and Use	Construction Guidelines	Evaluation Checklist	Instructional Outcomes and Items	Scoring
Selected-Response (Chapter 6)	Two-Choice					
	Multiple-Choice					
	Matching					
Free-Response (Chapter 7)	Essay					
	Short-Answer					

Figure 7.1
Presentation matrix illustrating the sequence of discussion for each item type in Chapters 6 and 7.

A common misconception is that free-response items require recall of information and selected-response items require recognition only and that, somehow, recall is better. Neither of these statements is necessarily true. Essay and short-answer items require recall, but selected-response items (with the exception of knowledge-level items) do also. In comparing two multiple-choice items, for example, identifying which of four formulas represents the Pythagorean theorem may involve only recognition, but identifying the correct solution to a problem involving the Pythagorean theorem requires recall as well as application of the theorem.

Before this last wave of interest in objective, selected-response assessment (which now appears to be waning somewhat), much student evaluation was done with free-response items, frequently oral. This was back in the days when paper was not so easily obtainable and school children wrote lessons on slabs of slate.[2] Poorly written free-response items can give unintended clues to the answer—an undesirable situation—or can be overly difficult, beyond the complexity of the related learning outcome. The major types of free-response items are short-answer and essay items. These will be discussed in turn, with essay items first.

[2] And walked 5 miles to school after doing their morning chores. I'm not kidding! Go ask your grandparents.

Essay Items

Understanding Essay Items and Using Them Appropriately

Essay items require the student to compose somewhat lengthy responses: ergo, the name *essay*. Good essay items typically require both recall and use of information in the demonstration of a higher-level learning outcome. For certain higher-level outcomes, especially those involving synthesis, the essay item can be especially appropriate. For example, you may want your students to be able to write letters that persuade the reader to take some particular action. A good way to see if they have achieved the outcome is to read letters they have written and assess the persuasiveness of tone and logic of argument or support of points made (depending on the intent of the learning outcome assessed). True-false items will not carry the day here. As you might have guessed, an English composition is an essay item, but so is an item requiring a student to generate budget items and amounts for a weekly budget for a family of four based on a given fixed income. Both require a lengthy answer (from a paragraph to a few pages, usually) composed in response to a well-described given task. We tend to think of essay items as written, but they can be oral or recorded in some other way than pencil on paper.[3]

Relative to other paper-and-pencil item types, essay items enjoy certain advantages. First, they are excellent for assessing certain learning outcomes at the higher levels of the cognitive domain. Second, due to their nature, they force students to exercise their thought composition and writing skills. Third, as compared to multiple-choice and matching items, essay items do not require the item writer to come up with the keyed correct answer or any attractive and plausible (not to mention homogeneous) wrong answers as distractors before administering the test. Thus, they can take less time to write than selected-response items.

Essay items also have their disadvantages. First, teachers who have given essay tests know that the real fun begins after the papers are turned in. Scoring essay items is a long process relative to scoring selected-response items. If you use essay items properly, you must create a model answer or list the points or characteristics for which you will give credit *before* you score the responses. Second, scoring is subjective, and the answers are open to at least some interpretation by the scorer regardless of the structure imposed by a model answer. This means that no "one and only one" correct answer or even "two and only two" correct answers exist. To cite an earlier example, any number of alternative family budgets could be equally acceptable as long as they budgeted appropriately for necessities and emergencies. Because of this variability in correct responses, essay items normally have to be scored by persons who know thoroughly both the content area and the learning outcome being measured. To a significant degree, the objectivity and accuracy of essay-item scoring is a function of the scope of the response elicited by the item. Correct responses are more clearly defined in an item such as the following:

List three major causes of the (U.S.) Civil War.

---

[3]More will be said about "nontraditional" essay items and other student products in Chapter 8.

The task is more difficult for broader responses such as the response to the following item:

> Do you think the current immigration policy of the U.S.A. is in the best interests of the country? Explain your reasons for your answer.

You might think that the problem of multiple interpretations could be solved with the use of more restricted response items, and that is true, but less restricted items are usually required for the assessment of higher-level outcomes. Examining the first essay item just presented, for example, you can see that the causes of the Civil War the item writer had in mind were probably those cited in a textbook. Asking the student to merely list them requires nothing above rote memory, legible handwriting, and reasonable spelling.

This calls to mind a third disadvantage: the fact that essay items usually involve a number of abilities, such as organization and expression of ideas, manuscript or cursive handwriting or typing, and spelling. All of these abilities and others may or may not be specified in the corresponding learning outcome. The major problem of this nature is the difficulty involved in separating quality and accuracy of response from pure writing ability. You have probably met people who know practically nothing and can say it eloquently, and others who know something and have great difficulty expressing what they know. Unless the outcome assessed is a writing outcome, emphasis in the scoring of essay items should *not* be on spelling, grammar, eloquence, or other such aspects of delivery. This is not to say that you should keep your corrective comments to yourself but, rather, that these factors should not affect your students' scores. This is also easy to say and tough to implement when you try to read a student's essay that tortures the language. When this happens, ask yourself if you would have awarded any more credit if the grammar and punctuation had been perfect. Adjust the score when the answer is yes.

A fourth disadvantage of essay items is that fewer items can be answered in the same amount of time than for any other paper-and-pencil item type. Thus, essay tests tend, in general, to be less content valid and reliable and have notoriously low scorer reliability. A large part of the problem, however, is due to faulty item development. If you construct a 30-minute, two-choice item test with one or two bad items, the reliability and content validity may not suffer too much. You have enough items (25 or so) to cushion the blow. If you construct a 30-minute *essay*-item test with one or two bad items, however, you practically guarantee a low-quality test. You have no such cushion with one or two bad items when there are only three to four items in the whole test. If you are aware of the potential pitfalls and include a number of clearly stated items, even if it takes two class periods to answer them, you increase your chances of producing a test with at least reasonable validity and reliability that assesses higher-level outcomes.

Bad essay items typically require nothing more from the student than stringing together a few facts; they are sometimes so ambiguous as to encourage students to bluff or "mind-dump"—write everything they can think of about a subject in the hope that you will see something you like in their answer and give points for it. Bad essay items are a waste of time for both you and your students (but you probably suspected that all along). But well-crafted essay items, administered in the right contexts, can prove to be a very effective method of assessment. Here are some guidelines for constructing useful essay items.

Using Guidelines to Construct Well-Designed Essay Items

The general guidelines for item construction presented in Chapter 5 apply to essay items and are summarized, along with additional guidelines listed here, in the Easy-Reference Checklist at the end of this section.

1. *Reserve essay items for higher-level learning outcomes not well assessed by other item types.* Although essay items can be used to measure just about any cognitive objective, they are best used when their advantages outweigh their disadvantages, because their disadvantages can be substantial. Use them when no other item type will do.

2. *Define the task completely and specifically.* With no response alternatives to help structure, limit, and clarify the item, it is crucial that the desired response be delineated as clearly as possible in the item. Do not tell your students to simply "discuss" (as in, "Discuss the Civil War"); tell them *what* to discuss, and use phrases that describe what the students are to do. Aspects of the expected performance should not be left to the students' imagination. If you want students to define terms or give examples, for instance, say so in the item. When you write an essay question, do not worry too much about separating the directions from the item. The basis for constructing an adequate answer is in the definition of the task, and you define that task. Specifying the number of words expected, telling the students how many points the question is worth, or giving a time limit are helpful additions that further define the scope of the answer you seek. As an example, you might present your students with a hypothetical 7-day diet for a 16-year-old male. You might intentionally include some undesirable items (such as cakes and cookies) and some desirable items (such as spinach and skim milk). The description of the diet would be accompanied by the following item:

> State whether you think the attached diet is more than adequate, adequate, *or* inadequate with respect to nutrition. Defend your position as follows:
>
> a. Identify any items in the diet that you think should be deleted or limited in quantity. Give reasons for your choices.
>
> b. Identify any items that you think should be added to the diet or increased in quantity. Give reasons for your answers.
>
> c. Make as many summary statements as you feel are necessary to describe the overall adequacy of the diet. For example, you might say: "This diet does not include enough leafy green vegetables" or "His bread, cereal, pasta, and rice requirements are met."
>
> Your answer should be stated in 75 words or less. (5 points maximum.)

When a student reads this item, she knows, for example, that she can earn five points in one item and that she must read and analyze a given diet, evaluate its adequacy nutritionally, then think of and write down concisely her responses to the three subitems (*a–c*). As no specific time limit is given, the student must gauge her test-taking time so she doesn't spend all of it on this one item but gets to the others on the test as well. This combination of time, points, words, and the defined task delineate and restrict the response appropriately. One way to tell if you have defined the task well enough is to examine the answers your students write after you administer the test. If the answers contain a wide range of detail, from too little to too much, for example, consider how you would revise the item to make it more clear. Your students—the ones who just took the test—are in the best position to help you do this. It may not help their scores, but it will help you improve the item for the next time. It also helps your students sharpen their inquiry skills—a key to good problem solving.

3. Do not provide optional essay items. Sometimes students are given a number of essay items from which to choose. They may be instructed, for example to answer any three of five given items. This business of students choosing items is interesting because I have never seen students given the same opportunity with selected-response items. The only possible reason for doing this is that students seem to like it (wouldn't you if you were a student?), so it may improve morale. It is *not,* however, good assessment practice. By allowing a choice of questions, you allow your students to, in effect, take different tests. Therefore, any comparison of performance on these tests is compromised due to the loss of a common measuring stick, rendering norm-referenced interpretation of the scores impossible. If the test is criterion-referenced, you are still not off the hook. With different students answering different items, it is not possible to determine the degree to which the students have achieved the objectives, only the degree to which *some* students have achieved *some* of the objectives. Further, each of the possible tests (from the combinations of items answered) has lower content validity because it is based on a smaller sampling of the behaviors (fewer items) than that represented by the total test. The task of estimating reliability will also be greatly complicated, and the reliability of each of the possible tests will, of course, be lower than if all students answered all items.[4] The only exception to this guideline would be if the items to choose from were assessing pure writing ability (English expression, grammar, syntax, and spelling) and how the response was crafted and presented—not its content. See the checklist on page 212.

Considering Related Instructional Outcomes

Essay items are useful for assessing achievement of higher-level instructional outcomes in the cognitive domain and those higher-level cognitive outcomes related to

[4]At this point you are to yell "uncle!" and vow to always require your students to answer all your carefully crafted, high-quality essay items.

✓ *Easy Reference Checklist*

Guidelines for Good Essay Items

- ❑ Corresponding outcome indicates higher-level behavior.
- ❑ Item calls for behavior stated in corresponding outcome.
- ❑ Item difficulty reflects difficulty/complexity of outcome.
- ❑ Task defined completely and clearly.
- ❑ Limits (time, words, space, and points available) restrict response appropriately.
- ❑ No optional items.

the affective and psychomotor domains. They can also be used to assess attitudes and opinions, as the following example illustrates:

> What would happen if the British had won the American Revolutionary War? Describe how life today would be if America were still a colony of the British Crown. Give at least three examples using your historical imagination. (Time Limit: 15 minutes, Points Possible: 4)

Below are listed some learning outcomes with a bit of context supplied in parentheses. Some are stated more clearly for assessment purposes than others. See if you can identify any of them as suitable for assessment with an essay item. Are there alternative item types that might be better?

1. Student will be able to explain in writing why stars shine. (eighth-grade advanced science)
2. Students will distinguish between the topic and the main idea of a paragraph. (fourth-grade language arts)
3. Compare the gravitational force of earth to that of other planets and the moon. (sixth-grade science)
4. Using logical argument, defend a position taken on a controversial issue. (ninth-grade English)
5. Students can explain the difference between density and mass. (sixth-grade science)

Let's look at each of them. The first outcome calls for the student to write something—the reason why stars shine. Now, the reason stars shine can get pretty detailed, having to do with nuclear fusion, a process in which some of the energy created during the change of hydrogen into helium passes into space from the surface of the star as light. The students are supposed to explain the process in writing, however, so the outcome is a candidate for an essay item. You may write an item that looks like this:

> Explain the reason why stars shine.

As written, it certainly captures the essence of the outcome. What it does not do, however, is present a clear, well-defined task to the students. The following possible answers illustrate the point:

a. They make their own light.
b. Stars have a lot of hydrogen. They turn this hydrogen into helium. This process is called nuclear fusion. Some of the hydrogen does not make it all the way into helium and becomes energy. The energy reaches the surface of the star and then goes into space as light. This light is what we really see when stars shine.

Both answers are "correct" in that they explain *why stars shine.* The student who wrote answer *a* may have known the process of nuclear fusion and so forth but decided to be concise instead. Answer *b* is certainly more detailed, but is it any better? If you expect such detailed answers from your students, how do you tell them so without giving away the answers? Well, adding a few *intended* clues to the correct answer might help define the task a little better, as illustrated below:

> Write a brief paragraph that explains the reason why stars shine. Use the following terms correctly in your answer: helium, hydrogen, nuclear fusion.

Only if the students are familiar with the process will they be able to put these words, listed alphabetically, into appropriate sentences. The words are also clues to the students that something beyond "they make their own light" is required for full credit. Knowing the capabilities of your students is key here. Answer *a,* which borders on being a short answer, might receive full credit if it came from a fifth-grader in a regular classroom, for example.

The second outcome states that "students will distinguish between the topic and the main idea of a paragraph." There are a number of ways of assessing this. One, you may have students write a few sentences that explained, in their own words, the difference between the two. Two, you may have students construct their own paragraphs, then underline the topic and circle the main idea. Three, you may present a brief paragraph followed by two short-answer or even multiple-choice items that ask, "What is the topic of this paragraph?" and "What is the main idea of this paragraph?" Get the picture? The point is that this is one of those rather common but rather vague learning outcomes that you must decide how to assess, keeping in mind the students, the curriculum, the grade level, and the level and intent of the outcome. You may even assess student performance regarding the outcome using a combination of item types. On the other hand, if the word *given* were added to the outcome right before the word *paragraph,* this would specify that you present the paragraph to the students rather than have them construct their own. As there are a number of ways to go about assessing student achievement of this outcome as written, an essay item might not be the most judicious use of either assessment time or your grading time. Remember guideline one regarding the best use of essay items: use only when no other item type will suffice.

Outcome three, regarding the gravitational force of the earth and other heavenly bodies, is similar to number two in that there are several ways to assess its achievement. Here is an essay item:

> The force of gravity on the moon is about one-sixth of that here on earth. Give two examples of how something that happens on earth would be different on the moon due to this gravitational difference.

For this to be a higher-level item, of course, the two examples given by the student must not be merely recalled from an earlier class discussion during instruction, typically referred to as the "regurgitation" method of assessment. If the class discussion or the teacher had produced examples of how something on earth, such as a 400-foot home run, would be different on the moon, then students should be cautioned in the item as follows:

> The force of gravity on the moon is about one-sixth of that here on earth. Give two examples, *not those discussed in class,* of how something that happens on earth would be different on the moon due to this gravitational difference.

In answering this item, a student would have to make the intended comparison and illustrate it in two original examples. But the outcome could, perhaps, be assessed just as well with the following multiple-choice item:

> Eliot can high jump 2 meters here on earth. Using the same amount of force, how high could Eliot jump on the moon, which has one-sixth the gravitational pull of earth?
>
> a. 0.3 meters
>
> b. 2.0 meters
>
> c. 12.0 meters

This item looks like a math problem, but it also calls for the student to make a comparison using a mathematical method.

The fourth outcome is a good candidate for assessment by essay if you wish the students to demonstrate their achievement of it in writing. (A non-writing alternative would be to stage a debate.) An essay item might look like this:

> Should convicted felons receive privileges in prison (such as physical exercise, television viewing, library book check-out, or job-skill training)? Take a position for or against privileges in prison and provide an argument that logically supports your position. Confine your final written answer to what will fit comfortably on the rest of this side of the page of your test paper.

Outcome five states that sixth-grade students should be able to explain the difference between density and mass. *Explain* usually implies verbal assessment, and there are two ways to do this—orally or in writing. Now you *could* summon each student to your desk and say, "Explain the difference between density and mass," but the land of small class sizes (say, a 10 to 1 ratio) is very tiny, and most of us do not teach there. Therefore, a written essay item, like the one below, is a more efficient way to assess this outcome.

Briefly explain the difference between mass and density. Use one original example to help your explanation.

The second sentence in the item elevates it from one that assesses at the knowledge level (repeating what is in the textbook) to an item that tests comprehension and understanding of concepts. The outcome was not specific with regard to level of the cognitive domain, so, in this case, it is left up to the teacher to decide at what level to test. For example, if this is the first time students have explored this area of physical science *and* they are likely to encounter more about these concepts at several points later in the district curriculum, it may be perfectly fine to test at the knowledge level now, knowing students will be assessed at a higher level later.

Short-Answer Items

Understanding Short-Answer Items and Using Them Appropriately

A *short-answer* item is essentially a short essay item, requiring a brief response—a word, a phrase, a sentence, or a short list of items, for example. As you might guess, the distinction between short-answer and essay items, based on this definition, is often blurred. Even experts do not all agree on exactly what the difference is, so you should not worry about it. Some distinction can be made, however, in providing some examples of short-answer items so you get the idea. Although short-answer items are often used for assessing knowledge-level outcomes, and essay items are most appropriate for synthesis and evaluation outcomes, short-answer items can easily be used for higher-level outcomes. "What is the area of floor (or table) space covered by your television set? ____________ sq. in." is an application-level item.

The *completion*-item subspecies of short-answer items is merely an incomplete sentence written so that the answer, written in the space by the student, accurately completes the statement; for example:

The name of the leader of the pirates in *Treasure Island* is ____________________.

The short-answer equivalent of this completion item would look like this:

What is the name of the leader of the pirates in *Treasure Island?* ____________________.

If you think they both look like multiple-choice stems without the options, congratulations on your perceptive eye. Short-answer items also include those in mathematics and science that require the student to solve a problem, derive a formula, balance a chemical equation, or otherwise supply the answer, which may be a symbol or a number. Occasionally, it may be appropriate to cluster several short-answer items together for greater efficiency, as the following examples illustrate:

After each title, write the last name of its author.

1. *Ivanhoe* ____________________
2. *Jane Eyre* ____________________
3. *Little Women* ____________________
4. *Oliver Twist* ____________________
5. *Wuthering Heights* ____________________

This saves repeating and reading "Who is the author of . . ." for five items.

Relative to other item types, short-answer items have some advantages. First, they avoid some of the criticism of selected-response items in that they require the student to produce an answer, not merely recognize one in a crowd. This also reduces the possibility of students guessing the correct answer using partial knowledge. Second, they are easier and less time consuming to construct than multiple-choice items, because teachers don't need to create distractors.

In their ease of construction, however, also lies a major limitation. Short-answer items are often difficult to score. The structure lent to a multiple-choice item by its options, for example, is not present in a short-answer item. The students are free to respond with any word, phrase, or symbol they can think of, not just the one you had in mind. Therefore, an item that seemed perfectly clear when you wrote it can turn into a nightmare when you score it. Multiple correct answers can abound if the item is not worded clearly.

Then there are the problems of legibility and spelling of the answers. What if a mere misspelling changes the nature of the answer? Should legibility count? What if you interpret a student's nervous scribbling differently than the student intended? If this is not a spelling test (that is, spelling is not specified in the outcome to be assessed), spelling should not count, should it? These are sticky questions, and novice item-writers do not usually think about them until they are faced with scoring short-answer items. This "morning-after" slap of reality tends to drive home the point that it is easier to score any type of selected-response item than it is to score short-answer items. Additionally, handwritten answers cannot be read by the optical scanning equipment usually available in schools. Short-answer items are thus more time consuming and less objective to score than selected-response items.

But don't let these challenges stop you; these major limitations can be overcome in some areas of physical sciences and mathematics where (1) there is only one correct answer, (2) it is expressed as a number or symbol, and, therefore, (3) spelling is not a problem. In these areas, short-answer items can be used to assess higher-level outcomes (like application) as well as knowledge. In other content areas, however, short-answer items are mainly used to assess knowledge of specifics (terminology and facts), knowledge of ways and means of dealing with specifics (conventions, trends and sequences, classification and categories, criteria, and methodology), and knowledge of universals and abstractions in a field (principles and generalizations, theories and structures): in other words, short-answer items can test most outcomes within the knowledge level of the cognitive domain.

Using Guidelines to Construct Well-Designed Short-Answer Items

Because of their limitations, it is important to know how to design or identify good short-answer items. The general guidelines presented in Chapter 5 regarding paper-and-pencil assessments also apply to short-answer items. In addition, some of the guidelines for selected-response items pertain also to short-answer items. As with good two-choice and multiple-choice items, short-answer items should be worded positively and should avoid tricky negatives. There should also be no unintended clues to the keyed correct answer. In addition, there are also some guidelines specifically for short-answer items.

1. *Use a direct question, rather than an incomplete statement.* The recent research on multiple-choice items logically holds here as well. Multiple-choice stems should be stated as grammatically complete questions and not as incomplete statements,[5] and so should short-answer items. They are preferred over completion items. A direct question helps structure the item for the answer you seek without giving students unintended clues to the correct answer. It also prevents you from lifting statements directly from the textbook and replacing a word or two with a blank, which is *not* good assessment technique. Here is an example:

During the Cuban missile crisis, the president of the United States was

____________________.

The answers could include "nervous," "a man," "angry with the Soviets," and "ready to bomb Cuba," in addition to "John Kennedy." A better way to structure the item is in a question:

Who was president of the United States during the Cuban missile crisis?

______Kennedy______

If you tend to think of items in incomplete sentences, try rewording them so that there is one blank and it is placed at the end. When written this way, it is usually easy to see how a question could just as easily be constructed. However you go about it, direct questions are preferred.

2. *Word the item so there is a single, unique, brief response.* Guideline one will help keep you out of the trap of multiple correct answers, but it is no guarantee by itself. One way to approach the item is to write it, then think of your students and how the more imaginative of them (regardless of their grades) might answer it. If you can come up with more than one answer, they surely can. Rework the item until you remove all possible responses except the keyed correct answer. Okay, you say, what if there really are two possible answers? Well, you can require both or accept either, as the following item illustrates:

Who was the author of *Tom Sawyer?* ____________________

---

[5]T. M. Haladyna, 1994. Author's personal communication with the researcher.

The two possibilities, of course, are Mark Twain and Samuel Clemens. If either will do, give full credit for whichever one of the two the student writes. If both are required, say so in the item:

> What was the pen name and the real name of the author of *Tom Sawyer?*
> Mark Twain, Samuel Clemens

3. Specify the response units or degree of precision required for the answer. In the item just above, the response unit was a name—an author's name. Primarily to simplify scoring, it is a good idea to tell students the units in which the answer should be written. This is especially true for items with numerical answers. If a math text is 8 inches by 10 inches, then the item "What is the perimeter of your math text?" has at least two correct answers: 36 inches and 3 feet. A single correct answer can be ensured by rephrasing the question:

> In inches, what is the perimeter of your math textbook? ____36____

Another way to accomplish this is to specify the response units at the end of the blank, like this:

> What is the perimeter of your math textbook? ____36____ inches

It is also advisable to specify the accuracy required of responses, unless being able to determine the appropriate accuracy is part of the outcome and, therefore, the item. For example, you might create this item:

> If a house that sold for $95,350 in 1989 has appreciated 5.5%, how much could it be sold for today? Round your answer to two decimal places. ________

The accuracy specified should be consistent with common practice. For example, there is usually no good reason for having students compute interest to five decimal places. Specifying response units or degree of precision can be done item-by-item or in the directions for all the short-answer items on a test if the response units are all the same. Directions may tell students, for example, to use their best handwriting for their answers or that spelling counts.

4. Arrange answer blanks so they accommodate handwritten answers. Just because you may type 10 letters to the inch does not mean your students write the same way. The blanks should accommodate the writers with the largest handwriting in your class—both in length as well as in the vertical space between items and response lines.

5. Arrange answer blanks so they are easily scored. Because scoring short-answer items can be tedious, make it easier on yourself by putting the answer blanks in some easy-to-scan arrangement—for example, along one side of the page. It can also make the entire set of items easier to read for your students.

6. Arrange answer blanks so they are equal in length. The length of the blank can be an unintended clue to the correct answer. To eliminate this, make all the blanks in a set of short-answer items equal in length, keeping in mind guideline four about accommodating handwritten answers. The following set of items does *not* take guidelines four, five, and six into consideration:

1. The Chinese use what type of farming to overcome steep slopes? (_____)
2. How were the islands of East Asia formed? (_______)
3. What percent of the world's population lives in China? (_) percent
4. In what region of the country is China's industrial heartland? (___)

Here is what the same set of items might look like when guidelines four, five, and six are followed:

1. The Chinese use what type of farming to overcome steep slopes? ____terrace____
2. How were the islands of East Asia formed? ____volcanoes____
3. What percent of the world's population lives in China? ____35____%
4. In what region of the country is China's industrial heartland? ____east____

✓ *Easy Reference Checklist*

Guidelines for Good Short-Answer Items

- ❑ Item calls for behavior stated in outcome.
- ❑ Item difficulty reflects difficulty/complexity of outcome.
- ❑ Higher-level (comprehension and above) items present novel material.
- ❑ Problem/task is stated clearly.
- ❑ Item is worded positively.
- ❑ Item is stated as a question.
- ❑ One and only one brief answer exists.
- ❑ Response units are specified.
- ❑ Blanks are long enough for handwritten answers.
- ❑ Blanks are equal in length.
- ❑ Blanks are arranged for easy scoring.

Considering Related Instructional Outcomes

Short-answer items are useful for assessing achievement of instructional outcomes in the cognitive domain and those cognitive outcomes related to the affective and psychomotor domains. Theoretically, as a free-response type, they can also be used to assess attitudes and opinions, but they are not as effective as essay items for this purpose. Short-answer items restrict expression, somewhat defeating the purpose of using free-response items to capture a student's attitude toward or opinion about something.

Knowledge-Level Outcomes

Knowledge-level outcomes in many content areas can be appropriate for short-answer assessment, especially where there is a single correct answer (labeling the parts of a flower or naming the main character of certain literary works, for example). Look at the following knowledge-level outcomes and identify those that are suitable for assessment with short-answer items.

1. Know the uses of the periodic table.
2. Without the use of the textbook or notes, the student will supply the correct term for a given definition for at least 75% of the given definitions.
3. Recall at least 67% of the major facts about cultures studied.
4. Name the type of a given angle. Angles will be from the student's math textbook and will be drawn on separate paper. Students may not use their textbook or notes.

Let's look at each of them. You could probably write a short-answer item for the first one pretty quickly:

List one use of the periodic table. ____________________

But there's a problem here. How many answers do you think are possible? For example, for one student, "use" might be interpreted as "What information can I get from the periodic table about an element?" Certainly, the periodic table can be used to determine the average atomic mass of an atom of an element or the number of protons (atomic number) in an atom of the element. Another student might interpret "use" to mean "Given the information in the periodic table, what can I determine about combinations of elements?" (a topic also discussed in class). This student's answer might be "To determine the molecular mass of a chemical compound." As you can see, there is no *one* correct answer or even just a few. Assessing achievement of this learning outcome may be sticky with short-answer items. The structure of a multiple-choice item would help here; so would a more clearly specified learning outcome.

The second outcome, on the other hand, is sufficiently specific. It is also generic enough to use with any subject matter for which there are terms and definitions to be learned. The outcome calls for the definition to be given to the student and for the student to provide the term. It also calls for enough items so that students can answer at least 75% of them. This would imply the following ratios of items answered correctly per number of items given for the student to reach criterion: 3/4, 6/8, or 9/12. The following examples are taken from the subject of art:

Directions: Fill in the blank with the art term that best fits the definition.

1. Picturing objects on a flat surface so that they appear three-dimensional. perspective
2. The part of a picture or scene that is nearest the observer. foreground
3. The horizontal line toward which receding parallel lines converge. horizon
4. The part of a picture or scene that is the farthest from the observer. background

The third knowledge-level learning outcome involves knowing information about cultures that are studied in classrooms across the land. The decision as to which cultures and which aspects of those cultures is usually left up to the district, the school, and the teachers but is influenced heavily by the textbook chosen. For a unit on the peoples of Canada, for example, these short-answer items could be used:

1. In about 1000 A.D. the Viking settled on the northern tip of which Canadian province? Newfoundland
2. These people are of mixed Native-American and French-Canadian heritage. Metis
3. What is the name of the group that is native to Canada and lives in the Arctic regions? Innuit

Outcome four specifies that angles from the students' math textbook are to be reproduced on paper (the test) and that students will be asked to name the angle. Presumably they could do this orally or in writing. If the test is written, they could also select the name of the angle in question (implying two-choice, multiple-choice, or matching items) or write the name of the angle on the test somewhere in the vicinity of the drawn angle. The students are not permitted, however, to use their text or notes in figuring this out. Achievement of this outcome could be assessed in all of the ways stated here. Examples of short-answer items for this outcome follow:

Directions: Write the name of the type of angle in the space to the right of the angle.

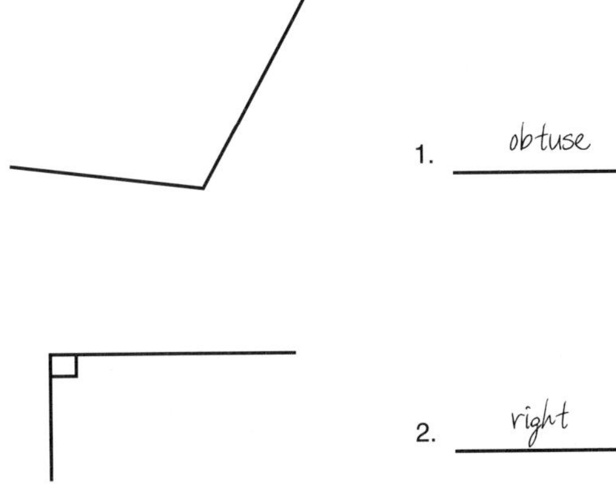

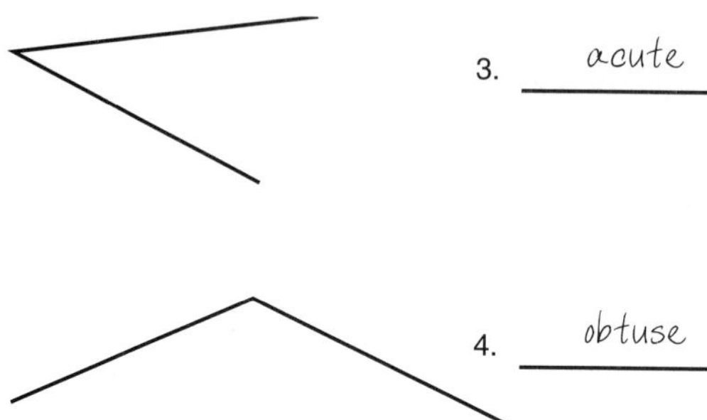

Higher-Level Outcomes

Included in this section are some examples of higher-level instructional outcomes from the cognitive domain and corresponding short-answer items. Keep in mind that more than one item type may be appropriate for assessing the outcome. This is not an exhaustive list, but it is intended to show some of the range possible with short-answer items. Keep in mind that short-answer items only tap higher-level thinking if they present students with new information or a novel task. To guard against the "We never went over that" complaint, prepare your students to think critically, and help them see critical thinking as an important skill and responsibility in our democracy.

Here are some sample higher-level outcomes from the cognitive domain that can be assessed using short-answer items:

Outcome: Corrects copy based on common proofreader's marks.

This outcome not only requires students to be able to interpret proofreader's marks but also to create new copy that incorporates the corrections. Here is what a short-answer set might look like:

Directions: For items 1–9, rewrite the correct copy in the space provided as indicated by the proofreader's marks.

Item	In Margin	In Copy	Rewrite
1.	tr	traesure	treasure
2.	[delete mark]	mealsure	measure
3.	tr	the in box	in the box
4.	sp	for 2 years	two
5.	l.c.	TOM SAWYER	Tom Sawyer
6.	caps	paradise island	Paradise Island
7.	stet	treasure	treasure
8.	r	you trust	your trust
9.	[close up mark]	Lo ne Point	Lone Point

Outcome: Solve problems involving computation of sales tax.

Directions: Solve and write your answer on the line next to the item. Round your answers to the nearest cent.

10. At the Taco Queen, Shawna bought a burrito special for $2.89. Tax in her state is 9%. What was her total bill? $3.15

11. Figure the total bill (including tax) for the following meal:

Salad	$3.50
Entree	8.95
Dessert	2.50
Coffee	1.00
Tax (11%)	

$17.70

12. Rudy's new coat cost $89.95 plus eight percent tax. What was the total cost of the coat? $97.15

Outcome: Students will punctuate unpunctuated sentences. Punctuation to be supplied may be internal, ending, or both.

Directions: Carefully rewrite each of the following sentences with the correct internal and ending punctuation. Write your answer on the blank line below the item.

13. Alexa will ride her new bicycle to school

Alexa will ride her new bicycle to school.

14. Stop it Jorge

Stop it, Jorge!

15. Will Li-wen come to my party

Will Li-wen come to my party?

Scoring Free-Response Items

Now that you know that scoring free-response items is difficult and a major disadvantage of the general item type, what to do? Well, you could decide to avoid free-response items altogether, but that would limit your assessment options. Rather than throwing the baby out with the bath water, here are some ways to make scoring free-response items more fair for the students and easier for you. The key here is to minimize the subjectivity of the scoring while increasing the objectivity and reliability of the test and maintaining its validity.

For any type of free-response item, having the "model" answer in mind when you create the item is imperative. A well-crafted item will ease the difficulty of scoring, so following the guidelines for item construction is key. Creating a scoring scheme based on what you've decided will count will help too.

Scoring Essay Items

You can make the scoring of essay items more objective to the degree that you can specify acceptable responses. If you can clearly spell out what factors should appear in the responses, then any knowledgeable scorer should be able to determine whether or not they are present. There are two basic approaches to scoring essay items: the analytic method and the holistic method.

The *analytic* approach to scoring essay items involves identifying all the aspects or components of a perfect answer and assigning a point value to each. This model answer would be one for which full points are awarded. In the earlier example about why stars shine, the total item could be worth, say, four points: one point each for correctly using the terms *helium, hydrogen,* and *nuclear fusion* and one point for including the release of energy into space as light. Your four-point, model answer (with portions *a* through *d* indicating the point-earning components) may look like this:

> "Stars make their own light. They turn (a) hydrogen, which they have a lot of, into (b) helium through a process called (c) nuclear fusion. Some of the hydrogen that does not make it all the way into helium becomes (d) energy that is released into space as light."

Further, you can create successive model answers, based on the components, for each reduced point value. Thus, a scoring rubric or scheme for the star shine essay item might look like the one in Figure 7.2.

Scoring Rubric for "Star-Shine" Essay Item

4 points maximum. 1 point each for correctly using the terms *helium, hydrogen,* and *nuclear fusion,* and 1 point for including the release of energy into space as light.

Model Answers and Points

4 points	"Stars make their own light. They turn (a) hydrogen, which they have a lot of, into (b) helium through a process called (c) nuclear fusion. Some of the hydrogen that does not make it all the way into helium becomes (d) energy that is released into space as light."
3 points	"They make helium out of hydrogen in a process called nuclear fusion." OR "Stars make helium during nuclear fusion and release the energy which is light."
2 points	"They make helium out of hydrogen." OR "They make their own light during nuclear fusion."
1 point	"They put helium and hydrogen into nuclear fusion."
0 points	"Helium, hydrogen, nuclear fusion." OR not attempted; erased.

Figure 7.2
Analytic scoring rubric for a sample essay item.

The answer to an essay item should be read twice, ideally by two different knowledgeable people (say, two eighth-grade science teachers for the previous example) with the model answer in mind. They each would assign points based on their analysis of the components in the response. The points for the two readings could then be compared. If there are any discrepancies, the item can be reread, or the points assigned for the two readings can be averaged. Using this approach, scoring can be more objective.

Where can you find the components that facilitate analytic scoring? They may sometimes be specified or implied in the learning outcome itself. They may also be determined from the model answer: Once you have written it, analyze the model answer for the several important pieces that make it a model answer. Then decide how many points each of them is worth.

The *holistic* approach (also called the global method) includes the rating approach and the primary trait approach and results in more-subjective, less-reliable scoring. But because it takes less time, holistic scoring is frequently used when a larger number of students or longer responses are involved. The holistic approach also includes identifying all of the aspects or components of a perfect answer, but point values are not assigned to each; instead, each response is judged as a whole, as a total unit, and points are awarded. Based on overall impressions, like the perceived completeness of the response, for example, points are assigned. The item is then reread and rescored and the scores compared and reconciled. If the item is worth 10 points, for example, then 0 to 10 points are assigned to the response as a whole. A variation of holistic scoring is the rating method. With the rating method, student papers are placed into piles representing the degree of quality in the response. Each pile represents a certain point value. In scoring an essay item worth 6 points, for example, you would use seven piles or boxes[6] representing 0 to 6 points. Of course, you may or may not end up with papers in each of the seven boxes. Rereading the papers in each point category helps you determine if they are all indeed worth the same number of points or if some should be moved to another pile. As you might imagine, without scoring criteria for each point category, this all becomes very norm-referenced.

Another variation of the holistic method is the primary-trait approach. The primary-trait approach involves analyzing responses and assigning points to them according to their underlying purpose. For example, consider the following learning outcome:

> The student will write a persuasive letter that logically supports a self-chosen point of view regarding a controversial issue.

"Persuasiveness" is a primary trait that a letter your students write to their congressional representative (arguing for or against stricter federal gun control, for example) should possess. In reality, the responses may range from those that take a strong stand and use compelling logic to those that are incomprehensible or make no effort to persuade. The more persuasive the response, the more points scored. Humor would be a primary trait for comedy skit scripts written by cooperative learning groups in language arts or drama. Balanced nutritional value may be a primary trait for diets constructed by students in science. Your job is to define the primary trait that is most important and assign points to it. Can there be more than one primary trait for one essay item? Yes, but ideally you would read each response once for each primary trait assessed, determining separately the degree of each primary trait present. If you were reading short stories your students had written for primary traits of character development and humor, you should read each one twice—once for the presence of character development and once for the presence of humor.

Usually, full credit in holistic scoring (and its variations) ranges from 4 to 10 points for each essay item. Most people (teachers included) do not possess the finer discrimination ability needed to go much beyond 10 points. How do you determine, for example, whether a response deserves 78 points or 79 points on a 100-point scale? Loading up points on essay items may also make them disproportionately important compared to the rest of the items on the test. As an example, assume you just created a test with 20 multiple-choice items (1 point each) and 2 essay items. It is *not* a good idea to assign 15 points to each essay just so the total adds to 50 points. A good question to ask in this case is, "Are the ideal essay responses really worth 15 multiple-choice answers?" If the answer is yes, then specify this on the test in the directions to the students. If the answer is no, then adjust the total-point scale accordingly.

Although both analytic and holistic approaches can be used for both criterion-referenced tests and norm-referenced tests, the analytic approach is clearly more ap-

---

[6]This method may be best done on the floor with the categories surrounding you. Although no actual boxes are required, dividing up the visual space around you helps separate the three-point papers from the four-point papers, and so forth.

propriate for criterion-referenced tests, and holistic approaches are more appropriate for norm-referenced tests. When the rating approach is used, for example, student papers tend to be compared to each other. A sample of responses may be read first to get a feel for the overall quality of responses, and then each response is judged to be very good, good, average, poor, or very poor (or just good, average, or poor), and finally corresponding points are assigned.

In scoring essay items, regardless of the method chosen for awarding credit, there are a few guidelines that, if followed, will make your life easier.[7]

1. Score each response without knowledge of who wrote it—that is, anonymously. This prevents scores from being biased by factors beyond the actual quality of the answers. Your personal feelings about the individual student should not enter into the scoring, and knowing the identity of the author can trigger these feelings. This is, of course, easier said than done. You get to know your students' handwriting and writing styles, and anonymity of authors is not always possible. Students' anonymity should be preserved as much as possible, however. One way to do this is to make sure that the pages on which students are to write answers to essay items are not pages on which they must also write their names. If a test included three essay questions and responses on pages two and three, for example, you could turn all the test papers to page two before scoring the essay portion. If necessary, use a coding system of some sort to avoid reading student names along with their essay responses.

2. Score essay items by item, not by student. Scoring one item at a time for all students (item one for all students and then item two for all students, and so on) helps to fulfill the anonymity guideline, to promote consistency of scoring, and to reduce scorer biases that can creep in when total tests are scored one at a time. If a student responds brilliantly to the first essay item, for example, scorers have a tendency to expect a good answer to subsequent items. This effect makes it likely that the student in this case will get a higher score than may be warranted by the actual responses. Of course, the reverse is also true. A poor response to one or more items leads to an expectation of poor performance on the remaining items. This undesirable phenomenon is reduced with item-by-item scoring.

3. Read and score essay items twice, independently, before assigning point totals. You may have groaned after reading this guideline, probably because you had a vision of the time that would be needed to follow it. Granted, it does require time, but it helps ensure consistency of scoring and reduces subjectivity and scorer bias. This is especially crucial in high-stakes assessment. The higher the stakes involved regarding the decisions made using the results, the more crucial it becomes to remove scorer bias and ensure consistency. To use a classroom example, a final unit exam with a lot of weight attached to it for a grade may have more grave consequences (higher stakes) for students than a weekly quiz or homework. A statewide test that is used to determine a student's eligibility for a special program is another example of high-stakes assessment.

[7]More specifics on scoring student products, of which essay responses are a part, in Chapter 8.

Teachers who participate as scorers for essay-item responses in statewide tests are typically trained to look for certain qualities so that scoring is consistent across scorers. On your own tests, at the very least, you should read the essay responses twice yourself, especially if the results are norm-referenced. A response that did not look good Friday afternoon when you first read it may look pretty good on Sunday, the second time around! The easiest way to do this is to score a response and put the point value in pencil on the back of the test so that it will not be visible the second time you score it. Then compare the points assigned at the two readings. If they are essentially the same, you can simply average them. If they are significantly different, you should go back and read the response another time and make your final decision. Ideally, responses should be scored by two independent, competent persons: you and another teacher, for example.

4. Prepare a model answer before you score the responses. This is especially useful for analytic scoring. If you wrote the item with a model answer in mind, then writing this model answer down somewhere (or writing it to another filename in your word-processing program) should be simple. Capturing the answer when you create the item saves you from doing it again when it is time to score the papers. For example, if an essay item is worth five points, create your top-notch, five-point answer at the same time you draft the item. Write the answer down, but not on the test. From that ideal answer you can then create a four-point answer, a three-point answer, and so on. If you are scoring analytically, a four-point answer may have one or more components fewer than a five-point answer, such as in the star-shine example used earlier. If you are scoring holistically, as in the case of the letter to the congressional representative, you may actually write a series of letters reflecting the degree of persuasiveness that corresponds to the six-point values possible (zero to five). You would then compare your students' responses to these point models to determine which model the response matched best. This would, in turn, determine the number of points awarded for the response. To score that same letter analytically, you might write down the following rubric to use in assigning points to the responses:

5 = strong stand *and* uses compelling logic
4 = moderate stand *or* logic slightly flawed *or* both
3 = weak stand *or* logic very flawed *or* both
2 = no stand taken *or* no logical argument presented
1 = incomprehensible *or* no stand taken *and* no logic detected
0 = not attempted/erased

The scoring rubric presented here can help you remember how many points to award the response that takes a moderate stand, but you still must decide whether the stand taken in the response was strong, moderate, or weak.

5. Use the appropriate scoring method for the item. This is a corollary to scoring guideline four, above. As you create the item and the model answer and consider the essence of the learning outcome, you will likely also decide how it should be scored. If you are not sure and it is a criterion-referenced test, try analytic scoring. If it is a norm-referenced test, try one of the holistic methods.

6. Decide how factors irrelevant to the learning outcome to be assessed are to be handled before scoring the responses. Sometimes, teachers have objectives (in written expression, for example) that not only span the curriculum but are also assessed the same way across the curriculum. Thus, an essay item response on a topic in science may be scored twice: once for its treatment of energy sources and their discovery and the second time for its demonstration of paragraph construction and English expression. A split score of 4/5, for example, might indicate four points for the "science" answer and five points for the "English" answer. The points may also be recorded separately in the teacher's gradebook for the two subjects. If split scoring is the case, students must be informed of this, preferably right on the test and orally by you, so they may compose their answers accordingly. Here are a few examples of language that could be used either in the items themselves or in the directions to the test:

In a well-constructed paragraph, . . .

Following the rules for good paragraph construction, . . .

Use your very best handwriting.

Follow the rules of business-letter writing.

If spelling is irrelevant to the learning outcome to be assessed with the essay item, then, theoretically, spelling should not count. A few words spelled wrong should not detract from an otherwise point-worthy answer. But what if the response is so badly spelled that it becomes difficult to grasp the student's meaning? At this point, spelling, indeed, counts whether you specifically take off points or not, for it does facilitate (or hinder) communication.

✓ *Easy Reference Checklist*

Guidelines for Scoring Essay Items

- ❑ Responses are scored anonymously.
- ❑ Responses are scored item by item across students.
- ❑ Each response is read twice, independently, before assigning point totals.
- ❑ Ideal answer is prepared before scoring responses.
- ❑ Appropriate scoring method for the item is used.
- ❑ How factors irrelevant to the learning outcome being assessed are to be handled is decided before scoring the responses.

Scoring Short-Answer Items

There are three basic guidelines for scoring short-answer items that parallel in many ways the guidelines for scoring essay responses.

1. *Prepare the correct answer(s) before scoring the responses.* Just as with essay items, it is a good idea to create short-answer items with the model answer in mind. Capture the model answer at the time the item is constructed by writing it down or saving it on disk so you do not have to do it again before scoring the responses. You can also use a blank test as an answer key and record the response(s) you will accept for credit in the answer blank.

2. *If unanticipated correct answers are discovered while scoring, give credit to all students who answered that way.* Consider this scenario: The test is over, you have collected the papers, and as you briefly scan the answers on the first few tests, you realize that your students have been more creative than usual in their interpretations or in their answers, and some of those answers look pretty good based on the question as you worded it. You realize that you may have to accept more than one answer as correct. Will you die? No. Will you be arrested and put in jail? No. Will you stop giving tests of any sort? Probably not. Will you learn from the experience and use that learning to improve your assessment skills? I hope so. Credible, accurate answers to the question deserve credit whether you anticipated them or not. If this happens, credit should be given to all students who wrote the same answer. You can fine-tune the item later based on what you learn about how your students interpreted it when you return the test papers. It is no sin, by the way, to throw an item out of the scoring entirely if it is a real bummer.[8] Just replace it next time with a better one that assesses the same learning outcome.

3. *Decide how factors irrelevant to the learning outcome to be assessed will be handled before scoring the responses.* Legible handwriting and reasonable (discernible) spelling may be the only requirements. If, on the other hand, spelling counts as part of the outcome to be assessed, for example, you must determine the point difference between the following answer situations:

   1. A right answer spelled correctly.
   2. A right answer spelled incorrectly.
   3. A wrong answer spelled correctly.
   4. A wrong answer spelled incorrectly.

You may decide to award two points (full credit) in situation number one, above, and one point in number two. You may also decide that a wrong answer is a wrong answer no matter how well it is spelled, so no points will be awarded in situations three and four. Of course, you could do this with one point for full credit and one-half point in situation two, but this could slow down the arithmetic in figuring the

---

[8]More about how to tell good items from bad using student assessment data in Chapter 10.

total score. An alternative is to split-score the item as described earlier for essay-item responses, recording two scores—one for the "content" answer and one for spelling, handwriting, or other such concerns.

✓ *Easy Reference Checklist*

Guidelines for Scoring Short-Answer Items

- ❑ Correct answer(s) are prepared before scoring responses.
- ❑ Unanticipated correct answers are given credit across students.
- ❑ How factors irrelevant to the learning outcome being assessed will be handled is decided before scoring responses.

Summary

Common to all *free-response* items is that the student is not forced to select an answer to an item from among those given, but, rather, is "free" to construct his own response. The teacher has built a task for the student in the free-response item but has left the answer for the student to supply. The structure and wording of the item regulate length (how many words, for example) of the response. A common misconception is that free-response items require recall of information and selected-response items require recognition only and that, somehow, recall is better. Neither of these statements is necessarily true. The two major types of free-response items are short-answer and essay items.

Essay Items

Essay items typically require the student to compose responses ranging from a paragraph to a few pages. Good essay items require both recall and use of information in the demonstration of a higher-level learning outcome. Advantages of essay items include the following:

1. They are excellent for assessing certain learning outcomes at the higher levels of the cognitive domain, especially synthesis.
2. They force students to exercise their thought-composition and writing skills.
3. They can take less time for teachers to write than selected-response items.

Disadvantages of essay items include the following:

1. Scoring essay items is a long and somewhat subjective process relative to scoring selected-response items.
2. Answers to essay items are open to at least some interpretation by the scorer.
3. They normally have to be scored by persons who know thoroughly both the content area and the learning outcome being measured.

4. Fewer essay items can be answered in the same amount of time than for any other paper-and-pencil item type.

Thus, essay tests tend, in general, to be less valid and reliable than other types, with notoriously low scorer reliability.

The general guidelines for item construction presented in Chapter 5 apply to essay items. Specific construction guidelines for essay items include:

1. Reserve essay items for higher-level learning outcomes not well assessed by other item types.
2. Define the task completely and specifically.
3. Do not provide optional essay items.

Essay items are useful for assessing achievement of higher-level instructional outcomes in the cognitive domain and those higher-level cognitive outcomes related to the affective and psychomotor domains. They can also be used to assess attitudes and opinions.

Short-Answer Items

Short-answer items are essentially short essay items, requiring a brief response—a word, a phrase, a number. A short-answer item resembles the stem of a multiple-choice item; a blank is provided for the student's answer. The *completion*-item subspecies is an incomplete sentence (rather than a question) written so that the answer, written in the space by the student, accurately completes the statement. Short-answer items are preferred over completion items based on research done with multiple-choice items.

Short-answer items have several advantages:

1. They require the student to produce an answer, not merely recognize one in a crowd, thus avoiding some of the criticism of selected-response items.
2. They are easier and less time consuming to construct than multiple-choice items.

They also have disadvantages:

1. Short-answer items are often difficult to score.
2. They are more time consuming and less objective to score than selected-response items.

The general guidelines for item construction presented in Chapter 5 also apply to short-answer items. Specific construction guidelines for short-answer items include:

1. Use a direct question, rather than an incomplete statement.
2. Word the item so there is a single, unique, brief response.
3. Specify the response units or degree of precision required for the answer.

4. Arrange answer blanks so they accommodate handwritten answers.
5. Arrange answer blanks so they are easily scored.
6. Arrange answer blanks so they are equal in length.

Short-answer items are useful for assessing achievement of instructional outcomes in the cognitive domain and those cognitive outcomes related to the affective and psychomotor domains. Short-answer items can also be used to assess attitudes and opinions, but they are not as effective as essay items for this purpose.

Scoring Free-Response Items

Scoring Essay Items

There are two basic approaches to scoring essay items: the analytical method and the holistic method. The *analytic* approach involves identifying all the aspects or components of a perfect answer and assigning a point value to each to create a scoring rubric. Components that facilitate analytic scoring may sometimes be specified or implied in the learning outcome itself. They may also be determined from the model answer.

The *holistic* approach, also called the global method, includes the rating approach and the primary-trait approach. The holistic approaches result in more subjective, less reliable scoring, but because they take less time than the analytical approach, they are frequently used when a larger number of students or longer responses are involved. The holistic approaches also include identifying all of the aspects or components of a perfect answer, but point values are not assigned to each; instead, each response is judged as a total unit, and points are awarded. With the rating method, student papers are placed into piles representing the degree of quality in the response. Each pile represents a certain point value. The primary-trait variation of holistic scoring involves analyzing responses and assigning points to them according to their underlying purpose. Full credit in holistic scoring (and its variations) usually ranges from 4 to 10 points for each essay item. Although both analytic and holistic approaches can be used for both criterion-referenced tests and norm-referenced tests, the analytic approach is clearly more appropriate for criterion-referenced tests, and the holistic approaches are more appropriate for norm-referenced tests.

These are specific scoring guidelines to keep in mind when scoring essay items:

1. Score each response without knowledge of who wrote it—that is, anonymously.
2. Score essay items by item, not by student.
3. Read and score essay items twice, independently, before assigning point totals.
4. Prepare a model answer before you score the responses.
5. Use the appropriate scoring method for the item.
6. Decide how factors irrelevant to the learning outcome to be assessed are to be handled before scoring the responses.

Scoring Short-Answer Items

There are three basic guidelines for scoring short-answer items that parallel in many ways those for scoring essay responses:

1. Prepare the correct answer(s) before scoring the responses.
2. If unanticipated correct answers are discovered while scoring, give credit to all students who answered that way.
3. Decide how factors irrelevant to the learning outcome to be assessed will be handled before scoring the responses.

Try These

I. Indicate which type of free-response item would be most appropriate for assessing each of the behaviors below:

E = essay

SA = short-answer

NFR = not appropriately assessed with any type of free-response item

_____ 1. Solves word problems involving percents with a four-function calculator.
_____ 2. States the main character of a given work.
_____ 3. Supports or refutes the position, "School attendance should be voluntary."
_____ 4. Discriminates among shapes of three dimensions.
_____ 5. Writes (or otherwise records) a weather forecast for an area, given a weather map of the area.
_____ 6. Lists, in chronological order, the steps in executing a chip shot in golf.
_____ 7. Identifies valid and invalid conclusions drawn from a given communication.
_____ 8. Calculates the square root of two-digit numbers.
_____ 9. Develops a plan for reducing household waste.
_____ 10. Names at least 75% of the countries on a given continent.
_____ 11. Given animal names (giraffe, turtle), classifies them as amphibian, bird, fish, mammal, or reptile.
_____ 12. Rewrites a previously written work based on given proofreader's marks.

II. Read each of the following items. If you think it violates one or more construction guidelines, on a separate sheet of paper state which of the guidelines the item violates and rewrite the item so that it is practically perfect and violates no guidelines. If it is practically perfect as it is written, state "OK as is."

Essay Items

1. *Outcome:* Students will explain the role chromosomes play in determining the sex of a human embryo.

   Explain how sex happens. Don't leave anything out. (20 min., 5 points)

2. *Outcome:* Students will know the basic characteristics of each of the following: capitalism, communism, and socialism as they were practiced in the 20th century.

   Describe the differences and similarities between communism and capitalism in their approach to ownership of such things as land, factories, service entities (e.g., transportation, mail).

3. *Outcome:* Using principles and guidelines in this chapter, students will create systematic procedures to be followed when scoring an important essay test in a subject of their choosing.

   Your colleague, Mr. Yakimura, has agreed to be the second scorer for an essay portion of an important exam you just gave. He has excellent content knowledge but does not have specific training in scoring essay responses. Create a set of specific procedures based on this chapter to guide him. List them in step-by-step fashion. Spend no more than 30 min. on this item. 10 points.

Short-Answer Items

1. What should all dieters do? ____________________
2. When a ____________________ is prepared, ____________________ always occurs.
3. What is the name of the highest mountain in the U.S.? ____________________
4. ____________________ is nicknamed the "Bluebonnet State."
5. What characteristic of a star is its color not related to? ____________________
6. What percent of 38 is 17? ____________________
7. What is the Pacific Ocean? ____________________

Answers

I. 1. SA, 2. SA, 3. E, 4. NFR (three-dimensional shapes imply a performance outcome, not assessed via paper and pencil), 5. E, 6. E (highly restricted—you might even argue SA), 7. NFR (a series of two-choice items following a brief written statement would work much better), 8. SA, 9. E, 10. SA, 11. Technically, SA, but matching would be more efficient, 12. E.

II. The rewrites of the following items should be taken as suggestions. Your rewrites may differ somewhat, but still should not violate any of the guidelines.

Essay Items

1. Guidelines violated: (1) The item does not call for the behavior stated in the corresponding outcome. By reading the item, the student has no idea that the role of chromosomes should be included anywhere in his or her answer. (2) The task is not defined completely or clearly. What *is* called for here is a

20-minute mind-dump. The item will also be interpreted in wildly different ways by individual students.

In a concise paragraph, describe the role chromosomes play in determining the sex of a human embryo. (20 min., 5 points)

2. Guidelines violated: (1) The corresponding outcome does not indicate higher-level behavior. "Knowing the basic characteristics" implies a knowledge-level outcome: Essay items are not efficient at all for assessing knowledge. (2) The item does not call for behavior stated in the outcome. Although one must know the characteristics to be able to explain the similarities and differences, one does not have to know the similarities and differences to list the characteristics of each type of economic system. (3) Few limits given to restrict the item. No time, word, or space limits given, nor points available.

   Rewrite: Set this up as a matching set with characteristics listed on the left-hand side and the "isms" listed in alphabetical order on the right-hand side. Directions might indicate that the "isms" may be used more than once or maybe not at all.

3. Guidelines violated: None. Wow, what an item! It appears to call for the behavior stated in the outcome, which, indeed, is a higher-level outcome. The task in the item reflects the difficulty and complexity of the outcome. The task is defined pretty completely—"create specific procedures based on this chapter . . . list in step-by-step fashion." A time limit is given and the points available are listed.

   Rewrite: None necessary. All that's left is for you to write your response and get it scored.

Short-Answer Items

1. Guidelines violated: (1) More than one brief answer. (2) The problem/task is not stated very clearly, which is what is causing the first violation to occur.

   Rewrite: Add structure to the item by providing alternative answers (make it a multiple-choice item, for example).

   What should dieters do to help lose weight?
   a. Consume 5,000 calories daily.
   b. Eat in cafeterias.
   c. Exercise regularly.

2. Guidelines violated: (1) Not a question. (2) Too many blanks, and, therefore, the task is not stated clearly. (3) Blank not at the end of the item.

   Rewrite: A chemical reaction always occurs when this is prepared. ____________________

3. Guidelines violated: None. OK as is.
4. Guidelines violated: (1) Not a question. (2) Blank not at the end of the item.

   Rewrite: Which state is nicknamed the "Bluebonnet State"? ____________________

5. Guidelines violated: (1) Item is not worded positively. As it is worded, any number of responses would be acceptable (e.g., circumference).

   Rewrite: What characteristic of a star is its color related to? ____________________

6. Guideline violated: (1) Response units not specified.

   Rewrite: In the directions, a statement such as the following should be inserted: "Round your answers to the nearest whole percent."

7. Guideline violated: (1) Problem/task is not stated clearly. A student might wonder whether this is intended to be answered metaphorically, chemically, or geographically. In none of these cases is the blank long enough to accommodate the answer!

   Rewrite: Knowing that the intended keyed correct answer was "the largest ocean in the world," we can improve it as follows:

   What is the name of the largest ocean in the world? ____________________

CHAPTER 8

Creating Performance and Product Assessments for the Classroom

Key Concepts:

- Understanding the nature of performance and product assessments and their appropriate uses.
- Identifying types of instructional outcomes that are typically assessed with performance and product assessments.
- Defining the process of constructing performance and product assessments.
- Using guidelines to construct good performance assessments.
- Scoring performance assessments using observation tools: checklists, rating scales, and anecdotal records.
- Making students assessors.
- Creating performance and product assessments or choosing pre-written ones.

Standards Addressed in This Chapter:

1. Choose assessment methods appropriate for instructional decisions.
2. Develop assessment methods appropriate for instructional decisions.

Before You Begin Reading, Consider This

Should students assess the work or performance of their peers?

YES Critically appraising others' work is a life skill. It should be taught to and required of students. They could even be evaluated on how well they assessed someone's performance. As they became skilled in evaluation, they would actually raise the standard of performance.

NO We should not teach students to be critical of others' work. As it is, students are cruel enough to each other without any help. Their assessment skills should be practiced on themselves, if anyone.

Understanding Performance and Product Assessment

Assessing student performances and products is not a new concept in education, although interest in the concept has been rekindled in recent years. Teachers have been observing students and evaluating their creations for hundreds of years, both formally for grades and informally during everyday instruction. Large-scale achievement testing, on the other hand, could not be accomplished cost effectively by such an approach, and so education borrowed a technique from the Army Alpha exam shortly after World War I: the multiple-choice item. In the years following, this approach eventually crept into the classroom assessment arena, in some cases to the point where it was the only form of assessment used—by the teacher *and* on statewide tests. Thus, a student could go through years of schooling, encountering little else but multiple-choice tests. Perhaps you were one of those students.

With such paper-and-pencil, objectively scored tests, teachers can assess whether students possess adequate knowledge of a given subject. With these assessments, teachers can also check whether the students grasp concepts and are able to apply rules in hypothetical situations presented in the test items. However, teachers can only infer from their students' scores whether they can perform adequately when confronted with real-life situations. As stated in Chapter 6, these objectively scored paper-and-pencil tools of assessment, especially multiple-choice tests, are very useful in some situations but not in others.

In recent years, our society has become much more interested in higher level thinking skills like problem solving and in real-life application of skills and knowledge outside the narrow context of the instructional setting. For example, where it may have once been appropriate for students to be able to list the steps in demonstrating a scientific principle (a test of memorization) or to select the principle demonstrated by the given steps (a test of their ability to choose correctly among several options), it now may be more appropriate for them to be able to perform a demonstration of their choice that illustrates the principle at work.

Efforts have also been under way in districts, in states, and at the national level to rewrite instructional outcomes to reflect this emphasis on higher-level learning and relevancy to the real world. That shift in interests, coupled with increasing dissatisfaction among some educators with extensive standardized multiple-choice testing, has caused many in education to reexamine their assessment practices. In the case of the scientific-principle example, a multiple-choice test will no longer match the objectives of the curriculum or the activities of the instruction. Forms of assessment must change in concert with shifts in the curriculum and instruction. In this case, assessments must provide students a structured opportunity to create and perform a demonstration. That performance must be observed by someone, most likely the teacher, if assessment is to take place and a judgment formed.

Assessing student performances and products cannot be adequately accomplished with true-false, multiple-choice, or even short-answer items. Some educators have accordingly expanded their repertoire of assessment tools with alternatives to standardized multiple-choice tests. A number of teachers have made similar changes in their classroom assessments. Some have known all along that assessment alternatives exist and have used them where appropriate.

Many terms have been used to describe different aspects of the assessment of a student's performance or a product of her creation. The terms *authentic assessment, alternative assessment, direct assessment, performance assessment,* and *portfolio assessment* all refer to alternatives to multiple-choice standardized achievement tests. These alternatives focus student assessment and evaluation on "examining and judging a student's actual (or simulated) performance on significant, relevant tasks."[1] The word *authentic* in the term *authentic assessment* refers to the context in which the response to the proposed task is performed. It suggests that the tasks should be relevant to learning and to real life as much as possible in order to produce a real instance of performance or ability, rather than an estimate. The term *alternative* assessment points out that these types of assessments are viable choices to the seemingly ubiquitous multiple-choice test. *Direct* assessment suggests that the assessment should require little or no inference to be drawn from something as nebulous as a test score.

The term *performance* assessment is used by some to designate the type of student response to be assessed. Whether the context is authentic or simulated, the teacher is interested in observing and assessing the student in action, in the process of performance. Others use the term *performance assessment* in a broader sense to mean a type of assessment other than a paper-and-pencil, objectively scored test. These alternate assessment methods may result in the creation of an authentic product and may even be preserved in a portfolio. A *portfolio* is an organized collection of student products and recorded performances. Herman, Aschbacher, and Winters describe portfolios as "collections of student work that are reviewed against criteria in order to judge an individual student or a program [of instruction]."[2] Experts dis-

---

[1]"Critical Issues That Will Determine the Future of Alternative Assessment" by B. Worthen, 1993, *Phi Delta Kappan,* 74, 444–454.

[2]*A Practical Guide to Alternative Assessment* (p. 72) by J. L. Herman, P. R. Aschbacher, and L. Winters, 1992, Alexandria, VA: Association for Supervision and Curriculum Development.

agree on whether portfolios are really authentic assessments. Although portfolios may contain products of authentic assessments, they are not necessarily authentic themselves.[3]

The range of what is considered a performance or a product is quite vast across the disciplines represented in the pre-K–12 curriculum. In most cases, the work assessed is that of the individual student, as in the case when each student produces a body of work for the teacher to review at the end of a grading period or term. In other cases, the performance or product may be that of a team of students working in a cooperative learning group. Other examples of performances include speeches, dances, sharing materials and toys, platform dives, typing speed tests, oral debates, plays, skits, basketball games, conversations in Russian, landing planes in a simulator, and conducting science experiments. Typically, the performance must be observed as it happens or, at least, recorded for later review. The task to be performed is structured so that it is relevant to the instructional outcome and is real or authentic in the sense that it represents a task performed by someone in everyday life or on the job and so is relevant to life outside school.

Products, on the other hand, are more tangible items of the students' creation that can be viewed or otherwise sensed by the teacher. Some examples of products include play critiques, poems, science projects, dioramas, a plaster cast of a hand, research reports and other such written assignments, a decorative mask, a tasty casserole dish, sculpture, a typed letter, a working V-8 engine, and the lines of code of a computer software program. The Florida Writing Assessment Program, a statewide test, requires students to produce a writing sample on a common topic to which all students can relate—for example, a favorite childhood toy. The purpose is not to assess knowledge of toys, of course, but to assess writing skills such as focus, organization, development of supporting ideas, sentence structure, punctuation, capitalization, and spelling.

Whether a teacher assesses a performance, a product, or perhaps both should depend on the instructional outcomes that are valued. For example, an art teacher may observe a student's technique in creating a clay sculpture (a performance) or assess the finished product based on several important criteria, depending on what is most important. The steps in creating a good assessment and the guidelines to accomplish it are the same whether the performance in process or the tangible product or both are of interest. For the purposes of clarity and brevity, I will use the broader term *performance assessment* in this chapter to mean the assessment of both student performances and the tangible products students create.

The Advantages and Disadvantages of Using Performance Assessment

As with any of the assessment techniques and item types presented so far in this text, there are advantages to performance assessment. First, it provides a way to assess complex and higher-level instructional outcomes—analysis, synthesis, evaluation,

[3]Portfolios are discussed in more detail in Chapter 9.

cognitive strategies, problem-solving, motor skills, and attitudes—much more directly than selected-response items can. Multiple-choice items, for example, can only indirectly assess affective outcomes through self-report. A student who can correctly answer all the items on the playground safety test may not necessarily follow the rules. If the important outcome is for students to follow the rules, then observation of actual performance is in order.

Another advantage is that performance assessment can be used to improve instructional practice. Analysis across students can pinpoint common weaknesses in the products or performances. Revisions to the instruction can be made on the basis of this analysis to eliminate the weaknesses. Thus, observing student performance is an excellent way of informally assessing learning and instruction. Additionally, students can be actively involved in the interaction of assessment and instruction. For example, armed with the criteria for assessment and a checklist or rating scale of the important dimensions, a student can evaluate his own performance. The increasingly important skills of self- and peer assessment can thus be taught. Moreover, with performance assessment, students and teachers are encouraged to move beyond the "one and only one right answer" mentality because multiple correct responses are possible as long as they meet the scoring criteria.

Performance assessment also has some disadvantages. As with multiple-choice items, some of the disadvantages stem from the nature of the assessment, and some from misuse of the type. First, performance tests take time to create and to score. You must think up an appropriate task for the learning outcome, structure it adequately, and create a scoring scheme to guide observation during the performance. The performance itself takes time to observe. When there is a product to assess, each one must be independently considered, much like an essay item. If a lot of weight is given to the assessment, in grading for example, you may want another teacher to score the performances in addition to yourself for purposes of averaging the scores. Further, you should refine a performance assessment once you have administered it for the first time. All of this takes time.

A second related disadvantage is that performance assessment is not a good way to assess knowledge and comprehension-level instructional outcomes. The nature of performance assessment and the time it takes makes it extremely cost-*in*efficient to use in assessing facts, definitions of words and concepts, and names of people, places, and things. Outcomes at these lower levels of the taxonomy are more efficiently assessed in other ways—with paper-and-pencil assessments, for example.

Third, performance assessments, like essay items, suffer from notoriously low reliability and for many of the same reasons. For example, because fewer performance assessments can be squeezed into the same amount of class time as, say, multiple-choice items, they typically yield a smaller sample of student behavior. You may find yourself questioning whether a student's performance on a given task was a fluke or was truly representative of how she will do in real life. This lack of generalizability of test results is a cause for concern with paper-and-pencil assessments also, but it is particularly troublesome for more direct assessments. Another part of the reliability problem is scoring *only* the performance or product, separating it from any prior learning. Interrater and intrarater reliability are a major concern in statewide performance assessment where the stakes tied to decisions are typically high. Experts continue to search for ways to increase these reliability coefficients. These problems with reliability have led to cautions that judgments about individual students based on performance assessments should be for formative or developmental purposes only, not for final grades or major placement decisions. A formative assessment is typically used during instruction to gauge the effectiveness of instruction, and it takes the form of practice and feedback. A further caution is that judgments regarding groups based on performance assessments should be used only for the purposes of continuous improvement of instruction due to the small sample of student behavior and the lack of generalizability of the results.

A fourth disadvantage to using performance assessments in the classroom is the difficulty of incorporating all the conditions relevant to real-life performance, thus rendering the assessment less than authentic. Finally, there may be little or no support for performance assessment in the school or community. Resources and trained personnel are necessary to create authentic tasks and reliable scoring procedures, and these resources may be scarce or non-existent in some districts, especially in times of tight budgets.

Using Guidelines to Construct Well-Designed Performance Assessments

Because of the time and other resources consumed in producing, conducting, and evaluating performance assessments, well-constructed performance assessments are a must. A haphazard approach to performance assessment will be much more costly than using a mediocre selected-response test. A quick listing of the steps in designing a performance assessment will be presented first, followed by a more detailed discussion of each step, including specific, relevant construction guidelines. The guidelines are summarized in checklists at the end of the sections. As you read the seven steps below, you will notice that they are similar to the steps in the design of a good paper-and-pencil test. Developing assessments, regardless of type, follow much the same strategy as developing good instruction: planning, creating, reviewing, and revising.

Here are the specific steps that constitute the design process for a performance assessment:

1. Determine the purpose of the assessment.
2. Determine what skills and outcomes the assessment will cover and specify these in some detail, including their taxonomy domain and level.
3. Develop a task that is illustrative of and calls for the behavior specified in the outcomes. The task should be recorded, along with the directions for the students.
4. Determine the criteria to use in judging the adequacy of the students' performance on the task.

5. Create a scoring scheme that enables the criteria from step four and your judgment to be applied consistently.
6. Pilot test the entire assessment to see where enhancements are needed.
7. Revise the outcomes, the task, the judging criteria, and the scoring scheme as necessary based on pilot-test data.

Although the process may appear linear, it is not. It is an iterative process, with each step being influenced by preceding and following steps. For example, it is important to think about judging criteria (step four) while creating the performance task (step three). Now that you know what the steps are, we will look at each step more closely and outline the guidelines that will help ensure a valid and reasonably reliable assessment.

Determining the Purpose

The first step in designing a performance assessment is to determine the purpose for which the results will be used, because the purpose drives other decisions in subsequent steps in the process. For example, the results of the assessment may be used to describe a student's "best" performance or to describe a student's "typical" performance. A performance may also be used for formative or summative purposes. A formative assessment, mentioned earlier, is rather informal and may not require generating a numerical rating scheme. Even if a rating scheme is used for giving feedback to the student, a formative assessment is not likely to be used as the basis for grades. A summative assessment, in contrast, is likely to figure into a grade and requires a more elaborate scoring scheme. By first thinking of the end of the process—how the results will be used—and then working backward, you create a more valid assessment, and you will also be less likely to create an assessment that does less or more than you need. Further implications of the purpose of the assessment will be discussed in the steps that follow.

Determining Skills and Outcomes and Their Taxonomy Level

Because classroom and assessment time are limited, you must define what the important, valued outcomes of instruction are, and among those, you must decide which require performance assessment and which are appropriate for paper-and-pencil testing. In this second step of the design process you determine the form and substance of the performance assessment. Thus, instructional outcomes play an important role in shaping good performance assessment. The "meaningful unit of instruction" discussed in Chapter 5 is a concept that is applicable to performance assessment as well, as a performance assessment may incorporate one or a meaningful cluster of outcomes from one or more disciplines or domains. As physical education teachers know, psychomotor outcomes typically lend themselves well to performance assessment. Affective outcomes at the receiving, responding, and valuing levels of the taxonomy can be observed as well. However, cognitive outcomes assessed using performances and products should be at the application level of the cognitive domain or higher; assessing lower-level outcomes in the cognitive domain is extremely time consuming and costly for the benefit gained. Thus, identifying the taxonomy level of the outcomes you assess, regardless of the method of assessment, is always an important step. As an exercise in determining important, valued outcomes that require performance assessment, consider the following instructional outcomes:

1. Select the correct verb form for four out of every five given simple sentences.
2. Judge an artwork according to the principles of composition and aesthetics.
3. Perform an original skit that communicates the effect humans have on the planet.
4. The student correctly names the following parts of a compound microscope: arm, base, body tube, coarse adjustment, diaphragm, fine adjustment, light source, objectives, nose piece, ocular/eyepiece, stage, and stage clips. The student misnames no more than twice.

As requested in the first outcome, being able to select correct verb forms (a measure of application) is certainly an important part of learning to manipulate the written language, but the way the outcome is written, a paper-and-pencil test is probably the most efficient way to determine a student's proficiency in the skill. Alternatively, students who are physically disabled might do this orally or on a computer. The second outcome is certainly higher level (it involves evaluation) and might appropriately be assessed by having the student write or record an evaluation of an artwork of his or her choice or of your selection, thus creating a product. Could the first two outcomes be included in one performance assessment activity? Certainly. They are both higher-level outcomes. Correct verb usage may be included as one of the dimensions in the scoring scheme when reviewing the student's evaluation report. It is important, however, to limit the dimensions included in a performance assessment to those that are most important. Otherwise, scoring the assessment may become overly complex, as you will see later in this chapter.

Outcome three seems custom-made for a performance assessment. It is written at the synthesis level, calls for a performance, and already defines at least one important dimension upon which scoring may be based—the degree to which the skit communicates the effect of humans on the planet. The fourth outcome calls for memorizing the parts of a microscope (a knowledge-level activity). Now, you *could* call a student to your desk, hand her a compound microscope, and say, "Please name and point to the 12 parts of this microscope," record the number right, then call the next student and repeat the process, and so forth. P-r-e-t-t-y slow assessment. This is why paper-and-pencil tests were invented: to facilitate speedy, low-cost assessment of groups of people. There is no need to spend the time it would take to individually assess each student's knowledge of the parts of the microscope.

Identifying the taxonomy domain and level of the outcomes to be assessed is as important for performance and product assessment as it is for the paper-and-pencil variety for two reasons. First, you know from Chapter 5 that different level outcomes have different assessment requirements. This is true for those outcomes slated for performance testing as well. If you know the taxonomy level of the outcome, you can more easily structure the performance task to bring forth in the student the behavior you wish to observe. You can also more easily determine the appropriate judging criteria when you know the level of skill involved. And, if you are working with other teachers to create a grade-level or department-wide assessment, knowing the taxonomy level will facilitate clear communication.[4]

Developing the Performance Task

Most teachers report that developing performance tasks for their students takes time to do well. Creating good performance tasks may take a little effort, but it is certainly worth the practice to produce tasks that are interesting, challenging, and fair for all students and that are congruent with the intended instructional outcome(s). Developing a performance task involves two processes: structuring the task by identifying the necessary sub-tasks and writing the directions to students. The performance task may take many forms: students may engage in an individual assignment, a long-term group project, or an in-class exercise, for instance. Suppose that among the instructional outcomes for your students are the following:

- The student will work cooperatively with others in a learning group (affective).
- The student will solve real-life, multi-part problems using learned arithmetic skills (math, application).
- The student will effectively communicate ideas to others in a variety of contexts, including presentations, small-group work, and student-teacher interaction (language arts, synthesis).

Also suppose that the class has been working on measurement in math (including perimeter, area, and problem-solving processes) and on written and oral communication skills in language arts. You decide to assess the above skills by setting up a group problem-solving task that is based on resurfacing and re-striping the school parking lot. You engage the help of your city or county planning department for pertinent information on striping conditions and their relative advantages and disadvantages. The task might involve the following sub-tasks:

1. Calculating the average or maximum car length based on measuring a sample of the cars currently in the lot.
2. Finding the overall area of the parking lot.
3. Calculating the amount of resurfacing compound needed.
4. Figuring the number of cars that can be parked safely in the lot based on different striping conditions (straight vs. angle parking; single vs. double stripes; one-way vs. two-way traffic between rows of cars, etc.).
5. Choosing a striping scheme.

[4]Chapter 4 provides sufficient detail on how to write clear instructional outcomes and how to identify what type of learning is involved in a given outcome.

6. Figuring the amount of striping paint needed for the striping arrangement chosen.
7. Drawing a diagram of the group's solution.
8. Presenting the group's solution and rationale to the rest of the class.

Clearly, this is a fairly complex task, encompassing not only a number of math skills but also group problem solving and both verbal and visual communication skills. You are in the best position to decide if the task facilitates transfer of learning and if all of these skills are important to assess and to assess in this way. You must consider all of this in light of the time it will take for the students to understand their task, gather their data, generate a solution, and make their presentation. You may, for example, forgo the presentation, deciding that it is more important to observe the students' communication skills as they naturally interact in their work groups. This modification would maintain congruency between assessment and outcome, yet eliminate any class time associated with working on and making a presentation. It would also mean, however, that the students must do at least some of their group work during class time and that you must observe each student for some period of time as he or she participates. In other words, you cannot be off in another part of the room with a student or group working on something else entirely while the learning groups meet if you are to perform your observations adequately. If there are many other opportunities to observe students' communication skills, this outcome might be eliminated from the assessment entirely.

In developing the task, then, it is important to consider a number of factors: the nature of your students (their developmental levels and disabilities, for example); the nature, domain, and taxonomy level of the outcomes; and the time available for assessment. You may wish, for example, to provide alternative tasks from which students select one, providing all the performance alternatives call for the same behavior and are all congruent with the outcome(s) that spawned them. It may sound tempting to create one gigantic performance task that enables assessment of practically all the outcomes in a given unit of instruction. This practice can lead to trouble, however. The task can become overly complex for the students and a nightmare for you to structure and judge. Keep it relatively simple and flexible, especially the first time you try performance assessment.

The second part of creating the task is writing the directions to the students. In practice, teachers typically think of the sub-tasks and directions together, each informing the other as both are created. As they do for good essay items, the directions or prompts for performance tasks include what is to be done, how it is to be done, and any special conditions (like adhering to a budget). The directions also provide the context and information necessary for successful task completion. A good task reflects the outcome(s) it assesses. Directions communicate the structure of the task to your students, helping to make it authentic—more "real-life"—in their minds.

For maximum effectiveness, directions should be tailored to your students' needs. Written directions are especially helpful if the students are expected to work on the task outside of class or any time or place you will not be immediately available to give assistance. Parents appreciate being given a written reference when they ask their panicked son or daughter the night before a project is due, "Just what is it you were *supposed* to do?" On the other hand, oral directions in small doses may work better for younger students or for those with reading difficulties. You may, depending on the dimensions of the outcomes assessed, reserve some of the directions to be given out to students as clues if they ask the "right" questions. However they are presented, your directions to the students should be clear and help them understand the nature of the task and know what is expected of them. One way to accomplish this is to keep several actual students in mind and write the directions for them specifically: a low-achieving student, an average student, and a high achiever, for example. This will help you create directions that are clear to all your students, not just to yourself. By thinking through what these students are apt to do in response to your directions, you can evaluate whether your directions are likely to bring forth the desired behaviors, skills, and attitudes that you and your outcomes intend.

A factor to consider in structuring the task and writing the directions is the degree of realism needed to make the performance authentic. In the task you design, what is realistic and what is abstract or symbolic? Is taking off, flying, and landing an airplane in a flight simulator real enough? The Federal Aviation Administration thinks so, because commercial airline pilots with a jet rating who perform capably in a simulator are certified to carry passengers in the type of aircraft represented by the simulator, without actually having to sit in the cockpit of the real thing. The various maneuvers or tasks a pilot performs in an airplane simulator are very highly structured, as are the simulated conditions (like lightning strikes and engine loss) and the environment itself. The simulator provides enough realism to dependably test performance without endangering lives or risking the loss of very expensive equipment.

Now consider a somewhat more mundane instructional outcome:

Adds two to five decimals. Decimals may range from .01 to 20.00.

At one extreme, you can devise a paper-and-pencil test with short-answer items such as the following:

Add:

```
                                     14.59
  .10        5.43        10.98        3.02
 +.15       +2.07        +5.99       +1.71
```

. . . and so forth.

At the other extreme, you could set up and operate a classroom "store" so that students could purchase inexpensive items (like school supplies). They would select items, figure the cost of their purchases, and verify their change. The "proprietor" would sell items, figure the cost of purchases, return change, and perhaps even order stock. Somewhere between the two extremes might be the following: (1) using photocopies of money on a paper-and-pencil test and (2) word problems along the lines of "Willie went to the store to buy some school supplies. He bought . . ." Certainly the class store has more realism than the above symbolic, short-answer items, and playing "store" is a lot more fun than taking a test, as any informal survey of school children will verify. The four addition problems on a paper-and-pencil test, however, take much less time to administer and can be given to all students at the same time. They also present the same four tasks to all students, and so students may be compared across tasks, if desired. Photocopying money could have the Secret Service after you,[5] and word problems must be read and understood in a particular language, sometimes two, before solving.

Which approach is better for the "adds two to five decimals" outcome? The outcome does not specify or imply any particular item type or assessment approach. By itself, the outcome does not make a compelling case for performance assessment. Even if it did, to go to the trouble to set up a store, run it, and observe each student as a shopper or proprietor for the sake of "adds two to five decimals" seems to waste time that could be put to better instructional use. Performance assessment using a class-store scenario could, perhaps, be justified if other instructional outcomes could also be adequately and efficiently assessed with the same general task. This is where your creativity and flexibility in combining outcomes for assessment can be brought to bear. As you saw in the parking lot task, you are not limited to one outcome per task, nor must the outcomes come from a single discipline or taxonomic domain.

Tasks can also vary to the extent that they are structured or natural. If you have just fixed a leak in the joint where the bottom of your kitchen sink meets the drain pipe, for example, you can test your handiwork in two ways. The natural way would be to wait until you have a naturally occurring sink full of water—old greasy dishwater, perhaps—and let it drain. Of course, if the seal doesn't hold, you may have to bail the sink, mop the floor, or both, not to mention reseal the joint. Another more structured test would be to put some clean water in the sink immediately after fixing it and then let it drain, watching for leaks around the seal. Both methods will test the performance of the seal, but the structured performance has advantages without sacrificing validity. Some occasions in the classroom for observing student achievement of affective outcomes (such as works cooperatively with others) will occur naturally. Other outcomes may require a more structured situation to ensure the opportunity for the performance to occur.

Developing Judging Criteria

Judging criteria form the measuring stick against which we evaluate a student's performance. The higher the stakes of the assessment, the more crucial this step becomes, for without criteria, any performance would do. As Herman, Aschbacher, and Winters put it, "Scoring criteria make public what is being judged and, in many cases, the standards for acceptable performance. Thus, criteria communicate your goals and achievement standards."[6] They are also an essential part of any scoring scheme

---

[5]The U.S. Secret Service advises that it is legal to photocopy U.S. currency and coins ONLY if (1) the copies are made at least 1 1/2 times larger or 1/4 smaller than the real thing, AND (2) the copies are black and white, not color. So much for realism.

[6]J. L. Herman, P. R. Aschbacher, and L. Winters, 1992, p. 44.

✓ *Easy Reference Checklist*

Guidelines for Good Performance Tasks

- ❑ Is congruent with the purpose of the assessment.
- ❑ Elicits the behavior(s) at the level(s) specified in the instructional outcome(s).
- ❑ Is interesting, challenging, and fair for all students.
- ❑ Is authentic; promotes transferability of learning to real world.
- ❑ Includes only important outcomes that are appropriately assessed via performance or product.
- ❑ Adequately reflects intended outcomes.
- ❑ Is appropriate for developmental level of students.
- ❑ Directions include what is to be done, how, and under what conditions.
- ❑ Directions give enough information and context for successful task completion by all students.

and, therefore, essential to promoting reliability. The following terms have been used interchangeably with judging criteria: *scoring criteria, scoring guidelines, elements, scoring rubrics, rubrics, scoring schemes,* and *performance dimensions.* Judging criteria describe the important dimensions you want to be sure to observe when a student performs a task for assessment. One colleague calls them the "look fors" for this reason. But it is also important to remember that a performance or product may be sensed in other ways than by observation. Although the term *observe* is typically used, it is meant in the broader sense. A product of a cooking class, for example, in addition to being observed, may be tasted, smelled, touched, and even heard in the case of sizzling fajitas.

Here is an example of judging criteria from a statewide product assessment. *The Florida Writing Assessment: Grade 8 Spring 1995* uses the following categories of student performance criteria:

- Focus on the topic
- Development of supporting ideas or examples
- Command of the language
- Sentence structure
- Punctuation
- Capitalization
- Spelling[7]

[7] *Florida Writing Assessment Grade 8 Student Report: Writing to Explain* by Florida Assessment Writing Program, 1995, Tallahassee, FL: Department of Education.

All judging criteria for a performance assessment, including those mentioned above, are created by examining the following:

1. The behavior and criterion components of the instructional outcomes chosen for the assessment.
2. The nature of the assessment task.
3. The nature of the students.

If you have written your instructional outcomes in three-component format, with a condition, behavior, and criterion, this step becomes much easier. Using the parking lot re-striping task and its three related outcomes, we can generate some criteria upon which we can base good judgment of performance. Assume for this exercise that your students (those in a grade for whom the outcomes would be appropriate) will present their results to the class. Because there are three outcomes to be assessed, we need judging criteria for each. One way to start is to brainstorm the qualities and characteristics we would expect to see in an ideal performance or product. Cover the candidate criteria list (Figure 8.1) so you cannot read it while you generate your own list of judging criteria. Keep in mind the target students, the seven steps in the performance assessment design process, and the three outcomes involved as you brainstorm. After you are finished, compare your list to the one in Figure 8.1.

Do our lists look anything alike? Depending on the group of students you had in mind, your list might look somewhat different than the one in Figure 8.1. High-school drafting students would probably perform differently than sixth-graders, for example. If we were working together on a grade-level assessment, we would need to discuss and agree on the dimensions and criteria that should be included. The criteria in Figure 8.1 can also be grouped to reflect the following performance dimensions or categories of judging criteria:

Mathematical skills (1–8)

Quality of the solution (6, 9, 10)

Communication qualities of the diagram (11–13)

Communication qualities of the presentation (15–16)

Working with others in a task group (14, 17, 18)

Thus, the list would be considered multidimensional. Your list probably is also, although your criteria may not be the same criteria enumerated in the above list or in Figure 8.1 and may be grouped differently.

Once you have a list of candidate judging criteria, review it to make sure that there are criteria for each outcome involved and that only essential criteria are used when you observe your students perform or assess their products. When you (or others) judge performance, you must be focused because you cannot capture everything, no matter how good your powers of observation may be. A short, focused list makes the job easier, and you are less likely to try to capture everything, thereby missing some essentials. This is especially critical when you are observing a performance as it happens that is not being recorded. A tangible product may be reviewed a num-

Candidate Judging Criteria

1. Maximum car length or average car length is based on a sample of at least 10 cars of different sizes. Average car length should be somewhere between 13 ft. (Miata) and 17 ft. (Cadillac).
2. Overall area is correct to within 30 square feet.
3. Number of containers of compound is specified.
4. Number of compound containers specified is enough to cover the calculated area with less than a whole container left over.
5. The number of cars to be parked is accurate based on the striping/traffic conditions chosen.
6. Striping scheme chosen includes number of handicapped slots required by law.
7. Number of striping paint containers needed is specified.
8. Number of paint containers is enough to stripe the lot based on the chosen striping scheme with less than a whole container left over.
9. Striping scheme chosen increases the number of cars that can be parked in the lot by at least one.
10. Cars can maneuver safely into and out of parking slots and the lot.
11. Diagram accurately depicts parking lot shape.
12. Diagram visually reflects selected striping scheme but does not have to be drawn to scale showing the placement of each and every slot.
13. Diagram should be big enough to be used as a visual aid in a presentation to the class.
14. Presentation includes participation of each group member.
15. Presentation summarizes group's findings and recommendations: lot area, average length, striping scheme and rationale, number of new slots generated, number of cans of compound and paint needed.
16. Group uses diagram as visual aid in presentation.
17. During group work, sharing and cooperation are evident. (Evidence: taking turns in speaking and using supplies; all members are included, none isolated; each member has responsibilities and works to complete them.)

For individuals:

18. During group work, observed student works in a give-and-take manner in speaking and using supplies, offers help to others, and asks others for help or accepts help when needed to complete a task.

Figure 8.1
A list of candidate criteria based on an envisioned ideal performance for the parking lot re-striping problem.

ber of times, perhaps, but that is not necessarily an effective use of time. As you review your brainstormed list of criteria, the following questions can help guide your decision as to whether to keep a criterion on the list:

- Does it render operational the outcome it is intended to reflect?
- Is it "observable"?
- Is it appropriate for the intended students?
- Does it apply across contexts that call for similar behavior?

- Does it focus on the instruction students have had, not on prior learning?
- Is the criterion an essential one for judging performance adequately?
- Does it communicate (to parents, students, or other judges) what constitutes excellence?
- Do all of the criteria associated with a particular outcome sufficiently describe the critical aspects of performance? Do they specify what behaviors are necessary for a teacher to observe in order to determine a successful performance?

The more questions answered with a "yes," the more likely the criterion is to be useful in assessing student performance.

Now apply the questions to the list of candidate criteria in Figure 8.1. There appear to be two criteria that could be improved. Criterion 10 is not directly observable—we would have to wait until after the lot is finished to watch cars actually maneuver and navigate through the lot. A workable alternative might be that a successful re-striping scheme conforms to accepted guidelines (obtained from the planning department, perhaps) for safety and maneuverability. That is directly observable and requires little inference on the part of the judge. This revised criterion might appear as follows:

10. Re-striping scheme conforms to accepted guidelines for automobile safety and maneuverability (guidelines to be supplied by the county planning department).

Additionally, criterion 14 does not communicate the concept of participation very well. For example, if you were a judge for this performance, would you know intuitively that all of the following qualify as participation?

- Holding the diagram for the class to see and pointing to information as a teammate orally presents.
- Answering questions from classmates or the teacher.
- Orally presenting data, results, or other information.
- Making other visual aids that enhance the presentation.
- Writing a "script" for group members to follow or otherwise "stage managing" the presentation.

Maybe not. The revised criterion might appear as follows:

14. Each group member actively participates in the presentation. Active participation includes any one or more of the following:
    a. Orally presenting information.
    b. Answering questions from the audience.
    c. Holding the diagram and pointing to information as someone else presents.
    d. Making other visual aids that enhance the presentation.
    e. Writing the presentation "script."

It may or may not be desirable to inform your students of the scoring criteria, depending on the purpose of the assessment. For most academic achievement purposes, giving them a copy of the criteria or the actual instrument you will use in judging their work as part of the directions can have a very positive effect on their performances because they will know what you expect of them. For the parking lot example, you might at least tell students that their performance was to be judged on the following dimensions:

- The correctness of their calculations.
- The quality of their solution.
- How well their diagram and presentation communicate.
- How well they worked with others in their groups and in their presentation.

By doing so, you communicate that they must pay special attention to these areas if they are to do well. You provide guidance and direction that keeps them focused on the task. It is similar to providing a study guide or review in preparation for a written test. Sharing the criteria with the students is also appropriate if your purpose is to assess best, rather than typical, performance. When the purpose is to assess typical performance, however, it may not be desirable to inform the students of the criteria at least until after the assessment. For example, when assessing attitudes, it is important that students feel free to choose to behave according to their attitudes, not according to someone else's wishes. Otherwise the results of your observations are less than valid. It may even be desirable that the students not know they are being observed on certain dimensions while engaged in the given task so that they reflect their true attitudes.

Creating the Scoring Scheme

As you have probably discerned by now, a student performance, especially one that results in a product, is like an essay item in many ways. In fact, an essay can be considered a student product. A scoring scheme or rubric in performance assessment is also similar to a scoring scheme constructed for essay items. Both use judging criteria, both inform the judges (and others) as to what counts and how much, and both can enhance the reliability of the assessment results. Both can follow either the analytic or the holistic approach, both often result in an instrument for recording scores and comments, both require teachers to determine ahead of time how they will deal with performance factors irrelevant to the assessed outcome(s), and both can be shared with the students. Using your familiarity with essay scoring, you will be able to select and create performance assessment scoring schemes that work in the classroom.

Regardless of the type of scoring scheme used, your observations should be noted or recorded in some way. Observation instruments can help capture important information regarding a student's performance or product. The two most common observation instruments for implementing scoring schemes for both school children and adults are checklists and rating scales. A third, less-common way to gather assessment information about a student's performance or behavior is the anecdotal record.

✓ *Easy Reference Checklist*

Guidelines for Good Judging Criteria

Use the following to evaluate each criterion:

- ❑ Communicates essential achievement standards of the outcome(s) assessed.
- ❑ Operationalizes the outcome it is intended to reflect.
- ❑ Applies across contexts that call for similar behavior.
- ❑ Focuses on current instruction, not prior learning.
- ❑ Criterion is observable.
- ❑ Criterion is essential for judging performance of the task adequately.
- ❑ Communicates to others (parents, students, other judges, etc.) what constitutes excellence.
- ❑ Criterion is appropriate for the students.

Use the following to evaluate the criteria as a whole:

- ❑ Criteria are present for each outcome assessed.
- ❑ All criteria associated with an outcome sufficiently describe the critical aspects of performance—what is necessary to observe to determine successful performance.
- ❑ Criteria are shared with students when appropriate.

Understanding and Using Checklists

Checklists are observation instruments that divide performance into two categories: adequate and inadequate. They are widely used in a variety of settings, including performance assessment. One advantage of using a checklist is that it works well in describing what students can do with respect to the selected outcomes. Checklists also work well for checking the process of learning. In a cooking exercise, for example, you might use a checklist like the one in Figure 8.2. Checklists are preferred over rating scales (described in the next section of this chapter) when many elements must be assessed, because the evaluative decisions are simpler to make and the assessment instrument is easier to read.

One major problem with checklists, whether completed by students or by teachers, is observer bias, or response set. When used by students as a self-report instrument, situations exist in which they may not want to report their true feelings or behavior, but would rather report responses that they perceive to be socially acceptable or desired. To escape the disfavor of a teacher, for example, certain students might indicate on a study skills checklist that they did read the previous night's assignment

Procedure	✓ If Observed	Comments
Recipe read before starting		
Correct equipment used		
Safety precautions followed		
Measurements accurate		
Sought help if needed		
Cleaned up area afterward		

Figure 8.2
A checklist for cooking.

when, in fact, they did not. Whether observer bias results from conscious or unconscious motivations, it can seriously affect the interpretation of results.

Teachers' decisions on performances or products may be influenced by factors other than those actually being observed. Two such factors are the halo effect and the generosity error. The *halo effect* is the tendency of an observer to let overall feelings about a student affect responses to individual checklist elements. A teacher who thinks that a person is a "terrific student" may make more favorable checks and positive comments even though in reality the student may not, for example, always be well prepared for class. The *generosity error* is the tendency of an observer to give the person being observed the benefit of the doubt whenever the observer does not have sufficient knowledge to make an objective decision. Both the halo effect and the generosity error can work for or against the person being observed, and such factors seriously hamper proper interpretation of results. Another limitation of checklists is that they do not separate the top performers from those whose performance is barely adequate. Fine discriminations in behavior regarding a judging criterion are not possible to detect with checklists.

A basic checklist consists of two parts: the elements and the check boxes or lines. You have seen many of them in this and the preceding chapters summarizing guidelines for item construction and other procedures (as in Figure 2.2). To create checklists for performance assessments, the judging criteria are paraphrased and listed as the elements of the checklist. This is done for two reasons: first, these phrases provide a memory jog for the judge so that he or she knows what to look for; second, the short descriptions (sometimes only one or two words) decrease reading time and maximize observation time. The box or line next to each element provides a place for the observer to indicate quickly with a √ whether the element was present during the performance. In addition to the yes-box format you see in this text, there are double-column formats with headings such as "yes/no" (see Figure 8.3) and "adequate/inadequate." Some checklists include a third column, usually titled "unobserved," to distinguish between situations where the observer had no opportunity to observe the behavior and where performance was observed but judged to be inadequate.

Regardless of the headings used, judges should be clear as to the basis for the distinction between decisions represented by the column headings. All of the people who judge performance using the instrument should know the criterion behind each element and what a "yes" decision and a "no" decision mean regarding that element. It is also important that the elements, paraphrased from the judging criteria, are worded so that a judge's mark in the yes column, for example, indicates a positive score and a mark in the no column indicates a negative score. This allows the judge to quickly tally the number of yes checkmarks for an overall score, if desired. For example, consider the following partial checklist for a student making a class presentation:

	Y	N
1. Establishes eye contact	✓	
2. Fidgets		✓
3. Modulates voice	✓	
4. Does not "read" notes	✓	

This student performed adequately on all four elements. Notice how much easier it would be, however, to score the same student's performance if the wording were as follows:

	Y	N
1. Establishes eye contact	✓	
2. Avoids fidgeting	✓	
3. Modulates voice	✓	
4. Avoids "reading" notes	✓	

Here, a mark in the no column is an indication of less-than-adequate performance for all of the elements, and the number of yes checks is easily tallied, even for long lists of elements. Element four is reworded to eliminate the double negative in the case of a no check.

For ease of use, the elements on a checklist are typically ordered in some logical or natural fashion. When a procedure is involved, the elements are typically arranged in chronological order so that those tending to occur early in the performance are listed ahead of those that occur later. For a student-product checklist, clustering the elements that naturally go together is helpful. The elements from criteria in a particular dimensional category, for example, may be listed together, followed by the elements from the next category, and so on. Figure 8.3, based on the judging criteria created for the parking lot re-striping problem, is such a checklist. Notice that Figure 8.3 includes both procedural and product elements and reflects a number of modifications from the original candidate criteria list in Figure 8.1. First, criterion candidate five is listed in the quality of solution category, as is the criterion regarding handicapped slots (number six in Figure 8.1). Notice also that candidate criteria 17 and 18

Checklist for the Parking Lot Task			
Directions: If the element (1–18) meets standard, check Yes. If not, check No.			
Correctness of Calculations		**Yes**	**No**
	1. Sample $\geq$ 10.		
	2. Avg. length 13 ft. to 17 ft.		
	3. Overall area $\pm$ 30 sq. ft.		
	4. Number of compound containers specified.		
	5. $<$ a whole compound container left over.		
	6. Number of paint containers specified.		
	7. $<$ a whole paint container left over.		
Quality of Solution			
	8. Number of slots matches striping scheme.		
	9. Required handicapped slots included.		
	10. Number of slots increased.		
	11. Cars can maneuver safely.		
Communication Quality of Presentation and Diagram			
	12. Diagram reflects lot shape.		
	13. Diagram reflects striping scheme.		
	14. Diagram is a good visual aid.		
	15. Diagram used in presentation.		
	16. Findings and recommendations summarized.		
Working with Others			
	17. Sharing and cooperation evident in work groups.		
	18. Each student participates in presentation.		
	Total Yes Checks: _______		

Figure 8.3
Checklist based on judging criteria for parking lot problem.

from Figure 8.1 were collapsed into one element (17) based on the teacher's decision to observe groups as wholes rather than to select individual students for observation at work in the group. The Working with Others section of the checklist contains elements that would be observed at both ends of the chronological spectrum. The pilot test of the checklist will determine whether this is the best order for the elements.

The checklist in Figure 8.3 is arranged for easy scoring (at least for right-handed judges) and provides a place for tallying the number of "yes" checks. There is, however, no way to inform a student as to why a particular performance was checked "no," meaning the performance did not meet your standards. If you want observers to go beyond making a simple mark, it is best to provide a place for comments on

Checklist for the Parking Lot Task			
Directions: If the element (1–18) meets standard, check Yes. If not, check No.			
Correctness of Calculations		**Yes**	**No**
	1. Sample $\geq$ 10.		
	2. Avg. length 13 ft. to 17 ft.		
	3. Overall area $\pm$ 30 sq. ft.		
	4. Number of compound containers specified.		
	5. $<$ a whole compound container left over.		
	6. Number of paint containers specified.		
	7. $<$ a whole paint container left over.		
Quality of Solution			
	8. Number of slots matches striping scheme.		
	9. Required handicapped slots included.		
	10. Number of slots increased.		
	11. Cars can maneuver safely.		
Communication Quality of Presentation and Diagram			
	12. Diagram reflects lot shape.		
	13. Diagram reflects striping scheme.		
	14. Diagram is a good visual aid.		
	15. Diagram used in presentation.		
	16. Findings and recommendations summarized.		
Working with Others			
	17. Sharing and cooperation evident in work groups.		
	18. Each student participates in presentation.		
Comments (indicate element #):	Total "Yes" Checks: _______		

Figure 8.4
A checklist with a place for comments. Observers are reminded to write the number of the element to which their comments pertain.

the front side rather than the back. Flipping the checklist back and forth to write comments and check elements slows down the process, distracts you, and annoys the students being observed. For example, you may provide another, wider column for recording comments for each element (see Figure 8.2), or you may provide a box or space at the bottom of the checklist. Figure 8.4 illustrates a checklist with a comment box. When writing in a comment box, it is helpful to identify the element to which the comment relates.

Understanding and Using Rating Scales

A *rating scale* is a checklist that allows the assessor to record information on a scale, noting a finer distinction than just the presence or absence of a behavior. The elements derived from paraphrasing the performance-scoring criteria are still present, as is the forced choice, but the decision the judge or respondent must make is expanded. For each element, a scale representing a continuum of categories between two extremes is presented. Observers respond to the elements by placing a mark to indicate their judgment on each element. You saw an early example of a rating scale in Figure 2.2.

Rating scales are used for a variety of purposes in education. In addition to classroom performance assessment, they are also used in opinion polls; student, parent, and teacher surveys; and on personnel performance appraisals. They are used heavily with statewide student assessments where the ratings of two or more judges may be averaged for a final score on one or more dimensions as well.

Rating scales are preferred over checklists when assessors want to do more than merely note the presence or absence of a behavior. For example, item 17 on the checklist for the parking lot task (Figure 8.4) might be improved by giving it a four-point scale to distinguish between inadequate sharing and cooperation (0), minimum level (1), good level (2), and high level (3). In contrast, item 15 on the same list would not be improved by the addition of a numerical scale. Either the students use the diagram in their presentation or they don't. Rating scales tend to look more "official" than checklists, perhaps because of the numerical scales. But more official looking does not necessarily mean more valid or reliable. An official-looking, invalid rating scale can be a very dangerous instrument if people take it more seriously than a simpler-looking but more satisfactory checklist. Rating scales suffer the same limitations as checklists: observer bias, the halo effect, and generosity error. The addition of a scale does not eliminate these problems.

Theoretically there is no maximum number of categories or scale points. In practice, however, more than seven require overly difficult discriminations. It is desirable to identify differences among students, to be sure, but too many scale points make it difficult to differentiate with any degree of confidence. The following rating scale elements should illustrate these points:

Circle the number that best represents your feelings.

A. The topic of calculus is

1	2
Very Boring	Totally Fascinating

B. The topic of calculus is

1	2	3	4	5	6	7	8	9	10	11	12	13	14	15
Very Boring														Totally Fascinating

In item A you are forced to express an extreme position, much like the all-or-nothing yes-or-no of a checklist. If you think that calculus is "fairly interesting," you would probably choose "totally fascinating" as best representing your attitude,

1	2	3	4	5
Scribbles				Adds details (hair, ears, hands, etc.)
1	2	3	4	5
Scribbles	Draws a face	Adds arms/legs	Adds body with arms/legs	Adds details (hair, ears, hands, etc.)

Figure 8.5
Two rating scales for assessing drawing skills of kindergarten-age children.

given the two choices, but your choice would not reflect your true feelings. But in item B you have too many choices. If you assume that 8 represents a midway or neutral point, then "fairly interesting" would fall somewhere between 8 and 15, but where? Furthermore, is there really any reliable difference between the feelings of those who mark 12 and those who mark 13? Most people cannot make such a fine distinction even once, much less consistently. The results from item B would be very difficult to interpret. The distinctions between the decisions as reflected in the scale points should, therefore, be clear to all raters. Anchoring each scale point with words can accomplish this if the words are descriptive and convey the meaning of the rating to the judges. To illustrate, consider the two product rating scales in Figure 8.5 using judging criteria from the Profile of Developmental Outcomes for Kindergarten Literacy and Numeracy Skills.[8] The first rating scale in the figure contains five scale points, but only two word anchors—at the extremes. The second scale contains word anchors for all scale points. Combining the qualitative description with a quantitative scale enhances the usefulness of the rating scale for student feedback purposes. The words give meaning to the numbers for both the observer and the student. A teacher may rate a student differently depending on which of the two scales is used.

A student's performance is usually rated once, if at all. But performance may be rated more than once. At the time the observation and rating are made, the scale provides a record that describes the student's current performance level. If the observation and rating are repeated at times throughout the school year, the student's progress over time can be documented. The two methods have different purposes and each is valuable in its own way. Of course, a student's current performance level may be expressed in norm-referenced terms or in criterion-referenced terms. The criterion—actually criteria—are the important instructional outcomes upon which the assessment is based. Thus you may document Jerome's progress in lengthening his episodes of on-task behavior within a 3-week intervention period or explain to

[8]*Profile of Developmental Outcomes for Kindergarten Literacy and Numerancy Skills* by E. Jones and J. M. Roberts, 1990, Soledad, CA: San Vincente School District.

LeeAnn's parents her developing ability to work cooperatively with others in a group by comparing ratings from May with earlier ones from September and January. These approaches can also be used with the class as a whole by averaging the ratings on each element across the class.

To give you an idea of how differently ratings might be done, the elements from *The Florida Writing Assessment: Grade 8 Spring 1995* have been recast into two different scoring schemes. As you examine them in Figures 8.6 and 8.7, notice the similarities and differences between the two approaches. Think about how you would use each to judge a writing assignment.

The two schemes are similar in a number of ways. The words used in both are essentially the same, so the elements are comparable: Both are evaluative and qualitative. Both approaches direct the judges to consider each element in their scoring decision. They both also involve numerical ratings, allowing two or more trained readers to rate the writing samples and average their ratings to determine a student's score.

There are also a number of differences between the two scoring schemes. First, the basis for how points are determined is different for each. Figure 8.6 represents a holistic scoring scheme. An overall level of writing is described for each score point using all of the scoring criteria. Although discernably different criteria are used, no separate points for each criterion are given. The implied assumption behind these score-point categories is that a writer's ability on each of the criteria at one level is essentially the same. In other words, students who can substantially develop supporting ideas or examples, for example, should also be able to choose precise words to express themselves, focus on the topic, vary sentence structure, and, therefore, score a 6.0. In a perfect world this may be so, but such consistency does not always happen, and teachers must decide which of the six paragraphs in the scoring scheme is the best fit for the writing sample based on the included elements. The use of two trained readers provides a system of checks and balances and improves reliability somewhat. The analytic scoring scheme in Figure 8.7 allows judges to score and report the dimensions separately for each paper. The individual word anchors for the scale points increase precision and facilitate feedback when desired.

A second major difference is that the approach in Figure 8.6 does not identify specific errors. Thus, a student who obtains a 3.0 receives no indication of whether it was focus, organization, word choice, structure, mechanics, or some combination that prevented a higher score. The criteria are lumped together and attached to one holistic score. As you have probably gathered, this scoring scheme is not well suited for instructional use. It is, however, efficient for high-stakes, large-scale testing, which is the assessment's actual purpose. In standardized performance testing, the students are not expected to learn from their mistakes and improve their writing based on the assessment results. The scheme in Figure 8.7, in contrast, uses a very analytical approach to scoring writing samples. Each sample is rated separately on each scoring dimension. This approach permits very targeted feedback for the students. For example, if Marla's actual score is expressed as points earned in each area (for example, 4/3/2/2/2), she can tell at a glance her strengths and weaknesses.

Writing Sample Scoring Scheme I

Student's Name ____________________ Reader ____________________

Circle the number that best describes the sample based on the elements observed.

6.0 The writing focuses on the topic, is logically organized, and includes substantial development of supporting ideas or examples. It demonstrates a mature command of language, including precision in word choice. Sentences vary in structure. Punctuation, capitalization, and spelling are generally correct.

5.0 The writing focuses on the topic with ample development of supporting ideas or examples. It has an organizational pattern, though lapses may occur. Word choice is adequate. Sentences vary in structure. Punctuation, capitalization, and spelling are generally correct.

4.0 The writing focuses on the topic, though it may contain extraneous information. An organizational pattern is evident, but lapses may occur. Some supporting ideas contain specifics and details, but others are not developed. Word choice is adequate. Sentences vary somewhat in structure, though many are simple. Punctuation, capitalization, and spelling are usually correct.

3.0 The writing generally focuses on the topic, though it may contain extraneous information. An organizational pattern has been attempted, but lapses may occur. Some of the supporting ideas or examples may not be developed. Word choice is adequate. Sentences vary somewhat in structure, though many are simple. Punctuation and capitalization are sometimes correct, but most commonly used words are spelled correctly.

2.0 The writing may be slightly related to the topic or offer little relevant information and few supporting ideas or examples. There is little evidence of an organizational pattern. Word choice may be limited or immature. Sentences may be limited to simple constructions. Frequent errors may occur in punctuation, capitalization, and spelling.

1.0 The writing may only minimally address the topic because there is little or no development of supporting ideas or examples. No organizational pattern is evident. Ideas are provided through lists, and word choice is limited or immature. Unrelated information may be included. Frequent errors in punctuation, capitalization, and spelling may impede communication.

Figure 8.6
A six-point scoring scheme for a writing product assessment. *Source:* From *Florida Writing Assessment Grade 8 Student Report: Writing to Explain* by Florida Assessment Writing Program, 1995, Tallahassee, FL: Department of Education. Reprinted by permission. In this assessment, student papers are rated by two readers and the scores averaged. Thus a student may obtain a score of 3.5, for example, if the writing was rated a 3 by one reader and a 4 by the other.

Better yet, if she is given the completed rating sheet along with her paper, the elements and ratings themselves provide the feedback and save the judge from writing extensive comments.

Writing Sample Scoring Scheme II

Student's Name ____________________ Reader ____________________

Circle the number of your rating for each element. Consider the elements independent of each other.

Focus on the topic:

5 Focuses on topic; no extraneous information.
4 Generally focuses on topic; may contain extraneous information.
3 May be slightly related to topic; may contain extraneous information.
2 Offers little relevant information.
1 Only minimally addresses topic.

Development of supporting ideas or examples:

5 Substantial development of supporting ideas or examples.
4 Ample development of supporting ideas or examples.
3 Some supporting ideas or examples may not be developed.
2 Offers few supporting ideas or examples.
1 Ideas are offered through lists, if at all.

Command of the language:

4 Demonstrates mature command of the language, including precision word choices.
3 Word choice is adequate.
2 Some word choices may be limited or immature.
1 Word choice is limited or immature.

Sentence structure:

4 Sentences vary in structure.
3 Sentences vary somewhat in structure, though many are simple.
2 Sentences may be limited to simple constructions.
1 Unrelated information may be included.

Punctuation, capitalization, spelling:

5 All are generally correct.
4 Usually correct.
3 Punctuation and capitalization are sometimes correct, but most commonly used words are spelled correctly.
2 Frequent errors may occur in punctuation, capitalization, and spelling.
1 Frequent errors in punctuation, capitalization, and spelling may impede communication.

Figure 8.7
A multi-element, multi-point scoring scheme with word anchors. *Source:* From *Florida Writing Assessment Grade 8 Student Report: Writing to Explain* by Florida Assessment Writing Program, 1995, Tallahassee, FL: Department of Education. Reprinted by permission.

If the rating is used for instructional purposes only (and not entered into your gradebook) or if student progress is reported in terms of instructional outcomes mastered, expressing a student's score as points earned in each area is an excellent option. If, on the other hand, the assessment will be used in determining an overall grade in writing, it may be best to record the total points (13), but still write separate sub-scores on the student's paper for feedback purposes. Either way, with a scoring scheme such as the one shown in Figure 8.7, students may learn from their effort and improve their writing.

Understanding and Using Anecdotal Records

Another observational tool for teachers is the anecdotal record (see sample in Figure 8.8). Although its main use in the past has been to facilitate the assessment of a student's psycho-social adjustment, it can be useful in assessing such important outcomes as work habits and attitudes. An *anecdotal record* is a continuous description of student behavior as it occurs, recorded without judgment or interpretation. It provides a factual recounting of an incident but is not as structured as a checklist or rating scale. The incident may be a critical one (Terry's behavior in class following a trip to the principal's office for fighting, for example), or it may be a sampling across time. A time sampling consists of observations of behavior at various pre-scheduled time periods. After collecting the samples, the teacher may add his or her interpretation of the behavior or discuss it with other staff. Time samplings help teachers document *typical* behavior in students and are usually conducted at intervals over a period of time such as a month or a semester. A teacher may use this technique in working with other staff to determine a student's eligibility for a pull-out program, for example. Anecdotal records document student behavior so that teacher judgment is not based on selective or incomplete recall of past events; in this case, the descriptions of behavior would be used as part of the information for making the eligibility decision.

Anecdotal records have certain advantages and disadvantages as an assessment tool. One advantage is that anecdotal records allow teachers to observe significant behaviors that may be missed in a more structured approach. If the behavior is not listed on a rating scale, for example, a teacher might disregard it although it could be very important under the circumstances. Another related advantage is that anecdotal records can sharpen teachers' powers of observation and increase their awareness of those significant, but hard to capture, behaviors. Also, anecdotal records are particularly useful with very young elementary students and with students whose communication skills are deficient, because teachers can observe their behavior in a natural or structured setting and the students do not need to write or communicate in any special way.

A serious limitation of anecdotal records is the amount of time they take to record and manage. Scheduling observations and limiting them to certain behaviors can ease this somewhat, but it is still a time-consuming process. Another disadvantage is the small sample of behavior that usually results from anecdotal records. You recall from Chapter 3 that the larger the sample of behavior, the more likely it is to be rep-

Anecdotal Record

Student Vannessa Scott Date 11/19/97

Time Start 10:45 Time Stop 11:15 Observer Ms. Brown

Location/Setting Classroom

Observations:

Today, as students transitioned from language arts to the science center, Vannessa continued to read the story to herself. She was the last to get into position for our science demonstration, taking a full five minutes to do so. Although this has been true for the past two days as well as today, it is contrary to her usual behavior. She used to be the first one ready for science and squealed with glee as we "blew up Mt. Vesuvius" (her words) in the last science unit. Today, she kept asking about the safety equipment and questions irrelevant to the task. This is also the third day of our unit on the human body and the material is getting more difficult. (Is there a connection??)

Figure 8.8
An observational anecdotal record.

resentative of the student's real functioning level and the more reliable the results tend to be. A single, or even a few, observations may not present a true picture of the observed student. A further limitation is the difficulty of being objective in recording behavior. Separating a student's behavior from your interpretation of that behavior is no easy task. The very words you choose to describe the behavior can sway interpretation by others, for example.

Judicious use and correct recording of anecdotal records will not only strengthen their credibility but provide documentation of student behavior that may not be captured any other way. It is toward this end that the following guidelines are presented.

Do not make anecdotal records of student performance on important instructional outcomes with the intent of determining the scoring criteria after all students have performed, for example. A checklist or rating scale would be much more efficient as well as make the results more valid.

Confine observations to a few areas at a time so that you do not feel compelled to record everything that happens. By limiting the length of time you observe and the areas on which you concentrate your observation, you increase the validity of the results. An elementary teacher might concentrate on the social interaction patterns of a student in a cooperative group. A middle-school science teacher may concentrate on the time it takes students to set up an experiment. A high-school teacher may observe small work groups to determine how each goes about selecting a leader.

Anecdotal records may be recorded in a variety of ways, but the method chosen should be unobtrusive to the person(s) being observed and convenient for the observer. A relatively unobtrusive 3″ × 5″ card is handy and may be kept in a pocket, ready for recording at any time. Several cards may be used for one observation, if needed. A three-ring binder may be useful for organizing a number of observations of one or more students recorded on standard 8 1/2″ × 11″ paper. Electronic help in recording is also available. Some teachers have used lap-top computers and hand-held electronic notebooks to record their notes. Others prefer standard size or micro-cassette audio-cassette recorders. Teachers who use audio recorders usually find them convenient for unobtrusively capturing behavior at the moment it happens. Later, they transfer their recorded observations to paper or disk.

Whether observing individuals or groups, it is important to record behavior and only behavior. Interpretations and judgments about the behavior may come later, usually after a number of observations, so that a sample of behaviors may be analyzed at one time. Objectivity in recording is the responsibility of the observer. As Sergeant Joe Friday would say, "Just the facts, Ma'am, just the facts." Below, on the left, is a recording of behavior as it might appear on an anecdotal record. To the right are some possible interpretations of that behavior. The range of possible interpretations illustrates why objectivity is a concern and why it is so necessary to capture the behavior and reserve judgment.

Recorded Behavior	*Possible Interpretations*
"Rik had slid far down in his seat so that he rested the base of his head on the back of the chair. The others in the group were hunched over their seats and talking among themselves."	Rik is tired, lazy, comfortable. Rik doesn't care. The group is talking about Rik. The others are engaged in learning; Rik is not. The group is gossiping, but Rik is thinking about the instructional activity. Rik can't see the monitor well. And so on.

Without the recorded behavior, judgments and interpretations may be perceived as having little basis in reality. "Behavior" may be interpreted broadly as the following examples illustrate:

- Behavior of the weather at the time of observation. (Example: "It was pouring down rain as the students ran to their buses.")
- Descriptions of physical arrangements and settings. (Example: "The desks were arranged so that in a group of four students, each sat next to a partner, across from another partner, and kitty-corner from the other—see diagram. There were 8 groups of 4 and 1 group of 3 = 35.")
- Descriptions of events as they happen. (Example: "On the first day of school after the storm, Marielo brought a small stuffed dog. He held it or dragged it practically everywhere he went: on the playground, to the cafeteria, to the library. When I asked him about it, he said that he didn't 'have a real one anymore.' He said he had lost his pet during the storm.")

✓ *Easy Reference Checklist*

Guidelines for Scoring Schemes

General:

- ❑ Scoring approach (analytic or holistic) is congruent with assessment purpose.
- ❑ Scoring scheme based on judging criteria for performance task.
- ❑ Scoring scheme uses instruments to record assessment information where possible.
- ❑ Judges are familiar with the scheme and any related instruments.
- ❑ Judges agree on meaning of criteria.

Checklists:

- ❑ Elements paraphrase yet convey the meaning of the judging criteria.
- ❑ Distinction between response categories is clear.
- ❑ "Yes" reflects a positive result.
- ❑ Double negatives are avoided.
- ❑ Elements are ordered logically.
- ❑ Checklist requires no writing.
- ❑ If used, comment box appears on front side.

Rating Scales:

- ❑ Elements paraphrase yet convey the meaning of the judging criteria.
- ❑ Distinction among response categories is clear.
- ❑ Word anchors are used for each rating-scale point.
- ❑ Judges agree on meaning of scale-point anchors.

Anecdotal Records:

- ❑ A more efficient observation instrument is not feasible or available.
- ❑ Method of recording works for observed individual(s) *and* observer.
- ❑ Record contains pertinent identifying information (names of observed and observer, date, location, etc.).
- ❑ Observation is limited to a few important areas.
- ❑ During observation, only behavior is recorded.
- ❑ Judgment and interpretation are reserved until after full observation period is complete.

Pilot Testing the Assessment

Once you have constructed a performance assessment, consider it a draft or prototype. It should be pilot tested to identify the "bugs" in the task and scoring scheme. Just as with a paper-and-pencil assessment, students may find directions unclear, you may encounter unanticipated student responses, or you may find your scoring scheme unworkable. Although it is best to try out your prototype with a few students and revise it before unleashing it on the larger group, this may not be feasible. As an alternative, submit the assessment documents—instructional outcomes, scoring criteria, task description/directions, and scoring scheme instruments—for review by a knowledgeable and trusted colleague who can suggest improvements. Even though you have worked very hard to create the perfect assessment, another pair of eyes (or two, or three) can enhance the final product. Consider the review as a developmental assessment of your product and give your colleagues the guidelines in this text for judging criteria to aid their effort.

Even if you have piloted the assessment or had it reviewed by colleagues, the first time you administer the assessment, do not put too much weight on the results. Even the best-conceived assessments, like good red wines, improve over time. Consider the assessment a work-in-progress and make notes every time you administer it so that you can refine it. During pilot testing and on initial full-scale use, be sure to do the following:

- Examine the actual match between the outcomes and the scoring criteria.
- Determine what type of trouble students had, if any, in understanding the task and directions.
- Note problems in observing students perform or in reviewing their products.
- Weigh the actual value of the observations in determining students' achievement or attitude or the usefulness of the scores for the intended audience(s).
- Consider the timing of the assessment in the instructional sequence.
- Note actual time, space, and other resource requirements.
- Think about what the other, non-observed students should be doing during the observations.

An effective way to gather this information is to ask questions. For example, after the assessment you may ask students what problems they had getting started and whether the task directions were clear or in a logical sequence for them. They may also be able to tell you the usefulness (to them) of the results. If the results are to be shared with a student's future teachers, you may ask a teacher in the next grade level to review the completed score sheet for ease of interpretation, value of the observations, and so forth. If other observers were involved, they should be asked for their input as well.

Revising Performance Assessments

When pilot testing a performance assessment, you gather data consisting of the notes you have taken on the administration of the assessment and on the assessment results of the students you have observed. Reflecting upon this information will help you determine what revisions are necessary to improve the assessment for the next group of students. You may find that incomplete student products or low scores stem from confusing directions, for example. Or, another teacher may not interpret the scores as you intended and may suggest a modification in the scoring scheme. When working with other teachers on a grade- or department-wide assessment, it is important to build consensus on the necessary revisions. The revisions should enhance the purpose, process, or results for all those who must use it. For example, if a particular revision will make scoring faster but also render the results uninterpretable, it probably should not be made.[9]

Creating Student Assessors

Understanding Self-Assessment and Peer Assessment

In the past, assessment was done typically by teachers and other school staff. A reading specialist, for example, would conduct an assessment of a student to diagnose a reading difficulty. A teacher would work with a school psychologist in observing a student's behavior to determine an individual educational program. Paper-and-pencil tests were administered by teachers to determine achievement levels of their students. All of this, of course, is still done today, but the pool of assessors has been expanded to include students themselves. Many students are now taught how to assess their own products and processes and how to assess those of others. They are also taught how to give meaningful feedback to their peers regarding their peers' performance. They even edit each other's written work, and not just in journalism class. Moreover, many are taught how to receive feedback and use it to improve their own work. These occurrences reflect a change from an individualistic, competitive classroom atmosphere to a more cooperative learning environment. Instead of students vying with each other for grades, they coach each other for optimum performance. Some teachers actually use the term *coach* to describe peer assessors and *coaching* to describe the peer-assessment process to their students. This is somewhat curious, as coaches assess, measure, and evaluate their charges all the time and can be extremely critical while doing so. Perhaps in certain circles the term *coach* has a more positive connotation than *peer assessor*.

Using Guidelines for Successful Self- and Peer Assessment

The notion of students as assessors carries with it a responsibility that should not be taken lightly by either the students or the teacher. Most people would agree that children should grow into self-regulating adults and that teaching self-assessment techniques to students can promote this type of growth. Not all experts agree,

---

[9]Using assessment data to improve the assessments is discussed in more detail in Chapter 10.

however, that students can or should evaluate their peers. Certainly if the outcome is that some students are picked on or if teachers never help their students accept feedback and other's suggestions, then students assessing students will be a negative experience both academically and emotionally for all involved. Teachers who feel that peer assessment is a worthy endeavor have the responsibility to provide the environment, the instruction, and the encouragement for students to succeed as discerning observers, tactful feedback givers, and gracious feedback receivers. The guidelines below should help teachers who wish to turn their students into competent assessors.

1. *Do not make peer assessments count for a grade.* Grading is a part of the teacher's job that should not be abdicated and certainly should not be loaded onto the students' shoulders. Peer assessments can be meaningful for developmental purposes and for improving work in draft stages. Students should not, however, be forced to assign a grade based on their assessment of another's work, nor should teachers rely solely on the observations of others in making a grading decision. For example, whether a student's performance was assessed by one or more of his peers, his teacher must also observe and assess his performance before assigning a grade.

2. *Foster a collaborative spirit.* Peer assessment, especially when coupled with a classroom atmosphere of individual competitiveness, can be viewed as a sniper's license by students who wish to eliminate the competition. If you have traditionally encouraged individual competition in your classroom, implementing this guideline will be a major change in your teaching approach. A collaborative atmosphere encourages students to work with others, helping and receiving help as appropriate. It also encourages students to see each other as partners in the learning enterprise rather than as competitors for a particular grade. If you still feel that a little healthy competition never hurt anyone, make the competition among teams of students rather than among individuals.

3. *Help students make continuous improvement a goal.* As teachers, we know that it is important for students to work toward high but achievable goals. If students can internalize the goal of continuous improvement, they may be more willing to critically appraise their own work and take seriously the suggestions offered by others. It may also help an overly self-critical student move away from always finding fault and toward self-affirmation and self-improvement.

4. *Focus the assessment on the product or performance, not on the worth of the student.* Being able to separate one's work from one's self is a mark of a mature person, regardless of age. Teachers can help students achieve this focus by asking, for example, "How can this be better?" rather than declaring, "You are not a very good student." The latter statement is a pronounced judgment. The former communicates several things: that improvement is desirable, that improvement is dependent in part on good feedback and suggestions, and that the focus is on the outcome, not the student. This focus can help students get past personality, popularity, and the like to use the judging criteria as they were intended.

5. Include strengths, weaknesses, and specific suggestions for improvement in assessment feedback. High-stakes assessments do not typically include this type of feedback. It is vital, however, for maximizing the instructional value of classroom performance assessments. This can be accomplished, in part, through the use of instruments like rating scales. The higher the rating on a criterion, the more of a strength it is for the student; the lower the rating, the more of a weakness. Suggestions can be written in an area reserved for that purpose. When instruments are not used, however, and students give feedback orally, they should begin with the strengths of the performance or product, followed by observed weaknesses, which should be stated as specifically as possible, and followed, in turn, with specific suggestions for improvement. Here is an example sequence of feedback that one student, Ron, might give to another student, Jon, who just finished delivering a speech to the class.

> Ron: I liked the joke you told at the beginning. It was funny, and it loosened us up a little. It was even related to your topic. I don't know whether you noticed it or not, but you kept jingling the change in your pocket. Maybe you were just nervous, but sometimes I would think about it and not about what you were saying. Maybe you could take all the stuff out of your pockets before you go up the next time.
>
> Jon: Thanks for the tip.

6. Provide the judging criteria to the students and discuss what they mean. If students are to judge performance with a discerning eye, they must acquire the skills necessary. They must know what to look at and what to look for. Regardless of who assesses, judging criteria should be provided to the performers in most cases, with a few exceptions previously discussed in this chapter. The criteria should be presented in terms meaningful to them so that there can be agreement among the students in their observations. The wording of the criteria and fineness of the discriminations appropriate for judgment will depend on the developmental level of the students. An alternative to the teacher creating the judging criteria alone is to guide the students in their generation. This promotes self-assessment and analytical skills, and it gives students a sense of ownership of the process and the criteria.

7. Teach students how to use observation instruments such as checklists and rating scales. If the assessment can be facilitated with one of these instruments, it should be provided and students should be trained in its use. These instruments are as helpful to student observers as they are to teachers. Be aware, however, that training students to be effective observers and assessors is an instructional enterprise itself and will take time. Herman, Aschbaker and Winters estimate that it takes 3 to 4 hours to train raters using a process that includes orientation to the assessment task, clarification of the scoring criteria, practice in observing/scoring and recording, and dealing with unanticipated responses.[10]

8. Teach self-assessment first and have students practice it before asking them to assess others. Students who are adept at assessing themselves and reflecting on their own work are more likely to do a good job assessing others. They already have some

[10] J. L. Herman, P. R. Aschbacher, and L. Winters, 1992.

training and practice. They learn these self-assessment techniques, as they do other skills, by observing a competent performer—you. You can guide them in acquiring evaluation-level skills by encouraging them to reflect upon their performance and identify what they did well and what specific things they might do differently next time to improve. You can demonstrate what to do by using the checklists and rating scales that you use when you are the assessor. Once they are successful using judging criteria and instruments on themselves and accepting feedback from you, they will have the prerequisite skills to assess others. You must still teach them how to look past personality, popularity level, personal relationships, and personal differences—and raging hormones, in the case of post-pubescent adolescents—to be as objective as possible in their appraisals of others' performance.

✓ *Easy Reference Checklist*

Guidelines for Students as Assessors

- ❑ Students work in a collaborative spirit.
- ❑ Students see continuous improvement as a goal.
- ❑ Assessment focuses on the product or performance rather than on the worth of the student.
- ❑ Strengths, weaknesses, and specific suggestions for improvement are included in the assessment.
- ❑ Students are aware of the judging criteria and what they mean.
- ❑ Students are trained in the use of observation instruments.
- ❑ Students have practiced self-assessment before assessing others.
- ❑ Peer assessments are used for developmental feedback purposes only (not for a grade).

Revisiting Validity and Reliability

Performance assessment can appear to have high congruency with instructional outcomes and can appear to provide a more direct measurement of those outcomes than more indirect, objective tests. These features are part of the attraction of performance assessment and give it the potential to increase the validity of the results. Appearances are not everything, however. Face validity does not ensure psychometric quality whether the assessment approach is direct or indirect. Linn, Baker, and Dunbar[11] propose eight evaluation criteria for judging the worth of

[11]"Complex, Performance-Based Assessment: Expectations and Validation Criteria" by R. L. Linn, E. L. Baker, and S. B. Dunbar, 1991, *Educational Researcher, 20*(8), pp. 15–21.

performance assessments. Although they were developed primarily through their experience with high-stakes, large-scale performance assessments, many of the criteria apply to classroom assessments either constructed specifically for the students and circumstances at hand or borrowed from another source. The criteria include:

Consequences—Having learned the hard way that standardized, objectively scored tests can be compromised, we cannot assume that performance assessments are immune to "teaching the test" or other corruption. The intended and unintended effects of the performance assessment approach should be examined to ensure that the former are achieved and the latter are not.

Fairness—The assessment task and the scoring procedures must be fair for all students regardless of race, socio-economic class, and other social constructs. Trained, impartial observers play a critical role in ensuring fairness.

Transfer and generalizability—Research[12] has found that performance is likely to be task dependent. Evidence must be gathered to justify the generalization from a highly specific task to a domain of achievement, in one discipline or across several disciplines.

Cognitive complexity—To ensure a cognitively complex task, teachers must attend to the intended taxonomic level of the outcomes on which the performance assessment is based, as well as analyzing the processes students use to complete the task. Like meaningless facts, processes too can be memorized.

Content quality—The tasks chosen should deserve the time and effort spent by all involved in designing, completing, and scoring them.

Content coverage—Both depth and breadth of coverage are important and contribute to transfer and generalizability of the results.

Meaningfulness—Because performance assessments are task dependent, teachers should consider whether the task has meaning from the students' perspective.

Cost and efficiency—The assessment should minimize cost and maximize efficiency.

Reliability issues are particularly nettlesome for performance assessment, due to the extent of human judgment required in the scoring and the number and type of assessments it may take to confidently estimate a student's true functioning level. If followed, the guidelines in this chapter will help ensure a reasonable degree of reliability in classroom performance assessments. Further research needs to be done to reveal improved techniques for increasing the quality and credibility of performance assessment.

---

[12]See, for example, *What Alternative Assessments Look Like in Science* by R. J. Shavelson, G. P. Baxter, and J. Pine, October 1990. Paper presented at Office of Educational Research and Improvement Conference, The Premise and Peril of Alternative Assessment, Washington, DC.

✓ *Easy Reference Checklist*

Guidelines for Valid and Reliable Performance Assessments

- ❑ *Consequences*—Intended effects are achieved. Unintended effects are avoided.
- ❑ *Fairness*—The assessment is fair for all students.
- ❑ *Transfer and generalizability*—Results generalize to a domain of achievement.
- ❑ *Cognitive complexity*—Task is sufficiently complex.
- ❑ *Content quality*—Task is worthwhile.
- ❑ *Content coverage*—Task is sufficiently deep and broad to facilitate transfer and generalizability of the results.
- ❑ *Meaningfulness*—Students regard the task as meaningful.
- ❑ *Cost and efficiency*—Performance assessment is the most efficient, cost-beneficial way to assess the outcome(s) in question.

Source: From "Complex, Performance-Based Assessment: Expectations and Validation Criteria" by R. L. Linn, E. L. Baker, and S. B. Dunbar, 1991, *Educational Researcher, 20*(8), pp. 15–21.

Selecting and Developing Performance Assessments

The middle-school science teachers and curriculum specialist in Mrs. Brubaker's district spent some of their summer reforming the curriculum to include more basic physics as a response to the new high-school curriculum. Their list of outcomes created for eighth grade included the following outcome: Demonstrate how simple machines (inclined plane, lever, pulley, wheel, and axle) work.

One August evening, as she sat in the audience watching a summer-stock production of a Broadway play, it occurred to Mrs. Brubaker that a theatrical stage incorporated many simple machines. She thought it might be exciting for her students to create a stage and set to demonstrate the use of various types of simple machines. Later, as she began to work on the details, she realized that 32 stage sets, each on a $2' \times 2'$ piece of plywood or other stiff platform, would get boring after about the second demonstration, so Mrs. Brubaker thought of other integrated uses of simple machines. Playground equipment immediately came to mind, followed by a house and a moving truck. All of these were suggestions she could list on a handout to start students' thinking about the project. They could use those ideas or come up with their own, as long as they met the criteria that she would also list in the handout. Mrs. Brubaker also realized that some students might not be able to afford the cost of materials, so she suggested to her students that they keep costs to a minimum, using scrap lumber and other materials from family attics, basements, garages, and sheds where possible.

In another middle school in the same district, Mr. Kerr, also a science teacher, remembered reading an article about assessing the learning of physics principles in a science teaching magazine to which he subscribed. In it the author described a performance assessment she had constructed that required students to invent new uses for simple machines by making a labor-saving or other useful device that incorporated at least three machines. After rereading the article and contacting the author to iron out some of the details, he used the assessment in his class. Both Mrs. Brubaker and Mr. Kerr felt that the outcome of demonstrating how simple machines work was an important one in the assessment of their students' achievement in physics. They both had choices in how they went about the assessment as no district-wide assessment had been created for their use.

If, as Mr. Kerr found for himself, perfectly good, uncopyrighted performance assessments exist for the valued outcomes you wish to assess, by all means use them or adapt them for use with your students. If, as Mrs. Brubaker found, a perfectly good assessment is in your head, then construct your own. The information contained in this chapter can help you select or create the assessment; the guidelines for constructing good performance assessments can also be used as criteria for judging the quality of existing assessments with potential for use in your classroom.

There are a number of sources of assessments in many disciplines and across disciplines you can use as resources when designing a curriculum that includes performance assessments. Although not exhaustive, a list of contacts regarding performance assessments might include the following:

- Your peers in your school and district.
- Your district's curriculum and assessment specialists.
- Curriculum and assessment specialists in a nearby district.
- The head of assessment for your state's department of education.
- Heads of assessment for states that have statewide performance assessments (California, Connecticut, Florida, Kentucky, and Vermont, to name a few).
- Professional educational journals and magazines.
- Professional educational associations such as:
  The Association for Supervision and Curriculum Development (ASCD)
  1250 N. Pitt St.
  Alexandria, VA 22314

  The National Council on Measurement in Education (NCME)
  1230 17th St. NW
  Washington, DC 20036-3078

  The Center for Research on Evaluation, Standards, and Student Testing (CRESST)
  UCLA Center for the Study of Evaluation
  10880 Wilshire Blvd., Suite 700
  Los Angeles, CA 90024-1394

  The U.S. Department of Education
  600 Independence Ave. SW
  Washington, DC 20202

Summary

Understanding Performance and Product Assessment

Assessing student performances and products is not a new concept in education, although interest in the concept has been rekindled in recent years. The shift in societal interest toward higher-level thinking skills (like problem solving) and real-life application of skills and knowledge outside the narrow context of the instructional setting, coupled with increasing dissatisfaction among some educators with standardized, multiple-choice testing, has caused many in education to reexamine their assessment practices and seek alternatives.

Many terms have been used to describe different aspects of the assessment of a student's performance or a product of his creation: *authentic* assessment, *alternative* assessment, *direct* assessment, *portfolio* assessment, and *performance* assessment all refer to alternatives to multiple-choice standardized achievement tests. The range of what is considered a performance or a product is quite vast across the disciplines represented in the pre-K–12 curriculum. Typically, the performance must be observed as it happens or at least recorded for later review. Products are the more tangible items of the students' creation that can be viewed or otherwise sensed by the teacher. Whether a teacher assesses a performance, a product, or both should depend on the instructional outcomes that are valued.

Performance assessment has many advantages:

1. Compared to selected-response and short-answer items, performance assessment provides a more direct way to assess many complex instructional outcomes.
2. The approach can be used to improve instructional practice.
3. Students can be actively involved in the interaction of assessment and instruction.
4. Students and teachers are encouraged to move beyond the "one and only one right answer" mentality because multiple correct responses are possible as long as they meet the scoring criteria.

Disadvantages of performance assessment include:

1. Performance tests take more time to create and to score.
2. It is an extremely cost-inefficient way to assess knowledge- and comprehension-level instructional outcomes.
3. Performance assessments, like essay items, suffer from notoriously low reliability for many of the same reasons.
4. It is difficult to incorporate all the conditions and elements relevant to real-life use, thus making the assessment less than authentic.
5. There may be little or no support or resources for performance assessment in the school or community.

Using Guidelines to Construct Well-Designed Performance Assessments

Because of the time and other resources consumed in producing and conducting performance assessments, it is especially important that they be well constructed. The steps in designing a performance assessment are:

1. Determine the purpose of the assessment.
2. Determine what skills and outcomes the assessment will cover and specify in detail, including taxonomic domain and level.
3. Develop a task that is illustrative of and calls for the behavior specified in the outcomes. Record the task and write directions for the students.
4. Determine judging criteria.
5. Create the scoring scheme.
6. Pilot test the assessment.
7. Revise the outcomes, the task, the judging criteria, and the scoring scheme as necessary based on pilot-test data.

The process of designing a performance assessment is iterative rather than linear. Performance assessment may be used for formative or summative purposes and may also be used to evaluate "typical" or "best" behavior. Clearly defined instructional outcomes are the backbone of good performance assessment, and performance assessment may incorporate one or a meaningful cluster of outcomes from one or more disciplines. Outcomes assessed using performance assessment should be at the application level of the cognitive domain or higher or in the psychomotor domain; otherwise, the method is too time consuming and costly for the benefit gained. Identifying the taxonomy domain and the level of the outcomes to be assessed is as important for performance and product assessment as it is for the paper-and-pencil variety of assessments.

Developing the task involves two processes: structuring the task by identifying the necessary sub-tasks and writing the directions to students. In developing the task, it is important to consider a number of factors: the nature of the students (their developmental levels or disabilities, for example); the nature, domain, and taxonomy level of the outcomes; and the time available for assessment. Specific guidelines for developing good performance tasks include:

1. Tasks should be congruent with the purpose of the assessment.
2. Tasks should elicit the behavior(s) at the level(s) specified in the instructional outcome(s).
3. Tasks should be interesting, challenging, and fair for all students.
4. Tasks should be authentic and promote transferability of learning to the real world.
5. Tasks should include only important outcomes that are appropriately assessed via performance or product.

6. Tasks should adequately reflect the intended outcomes.
7. Tasks should be appropriate for the developmental level of the students.
8. Include in the directions what is to be done, how, and under what conditions. Give enough information and context for successful task completion by all students.

Judging criteria form the measuring stick against which we evaluate a student's performance. Judging criteria for a performance assessment are created by examining the behavior and criterion components of the instructional outcomes chosen for the assessment, the nature of the assessment task, and the nature of the students who must perform. Specific guidelines for individual judging criteria are that each criterion should:

1. Communicate essential achievement standards of the outcome(s) assessed.
2. Operationalize the outcome the criterion is intended to reflect.
3. Apply across contexts that call for similar behavior.
4. Focus on current instruction, not prior learning.
5. Be observable.
6. Be essential for judging performance of the task adequately.
7. Communicate to others (parents, students, and other judges) what constitutes excellence.
8. Be appropriate for the students.

Further, the set of judging criteria associated with a performance assessment should:

1. Be present for each outcome assessed.
2. Sufficiently describe the critical aspects of performance—what is necessary to observe to determine successful performance.
3. Be shared with students when appropriate.

Some general guidelines for scoring schemes are:

1. Make the scoring approach (either analytic or holistic) congruent with the assessment purpose.
2. Base the scheme on judging criteria for the performance task.
3. Use observation instruments to record assessment of performance where possible.
4. Familiarize judges with the scheme and any related observation instruments.
5. Ensure agreement among judges on meaning of criteria.

The two most common scoring schemes for both school children and adults are checklists and rating scales. A third, less-common observational tool is the anecdotal record.

A *checklist* divides performance into two categories: adequate and inadequate. Advantages of checklists include:

1. They work well in describing what students can do with respect to the selected outcomes.
2. They are good for checking the process of learning.
3. They accommodate a large number of elements.

Disadvantages of checklists include:

1. Observer bias or response set.
2. They do not separate the top performers from the barely adequate performers.
3. They do not permit fine discriminations in behavior.

Checklists are preferred over rating scales when many elements must be assessed because the decisions are not as difficult to make and checklists can be read more quickly. A basic checklist consists of two parts: the elements and the check boxes or lines. A place for comments may also be included. Specific guidelines for creating good checklists are:

1. Paraphrase yet convey the meaning of the judging criteria in the elements.
2. Clearly distinguish between response categories.
3. "Yes" should reflect a positive result.
4. Avoid double negatives.
5. Logically order the elements.
6. The checklist should require no (or very little) writing.
7. If used, the comment box should appear on front side of the checklist.

Rating scales are used for a variety of purposes in education in addition to performance assessment: surveys, opinion polls, personnel performance appraisals, and statewide student assessments. A rating scale is an expanded checklist that includes for each element a numbered scale representing a continuum of categories between two extremes. The extremes and the scale points are usually attached to word anchors. Advantages of rating scales include:

1. They permit finer discriminations in behavior.
2. Numerical scales permit numerical scores for students.

One disadvantage of rating scales is that, like checklists, rating scales suffer from observer bias, the *halo effect,* and *generosity error.* Specific guidelines for creating rating scales are:

1. Paraphrase yet convey the meaning of the judging criteria in the elements.
2. Clearly distinguish among response categories.
3. Use word anchors for each rating-scale point.
4. Ensure agreement of judges on the meaning of the scale-point anchors.

An *anecdotal record* is a continuous description of student behavior as it occurs, recorded without judgment or interpretation. It provides a factual recounting of an incident but is not as structured as a checklist or rating scale. Anecdotal records document student behavior so that teacher judgment is not based on selective or incomplete recall of past events. Advantages of anecdotal records are:

1. They allow teachers to observe significant behaviors that may be missed in a more structured approach.
2. They can sharpen teachers' powers of observation and increase their awareness of those significant but difficult-to-capture behaviors.
3. They are particularly useful in natural settings with very young elementary students and with students whose communication skills are deficient.

Disadvantages of anecdotal records are:

1. They are tremendously time consuming and labor intensive to record and manage.
2. They typically yield a small sample of behavior.
3. It is difficult to be objective in recording behavior.

Specific guidelines for anecdotal records include:

1. Do not use an anecdotal record if a more efficient observation instrument is feasible or available.
2. Ensure that the method of recording works for observed individual(s) *and* the observer.
3. Include pertinent identifying information (names of observed and observer, date, and location, for instance).
4. Limit observation to a few important areas.
5. During observation, record only behavior.
6. Reserve judgment and interpretation until after the full observation period is complete.

It is best to try out the prototype assessment with a few students first and revise it before unleashing it on the larger group, but submitting the assessment documents for review by a knowledgeable and trusted colleague who can suggest improvements is a practical alternative. The results of a performance assessment should be given little weight, if any, the first time it is administered. The following types of data are important to collect during pilot testing and on initial use:

1. The actual match between the outcomes and the scoring criteria.
2. The type of trouble students had, if any, understanding the task and directions.
3. Problems in observing students perform or in reviewing their products.
4. The actual value of the observations in determining students' achievement or attitude.

5. Logistical issues, such as the timing of the assessment in the instructional sequence; the actual time, space, and resource requirements; and what the other, non-observed, students should be doing during the observations.

When working with other teachers on a grade- or department-wide assessment, building consensus on the necessary revisions is important. Revisions to an assessment should enhance the purpose, process, or results for all those who must use it.

Creating Student Assessors

Many students are currently being taught how to assess their own products and processes, how to assess those of others, how to give meaningful feedback to their peers regarding their peers' performance, how to receive feedback, and how to use feedback to improve. Not all experts agree that students can or should evaluate their peers. Teachers who feel that peer assessment is a worthy endeavor have the responsibility to provide the environment, the instruction, and the encouragement for students to succeed as discerning observers, tactful feedback givers, and gracious feedback receivers. Specific guidelines for assessment by students are:

1. Do not make peer assessments count for a grade.
2. Foster a collaborative spirit.
3. Help students make continuous improvement a goal.
4. Focus the assessment on the product or performance, not on the worth of the student.
5. Include strengths, weaknesses, and specific suggestions for improvement in the assessment feedback.
6. Provide and discuss the judging criteria with the students.
7. Teach students how to use observation instruments such as checklists and rating scales.
8. Teach self-assessment first and have students practice it before asking them to assess others.

Revisiting Validity and Reliability

Face validity does not ensure psychometric quality, whether the assessment approach is direct or indirect. Criteria for judging the worth of performance assessments include evaluations of their *consequences, fairness, transfer and generalizability, cognitive complexity, content quality, content coverage, meaningfulness,* and *cost and efficiency*. Reliability issues are particularly nettlesome for performance assessment, due to the extent of human judgment required in the scoring and the number and type of assessments it may take to confidently estimate a student's true functioning level. Further research needs to be done to reveal improved techniques for increasing the quality and credibility of performance assessment.

Selecting and Developing Performance Assessments

There are a number of sources of assessments in many disciplines and across disciplines. The criteria for quality performance assessments presented in this chapter apply whether the teacher creates or selects from among pre-existing assessments.

Try This

I. Create your own performance assessment. Choose a setting (early childhood, elementary, middle, or high school), then write or select higher-level outcomes that are appropriate for performance assessment. The purpose of your assessment will be to determine if students have achieved the stated outcomes. If the outcomes are not available or easily forthcoming, try using the following ones:

> Given the appropriate equipment and instruction on propaganda tactics in media advertising, students will apply one or more of the tactics in producing a commercial about a fictional product or service of their own creation. Propaganda tactics include bandwagon, testimonial, and sweeping generality.
>
> Students will work cooperatively with their peers toward a common goal.

Answer

I. A wide variety of responses would be considered appropriate for this performance. Here is how a middle-school teacher might respond.

Sub-tasks:

- Create product or service
- Generate ideas for a commercial including propaganda tactic(s)
- Write script
- Cast characters, crew
- Arrange/select set
- Videotape commercial
- Play commercial in class

The task:

Students will form groups of four or five to work on this project. They will be given some class time to work on the earlier sub-tasks, but they are expected to work outside of class as well. All commercials will be videotaped outside of class. At least one student in each group has access to a camcorder or other video camera that uses VHS format tape. The teacher's camcorder will be made available in the case of equipment failure or uncooperative parents. The videos will be shown to the class to celebrate their accomplishment. The teacher will evaluate the videos privately using the judging criteria.

Directions to students:

Madison Avenue needs your help! Your group has been assigned to create a new product or service and create a commercial for it. Your group is responsible for the following activities: creating the product or service, generating ideas for the commercial including one (or more) propaganda tactics, writing the script, casting the characters and crew, selecting and arranging the set, videotaping the commercial, and presenting the commercial in class. You may divide up the work in many ways, but two things are key—collaboration and the proper use of a propaganda tactic in commercial advertising. You will be given class time to meet and work on your projects, but out-of-class meetings will be necessary, so exchange phone numbers. Your group should be prepared to air its video at our annual Video Commercial Festival on November 19 (popcorn will be supplied). The judging criteria for your project are as follows:

1. Commercial is videotaped.
2. Product or service is of the students' creation.
3. At least one propaganda tactic is used in selling the product or service.
4. The propaganda tactic(s) used is (are) used appropriately (for example, person giving testimonial has credibility with the audience).
5. Students work together on their group's project.

Judging criteria:

Judging criteria (1–5, above) will be written on a checklist that also lists the names of the participants in each group. Each criterion will be judged as met (with a ✓) or not met (no mark).

CHAPTER 9

Using Portfolios in the Classroom

Key Concepts:

- Making decisions regarding portfolios: purpose, audience, contents, and assessment options.
- Considering the advantages and disadvantages of using portfolios in the classroom.
- Planning, using, and assessing student portfolios.

Standards Addressed in This Chapter:

1. Choose assessment methods appropriate for instructional decisions.
2. Develop assessment methods appropriate for instructional decisions.

Before You Begin Reading, Consider This

Should portfolios of student work replace traditional grades and transcripts for decisions such as promotion to the next grade or college admission?

YES A portfolio is a much more information-rich source than a grade or even a grade-point average. With a portfolio, a college admissions officer or classroom teacher has a fuller profile of the whole student and thus has a greater likelihood of making the "right" decision.

NO Not only can portfolio contents be faked (well-written papers can be purchased), they are much more limited than grades. If a portfolio is limited enough in scope so as not to overburden the person who has to review it, it may not represent the student well. If it is comprehensive enough to represent the student well, it may be impossible for reviewers to wade through. Grades are much simpler; everyone understands them, and report cards and transcripts that reflect many grades over the course of time give teachers and admissions officers more information than the fattest of portfolios, and in less space too.

Understanding Portfolios

Products and recordings of performances may be kept over time by teachers to document their students' development or achievement during that period. A teacher, for example, may wish to compare a student's September writing assignment with one produced in May on any number of dimensions and summarize the findings in a statement of progress for the year. One way to keep track of the student's actual work is to place the representative pieces in a portfolio. A *portfolio* is a collection of student work gathered together for a purpose. The idea is to collect samples of work in one place that illustrate something about the person, much like an artist's portfolio. The following vignette illustrates the point:

> Alejandro jumped into the air, shot his fist into the sky, and shouted, "Yes!" as he hung up the phone. He had just secured a hard-won appointment with the hiring manager of a local firm. Now all he had to do was impress the manager with his work skills and abilities and hope there was a match somewhere in the company between him and a job. Alejandro puzzled a bit about how he would dazzle the hiring manager in some unique way—show her that he was not just another recent high-school graduate with car payments and insurance premiums to cover. Then he thought of the expandable folder sitting on his bookshelf that was crammed full with papers he had written, a video-taped presentation he made to the PTSA on school overcrowding, and who knew what else. He had spent a portion of the last four years assembling and refining that high-school portfolio. Now, maybe, it could be put to some use. He decided to use it in his interview to illustrate some of his capabilities. The work in the portfolio reflected, among other things, Alejandro's abilities in writing, critical thinking, and teamwork on projects. He pulled it from the shelf, dusted it off, and began to cull and reorganize the contents for

> a new audience: the hiring manager. He threw out some papers, replayed the tape and decided to keep it in because it revealed some of his showmanship and poise in a mostly adult group, and vowed to replace the battered folder with something a little more business-like from the office supply store. When he thought of Mrs. Francis, one of his English teachers who was always after him to keep his portfolio current, he smiled.

The purpose of Alejandro's high school portfolio was to document his acquisition of various skills and abilities considered desirable in the workplace. In addition to graded assignments and test papers, it also contained the following:

- A record of his academic and non-academic plans beyond high school.
- Four years of academic transcripts.
- A record of his career preparation.
- A record of recognition for his accomplishments both in and out of school.

Portfolios are not limited to high-school or professional use. They may be used in any grade and for a variety of purposes. Depending on the purpose of the portfolio, a number of other variables must also be decided, such as the contents, who chooses the contents, the audience(s), and assessment options.

Typically, a portfolio chronicles progress, effort, or achievement in one or more given areas. For example, a student may compile a language-arts portfolio containing written work and audio-recorded oral readings to document her progress on important dimensions throughout the term and to practice self-reflection. Another student, along with his teacher, may compile a portfolio of work done in several academic areas in grade 3 to celebrate his accomplishments. Student participation is a major feature of most portfolios and is what distinguishes them from cumulative folders and permanent records, which are assembled by teachers and other school staff. Whereas a student's cumulative or permanent folder has traditionally been the repository for standardized test results, pertinent medical and immunization records, grade transcripts, results of psychological and educational assessments, and other formal records, a portfolio has a different purpose. Arter and Spandel contend that for a collection of student work to qualify as a portfolio rather than a work folder, it must have a specific purpose, and the student must be involved in deciding on the contents of the portfolio and must actively engage in self-reflection.[1]

Making Decisions Regarding Portfolios

Determining the Purpose

Portfolios vary widely in the forms they take due to the number of variables that must be decided and the people involved in those decisions. For example, Batzle differentiates among three types of portfolios for the K–6 classroom—working,

[1] "Using Portfolios of Student Work in Instruction and Assessment" by J. A. Arter and V. Spandel, 1992, *Educational Measurement: Issues and Practice, 11*(1), pp. 36–44.

showcase, and record keeping—based on combinations of these variables.[2] The first decision, which is usually the teacher's to make, is about the purpose of the portfolio. A portfolio of student work may be collected for instructional purposes—as a monitoring tool, for example. With enough entries across time in such portfolios, a teacher may examine the progress of one student or a group of students along a continuum of development. The teacher may track the progress of the group, looking for ways to enhance instruction. Individual students may reflect on their own progress and identify their own strengths and weaknesses. In fact, one of the most powerful aspects of portfolios is that the students' work is collected in one place, where they can actually see it all together and review it. Students whose work usually is returned to them in a piecemeal fashion are often astonished at its quantity and increasing quality when it is gathered into a portfolio over a period of time.

A second purpose for which portfolios are useful is to celebrate or showcase accomplishments (such as a student's class-published books, poetry, and personal statements of how her writing has changed during the term). A third purpose is to pass on information and examples to the next teacher regarding each student's progress. A second-grade teacher may pass on portfolios of her students' typical and best work to the third-grade teacher, who can then examine them to gauge his own teaching efforts.

Portfolios may also be used to facilitate communication between teachers and parents regarding their child's achievement and progress, providing examples to illustrate the points teachers want to make. Students in the upper grades may use portfolios for purposes of college admission or prospective employment, as Alejandro did. Administrators may use portfolios for statewide competency testing (as is done in Vermont), to grant high-school credit, or to evaluate educational programs. Portfolios may also be assembled for combinations of purposes. For example, instructional enhancement and progress documentation are both served when the second-grade teacher, mentioned just above, also reviews her students' portfolios periodically and makes notes for revising her instruction for next year.

Identifying Audiences

Once the purpose of the portfolio is decided, the next decision is the intended audience. Who is the portfolio for? There are a number of possible answers to this question. Each possible audience, combined with the purpose of the portfolio, guide further decisions such as content and containers. There may be more than one audience for a particular type of portfolio. Audiences typically include the students themselves, teachers, parents, prospective employers, state assessment officials and staff, program evaluation staff, and college admissions officers.

---

[2] *Portfolio Assessment and Evaluation: Developing and Using Portfolios in the K–6 Classroom* by J. Batzle, 1992, Cypress, CA: Creative Teaching Press.

Deciding on the Contents

A portfolio may contain almost anything. What actually goes into one is determined, in part, by the purpose and audience for which it is designed and by those making the inclusion decisions. A portfolio may be assembled for a singular discipline such as language arts, mathematics, or science, or the contents may be cross-disciplinary and contain information and work gathered from scored or graded assignments and tests. Alejandro's high-school portfolio would, most likely, contain samples across disciplines. Observations and comments by teachers (such as anecdotal records), students, and parents are also common portfolio contents, as are conference records.

Who makes those inclusion decisions on the contents of a portfolio? For most classroom portfolio purposes, the answer to this question is the teacher and the students. Representative members of the audience may help set the criteria for selection, but those closest to the work are usually the ones in the best position to decide whether a particular test, paper, project documentation, or performance recording should be included. For example, a group of parents of second graders may be asked for their ideas on what would be important evidence to them of their child's progress on various dimensions. This information could be combined with the teachers' ideas and those of the students and reduced to some manageable number that reflects the purpose. During the year, these criteria would be applied to candidate pieces for inclusion. Using the criteria for selection, the inclusion decision might be made by any of the following:

- Each student alone.
- The students with guidance from the teacher.
- The students and teacher in collaboration.
- Individual students with input from their peers.
- The teacher alone.

Portfolios come in all shapes and sizes, as you can imagine from the range of contents. Figure 9.1 illustrates some of the many options. Some are quite large (like plastic crates), and others are quite thin (like manila file folders). Some teachers prefer expandable folders with gusseted sections that facilitate organizing the contents. Others prefer a three-ring binder or closable container so that contents are not loose. Compact disks (CD-ROM) have also been used for the ultimate in storage capacity for the variety of products and performances typically included in a portfolio.[3] In fact, multimedia portfolios and résumés have been posted on the Internet for worldwide access.[4] What works depends on the portfolio management skills of those entrusted with its care. Containers are usually personalized in some way by their owners. In one first-grade classroom, the first art project of the year was to find, buy, or make, then decorate, a container that met the specifications necessary. The students engaged the help of their parents in the project, and a "spec sheet" was sent home so that parents knew the portfolio's purpose and the necessary features of the container.

---

[3]"Laser Disk Portfolios: Total Child Assessment" by J. Campbell, 1992, *Educational Leadership,* pp. 69–72. There are several "personal testimony" articles regarding portfolios in this issue.

[4]"New Job May Be a Click Away" by R. Kanaley, October 23, 1995, *The Herald,* pp. BM31–32.

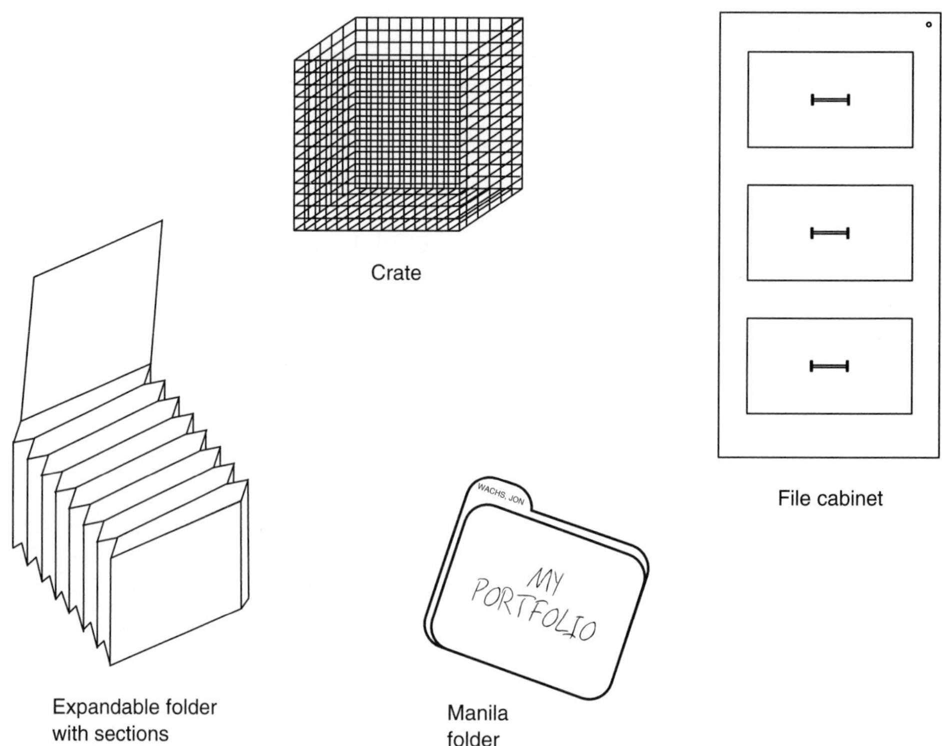

Figure 9.1
Examples of containers for portfolios and holding files.

Considering Assessment Options

Portfolios provide two assessment options to teachers. First, the portfolio may serve as a repository of work, comments, and observations for the student's reflection. Each piece in the portfolio may be assessed or not, individually, prior to inclusion. In this case, there is usually no assessment of the portfolio as a whole, for it is unnecessary. This repository option is commonly used when the chief purpose of the portfolio is celebratory or instructional, whether or not it is passed on to the next teacher, and when it is used to communicate with parents. The items in the portfolio may be graded or ungraded, but they are examples that help tell a purposeful story about the student over the period of time the work was collected.

A second option is to assess the entire contents as one body using judging criteria developed expressly for that purpose. Although the judging criteria and scoring scheme may be analytic or holistic, most are holistic in nature, due to the sheer number of criteria and portfolio items usually involved. The process of creating the scoring scheme or rubric for a portfolio is the same as for other multifaceted student products; therefore, the guidelines in Chapter 8 for judging criteria and observation instruments are useful here. With this option, also, the contents may or may not have been scored individually before inclusion. If they were scored previously, the scores would be removed or covered so as not to influence judgment. What is important here is that the contents, together, are considered a singular expression of student achievement, effort, or disposition. This option is sometimes used for purposes of college admission, employment, and statewide competency testing. For example, an art student may be accepted into a college program in commercial art based on the overall strength of her portfolio. This option is also used at times when the contents of the portfolio are from a single discipline, perhaps from a particular unit, or are separated into disciplines. A student's term grade in math may be generated, either wholly or in part, from an assessment of his math-related portfolio contents, for instance.

Considering the Advantages and Disadvantages of Portfolios

Many benefits of portfolios cited in the literature stem from benefits of performance and product assessment. In addition to those, there are some that pertain specifically to portfolios. A primary advantage of using portfolios is that portfolios are consistent with theories of instruction and philosophies of schools that promote student involvement with their learning. Portfolios are a powerful way to articulate the philosophy of the school and what is valued in terms of student growth and achievement. Further, assessment and instruction can be blended through the use of portfolios so that students are actively engaged in, responsible for, and in control of their learning.

Another important advantage is that portfolios are an excellent way to document developmental growth over time. Comparisons can be made among products across time for a particular student or across students for instructional enhancement purposes. Portfolios can also bring together staff to discuss and reach consensus on decisions such as the purpose, audience, and contents. For students involved in their use (by selecting the contents, for instance), portfolios can foster a sense of ownership of the work and skill in critical self-reflection and decision making—increasingly important outcomes themselves. Additionally, portfolio contents may be used to illustrate the processes and procedures students follow in their performances and in producing work. These are important for teachers to be aware of in helping students acquire cognitive strategies and critical-thinking skills. Illustrative contents work extremely well in structuring conferences with students and parents and in guiding parental assessment with open-ended questions. As portfolios favor no particular assessment strategy, they facilitate combining paper-and-pencil tests with performance and product assessments for more complete data on what students know, think, feel, and can do.

There are also a number of disadvantages or tradeoffs in using portfolios. First, and very important, are the logistics involved in a portfolio system. In addition to any time and effort needed to design and implement performance assessments, which typically produce the bulk of portfolio contents, are the time and effort needed to design, create, and manage the portfolios, often with little or no institutional support. Also, classroom storage space is limited. Without advance planning, the entire system may collapse under the weight of unwieldy containers, jumbled contents, and frustrated participants. This leads to a second disadvantage: Proper training is necessary for all people involved with portfolios so that they know how to carry out their roles as (1) members of the target audience, (2) system designers/managers, or (3) content evaluators. Students are not congenitally predisposed to self-reflection, and teachers do not "just know" how to design a workable portfolio system, even if they are enthusiastic about the concept. A third disadvantage is that portfolios carry no inherent insurance against being used for purposes for which they are not intended. As with high-stakes standardized tests, high-stakes portfolio assessment results may end up being used to rank schools, buy and sell real estate, and evaluate teachers.

As an assessment strategy, portfolios are a relatively new approach. As time passes, more research will be conducted on the design, use, and scoring of portfolios, but many issues are still to be resolved. Teachers (and others) can be misled, for example, about what students know and can do by murky judging criteria, ill-conceived tasks and performance requirements, and poor sampling of performances and products. Teachers must keep informed as research results are reported to make the best use of portfolios, because "best use" is still being defined.

Using Guidelines to Implement Portfolios Effectively

Guidelines for Using Portfolios

The following guidelines will help teachers reap some of the benefits of portfolios while avoiding some of the pitfalls associated with them. The guidelines for portfolios in general are presented first, followed by guidelines that are useful if the portfolios will be scored as a whole.

1. *Clearly articulate the purpose of the portfolio.* The importance of this guideline is paramount. Because it drives everything else (the selection of contents, for example), the purpose must be well conceived and written in unambiguous language. A clear purpose contains a statement of what will be done with the portfolio and at least a general indication of the contents and the stakeholders (those who will use or contribute to the portfolio in some way). Consider the two statements of purpose below:

> Purpose: Students in fourth grade will assemble portfolios of work to pass on to their teachers next year.
>
> Purpose: Each student in fourth grade will assemble a portfolio of work to pass on to his or her teacher next year. The portfolio will emphasize the following:
>
> - Growth, development, and academic progress over the course of the year in arithmetic, language arts, social studies, and science.
> - The cognitive processes the student uses in critical thinking and in solving problems, whether real or simulated.

The first statement says that fourth-graders will be responsible for putting together portfolios of work that will be given to their fifth-grade (presumably) teachers. Who the stakeholders are is relatively clear. After reading the first statement, however, you might ask, "Why? What is the purpose?" and you would be right to do so. Some fifth-grade teachers might think that the fourth-grade teachers were cleaning house this year and dumping the trash next year on them! The point is that the purpose should be clear to any stakeholder who reads it, whether that person is a member of the audience, the selection criteria committee, the teacher, or the students. The second statement does a much better job of articulating the type of contents that are appropriate for selection without being overly prescriptive. For example, the fifth-grade teachers might want to review the portfolios once they receive them. The second purpose specifically states that these portfolios are to be multi-disciplinary and that the documentation should include an identification of the critical-thinking processes students use.

2. *Communicate the articulated purpose to all stakeholders.* Rarely is it the case where a teacher uses student portfolios and is also the only person interacting with them. Therefore, it is necessary to ensure that all who have access to the portfolios are clear about their purpose. Some teachers make the statement of purpose the first document in the container. Others have pasted it right on the outside of the container so that it could not be missed. In any case, it is important that all who come in contact with the portfolio know of its purpose and the expectations surrounding the included work.

3. *Use only content-selection criteria that are congruent with the articulated purpose.* The criteria used for selecting pieces for inclusion in the portfolio are important because they directly affect the contents. They also render the purpose operational. Those responsible for selecting the pieces should be able to see a relationship between the basis for selection and the purpose. If the purpose is formative or for redesign of instruction, for example, a teacher might include "commendations" and "recommendations."[5] All of the selection criteria together should cover all facets of the purpose. For example, the selection criteria for the second purpose statement, above, might include the following:

- At least five products (or performances) from each of the listed disciplines.
- Works selected at times over the year (book reports written in September, December, February, and May, for example).
- Records of teacher-student interviews or students' audio-taped self-reports of the cognitive processes they used in critical thinking.
- Examples of best work.
- Examples of work in progress (such as an outline, rough draft, and final report on some topic).

---

[5] *Writing Portfolios: Potential for Large Scale Assessment. Project 2.4: Design Theory and Psychometrics for Complex Performance Assessment. Design and Analysis of Portfolio and Performance Measures,* ERIC Document # ED 350 312, by E. L. Baker and R. Linn, 1992.

4. *Choose only portfolio contents that are congruent with the selection criteria.* If not carefully managed, portfolios may become overstuffed or neglected. By adhering to the selection criteria, extraneous material is avoided and what is important is more likely to be included, provided you and your students have also followed guideline three, above. A working file, such as that described later in this chapter in the case study, can help organize this process. At scheduled times throughout the grading period, term, or academic year, the students can use the selection criteria to cull portfolio contents from the file.

5. *Ensure that the role of each stakeholder group is congruent with the purpose.* This guideline is stated broadly to include all of the people who interact in some way with the portfolios. For most classroom purposes, the teacher and the students are the major stakeholders. From the example purpose stated in guideline one, it is clear that the fifth-grade teachers are a major audience and that the students are actively involved in the content selection process. What is less clear in that statement is the role of the fourth-grade teachers. They are not mentioned in the statement, but presumably they will be involved in some way. Roles for them that are congruent with this purpose include supervising content selection, periodically reviewing the contents with each student, and contributing such things as summary statements, anecdotal records, and recorded interviews with the students. For the fourth-grade teachers to be solely responsible for portfolio content selection is, however, incompatible with the stated purpose.

6. *Familiarize all stakeholder groups with the responsibilities and activities associated with their roles.* For portfolios to succeed in your school, people who will interact with them must know how to use them. The fifth-grade teachers in the previous example must be able to interpret the contents of the portfolios they receive in light of the stated purpose. The students must understand and apply the selection criteria to their work as well as explain (orally or in writing) their cognitive processes. This may require training audiences, students, and others in their roles. To do otherwise leads to disappointment and confusion when the portfolio process does not live up to their expectations.[6]

7. *Involve students in the process appropriate to their developmental and maturity levels.* This may sound obvious as students are the producers of the work in classroom portfolios, but this guideline goes beyond mere production. To foster the sense of ownership cited as an advantage of portfolios, students might participate in the following activities: (a) select work for inclusion or collaborate with others in this decision, (b) critically appraise their work based on the judging criteria, (c) self-reflect on the processes they use, and (d) make or personalize the container.

8. *If documenting process in the product, the student must articulate it.* Proponents of portfolios cite as an advantage the fact that they can be used to document processes such as thought, revision, and problem solving. Remember, however, that students also use internal processes to come up with answers to multiple-choice and

---

[6]J. A. Arter and V. Spandel, 1992.

completion items. In either case, the student must articulate the process—explain it in some way—in order for it to be documented. The process can be captured in any of a number of ways, including the following:

- Recorded by the teacher on paper in an interview with the student.
- Recorded on audiotape or videotape, either by the student or in an interview.
- Written by the teacher in an anecdotal record.
- Written by the student in a journal entry.
- Entered onto a computer disk by the student or teacher.

9. Use cover sheets, sticky notes, or cards attached to portfolio items to describe them and why they were chosen. A description of the item and rationale for including it are helpful to the audiences (and raters) in understanding the importance and meaning of the chosen work. Some teachers have their students create an annotated "table of contents" (see Figure 9.2) as a first document that lists three things in columns: item identification information, selection criteria the item represents, and the reason for including it. Batzle suggests an 8 1/2″ × 11″ cover sheet for each item that has space set aside for students, parents, and teachers to write comments.[7]

10. Do not include scores on portfolio items. Portfolios may certainly contain previously scored works, but the score is not the important issue. What is important is the story the item tells about the student regarding the selection criteria and the purpose

Table of Contents

Item	Criteria	Why included
Science journal 10/19 - 11/6	Shows cooperation with others in reaching a common goal.	I didn't know Franz before this. Now we're friends.
Letter to Congress about the environment	Shows writing process of planning, drafting, and revising.	It was better after I rewrote it. It was important.
Great mathematician report	My best work.	I liked it

Figure 9.2
Partial table of contents for a portfolio. The item selection criteria were listed by the teacher. The student filled in the item along with her reason for choosing it.

---

[7]J. Batzle, 1992.

of the portfolio. Scores and grades may distract the audience from that story. This guideline is doubly important to follow if the portfolio as a whole will be scored. Raters may be influenced by previously assigned grades, whether high or low. Some teachers who use portfolios in their classrooms write grades and scores on separate cards or note sheets and attach them to student papers and such so that they may be removed if the work is later chosen for inclusion in a portfolio.

11. Choose a storage container and classroom space large enough to accommodate the contents and facilitate easy use. If a portfolio is to follow a student from kindergarten through sixth grade, it must be large enough to fit everything and must be easy to work with. Performances may be recorded on videotape, and bulky products (like dioramas and science project displays) may be video recorded or photographed. All of the papers, folders, and objects take up space. Teachers can plan the space necessary by keeping in mind the purpose of the portfolios, the selection criteria, and the nature of the tasks likely to be included. An expandable file folder might be kept in a student's desk. A plastic crate might be kept under the student's desk or stacked with others in cubbyholes along a wall. Depending on the stakes involved and the nature of the students, portfolio security measures may need to be taken.

12. Follow through. Ensure that portfolios are passed on to their audience(s). Students who have spent a considerable amount of time assembling, reflecting on, and reviewing the contents of their portfolios may become frustrated and disheartened if they find them tossed in the dumpster at the end of the year. If, for example, a teacher has told his students that their ninth-grade writing portfolios will be forwarded to their 10th-grade English teachers, he has the obligation to do so. If parents are the audience and the portfolios never go home with the students or are never used in a parent-teacher conference, then they have not achieved their purpose.

Guidelines for Assessing Portfolios

In addition to the above general guidelines for working with portfolios, there are guidelines that are useful to follow when working with portfolios that will be assessed as a single work with many facets. These guidelines pertain to the contents of the portfolio and the scoring process. They are summarized in a checklist on page 301.

1. Include enough documents (items) on which to base judgment. As with other types of assessment, portfolios merely sample what students know and can do. Recall from Chapter 3 that a small sample of items is more likely to yield a nonrepresentative and invalid profile of the student than a larger sample, although a large sample, in itself, is no guarantee. A decision must be made as to the minimum number of pieces necessary for the raters to make a sound judgment. A minimum of six for any one scoring dimension is probably workable—enough for judgment without over-stuffing the portfolio.

2. Structure the contents to provide scorable information. Baker and Linn found that "comparing an October folk tale with a December fantasy, a January haiku, a March whale report, a May letter to a pen pal, and a June summary of a field trip was an impossible task"[8] when raters tried to judge portfolios on writing competencies such as mechanics, organization, and style using an analytic scoring scheme. A problem with structuring the contents for analytic scoring is that it may interfere with a teacher's instructional practices. Holistic scoring techniques, in contrast, may reduce the necessity for structure. Although it appears that analytic scoring schemes have some potential, further research is necessary to determine their best use with scored portfolios in the classroom.

3. Develop judging criteria and a scoring scheme for raters to use in assessing the portfolios. The guidelines presented in Chapter 8 may also be used for collections of performances and products. Do not, however, try to use the same criteria and scheme that you might have used to previously score individual pieces. This is redundant. The collection is viewed differently from the individual pieces, whether they have been individually scored or not.[9] The scoring scheme may include which items are to be considered for scoring along a particular dimension to inform the raters. For example, in Figure 9.3, Lamar has selected six works for each dimension to determine his progress in developing some of his writing skills over the course of the school year. To facilitate rating, the selected items are listed for each scoring dimension. Optimally, the scoring scheme design should be coordinated with the design of the portfolio collection so that each process informs the other. By thinking

✓ *Easy Reference Checklist*

Guidelines for Using Portfolios

- ❑ Purpose clearly articulated.
- ❑ Purpose communicated to all stakeholders.
- ❑ Selection criteria congruent with purpose.
- ❑ Contents congruent with selection criteria.
- ❑ Stakeholder roles congruent with the purpose.
- ❑ Stakeholders familiar with their responsibilities and activities.
- ❑ Students involved in the process appropriate to their developmental level.
- ❑ Students articulated processes in products where necessary.
- ❑ Cover sheets/cards used to identify and describe items.
- ❑ Scores and grades removed from items.
- ❑ Storage space and containers accommodate the contents.
- ❑ Portfolios passed on to their audience(s).

[8]E. L. Baker and R. Linn, 1992, p. 12.

[9]E. L. Baker and R. Linn, 1992. In this study, Baker and Linn also found that portfolios scored as single works received higher ratings than when the contents of those same portfolios were scored individually and added together for a total score.

Dimension (To assess this...)	Selected Works (. . . see these.)
Writes in complete sentences.	Letter to Joey "Sacagawea, Indian Guide" "Recycling" "My Favorite Reptile" Social studies homework – 3/26 "The Minutemen"
Creates more interesting, more complex sentences.	Letter to Joey "The Most Fun I Ever had Was . . ." "Martin Luther King, Jr." report "The Minutemen" "Recycling" Science lab journal – 4/6 – 4/9

Figure 9.3
Part of a selection criteria worksheet for Lamar Jenkins. Selected works include a friendly letter to a pen pal, a paragraph recounting events, biographical reports, other reports, a persuasive letter, and a journal entry.

through both processes at the same time, even though actual scoring may take place much later than the design of the portfolios, teachers can avoid rater frustration.

4. Use observation instruments such as checklists and rating scales when possible to facilitate scoring. The task of a portfolio rater is not an easy one, even when there are judging criteria and a scoring scheme to follow. Remove as much of the labor and guesswork as possible with these instruments. They summarize performance, and the data they yield may be aggregated for further analysis, if that is desired.

5. Use trained raters. This is a corollary to the earlier guideline about stakeholders and their roles. Raters are, of course, a major stakeholder group. Trained raters increase the credibility of the results by enhancing the inter- and intrarater reliability. Training might include such topics as (a) understanding the teachers' expectations, perhaps by presenting and discussing a description of the tasks and the quality indicators used to evaluate competent performance, (b) the difference between score points, such as discussing what constitutes a "3" portfolio versus a "4," and (c) what the item wording on the observation forms means and how to use the forms effectively.

✓ *Easy Reference Checklist*

Guidelines for Assessing Portfolios

- ❑ Enough items included to base judgment on.
- ❑ Contents provide scorable information.
- ❑ Judging criteria and scoring scheme developed specifically for assessing the portfolios.
- ❑ Observation instruments used to facilitate judgment/scoring.
- ❑ Trained raters used.

Implementing Portfolios in the Classroom: A Case Study

The portfolio guidelines listed in this chapter give you a general sense of the process of establishing portfolios in your classroom and integrating them into your curriculum. The following case study, "Anatomy of a Year" by Robyn S. Lane, describes specific challenges and solutions that one teacher encountered when she introduced the use of portfolios, based on the guidelines listed above, to her fourth- and fifth-graders. These students were from diverse economic backgrounds and demonstrated a variety of reading levels.

Lane, a teacher in the Bedford Central School District in New York State, moved to the use of portfolios in an effort to increase authenticity of assessment in her classroom (a district-wide goal) and to have students value their work and her own more highly (a personal goal). Her experience using portfolios over the course of 3 years led to these insights.

ANATOMY OF A YEAR: ONE TEACHER'S EXPERIENCE WITH LONG-TERM PORTFOLIOS

By Robyn S. Lane

My initial interest in portfolio assessment had less to do with my professional curiosity than it had to do with my maternal awareness. My daughters, who were then in elementary and middle school, would bring home evidence of great learning. Test papers, graded reports, homework assignments—all the traditional indicators parents crave—were neatly presented and commented upon by wonderful teachers. Yet, why were these papers being tossed in the trash so quickly? Why didn't my own kids seem to value what I as a professional wanted them to value? After all, hadn't they worked hard for all this feedback? What was the missing link that connected what they *did* with care to what they *cared* to do? What implications did this have for me as a teacher of 9- and 10-year-olds? Was all of my students' hard work and my belabored comments also going quickly into the trash in their homes? Were students, even the most motivated ones, only interested in short-term gratification? Could it be that I wasn't doing the job I wanted to believe I was doing?

Establishing a Purpose

As Donald Graves has been known to say, "Good questions don't go away." I knew from the start of my involvement in creating and maintaining portfolios in my classroom that I was searching for a way to make my students' products and efforts more meaningful to *them.* I was deriving a great deal of both pleasure and frustration from their accomplishments, but there was a definite disparity in the degree of investment by me, my students, and their parents. That nagging feeling was what led me to define the three-fold purpose of using portfolios in my classroom: to demonstrate growth in the ability of my students to communicate for a variety of purposes, to make this growth more apparent to all invested parties, and to engage students in the process of reflection.

In my opinion, the most critical part of the entire process lies in answering that question of purpose for yourself. What is it you want to document or achieve with a portfolio? For many of us, answering this question means making choices. There are many different kinds of portfolios. Some portfolios serve as a "showcase" of students' best work, either from a unit of study or from a year's worth of work. Some portfolios document growth within a specific content area or with regard to reading and writing skills. Some portfolios are used to evaluate students, and some are designed to reveal additional information about students, but not for evaluative purposes.

As I reflected on my own instructional goals and the goals I had set for my students, I decided it would be best for me to implement a *communications portfolio,* designed to document growth over time in the language arts by representing students' writing activities that occurred in the classroom throughout the year.

The Process of Implementing a Long-Term Communications Portfolio

To begin this huge undertaking, I looked at the "blueprint" or scope of my school year and recorded student experiences that provided writing opportunities and enabled data collection. I planned to use the learning experiences so that the portfolios mirrored the year instead of "driving" it. The language-arts activities I planned included experiences that spanned many curriculum areas and focused on student writing using these forms: personal narratives, descriptive paragraphs, persuasive essays, point-of-view pieces, business letters and letters to friends, personal journals, content-response journals, literature-response activities, news summaries, book reports, projects in different curriculum areas, and research reports. All of these experiences provided opportunities for students to write and produce work that they could consider for inclusion in their portfolios.

Once I felt comfortable with the focus for the portfolio, the process began. I was still faced with both philosophical and pragmatic questions: What would these portfolios look like at the end of the year? Was there a right or wrong way to do this? How would I handle a year's worth of paper? How would I guide students through the process? Could children at this age be reflective enough to make the portfolio a useful tool? This stage of teacher insecurity is to be anticipated, and I learned that students will benefit from the portfolio experience even if there are some logistical errors. The process is really similar to taking a journey together. Sharing errors with students along the way created an atmosphere of trust. I had to be prepared to change what wasn't working, as teachers routinely do for class lessons. The main advantage of this long-term portfolio as compared to a short-term content portfolio was that I was *not* using it to evaluate or grade students but to document their growth and provide the opportunity to establish learning goals. The real challenge of this long-term portfolio, however, was keeping it from becoming overwhelming to me and my students. Even after using this long-term portfolio for 3 years, I am still looking for ways to refine it by reducing paperwork and increasing authenticity.

There were a number of logistical issues to tackle in implementing portfolios in my classroom. First, I decided that work could not go home without it returning to school. I created a file of manila folders and placed them in hanging files to store daily work. The students and I referred to these as *holding folders.* Their purpose was to contain everything for us to consider until we made decisions about portfolio contents. Students also maintained individual writing folders that held works in progress. This system worked well for me as long as I took the time early in the year to create a "think portfolio" mindset. Students needed reminding to date and store their work in the folders, especially when they worked with specialty-area teachers in subjects other than language arts. The work from these subject classes also "counted" as part of portfolio contents. As the year progressed, students generally began to internalize the system and the holding folders became delightfully full and never dusty!

The "think portfolio" environment was most important. I found that students may not initially understand the portfolio concept, and I needed to introduce it to them in a tangible way. One way is to share an actual artist's portfolio or one that you have created yourself. In our school we have been fortunate to have a few grade levels involved in portfolios, and our fifth-graders share their work with younger students. In the beginning of the year, students really only collect work without understanding the true notion of a portfolio collection, but this soon changes.

In addition to setting the stage at the beginning of the year, I discovered that other activities can be completed to create the foundation of a portfolio. Our students were asked to complete a writing sample for their permanent writing folders, a district requirement. I made copies of each student's piece and used these as a baseline for individual portfolios, because I wanted to demonstrate growth in writing through the year. Fortunately, the writing sample the district required was a friendly letter to the teacher in which the students were asked to describe themselves and tell of their expectations for the year. Not only did this give me a baseline of the students' writing ability, it provided me with information about the students' backgrounds and put me in touch with their personal goals.

Portfolios also provided a golden opportunity to enhance the school-home connection. Periodic parent feedback is invaluable. It provides students with the realization that teachers do not work in isolation and that each child's success is orchestrated and celebrated by all who care about him or her. Of course, not all parents participate as much as we would want them to, but we need to consistently provide opportunities for them to do so. I send home a portfolio questionnaire at the beginning of the year, focusing on how each child learns. A similar questionnaire is sent home in June, and it's quite interesting to compare the two. Figure 9.4 is a sample of a completed parent questionnaire. Students also complete a questionnaire at the beginning of the year, shown in Figure 9.5. It is also interesting to compare the parents' responses with those of their children.

Once we collected initial information, the students and I needed to start making portfolio selections. After my first year's experience, I established a goal of making portfolio selections more frequently. This is easier said than done because the process takes time, and we all know how little time we have in the classroom. I was able to plan 3 selection days, even though I had wanted to have students make selections every 6 weeks. The first round of making selections was the most difficult. It helped to first model the process with my class and discuss the purpose for making selections early in the school year. I acted as if I were a student making piles of work and narrowing down the choices to what I felt very strongly about according to the selection guidelines.

During my first year of using the portfolio process several issues arose:

- Would students always select pieces of work that I, their teacher, have responded favorably to? If so, how could I avoid my evaluation being substituted for theirs?
- What if the students chose selections from their on-going journals or the selections were otherwise not easily accessible on selection day?
- What should I do with the work the students did (or didn't) select?
- How should I guide the students but not direct them through this process?
- How many selections should be made? Must they be in final form?
- Is all work potentially portfolio material, or are there limits?
- What about the child who doesn't want to participate?

A general answer to each of these questions is "It's entirely up to you!" and there is no simple right or wrong answer, although the stakes for wrong answers are low if you are not using portfolios to evaluate your students. Teachers should refer back to their purpose for doing a portfolio and try to answer each question in relation to it. I learned that there is no single exemplary portfolio design, although I spent much time looking for one. I also learned a few other things that may be helpful for other teachers considering using portfolios in their classrooms.

Some Recommendations Based on Experience

After reflecting on the process based on my experience, here are some recommendations for making portfolios successful. First, try to live with life's imperfections. Students are insecure when they make their first selections, and they want indicators of success. For many, this may mean selecting a piece for which they received a good grade or one that looked neat. The students' ability to make choices develops over time based on their use of more appropriate criteria. As teachers, we can provide them with helpful information such as the realization that not everything in a portfolio has to be in final form. Second, students

PARENT RESPONSE FORM
(pre-portfolio)

Student's name: Caitlyn Taylor **Date:** Sept. 16, 1997

1. What would you identify as a strength of your child's writing?
   Creative expression — that she enjoys writing and research for writing.

2. What would you identify as an area for most improvement in your child's writing?
   To take time - the process is as important as the final product

3. If you could improve something about the way your child reads, what would it be?
   That she takes Challenges to read different types of books.

4. My child does his/her best when She can work by herself or in a small group. Large group is very risky for her.

Please feel free to provide additional information on the back of this form. THANK YOU!!!

Figure 9.4
Pre-portfolio parent response form.

Name: Caitlyn Taylor Date: 9/21/97

PRE-PORTFOLIO QUESTIONNAIRE

1. Do you like to write? (Check one answer)
   ✓ I enjoy writing
   ___ I sometimes enjoy writing
   ___ I write only when I have to

2. On the following list, place a check next to the writing skills you most want to improve this year. (choose no more than 5):

   A. Spelling ✓
   B. Making paragraphs ___
   C. Punctuation (commas, periods, question marks, quotation marks) ___
   D. Having an interesting introduction ___
   E. Having a strong concluding paragraph ___
   F. Putting events in the correct order ___
   G. Keeping to the topic ___
   H. Using more interesting words ✓
   I. Starting sentences in a variety of ways ___
   J. Thinking about what to write/starting ✓
   K. The revising stage of the writing process ✓
   L. Other: Picking the title

3. Please explain the kinds of things that help you when you're writing.
   Quiet.
   Time.

4. What kinds of problems do you have when you write?
   Remembering what I was going to do like When we stop and I get my mind on something else.

5. Check your 2 favorite kinds of writing:

   1. personal narrative (about yourself) ___
   2. make-believe stories ✓
   3. factual reports ✓
   4. letters ___
   5. poetry ___
   6. journals ___

Figure 9.5
Pre-portfolio questionnaire.

6. What do you read in your free time? (check one or more)

____	short stories	____	poems
____	magazines	____	comics
✓	fiction books	____	biographies about famous people
✓	non-fiction books	____	I don't read in my free time

7. I like to read books and stories about people for instance the Babysitter Club (is my favorite)

8. When I read by myself, I feel independent. I am doing something good

9. When I read with a group of other students, I feel like I'm doing something fun. Can't wait to find out what happens

10. When I come to a word I do not know, I try to sound it out ask a teacher

11. When I don't understand something I've read, I read it over. again a try to understand it

12. The time of day when I most enjoy reading is night - before bed

13. How do you think I might help you become a better reader or writer? Maybe you could let us read any kind of books we want?

Figure 9.5
Continued

choose different pieces for a variety of reasons. If students chose a test to keep in the portfolio, it might mean that they studied especially hard for the test and the success meant a great deal to them. The important issue here is to inform the students that they are the decision makers about selections, but they must be able to explain why they made their choices. One tip I can never stress enough is to make sure that the students put the date on all their work, because this saves time and aggravation later in the year.

Third, work that is contained outside of the holding folders (in journals, for instance) needs to be managed. I gave students a worksheet (see Figure 9.6) that listed suggestions for choices and had the students write down some information about each of their choices. If an entry came from a journal, the students listed the selection on the worksheet and put a sticky note on their journal. They turned the journal in with their other selections, and I copied or extracted the work for them. The selection worksheet also provided a framework for the class to use to help them make selections. I reinforced the concept that the final decision is always theirs. I reminded the students that the purpose of the portfolio was to show their ability to write for a variety of purposes, and, therefore, I advised them to include different forms of writing when they made their selections. I urged them not to choose too many pieces and to be selective. Some teachers may want to be more direct about the type and number of selections for a portfolio. Again, the decision should be made based upon the portfolio's purpose and intended audiences.

It's also important to discuss "ownership" with the students. In my class it's quite clear that the students own their portfolios, and the audience consists of their parents and me. The students are aware of this, and they end the school year by taking their portfolio treasures home. I don't grade their work and the portfolios are not given to the next year's teacher, because I want the students to enjoy them without being concerned about evaluation. A number of school districts now, however, require portfolio assessment for student evaluation throughout elementary school.

Reflections on Self-Reflection

It's important to think about ways to help students reflect about themselves and learn to set goals. I know how difficult this can be for my students. Learning to be self-analytic is a developmental process, and as with other skills, guidance and practice does lead to improvement. It's important to provide lots of opportunities for self-reflection and to model the behavior. Teachers should also be reminded to listen to their students because there may be more reflection occurring than they think. I found this out the first year I attempted to document self-reflection. I had asked students to complete a reflection form for each piece they selected for their portfolios (see Figure 9.7). However, I was disappointed in the quality of their responses: for example, *"I chose this piece because it was good"* and *"I liked my handwriting that day."* I was almost convinced that students of this age were limited in their ability to be reflective about their work. I discussed the problem with the project facilitator who advised me to change the way I was looking at reflection. Consequently, I decided to videotape my class on the next selection day. When I viewed the tape, I wrote down words and phrases that my students said as they made their selections, and what a difference I found. Typical comments were: *"Wow! I can't believe I used so many descriptive words in this"* and *"This is interesting to read."* Wasn't this reflection? The students may not have written insightfully on their forms, but their oral comments showed me that they were invested in the process.

Because of these comments, I decided to document reflection in a less restrictive fashion. Although I still required students to complete a reflection form (Figure 9.7) for at least

Name: ____________________

PORTFOLIO SELECTION WORKSHEET
(to be used for selection days that precede
mid-year and final selection days)

POSSIBLE CATEGORIES:

friendly letters
business letters
descriptive
persuasive
literature wkshp.
Book-It
mini-report
social studies
science
other
personal narrative
point of view
poetry
journals-content
journals-personal
fantasy
research
reading
math

Title	Category	Date Written	Date Selected

Figure 9.6
Portfolio selection worksheet

STUDENT REFLECTION FORM

(To be filled out by student after making a selection for the Portfolio and then discussed during student/teacher conference)

NAME: ____________________ DATE PIECE WAS WRITTEN: ____________

1. I think this is my best sample of a ________________ because __________

____

____

2. Some of the things I learned from completing this writing sample are ______

____

____

3. One way I think I have improved is ___________________________________

____

4. Some things I still have to improve on are _____________________________

____

Figure 9.7
Portfolio student reflection form.

one piece of work, I also asked them to assess any final piece of writing with a rubric that we devised together in class (see Figure 9.8).

To develop this rubric we talked a great deal about what constitutes good writing. Figures 9.9, 9.10, and 9.11 show three samples of students' writing that we jointly agreed represented a 3, 2, and 1 on the rubric. By applying the rubric in this concrete fashion students clearly understood how they were to apply the criteria to their work.

In addition to these reflective activities, students were required to complete a mid-year reflection sheet once they had the experience with two separate portfolio selection sessions. I tried to have this coincide with mid-year, because I have found that the second selection day is best done after the December vacation. I also find that these forms are valuable when I meet with parents during conferences. Figure 9.12 contains a sample of a completed mid-year reflection sheet that reveals good insights not only about the work but about the learning process as well.

I find that the most valuable form of reflection is the "Dear Reader" letter. This letter introduced the student to the reader and provided a forum for sharing information about themselves and their accomplishments. Figure 9.13 is a letter done by a fifth-grade student, and Figure 9.14 contains one done by a fourth-grade student. Although there is clearly a wide difference in these students' abilities, both pieces provide evidence of self-reflection, which was one of my goals for them.

Final Thoughts on Using Portfolios in the Classroom

Once the students reflected on the year's efforts, it was time for a response from both me and the parents. The students and I planned a portfolio party. In preparation, they practiced ways in which they could present their portfolios to their families. Parents were also asked to complete an end-of-year questionnaire, a sample of which is shown in Figure 9.15. I personally responded in each student's portfolio and related how I'd seen him or her grow in communication ability, and I identified areas in which I thought the student could improve. I also included a statement about how I enjoyed a specific experience working with the student. This collection, which contained a blend of student and teacher selections, was then turned over to the rightful owners: the students.

The true compensation for keeping portfolios comes during the final hours of the school year. I will never forget the silence when my students opened their final portfolios that were complete with their selections, my reflections, and responses from other teachers and their family. I now realize that, without my ever intending it, these folders became a great equalizer in my classroom, which was made up of students from a diverse array of backgrounds, some of whom were advanced readers and some of whom could barely get by. There was a smile on each student's face, whether the student was a high achiever or always seemed to be struggling. For some, this smile represented validation of ability, and for others, it meant recognition that they too had come far during the year. All held tangible examples of success in their hands.

I join with many other educators who continue to experiment with more effective ways of educating students, and I offer this encouragement to those who are interested in beginning a portfolio process. Keep it simple and follow your instincts; they're probably correct. Share with others; it really helps a lot. When you have questions or problems, discuss the issues with your students; their answers may surprise you. My students and I both learned a great deal from our use of portfolios. I end with this quotation from one of my fifth-grade students: "Keeping a portfolio is like having a reminder to not be too hard on yourself. You can see the whole picture better."

WRITING RUBRIC

3

My writing...

* stays on the topic (is focused) from beginning to end
* has a strong introduction that interests the reader
* is developed enough to cover the topic
* has a strong concluding paragraph
* uses descriptive language in a way that makes the piece more interesting
* has sentences that start in a variety of ways
* has few mechanical or grammatical errors (spelling, punctuation, paragraphs, capital letters)
* is neatly presented / legible handwriting

2

My writing...

* stays on the topic (is focused) for most of the piece but parts could be taken out or changed
* has an introduction
* covers the topic but could be more developed to include more details or information
* has a concluding paragraph
* uses some descriptive language
* has a few sentences that start in an interesting way
* has some mechanical and grammatical errors (spelling, punctuation, paragraphs, capital letters)
* is mostly neat and easy to read

1

My writing...

* gets off the topic or includes details that are not related to the topic
* does not have a clear introduction
* does not give the reader enough details or information
* does not have a clearly written conclusion
* does not use descriptive language
* has most sentences that start in the same way

Figure 9.8
Portfolio writing rubric.

What I Want to Be When I Grow up

I am a person who has many interests. I like to sing, play the clarinet, do hand work, and write. I like to write because it lets all the thoughts that are bottled up inside of me be put on paper. Writing allows me to express myself in a way that sometimes only I understand. When I grow up I want to be a writer.

Writing is a special magic that we all have inside of us, but can only be used when you set your mind to it. Many people must take classes to learn how to use this magic, but there are some of use who are born with the talent of writing and need no classes to use it.

Some people who write can feel the power of words, and when they express them on paper the words will seem to dance. They can make people feel so happy that the world seems to want to join in the happiness also. If you are a pauper who is so sad, and he reads a paper whose words are written with the magic inside of you, he will feel a joy inside of him.

I want to write so I can express all the thoughts of me so they make the paper seem like it's dancing. I want to make a pauper whose never smiled smile, and I will do this by writing.

Figure 9.9
Student writing sample: 3 on rubric.

The Big Gust of Wind

My family decided to go to Flanagans. My mom told me to get my dad. I got out of the car and started to walk down the street. It was cold, but I felt safer

All of a sudden a big gust of wind came and knocked me over. I wanted to get back to the car. Then I started to ride down the sidewalks I couldn't breath. Then my dad picked me up and asked me why I was on the groand. I told him the story while I was walking up the street. When I got to the car, I was excited because we were going to flanagans.

Figure 9.10
Student writing sample: 2 on rubric.

What a day

Oh my god in late in late!!!
in late to go baby sitting.
I ran out the door as
fast as a tiger. zoom!!!!!
i got on my bike and
rode to beford Hills, In
here i yelled when i got
there. Good thing she was
runing late she did not even
know i was late. After 7
have fron runing all over
town i was very tried
What a day.

Figure 9.11
Student writing sample: 1 on rubric.

Name: Jamal Moore **Date:** April 4, 1997

MID-YEAR REFLECTION

1. As I look at my portfolio selections, the piece I like best is Cheesecake and My Crave for it I like this piece because it is descriptive, funny and had no errors.

2. The hardest piece for me to write was My Isebel piece because it took alot of time to write what would happen to Isabel when she got to the whitches bee

3. After reviewing my mid-year portfolio, I feel that I have grown better at spelling and breaking my story up into paragraphs

4. I was pleased with the way have become more descriptive in my pieces like in Cheese Cake and my crave for It.

5. I was not pleased with the way I made some Spelling errores in Some pieces.

6. My goal for the next part of the school year is to write a really adventures Story and alot more poems.

7. I think I can achieve this goal by putting time every day to write my story, and make one of the best stories I have ever writen.

Figure 9.12
Sample mid-year reflection sheet.

Dear Reader,

You are now looking at my portfolio, throughout the year I have written many writing pieces, such as descriptive, short stories, and point of view, ect. Now I would like to share this work with you. A portfolio, though, does not just contain all your work, it is made up of special writing pieces and shows growth throughout the year.

You will read everyihing I'm sure, yet I would like you to notice my growth and how much more descriptive I have become. Not to mention how much longer my writing has become!

I am very proud of this accomplishment and I feel special to be able to say "I have a portfolio." I hope you will feel the same way and mabey start a portfolio of your own since you look over the contents in it!!!

Sincerely,

Anthony Blake

Figure 9.13
Fifth-grade student's letter to the reader.

5/31/97

Dear Reader,

This portfolio show the work I have been working on in the 96-97 schod year, It reresents some of my best. work.

You will find a lot of my work from this school year. You can tell which was wnten in Setember and Which was writin in May You will find a lot of persanal nartive becase I feel I put a lot of effurt into them

I want you to notice The leanghs of my work and look at the effort I put into them.

Singerely

Alicia

Martinez

Figure 9.14
Fourth-grade student's letter to the reader.

PARENT RESPONSE FORM

Student's name:______________________________ **Date:**____________

Dear Parent,

Enclosed is your child's final portfolio representing student and teacher selected samples of his/her growth as an effective communicator this year. As we discussed earlier in the year, the purpose of this portfolio is to document how your child's ability to communicate for a variety of purposes has developed over the past ten months. The portfolio also gives your child an opportunity to select, evaluate and reflect upon his/her own progress as a communicator. This will hopefully enable him/her to set goals for improving skills and see more clearly how much has been accomplished.

Your child has practiced the way in which he/she will present the portfolio to you. I encourage you to spend some time with them as they share this new adventure with you. I am sure that you will enjoy every moment of the trip!

I would greatly appreciate feedback from you and would find your responses to the following questions extremely helpful. Thank you for your continued enthusiasm and support.

Sincerely,
Robyn Lane

1. After viewing the portfolio, I found evidence of growth in the following areas:

   A. Expression of ideas ________
   B. Focus (staying on topic) ________
   C. Vocabulary/language ________
   D. Spelling ________
   E. Punctuation (commas, capitals, periods, etc.) ________
   F. Ability to revise from first to final draft ________
   G. Organization ________

2. I feel my child has shown the greatest growth in the following area:
____
____
____

Figure 9.15
End-of-year parent response form.

3. I would like to see my child further improve in ____________________
____
____

4. Please explain if, and in what ways, you have seen growth in your child's reading ability and/or interests: ____________________
____
____

5. Additional comments: ____________________
____
____
____
____

Parent/Guardian signature: ____________________

Figure 9.15
Continued

Summary

Understanding Portfolios

A *portfolio* is a collection of student work, gathered together for a purpose. Portfolios may be used in any grade and for a variety of purposes. Depending on the purpose of the portfolio, a number of other variables must also be decided, such as the contents, who chooses the contents, the audience(s), and assessment options. Student participation is a major feature of most portfolios, and it is what distinguishes portfolios from cumulative folders and permanent records, which are assembled by teachers and other school staff.

Making Decisions Regarding Portfolios

Purposes of portfolios include instructional monitoring, celebrating or showcasing accomplishments, passing on information, facilitating communication between teachers and parents, and providing materials to college admissions officers or prospective employers. Audiences typically include the students themselves, teachers, parents, prospective employers, state assessment officials and staff, program evaluation staff, and college admissions officers. Common portfolio contents include recordings of student performances, products, projects, written work, tests, observations and comments by teachers and parents, and conference records. The decision to include a particular item in the contents of a portfolio may be made by each student alone, the students with guidance from the teacher, the students and teacher in collaboration, individual students with input from their peers, or by the teacher alone. Portfolios come in all shapes and sizes, some incorporating computer technology, to accommodate their contents. Portfolios provide two assessment options: (1) each piece in the portfolio may be assessed individually prior to inclusion, or (2) the entire contents may be assessed as one body using judging criteria developed expressly for that purpose.

Considering the Advantages and Disadvantages of Portfolios

Advantages of portfolios include the following:

1. Portfolios are consistent with theories of instruction and philosophies of schools promoting student involvement with their learning.
2. They are an excellent way to document developmental growth over time.
3. Portfolios can bring together staff to discuss and reach consensus on such decisions as the purpose, audience, and contents.
4. For students involved in their use, portfolios can foster a sense of ownership of the work and the skills of critical self-reflection and decision making.

5. Portfolio contents may be used to illustrate the processes and procedures students follow.
6. Portfolios facilitate combining paper-and-pencil tests with performance and product assessments.

Disadvantages include:

1. Logistics involved in designing and maintaining a portfolio system may be overwhelming with little or no support.
2. All stakeholders need training to design, implement, manage, and assess portfolios.
3. Portfolios carry no inherent insurance against being used for purposes not intended.
4. Portfolios are a new assessment strategy to most teachers, relative to previous approaches, with many unresolved issues.

Using Guidelines to Implement Portfolios Effectively

Guidelines for using portfolios are as follows:

1. Clearly articulate the purpose of the portfolio.
2. Communicate the articulated purpose to all stakeholders.
3. Use only content-selection criteria congruent with the articulated purpose.
4. Choose only portfolio contents congruent with the selection criteria.
5. Ensure that the role of each stakeholder group is congruent with the purpose.
6. Familiarize all stakeholder groups with the responsibilities and activities associated with their roles.
7. Involve students in the process appropriate to their developmental and maturity levels.
8. If documenting process in the product, the student must articulate it.
9. Use cover sheets, sticky notes, or cards attached to portfolio items to describe the items and why they were chosen.
10. Do not include scores on portfolio items.
11. Choose a storage container and classroom space large enough to accommodate the contents and facilitate easy use.
12. Follow through. Ensure that portfolios are passed on to their audience(s).

Guidelines for assessing portfolios include:

1. Include enough documents (items) on which to base judgment.
2. Structure the contents to provide scorable information.
3. Develop judging criteria and a scoring scheme for raters to use in assessing the portfolios.

4. Use observation instruments such as checklists and rating scales when possible to facilitate scoring.
5. Use trained raters.

Try This

I. Assume that the staff and administration at your school have decided to implement portfolios, as they are consistent with the school's philosophy of students' involvement in their learning. Choose a setting (early childhood, elementary, middle, or high school) and make the necessary decisions. If possible, do this exercise in a small group with your peers. Discuss and answer the questions in the areas listed below. Read through all the questions before beginning discussion.

Purpose: What is the major purpose? Are there other, lesser purposes? If so, list in rank order.

Audience: Who are the audience(s) for the portfolios? What will be the students' role and responsibilities regarding the portfolios? What are your responsibilities as the teacher? What training will the students need to successfully implement the portfolio system? Are the audiences and their roles consistent with the purpose(s) of the portfolios?

Contents: What are the contents of the portfolios likely to include, given your knowledge of the curriculum and typical instructional activities in this setting? How do the projected contents relate to the purpose(s)?

Storage: What types of storage containers might work for the setting and the students? Where will they be kept? Is access or security a concern? If so, what can be done? Are the containers consistent with the students' needs, the contents, and the purpose(s)?

Scoring: Will the portfolios be assessed as a unit (assessment option two)? If so, is this consistent with the purpose(s)? What are the judging criteria likely to be? Who will rate the portfolios? Who will train the raters?

CHAPTER 10

Improving Classroom Assessment

Key Concepts:

- Understanding the benefits of item analysis and when to use it.
- Applying the item-analysis process to non-mastery assessments.
- Understanding item-achievement charts and how to use them.
- Understanding item-achievement rates and discriminating power.
- Analyzing responses to multiple-choice items.
- Analyzing multi-point essay items, performance tasks, and judging criteria.
- Improving assessments and instruction using item-analysis data.
- Determining the outcome-achievement rate for mastery assessments.
- Adjusting scores and organizing and storing item-analysis data.

Standards Addressed in This Chapter:

1. Choose assessment methods appropriate for instructional decisions.
2. Develop assessment methods appropriate for instructional decisions.
3. Use assessment results when making decisions about individual students, planning teaching, developing curriculum, and school improvement.

Before You Begin Reading, Consider This

Is it better to stand firm behind an assessment score you know is partially due to faulty items or performance tasks, rather than discuss the matter with your students?

YES Otherwise, students will challenge anything they get wrong and chaos will reign whenever assessments are returned. It sets a bad example and costs instructional time. The scores all average out, anyway.

NO How else can we know how to fix bad items and performance tasks but by understanding our students' thinking and asking for their input? Clinging steadfastly to an assessment result we know is not accurate sets a bad example for students, too.

Understanding Item Analysis

Veteran teachers know that when they try new materials or instructional strategies with their students, it is important to pay attention to how the materials and strategies are working. If they are confusing, incomplete, or just plain ineffective, they must be adjusted or replaced by something that does work. The same is true for classroom assessments that teachers create or select for use, especially if they will be used again. Even if teachers follow all the guidelines for assessment design and construction to the letter, it is sometimes difficult to identify problems with items, performance tasks, and scoring schemes before the assessment has actually been given.

What is the point of analyzing the adequacy of an assessment after it has already been given? Good question. I'm glad you asked. It is true that validity should be a paramount consideration during test construction. But remember, validity for classroom assessments is basically a judgmental process. Analysis of test results supports or does not support initial validity judgments. Use of techniques such as item analysis helps us to identify the trouble spots (if any) of a given assessment so that we can reduce them. Further, analysis of results can help us to better interpret the scores and to use them more wisely.[1] We would not, for example, make any important decisions concerning students based on the results of an assessment found to have serious defects.

Item analysis involves examination of the pattern or type of student responses for each item or performance task in order to assess its effectiveness. The results of item analysis permit better interpretation of test results and provide guidance for item revision. If many students miss the same item or perform a certain task inadequately, for example, it does not necessarily mean that they did not achieve the corresponding instructional outcome; the item or the task itself may be defective. Item analysis also indirectly provides feedback to the teacher concerning factors related to good

[1]More on interpreting assessment results in Chapters 11 and 14.

and poor items, which can be useful in future assessment development efforts. It does not tell a teacher *how* to improve an item; however, it does identify potential problem items and provide clues as to the source of the problem.

In the past, item analysis was associated with standardized, multiple-choice tests. The goal was to maximize the capability of the assessment to spread people out on a continuum of performance so that norm-referenced interpretations of the results could be made with confidence. The basic thought process involved in item analysis may, however, be applied to the results of any assessment: yes, even an essay test. The major aspect of item analysis—item-achievement rate—applies to all types of items and performance-scoring criteria.

Some experts advocate the use of item-analysis procedures more tailored to criterion-referenced assessment such as a pretest-posttest sensitivity index or an uninstructed-instructed sensitivity index to judge the quality of criterion-referenced items.[2] These procedures have difficulties, however, that make them impractical for most teachers. With the pretest-posttest sensitivity index, for example, a pretest must be administered, and no analysis may be done until instruction is completed and the posttest administered. Students must, therefore, endure bad items twice. Furthermore, it may not always be feasible or advisable to administer a pretest. The uninstructed-instructed sensitivity index requires the assessment to be given to two groups that can be tested at the same time, but only one group receives instruction. The test results from both groups must then be compared, thus creating double computational work.

As you read on, item analysis may begin to sound like a lot of trouble. It is true there is a learning curve that comes with item analysis, just as there is with learning any new thought process. Part of the problem is that item analysis takes longer to explain than to do. Nevertheless, item analysis is an excellent assessment-strengthening process that should be performed on at least the more heavily weighted assessments you use in the classroom and any others that you suspect are not working as well as you would like. Once you get reasonably accustomed to analyzing items and tasks, visual inspection of results may be enough to obtain the desired information, eliminating the need for computations. Item analysis is not a cure-all that subsequently results in perfect tests; however, it can provide a splendid basis for a classroom discussion with students concerning assessment results. When students complain that item five "wasn't fair!" instead of being defensive you can agree with them and show them why. Sharing the results of item analysis also provides opportunities to clarify misconceptions and points of confusion. You may say, "Some of you selected *b,* probably because you thought. . . ." When these students see that most of the class selected the correct response, they realize that they were in error and that the item was not at fault. To summarize, item analysis can save time and enhance your teaching by:

- Improving assessments for later administration.
- Improving future assessment development (reducing the need for revision).

---

[2]See, for example, *Principles of Educational and Psychological Measurement and Evaluation* (4th ed.) by G. Sax, 1997, Belmont, CA: Wadsworth.

- Reducing arguments over "unfair" items and performance tasks (you already know which ones are suspect).
- Increasing your confidence in the assessments on which grades are based.
- Promoting better interpretation and use of results.

Not only is it worth the time and effort in terms of benefits to be derived, but many teachers actually think that the process is fun!

Item analysis can be performed on a paper-and-pencil assessment or a performance assessment and for a criterion-referenced mastery test or a norm-referenced non-mastery test. Types of results on which item analysis can be successfully performed include:

- Dichotomously scored test items, in which answers are either correct or incorrect. This includes multiple-choice, short-answer, matching, and two-choice formats.
- Analytically scored essay items where each aspect or component is scored dichotomously.
- Performance task scoring rubrics and holistically scored essay items where a judgment is made as to acceptable and unacceptable performance. For example, you may decide that a score of 3 or higher is acceptable, whereas a score of 2 or lower is unacceptable for a multi-element, multi-point scoring scheme (see Figure 8.7).
- Performance checklist "items" (see Figures 8.3 and 8.4).

Item analysis is appropriate to perform whenever you have assessment results, but that could get cumbersome. To keep your workload to a minimum, consider the following guidelines in deciding whether to analyze all the items, only certain items, or no items. Item analysis is especially appropriate when you are pilot testing a new assessment instrument: a new checklist, perhaps. It is also beneficial when you have administered an assessment that counts for a substantial part of a grade or one on which students did not do as well as expected. Finally, item analysis can be used on any assessment related to instruction that you have targeted for improvement. It helps pinpoint the trouble spots. The process of item analysis for non-mastery assessments will be explained first, followed by an explanation of the process for mastery assessments.

Applying the Item-Analysis Process to Non-Mastery Assessments

Item analysis of classroom assessments that are either criterion-referenced, non-mastery tests or norm-referenced assessments involves a series of steps carried out after the tests or performances are individually scored. The following steps will be discussed more fully in turn:

1. Prepare an item-achievement chart indicating correct (or acceptable) responses with a symbol (such as •, 1, or /). List students on the chart in order based on total score, highest to lowest.

2. Calculate the item-achievement rate (IAR) for each item using the results from all students in the calculations.
3. For each item, make a judgment concerning the acceptability of the item-achievement rate. The criterion of acceptability of the item-achievement rate will vary depending on the difficulty of the concept or skill measured. Thus, for example, for certain items, IAR = 70 might be considered acceptable.
4. For items with unacceptable item-achievement rates (and *only* for items with unacceptable item-achievement rates), calculate discriminating power (DP), based on the results for high- and low-scoring subgroups (the top third and bottom third of the class).
5. Logically analyze the results to pinpoint the problem and suggest revisions for later administrations of the assessment or for related instruction.

Item-Achievement Charts

An *item-achievement chart* is a visual tool that helps teachers discern response patterns and identify possible defective items. Students are listed down the left column in order of their total assessment performance, highest to lowest. Thus, in the far right column the total scores (TS) are listed in descending order. The individual items on the test head the intervening columns. Figure 10.1 is a sample item-achievement chart for a 20-item assessment for 18 students. The grid is easily constructed by most word-processing computer software that produces tables and by spreadsheet programs. Across the bottom are two rows for writing in item-analysis data—item-achievement rate (IAR) and discriminating power (DP).

Item-Achievement Rate

Item-achievement rate (IAR) refers to the percentage or proportion of students who get the individual item correct or, in the case of a multi-point scale, muster enough points for "acceptable" performance. In the past, item-achievement rate was also called *item difficulty* (you may still hear the term), but item-achievement rate is a more apt description of a percentage that increases as more students achieve the item. There is a simple formula for calculating it:

$$IAR = (R \div T) \times 100$$

where IAR = item-achievement rate

R = the number of students who took the test who got the item correct or achieved "acceptable" performance (R is for *right*)

T = the total number of students who took the test (T is for *total*)

If 30 students took the test and all got the item right, the IAR would be 100:

$$IAR = (30 \div 30) \times 100 = 1 \times 100 = 100$$

If 30 students took the test and all got the item wrong, the IAR would be 0.

$$IAR = (0 \div 30) \times 100 = 0 \times 100 = 0$$

Item / Student	1	2	3	4	5	6	7	8	9	10	11	12	13	14	15	16	17	18	19	20	TS
1	•	•	•	•	•	•	•	•	•	•	•	•	•	•	•	•	•	•	•	•	20
2	•	•	•	•	•	•	•	•	•	•	•	•	•	•	•	•	•	•	•	•	20
3	•	•	•	•	•	•	•	•	•	•	•	•	•	•	•	•	•	•	•	•	20
4	•	•	•	•	•	•	•	•	•	•	•	•	•	•	•	•	•	•	•	•	20
5	•	•	•	•	•	•	•	•	•	•	•	•	•	•	•	•	•	•	•	•	20
6	•	•	•	•	•	•	•	•	•	•	•	•	•	•	•	•	•	•	•	•	20
7	•	•	•	•	•	•	•	•	•	•	•	•	•	•	•	•	•	•	•	•	20
8	•	•	•	•	•	•	•	•	•	•	•	•		•	•	•	•	•	•	•	19
9	•	•	•	•	•	•	•	•	•	•		•	•	•	•	•	•	•	•	•	19
10	•	•	•	•	•	•	•	•	•	•	•	•		•	•	•	•	•	•	•	19
11	•	•	•	•	•	•		•	•	•	•	•	•	•	•	•	•		•	•	18
12	•	•	•	•	•	•		•	•	•	•		•	•	•	•	•	•	•	•	18
13	•	•	•	•	•	•	•	•	•	•		•		•	•	•	•	•	•	•	18
14	•	•	•	•	•	•	•		•	•		•	•	•	•	•	•	•	•	•	18
15	•	•	•	•	•		•	•		•	•	•	•	•	•	•	•	•	•	•	18
16	•	•	•	•	•	•	•	•		•	•	•	•	•		•	•	•	•		17
17	•	•	•	•	•	•		•	•	•						•		•	•		12
18	•	•		•				•		•											5
IAR																					
DP																					

Figure 10.1
An item achievement chart for 18 students and a 20-item nonmastery assessment. A dot (•) indicates the student answered the item correctly or earned enough points (in the case of a multi-point item) to "pass" the item.

What would the IAR be for item six in Figure 10.1? Looking down the column for item six, we count 16 dots, so R = 16. Looking down the student column, we see that 18 students took the test, so T = 18. Inserting these values into our formula and our calculator, we get:

$$\text{IAR} = (16 \div 18) \times 100 = .8888888 \times 100 = 88.88888, \text{ which rounds to } 89$$

One way to interpret this is to say that 89% of the students who took the test achieved item six. Now fill in the rest of the IAR row in Figure 10.1. Once you have calculated a few, it goes much faster. When finished with Figure 10.1, compare your answers to those in Figure 10.3. Try not to peek before you finish.

Now the question is, "What is a good item-achievement rate?" Generally, if the item-achievement rate is high, we say that students found the item easy. If the item-achievement rate is low, we say that the item was difficult. But "good" goes beyond this. For most classroom assessments that are curriculum-based and criterion-referenced, the difficulty of the item should reflect the difficulty of the instructional outcome it is designed to measure. That is, if the outcome to be assessed is of low difficulty and the students have been given sufficient instruction on it, we could expect that the items related to it to have high item-achievement rates: 100 would not be uncommon. If the outcome assessed is a difficult one to achieve or if it is the first time students have encountered it in the curriculum, we might expect the item-achievement rates to be lower, say 65, for example. Of course, the quality of the teaching and time on task are important factors as well.

Given these variables, the teacher's judgment should prevail when determining acceptable item-achievement rate values. What is "acceptable" may vary by instructional outcome or, perhaps, by assessment. For the math test in Figure 10.1, the teacher selected 75 as the item-achievement rate standard for each of the items—if at least 75% of the students achieved it, no further analysis was necessary. Any item with an item-achievement rate below 75 would be further analyzed (using discriminating-power calculations, discussed below) and perhaps considered defective. For some items assessing certain complex instructional outcomes, a teacher may choose an item-achievement rate as low as 30 for the lower limit of the acceptable range. Within the range of 30 to 100, teachers have great latitude in deciding where to set the level of acceptability for the items on any given classroom assessment. Assuming the item or performance task parallels the outcome it measures, the question to ask in setting minimum acceptable item-achievement rate values is, "What is the proportion of students I reasonably and fully expect to achieve this item?" The answer to this question and the resulting minimum item-achievement rates may be determined either individually or in collaboration with other teachers.

Discriminating Power

Discriminating power (DP) refers to the degree to which an item discriminates between high and low achievers on the assessment. In other words, if an item has high, positive discriminating power, then the high achievers in the class tended to get it right (or to get enough points to meet criterion following the scoring rubric) and the low achievers did not. Because the best measure of overall achievement is the test itself, we determine how an item on the test relates to performance on the total test. If the performance pattern of a given item is similar to that of the total test—that is, high scorers get it right and low scorers get it wrong—then the item has good discriminating power. If the assessment is indeed a valid measure of the intended outcomes, then the process of determining discriminating power does validate the items. Without verification of the total test validity, however, the most we can really say is that a given item does or does not measure whatever the total test measures (or, more precisely, that it measures it to a certain degree), which means that we are really analyzing an index of internal consistency. It is fairly safe to assume, however, that most classroom assessments are at least adequately valid and, therefore, that indices of discriminating power are indices of item validity.

The steps in estimating discriminating power are simple and proceed from the same item-achievement chart used for finding item-achievement rates. It is not necessary to use data from all of the students on the chart, however. For estimating discriminating power, only the information from the top and bottom thirds of the students are required. That is why it is important to enter the data into the chart in rank order, from best performance to worst. Recall also that it is only necessary to estimate discriminating power for items with unacceptably low item-achievement rates. The first step in estimating discriminating power, then, is to split the rows into thirds: In Figure 10.1, students 1 through 6 become the upper group and students 13 through 18 become the lower group. An easy way to do this is to draw a thick, horizontal line between the data for students 6 and 7 and for students 12 and 13. The middle third is not needed in this part of the analysis. If you *did* use the item results for all the students, you would increase the accuracy of the discriminating-power values calculated, but you would also increase computational time. Discriminating power is estimated using the following fairly simple formula.[3]

$$DP = (R_U - R_L) \div .5T$$

where

DP = discriminating power

R_U = the number of students in the upper group who responded correctly (again, R is for *right*)

R_L = the number of students in the lower group who responded correctly

T = the total number of students in the item analysis (the high group and the low group added together)

As the formula suggests, there are three possible relationships between R_U and R_L:

$R_U > R_L$ (more students in the upper group responded correctly),

$R_U = R_L$ (the same number of students in the two groups responded correctly), or

$R_U < R_L$ (more students in the lower group responded correctly).

---

[3]This formula actually represents a method of estimating point-biserial correlations. For many purposes, however, especially when discriminating power is calculated by hand, the estimates are adequate.

When $R_U > R_L$, the item is behaving the same way as the total test and has positive discriminating power. When R_U and R_L are essentially the same or very close, the item has discriminating power near .00, which means that the item does not discriminate. When $R_U < R_L$, the item is behaving in a manner opposite to that of the total test and has negative discriminating power; the "wrong" students (those who did poorly on the total test) are getting the item correct. Figure 10.2 summarizes these concepts.

If everyone in the upper group got the item correct and no one in the lower group got the item correct, what would the discriminating power be? Right, DP = +1.00. For example, for a class of 30 students, if $R_U = 10$, $R_L = 0$, and T = 20 (there are 10 each in the upper and lower groups):

$$DP = (R_U - R_L) \div .5T = (10 - 0) \div .5(20) = 10 \div 10 = +1.00$$

Note that if the opposite were true, $R_U = 0$, $R_L = 10$, then DP would equal −1.00:

$$DP = (R_U - R_L) \div .5T = (0 - 10) \div .5(20) = -10 \div 10 = -1.00$$

Any time the discriminating power is negative, the item is said to be "negatively discriminating." Using the teacher's criterion of 75 as the lowest acceptable item-achievement rate for the items in Figure 10.1, we see that items 11 and 13 are unacceptable. With their item-achievement rates of 72, they are to be investigated further. Using the data from the upper and lower thirds of the group, the discriminating power for item 11 is:

$$DP = (R_U - R_L) \div .5T = (6 - 2) \div .5(12) = 4 \div 6 = .6666666 = .67 \text{ (rounded)}$$

and the discriminating power for item 13 is:

$$DP = (R_U - R_L) \div .5T = (6 - 3) \div .5(12) = 3 \div 6 = .50$$

Both of these values have been entered into the completed item-achievement chart in Figure 10.3.

The Relationship Between Item-Achievement Rate and Discriminating Power

Note that discriminating power is related to item-achievement rate. In other words, if half of the students in the item analysis get the item correct, IAR = 50, and if that half is the upper half, then discriminating power will be +1.00. For most classroom

Situation	Resulting DP	Examples of DP
$R_U > R_L$	Positive	.92, .80, .67, .59, .44
$R_U = R_L$ or nearly so	At or near zero	.05, .11, .08, .00
$R_U < R_L$	Negative	−.10, −.23, −.39, −.57

Figure 10.2
Summary of possible item-analysis data and resulting discriminating power.

Item / Student	1	2	3	4	5	6	7	8	9	10	11	12	13	14	15	16	17	18	19	20	TS
1	●	●	●	●	●	●	●	●	●	●	●	●	●	●	●	●	●	●	●	●	20
2	●	●	●	●	●	●	●	●	●	●	●	●	●	●	●	●	●	●	●	●	20
3	●	●	●	●	●	●	●	●	●	●	●	●	●	●	●	●	●	●	●	●	20
4	●	●	●	●	●	●	●	●	●	●	●	●	●	●	●	●	●	●	●	●	20
5	●	●	●	●	●	●	●	●	●	●	●	●	●	●	●	●	●	●	●	●	20
6	●	●	●	●	●	●	●	●	●	●	●	●	●	●	●	●	●	●	●	●	20
7	●	●	●	●	●	●	●	●	●	●	●	●	●	●	●	●	●	●	●	●	20
8	●	●	●	●	●	●	●	●	●	●	●	●		●	●	●	●	●	●	●	19
9	●	●	●	●	●	●	●	●	●	●		●	●	●	●	●	●	●	●	●	19
10	●	●	●	●	●	●	●	●	●	●	●	●		●	●	●	●	●	●	●	19
11	●	●	●	●	●	●		●	●	●	●	●	●	●	●	●	●		●	●	18
12	●	●	●	●	●	●		●	●	●	●		●	●	●	●	●	●	●	●	18
13	●	●	●	●	●	●	●	●	●	●		●		●	●	●	●	●	●	●	18
14	●	●	●	●	●	●	●		●	●		●	●	●	●	●	●	●	●	●	18
15	●	●	●	●	●		●	●		●	●	●	●	●	●	●	●	●	●	●	18
16	●	●	●	●	●	●	●	●		●	●	●	●	●		●	●	●	●		17
17	●	●	●	●	●	●		●	●	●						●		●	●		12
18	●	●		●				●		●											5
IAR	100	100	94	100	94	89	78	94	83	100	72	83	72	89	83	94	89	89	94	83	
DP											.67		.50								

Figure 10.3
An item achievement chart for 18 students on a 20-item criterion-referenced nonmastery test, with item achievement rates for each item calculated, and discriminating power for selected items estimated.

assessments, however, the items have an average item-achievement rate higher than 50. To the degree the average item-achievement rate is greater than 50, to that degree the maximum discriminating power is less than +1.00.

The point of using discriminating power along with item-achievement rate in analyzing classroom non-mastery assessments is to see if an item appearing at first to be overly difficult due to its low item-achievement rate is at least positively discriminating between those who did well on the assessment and those who did not. It is not a good idea, however, to label an item defective just because it has low discriminating power. Discriminating power estimates are not *that* precise, and if the item is measuring something different from the assessment as a whole, low discriminating power is to be expected. Eliminating several such items on the basis of their discriminating powers might actually result in the validity of the assessment being lowered. Further, maximum discrimination is possible only when items are of "medium" difficulty (IARs = 50). Because we may intentionally include some very easy items due to the outcomes they assess, we know in advance that these will have low discriminating power. As with item achievement, common sense must be used in interpreting indexes of discriminating power.

A low item-achievement rate coupled with a negative discriminating power is an automatic call for further analysis. Recall that item analysis does not tell you *what* is wrong, only that something appears amiss. You may have to inspect the individual item and the various responses of your students to determine its true adequacy. After doing this, you may come to the conclusion that the item is fine but that more time on task or a different instructional strategy is needed. Item analysis thus gives you a place to start and data to work with in a critical-thinking process that leads to improved assessment and instruction. The general procedure can be summed up in a series of "if, then" statements that you can use after calculating the item-achievement rates.

If . . .	**Then . . .**
IAR is suspiciously high,	verify match between outcome and item; check for possible violation of item/task construction guidelines.
IAR is acceptable,	no DP check needed.
IAR is too low,	check DP.
IAR is too low, but DP acceptable,	verify match between outcome and item.
IAR is too low and DP at or near zero,	verify match between outcome and item; check for possible violation of item/task construction guidelines.
IAR is too low and DP negative,	verify match between outcome and item; check item response pattern across students; check for possible violation of item/task construction guidelines.

You may have noticed that on the previous item-achievement charts, the more marks missing from cells in the column for an item, the lower the item-achievement rate. Some teachers, after they become comfortable creating item-achievement charts, no longer need to calculate item-achievement rates for every item. They visually inspect the chart to determine those items with "too few marks." After a visual inspection, these teachers may calculate item-achievement rates for the several items with the most missing marks. If any of the item-achievement rates are unacceptable, estimates of discriminating power can also be calculated if it cannot be determined visually that they are negative. If an overabundance of the empty cells for an item occurs in the upper third of the assessed group as opposed to the lower third, then the calculated discriminating power will be negative.

Distractor Analysis

Remember that item-achievement rate and discriminating power merely indicate whether an item is doing its intended job, not why or why not. If an item is found to be defective, we have to examine possible reasons. The cause might be something as simple as an incorrect scoring key, but not very often. The problem may be the result of misunderstanding on the part of students, or there may actually be something wrong with the item. If the scoring key checks out, the next logical place to look is at the item itself. The examination of incorrect responses, or *distractor analysis,* often provides clues concerning the source of the problem. This is not very helpful for simple true-false tests, but it is for other types of items, especially multiple-choice items. If distractors are not doing their job—that is, they are not all plausible to a student who does not "know" the answer—the result may be an exceptionally easy item and a low estimate of discriminating power.

There are any number of other undesirable possibilities. A good distractor is one selected by more students in the lower group than in the upper group. Thus, a good distractor has distractability; the ability to distract certain students from the correct answer. If no one selects a given distractor, it has no distractibility and is ineffective and useless, and it should be replaced. If a distractor is selected by more students in the upper group than the lower group, it has negative distractibility—not a good attribute. The fault may lie in the stem (it could have been ambiguous), for example, or in the instruction that preceded the assessment (which also could have been ambiguous!).

Analysis of distractors does not require the application of any formula. Examination of the alternatives selected by each group in the item analysis makes it fairly evident how the distractors worked. For example, suppose that on a 50-item, multiple-choice test 10 students are in the upper group and 10 in the lower group out of your class of 30. Suppose that *b* is the correct alternative for item 18 and that 7 of the 30 students answered it correctly. The pattern of responses for the upper and lower groups is shown below.

Item	IAR	DP	Alternative	Upper 10	Lower 10
18	23	+.30	a.	0	0
			b.	4	1
			c.	4	6
			d.	2	3

From the information about item 18 we can see the following:

1. Overall, the item appears to be too difficult; IAR = (7 ÷ 30) × 100 = 23.
2. The DP of this item can be calculated from the upper 10 and lower 10 data. It is minimally acceptable; (4 − 1) ÷ 10 = +.30.
3. Distractor *a* is not working at all; no one chose it.
4. Distractors *c* and *d* are working in the right direction; they attracted more of the students in the lower group. Distractor *c*, however, attracted as many students from the upper group as the correct answer; this bears looking into.

If we wanted to improve this mediocre item, we would first try to determine why alternative *c* was so attractive to both groups. Perhaps the stem needs rewording. We would also eliminate distractor *a* or replace it with a more plausible and attractive, but wrong, choice.

Because the number of students in each group is generally small and we are working with general trends anyway, we do have to be careful not to be overly influenced by small differences. We can be satisfied if all of the alternatives are functioning reasonably well and are leading students in the right direction. Just to be sure you have a basic understanding of the concepts discussed, we will look at two more examples, both of which have item-achievement rates of 50. Of the two sets of item data below, see if you can tell which item is terrific and which is terrible. Use the upper and lower group data to calculate discriminating power and write it in the blank indicated in the DP column.

Item	IAR	DP	Alternative	Upper 10	Lower 10
4	50	_____	a.	1	3
			b.	0	2
			c.	1	3
			d. (underlined)	8	2
5	50	_____	a.	0	0
			b.	5	2
			c. (underlined)	3	7
			d.	2	1

If you did not pick item four as the good one, go back to the beginning of this discussion! Although both items have the same item-achievement rate, their discriminating powers are v-e-r-y different.

Item 4	Item 5
DP = (8 − 2) ÷ 10 = 6 ÷ 10 = +.60	DP = (3 − 7) ÷ 10 = −4 ÷ 10 = −.40

The discriminating power of each item tells the real story. For item four, the DP of +.60 is quite good and all of the distractors are working. All distractors were chosen by members of the lower group, and, in fact, the pattern of responses makes it appear that they were equally plausible to members of that group. In item five, the DP of −.40 is terrible and the distractors are clearly not working. Distractor *a* was chosen by no one and distractor *d* was chosen by the "wrong" students. The real problem, however, is distractor *b*. For some reason, a number of the higher achievers thought that it was the correct choice, whereas the low achievers had little difficulty in identifying *c* as the correct response. Got the idea?

Item Analysis for Performance Assessments and Multi-Point Essay Items

Item analysis can be performed on essay items without too much difficulty provided that the desired response for each item has been clearly defined and that the analytical method of scoring is used. We *can* do item analysis on an assessment with broader, globally scored items, but the information is not nearly as useful. If point values are assigned to each sub-part of an essay item, then we can treat each sub-part as a separate item. The major problem is that by their very nature these "items" tend to be non-independent because degree of success on one may be related to degree of success on another.

As an example of how such an analysis can be done, suppose essay item four has five parts (*a–e*) and each part is worth three points; for our purposes part *d,* for example, would be an item worth three points, and the results for it could be analyzed as follows:

Item Part	Points	Upper 12	Lower 12
d.	0	0	4
	1	3	6
	2	4	2
	3	5	0

From this we can determine, for example, that the upper group received much higher scores than the lower group. In each of the pairs of parentheses below, the first number refers to the number of points and the second number refers to the number of students who earned that many points:

$$\text{Upper group} = (0 \times 0) + (1 \times 3) + (2 \times 4) + (3 \times 5)$$
$$= 0 + 3 + 8 + 15 = 26.$$

$$\text{Lower group} = (0 \times 4) + (1 \times 6) + (2 \times 2) + (3 \times 0)$$
$$= 0 + 6 + 4 + 0 = 10.$$

When we compare 26 points for the upper group to 10 points for the lower group, we see that the item is performing as expected.

Using the multi-element, multi-point scoring scheme in Figure 8.7, we can submit each of the five elements of a performance assessment to the same analysis as the previous essay item. Five points were available for elements one, two, and five, and a dot (●) in the cell indicates that the student received at least three points. Four points were available for elements three and four, and a dot (●) in the cell indicates that the student received at least two points. For item-analysis purposes, we may decide to turn each of the elements in Figure 8.7 into a dichotomous "item" and, in effect, create an item-achievement chart for a five-item assessment. The chart may look like Figure 10.4. A checklist, of course, is already a list of dichotomously scored (yes/no) elements or items. In Figure 10.4 there are no items for which there are more dots for the lower group (students seven, eight, and nine) than there are for the upper group (students one, two, and three), so there are no negatively discriminating items for these students. In terms of this non-mastery performance assessment, this means that students who did well on the assessment overall also tended to do well on the individual scoring components.

What is more important, however, is the distribution of the cell marks. If other writing tasks are assigned and the same rubric is used to score them, a teacher may compare item-achievement charts across assignments to see strengths and weaknesses in the class. If, for example, development of supporting ideas or examples ("item" two in Figure 10.4) gets consistently low item-achievement rate values on other assignments as well, the teacher may wish to examine the instructional activities and materials he or she uses to teach students this skill.

There are a number of places to look when determining the causes of unacceptable item-achievement rates and discriminating-power values that have been mentioned individually throughout this chapter. They are summarized in the checklist for your reference.

✓ *Easy Reference Checklist*

Possible Causes of Unacceptable IAR and DP Values

- ❑ Mis-keyed correct answer.
- ❑ Violation of construction guidelines for tests, items, performance tasks, scoring schemes, checklists, or rating scales.
- ❑ Spelling errors that change the meaning of the words used in the item or to present the task.
- ❑ Reproduction problems (light copies, missing pages, smudges, etc.).
- ❑ Mismatch between outcome and item or task—item or task too hard or too easy as compared to the outcome it assesses.
- ❑ Minimum IAR is unrealistic.
- ❑ Not enough practice or time on task.
- ❑ Method of instruction and/or instructional materials not effective for students and outcome.

Item / Student	1 Focus	2 Support	3 Language	4 Structure	5 Mechanics	Total Score
1	•	•	•	•	•	20
2	•	•	•	•	•	19
3	•	•		•	•	17
4	•		•	•	•	14
5			•	•	•	13
6	•		•	•		13
7			•	•	•	13
8				•		11
9						10
IAR	56	33	67	89	67	
DP						

Figure 10.4
Item-achievement chart for a multi-component, multi-point, non-mastery performance assessment scoring rubric. Note that the "items," from the Writing Sample Scoring Scheme II (Fig. 8.7), are 1. focus on the topic, 2. development of supporting ideas or examples, 3. command of the language, 4. sentence structure, and 5. punctuation, capitalization, and spelling.

Determining the Outcome-Achievement Rate for Mastery Assessments

When items assess a particular outcome, as they typically do on a mastery assessment, we are more interested in how the items related to a certain outcome performed than how all of the items may have performed individually. We can analyze all the items that measure a given outcome together, independently from the rest of the assessment, by calculating the outcome-achievement rate (OAR). *Outcome-achievement rate* is the percentage of assessed students who reached criterion on the outcome based on their performance on the items related to that outcome. Reviewing items in context this way gives us the information we need for mastery assessments. We are interested in the pattern and total marks for a given outcome even more so than we may be for the item-achievement rate. Here are the steps in analyzing items for mastery assessments:

1. Prepare an item-achievement chart for the outcome which indicates correct (or acceptable) responses with a symbol (such as ●, 1, or /). List students on the chart based on their score for the outcome, highest to lowest.
2. Calculate the outcome-achievement rate using the results of all students in the calculation.
3. For each outcome analyzed, make a judgment concerning the acceptability of the outcome achievement rate. The criterion of acceptability of the outcome-achievement rate will vary depending on the difficulty of the outcome assessed and the proportion of students you reasonably expect to master it.
4. For outcomes with unacceptable outcome-achievement rates, calculate the item-achievement rates for each constituent item using the results of all students in the calculations.
5. Logically analyze the results for the related item(s) with the lowest item-achievement rate(s).

Discriminating power estimates are not calculated for mastery assessments because they are not precise enough to be worth the effort.

As an example, here is how one teacher, Mr. Washington, interpreted item-analysis data from a five-item mastery assessment (actually a portion of a test) that measured the following application-level outcome:

> **Given accurate drawings of a variety of triangles, each having all the needed dimensions shown, the student will use the memorized formula to correctly compute the area of each to the nearest whole number, four out of five times.**

This outcome represents a higher-level outcome, but Mr. Washington anticipated that at least 80% of his students would master it. He wrote short-answer items, each consisting of a triangle with necessary dimensions identified and a blank in which to write the computed area to measure this outcome. The items represented different kinds of triangles (such as scalene and isosceles). Mr. Washington was interested specifically in this outcome because, as he scored the tests, it appeared to him that "too many" students struggled with these items. He decided to check out the items for this outcome only.

Figure 10.5 presents the results for the five items associated with the instructional outcome. A dot (●) in the cell indicates a correct response. Mr. Washington used all 10 papers and arranged the student data in order of performance on the entire out-

Outcome	1				
Item / Student	1	2	3	4	5
Lyons, A.	•	•	•	•	•
Kaylo, S.	•		•	•	•
Apps, H.	•		•	•	•
Arch, Z.	•	•		•	•
Griswold, M.	•	•	•		•
Drexler, C.	•	•	•		•
Rogers, L.	•			•	•
O'Hara, C.	•		•		•
Wiley, W.			•		•
Ziff, S.					
OAR	60				
IAR	80	40	70	50	90

Figure 10.5
Item-achievement chart, outcome-achievement rate, and item-analysis data for a five-item mastery assessment of a particular instructional outcome.

come. Recall that for item analysis by outcome and for outcome-achievement rates, best results require ordering student performance by outcome and not by total test score. In the figure, Lyons through Drexler answered correctly at least four out of five times, thus reaching criterion on the outcome. Rogers through Ziff did not reach criterion. For item analysis by outcome, a total-score column is not necessary.

Now, first question: How many students achieved the outcome? The answer is six. The number of students who achieved the outcome in relation to the number of students assessed is expressed as a percentage. Thus the outcome-achievement rate for this outcome is 60. The outcome stated four out of five as the criterion of performance, and the first six students (Lyons through Drexler) did get at least four out of five items correct. Ten students were assessed.

$$\text{OAR} = (6 \div 10) \times 100 = .60 \times 100 = 60$$

Mr. Washington decided that 60% was not too terrific, especially as he chose 80% as the acceptable outcome-achievement rate for that outcome.

Next question: Which items did students have trouble with? The item-achievement rates point to the answer: items two and four. Only one student missed item five; it presented a right triangle, and apparently the students know how to compute the area of a right triangle. They also did well on item one and not too badly on item three, so apparently they know how to compute the area of the triangles represented, though a little review probably would not hurt if time permits. At least half the class, however, does not know how to compute the area of the triangles represented by items two and four. Item two presented an isosceles triangle. The first thing Mr. Washington did was check these items to see if there was anything ambiguous about the drawings. He found that both of the suspect items were poorly labeled and that one was light on some copies of the test. These flaws may have prevented some students from demonstrating their true ability regarding the outcome.

If the drawings for these items *were* at least equally as accurate as for the other items, then a logical explanation for the poor performance is that the students do not possess the assessed skill. A need for further instruction and review would be indicated. Of course, it is always possible that the problem lies with the outcome, especially the criterion. On Mr. Washington's test, if the criterion for the outcome were three out of five correct, then 80% of the students would have achieved the outcome. Adjusting the criterion, however, is tricky business. There is a fine line between adjusting unrealistically high standards and lowering standards to the level of the students' performance. Thus, Mr. Washington must decide whether four out of five correct is too high an expectation. If he believes that it is not, then he should prepare his students further, providing more instruction before assessment. Without in-depth knowledge of the students and their typical abilities, this decision may be ill informed. If you are new to a grade level or school, ask the other grade-level or subject-matter teachers to share their experience in this area.

Adjusting Scores

If, through item analysis, you have eliminated some poor items from a test or revised your scoring scheme or task for a performance assessment, avoid the "assessment feedback blues" by adjusting the students' scores *before* returning papers and grades. For example, if you eliminate two bad items from a 50-item written exam, it becomes a 48-item exam and percentages, grades, and so forth should be figured on the basis of those 48 items. Change the percentage scores or grades you penciled in on the students' papers before you hand them back so that students do not feel they have to argue their case with you. Whether you do item analysis with a calculator, computer, or by hand, to avoid having to change grades after the fact, follow these easy steps:

1. For each student, mark the individual test items or scoring criteria that she or he achieved.
2. Write the total raw score *in pencil* on the test, answer sheet, checklist, or rating scale.
3. Arrange the papers in rank order, highest to lowest either by total score or by outcome (depending on the type of item analysis you are doing).
4. Perform item analysis.
5. Adjust total raw scores and total possible raw scores, if necessary.
6. Write adjusted total raw scores on students' papers in pen. Erase penciled scores.
7. Convert final raw scores to percentages and grades if appropriate, based on adjusted total possible score, and write them in pen on students' papers.
8. Return assessment results to students and discuss.

When you hand the papers back, take the opportunity to explain your item-analysis findings and what you did about it at a level that is suitable for your students. For example, if you teach secondary math, you might explain the mathematics involved and how the comparisons (division problems) were used for making decisions. Ask the students, if appropriate, how the items might be improved or what would have helped them do better.

Keeping Track of Item-Analysis Data

Teachers have their own ways of storing important materials. Some keep everything in loose-leaf notebooks or manila folders. Some prefer to use a computer for easy access and manipulation of files. Still others prefer to throw everything in a drawer. Whichever your preference (and let's hope it's not the drawer!), you need to organize and store the information resulting from your item analyses. You obviously want to keep all the information about a given assessment together, and all the information concerning a given item or outcome should be together. There are several good ways to do this. One way is to put all the information for a particular item on a large index card and file the cards in a file box. Some teachers have made an extra copy of a test, cut out the individual items and pasted them on index cards, adding item-analysis data on the back. In this way, cards can be redone, replaced, and added to easily. Another good way (and for the same reasons) is to put all the information for a particular item on a sheet of notebook paper and to file all the sheets for a given test in a loose-leaf notebook. Still another way is to keep a record of the item/out-

Unit: Basic Economics

Outcome: Ability to apply principles of supply and demand to given market conditions.

Test date: 4/20/97

According to the principles of supply and demand, what will happen to the price of coffee if there is a shortage of coffee beans?

Options	Upper Third	Lower Third	IAR	DP
a. Decline	2	4	55	.50
b. Stay the same	0	3		
c. Rise	8	3		

Figure 10.6
An example of an item-analysis data card.

come achievement chart for an assessment along with any revisions that were made as a result of item analysis. If assessment items, tasks, and scoring criteria are systematically revised, they will get progressively better. Even if they are not used again, a record of the revisions and item-analysis data will alert you to pitfalls to avoid in the development of future assessments.

The information recorded for a given test item or performance judging criterion is fairly standard. First you should record some identification data, such as the instructional outcome measured (preferably expressed in behavioral terms) and the assessment date. The actual item or criterion should also be recorded, along with all the analysis data. For a multiple-choice item, you should include the stem and all the alternatives, item-achievement rate, discriminating power, and distractor-analysis data. How you organize and arrange the data are up to you. Figure 10.6 illustrates one way.

Computers have reduced a lot of the tedium of computing item-achievement rates and discriminating power and of keeping record of item-analysis data over time. In addition to software custom-made for item analysis (such as ITEMAN®), word-processing programs can be used to store items and analysis data; spreadsheet software can be programmed to calculate outcome-achievement rate, item-achievement rate, and discriminating power. If your school is equipped with an electronic scanner to score machine-readable answer sheets, it may have item-analysis capabilities, depending on the software package used. If so, the item-achievement rate is likely to be presented as "item difficulty" or "*p*" for proportion of students who got the item correct. Additionally, item-achievement rate may be presented as a decimal, rather than a whole number: .87, rather than 87, for example. Discriminating power may be listed as "item discrimination," but it will still yield positive and negative decimal values. You still may have to calculate outcome-achievement rates. Regardless, the information is useful in the same way to improve assessments. If your school has an electronic scanner, you may be able to take advantage of possible existing item-analysis capabilities. You may even use a separate, scanable sheet to use with a performance checklist. The computer will treat it the same as it would a true-false test. To find out what is available and how you might use it with the type of assessments you administer, check educational software catalogs or other educational desk references, or consult with the person in charge of your school's or district's assessment program.

Summary

Understanding Item Analysis

Even if teachers follow all the guidelines for assessment design and construction to the letter, identifying problems with items, performance tasks, and scoring schemes before the assessment has actually been given is sometimes difficult. Analysis of test results supports or does not support initial validity judgments. Using item-analysis techniques helps us to (1) identify the trouble spots (if any) of a given assessment so that we can improve it, (2) better interpret the scores, and (3) use the scores more wisely.

Item analysis involves examining the pattern or type of student responses for each item or performance task to assess its effectiveness. Item analysis does not tell a teacher how to improve an item. It does, however, identify possible problem items and provide clues as to the source of the problems. The basic thought process involved in item analysis may be applied to the results of any assessment, including performance/product and paper-and-pencil types. Although there are other approaches to assessment item analysis, these procedures have difficulties that make them less than practical for most teachers. Once you get reasonably accustomed to analyzing items and tasks, visual inspection of results may be enough to obtain the desired information. Item analysis can save time and enhance your teaching by (1) improving future assessment development, (2) reducing arguments over "unfair" items and performance tasks, (3) increasing your confidence in the assessments on which grades are based, and (4) promoting better interpretation and use of results.

Item analysis can be successfully performed test data that include (1) dichotomously scored test items that are either correct or incorrect, (2) analytically scored essay items where each aspect or component is scored dichotomously, (3) performance-task scoring rubrics and holistically scored essay items where a judgment is made as to acceptable and unacceptable performance, and (4) performance checklist "items." Performing item analysis is especially appropriate when you have (1) pilot tested a new assessment instrument, (2) administered an assessment that counts for a substantial portion of a grade, (3) administered an assessment on which students did worse than expected, or (4) gathered results for an assessment related to instruction that you have targeted for improvement.

Applying the Item-Analysis Process to Non-Mastery Assessments

Item analysis of classroom non-mastery assessments involves carrying out the following steps after the tests or performances are individually scored:

1. Prepare an item-achievement chart.
2. Calculate the item-achievement rate (IAR) for each item using the results from all students in the calculations.
3. For each item, make a judgment concerning the acceptability of the item-achievement rate.
4. For items with unacceptable item-achievement rate values (and *only* for items with unacceptable item-achievement rate values), calculate discriminating power (DP) based on the results for high- and low-scoring subgroups.
5. Logically analyze the results to pinpoint the problem and suggest revisions.

Item Achievement

An *item-achievement chart* is a visual tool that helps teachers discern response patterns and identify possible defective items; it is a student-by-item matrix listed from highest ranking student to lowest, based on either total scores or scores on particular outcomes. *Item-achievement rate* (IAR) refers to the percentage or proportion of students who get the item correct or, in the case of a multi-point scale, muster enough points for "acceptable" performance. Percentage, item-achievement rates range from a low of 0 to a high of 100. The formula is $IAR = (R \div T) \times 100$. For most classroom assessments that are curriculum-based and criterion-referenced, the difficulty of the item should reflect the difficulty of the instructional outcome it is designed to measure: It is the teacher's judgment that should prevail when determining acceptable item-achievement rate values.

Discriminating Power

Discriminating power (DP) refers to the degree to which an item discriminates between high and low achievers on the assessment: high, positive discriminating power indicates that the high achievers in the class got the item right (or got enough points to meet criterion following the scoring rubric) and the low achievers did not. For estimating discriminating power, only the top and bottom thirds of the students in an item-achievement chart are required, assuming they are entered into the chart in rank order, from best performance to worst. Discriminating power values range from -1.00 through 0 to $+1.00$. Discriminating power values are calculated only for those items with item-achievement rates that are less than acceptable. The formula is $DP = (R_U - R_L) \div .5T$.

Discriminating power is related to item-achievement rate. Only with an item-achievement rate of 50 can an item perfectly discriminate ($DP = +1.00$), and then only if the half of the students that got the item right were also those in the upper group. Using discriminating power along with item-achievement rate in analyzing classroom assessments determines if an item that appears at first to be overly difficult due to its low item-achievement rate is at least positively discriminating between those who did well on the assessment and those who did not. It is not a good idea to label an item defective just because it has low discriminating power. As with item achievement, common sense must be used in interpreting indexes of discriminating power. A low item-achievement rate coupled with a negative discriminating power is an automatic call for further analysis. Teachers can visually inspect the chart to determine those items with "too few marks." The more marks missing from cells in the column for an item, the lower the item-achievement rate. If an overabundance of the empty cells for an item occurs in the upper third of the tested group as opposed to the lower third, then the discriminating power will be negative.

Distractor Analysis

Distractor analysis is the examination of incorrect responses to multiple-choice items. A good distractor is one that is selected by more students in the lower group than in the upper group. If no one selects a given distractor, it is ineffective and should be replaced. If a distractor is selected by more students in the upper group than the lower group, it is confusing to the wrong students—not a good attribute. No formula is required to calculate the effectiveness of the distractors; an examination of the alternatives selected by each group in the item analysis makes it fairly evident how well the distractors worked.

Item Analysis for Performance Assessments and Multi-Point Essay Items

Item analysis can be performed on essay items without too much difficulty provided that the desired response for each item has been clearly defined. The analytical method of scoring is preferred. For item-analysis purposes, each element in a multi-element, multi-point scoring scheme may be turned into a dichotomous "item" for use in an item-achievement chart. A performance or product checklist is also dichotomously scored. When using the same scoring scheme for multiple assignments, teachers may compare item-achievement charts across assignments to see strengths and weaknesses in the class. The item-analysis data can also be pooled for interpretation.

Possible causes of unacceptable item-achievement rate and discriminating power values include:

1. Mis-keyed correct answer.
2. Violation of construction guidelines for tests, items, performance tasks, scoring schemes, checklists, or rating scales.
3. Spelling errors that change the meaning of the words used in the item or to present the task.
4. Test-reproduction problems.
5. Mismatch between outcome and item or task.

6. Minimum item-achievement rate is unrealistic.
7. Not enough time on task.
8. Method of instruction and/or instructional materials is not effective for students and outcome.

Determining the Outcome-Achievement Rate for Mastery Assessments

For classroom mastery assessments where a number of items or tasks assess a specific outcome, all the items that measure a given outcome should be analyzed together. The number of students who achieved an outcome in relation to the number of students assessed on that outcome is expressed as a percentage called the *outcome-achievement rate* (OAR). When combining the analysis of outcomes and their constituent items, the process is as follows:

1. Prepare an item-achievement chart for the outcome, ranking students highest to lowest on the outcome.
2. Calculate the outcome-achievement rate using results of all students.
3. For each outcome, judge the acceptability of the outcome-achievement rate.
4. For outcomes with unacceptable outcome-achievement rates, calculate the item-achievement rates for constituent items using the results of all students.
5. Logically analyze the results for items with lowest item-achievement rates to pinpoint the problem and suggest revisions.

The item results, then, are not divided into thirds but are categorized by whether the student reached criterion. Discriminating power is not estimated for mastery items. Adjusting the criterion of performance for an outcome due to low outcome-achievement rate values is tricky business: There is a fine line between adjusting unrealistically high standards and lowering standards to the level of the students' performance.

Adjusting Scores

If poor items are eliminated from a test or the scoring scheme or task for a performance assessment is revised, adjust the students' scores *before* returning papers and grades. Ask the students, if appropriate, how the items might be improved or what would have helped them do better.

Keeping Track of Item-Analysis Data

There are several good ways to organize and store the information resulting from your item analysis:

1. Put all the information for a particular item on a large index card and file the cards in a file box.
2. Put all the information for a particular item on a sheet of notebook paper and file all the sheets for a given test in a loose-leaf notebook.

3. Keep a record of the item/outcome-achievement chart for an assessment along with any revisions that were made as a result of item analysis.
4. Use a computer word-processing, database, spreadsheet, or item-analysis program. If assessment items, tasks, and scoring criteria are systematically revised, they will get progressively better.

Try These

I. Figure 10.7 is an item-achievement chart for a non-mastery performance assessment with five judging criteria. Perform an analysis on the data provided. Use a minimum item-achievement rate of 50. Write the total scores, item-achievement rates, and discriminating power estimates in the table. Determine which of the five criteria, if any, are troublesome for the students. The performance was an individual speech. A dot (●) indicates the student received an acceptable rating—at least six points out of a possible 10—for the individual scoring criterion. The criteria, summarized in the boxes at the top of the table, are as follows: (1) speech met the 2-1/2-minute time limit, (2) an appropriate introduction was used effectively, (3) the thesis was clearly explained, (4) the speaker gained and kept the audience's attention during the speech, and (5) delivery—voice, eye contact, body language—was effective.

II. Figure 10.8 is an item-achievement chart for a 10-item paper-and-pencil mastery test covering a single instructional outcome—number 16. Calculate the outcome-achievement rate on the data provided. Use a minimum outcome-achievement rate of 70. Write the outcome-achievement rate in the table and item-achievement rates, if appropriate. Determine which items, if any, were troublesome for the students.

III. Construct an item-achievement chart for a classroom assessment you have (or someone else has) recently administered and perform item analysis on the data. Choose the appropriate analysis procedure based on whether the assessment is for mastery or non-mastery. Your analysis for a non-mastery assessment should include:

1. The minimum item-achievement rate you chose.
2. Item-achievement rate values for all items or sub-tasks.
3. Discriminating power for all items/sub-tasks that have unacceptable item-achievement rates.
4. Your interpretation of the results.
5. Indication of what items may need revision and why.
6. Your suggestions for improving assessment and/or instruction based on the analysis.

Your analysis for a mastery assessment should include:

1. The minimum outcome-achievement rate you chose.
2. Whether the minimum outcome-achievement rate was reached.

Student \ Item	1 Time	2 Intro	3 Clr Thesis	4 Attention	5 Delivery	Total Score
1	•	•	•	•	•	
2	•	•		•	•	
3	•	•	•	•		
4	•	•		•		
5	•		•	•		
6	•		•	•		
7	•	•		•		
8	•	•		•		
9	•	•	•			
10	•	•	•			
11	•	•	•			
12	•	•				
13	•	•				
14	•		•			
15						
IAR						
DP						

Figure 10.7
Item-achievement chart for 15 students on a nonmastery performance assessment.

3. If not reached, item-achievement rates for all items or sub-tasks.
4. Your interpretation of the results.
5. Indication of what items may need revision and why.
6. Your suggestions for improving assessment and/or instruction based on the analysis.

Outcome	16									
Item / Student	1	2	3	4	5	6	7	8	9	10
Mosby	•	•	•	•	•	•	•	•	•	•
Brown	•	•	•	•	•		•	•	•	•
Strickert	•		•	•	•		•	•	•	•
Smolev	•	•		•		•	•	•	•	•
Lanman	•			•	•	•	•	•	•	•
Wong	•			•	•	•	•		•	•
Cat	•		•	•		•	•	•		•
Allison	•			•	•		•	•	•	•
O'Neill	•	•	•	•			•	•	•	
Gupta	•	•	•		•	•		•		
Williams	•	•	•		•		•	•		
Haygood	•	•	•	•				•		
Felzer	•	•	•	•	•					
Simpson	•	•								
Vincent										
OAR										
IAR										

Figure 10.8
An item-achievement chart for 15 students on a 10-item mastery assessment covering outcome 16. A dot (•) indicates the student answered the item correctly. The criterion of individual performance for the instructional outcome was 7/10.

Answers

I. Total scores: 1 = 5, 2 = 4, 3 = 4, 4 = 3, 5 = 3, 6 = 3, 7 = 3, 8 = 3, 9 = 3, 10 = 3, 11 = 3, 12 = 2, 13 = 2, 14 = 2, 15 = 0.

Item	IAR	DP
1	93	+.20
2	73	+.20
3	57	+.20
4	57	+1.00
5	13	+.40

The item-achievement rates indicate that the class did well on all but one of the sub-tasks as summarized in the scoring criteria. Delivery (item five) appears to be a problem for these high-school students. Its discriminating power of +.40, however, indicates that the students who do well overall tend to have better speech delivery skills than those who don't do so well overall. If the teacher wishes to do anything, he or she may review written comments to students to determine whether voice, eye contact, body language, or some combination of these may benefit from further attention.

II. OAR = $(9 \div 15) \times 100 = 60$. Outcome-achievement rate is below minimum acceptable OAR of 70.

Item	IAR
1	93
2	60
3	60
4	73
5	60
6	40
7	67
8	73
9	53
10	53

Item six was too difficult for a full 60% of the class (only 40% got it right). Items 9 and 10 appear difficult as well with their item-achievement rates of 53. Perhaps checking the match between the items and the outcome will shed some light on the reasons for these low values.

If you were the teacher, you may wonder why the students did so poorly compared to your expectations. Of course, you would have some contextual clues such as knowledge of your students and test administration conditions to help you. Some suggestions beyond checking the scoring key might include:

1. The test was administered too early; students needed more practice.
2. Some of the items (six, nine, and 10) may have violated construction guidelines.
3. Some of the test items, or the instruction, or both were out of alignment with the intended outcome.
4. Something (an outside event, perhaps) distracted a number of students.
5. Your expectations of mastery were too high for these students at this time.

III. Products will vary, but should meet criteria one through six for the type of assessment chosen.

CHAPTER 11

Describing Group and Individual Assessment Performance

Key Concepts:

- Describing performance using nominal, ordinal, interval, and ratio scales.
- Describing the average or typical score using measures of central tendency.
- Describing the spread of scores using measures of variability.
- Understanding characteristics of the normal curve and normal distributions.
- Describing group performance with outcome/item-achievement charts.
- Describing individual performance with measures of relative position.
- Describing individual performance with outcome/item-achievement charts.

Standards Addressed in This Chapter:

3. Administer, score, and interpret the results of both externally produced and teacher-produced assessment methods.
6. Communicate assessment results to students, parents and other lay audiences, and other educators.

Before You Begin Reading, Consider This

With all the emphasis on individual educational plans and on students as individuals, should teachers also be concerned with describing the assessment performance of their students as a class?

YES Teachers who only concentrate on individual performance cannot see the forest for the trees when it comes to instructional planning and improvement. Individual students also like to know "how the class did" on an assessment.

NO It is unnecessary to worry over the performance of a class or a group of classes if the emphasis is on student accomplishment of individual educational plans. Students do not care how the other students did as long as they know how *they* did.

Many of the assessments teachers construct and use, as well as standardized tests, yield scores of one type or another that are then analyzed and summarized to describe the students' collective and individual performance. Regardless of whether these scores are interpreted in relation to a criterion or a norm group, it is important to understand the different types of scores and scales used. This understanding is essential to correctly interpreting and explaining assessment results, as well as using them in instructional planning and revision.

Describing Assessment Performance Using Measurement Scales

The assessment of students on one or more variables results in data for analysis. Depending upon the variables and the way in which they are assessed, different kinds of data result, representing different scales of measurement. There are four types of measurement scales: nominal, ordinal, interval, and ratio. It is important to know which type of scale is represented by your data because different mathematical procedures and scores are appropriate for different scales of measurement.

Nominal Scales

A *nominal scale* classifies people (or objects) into two or more categories. Such a scale represents the lowest level of measurement. Whatever the basis for classification, a person can be in only one category, and members of a given category have a common set of characteristics. Classifying students as male versus female, master versus non-master, or introverted versus extroverted are all examples of nominal scales. When a nominal scale is used, the data simply indicate how many people are in each category. For 100 first-graders, for example, it might be determined that 60 attended kindergarten and 40 did not. For outcome-achievement purposes, a teacher

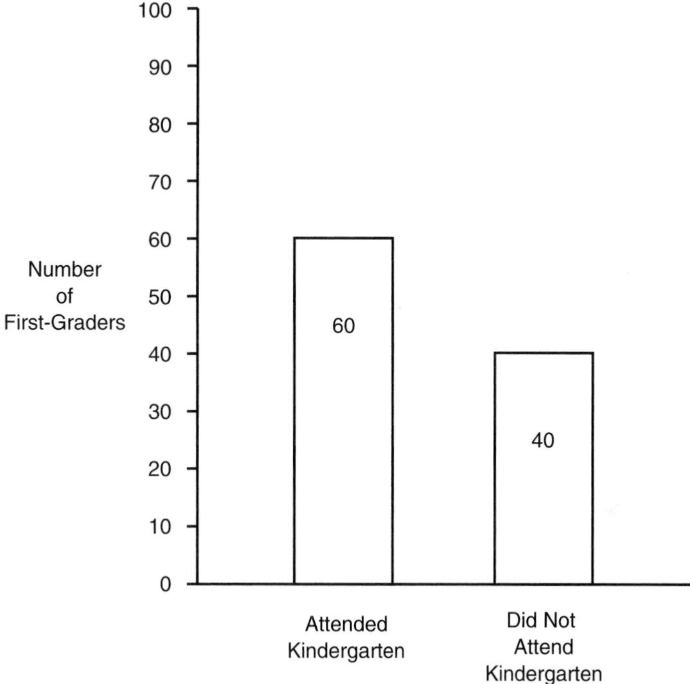

Figure 11.1
Bar chart illustrating kindergarten attendance for 100 first-graders.

may want to know how many students can label the parts of a microscope and how many cannot. Nominal data can be displayed in a bar chart (see Figure 11.1) where each bar represents a category and the length of the bar indicates how many are in the category.

For identification purposes, categories are sometimes numbered from one to however many categories there are, say four. It is important to realize, however, that the category labeled four is only different from the category labeled three; four is not more or higher than three, only different from three. To avoid confusion, categories are sometimes labeled with letters instead of numbers—A, B, C, D instead of one, two, three, four, for example. A nominal scale also replaces names with numbers. The Spanish word *nombre,* meaning name, comes from the same Latin root as *nominal.* Sometimes the data represent *true categories.* Gender, race, and the state in which you live (New York, for instance) are examples of true categories. Other times continuous data are divided into *artificial categories.* For example, we could say that everyone whose height was over 5′6″ would be placed in the "tall" category, and everyone whose height measured 5′6″ or less would be placed in the "short" category. Although nominal scales are not very precise for continuous data such as test scores, their use is sometimes necessary.

Ordinal Scales

An *ordinal scale* not only classifies people or objects but also ranks them in terms of the degree to which they possess a characteristic of interest. Ordinal implies order: An ordinal scale puts people in order from highest to lowest, from most to least. With respect to height, for example, 50 students might be ranked from 1 to 50; the student with rank 1 would be the tallest and the student with rank 50 would be the shortest. It would then be possible to say that one student was taller or shorter than another student. A student's rank in a graduating class and the expression of a test score as a percentile rank both describe relative standing and represent ordinal scales.

Although ordinal scales do indicate that some persons are higher or possess more of a trait than others, they do not indicate how much higher or how much more. In other words, intervals between ranks are not necessarily equal. The difference between rank one and rank two is not necessarily the same as the difference between rank two and rank three, as the example below illustrates:

Rank	Height
1	6′2″
2	6′1″
3	5′11″
4	5′7″
5	5′6″
6	5′5″
7	5′4″
8	5′3″
9	5′2″
10	5′0″

The difference in height between the person with rank one and the person with rank two is 1 inch; the difference between rank two and rank three is 2 inches. In the example given, differences in height represented by differences in rank range from 1 inch to 4 inches. Similarly, differences in achievement represented by differences in rank may vary greatly. An ordinal scale results in more precise measurement than a nominal scale, but there are others that are even more precise.

Interval Scales

An *interval scale* has all the characteristics of a nominal scale and an ordinal scale (classification and order). In addition, it is based upon predetermined equal intervals. Most of the tests used in educational assessment, such as achievement tests and aptitude tests, represent interval scales. Therefore, as a teacher you will often work with interval data. For example, when scores have equal intervals, it is assumed that the difference between a score of 30 and a score of 40 is essentially the same as the difference between a score of 53 and a score of 63. Similarly, the difference between

81 and 82 is approximately the same as the difference between 82 and 83. If height is considered as an interval scale, then clearly the difference between a height of 5′6″ and 5′5″ (1 inch) is the same as the difference between 5′4″ and 5′3″. Thus, with an interval scale we can say not just that Egor is taller than Iago, but also that Egor is 7 feet tall and Iago is 5 feet tall.

Interval scales, however, do not have a true zero point. Such scales typically have an arbitrary maximum score and an arbitrary minimum score, or zero point. If an intelligence test produces scores ranging from 0 to 200, a score of 0 does not indicate the absence of intelligence, nor does a score of 200 indicate possession of the ultimate intelligence. A score of 0 only indicates the lowest level of performance possible on that particular test, and a score of 200 represents the highest level of performance. Thus, scores resulting from administration of an interval scale can be added and subtracted but not multiplied or divided. We can say that an achievement test score of 90 is 45 points higher than a score of 45, but we cannot say that a person scoring 90 knows twice as much as a person scoring 45. Similarly, a person whose intelligence is assessed at 140 is not necessarily twice as smart or twice as intelligent as a person whose intelligence measures 70. For most educational assessment, however, such generalizations are not needed.

Ratio Scales

A *ratio scale* has all the characteristics of the other types of scales, and it has a meaningful, true zero point. A ratio scale represents the highest, most precise level of measurement. Height, weight, and time are examples of ratio scales. The concept of "no time," for example, is a meaningful one. Because of the true zero point, we can say not only that the difference between a height of 3′2″ and a height of 4′2″ is the same as the difference between 5′4″ and 6′4″, but also that a person 6′4″ is twice as tall as a child 3′2″. Similarly, 60 minutes is three times as long as 20 minutes, and 40 pounds is four times as heavy as 10 pounds. Thus, with a ratio scale we can say the following:

- Egor is tall and Iago is short (nominal scale).
- Egor is taller than Iago (ordinal scale).
- Egor is 7 feet tall and Iago is 5 feet tall (interval scale).
- Egor is seven-fifths as tall as Iago (ratio scale).

As most physical measures represent ratio scales, but psychological measures do not, ratio scales are not used very often in educational assessment.

A descriptive statistic appropriate for a lower level of measurement may be applied to data representing a higher level of measurement. A statistic appropriate for ordinal data, for example, may be used with interval data, because interval data possess all the characteristics of ordinal data and more. The reverse, however, is not true. A statistic appropriate for interval data, for example, cannot be applied to ordinal data because such a statistic requires equal intervals.

Describing Group Performance

Two major concepts in describing the assessed performance of a group are central tendency and variability. Measures of central tendency are used to determine the typical or average score of a group of scores; measures of variability indicate how spread out a group of scores are. Both concepts help us understand the performance of the group—a class of eighth-graders, for example—as a whole.

Measures of Central Tendency

Measures of *central tendency* provide a convenient way of describing a set of data with a single number that describes the typical performance of the group. When you compute a measure of central tendency for your class on an assessment, you get a number that represents the average or typical score attained by the class. Another way to think about it is, if the class were a single person, how might you describe the performance of that person? The three most frequently encountered expressions of central tendency are the mode, the median, and the mean. Each of these indices is appropriate for a different scale of measurement. The mode is appropriate for nominal data, the median for ordinal data, and the mean for interval or ratio data (see Figure 11.2). Because many classroom assessment and standardized test scores represent an interval scale, the mean is the most frequently used measure of central tendency in education.

The Mode

The *mode* is the score attained by more people than any other score or the category into which more people fall than the other available categories. When we vote, for example, we place ourselves into categories based on who we support for election. The modal candidate—the one who receives the most votes—wins. The mode is not established through calculation; it is determined by looking at a set of scores or at a graph of scores to see which score occurs most frequently. When analyzing assessment results by item or performance-task dimension, we may be more interested in how many students selected a particular answer choice or scored three points versus four on a project.[1] In these cases, we use categorical data and are interested in the modal answer or score.

For this type of data . . .	Use this central tendency measure . . .
Nominal	Mode
Ordinal	Median
Interval or Ratio	Mean

Figure 11.2
Summary of types of data and their appropriate central tendency measures.

[1] More information on analyzing assessment results by item or performance task appears in Chapter 10.

There are several problems associated with the mode, and it is, therefore, of limited value and seldom used. For one, a set of scores may have two (or more) modes, in which case the score set is referred to as bimodal (or multimodal). Another problem is that the mode is an unstable measure of central tendency. Equal-sized groups of students randomly selected from the same accessible population are likely to have different modes. When nominal data are involved, however, the mode is the only appropriate measure of central tendency.

The Median

As a highway median strip divides lanes of traffic, the *median* of a score distribution is the point at which the scores both above and below it are equal in number. In other words, the median is the midpoint, or middle score, when the scores are arranged from highest to lowest. If there is an odd number of scores, the median is the middle score (assuming the scores are arranged in order). For example, for the following scores, the median, 82, is circled:

75 77 80 (82) 83 84 87

If there is an even number of scores, the median is the point halfway between the two middle scores. For example, for the scores 21, 23, 24, 25, 26, 30, the median is 24.5, halfway between 24 and 25; for the scores 50, 52, 55, 57, 59, 61, the median is 56, halfway between 55 and 57. Thus, the median is not necessarily the same as one of the scores.

The median is only the midpoint of the scores and does not take into account the absolute value of each and every score but, rather, their ranking in the distribution. Two quite different sets of scores may have the same median. For example, for the scores 60, 62, 65, 67, 72, the median is 65; for the scores 40, 62, 65, 67, 89, the median is also 65. As you will see shortly, this apparent lack of precision may be advantageous at times.

The median is the appropriate measure of central tendency when the data represent an ordinal scale. For certain distributions, the median may be selected as the most appropriate measure of central tendency even though the data represent an interval or ratio scale. The median appears to be a rather simple index to determine, but it cannot always be arrived at by simply looking at the scores; it does not always neatly fall between two different scores. For example, determining the median for the scores 80, 82, 84, 84, 84, 88 would require application of a relatively complex formula. Fortunately, this situation does not arise very often with classroom results. When it does, an estimate of the median is usually sufficient. If we consider the median of 80, 82, 84, 84, 84, 88 to be 84, for example, subsequent analyses and interpretations will be very close to what they would have been had the exact value of the median been determined.

The Mean

The *mean* is the arithmetic average of the scores and is the most frequently used measure of central tendency. It is calculated by adding up all of the scores and dividing that total by the number of scores. For example, to find the mean for the following scores—21, 23, 24, 25, 26, 30—you would add the six scores together and divide the sum by 6 to get 24.8. By the very nature of the way in which it is computed, the mean takes into account or is based on each and every score. Unlike the median, the mean is definitely affected by extreme scores. Thus, in certain cases, the median may actually give a more accurate estimate of the typical score.

In general, however, the mean is the preferred measure of central tendency for interval or ratio data and is a more precise, stable index than both the median and the mode. If equal-sized groups of students are randomly selected from the same population, the means of those groups will be more similar to each other than either the medians or the modes. Although the mode is almost never the most appropriate measure of central tendency when the data represent an interval or ratio scale, the median may be appropriate in some cases. In the situation described previously in which there are one or more extreme scores, the median will not be the most accurate representation of the performance of the total group, but it will be the best index of typical performance. As an example of this concept, consider the following test scores: 46, 47, 47, 48, 49, 50, 51, 52, 53, 54, 99. For this set of scores, the measures of central tendency are:

Mode = 47 (most frequent score)

Median = 50 (middle score)

Mean = 54.18 (arithmetic average)

In this case, the median clearly best represents the typical score. The mode is too low, and the mean is higher than all of the scores except one. The mean is "pulled" or *skewed* in the direction of the 99 score, whereas the median essentially ignores it. The different pictures presented by the different measures are part of the reason for the phrase "lying with statistics." And, in fact, by selecting one index of central tendency over another, one may present a particular point of view in a stronger light. In student assessment, we are not interested in "making a case" but rather in describing the data in the most accurate way. For the majority of classroom test scores, the mean is the most appropriate measure of central tendency. If there are one or two extremely low or high scores in a data set, however, it is wise to compute both the median and the mean for the most complete picture.

Measures of Variability

Measures of central tendency are very useful for describing a set of assessment scores, but they only tell part of the story. Two sets of very different test scores can have identical means or medians. As an example, consider the sets of scores and their frequency distributions in Figure 11.3. The mean of both sets of scores is 60 and the median of both is 60, but set A is very different from set B, as you can see in the score distributions in Figure 11.1. In set A the scores are all close together and clustered around the mean. In set B the scores are much more spread out; that is, there is much more variation or variability in set B. Thus, there is a need for a measure indicating how spread out the scores are, how much *variability* there is.

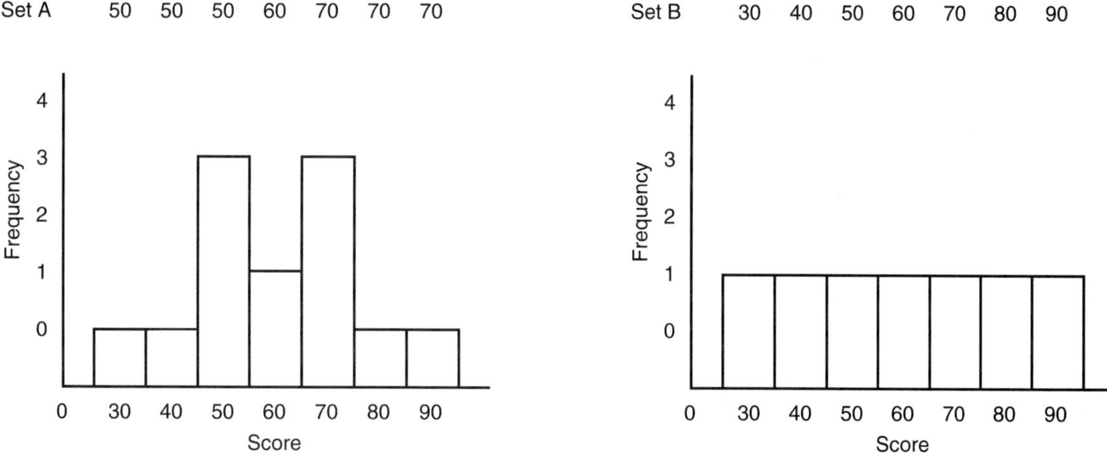

Figure 11.3
Two sets of scores and their frequency distributions.

There are several ways of describing the spread of scores; collectively, they are referred to as measures of variability. The three most frequently encountered measures of variability are the range, the quartile deviation, and the standard deviation. Although the standard deviation is by far the most often used, the range is useful when a "quick and dirty" estimate of variability is needed. The quartile deviation is the appropriate index of variability for ordinal data. As with measures of central tendency, measures of variability appropriate for ordinal data may be used with interval or ratio data even though the standard deviation is generally the preferred and more precise index for such data (see Figure 11.4).

The Range

The *range* is defined as the difference between the highest score and the lowest score (R = H − L). For example, the range for the scores 50, 50, 50, 60, 70, 70, 70 is 20, whereas the range for the scores 30, 40, 50, 60, 70, 80, 90 is 60. Thus, if the range is small, the scores are close together; if the range is large, the scores are more

For this situation . . .	Use this variability measure . . .
Need a "quick and dirty" estimate	Range
Ordinal data	Quartile deviation
Interval or ratio data	Standard deviation

Figure 11.4
Summary of types of data and their appropriate variability measures.

spread out. Like the mode, the range is not a very stable measure. It only considers two scores—the two most extreme. Its chief advantage is that it gives a quick, rough estimate of variability.

The Quartile Deviation

In "statistics talk," the *quartile deviation* (also referred to as the semi-interquartile range) is one-half of the difference between the upper quartile and the lower quartile in a distribution. In English, *quartiles* are the three points that divide a score distribution into four equal parts: the upper quartile is the 75th percentile, that point below which are 75% of the scores, and the lower quartile, correspondingly, is the 25th percentile, that point below which are 25% of the scores. By subtracting the score at the lower quartile from the score at the upper quartile and then dividing the result by two, we get a measure of variability:

$$QD = \frac{Q3 - Q1}{2}$$

As an example, if there are 60 scores, Q1 is the score below which are 15 of the scores (15 = 25% of 60), and Q3 is the score below which are 45 of the scores (45 = 75% of 60). If the quartile deviation is small, the scores are close together; if the quartile deviation is large, the scores are more spread out. The quartile deviation is a more stable measure of variability than the range and is appropriate whenever the median is appropriate. Calculation of the quartile deviation involves a process very similar to that used to calculate the median, which just happens to be the second quartile, Q2. A quartile is, therefore, a point in the distribution, not a group of scores: we might say that a particular score is *at* the third quartile (Q3), but not *in* the third quartile.

The Standard Deviation

The *standard deviation* is a measure of variability appropriate when the data represent an interval or ratio scale. It is by far the most frequently used index of variability. Like the mean, the measure of central tendency that is its counterpart, the standard deviation is expressed in the same units as the scores used to calculate it. If you use raw scores in the formula, you get the standard deviation expressed in raw score points. If you use percentages, the standard deviation will be expressed in percentage points. Also like the mean, the standard deviation is the most stable measure of variability and takes into account each and every score. In fact, the first step in calculating the standard deviation involves finding out how far each score is from the mean—that is, subtracting the mean from each score. For the raw score formula for calculating the standard deviation, turn to Appendix D. A small standard deviation indicates that scores are close together, and a large standard deviation indicates that the scores are more spread out.

If you know the mean and the standard deviation of a set of scores, you have a pretty good picture of what the distribution looks like. An interesting fact associated with the standard deviation is that if the distribution is relatively normal (more about normal distributions shortly), then the mean plus three standard deviations and the mean minus three standard deviations encompasses just about all the scores (over 99% of them, actually). In other words, each distribution has its own mean and its own standard deviation, which are calculated based on the scores in that distribution. Once they are computed, three times the standard deviation added to the mean and three times the standard deviation subtracted from the mean gives you a range that includes just about all the scores in the distribution.[2] The symbol for the mean is $\overline{X}$ (sometimes referred to as "X-bar"), and the standard deviation is usually abbreviated as SD. Thus, the above described concept can be expressed as follows:

$$\overline{X} \pm 3SD = 99+\% \text{ of the scores}$$

For example, suppose that for a set of scores the mean ($\overline{X}$) is calculated to be 60 and the standard deviation (SD) to be 1. In this case the mean plus three standard deviations, $\overline{X} + 3SD$, is equal to $60 + 3(1) = 60 + 3 = 63$. The mean minus three standard deviations, $\overline{X} - 3SD$, is equal to $60 - 3(1) = 60 - 3 = 57$. Thus, almost all the scores fall between 57 and 63. This makes sense since such a small standard deviation (in this case SD = 1) indicates that the scores are close together, or not very spread out.

As another example, suppose that for another set of scores the mean ($\overline{X}$) is again calculated to be 60, but this time the standard deviation (SD) is calculated to be 5. In this case the mean *plus* three standard deviations, $\overline{X} + 3SD$, is equal to $60 + 3(5) = 60 + 15 = 75$. Here is another way to express the concept:

$$60 \text{ plus } 1SD = 60 + 5 = 65;$$
$$60 \text{ plus } 2SD = 60 + 5 + 5 = 70;$$
$$60 \text{ plus } 3SD = 60 + 5 + 5 + 5 = 75.$$

Or, $60 + 1SD = 60 + 5 = 65$, plus another $SD = 65 + 5 = 70$, plus one more (the third) $SD = 70 + 5 = 75$. The mean *minus* three standard deviations, $\overline{X} - 3SD$, is equal to $60 - 3(5) = 60 - 15 = 45$. In other words, 60 minus $1SD = 60 - 5 = 55$; 60 minus $2SD = 60 - 5 - 5 = 50$; 60 minus $3SD = 60 - 5 - 5 - 5 = 45$. Thus, almost all of the scores fall between 45 and 75. This also makes sense because a larger standard deviation (in this case SD = 5) indicates that the scores are more spread out.

Clearly, if you know the mean and standard deviation of a set of scores you have a pretty good idea of what the scores would look like if you were to plot them on a graph. You know the average score, and you know how spread out or how variable the scores are. Thus, together the mean and the standard deviation describe a set of data quite well. If you administer the same assessment to different classes of students (across years or teachers for elementary grades, or across the schedule for secondary grades, for example), you can compare the performance of the classes by

---

[2]The number 3 is a constant. In other words, for any normal distribution of scores, the standard deviation multiplied by 3 and then added to the mean and subtracted from the mean will yield two scores, between which will be included almost all the scores in the distribution.

comparing the means and standard deviations of the classes. For example, the means and standard deviations (in percentage points) for two fifth-grade science unit tests are listed below for two classes. N = number of students in the distribution:

	$\overline{X}$	SD	N
Ms. Adams	61.22	12.50	32
Ms. Baker	82.45	11.02	18

Let's compare the means first. There would appear to be a clear difference between the two because 21 percentage points separate them (82.45 − 61.22 = 21.23). The standard deviations are different, also, but not by much (12.50 − 11.02 = 1.48), so the scores are spread similarly around their respective means.[3] We also notice that Ms. Adams has 14 more students in her class than Ms. Baker. What might account for the big difference in performance as indicated by the means? The means and standard deviations for the two groups do not tell us the cause of the difference, only that there is one. Although we cannot tell whether class size is a factor from these numbers, it warrants investigation.

The Normal Curve

The ±3 concept is valid only when the scores are normally distributed—that is, form a normal or bell-shaped curve. Many, many variables, such as height, weight, general aptitude scores, and achievement scores, do yield a normal curve if a sufficient number of people are assessed. If enough scores are used in the distribution, several hundred at least, then the scores may be norm-referenced based on the normal curve concept.

A *normal curve* is essentially a frequency distribution constructed for a set of normally distributed scores. Thus, Figure 11.5 is based on a vertical axis labeled *frequency* and a horizontal axis labeled *scores*. If a variable is normally distributed—that is, forms a normal curve—then the following statements are true:

- The area under the curve represents all (100%) of the scores.
- 50% of the scores are above the mean and 50% of the scores are below the mean.
- The mean, the median, and the mode are the same.
- Most scores are near the mean, and the nearer the mean a score is, the larger the number of people who attained that score.
- The farther from the mean a score is, the fewer the number of people who attained that score.
- The same number or percentage of scores is between the mean and plus one standard deviation ($\overline{X}$ + 1SD) as between the mean minus one standard deviation ($\overline{X}$ − 1SD), and likewise for $\overline{X}$ ± 2SD and $\overline{X}$ ± 3SD (see Figure 11.5).

[3]Remember that out of a possible 100 percentage points, 1.48 is a small amount.

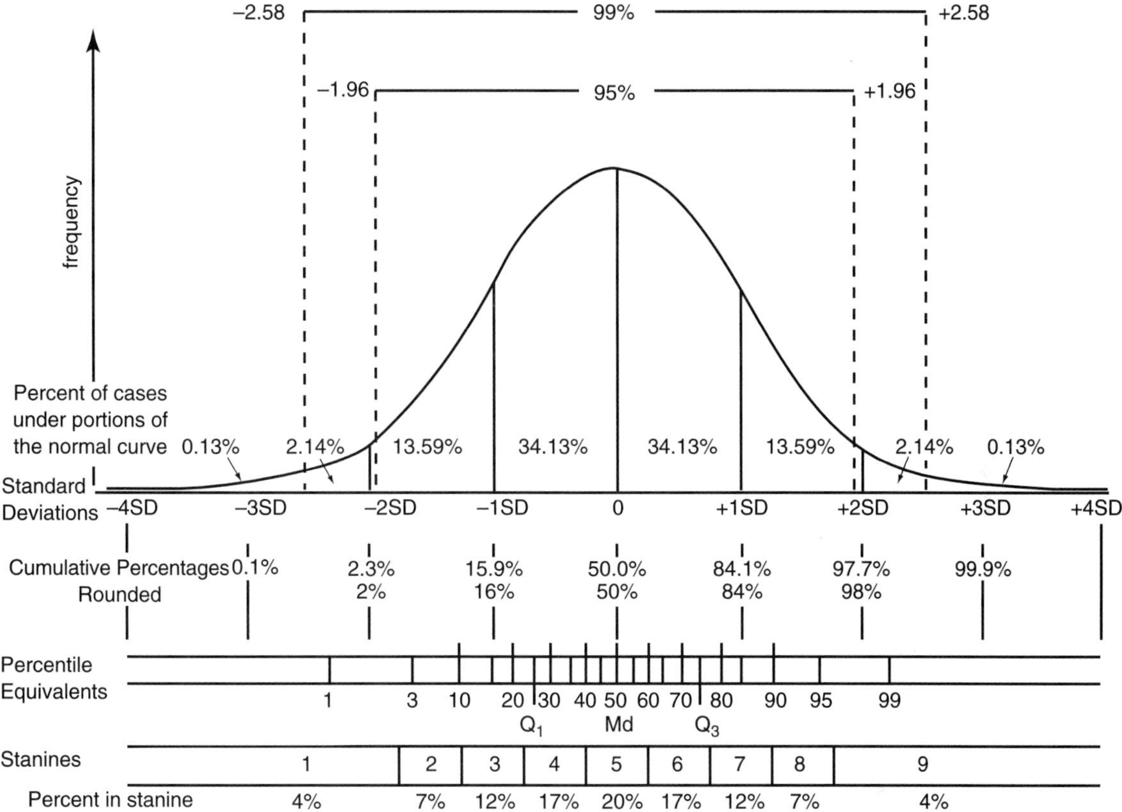

Figure 11.5
The normal curve and its characteristics. *Source:* From *Test Service Bulletin 48,* by the Psychological Corp. Reprinted by permission.

The vertical lines at each of the SD points in Figure 11.5 delineate a certain percentage of the total area under the curve. As Figure 11.5 illustrates, if a set of scores forms a normal distribution, then the $\overline{X}$ + 1SD includes 34.13% of the scores and the $\overline{X}$ − 1SD also includes 34.13% of the scores. Each succeeding standard deviation encompasses a constant percentage of the cases. Since the $\overline{X}$ ± 2.58SD (approximately 2 1/2 SDs) includes 99% of the cases, we see that $\overline{X}$ ± 3SD includes almost all the scores, as pointed out previously.

Below the row of SDs in Figure 11.5 is a row of percentages. As you move from left to right, from point to point, the cumulative percentage of scores falling below each point is indicated. Thus, at the point corresponding to −3SD, we see that only .1% of the scores fall below this point. The numerical value corresponding to +1SD, on the other hand, is 84.1% (rounded to 84% on the next row) of the scores. Relatedly, the next row, percentile equivalents, also involves cumulative percentages. The figure 20 in this row, for example, indicates that 20% of the scores fall below this point. We will discuss percentiles and the remaining row further as we proceed through this chapter. Note that the mean always corresponds to the 50th percentile. In other words, the average score in a normal distribution is always that point at which 50% of the cases are above it and 50% of the cases are below it. Thus, if scores are normally distributed, the following statements about the standard deviation are true:

- $\overline{X} \pm 1SD$ = approximately 68% of the scores.
- $\overline{X} \pm 2SD$ = approximately 95% of the scores (1.96SD is exactly 95%).
- $\overline{X} \pm 2.5SD$ = approximately 99% of the scores (2.58SD is exactly 99%).
- $\overline{X} \pm 3SD$ = approximately 99+% of the scores.

And similarly, the following statements are always true when the distribution is normal:

- $\overline{X} - 3SD$ = approximately the .1 percentile.
- $\overline{X} - 2SD$ = approximately the 2nd percentile.
- $\overline{X} - 1SD$ = approximately the 16th percentile.
- $\overline{X}$ = the 50th percentile.
- $\overline{X} + 1SD$ = approximately the 84th percentile.
- $\overline{X} + 2SD$ = approximately the 98th percentile.
- $\overline{X} + 3SD$ = approximately the 99th+ percentile.

These equivalents are generalizable to the scores of any group on any measure to the degree that the scores approximate a normal curve.

You may have noticed in Figure 11.5 that the ends of the curve never touch the baseline and that there is no definite number of standard deviations which corresponds to 100%. This is because the curve allows for the existence of unexpected extremes at either end and because each additional standard deviation includes only a tiny fraction of a percent of the scores. Thus, although ±3SDs includes just about everyone, the exact number of standard deviations required to include every score changes depending on the variable assessed.

As mentioned earlier, many variables form a normal distribution, including physical measures, such as height and weight, and psychological measures, such as intelligence and aptitude. In fact, most variables measured in education form normal distributions *if enough people are tested.* In other words, a variable that is normally distributed in a large population (for example, all fourth-graders in the U.S.) may not be normally distributed in a small group (for example, the fourth-graders in your class). Depending upon the size and nature of a particular group, the assumption of a normal curve may or may not be a valid one. Because classroom assessment, for example, deals with a finite number of students and often not a very large number, data only more or less approximate a normal curve. Likewise, all of the equivalencies (such as standard deviation and percentiles) are also only approximations. This is an important point, because many statistics used in education are based on the assumption that the variable is normally distributed. In general, however, the fact that most variables are normally distributed allows us quickly to determine many useful pieces of information concerning a set of assessment data.

Outcome/Item-Achievement Charts and Group Performance

Total scores on tests, be they written or performance based, do not always describe students' status in ways useful to teachers. When the desire is to describe exactly what students can and cannot do, either collectively or individually, an outcome/item-achievement chart can be very useful (see Figure 11.6). You may remember using this chart in Chapter 10 for item analysis and assessment improvement. But when describing group performance on a classroom assessment, we are usually more concerned with outcome achievement than with individual item achievement. An outcome/item-achievement chart can help you describe, for example, the following:

- The number or percentage of students who achieved each outcome.
- The number or percentage of students achieving mastery.
- Specific outcomes that are relative strengths and weaknesses for the class.
- The mean total number or percentage of items correct.
- The mean total number or percentage of outcomes achieved.
- The median number or percentage of outcomes achieved.

Outcome	1				2				3				4			5		
Item / Student	1	2	3	4	5	6	7	8	9	10	11	12	13	14	15	16	17	18
Barney	•	•	•	•	•	•	•		•	•	•	•				•	•	•
Betty	•		•		•		•		•		•	•	•	•	•		•	•
Bam Bam											•	•	•	•	•			•
Fred	•				•				•		•	•				•	•	•
Pebbles									•		•	•	•	•	•			•
Wilma		•	•	•		•			•		•	•	•	•	•	•		•
Dino		•	•	•		•	•	•		•	•	•						•

Figure 11.6
A simple outcome/item-achievement chart for seven students on an 18-item test covering five instructional outcomes. A dot indicates the student answered the item correctly or earned enough points (in the case of a multi-point item or task) to "pass" it. For outcomes 1, 2, and 3 the performance standard is 3/4; for outcomes 4 and 5 the standard is 2/3.

For the students in Figure 11.6, we can figure the outcome achievement rates—percentage of students who achieved each outcome. For outcome one, which has a performance standard of 3/4 (three out of four items), first count the number of students who received at least three dots for items one through four. The chart indicates that Barney, Wilma, and Dino (three students) achieved the first outcome. Divide this number by the total number of students who took the test and multiply the result by 100 to get the percentage ($3 \div 7 = .4285714 \times 100 = 42.85714$ or 43%). Completing the same operations for the rest of the outcomes using their respective performance standards, you get the following percentages using a handheld calculator:

1. $3 \div 7 = .4285714 \times 100 = 42.85714$ or 43%
2. $2 \div 7 = .2857142 \times 100 = 28.57142$ or 29%
3. $6 \div 7 = .8571428 \times 100 = 85.71428$ or 86%
4. $4 \div 7 = .5714285 \times 100 = 57.14285$ or 57%
5. $3 \div 7 = .4285714 \times 100 = 42.85714$ or 43%

These outcome-achievement rates can help determine the relative strengths and weaknesses of the class. From them we can see that the students in Figure 11.6, as a class, did their best on outcome three because it has the highest rate of achievement (86%). They did their worst on outcome two because it has the lowest rate of achievement (29%). Once you become accustomed to using outcome/item-achievement charts, you may not always need to perform all the calculations. Sometimes the pattern and density of dots for the students on an outcome/item-achievement chart can tell you all you need to know.

Looking across the columns for each student, we can determine the mean total number and percentage of outcomes achieved. All we need to do is count the dots for each student for each of the five outcomes. Thus, the number and percentage of outcomes achieved by each student is as follows:

Barney	4 out of 5 or 80%
Betty	3 out of 5 or 60%
Bam Bam	1 out of 5 or 20%
Fred	2 out of 5 or 40%
Pebbles	2 out of 5 or 40%
Wilma	4 out of 5 or 80%
Dino	3 out of 5 or 60%

The mean or average number and percentage of outcomes achieved for the class is 2.71 or 54%:

$$4 + 3 + 1 + 2 + 2 + 4 + 3 = 19$$
$$19 \div 7 = 2.71$$
$$2.71 \div 5 = .542$$
$$.54 \times 100 = 54\%$$

In other words, the average student in this class achieved a little over half the outcomes assessed.

So far, we have treated Figure 11.6 as if it represented the 18 individual items on a written test, but the same type of chart can help describe scores on a performance assessment just as easily. Consider Ms. Shapiro's fourth-grade class as an example. Ms. Shapiro constructed a series of three performance tasks to comprise a unit assessment on electrical circuits. The three tasks call for the behaviors listed in outcomes 1.0, 2.0, 3.0, 4.0, and 5.0 in Figure 11.7, and the sub-tasks (for example, 1.1, 1.2, 1.3, and 1.4) were used as performance dimensions or "items" on a checklist that she used to score the tasks. She decided to assess outcomes 4.0 and 5.0 as she observed each performance task so that each student had three opportunities to perform each to criterion. The results in Figure 11.8 are presented for seven students as an example chart. You would, of course, for your own class list all students and all tasks assessed. Do these results look familiar? The results—dot density and pattern—are the same as those in Figure 11.6. The chart in Figure 11.8 is different only in that it identifies performance dimensions as they relate to each outcome. As you work with outcome/item-achievement charts, you should modify the system to fit your particular needs (you might, for example, add a total-points column).

Performance Outcomes for "Fun with Circuits"

1 .0 Demonstrates that a battery (cell) produces energy by forming a complete circuit with a light bulb, aluminum foil, and a dry-cell battery.

- 1.1 Gathers materials and prepares work area.
- 1.2 Writes prediction on lab sheet as to whether drawing represents a circuit that will light the bulb.
- 1.3 Creates a complete circuit using given materials.
- 1.4 Verifies predictions.

2.0 Demonstrates the difference between open and closed electrical circuits.

- 2.1 Gathers materials and prepares work area.
- 2.2 Makes an on/off switch using two fasteners.
- 2.3 Creates a complete circuit with a switch.
- 2.4 Demonstrates open/closed circuits with the switch.

3.0 Classifies given objects as conductors or insulators.

- 3.1 Gathers materials and prepares work area.
- 3.2 Predicts which objects are conductors and which are insulators.
- 3.3 Creates circuit that will test objects.
- 3.4 Tests each object for conductivity using circuit.

4.0 Demonstrates proper safety procedures while working with electricity.

5.0 Works cooperatively with others in a learning group.

Figure 11.7
Performance outcomes for Fun with Circuits for Ms. Shapiro's fourth-grade class.

Outcome	1				2				3				4			5		
Subtask / Student	1	2	3	4	1	2	3	4	1	2	3	4	1	2	3	1	2	3
Barney	•	•	•	•	•	•	•		•	•	•	•				•	•	•
Betty	•		•		•		•		•		•	•	•	•	•		•	•
Bam Bam											•	•	•	•	•			•
Fred	•				•				•		•	•				•	•	•
Pebbles									•		•	•	•	•	•			•
Wilma		•	•	•		•			•		•	•	•	•	•	•		•
Dino		•	•	•		•	•	•		•	•	•						•

Figure 11.8
Outcome/item-achievement chart for seven students and five instructional outcomes on a performance-based assessment. A dot indicates the student performed to criterion on the corresponding dimension as indicated by a $\surd$ on the scoring checklist. For outcomes 1, 2, and 3 the performance standard is 3/4; for outcomes 4 and 5 the standard is 2/3.

Because the needed calculations are the same as those already performed, we will use them to interpret the results for this class of seven. With regard to the performance assessment on electrical circuits, we can say a number of things, some of which are variations of one another:

1. Students achieved a little more than half the outcomes assessed (54%).
2. The "average" student achieved just over half the outcomes assessed (54%).
3. No one achieved all (100%) of the outcomes: Barney and Wilma tied at 80%.
4. The fewest outcomes achieved was 20% (by Bam Bam).
5. The number (and percentage) of outcomes achieved ranged from 1 to 4 (20%–80%).
6. Median achievement was 3 (60%) of the outcomes.
7. The relative strength of the class was in classifying given objects as conductors or insulators (outcome 3.0).

8. The relative weakness of the class was on performance task two, relating to outcome 2.0—demonstrating the difference between open and closed electrical circuits.

Describing Individual Performance

Measures of Relative Position

A numerical value summarizing the responses actually made on a test by an individual is called a *raw score*. This value is usually the total number of correct answers but may be some other index, like the total number of typographical errors in a business letter. Raw scores have essentially no meaning in and of themselves. Knowing that Linus scored 35 on a test tells you practically nothing about how well he did on the test in relation to either a criterion score or the performance of others who took the same test. If you also know the highest possible score on the test, you can convert the raw scores to a percent. For a 50-item test, for example, a score of 35 would equal 70%. This information may be helpful for a criterion-referenced test, but it still tells us nothing about performance in relation to that of others who took the test. Clearly there is a need for methods of transforming raw scores into values facilitating the interpretation of scores on both an individual and group basis. Measures of relative position fill this need. Classroom teachers typically encounter measures of relative position when they examine the results of norm-referenced standardized tests.

Measures of relative position indicate where a score is in relation to all other scores in the distribution. In other words, measures of relative position permit you to express how well an individual has performed as compared to all other individuals in some group who have been given the same test. An individual's performance may be compared to the performance of a norm group or to the performance of the group of which he is actually a member. A major advantage of such measures is that they make it possible to compare the performance of an individual on two or more different tests (or sub-tests). For example, if Xavier's raw score in reading is 40 and his raw score in math is 35, it does not follow that he did better in reading; 40 may have been the lowest score on the reading test and 35 the highest possible score on the math test! By the same token, the same raw score on two different tests does not necessarily indicate equal levels of performance. A raw score of 40 on one test may correspond to a low rank, whereas a raw score of 40 on another test may correspond to a very high rank. Measures of relative position express different scores on a common scale, providing a common frame of reference and thus permitting valid comparisons of scores on different tests.

Raw scores that have been transformed systematically into equivalent values that indicate relative position are referred to as *derived scores*. The most common type of derived scores used by teachers are percentile ranks, standard scores, and grade equivalents. The most frequently reported and used standard scores are stanines. Standardized test manuals almost always provide norms tables containing raw scores and one or more equivalent derived scores. A good standardized test manual is quite comprehensive. In addition to providing complete information related to test development and validation, directions for administering and scoring the test, and a description of the norm group, it provides detailed instructions for interpretation of given scores. These instructions usually take the form of one or more norms tables and accompanying explanatory material. A number of manuals provide separate tables for each of a number of levels of a given test. The term *level* refers to the grade or age range for which the test is supposedly appropriate. The Stanford Achievement Test, for example, has 13 level tests, each appropriate for a given grade range (indicated in parentheses):

TASK 3 (11.0–13.0)

TASK 2 (10.0–10.9)

TASK 1 (9.0–9.9)

Advanced 2 (8.5–9.9)

Advanced 1 (7.5–8.5)

Intermediate 3 (6.5–7.5)

Intermediate 2 (5.5–6.5)

Intermediate 1 (4.5–5.5)

Primary 3 (3.5–4.5)

Primary 2 (2.5–3.5)

Primary 1 (1.5–2.5)

SESAT 2 (K.5–1.5)

SESAT 1 (K.0–K.5)

Separate tables are also frequently provided for each of a number of subtests. Local norms tables can be created for districts with large student populations as well.

Occasionally, although fortunately not very often, a norms table does not provide derived scores for each and every raw score. Some systematic portion of the raw scores and their equivalents is presented, such as every other or every third raw score. In such cases it is necessary to estimate missing values. In other words, if a particular raw score of interest is not included in the table, then desired derived scores must be estimated using values that are given. As an example, suppose a table indicates that a raw score of 20 corresponds to a percentile rank of 46 and a raw score of 22 corresponds to a percentile rank of 50. If a student scores 21 correct, the percentile rank has to be estimated. In this case the best estimate would be a value halfway between 46 and 50 (48). Although estimating missing values does not represent the ideal situation, it is necessary at times and it does not alter subsequent interpretations to any significant degree.

All of the types of derived scores to be discussed in this chapter are depicted in Figure 11.5 (the diagram of the normal curve) and are based on the concept of a normal distribution. Keep in mind that the equivalencies between derived scores indicated on the normal curve figure are accurate to the degree that the distribution upon which they are based is normally distributed. Although it is not likely that classroom distributions will be normal, it is also true that teachers are not likely to need all of those derived scores anyway. The norms tables for major standardized tests are invariably based on a large sample, thus ensuring a relatively normal distribution. Therefore, the normally distributed/not normally distributed problem is really not much of a problem in practice after all.

Percentile Ranks

Because percentile ranks are virtually always reported, it is important for anyone involved with interpretation of standardized test results to be familiar with their symbolism and meaning. Although the percentile rank concept is a fairly simple one, there are a number of misconceptions associated with interpretation of percentiles and percentile ranks. For one thing, percentile ranks tell us nothing about percentages of correct answers. *Percentile ranks* indicate the percentage of persons who scored as well as or lower than a given score. They do not indicate the percentage of items a student answered correctly. Also, although the terms *percentile* and *percentile ranks* are often used as if they are synonymous, there is an important distinction between them. A percentile is a point in a distribution, whereas a percentile rank indicates the relative position of a score in a distribution.

A *percentile* is a point that cuts off a given percentage of a distribution. There are 99 percentiles and thus a distribution is divided into 100 equal parts. The first percentile, symbolized as P1, is the point below which are 1% of the scores. Similarly, P50 is the point below which are 50% of the scores, and P90 is the point below which are 90% of the scores.

A percentile rank (PR) indicates the percentage of scores equal to or less than a given score. Thus, if a raw score of 48 corresponds to a percentile rank of 80 (symbolized PR80), this means that 80% of the scores are equal to or less than 48. In other words, if Beulah Bright had a PR of 98, this would mean that she did as well, or better than, 98% of the members of some group who took the same test. Conversely, if Vera Verislow had a PR of 2, this would mean that Vera only did as well as, or better than, 2% of the members of the comparison group. Percentiles and percentile ranks are appropriate for data representing an ordinal scale, although they are frequently computed for interval data. The median of a set of scores corresponds to the 50th percentile, which makes sense because the median is the middle point and therefore the point below which are 50% of the scores. Thus, percentile ranks allow us to determine how well an individual did in relative terms, as compared to others who took the same assessment. If percentile ranks are given for a number of subtests, they also provide a rough means of comparing an individual's relative performance in a number of different areas.

Percentiles can also be combined with the standard error of measurement (SEM) to form percentile bands. Recall from Chapter 3 that the standard error of measurement provides an estimate of how often you can expect certain errors of a given size, errors in estimating a student's true score, and errors resulting from the fact that no assessment is perfectly reliable. Using percentile bands, you can compare the percentile ranks of individual students in your class on a standardized test or the percentile ranks of a single student on various subtests of an achievement series.[4]

One point to keep in mind when interpreting percentile ranks is that they are ordinal, not interval, measures. Therefore, intervals between percentile points are not equal. An increase of a given number of percentile points corresponds to a different number of raw score points depending upon where we are in the distribution. The difference between the 45th and 50th percentiles, for example, does not represent the same increase in raw scores as the difference between the 90th and 95th percentiles. As Figure 11.5 indicates, the percentiles are much closer together at the middle of the distribution, near the mean, than at the ends of the distribution. An increase in 5 raw score points, for example, will increase the corresponding percentile much more if the score is near the middle of the distribution than if it is at either end. The reason, as Figure 11.5 illustrates, is that there are more people near the middle than at the extremes. Therefore, an increase of a given number of raw score points results in more people "being passed"—that is, in more scores being surpassed. To put it another way, if you increase your raw score a few points, you overtake or do better than a lot of people if your score is near the middle, but very few people if your score is at either end, simply because there are more people near the middle or average score.

Another alleged drawback associated with percentile ranks is that, theoretically, you cannot perform arithmetic operations on them. You might wish, for example, to average a student's percentile ranks on a number of subtests to produce an average percentile rank. Mathematically speaking, you cannot do this and still have an interpretable result. In reality, however, averaging percentile ranks often provides a fairly reasonable estimate of typical performance. However, since the practice is questionable and because there are other derived scores that permit such manipulations, it is probably wise to avoid tampering with percentile ranks.

Although percentiles are 99 points that divide a distribution into 100 parts, quartiles (discussed previously in the Measures of Variability section) are three points that divide a distribution into four equal parts. Figure 11.5 shows the relationship between percentiles and quartiles. The first quartile (symbolized as Q1) corresponds to the 25th percentile, the second quartile (Q2) corresponds to the 50th percentile (the median), and the third quartile (Q3) corresponds to the 75th percentile. Quartiles are not used very often. Functions that they once served, such as providing a basis for grouping, have largely been taken over by stanines, which are discussed next.

---

[4]We will do just that in Chapter 14.

Standard Scores and Stanines

A *standard score* is a derived score expressing how far a given raw score is from some reference point, typically the mean, in terms of standard deviation units. A standard score is a measure of relative position, which is appropriate when the test data represent an interval or ratio scale of measurement. The most commonly reported and used type of standard scores are stanines. Figure 11.5 depicts stanines and their relationship to the normal curve. Standard scores allow scores from different tests to be compared on a common scale and, unlike percentiles, we can validly perform mathematical operations on standard scores—to average them, for example. Averaging scores on a series of classroom tests to arrive at a final grade is like averaging apples and oranges and getting an "orapple." Such tests are likely to vary in level of difficulty and variability of scores. By converting test scores to stanines, however, you can average them and arrive at a valid final grade based on relative position. Or, in order to determine a student's general level of functioning, for example, you could average his subtest stanines from the most recent standardized test administration.

Stanines are standard scores that divide a distribution into nine parts. Stanine is short for *standard nine*. Stanines two through eight each represent one-half a standard deviation (1/2SD) of the distribution; stanines one and nine include the remainder. In other words, stanine five includes 1/2SD around the mean ($\overline{X}$); that is, it equals $\overline{X} \pm 1/4SD$. Stanine six goes from +1/4SD to +3/4SD (1/4SD + 1/2SD = 3/4SD), and so forth. Stanine one includes any score that is less than −1 3/4SD (−1.75SD) below the mean, and stanine nine includes any score that is greater than +1 3/4SD (+1.75SD) above the mean. As Figure 11.5 indicates (see the row of figures directly beneath the stanines), stanine five includes approximately 20% of the scores, stanines four and six each contain approximately 17%, stanines three and seven each contain approximately 12%, two and eight each contain approximately 7%, and one and nine each contain approximately 4% of the scores.

Using these theoretical percentages, you can translate a set of scores from any assessment into stanines. To do this, first simply arrange the scores in ascending order and identify the median (midpoint). Then assign the 10% of the scores just above the median and the 10% just below the median to stanine five (stanine five contains 20% of the scores). Then assign the next 17% on either side of the scores to stanines four and six respectively, and so forth. Of course, unless the raw score distribution is normal, which is not likely in many local situations, the percentages in each category will only more or less approximate the identified percentages. For most purposes, however, this is not a serious problem and the resulting stanines are useful. The only matter you must guarantee is that all persons with the same score end up in the same stanine. If, for example, four students have the same score, the percentages may indicate that two of the students should be in stanine six and two of them should be in stanine seven. Logically, however, this does not make any sense; students with the same raw score cannot have different derived scores. All four students must be assigned to the same stanine, six or seven, and the necessary adjustments made.

Like percentiles, stanines are almost always reported in norms tables for standardized tests. They are very popular with school systems because they are so easy to understand and to explain to others. Although they are not as exact as other standard scores, they are useful for a variety of purposes. As mentioned earlier, they are frequently used as a basis for flexible grouping. They are also used as a criterion for selecting students for special programs. A reading program, for example, may select students who scored in stanines one and two (and perhaps three) on a standardized reading test. In many districts, stanines operationally define "average." Students in stanines four, five, and six are considered average with regard to the variable assessed. Students in stanines one, two, and three are considered below average, and students in stanines seven, eight, and nine are considered above average.

Grade Equivalents

A *grade equivalent* or grade score of a given raw score is the grade level of students whose typical (mean or median) score is the same as the given raw score. For example, if the median raw score on a reading comprehension test is 29 for a norm group of students beginning the fourth grade, then any student who scores 29 will have a grade equivalent of 4.0, regardless of what grade the student is actually in. A grade equivalent expresses both the grade and the month in the grade. Thus 4.0 indicates the beginning of the fourth grade, 4.5 indicates the fifth month of the fourth grade, and 4.8 indicates the eighth month of the fourth grade. The year is typically divided into 10 parts such that the first nine parts (4.0 through 4.8) correspond to the months of the school year and the 10th part corresponds to summer vacation.

Interpretation of grade equivalents is tricky, mainly because so many values are based on estimation. Typically, a test being normed is administered to large groups of students in each of several successive grade levels at the beginning of a school year and again at the end. For example, a test may be administered in September and May to third-, fourth-, fifth-, and sixth-grade students. Intermediate values within each grade level (for example, the score corresponding to 4.4) and sometimes values for grade levels above and below those actually tested (like the seventh grade) are estimated. Such estimations, especially those that extend beyond the grade levels actually tested, are not very sound and are a source of much misinterpretation. If Cal Culator, currently completing the fourth grade, takes the Mathematics: Problem Solving and Mathematics: Procedures subtests of the Stanford Achievement Test for fourth-graders and earns grade equivalents of 7.4 and 7.2, respectively, does this mean that we should schedule Cal into seventh-grade math classes in September? No. All these grade equivalents tell us is that Cal is very advanced for a fourth-grader. It is extremely unlikely that he actually has achieved all of the arithmetic competencies taught in the fifth and sixth grades. It is also unlikely that he would do well on a test designed for a higher grade level. Further, grade-equivalent estimations are based on the assumption that scores increase evenly, or by the same amount, from month to month and from year to year.

This may be essentially true in lower grades in which instruction in certain content areas (like reading) is continuous from grade to grade, but it becomes a progressively less valid assumption at higher grade levels. Thus, the use of grade-equivalent scores in high school is questionable, at best.

Another interpretation problem associated with grade equivalents arises from the fact that the same grade equivalent on two different tests or subtests does not necessarily indicate the same relative position (such as percentile rank). In fact, it is entirely possible for a student to have a higher grade equivalent on one subtest than on another and yet have a lower percentile for that subtest. The reason is that the distribution of scores is different for each test or subtest, and some have greater variability than others. It is easier, for example, to score very highly in verbal areas than in mathematical areas; achievement in math is more dependent on instruction.

All in all, grade equivalents leave much to be desired. We could probably do without them very easily, given the variety of alternative equivalents available to us, but their popularity persists because they are considered to be fairly easy for most people to understand when accompanied by a bit of helpful explanation. In your own practice you may either choose not to use them or to interpret them intelligently, realizing that they are rough indicators at best. You should, however, be able to help parents understand grade equivalents and correct any misunderstandings they may have about them.

Outcome/Item-Achievement Charts and Individual Performance

To describe individual student performance on a classroom assessment, measures of relative position are often inadequate. This is especially true when we wish to describe (to a parent, for example) what skills and abilities a student has and has not acquired. Outcome/item-achievement charts again come to our aid. When specific individual performance data for each student is spread out visually in such an organized fashion, the task of describing a student's achievement status becomes much easier. In some cases, depending on the assessment, it may be more desirable to describe specific outcomes achieved rather than total points earned. In other cases, total points earned may be recorded by the student for grading purposes, and specific strengths and weaknesses of individuals and the class are recorded elsewhere for instructional planning. In any case, the outcome/item-achievement chart may be customized to produce the necessary information. Using the chart in Figure 11.8, for example, Ms. Shapiro can determine for each student whichever of the following are appropriate:

- Percentage of checklist or rating-scale items performed to criterion for each outcome.
- Which outcomes were and were not achieved.
- Percentage of outcomes achieved.
- Which performance dimensions or items relating to a specific outcome were missed.
- Whether mastery was attained.
- Relative strengths and weaknesses with regard to very specific behaviors.

The pattern of dots can also be enlightening with regard to individual performance. Take Dino for example (see Figure 11.8). It appears that he can perform the critical parts of the three performance tasks, but he may let others set up materials for him. He doesn't seem to follow safety procedures, either. Bam Bam, on the other hand, appears to be safety conscious but cannot do much else. Fred may be the cooperative and helpful one who gets things ready then lets others take over. All of these, of course, are *possible* explanations and would need to be corroborated (or disproved) through careful observation. The dot pattern can also help identify students and behaviors to observe further. For example, Ms. Shapiro may want to keep a vigilant eye on Dino during the next lab experiment, especially if it has the potential to be dangerous.

Summary

Describing Assessment Performance Using Measurement Scales

Depending upon the variables and the way in which they are assessed, different kinds of data can result, representing different scales of measurement. A nominal scale represents the lowest level of measurement. A *nominal scale* classifies people (or objects) into two or more categories. Whatever the basis for classification, a person can be in only one category, and members of a given category have a common set of characteristics. Gender, race, and the county in which you live are examples of *true categories,* whereas low, medium, and high are examples of *artificial categories*. An *ordinal scale* not only classifies people (or objects) but also ranks them in terms of the degree to which they possess a characteristic of interest—that is, an ordinal scale puts people in order from highest to lowest, from most to least. Intervals between ranks are not necessarily equal.

An *interval scale* has all the characteristics of a nominal scale and an ordinal scale, but in addition it is based upon predetermined equal intervals. Most of the tests used in educational assessment, such as achievement tests and aptitude tests, represent interval scales; therefore, you will often work with interval data. Interval scales typically have an arbitrary maximum score and an arbitrary minimum score; they do not, however, have a true zero point. A *ratio scale* represents the highest, most precise level of measurement and has all the characteristics of the other types of scales, as well as a meaningful, true zero point. Because most physical measures represent ratio scales but psychological measures do not, ratio scales are not used very often in educational assessment. A descriptive statistic appropriate for a lower level of measurement may be applied to data representing a higher level of measurement, but the reverse is not true.

Describing Group Performance

Measures of central tendency are used to determine the typical or average score of a group of scores. They provide a convenient way of describing a set of data with a single number. Each index of central tendency is appropriate for a different scale of measurement: The mode is appropriate for nominal data, the median for ordinal data, and the mean for interval or ratio data.

The *mode* is the score that is attained by more people than any other score or the category into which more people fall than any other available category. The mode is not established through calculation; it is determined by looking at a set of scores or at a graph of scores to see which score occurs most frequently. Because of problems associated with the mode, it is usually used as a measure of central tendency only when nominal data are involved.

The *median* of a score distribution is the point at which the scores both above and below it are equal in number, or the midpoint or middle score when the scores are arranged from highest to lowest. The median does not take into account each and every score. It ignores, for example, extremely high scores and extremely low scores.

The *mean* is the arithmetic average of the scores and is the most frequently used measure of central tendency. The mean takes into account or is based on each and every score. The mean is the preferred measure of central tendency for interval or ratio data and is a more precise, stable index than either the median or the mode. For *skewed* distributions (in which there are one or more extreme scores), the median will not be the most accurate representation of the performance of the total group, but it will a better index of typical performance than the mean.

Two sets of test scores that are very different can have identical means or medians; thus, there is a need for a measure indicating how spread out the scores are, how much *variability* there is. Although the standard deviation is by far the most often used measure of variability, the range is useful to estimate variability when a rough measure is needed. The quartile deviation is the appropriate index of variability for ordinal data. As with measures of central tendency, measures of variability appropriate for ordinal data may be used with interval or ratio data even though the standard deviation is generally the preferred and more precise index for such data. The *range* is defined as the difference between the highest score and the lowest score ($R = H - L$). Like the mode, the range is not a very stable measure of variability, and its chief advantage is that it gives a quick, rough estimate of variability.

The *quartile deviation* (also referred to as the semi-interquartile range) is one-half of the difference between the upper quartile (75th percentile) and the lower quartile (25th percentile) in a distribution. The quartile deviation is a more stable measure of variability than the range and is appropriate whenever the median is appropriate. The standard deviation is the measure of variability appropriate when the data represent an interval or ratio scale and is by far the most frequently used index of variability. Like the mean, the measure of central tendency that is its counterpart, the *standard deviation* is the most stable measure of variability and takes into account every score. If you know the mean and the standard deviation of a set of scores, you have a pretty good picture of what the distribution looks like. If the distribution is relatively normal, then the mean plus three standard deviations and the mean minus three standard deviations encompass just about all the scores, over 99% of them; that is, $\overline{X} \pm 3SD = 99+\%$ of the scores.

A *normal curve* is essentially a frequency distribution constructed for a set of normally distributed scores. If a variable is normally distributed—that is, if it forms a normal curve—then the following statements are true:

1. The area under the curve represents all—100%—of the scores.
2. Fifty percent of the scores are above the mean and 50% of the scores are below the mean.
3. The mean, the median, and the mode are the same.
4. Most scores are near the mean and the nearer the mean a score is, the larger the number of people who attained that score; the farther from the mean a score is, the fewer the number of persons who attained that score.
5. The same number or percentage of scores is between the mean and plus one standard deviation ($\overline{X}$ + 1SD) as between the mean minus one standard deviation ($\overline{X}$ − 1SD), and likewise for $\overline{X}$ ± 2SD and $\overline{X}$ ± 3SD.

If scores are normally distributed, the following statements about the standard deviation are true:

$\overline{X}$ ± 1SD = approximately 68% of the scores
$\overline{X}$ ± 2SD = approximately 95% of the scores (1.96SD is exactly 95%)
$\overline{X}$ ± 2.5SD = approximately 99% of the scores (2.58SD is exactly 99%)
$\overline{X}$ ± 3SD = approximately 99+% of the scores

And similarly, the following statements are always true when the scores are normally distributed:

$\overline{X}$ − 3SD = approximately the .1 percentile
$\overline{X}$ − 2SD = approximately the 2nd percentile
$\overline{X}$ − 1SD = approximately the 16th percentile
$\overline{X}$ = the 50th percentile
$\overline{X}$ + 1SD = approximately the 84th percentile
$\overline{X}$ + 2SD = approximately the 98th percentile
$\overline{X}$ + 3SD = approximately the 99th+ percentile

These equivalents are generalizable to the scores of any group on any measure to the degree that the scores approximate a normal curve. Most variables measured in education form normal distributions *if enough people are tested.* Because classroom assessment deals with a finite number of students and often not a very large number, data only more or less approximate a normal curve; likewise, all of the equivalencies (such as standard deviation and percentiles) are also only approximations.

When the desire is to describe exactly what students can and cannot do, either collectively or individually, an outcome/item-achievement chart can be very useful. Such a chart can help describe (1) the percentage of students who achieved each outcome, (2) the percentage of students achieving mastery, (3) specific outcomes that are relative strengths and weaknesses, (4) the average total number or percentage of items correct, (5) the average total number or percentage of outcomes achieved, and (6) the median number or percentage of outcomes achieved. The outcome/item-achievement chart can help describe scores on a performance assessment or a paper-and-pencil test with equal ease.

Describing Individual Performance

A numerical value summarizing the responses actually made on a test by an individual is called a *raw score,* which is usually the total number of correct answers and has essentially no meaning in and of itself. There is a need for methods of transforming raw scores into values that facilitate the interpretation of scores on both an individual and group basis; measures of relative position fill this need for norm-referenced assessments. Measures of relative position indicate where a score is in relation to all other scores in the distribution. Measures of relative position permit you to express how well an individual has performed as compared to all other individuals in some group who have been given the same assessment. A major advantage of such measures is that they make it possible to compare the performance of an individual on two or more different tests (or subtests); measures of relative position express different scores on a common scale, giving a common frame of reference and thus permitting valid comparisons of scores on different tests. Raw scores that have been transformed systematically into equivalent values indicating relative position are referred to as *derived scores*. Standardized test manuals almost always provide norms tables containing raw scores and one or more equivalent derived scores. Occasionally, a norms table does not provide derived scores for each and every raw score; in such cases it is necessary to estimate missing values. The equivalencies between derived scores based on the normal curve are accurate to the degree that the distribution upon which they are based is normally distributed.

Percentile ranks indicate the percentage of persons who scored as well as or lower than a given score. A *percentile* is a point that cuts off a given percentage of a distribution; there are 99 percentiles, and thus a distribution is divided into 100 equal parts. Percentiles and percentile ranks are appropriate for data representing an ordinal scale, although they are frequently computed for interval data. The median of a set of scores corresponds to the 50th percentile. Percentiles can also be combined with the standard error of measurement (SEM) to form percentile bands. As ordinal measures, percentile points do not have equal intervals between them; an increase of a given number of percentile points corresponds to a different number of raw score points depending upon where we are in the distribution. Percentiles are 99 points dividing a distribution into 100 parts; quartiles are three points which divide a distribution into four parts.

A *standard score* is a derived score that expresses how far a given raw score is from some reference point, typically the mean, in terms of standard deviation units. A standard score is a measure of relative position that is appropriate when the test data represent an interval or ratio scale of measurement. Standard scores allow scores from different tests to be compared on a common scale, and, unlike percentiles, we can validly perform mathematical operations on them, like finding the average. *Stanines* are standard scores that divide a distribution into nine parts; stanine is short for *standard nine*. Stanines two through eight each represent 1/2SD segments of the distribution; stanines one and nine include the remainder. Stanine five includes 20% of the scores, stanines four and six each contain 17%, stanines three and seven each contain 12%, two and eight each contain 7%, and one and nine each contain 4% of the scores (with all percentages being approximate). Using these theoretical percentages you can translate a set of scores from any assessment into stanines. Although stanines are not as exact as other standard scores, they are useful for a variety of purposes such as flexible grouping and selection of students for special programs; in many districts they operationally define "average."

A *grade equivalent* (or grade score) of a given raw score is the grade level of students whose typical (mean or median) score is the same as the given raw score. A grade equivalent expresses both the grade and the month in the grade. Grade-equivalent estimations are based on the questionable assumption that scores increase evenly, or by the same amount, from month to month and from year to year. The same grade equivalent on two different tests or sub-tests does not necessarily indicate the same relative position (such as percentile rank). All in all, grade equivalents leave much to be desired. Their popularity persists, however, because they are considered to be fairly easy for most people to understand.

When specific individual performance for each student is organized visually in an outcome/item-achievement chart, the task of describing a student's achievement status becomes much easier. Using an outcome/item-achievement chart, a teacher can determine for each student whichever of the following are appropriate: (1) percentage of checklist or rating scale items performed to criterion for each outcome, (2) which outcomes were and were not achieved, (3) percentage of outcomes achieved, (4) which performance dimensions or items relating to a specific outcome were missed, (5) whether mastery was attained, and (6) relative strengths and weaknesses with regard to very specific behaviors. The pattern of dots can also be enlightening with regard to individual performance; it can help identify students and behaviors to observe further.

Try These

I. Circle the letter of the response that best answers the question.

1. Which of the following can we best accomplish with measures of relative position?
   a. Compare an individual's score with that of his or her peers who took the test.
   b. Calculate the mean, median, and mode for a set of scores.
   c. Determine the number of outcomes achieved by each student who took the test.

2. What do norms tables help us do?
   a. Convert norm-referenced scores into criterion-referenced scores.
   b. Construct outcome/item-achievement charts.
   c. Interpret scores on tests.

3. Why are grade equivalents tricky to interpret?
   a. The year is divided into 10 parts instead of the normal 12.
   b. Many of the equivalents are estimated rather than calculated from actual scores.
   c. Not all grades are represented in the norms tables.

II. For each of the following items, circle T if the statement is true; circle F if it is false.

1. Measures of relative position are used with norm-referenced test scores. T F
2. An outcome/item-achievement chart is used with paper-and-pencil tests but *not* with performance assessments. T F
3. The most commonly reported standard score is the stanine. T F
4. Percentile rank is another way of saying percentage correct. T F
5. There are equal intervals between percentile points. T F
6. The lower the standard deviation, the less variability there is in the scores. T F

III. Matching

Set A: Match the type of data on the left with the type of measurement scale it is appropriately associated with. Write the letter of your answer in the blank to the left of the statement. Answers may be used once, more than once, or not at all.

Data

_____ 1. Jersey numbers on a sports team.
_____ 2. Written test scores on lacrosse rules.
_____ 3. Which after-school care program the parents like best.
_____ 4. Prizes in a competition (second prize in a pie-eating contest, for example).
_____ 5. Golf score.
_____ 6. A final exam score on the mechanics and principles of drafting.
_____ 7. Jordan's percentile rank in reading comprehension.
_____ 8. Sylvie's stanine score in math application.

Scales

a. Nominal
b. Ordinal
c. Interval
d. Ratio

Set B: Match the measure of central tendency or variability with the scale it is generally best used with. Write the letter of your answer in the blank to the left of the measure. The scales may be used once or more than once.

Measures of Central Tendency and Variability

_____ 1. Median.
_____ 2. Standard deviation.
_____ 3. Mode.
_____ 4. Mean.
_____ 5. Quartile deviation.
_____ 6. Range.

Scales

a. Nominal
b. Ordinal
c. Interval or Ratio

IV. For the following short-answer items, write your answer on a separate sheet of paper or in the space provided.

1. Briefly list the steps in figuring the average percentage of outcomes achieved for a class of 30 students.
2. Complete the following chart by filling in the blanks:

Quartile 1	__________ Percentile
Quartile __________	50th Percentile
Quartile 3	__________ Percentile

V. From the outcome/item-achievement chart data in Figure 11.9, find or calculate the answers to the following items.

1. For the scores (Total column), find the:
   a. $\overline{X}$ = __________________
   b. Median = __________________
   c. Mode = __________________
   d. Range = __________________
2. Use the criteria stated in the outcomes to determine for each student whether an outcome was achieved. Write a "Y" in the Achieved column for each outcome so achieved. Determine the number of outcomes achieved for each student and write the number in the Total Outcomes column.
3. For the outcomes (Total Outcomes column), find the:
   a. Mean number of outcomes achieved = __________________
   b. Median number of outcomes achieved = __________________
   c. Outcomes achieved by the group = __________________
   d. Outcomes that were relative strengths/weaknesses of the group =
   Strength(s) __________________ Weakness(es) __________________
4. On a separate sheet of paper, explain how you would interpret Alfie's performance on this assessment given that he is usually in the top third of the class in most subjects and especially in geography.

Answers

I. 1. a, 2. c, 3. b.

II. 1. T, 2. F, 3. T, 4. F, 5. F, 6. T.

III. Set A: 1. a, 2. c, 3. a, 4. b, 5. d, 6. c, 7. b, 8. c.

Set B: 1. b, 2. c, 3. a, 4. c, 5. b, 6. b.

Outcome	1							2							3										
Item / Student	1	2	3	4	5	6	Ach	7	8	9	10	11	12	Ach	13	14	15	16	17	18	19	20	Ach	Total Items	Total Outcomes
Ursula	•	•	•	•	•	•		•	•	•	•	•	•		•	•	•	•	•	•	•	•		20	
Baxter	•	•	•	•	•	•		•	•	•	•	•	•		•	•	•	•		•	•	•		19	
Clarice	•	•	•	•	•	•		•	•		•	•	•		•	•	•	•		•	•	•		18	
Vicki	•	•	•	•	•			•	•	•		•	•		•	•	•	•		•	•	•		17	
Lucy	•	•	•	•	•	•		•	•		•	•	•		•		•	•	•	•	•			17	
Shayna	•	•	•	•	•			•	•	•		•	•		•		•	•		•	•	•		16	
Neri	•		•	•	•	•		•	•	•		•	•		•		•	•	•	•	•			16	
Owen	•	•	•	•	•			•	•	•		•	•		•		•	•		•	•	•		16	
Morris		•	•	•	•	•		•	•	•	•	•	•		•	•		•		•				15	
Tony	•		•		•	•		•	•	•	•	•	•		•		•	•		•	•			15	
Alfie	•	•	•	•	•	•		•	•	•	•	•			•		•							13	
Doreen	•	•	•	•				•		•	•		•		•		•	•			•			12	

1. Given a political map of South America, students will write in the correct names of countries with at least 67% accuracy.
2. Given a political map of Asia, students will write in the correct names of countries with at least 67% accuracy.
3. Given a geographical features map of a continent, students will write in the correct names of major rivers with at least 60% accuracy.

Context: The above outcomes are part of a unit on map-reading skills and knowledge of countries and physical features. The teacher decided that if at least 70% of the students achieved all three outcomes, the instruction could be considered a success and no major revisions would be needed.

Figure 11.9
Outcome/item-achievement chart, outcomes, and context for determining achievement.

IV. 1. a. Determine the number of outcomes achieved by each student.
   b. Add the number of outcomes achieved by each student.
   c. Divide by the number of students assessed.
   d. Multiply answer by 100 to turn the decimal into a percentage.

2.

Quartile 1	25th Percentile
Quartile 2	50th Percentile
Quartile 3	75th Percentile

V. 1. a. $\overline{X} = 16.16$
   b. Median = 16
   c. Mode = 16
   d. Range = 8 (20−12)

2. See Figure 11.10.

3. a. Mean number of outcomes achieved = 2.75
   b. Median number of outcomes achieved = 3
   c. Which outcomes were achieved by the group = 1, 2, and 3 (all)
   d. Outcomes that were relative strengths/weaknesses of the group = Strengths = 1 and 2. Weakness = 3.

4. Your explanation may be in different words, but should include the following points: Alfie did not do as well individually as the students did as a group. He achieved two outcomes, whereas the typical performance (median) was three outcomes achieved. Alfie achieved outcomes one and two and did very well on them. His performance on outcome three, however, was the worst in the class (only two items correct out of eight). Since Alfie usually performs at a higher level in geography, this may be considered an anomaly. Perhaps he forgot that major rivers were going to be on the test. The teacher might inquire further to determine his true performance with regard to outcome three.

Outcome	1							2							3										
Item / **Student**	1	2	3	4	5	6		7	8	9	10	11	12		13	14	15	16	17	18	19	20		**Total Items**	**Total Outcomes**
Ursula	•	•	•	•	•	•	**Y**	•	•	•	•	•	•	**Y**	•	•	•	•	•	•	•	•	**Y**	20	**3**
Baxter	•	•	•	•	•	•	**Y**	•	•	•	•	•	•	**Y**	•	•	•	•		•	•	•	**Y**	19	**3**
Clarice	•	•	•	•	•	•	**Y**	•	•		•	•	•	**Y**	•	•	•	•		•	•	•	**Y**	18	**3**
Vicki	•	•	•	•	•		**Y**	•	•	•		•	•	**Y**	•	•	•	•		•	•	•	**Y**	17	**3**
Lucy	•	•	•	•	•	•	**Y**	•	•		•	•	•	**Y**	•		•	•	•	•	•		**Y**	17	**3**
Shayna	•	•	•	•	•		**Y**	•	•	•		•	•	**Y**	•		•	•		•	•	•	**Y**	16	**3**
Neri	•		•	•	•	•	**Y**	•	•	•		•	•	**Y**	•		•	•	•	•	•		**Y**	16	**3**
Owen	•	•	•	•	•		**Y**	•	•	•		•	•	**Y**	•		•	•		•	•	•	**Y**	16	**3**
Morris		•	•	•	•	•	**Y**	•	•	•	•	•	•	**Y**	•	•		•		•				15	**2**
Tony	•		•		•	•	**Y**	•	•	•	•	•	•	**Y**	•		•	•		•	•		**Y**	15	**3**
Alfie	•	•	•	•	•	•	**Y**	•	•	•	•	•		**Y**	•		•							13	**2**
Doreen	•	•	•	•			**Y**	•		•	•		•	**Y**	•		•	•			•			12	**2**

Figure 11.10
Completed outcome/item-achievement chart.

CHAPTER 12

Creating and Using Grading and Reporting Systems

Key Concepts:

- Understanding purposes, criticisms, and general principles of grading.
- Deciding bases for grading and reporting.
- Establishing frames of reference and understanding methods and symbols used in grading.
- Designing a personal grading system.
- Using electronic gradebooks.
- Developing communication alternatives to grades.

Standards Addressed in This Chapter:

5. Develop valid grading procedures that use student assessments.
6. Communicate assessment results to students, parents and other lay audiences, and other educators.

Before You Begin Reading, Consider This

Should grades be used to regulate student behavior? For example, should a student's grade in math be lowered as a result of his or her disruptive behavior? Or should a student's academic grade be raised because of a perceptible increase in effort, although the effort did not produce a perceptible increase in performance?

YES Grades are one of the main ways teachers have of getting students to follow the rules. Without grades, there are few consequences of significance to the student. Slightly lowering a grade for disruptive behavior or work turned in continually late, for example, is also more the way things operate in real life. A million-dollar sale may be lost because a high-quality proposal missed a deadline. An increase in effort should be rewarded.

NO Achievement is not attitude. Mixing them up in the same grade is confusing. Achievement and other things such as attitude, citizenship, effort, and conduct should be kept distinct and reported separately. If an academically adept student continually acts up in class, he or she should be dealt with in other ways. Disruptive behavior has nothing to do with math. Likewise: no increase in performance, no increase in grade. Reward good effort in other ways.

Re-Introducing Grading

Think for a moment about the number of grades you received over the course of your K–12 career. The total is likely to be well over 300! Even if your K–3 years were in a non-graded environment, the total is still likely to be over 200. Those grades represented a lot of painstaking work your teachers performed to communicate to you, your parents, and others how well you were doing in that academic situation. Of those hundreds of grades, did you ever receive one you thought was unfair? Probably, and probably more than once. Perhaps you thought the standards were too tough or that the objectives were never made quite clear to you. Maybe you thought that the assessments upon which the grades were based were not a match with what you were studying.

As a teacher, no doubt you have acquired a new perspective on the whole process of grading. Grading, to anyone who has had to do it, is not easy, requires a lot of thought and planning, and must be defensible to various audiences. Moreover, grading is a tremendous responsibility. Grades assigned to students have both short- and long-term effects on their lives. This is painfully obvious to students and their parents, and the pressure to do well fills the process with emotion. It is difficult to discuss grading because it is far from being a clear-cut issue. Strong written opinions on grading have been in print since Horace Mann in the mid-1800s, and these opinions differ widely according to personal and institutional philosophy. In this chapter we will consider various grading practices and their consequences for practice in the classroom.

A *grade* is an expression of judgment, usually a symbol—letter, number, or mark—that indicates the degree to which intended outcomes have been achieved. A grade represents and is derived from data gathered by the teacher in the variety of ways discussed in the earlier chapters of this book. The teacher analyzes the data and renders a judgment, filling in the report card directly, "bubbling in" the grade on a computer data entry sheet, or entering it into a computer file.

A major purpose of grades is to communicate how well a student is doing in the several academic (subject) areas and in non-academic, affective areas such as citizenship, conduct, and effort. The idea is to periodically, succinctly, and meaningfully inform a student, his or her parents (or guardian), and his or her counselor of the student's progress. These snapshots-in-time are typically recorded in cumulative folders, electronic or paper, that follow the students through their academic career to communicate their levels of achievement at various points in time to interested people. Typically, a copy is also sent home to parents via the student delivery system. If a student moves to a new school, the cumulative folder will communicate past achievement to the staff at the new school. The record of grades over a number of years communicates to post-secondary admissions officers and employers a student's pattern of past achievement.

Understanding General Principles of Grading

Matching Instructional Philosophies with Grading Practices

Planning for grading requires the same careful thought as producing effective instruction and assessment procedures. Different grading methods have different strengths, and some are more compatible with certain purposes of assessment and instructional philosophies than others. For example, criterion-referenced assessment, which is appropriate for mastery learning, calls for criterion-referenced grading and reporting. Grading on the curve, a norm-referenced grading system, would be out of place here. When teachers use a grading system that is not consistent with their teaching philosophy or that of the school, miscommunication results and grades are rendered meaningless. Therefore, when choosing or modifying an existing grading system, it is important to consciously consider the following:

- The teaching philosophy or approach that prevails at your school,
- The purpose of assessment as it applies to your classroom, and
- The philosophy underlying the proposed grading system.

A grading system that promotes congruency among these three factors is defensible, workable, and less stress producing for both you and your students. Grading methods are introduced and discussed in this chapter, along with their compatible philosophies and assessment purposes, to help you make informed decisions. The principles and suggestions for good grading and reporting systems are listed in the checklist toward the end of this chapter.

Ensuring Sufficient, Valid Data

A student's grade in a subject should not be based on subjective impressions or on one hastily developed assessment at the end of the term. Grades should be based on a sufficient amount of data systematically collected over the course of the grading period. A teacher's judgment is subject to all sorts of biases, including the influence of personal feelings. Although you might have a fairly accurate general picture of the level of a student's performance, the importance of grades demands a level of precision achieved only through systematic collection of valid data over time.

Recall from the discussion on reliability that there is no way that one randomly selected student can represent an entire population of students. The more students selected, however, the more likely it is that the sample is representative of the population. Also remember that tests with more items are more reliable than those with fewer items because they better represent the domain of all possible items. The same is true for assessments used as components of grades: The more valid components used to figure a grade, the more likely the grade is to be representative of the student's performance for the term—that is, reliable. The combination of the scores on all the components, in effect, represents the score on a "longer," more inclusive assessment.

Before you vow to grade everything in sight to achieve perfect reliability, realize that grading should not be overdone. Grading all seatwork, homework, responses to oral questions, and problems worked at the chalkboard is not a good practice. You must balance time given to assessment with time given to instruction. Students need a number of non-threatening opportunities to try out new skills or otherwise practice new learning. A major instructional event in many types of learning is practice with feedback. There is nothing wrong with "scoring" a worksheet or homework paper and providing corrective comments *for the sake of feedback* when the teacher's comments *are* the feedback. These scores and such should *not* be recorded in a gradebook or included in figuring the final grade for the term or grading period, however, and students should be informed of this. It is one thing to say, "I score homework to give you feedback." It is quite another to say, "Your homework will be graded, and these grades will figure into your academic grade for the marking period." The latter statement turns an originally non-threatening opportunity to risk being wrong for the sake of learning into a threatening one.

But, you may argue, if homework is not graded, the students may not feel the need to do it. And if they do not do it, shouldn't they be penalized? Students tend to feel homework is a waste of time if they see that nothing happens as a result. If they see that the teacher doesn't look at it anyway, why bother? Offering homework scores only for feedback purposes does two things: It shows your students that you do look at their homework and are concerned about their learning, and it lets them know how they might perform under assessment conditions if they were to be assessed at that time. And for students who do not do the homework? Some students need less practice and feedback to learn and will do well on assessments without the homework practice. They should not be punished for this. Others who need the practice but choose not to do it will see that need in their low grades that are based on assessments. You can help them see the link between practice and assessment without having to resort to including grades for practice as a component of the grade. In a sense, the link is already included, because for many students, if they do not practice, they will not do well in the subject.

Moreover, students should know *in advance* which grades "count" toward their final grade and which ones do not. They should be informed as to how final grades will be determined and on what basis. Keeping students in the dark about it or making requirements up as the term progresses is anxiety producing—some might say downright sneaky. This is especially important to older students who may have a number of out-of-class assignments, activities, or jobs and who must allocate time wisely. It is simply not fair to announce a week before it is due that you want a biology lab journal from everyone that includes a report on every lab project and procedure completed throughout the term. The requirement for such a journal should be announced at the beginning of the term and detailed instructions given (written *and* oral preferably) concerning its purpose, contents, and how it will be evaluated. Also, if six weekly quizzes are to be averaged and that average will constitute one-third of the students' grade, the 3-week cumulative test one-third, and the final 6-week cumulative test one-third, students should know this from day one. One way to do this is to hand out a sheet that has your grading policy on it, summarizes what counts and how much by listing components and their respective weights, and provides a place for students to track their performance. An example of this is shown in Figure 12.5 later in the chapter.

Separating Dimensions

There is general consensus that a final grade should be based on a combination of components such as written tests, projects, oral reports, procedural demonstrations, and products. There is some difference of opinion, however, concerning whether grades should be based on actual academic achievement only or also on such factors as effort and conduct. Although most would agree that the purpose of grades is to communicate level of achievement, this does not imply that student progress in other areas should not be reported. Depending on the grade level of the students and the grading policy in force, any of the following may be reported along with, but determined and listed separately from, academic achievement grades:

Citizenship	Attendance
Tardies	Effort
Work habits	Social skills
Conduct	Attitude
Respect for teacher	Class participation

Many school systems use a multi-symbol grading system, allowing progress in non-academic areas to be reported independently. An example is a three-symbol grading system that allows effort and conduct to be reported independently on the same report card. Thus, a B–2–C in Spanish might indicate an achievement grade of

B, an effort level of 2 (1 being maximum and 3 being abysmal), and a conduct level of C (on an A, B, C, D, F scale). Other school systems reserve the A, B, C, D, F scale for academic achievement only and use other codes to indicate teacher comments regarding dimensions, such as:

Completes work/class participation

Follows directions/uses time wisely

Is responsible

Is courteous

Respects the rights and property of others

Shows self-control

There may also be an indication by the teacher of whether a conference with the parent is suggested or requested. In each case, important areas of communication between teachers and parents should be well defined and separated from academic achievement.

Recognizing Faulty Practices

There are a number of faulty practices that can make the imperfect process of determining grades even worse and that lead to criticism of the use of grades. First, some teachers abdicate their responsibility for grading and turn the process over to the students, claiming that the only worthwhile evaluation is self-evaluation. Teaching students to apply critical-thinking skills to themselves is not a bad practice, but unless students are at a developmental level such that they can (1) judge the quality of the assessments they have had and (2) objectively observe themselves and compare that observation to some given standard or judging criterion, teachers have relinquished their responsibility for helping students learn to think critically. Students may also see this as an attempt on the teacher's part to avoid any confrontation that might arise as a result of assigning a particular grade to a student or as just plain laziness.

A second faulty practice is grading everything. Some teachers feel that if they do not count everything, it will not get done. This tends to turn the classroom into a place where a lot of grading and checking go on but not much instruction. Practice, as such, ceases to exist, and risk-taking is forsaken when students are required to do everything "for a grade." Grading everything is a way to police student behavior, but there are other ways to do this that do not cost as much precious instructional time.

The third faulty practice is grading on sight. Some teachers feel they have a sixth sense in determining term grades for students. One teacher I worked with actually told me a few weeks after the beginning of classes, "I know a D student when I see one, and I do not need a test or a cumulative record to tell me. I can spot them at the beginning of the year." Seasoned teachers do recognize behavior patterns and informally assess their students all the time, but this does not give them permission to forego appropriate assessment and assign a grade based on the thickness of a student's glasses or the number of sports letters on his or her school jacket. This is an unethical practice that can lead to lawsuits and is certainly not in the students' or teachers' best interests.

The fourth faulty practice is the teacher's imposition of impossible standards on students. High standards are one thing. It is quite another for a teacher to tell students that no one has the brains to get an A in her class and that precious few even make a B. Teachers who do this may also be abdicating their instructional responsibilities, citing that the high number of failures and low grades in their class are due to their high standards and the "fact" that the students just were not up to them, and not due to the teachers' less-than-stellar teaching.

Considering Criticisms of Grading

Surprisingly, not all of the critics of grading are students. Many view grading as unnecessary or, worse, harmful. Some have even called for an end to grading practices altogether. Although this may be an extreme position, critics make some valid points worth consideration. Here are some of those major points, along with some refutations of those criticisms.

Grades Are Interpreted Differently by Different People

One major objection to grades is that there is considerable variability in the interpretation of their meaning. An A is an A, right? Well, yes and no. Consider the following three scales for equating percentage scores or averages with a letter grade, all of which are used in schools today:

95–100 = A	93–100 = A	90–100 = A
88–94 = B	85–92 = B	80–89 = B
81–87 = C	77–84 = C	70–79 = C
75–80 = D	69–76 = D	60–69 = D
0–74 = F	0–68 = F	0–59 = F

Depending on the conversion scale used, an 80 could be a B, C, or D. Grading criteria can vary from teacher to teacher, school to school, and district to district. Of course, the letters A, B, C, D, F are not the only set of symbols used, which can complicate matters further. It is difficult to interpret precisely what is meant by a given set of grades, even with the help of a conversion scale. For example, 87% of *what* is a B? Some critics propose communication alternatives such as parent-teacher conferences and written reports to more fully communicate to parents how their child is doing. They are not without their own flaws, however, such as scheduling problems and language barriers. These strategies are discussed in greater detail later in this chapter.

The surprising fact is that there is a lot of consistency in students' grades across time. Students do not usually go from being B students to D students just because they change teachers or schools. There is also a high degree of agreement between a student's grades and his or her performance on standardized tests. Students who score well on these tests tend to get good grades, and students with low standardized test scores tend to get low grades also. This fact underscores the notion that there is consistency across grading practices—more so than critics allege.

Grading Has Negative Effects on Students

Some critics of grading have concluded that grading is an inhumane process with negative effects, pointing to consequences such as cutthroat competitiveness, cheating, plagiarism, resignation to failure, anxiety, depression, and even suicide. Some parents punish their children for not getting grades that meet their expectations. Some teachers also punish their students academically for misbehavior ("A zero in my gradebook for your outburst, Terry!"). These consequences are due to the abysmal behavior of some parents and teachers, not to the use of grades. Abolishing grades would not solve the problem of parents and teachers who punish students with grades. The parents and teachers would find another way to penalize students, and the negative effects would remain. Also, if we didn't possess at least a little anxiety, we might stay in bed all day. A reasonable amount of pressure—emphasis on the word *reasonable*—leads to increased achievement. As for failure, no one succeeds at everything he or she attempts. In real life, people lose sales deals, get fired, and go bankrupt. Bizarre student responses to grading pressures are frequently symptomatic of other adjustment problems, and low grades can be an indicator of such problems. Students who exhibit such behaviors need counseling to help them deal with the pressure from grades and perhaps other parts of their life in general. Finally, if the curriculum and program of instruction are properly designed to meet the needs of all students, no one is doomed to failure, because in good curricula students are assigned tasks at which they can be successful.

There are a number of less serious criticisms of grades. People frequently claim that some teachers are too cavalier about grading, that they do not base the grade on valid, sufficient data, and that they do not assign grades on any rational, justifiable basis. As a student, you may have had a teacher you suspected of doing just this. As with the variability of meaning criticism, however, the observed consistency of grades across time and teachers indicates that, at least on the average, teachers do a pretty good job of grading, as students do a pretty consistent job of performing. As for mastery learning and outcome-based education (OBE), students definitely differ with respect to the time they take to achieve mastery and the number of attempts they require. Some grading systems can take these differences into consideration, as you will see later in this chapter.

There is no one perfect grading system. Neither are there any national or statewide laws mandating a particular system of grading. These are probably major reasons why so many different grading systems are used. But grading is serious business. Even if you do not personally believe in grades, you must accept the fact that other people take them seriously and use them to make decisions about students.

Considering Achievement, Effort, and Other Components of Grading and Reporting

Before you determine a student's grade in a subject, you must decide what assessment opportunities will be given and which of these will be used as components of the final grade. You can review your master lesson plan for the grading period or year to spot these opportunities. The components for grading and reporting stem from the same valued outcomes that drive instruction and assessment. For the components, you then decide whether all are equally important in determining the grade or whether there are some components that may be weighted more heavily than others. In practice, teachers tend to place more weight on assessments that require students to work on their own, without possible help from classmates or parents, siblings, and friends outside school. Thus, Jessica's individual essay written in class or her unit test on early settlers of North America may be worth two or even three times as much as her made-at-home diorama depicting American colonial life. The grades on all three components (essay, test, and diorama) and others might count toward her social studies grade for that marking period. Keep in mind that you do not have to count everything, and what you do count for a grade should be highly related to the instructional outcomes you have selected for assessment.

A corollary to the "achievement only" position is that every component score that contributes to the academic grade should also be based on achievement only. Thus, if a science project represents a component of the final academic grade, it should be graded on demonstrated understanding of scientific concepts and application of scientific principles stated in the instructional outcomes, not on effort. The amount of effort the student put forth to produce the science project should be reported separately if effort is important to you. Figure 12.1 is a schematic representing a way to separate your thinking when planning for grading and in determining grades. The figure uses the academic area of science as an example. Suppose that the grading policy at a particular school states that the separation of academic achievement and effort is important, but that both are also important to report accurately to parents. Suppose also that the teacher assigns an essay and a project (among other things), both of which count toward students' grades for a particular marking period. The teacher issues two scores for each component, one for achievement of instructional outcomes and one for evident effort put forth. This is represented schematically in the figure. Both scores on each would be reported to the student. When it comes time to determine grades for the term, the teacher can then concentrate on the achievement grade for all components and then on the effort grade to arrive at two separate grades that will appear on the report card. This is represented at the bottom of Figure 12.1.

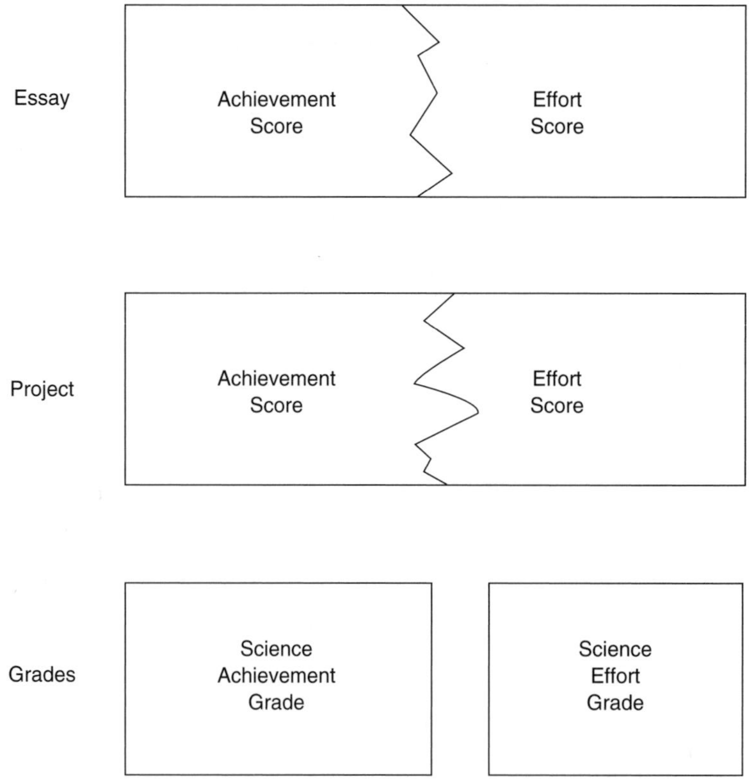

Figure 12.1
A schematic representing the contributions of essay, project, and other achievement scores to the science achievement grade, and the contribution of effort on these assignments to the effort grade in science. The two marks in science are then entered separately on the report card for the student.

Elementary-school teachers may argue that affective outcomes such as positive attitudes toward school are just as important as cognitive outcomes and, therefore, so is effort. If putting forth sustained effort to complete assignments is a valued instructional outcome, then it should be assessed, and components should be designated so that the teacher can make an informed judgment about whether the student has achieved it. In reality, effort cannot be separated entirely from achievement, because one begets the other to a large degree. Thinking about them separately, however, can make grading a less arduous task for teachers. At the high-school level, students are preparing to enter society in one capacity or another, and the real world evaluates actual performance, not effort or whether the person means well. Effort in the workplace counts only if it produces desired results. Employers, for example, do not look favorably on computer programmers who make 20 errors per 100 lines of code written, regardless of how hard they try. But increased effort usually results in increased achievement, and few students get good grades without effort. Those who do should not be penalized for being bright.

Considering Frames of Reference and Methods of Grading

Another issue that teachers must resolve for themselves is that of interpretation—the frame of reference or context within which a certain level of achievement should be judged. Achievement is labeled "good" or "poor" in relation to something. That something should be defined and communicated to users of grades so that the meaning of the grade is clear. Should a student's achievement be compared to previous levels of achievement? Should it be assessed relative to his or her ability? Should it be compared to the achievement level of other students? And if so, which ones? Would it be better to compare a student's achievement to pre-specified standards of performance? How about grading on the basis of improvement—from the beginning of the term to the end? All of these questions deal with the process of comparison. Users of grades such as college admissions personnel and employers often prefer norm-referenced grades, perhaps due to tradition more than anything else. Educators, on the other hand, have more diverse views on the subject. Although there are many alternative grading systems from which to choose, most of them are variations on one of three basic approaches: percent grading, criterion-referenced grading, and norm-referenced grading. We will consider each in turn.

Percent Grading

In *percent grading,* a student's raw scores on the assessments used as components of the final grade are tallied and divided by the total number of points available for those same assessments. That decimal is multiplied by 100 to obtain a percent. The percent itself may be reported as the grade (for example, Science, 78%) or converted to a letter-grade equivalent (94%–100% = A, and so forth). This system is used by teachers who view percent-to-letter-grade conversion scales (shown earlier in the chapter) as pre-specified standards of performance.

An advantage of the percent system is that no one has to fail; an F is not assigned to a student simply because he is at the bottom of the class, provided he amasses a large number of possible points. In addition, because no one has to fail, student anxiety may be reduced. A second advantage claimed by proponents of percent grading is that the basis for assigning grades is clear and easily communicated among teachers, students, and parents. This is a seductive statement, however, because the meaning of such grades is, in reality, very obscure.[1] The system of percent grading may be very familiar, but familiar does not equal clear. There are other problems with percent grades that should also be considered. A grade of 75%, for example, often means nothing more than the student answered 75% of all test items correctly. Such a grade tells us nothing about how much the student learned, either in relation to the intended learning outcomes—of which there are usually many—or in relation to what other students achieved. A grade of 75% might look all right, but it might also be the lowest in the class.

Also implicit in this system is the notion that academic achievement can be measured in much the same way as height, weight, or time and that classroom assessment instruments, like meter sticks, scales, and clocks, are well calibrated against some commonly defined unit. This is, of course, not true. Percentages are not true ratio scales for assessments and do not enable teachers to say, for example, that Shelly, with her score of 90%, knows exactly twice as much as Byron, with his score of 45%. The units of classroom assessment—questions, problems, items, scoring dimensions—are anything but equal and should not be thought of as such. Percent grading is sometimes referred to as absolute grading. The term *absolute* is a misnomer, however; a grade of 100% does not mean that the student knows 100% of the content domain, because the assessments on which the grade is based are but a sample of that domain.

Another problem with percent grading lies in the determination of the grading categories. There is usually no good justification, other than tradition, for using 93%–100% as the range for an A, for example. The determination of the ranges for converting a final percent into a letter grade should be based on knowledge of how students *typically* perform on the assessments that count toward a final grade. Only then can you determine the percent score achieved by the students who are considered minimally competent and thus determine the cut-off between D and F. On some grading scales this cut-off may be 60%; on others, 76%. This makes an "absolute" system somewhat relative. Even so, the nature of your assessment procedures should determine your standards or grade categories, not the other way around. One way to enhance the utility and defensibility of a percent system is for elementary teachers for a particular grade level or secondary teachers in a particular department to use common assessments as components of grades and to agree among themselves on the cut-offs for each category based on their collective knowledge of how students typically perform on these components.

Teachers have found the percent grading system useful and consistent with the philosophy of a mastery system of learning. The hallmarks of mastery learning—a set of clearly bound and defined learning tasks stated in performance terms, instructional outcomes that include performance standards, and criterion-referenced assessments—are conducive to absolute grading. Keep in mind, however, that the

---

[1] "Testing and Grading Practices and Opinions of Secondary Teachers of Academic Subjects: Implications for Instructions in Measurement" by R. B. Frary, L. H. Cross, and L. J. Weber, 1993, *Educational Measurement: Issues and Practice, 12* (3), pp. 23–30.

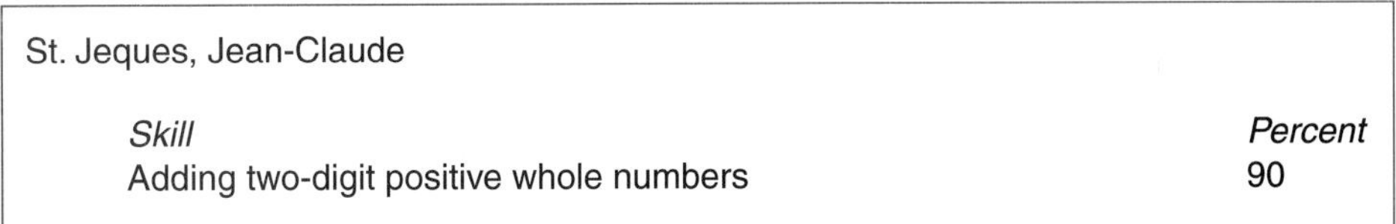

St. Jeques, Jean-Claude

Skill	*Percent*
Adding two-digit positive whole numbers	90

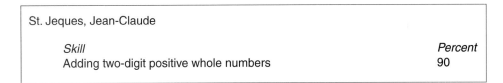

Figure 12.2
An example of mastery reporting using percent grading.

assessments must be constructed and used in such a way that you can determine the student's performance on each and every pre-specified learning task, for this is often how the grades are reported for mastery systems (see Figure 12.2). A given percent must have real meaning; for example, "of the 20 opportunities Jean-Claude has had to add two-digit integers, he has done so correctly 18 times or 90%." Such a system requires that the individual tasks and items on an assessment must be traceable back to the instructional outcome of origin. Only then can you figure a number correct/number attempted ratio or percent. Otherwise, the grades become meaningless. In most other contexts, however, a percent grade may mean any number of things.

Using the first conversion scale for grades at the beginning of this chapter (95%–100% = A, and so forth), consider the following scenario. You have judiciously constructed an assessment that parallels the learning outcomes on which you have concentrated your instruction. You intend to use the scores students earn on this assessment as a component of their grade for the marking period. After administering it, you find that the average performance of your class was 73%, ranging from a high of 87% to a low of 46%. What can you do? You have some options:

- Fail a large portion of your students.
- Redefine the ranges of grades to better reflect the difficulty of the outcomes and assessment (such as 86–100 = A, 76–85 = B, 66–75 = C, 55–65 = D, and 0–54 = F).
- Add 10 points to everyone's score this time.
- Throw out the assessment altogether and reconstruct it for next time to yield scores more in keeping with the pre-specified standards; in other words, make the test easier.

The first option is consistent with an absolutist view but is rarely justified unless your teaching has been consistently above reproach or you just happen to get an overabundance of slower learners in the class. Be aware that public relations may suffer for a while if you choose this option: You may be accused of not adjusting your teaching to the level of your learners, for example. The second alternative involves going against the ingrained beliefs about what the specific standards of performance mean and also, possibly, going against district policy. The third choice is the path of least resistance from others, but may be unsettling to you if you take pride in putting into practice the principles of good instruction and good assessment.

Also, adding 10 points to everyone's score does not change their respective ranking, and it may cause more confusion. Throwing out the assessment as a grade component is a good option if, in fact, the assessment was overly difficult or if your teaching strategies were less than optimal for your students and the content. Making the assessment easier is a good option only if, upon reflection, it does not match the instructional outcomes well.

Percent grading is most useful where student performance can be expressed in standard physical units of measurement, because this facilitates the setting of uniform absolute standards that can be divided into categories for grades.[2] The following are examples of these units: percent of words spelled correctly on a spelling test, percent of lines in a computer program coded without error, percent of tennis serves within the opposing player's service court, percent of baseballs thrown accurately from second to first base, percent of words correctly typed per minute, percent of successful goals shot in a timed hockey drill, percent of arrows that hit the target within the blue circle, and percent of shapes correctly placed in a form in one minute.

Criterion-Referenced Grading

Criterion-referenced grading involves expressing a student's achievement in relation to pre-specified criteria rather than in relation to the achievement of others in the class. The standards are absolute, in contrast to relative, in that the students who achieve the same standards achieve the same grade. No student is failed simply because he or she achieved lower than other students, provided the student achieves the criterion. Criterion-referenced grading came into wide usage a few decades ago along with the advent of competency-based education and behavioral objectives. The criterion-referenced grading system is best used with a mastery system of learning where specific learning targets can be set and assessed with criterion-referenced tests. Systematically designed instruction is also an example of the type of instruction that is congruent with a criterion-referenced grading system. It is also very compatible with outcomes-based education and facilitates accountability.

Proponents of criterion-referenced grading claim a number of advantages of the approach relative to other grading systems. First, as with percent grading, no one has to fail. Second, criterion-referenced grading removes most of the cutthroat competition among students fostered by a norm-referenced approach. Third, a criterion-referenced system facilitates reporting of student achievement by outcome so that it is abundantly clear just what the student knows and can do.

Just as with percent grading, a criterion-referenced system requires that:

- The intended learning tasks are clearly described and defined,
- The criteria for acceptable performance are specified for each task, and
- Criterion-referenced assessments are used to assess student performance.

---

[2] *Assigning Students Grades* by J. S. Terwilliger, 1971, Glenview, IL: Scott, Foresman.

For example, each outcome may be listed on a report card along with space for recording (1) the specified criterion of achievement or mastery, (2) the student's performance, and (3) an indication of whether the student's performance was enough to achieve the criterion. This may also include percent scores, such as in the following example:

Bobby Ten-Pow

Outcomes	Student's Percent	Criterion Level (%)	Criterion Reached?
1. Reduces proper fractions to lowest terms	90	80	Yes
2. Reduces improper fractions to lowest terms	75	80	No

Bobby's performance indicates that, for the outcomes listed, the criterion level is 80% for each—the student must perform to criterion at least 80% of the time. This may mean that there are 10 items on a paper-and-pencil test for a particular learning outcome, and Bobby must answer at least eight of them correctly to demonstrate mastery of the outcome (8/10 = 80%). It may also mean that his teacher will provide five opportunities to demonstrate achievement under performance assessment conditions and that Bobby must perform to criterion at least four times (4/5 = 80%). A variation on this is to use actual numbers and ratios, rather than percents, as illustrated below:

Bobby Ten-Pow

Outcomes	Student's Performance	Criterion Level	Criterion Reached?
1. Reduces proper fractions to lowest terms	4	4/5	Yes
2. Reduces improper fractions to lowest terms	3	4/5	No

In this case, the criterion level is expressed as 4/5 or "four out of five," which specifies that at least five opportunities for demonstrating achievement will be provided to the students and that they must perform to criterion four or all five times in order to reach criterion. In both cases, the student's actual performance with regard to the individual outcome is expressed. Criterion levels may vary by outcome—2/3, 7/10, and 5/5 are not uncommon.

Recall that a paper-and-pencil test, for example, may assess learning with regard to a number of outcomes. For criterion-referenced grading purposes, the performance or percent correct on the overall test is not as important as performance in relation to the specific outcomes covered by the test. Such a report communicates specific information to parents about the areas in which their children are achieving, areas in which they are having minor difficulties (as Bobby is having with outcome 2, above), and areas in which they are having major difficulties. Detailed reports such as these also make it easy for concerned parents to help their children at home on problem areas.

Expressing the student's actual performance with regard to each individual outcome is one of the hallmarks of a mastery learning system. Such a system may list the outcomes for the year or for several years in the case of a non-graded mastery

Periodic Mastery Chart

Student: Pamela Gouthrow **Teacher:** Ms. Butler

Outcome	Instruction Date Began	Date Mastery Achieved
Identify place value of ≤ 6-digit whole numbers.	9/23	10/7
Read numbers: word names of ≤ 6-digit whole numbers.	9/27	10/7
Add 6-digit numbers.	10/8	10/16
Subtract 6-digit numbers.	10/17	10/29
Read Roman numerals: I through CCCXCIX.	No*	
Multiply: 3- or 4-digit number by 1-digit number.	11/2	P**
Divide: 2-, 3-, or 4-digit number by 1-digit number, remainder as fraction.	No	
Compute averages: 2 through 6 numbers of ≤ 2 digits.	No	

*A "No" in this column indicates that instruction has not yet begun.
**A "P" in this column indicates that, although instruction has begun and the student has made progress toward the outcome, he or she has not yet been called upon to demonstrate mastery.

Figure 12.3
A partial periodic mastery report for a student in a non-graded system.

system. The student's performance may also be recorded in terms of the date mastery was achieved or demonstrated. Other information, such as the criterion for acceptable achievement, may also be included. A periodic report "card" thus provides a snapshot-in-time of what is actually a running account of the student's progress toward mastery, as in Figure 12.3. Thus it provides a way to take differential performance along a time continuum into consideration. The report is then signed by the student's parent or guardian and returned to the teacher for further entries.

A major disadvantage of criterion-referenced grading, especially in reporting mastery, is the tendency to list *every single* performance outcome, even those of the most minute proportions. This practice fragments learning into small meaningless bits that causes parents to ask, "So what does this all mean? Is it good or is it bad? I can't tell." Parents should be thoroughly informed of the process so they can correctly interpret their children's progress with the proper frame of reference. This can be accomplished through normal channels of communication with parents such as flyers with sign-offs, open houses, PTA meetings, and conferences.

Regardless of whether numbers or percents are used in criterion-referenced grading, setting the criterion for acceptable performance or mastery is the most difficult task. Whether set collectively by curriculum experts and included in a curriculum guide or set by teachers, standards may be difficult to defend because they are based primarily on judgment. One way to improve the defensibility of standards is to involve the stakeholders, like parents and potential employers of students, in the process of decision making. If setting standards is a district-level decision, for example, parents could be involved as part of the decision-making team in deciding mastery levels. At the very least, parents should be informed of the outcomes and the criteria for acceptable performance. As a teacher, you should also be prepared to show them their child's test papers, products, and so forth so they can see exactly what their child did. Standards can also be defended by showing parents the distribution of scores. You can point out that the majority of students scored at or above the level of acceptable performance. Such information enhances the validity of the standards.

Setting the criterion for acceptable performance can be done in a number of different ways. The following is one example of how you might successfully do this. First, you and the other teachers of your subject or grade review the learning outcomes for your classes for the year. For the purposes of this example, let's say there are 50 of them. You collectively decide that 35 of them are mastery objectives, meaning that all students should be able to achieve them by the end of the year. You also decide as a group that a student who mastered the minimum 35 competencies would receive a D, indicating minimal achievement. The achievement of the other 15 outcomes would be used to separate A, B, and C performance. For example:

A = all mastery outcomes and at least 10 nonmastery outcomes achieved.

B = all mastery outcomes and at least 5 nonmastery outcomes achieved.

C = all mastery outcomes and at least 1 nonmastery outcome achieved.

D = all mastery outcomes and no nonmastery outcomes achieved.

F = not all mastery outcomes achieved.

Norm-Referenced Grading

Norm-referenced grading is consistent with norm-referenced assessment procedures, which, you might recall, are designed to spread individuals out on a continuum of performance so that their rank can be determined with confidence. Student achievement is expressed in relation to the achievement of the rest of the norm group. In such a system most students in a class receive a grade indicating average achievement (*C*, for example), a few students fail, and a few students receive *A*s. A norm-referenced grade does not communicate what a student has actually achieved, but rather demonstrates how a student's achievement compared to the achievement of others in a comparable group. A student receiving a grade of B, for example, performed better than most but not as well as a few. With the norm-referenced system it is easy to determine if Geraldine is in the top fourth of her class or if Zach is doing better or worse than his twin sister, Zelda. Norm-referenced grading is more prevalent in schools where rank in class assumes more importance and there is less emphasis on mastery of specific, discrete skills. These conditions are more typically found in high schools than in others. Some of the recent research on grading systems, however, indicates that, at least in some secondary schools, teachers are more likely to use a percentage or even a criterion-referenced approach.[3] Norm-referenced grading is used much less frequently in elementary schools.

Norm-referenced grading requires norm-referenced assessments to maximize accuracy in detecting individual differences necessary for rank-ordering students. Recall that the item-achievement rates of norm-referenced assessment items, problems, and tasks should range in difficulty from about 30 to 90 with an average of 50 to maximize the spread of scores. Norm-referenced grading is, therefore, inconsistent with mastery learning and outcomes-based education. It is also more difficult to consistently rank order a homogeneous group than a heterogeneous one because a more variable group is easier to classify into different achievement levels. Therefore, norm-referenced grading is consistent with heterogeneous, untracked classes and is not consistent with entire classes that are homogeneously grouped for ease of instruction. Not only must the norm group be heterogeneous for norm-referenced grading, but it must also be large enough (several hundred scores at least) to produce a normal distribution of performance with which to compare. In practice, however, the distribution is rarely this large, and the assumption of a normal distribution is likely to be invalid. Imagine the high school where there are 300 or more 10th-grade students, all in heterogeneous English classes (no honors or remedial sections). Imagine also that the teachers of these 10 or so classes have all agreed to use the same assessments and have constructed each of them of such difficulty that the typical range of scores is 30% to 90% of the points available. This scenario seems difficult to imagine given the nature of most secondary schools, yet this scenario describes appropriate circumstances for the use of a norm-referenced grading system.

Sometimes, especially at the elementary level, an achievement grade not determined on a norm-referenced basis is accompanied by a ranking on any number of affective variables. Thus, a student might be rated as above average, average, or below average on such things as neatness, initiative, respect for teacher, and so forth. Such ratings are, of course, subjective, and biases such as the halo effect are possible.

Normal Curve Grading

In its extreme form, norm-referenced grading, or grading "on the curve," is based on an assumption of a normal distribution, and a fixed percentage of students receive each grade. These percentages, called *grade ranges,* are determined by the teacher(s), the school, or the district. A commonly used percentage scheme assigns

---

[3]R. B. Frary, L. H. Cross, and L. J. Weber, 1993. The data reported in this study indicate that the confusion over grading philosophies and system implementation realities may not have improved much over that indicated in an earlier study by James Terwilliger. See "Self Reported Marking Practices and Policies in Public Secondary Schools" by J. Terwilliger, March 1966, *Bulletin of the National Association of Secondary-School Principals,* pp. 5–37.

the top 7% of the scores an A, the next 23% a B, the middle 40% a C, the next 23% a D, and the bottom 7% a failing grade. Although percents are used, this grading system is not the same as percent grading. Thus, if Ms. Villadares, a history teacher, decides to base her grades on the normal curve, she might equate total achievement with points amassed on all tests, all quizzes, two term projects, and a research paper. She could then rank order the students by total points amassed from highest to lowest. If there are 33 students, the top two receive an A (7% of 33 is 2), the next eight students would receive a B, and so on. Following this logic, it is clear that some students must receive a failing grade. This may happen regardless of their actual achievement because the grade is due to their status at the bottom of the grade distribution. If overall points earned range from 80% to 100% of those possible, for example, giving out Ds and Fs does not make much sense. Imagine being told that no matter how effective your teaching may be, you must fail a given percentage of the students in your class. This provides no incentive for improving your teaching, not to mention what it does to the students. As another example, if all but one of the point percentages are between 70% and 100% and there is one student who garnered 50% of the points available, awarding the 70 and the 50 the same failing grade even if they are the bottom two in the distribution is probably not justified. Also, neither a magic nor a scientific formula exists for determining what the grade ranges should be for any given situation. Any local school staff can do it well for their purposes by taking into consideration the school's philosophy, the students, and the purposes of the grades generated.

A related problem is the shifting nature of the meaning of the grade based on the make up of the norm group. Recalling the earlier example of the 10th-grade English students, last year's 10th graders may have included five potential merit scholars and a record number who will attend college after they graduate. This year's 10th-grade class may be considerably less academically blessed. A student accumulating the same number of points might receive a different grade depending on which class is used as the norm group. The grade also tells nothing about what the student actually knows or can do. Terwilliger cites two major weaknesses of grading on the curve:

1. A normal distribution cannot be assumed and is, in fact, highly unlikely in classroom assessment.
2. The number of students who can comprise a norm group is too small to expect a normal distribution.[4]

These problems with grading on the curve are so strong and so serious that basing grades on the normal distribution curve is rarely justified.

Pass-Fail Grading

Another form of norm-referenced grading is *pass-fail grading* or credit/no-credit grading in which everyone who achieves the criterion of acceptable performance passes, and everyone who does not, fails. Usually when we think of pass-fail grad-

[4]J. S. Terwilliger, 1971.

ing, we think of criterion-referenced assessment. Pass-fail grading is norm-referenced, however, in that minimum competence in the course—the point at which everything below it is designated "fail"—is usually determined *relative* to typical student performance in the subject.

The pass-fail option is used mostly at the college level for courses for non-majors and occasionally at the high-school level. Students are typically given an option to take a certain number of courses on a pass-fail basis. Students who choose this option are usually in a class with students who are working for letter grades. If a pass-fail student achieves a level of performance that is no lower than the minimum for the course (a D or C depending on policy), the student passes.

The rationale behind offering this option is to entice students to take courses for which they might not otherwise risk their grade-point averages. In practice, such a system usually results in a reduction of achievement levels. Quite naturally, a student is less motivated to do well in a course where the grading option is pass-fail and devotes more energy to courses in which he or she will receive a letter grade. Moreover, if at some point in the future a student's "pass" grade is translated into a letter grade, it is usually lower than the student's typical grade. A student who has received "credit" for a class may receive a grade of C when translated into a letter system, for example, even if her level of achievement was equivalent to a B or an A.[5] Pass-fail grading is used on a very limited basis, if at all, and for good reason. A grade of "pass" communicates nothing except that the student achieved some minimum level of performance. In some extreme cases it may even communicate one of the following:

- The teacher's inability or unwillingness to separate achievement from effort and that the student, regardless of his or her failing performance, tried very hard in class and thus does not "deserve" to get a failing grade, or
- The teacher's unwillingness to challenge a prevailing myth that good teachers do not fail students.

Typically, the final grade is reported without the helpful context of what constitutes minimum performance; therefore, the pass-fail grade does not fulfill its promise of unambiguous communication. Its use is discouraged generally and justified only on a limited basis, for some electives in higher levels of education, for example.

Expanded Norm-Group Grading

Secondary-school teachers who find normal curve and pass-fail grading problematic but who work with a norm-referenced grading policy may find hope in a third approach. This approach makes no assumption of a normal distribution and can thus be used with negatively skewed distributions; it also maximizes the comparability of grades over different classes and over different years, thus enhancing the communication properties of grades and their utility to college admissions personnel and other users. The method, called *expanded norm-group grading* involves expanding

---

[5]Personal experience and communication with former students.

the norm group to include all students who have taken the subject under similar conditions. In high schools where the student population may be over 3,000, a large enough norm group may be found. In addition, the method requires the teachers of such courses to decide what these similar conditions will be and to render comparable such things as the following:

- Concepts and other content to be covered in the several sections or classes.
- Type and amount of coverage of relevant concepts through the teachers' instructional strategies.
- The quantity, quality, and scope of textbooks and other resource materials used.
- The methods and instruments used to assess achievement.

This grading method requires standardization of courses to a certain extent. For example, a common course syllabus based on common instructional outcomes, which are also the basis for common assessments, is preferred. Also, as the course is taught from year to year, the last 3 to 5 years of student scores and grades can be combined to provide a rolling data base large enough to accommodate norm-referenced grading. Terwilliger presents three ways to do this, using either raw scores, percentile scores, or standard scores.[6] With the increasing availability of computers to do the more tedious calculations and sorting tasks, the standard-score approach to expanding the norm group becomes feasible for busy classroom teachers. Of course, slavishly following strict standard-score, letter-grade equivalencies is as unwise as strictly following normal-curve percent, letter-grade equivalencies. The point to remember is that norm-referenced grading simply rank orders the students; it indicates nothing about actual achievement. Finally, grades have to be based on a combination of scores, points, and judgment.

Using Grading Symbols

Many grading symbols are used to communicate student progress in cognitive and affective areas. Many schools use the A, B, C, D, F or A, B, C, D, E system to indicate four categories of passable performance and one category of failure. Other schools use an expanded version with plus and minus signs to increase the number of categories of passable performance. The following set of symbols has 12 categories: A, A−, B+, B, B−, C+, C, C−, D+, D, D−, F. The increased number of categories allows teachers to indicate whether a B grade is high (B+), low (B−), or "solid" (B). These finer discriminations in performance are more difficult to perceive, however. For example, the difference between a C− and a C+ may only be four points on a single test. The symbols E, S, and U are also used to indicate Excellent or Exemplary, Satisfactory, and Unsatisfactory achievement. In addition to the 1, 2,

[6] J. S. Terwilliger, 1971.

3 system for indicating effort level mentioned earlier, there is the +, S, and − system which may be used to indicate performance in the affective domain. Even smiley faces (☺☻☹) have been used to communicate to very young students their status with regard to important outcomes. Regardless of the actual symbols used, there must be general agreement on and mutual understanding of the symbols by the users of grades; otherwise, communication does not take place and confusion reigns. Users of grades include students and parents, not just teachers.

Some teachers make the mistake of converting test and performance assessment scores to symbols in their gradebook during the course of a grading period. Not only may this distort the true performance level of the students, but it is also an inefficient use of teacher time. At the end of the marking period, the teachers must re-convert the letters or symbols to numbers for averaging. To maximize efficiency and avoid distorting the picture of student performance, record either the actual raw scores—the number of items answered correctly or performance points earned—or percentage scores rather than a letter grade. A raw score or percent score is more accurate and is easier to work with at the end of the grading period. Raw or percent scores also reduce the tendency to think of a student as a letter (a "D" student, for example), at least until all the evidence is in. For feedback purposes, you may give students a chart for converting raw scores to grades or percentages to use in answering the question, "Based on what I have done so far, what grade am I likely to get when report cards come out?" Depending on the level of your students, you may teach them the math involved and have them track their own performance unofficially. In some schools, students track their performance via computer and can display their personal data in a variety of charts and graphs.

Creating Personal Grading Systems

The Process and Decisions Involved in Designing a Grading System

Designing a grading system is a very personal act for a teacher. The process is filled with questions about philosophical issues, beliefs, and values due to the high emotion associated with grades and the various uses to which they are put. The six steps in the process are briefly listed here and described more fully in the following paragraphs.

1. Develop a personal grading philosophy.
2. Implement district policy, if one exists.
3. Choose an appropriate frame of reference for interpreting what the grading symbols mean.
4. Develop benchmarks for your grading system from the practices of your colleagues.

5. Decide on the types and number of grading components.
6. Weight the components.

The first step in creating a grading system is to develop a personal grading philosophy. Frisbie and Waltman summarize the philosophical issues teachers must face in assigning grades in their list of nine questions:

- What meaning should each grade symbol carry?
- What should *failure* mean?
- What elements of performance should be incorporated in a grade?
- How should grades in a class be distributed?
- What should the components be like that go into a final grade?
- How should the components of the grade be combined?
- What method should be used to assign grades?
- Should borderline cases be reviewed?
- What other factors can influence the philosophy of grading?[7]

The second step is to implement district policy. If one exists, you are obliged to use it. This is not a difficult task if the district policy is compatible with your personal grading philosophy. If no policy exists or the one that does is incompatible, a change is in order—in your philosophy, in the district's policy, or in your place of work. A district-wide policy is also likely to be general and not much help for a beginning teacher who would like more structure. On the other hand, a general policy gives teachers greater latitude. You must ensure that whatever system you implement is within policy guidelines where they exist.

The third step in creating a personal grading system is to choose an appropriate frame of reference for interpreting what the grading symbols mean. Whichever method is used, it should be consistent with your grading philosophy and instructional approach. A mastery learning approach to instruction is less consistent with norm-referenced grading than with criterion-referenced grading, for example.

The fourth step is to check with colleagues who teach the same subject or grade. After examining their grade distributions, grading components, and weights, you will see the range of possibilities for creating a grading system that may borrow the best features and still fit in with the rest. Quality experts call this benchmarking. This step is especially important if no district policy exists because most recent experience is the norm. If you are new to the school, the experience lies in your colleagues who are more familiar with the curriculum, the students, and the community. Your colleagues can, for example, help with the customary comments used to communicate non-academic performance or with the meaning of teacher comment codes used in the computer system of larger districts.

---

[7]"Developing a Personal Grading Plan" by D. A. Frisbie and K. K. Waltman, 1992, *Educational Measurement: Issues and Practice, 11* (3), p. 36.

Science Grade Component	Total Score	Weight	Weighted Total Score
Test 1	100	2.5	250
Test 2	100	2.5	250
Quiz 1	100	2	200
Quiz 2	100	2	200
Quiz 3	100	2	200
Quiz 4	100	2	200
Written Assignment	100	1	100
Project	100	1	100
Total Points Available	—	—	1,500

Figure 12.4
A grading system chart of components and weights.

The fifth step is to decide on the types and number of grading components you will use in assigning each grade. Elementary teachers must do this for each subject matter area on the report card. There may be separate grades for math computation and math problem solving, for example, each one with its own grading components. Secondary teachers will do this for each course taught. For example, a high-school teacher who teaches three sections of 10th-grade general English and two sections of ninth-grade honors English has two sets of components to develop.

Finally, the sixth step is to weight the components to reflect their importance. If they are all of the same importance, then there is no need to weight anything and add steps to the computation. It is more likely, however, that your system will use differential weights to reflect the relative importance of the components. The easiest way to weight components is to use whole numbers. The chart in Figure 12.4 reflects a science teacher's choice of components, the total number of points available for each component, the relative weight of each component, and a weighted total score for each component. The total number of points available for the grading period in science is the sum of the weighted total scores, in this case 1,500. The table reflects that the test components are valued two and one-half times as much as a take-home written assignment and half again as much as a quiz. This system of whole number weights is less cumbersome to compute than weights expressed as percentages. The only time decimal points are entered is if the weight is not a whole number (like 2.5). As arranged, it becomes a handy chart for the teacher in calculating a student's total earned points and can be printed in a handout for students when you communicate your grading system at the beginning of the term. With some minor adjustments, it may be expanded into a grade-tracking system that students can use during the marking period to monitor their performance, such as that in Figure 12.5. If used with a points-to-grade conversion chart, a student can determine her grade as soon as the final component is scored and returned, before report cards are issued.

Component	Total Score	Your Score	Weight	Your Weighted Score	Weighted Total Score
Test 1	100		2.5		250
Test 2	100		2.5		250
Quiz 1	100		2		200
Quiz 2	100		2		200
Quiz 3	100		2		200
Quiz 4	100		2		200
Written Assignment	100		1		100
Project	100		1		100
Total Points	—	—	—		Available 1,500

Figure 12.5
Chart for student tracking of grading components for a marking period. Blank cells may be filled in as components are completed.

Once the system is in place and communicated to students and parents, you can record in your gradebook the scores earned by students on the components for grading as the papers, projects, and other assessments are completed. Some teachers highlight these columns in their gradebooks so they are easier to distinguish from other entries. Using the gradebook entries for Will Twombley, in Figure 12.6, we can see how Mr. Knight, Will's science teacher, figured his grade. Using the expanded chart from Figure 12.5, Mr. Knight listed Will's earned scores, then multiplied each one by its respective weight to establish Will's weighted scores. Mr. Knight then summed the weighted scores. The completed chart in Figure 12.7 shows that Will earned 1,302 points out of a possible 1,500.

Those 1,302 points sound pretty good, but we need some way to convert this point total to a letter grade, which is required for report cards in Mr. Knight's school district. Mr. Knight chooses to use percent grading where students' total points earned are compared to the total available points and expressed in a percentage. For Will, 1,302 is 86.8% of 1,500 [(1,302 ÷ 1,500) × 100 = 86.8]. This final figure may be rounded to 87%, which can be converted, via the science department's percent-to-grade conversion scale, below. Thus, Will earned a B for the marking period.

Percent-to-grade conversion scale:	*Will's % of points earned:*
93–100 = A	
85–92 = B	87 = B
77–84 = C	
69–76 = D	
0–68 = F	

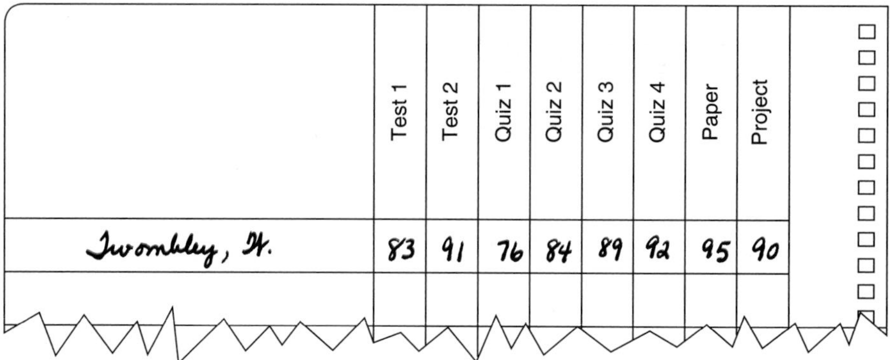

Figure 12.6
Gradebook entries for Will Twombley.

Component	Total Score	Will's Score	Weight	Will's Weighted Score	Weighted Total Score
Test 1	100	83	2.5	207.5	250
Test 2	100	91	2.5	227.5	250
Quiz 1	100	76	2	152	200
Quiz 2	100	84	2	168	200
Quiz 3	100	89	2	178	200
Quiz 4	100	92	2	184	200
Written Assignment	100	95	1	95	100
Project	100	90	1	90	100
Total Points	—	—	—	1,302	Available 1,500

Figure 12.7
Table of grading components filled in for Will Twombley.

Some teachers prefer to keep everything in points amassed, rather than percentages, even though they use a percent grading method. An alternative, then, to the above *percent*-to-grade scale is to prepare a *points*-to-grade conversion scale based on the same proportions. Thus, Mr. Knight would see in the following conversion scale that 1,302 points is in the B range, just as it should be. The two conversion scales are equivalent in proportions of earned points or percentage points within each grade range.

Points-to-grade conversion scale

1,395–1,500 = A

1,275–1,394 = B

1,155–1,274 = C

1,035–1,154 = D

1,034 or below = F

As you can see, 1,395 is 93% of 1,500; 1,275 is 85% of 1,500; 1,155 is 77% of 1,500; and so forth.

The Actual and Intended Weights of Scores

Most teachers feel that some components of grades (activities, tests, and products) are more important than others, meaning that some grades are "worth more" than others. For example, you may feel that a test grade or one received on an in-class solo performance should be weighted more heavily than an out-of-class project on which the students could receive outside help. Your goal in weighting grades, then, is to reflect their differential importance in your students' composite grade. Regardless of the weight you assign a particular component, however, its actual weight depends on the variability of the scores students received on that component. It depends neither on the average score nor on the number of times you add it to the composite. This also means that the actual weight of a particular component is likely to be different for different groups of students (your third-grade class this year versus your third-grade class last year, for example). Also, the more variability in the scores, the more weight the component contributes to the composite. For example, assume you have decided to give double weight (count it twice) to a unit test and single weight (count it once) to an out-of-class project. If the range of scores for the project is quite wide and the range of scores on the unit test very narrow, the actual weight of the components comes out in favor of the project. Your differential weighting has the effect of making them more equal, but this is not what you intended.

One way to avoid most of the effects of this pesky situation that is consistent with criterion-referenced assessment and mastery learning is to base all scores on all components on the same number of points (as the teacher did in Figure 12.7). With percents this is easy because the maximum is always 100 and the minimum is always 0, but the maximum points available before weighting should be consistent across components, whether that number is 100, 50, 27, 19, or whatever.

If you choose a norm-referenced grading system and record raw scores in your gradebook, a number of assessment experts advise following a "simple" rule to eliminate unintended weighting—equating the scores before weighting them.[8] The implementation requirements of this rule, however, make it less than practical for most teachers unless equating scores before weighting them is part of an electronic or automated grading system. Equating scores before figuring final grades involves determining the standard deviation of the scores for each component, identifying the component with the largest standard deviation, and then using that standard deviation to determine equating factors for each of the other components. Once the equating factors are determined, each student's score must be multiplied by each factor for each component, in addition to being multiplied by the weights the teacher determines. Some experts advocate using the score ranges to ease computation, but the same number of steps—and opportunities for error—remain. The degree of precision gained from equating scores is in the accuracy of the final average (a 70 vs. a 69 or 71, perhaps).

Equating before weighting is not necessary if all students are consistent performers who earn consistent rankings across components. Equating before weighting makes a difference when individual students perform differentially across components—students like Jen, who rank higher on the heavily weighted components than they do on the lesser-weighted ones, and like Ben, who rank higher on components of lesser weight than they do under testing conditions. Many teachers have a few students like Jen and Ben in their classrooms in addition to a vast majority of consistent performers; therefore, equating before weighting appears to make sense. In practice, however, equating rarely affects any student's final average, and if it does it will only raise or lower it by a point or two. This will only affect a student's grade if his or her average is within a point or two of the next grade category—higher or lower. If a student's average is near a cut-off, you may reach a justifiable conclusion and save a lot of computational time by looking at the component scores and asking yourself, "Which of the two grades is the better descriptor of the student's achievement status this marking period?" Combine what you know of the student's performance with what you know of the concept of assessment error to make a sound judgment. Thus, in practice, equating before weighting is worth doing if you use a norm-referenced grading system and a computer program to equate the scores for you.

The Use and Misuse of Zeros in Figuring Grades

Suppose you were to look in a teacher's gradebook and see the following set of scores for Maria Garcia: 89, 78, 84, 0, 91, and 88. What do you suppose the zero is for? Could it be that she was absent the day of the test? Maybe she was annoying the teacher that day more than usual. Perhaps she did not turn in a graded assignment.

---

[8]See, for example, "Obtaining Intended Weights When Combining Students' Scores" by A. C. Oosterhof, 1987, *Educational Measurement: Issues and Practice, 6*(4), pp. 29–37.

All of these reasons are ones given for entering zeros in teachers' gradebooks. Rarely does a zero in a gradebook represent actual performance on an assessment. This is interesting, because that is exactly what a zero for an academic grading component should represent. Zeros should not be used for other purposes because they distort the picture of the student's true performance, thus introducing measurement error into the set of scores. In Maria's case, she was absent the day of a test. Let's see what that one zero can do to distort the story told by the other component scores. Below are two different ways of figuring Maria's grade:

Method A		Method B	
	89		89
	78		78
	84		84
	0		91
	91		88
	88		430
	430		

430 ÷ 6 = **72** (average of six scores) 430 ÷ 5 = **86** (average of five scores)

In method A, the zero is figured into the grade and counted as one of the components. The total points earned by Maria are divided by 6 to arrive at an average of 72. In method B, the zero and the component it represented are left out of the calculations altogether to yield 86 as Maria's average over five components. Which average (72 or 86) appears to best represent Maria's performance status? In method A, her average of 72 is *lower* than any of her individual scores! The zero had a devastating effect, rendering the final average meaningless for the purposes for which it was intended. If you were her teacher and used one of the three grade-conversion scales at the beginning of this chapter, you would be compelled to assign an F, a D, or a C. How would you explain any one of those grades to Maria and her parents? There is at least one letter grade difference, sometimes two, between the results of the two methods of averaging. In method B, the resulting average is 86, and although it is based on fewer components, it appears to be more in line with her actual performance as reflected in the other component scores.

The fact remains that Maria missed an assessment opportunity, however. Teachers can deal with these missed opportunities in a number of ways. One way is to provide parallel make-up tests so that students who have excused absences may still be appropriately assessed. Another is to extend due dates for assignments under certain circumstances. Some teachers have parallel performance tasks covering the same outcomes as the original assessment that can be assigned if a student misses a group presentation that cannot be made up. Other teachers have a policy, based on the rationale that everyone bombs an assessment once in a while, where students can eliminate their lowest score from grade calculations. The point is that unless a zero truly represents a student's performance status, it should be left out of the calculations for grades altogether.

Easy Reference Checklist

Guidelines for Good Grading Practices

- ❑ Grading system is consistent with purpose of assessment and instructional philosophy.
- ❑ Grades are based on sufficient data systematically collected throughout the term.
- ❑ Grades are based on a variety of components.
- ❑ Students are informed at the beginning what counts and how much.
- ❑ Non-academic achievement factors are kept out of academic achievement grades.
- ❑ Students understand that academic grades are based on achievement only.
- ❑ Students understand what non-academic factors will be reported and how.
- ❑ Practice opportunities are not counted for grades.
- ❑ Grading components are tied to valued instructional outcomes.
- ❑ Component weights are based on component's relative importance in composite grade.
- ❑ Grading system uses common assessments across similar courses (secondary) or classrooms (elementary).
- ❑ Grading system uses consistent criteria agreed upon by the teachers involved.
- ❑ Raw scores or percentages are recorded and reduced to symbols or marks at the end of the grading period.
- ❑ Zeros are kept out of the academic average unless for actual performance.

Using Electronic Gradebooks

Grading is one of the tasks for which computers have lessened the drudgery for teachers. An electronic gradebook, the popular term for these computer programs, can quickly calculate composite point totals, print reports, and compile class and student statistics, among other things. If you are proficient in a popular spreadsheet or database program, buying specialized software especially for grading may not be necessary. Your user support group or software help line can usually assist in constructing one if you know what you want it to do. If you do not already have a spreadsheet or database package or you are not proficient in it, it may be wiser to buy a dedicated electronic gradebook. Electronic gradebooks are more specialized than spreadsheets but also more limited in range of application. They are built only for grading, but they may be easier to learn as a result. Electronic gradebooks are also cheaper than large spreadsheet or database packages. If you are proficient in a programming language, you may be able to build your own customized electronic gradebook.

Most electronic-gradebook programs allow teachers to enter assigned weights for their chosen grading components and enter each student's scores. The typical program then totals the scores, applies the weights, and figures a composite score for each student, all in the blink of an eye. An electronic gradebook does not relieve you of the philosophical soul searching or decision making involved in assigning and reporting grades, but it does remove a lot of computation tedium. The higher-end, more expensive electronic gradebooks provide options such as handling missing scores, equating, displaying data for a single student (a great idea for in-classroom conferences), automatic data entry when coupled with a desktop scanner for scoring paper-and-pencil tests, and item analysis.

If you only use an electronic gradebook to record student names and component scores, and you do not use it to perform such tasks as averaging, class and student statistics, reports, and item analysis, then it is probably cheaper in both time and money to stay with a paper gradebook. These tasks are where an electronic gradebook can save time because speed and accuracy of calculations are an electronic gradebook's strong suit. The time it saves can be used to analyze the reports to enhance your assessments and instruction.

If you are a pre-service teacher, it may be wise to wait and see if the school you will work in has a specified electronic gradebook for use by its teachers. It may also be wise to teach for a while using a paper gradebook until you and your grading system have adjusted to each other. Then you will have a better idea of your grading needs and what the software must do to meet them. If the school has administrative software, it may contain a grading feature or sub-program that few know about. Check with the manufacturer to determine whether it may be useful in grading. Many school districts and individuals (myself included) have purchased software beyond their present level of computer sophistication with growth in mind.

Buying an electronic gradebook is a lot like buying a car, only less expensive. You are going to have to live with it for a while. Shop around for the package that is likely to meet your projected needs a few (say, 2 to 3) years from now as well as the immediate ones. Also like a car, the more "bells and whistles" in the software, the more it will cost. The more expensive ones will also take up more computer memory. One preferred bell (or is it a whistle?) for electronic gradebooks used with norm-referenced grading systems is a score-equating procedure based on the standard deviation. It is worth it to "equate before you weight" *if* the computer will do it for you, and the most precise method uses the standard deviation. Another desired feature is the ability to handle missing scores without equating them to zeros. The general principles of grading presented in this chapter apply whether you select an electronic gradebook or construct one. It should be compatible with both your school's grading policy and your philosophy and able to perform the duties necessary. For example, if you teach multiple sections of a course (general biology, for example) and your grading procedure is norm-referenced, be sure the program can accommodate the several sections as the norm-group. Read up on the alternatives and find out if they reflect sound assessment practice.

There are many sources of information about electronic gradebooks and other computer applications in the classroom. Teacher- and instruction-oriented magazines and journals advertise and review software regularly. Database and spreadsheet user groups trade programs and information regarding them through meetings, newsletters, and other communication channels. You may also try software stores with educational departments and educational stores with software departments.

Using Communication Alternatives

Grades on report cards are only one form of communication regarding student progress and achievement. Reports similar to those for Bobby Ten-Pow and Pamela Gouthrow (shown in Figure 12.3) have been used by many schools to expand reporting to parents and students. Teachers also communicate student progress to families in other ways, using face-to-face conferences, narrative reports, and telephone calls. These may be used along with grades to provide a more complete profile of the student than can be packed into a few symbols. They have also been used in place of grades.

Conferences

Conferences are opportunities for those most responsible for a student's learning to interact—sharing concerns, strategies, and triumphs and solving problems. Therefore, conferences are not only for discussing grades. Classroom behavior, portfolio contents, standardized assessment scores, post-secondary study, curriculum, study skills, and instructional strategies advantageous for the student are just some of the topics that may be discussed in a parent-teacher conference. Parent-teacher conferences in the elementary grades are typically a regularly scheduled event where the progress and current status of the student are discussed. As the student moves into the secondary grades, these conferences may occur only when there is a problem to discuss. Teachers may also confer with students individually in the classroom. Together they might review portfolios, discuss cognitive strategies, or work on problematic areas. Teacher-student conferences, like performance reviews in the workplace, may concentrate on current performance level and goals for the future.

Face-to-face conferences help both teachers and parents put faces with names and get to know each other better. They also provide the opportunity to work together for a common goal—the scholastic well-being of the student—and to eliminate any misunderstanding that may otherwise occur. Conferences also have some drawbacks. It is not always possible to schedule conferences at times convenient to everyone. In these times of dual working parents and split families, teachers count themselves lucky if they get to meet one of a student's parents, let alone two. Some dedicated teachers have met parents at convenient malls or even at the student's home in the evening to be sure the conference took place. Others use the telephone when a face-to-face conference is not feasible or necessary. Another disadvantage of conferences is that the parents and the teacher might not speak the same language. Language barriers may be somewhat overcome with the use of an interpreter, but the situation is still a bit awkward, and interpreters may not be readily available. A drawback to at least some parents is that conferences usually take place on school grounds. Not all parents had the wonderfully positive experiences you did (you did, didn't you?) when they were in school, and being back in that atmosphere may conjure up some dreadful memories. If the mood is already sour before the conference begins, the meeting may be less than productive.

Assuming you have overcome all the scheduling barriers and arranged a parent-teacher or student-teacher conference, how can you make it a positive, productive experience? The following guidelines will help whether the conference is face-to-face or over the telephone:

1. *Do your homework.* Plan ahead by reviewing all pertinent documents—cumulative folder, assessments, assignments, portfolio—and have them ready for easy reference during the conference to back up the points you make. In your review, make note of your concerns and any you think the parents or student are likely to have.

2. *Know what you want to achieve as a result and work toward it during the conference.* The goal, for example, may be to gain a better understanding of the home life of the student or to recommend some study skills. Plan and conduct the conference with this in mind.

3. *Balance your goals for the conference with those of the parents or student.* You want the conference to be a win-win situation for all parties. As the teacher, you are in charge of the conference and so are the main facilitator for achieving those goals.

4. *When giving negative feedback to parents or students, balance bad with good.* Start with something positive, then lead to the negative behaviors. Use tact, but do not appear afraid to discuss what is wrong.

5. *Manage the "air time" so that everyone's perspective may be heard.* Let parents and students talk. This might include asking a more reticent conference participant for his or her opinion.

6. *Make summary notes.* Near the end of the conference it is helpful and clarifying to summarize the discussion and restate who is responsible for doing what if there is any action to be taken. A brief note as to the nature of the conference, the issues discussed, and the agreed-upon action to be taken should be placed in the student's folder for reference. Many schools and districts offer inservice workshops for practice in conducting conferences for maximum productivity. These can help, too.

Narrative Reports

Narrative reports document what the students have been learning by having them write it down in their own words. The teacher may also write what the students have been learning, exploring, and researching, thus providing two perspectives. Narrative reports are frequently used with portfolios although there is no law that

✓ *Easy Reference Checklist*

Guidelines for Conducting Effective Conferences

- ❑ Teacher's homework is completed before conference.
- ❑ Objective of conference is known and worked toward.
- ❑ Teacher's goals are balanced with the students' or parents' goals.
- ❑ Positive and negative feedback are given and balanced.
- ❑ Everyone's perspective is heard.
- ❑ Summary notes are made.

says that they cannot be used with report cards. They may describe a student's strengths and weaknesses or his developmental progress. Most narrative reports are organized around subject areas or ability areas. For example, students might be asked to write about what they have been learning in science, or a teacher may report on a student's intra- and interpersonal relationships as they pertain to development of appropriate social and emotional attitudes.

Narrative reports have a number of advantages. By definition, a narrative report requires of the writer reflective thinking, which, in turn, helps to solidify learning. The depth and quality of the reflection is dependent, in part, upon the developmental level of the student; nevertheless, the practice is a good one and can be initiated at a fairly young age. The documentary nature of narrative reports is another positive aspect. What is actually going on in the classroom from the writer's perspective is documented for all to see. Another advantage is that the students' perspectives are captured and communicated to their parents and teacher. This, in itself, can be an eye-opening experience and informative for your teaching.

There are also some drawbacks to using narrative reports. First, the quality of the writing may render the narrative meaningless other than to document the poor writing skills of the author. Obviously, written narrative reports are not a good exercise for students who don't write yet or who are physically incapable of doing so. A related issue is the writing skill of the teacher. For years in many districts, teachers selected codes as part of their grading procedure that caused the computer to print pre-specified messages on report cards. Teachers who are out of the habit of writing may need some practice sharpening their syntax, grammar, and spelling. Proficiency in a word-processing program can help, but Emily Dickinson or Robert Frost will not flow from the printer on command. Another drawback is that the audience (parents or guardians, for instance) may not read the language of the narrative. An eloquently written summary statement may not communicate at all if it cannot be read or is uninterpretable.

Despite some of their limitations, narrative reports can enrich the profile of the student to those who are most interested. Here are a few suggestions for making them work:

1. The report should have a clear purpose that is communicated to all who must write and read one. If students are to write a narrative about what they have been learning in a particular area, for example, guiding statements or questions can help—"In science, we have been discovering . . ."

2. The narrative should be integrated with the rest of the assessment, grading, and reporting strategy. It should not overlap in purpose or content with another element of the strategy, for this is wasteful. On the other hand, it should fill a need that if not met would be consequential.

3. The narrative report should be appropriate for the students' developmental level. Primary-grade teachers should keep in mind that the language development of children may not match their assessment needs. In the early grades, students can answer who, what, and where questions but do not answer well questions of when, why and how until around age 6, 7, or 8. This is partly due to the type of thinking required (such as understanding time and cause-effect relationships).

4. Oral narrative may work as well or better than written narrative for certain audiences. Keep in mind, however, that oral narrative requires a tape recorder/player, equipment that may be scarce.

The Garfield Avenue School (Milwaukee, Wisconsin) devised an integrated assessment, grading, and reporting strategy for grades K–3 that included the following:

1. An abilities checklist (filled out by the teacher).
2. A portfolio cover sheet listing required and supporting data.
3. An activity summary sheet.
4. A student progress report (report card) listing specific skills.
5. Narratives from both the student and the teacher on what the student had learned in each of the content areas.
6. A progress report cover that contains "I'm proud because" statements on front and "My goals" statements on back.[9]

✓ *Easy Reference Checklist*

Guidelines for Using Narrative Reports

- ❑ Narrative report has a clear purpose communicated to all who must write and read it.
- ❑ Narrative report is integrated with the rest of the assessment, grading, and reporting strategy.
- ❑ Narrative report is appropriate for the students' developmental level.
- ❑ Oral narrative reports are used when appropriate.

[9] *Understanding Assessment and Evaluation in Early Childhood Education* by D. F. Gullo, 1994, New York: Teachers College Press.

Summary

Re-Introducing Grading

Grading is not easy; it requires a lot of thought and planning and must be defensible to various audiences. It is a tremendous responsibility. Grades assigned to students have both short- and long-term effects on their lives. A *grade* is an expression of judgment, usually a symbol—letter, number, or mark—that indicates the degree to which intended outcomes have been achieved. A major purpose of grades is to communicate how well a student is doing in the several academic (subject) areas and in non-academic, affective areas such as citizenship, conduct, and effort.

Understanding General Principles of Grading

When choosing or modifying an existing grading system, it is important to consciously think of (1) the teaching philosophy or approach that prevails at the school, (2) the purpose of assessment as it applies to the classroom, and (3) the philosophy underlying the proposed grading system. A system that promotes congruency among these three factors is defensible, workable, and less stress producing for both teachers and students.

Grades should be based on a sufficient amount of data systematically collected over the course of the term. The more valid the components used to figure a grade, the more likely the grade is to be representative of the student's performance for the term and, therefore, reliable. Grading should not be overdone. Students need a number of non-threatening opportunities to try out new skills or otherwise practice new learning. Offering homework scores only for feedback purposes does two things: It shows your students that you do look at their homework and are concerned about their learning, and it lets them know how they might perform under assessment conditions if they were to be assessed at that time. Students should be informed in advance which grades "count" toward their final grade and which ones do not, how final grades will be determined, and on what basis.

There is general consensus that a final grade should be based on a combination of components such as written tests, projects, oral reports, procedural demonstrations, and products. Many school systems use a multi-symbol grading system allowing progress in non-academic areas to be reported separately from achievement, a desirable practice.

The following faulty practices can make the imperfect process of determining grades even worse and can lead to criticisms of grading:

1. Teachers abdicating their responsibility for grading and turning the process over to the students.

2. Grading everything.
3. Grading on sight.
4. Imposing impossible standards on students.

Considering Criticisms of Grading

Many view grading as unnecessary or harmful and have called for an end to grading practices altogether. Grading criteria can vary from teacher to teacher, school to school, and district to district. Some critics propose communication alternatives such as parent-teacher conferences and written reports to more fully communicate to parents how their child is doing. In practice, however, there is consistency across grading practices—more so than critics allege.

Some critics of grading have concluded that it is an inhumane process with negative effects, pointing to consequences of grading such as cutthroat competitiveness, cheating, plagiarism, resignation to failure, anxiety, depression, and even suicide. The negative consequences are more due to the abysmal behavior of some parents and teachers; they are not due to the use of grades. People frequently claim that some teachers are too cavalier about grading, that they do not base the grade on valid, sufficient data and do not assign them on any rational, justifiable basis. No one perfect grading system exists. Neither are there any national or statewide laws mandating a particular system of grading.

Considering Achievement, Effort, and Other Components of Grading and Reporting

Before a teacher can determine a student's grade in a subject, he or she must decide what assessment opportunities will be given and which of these will be used as components of the final grade. Teachers must decide whether all components are equally important in determining the grade or whether there are some components that may be weighted more heavily than others. The components for grading and reporting stem from the same valued outcomes that drive instruction and assessment and should be highly related to those outcomes. Every component score that contributes to the academic achievement grade should also be based on achievement only. The teacher can issue two scores for each component, one for achievement of instructional outcomes and one for evident effort put forth.

Considering Frames of Reference and Methods of Grading

Achievement is labeled "good" or "poor" in relation to something. That something should be defined and communicated to users of grades so that the meaning of the grade is clear. Although there are many alternative grading systems from which to choose, most of them are variations on one of three basic approaches: percent grading, criterion-referenced grading, and norm-referenced grading.

In *percent grading,* a student's raw scores on the components of the final grade are tallied and divided by the total number of points available for those same assessments. That decimal is multiplied by 100 to obtain a percent. Advantages of percent grading include:

1. No one has to fail.
2. The basis for assigning grades appears to be clear and easily communicated among teachers, students, and parents.

The disadvantages of percent grading are:

1. The meaning of grades is, in reality, very obscure.
2. Percent grades tell nothing about how much the student learned, either in relation to the intended learning outcomes or in relation to what other students achieved.
3. Percentages are not standardized units for assessments.
4. There is usually no good justification for the determination of the grading categories.

One way to enhance the utility and defensibility of a percent system is for teachers of similar students or subjects to use common assessments as components of grades and to agree among themselves on the cut-offs for each category based on their collective knowledge of typical student performance on these components. Percent grading is consistent with the philosophy of a mastery system of learning. Percent grading is most useful where student performance can be expressed in standard physical units of measurement.

Criterion-referenced grading involves expressing a student's achievement in relation to pre-specified criteria or standards. The criterion-referenced grading system is best used with a mastery system of learning where specific learning targets can be set and assessed with criterion-referenced tests. Criterion-referenced grading is also compatible with systematically designed instruction and outcomes-based education. Advantages of criterion-referenced grading are:

1. No one has to fail.
2. It removes most of the cutthroat competition among students fostered by a norm-referenced approach.
3. It facilitates reporting student achievement by outcome.

Disadvantages of criterion-referenced grading include:

1. The tendency of teachers to list *every single* performance outcome, even those of the most minute proportions.
2. The difficulty of setting the criterion for acceptable performance or mastery.

A criterion-referenced system requires three things:

1. The intended learning tasks are clearly described and defined.
2. The criteria for acceptable performance are specified for each task.
3. Criterion-referenced assessments are used to assess student performance.

Criterion cut-offs may be expressed as percentages or ratios. For criterion-referenced grading purposes, the performance or percent correct on the overall test is not as important as performance in relation to the specific outcomes covered by the test. The student's performance may also be reported in terms of the date mastery of the outcome was achieved or demonstrated. A periodic report card, if issued, provides a snapshot in time of what is actually a running account of the student's progress toward mastery. To overcome the disadvantages of criterion-referenced grading, it is important to help parents make proper interpretations and involve stakeholders in setting the performance standards.

Norm-referenced grading is consistent with norm-referenced assessment procedures, which are designed to spread individuals out on a continuum of performance so that their rank can be determined with confidence. A norm-referenced grade does not communicate what a student has actually achieved but rather how a student's achievement compared to the achievement of others in a comparable group. Norm-referenced grading is more prevalent in schools where rank in class assumes more importance and there is less emphasis on mastery of specific, discrete skills—conditions more typically found in high schools. Some recent research on grading systems indicates that, at least in some secondary schools, teachers are more likely to use a percentage or even a criterion-referenced approach than to use norm-referenced grading.

Norm-referenced grading requires norm-referenced assessments to maximize accuracy in detecting individual differences necessary for rank-ordering students. Norm-referenced grading is inconsistent with mastery learning, outcomes-based education, and classes that are homogeneously formed for ease of instruction. Norm-referenced grading is consistent with heterogeneous, untracked classes. The norm group must be heterogeneous and large enough (several hundred scores at least) to produce a normal distribution of performance with which to compare. Sometimes, especially at the elementary level, an achievement grade that is not determined on a norm-referenced basis is accompanied by a norm-referenced ranking on any number of affective variables.

In its extreme form, norm-referenced grading is based on an assumption of a normal distribution, and a fixed percentage of students receive each grade; this is called normal curve grading or grading "on the curve." A commonly used percentage scheme of *grade ranges* assigns the top 7% of the scores an A, the next 23% a B, the middle 40% a C, the next 23% a D, and the bottom 7% a failing grade. The advantage of normal curve grading is that performance is described in relation to that of others in the comparison group. Disadvantages of normal curve grading include:

1. Some students must receive a failing grade.
2. The nature of the meaning of the grade based on the make up of the norm group shifts with each class.

3. The grade tells nothing about what the student actually knows or can do.
4. A normal distribution cannot be assumed and is, in fact, highly unlikely in classroom assessment.
5. The number of students who can comprise a norm group is usually too small a number to expect a normal distribution.

Pass-fail grading is a system in which everyone who achieves the criterion of acceptable performance passes, and those who do not, fail. Minimum competence in the course—the point below which is designated "fail"—is usually determined relative to typical student performance in the subject. The rationale behind offering this option in college and some high schools is to entice students to take courses for which they might not otherwise risk their grade-point averages. A pass-fail system usually results in a reduction of achievement levels due to students' reduced motivation. The pass-fail grade does not fulfill its promise of unambiguous communication. Pass-fail grading is discouraged generally and justified only on a limited basis, for some electives, for example.

Expanded norm-group grading makes no assumption of a normal distribution and can thus be used with skewed distributions. The method involves expanding the norm group to include all students who have taken the subject under similar conditions. This grading method requires standardization of courses to a certain extent. Three types of scores may be used with the expanded norm-group method: raw scores, percentile scores, or standard scores. With the increasing availability of computers to do the more tedious calculations and sorting tasks, the standard score approach to expanding the norm group becomes feasible for busy classroom teachers.

Using Grading Symbols

There are many grading symbols used to communicate student progress in cognitive and affective areas. Schools may use actual percentages, letters, a combination of letters with plus and minus signs, and other symbols. Regardless of the actual symbols used, there must be general agreement on and mutual understanding of the symbols by the users of grades.

Creating Personal Grading Systems

Designing a personal grading system is a six-step process:

1. Develop a personal grading philosophy.
2. Implement district policy that teachers are obliged to use, if one exists.
3. Choose an appropriate frame of reference for interpreting what the grading symbols mean.
4. "Benchmark" or check the grade distributions, grading components, and weights of colleagues who teach the same subject or grade.
5. Decide the types and number of grading components needed for each grade reported.
6. Weight the components to reflect their importance.

Once the system is in place and communicated to students and parents, scores can be recorded in the gradebook for the components as the papers, projects, etc. are completed. An alternative to the *percent*-to-grade scale is a *points*-to-grade conversion scale based on the same proportions.

The goal in weighting grades is to reflect their differential importance in the students' composite grade. Regardless of the weight assigned a particular component, its actual weight depends on the variability of the scores students received on that component. The more variability in the scores, the more weight the component contributes to the composite. One way to avoid most of the effects of this situation that is consistent with criterion-referenced assessment and mastery learning is to base all scores on all components on the same number of points. If you use norm-referenced grading and record raw scores in your gradebook, you can equate the scores to remove unintended weights. Equating before weighting is usually not practical for most teachers unless it is part of an electronic or automated grading system. Equating before weighting is not necessary if all students are consistent performers. Equating before weighting makes a difference when individual students perform differentially across components and doing so will affect a student's grade only if his or her average is within a point or two of the next grade category—higher or lower. Teachers can do just as well and save a lot of computational time by looking at the component scores and asking themselves, "Which of the two grades is the better descriptor of the student's achievement status this marking period?"

Rarely does a zero in a gradebook represent actual performance on an assessment, which is interesting, because that is exactly what a zero for an academic grading component should represent. Misused zeros distort the picture of the student's true performance, and they introduce measurement error into the set of scores. Unless a zero truly represents a student's performance status, it should be left out of the calculations for grades altogether.

Using Electronic Gradebooks

Grading is one of the tasks for which computers have lessened the drudgery for teachers. Most electronic gradebook programs allow teachers to enter assigned weights for their chosen grading components and enter each student's scores. The program then totals the scores, applies the weights, and figures a composite score for each student. An electronic gradebook does not relieve teachers of the responsibilities of philosophical soul searching or making decisions about the components of grades. In addition to performing the basic functions, two desired features of electronic gradebooks are a score-equating procedure based on the standard deviation (for norm-referenced grading) and the ability to handle missing scores without equating them to zeros. The best electronic gradebook is one that is compatible with both the school's grading policy and the teacher's instructional philosophy and can perform the duties necessary.

Using Communication Alternatives

Teachers communicate student progress to families in ways other than grades, using methods such as face-to-face conferences, narrative reports, and telephone conferences.

Conferences are opportunities for those most responsible for a student's learning to interact, to share concerns, strategies and triumphs, and to solve problems. Classroom behavior, portfolio contents, standardized assessment scores, post-secondary study, curriculum, study skills, and instructional strategies advantageous for the student are some topics that may be discussed in a parent-teacher conference. Teachers may also confer with students individually in the classroom, reviewing portfolios, discussing cognitive strategies, or working on problematic areas. Advantages of conferences:

1. They help teachers and parents put faces with names and get to know each other better.
2. They provide the opportunity to work together for the benefit of the student and to eliminate any misunderstanding that may otherwise occur.

Disadvantages of conferences:

1. It is not always possible to schedule conferences at times that are convenient for everyone.
2. The parents and the teacher might not speak the same language.
3. Conferences usually take place on school grounds, which may make some parents ill at ease.

The guidelines for effective face-to-face and telephone conferences:

1. Plan ahead by reviewing all pertinent documents and having them ready for reference during the conference to back up the points you make.
2. Set a goal—know what you want to achieve as a result and work toward it during the conference.
3. Balance your goals for the conference with those of the parents or student.
4. When giving negative feedback, balance bad with good.
5. Manage the "air time" so that everyone's perspective may be heard.
6. Make summary notes.

Narrative reports document what the students have been learning by having them write it down in their own words. The teacher may also write what the students have been learning, exploring, and researching, thus providing two perspectives. Most narrative reports are organized around subject areas or ability areas. Advantages of narrative reports:

1. By definition, a narrative report requires of the writer reflective thinking, which helps to solidify learning.
2. What is actually going on in the classroom from the writer's perspective is documented for all to see.
3. The students' perspectives are captured and communicated to their parents and teacher.

Disadvantages of narrative reports:

1. The quality of the writing may render the narrative meaningless other than to document the poor writing skills of the author.
2. The writing skill of the teacher may not be up to the task.
3. The audience (parents or guardian, for example) may not read the language of the narrative.

Some guidelines for making narrative reports work:

1. The report should have a clear purpose that is communicated to all who must write one.
2. The narrative should be integrated with the rest of your assessment, grading, and reporting strategy.
3. The narrative task should be appropriate for the students' developmental level.
4. Oral narrative reports may be more appropriate than written narrative reports in some situations.

Try This

I. For a school in your district, obtain copies of the following documents regarding grading:

The district's policy.

The school's policy.

Another teacher's personal grading system (not your own).

Answer the following questions about the documents:

1. Do the policies and personal system appear to be congruent? What evidence can you cite to support your claim?
2. In what ways is the teacher's system
   a. norm-referenced?
   b. criterion-referenced?
   c. percent-based?
3. Of the three general approaches, which is the best descriptor of the teacher's system?
4. How would you modify the school's policy and the district's policy to better reflect the principles you have learned in this chapter?

Assume you are a consultant to the teacher. Use both Frisbie and Waltman's nine questions designed to help teachers develop grading philosophies and the checklist for good grading practices to evaluate his or her stated grading system. You may wish to interview the teacher for more information. The following questions can guide your review:

1. What are its strengths and weaknesses?
2. How is the system communicated to students?
3. What questions do you think students or parents are likely to have as a result of this communication?
4. What recommendations would you make to the teacher to enhance the system according to the principles of good grading?

Note: This exercise may be done as an individual or small group exercise in several different ways:

1. Individually gather and review documents, then discuss in a large group.
2. Individually gather and review documents, then discuss in small groups.
3. Teams gather and review documents—one school per team and each person obtains a different teacher's grading system. Discuss findings in teams. Team reports summary findings to the larger group.

Answer

I. The systems and policies are context specific but the general performance criteria applied to the ones reviewed should be (1) clear communication to students and (2) conformity to principles of good grading.

CHAPTER 13

Preparing Students and Administering Assessments

Key Concepts:

- Preparing students for classroom assessments.
- Administering paper-and-pencil and performance assessments.
- Discouraging cheating.
- Assessing students with disabilities in the classroom.
- Recognizing ethical and unethical preparation practices for standardized assessments.
- Teaching test-taking skills.
- Administering standardized instruments.

Standards Addressed in This Chapter:

3. Administer, score, and interpret the results of both externally produced and teacher-produced assessment methods.

7. Recognize unethical, illegal, and otherwise inappropriate assessment methods and uses of assessment information.

Before You Begin Reading, Consider This

Should test-taking skills or test-wiseness (how students can use their knowledge of the characteristics and formats of an assessment and/or the assessment situation to receive a higher score) be taught?

YES Test-wiseness can and should be taught to every student to give all the opportunity to earn their highest score. That earned score will also be closer to her or his true score, dependent only on what the student knows and can do regarding the content assessed.

NO It is naive to think that all schools will have the resources (the budget, for example) to teach students how to be test-wise; therefore not all students will get the benefit. That is unfair and clouds up the picture of true performance even further.

Preparing Students for Classroom Assessments

Taking tests, performing tasks in class, and completing projects are a way of life for children of school age. Some would argue that expertise in assessment is a life skill to be acquired in school in preparation for the tests we endure in adult life. For example, a job applicant may be required to take a keyboarding skills performance test in consideration for a job as an office worker; a newly minted lawyer must pass a state's bar exam in order to practice law in that state; and prospective condominium and homeowners' association managers are required in some states to pass a licensing exam. This chapter discusses some of the ways teachers can prepare their students for assessments and the considerations involved in conducting assessments. Checklists at the end of the respective sections summarize the guidelines for preparing students for classroom and standardized assessments.

For students, proper preparation for a quiz, test, exam, performance, or project involves (1) having the opportunity to interact with the content to acquire the intended skills and knowledge and (2) psychologically approaching the assessment situation with a sense of calm and confidence. The following guidelines are meant to assist you in helping your students achieve both of these goals. They are also summarized in the Easy Reference Checklist on page 439.

1. *Provide adequate instruction, including appropriate opportunities to practice the skill or apply the knowledge.* That may seem rather obvious, but it is surprising how often the second part of that statement—the practice part—is inadequate or missed entirely. There is no magic to this, however, and no substitute for it. In addition, the instruction and application opportunities you provide to your students should be congruent with the intent of the related instructional outcomes. The interaction of instructional outcomes, instructional activities, and assessments (refer to Figure 4.1) is a necessary consideration, because by keeping the three in alignment, you are also preparing your students to perform their best.

2. *Familiarize students with the type of assessment, including item formats and conditions under which they will be required to perform.* It is appropriate, for example, to inform your students that: the math test they will take on Thursday will be timed; although the items are relatively easy, there will be too many of them for any student to finish; they should work as quickly as they can to finish as many items as possible in the time they are given; and their scores will be based on how many correct answers they produce. Informing your students of how their learning will be evaluated helps reduce their anxiety to manageable proportions and operationally defines your instructional outcomes for them. An excellent way to do this for performance assessments is to provide the judging criteria, either in a checklist or rating scale or along with a written task description. Another way to inform your students is through practice tests and tasks that acquaint students with your particular methods of assessment and item types; this method also complies with guideline one, above.

3. *Facilitate review.* In-class reviews and take-home study guides (see Figure 13.1) help students decide study priorities for whatever time they have available. These activities and instruments let students know what you think is important, not just what the textbook authors think. A teacher-led review of the more important material covered will refresh students' memories and give them one last opportunity to ask questions. The review can promote both retention and transfer of the material to the next unit or course of study. Study guides typically list areas, topics, skills, concepts, and knowledge that you deem important to help students focus their at-home review. Study guides may be provided in addition to or in place of in-class reviews, depending on class time available, the scope of the assessment, and the stakes involved in the use of the results. The higher the stakes and the larger the body of content covered by the assessment, the more necessary pre-assessment review becomes.

4. *Approach the assessment positively.* You set the tone for how your students are to approach tests. For example, if you use assessment as punishment ("I see that no one has read the story so we are going to have a test. Take out a sheet of paper . . ."), then the students will see them as such. If you approach tests positively, as opportunities to use new skills and knowledge, for example, then students are likely to see them more positively.

5. *Help students manage their assessment anxiety.* Some students have overly heightened anxiety levels and may need extra coaching before big exams or important presentations to calm fears. You can share with them techniques that you or other students have found effective in overcoming pre-exam nervousness.

Administering Classroom Assessments

Administering Paper-and-Pencil Assessments

If you have followed the guidelines presented in earlier chapters in creating your paper-and-pencil assessments, you will have a well-organized test with easy-to-follow

Biology I

Final Exam Review Sheet

2nd Semester

Mr. Glazer

Chapter 5—The Cell

1. Know the cell theory.
2. Distinguish prokaryotic from eukaryotic.
3. Know all the cell organelles (and their functions) of a plant and animal cell.
4. How does an animal cell differ from a plant cell?
5. What is homeostasis?
6. What is diffusion?
7. Distinguish active transport from passive transport.
8. What are the different levels of organization?

Chapter 20—Mitosis and Asexual Reproduction

1. What is mitosis and how is it significant to living things?
2. Diagram mitosis with varying numbers of 2n numbers.
3. How are plant and animal cell mitosis different?

Figure 13.1
A portion of Mr. Glazer's final exam review sheet for Biology I.
Used with permission from the author.

✓ *Easy Reference Checklist*

Guidelines for Preparing Students for Classroom Assessments

- ❑ Adequate instruction provided.
- ❑ Adequate amount of practice/application provided.
- ❑ Practice/application congruent with instructional outcomes.
- ❑ Students familiar with type/conditions of intended assessment.
- ❑ Judging criteria provided to students in advance.
- ❑ Review facilitated.
- ❑ Pre-assessment anxiety managed.

general and specific directions that matches both the intended learning outcomes and your instruction. Almost all that is left for you to do is to create the proper assessment atmosphere prior to administration. The proper assessment atmosphere is one that:

- Is distraction-free,
- Provides adequate tools and space for working,
- Does not increase student anxiety, and
- Discourages cheating.

A completely distraction-free classroom is difficult to achieve but, nevertheless, should remain a goal to work toward. Noise and interruptions should be kept to a minimum. Students should not wander about the classroom when finished or walk to your desk to ask questions. If separate answer sheets require number 2 pencils, keep a "loaner" set for those students without them and collect them when finished.

Depending on the stakes involved and the perceived anxiety levels of your students, you may actively try putting their minds at ease before assessment. One way is to lead deep-breathing exercises or emphasize that they now have the opportunity to show off their newly acquired knowledge and skills just as they might a new pair of shoes. Another approach is to answer any last-minute questions students may have about their learning just before the assessment to identify and clear up any confusion. For younger students who are learning how to take tests, you may lead them in the process of getting ready for assessment: putting books away, getting out a writing instrument, concentrating on listening to your directions, and so forth. If students have a routine for getting ready for a test, it can have a calming effect and help them transfer the emphasis in energy from physical to mental. After all, if professional baseball players can have a pre-game ritual to prepare themselves, so can your students. Going over the directions to the test can be especially helpful if the items are of a different type than the students have previously encountered or if this is the first test of the term. Students should be put at ease with regard to item format and should be told about what they are likely to encounter that is unrelated to content but important to their success. For example, you may tell students that they may (or may not) write on the back of the page if their essay response takes more than the space you allotted.

Discouraging Cheating

Cheating is a source of error that all teachers would like to erase. You can do many things to discourage both the inadvertent type and the deliberate type of cheating, but you must start early in the year and early in the students' academic careers to be effective. You should be familiar with your school's policy on cheating and the consequences for it. The policy should be communicated in language appropriate to your students and their parents at the beginning of and regularly throughout the year. In addition, here are some suggestions from teachers in the field at various levels of the K–12 curriculum that they have found useful:

- Arrange desks in rows (one behind the other) with adequate space between rows.
- Use multiple forms of the test—either scrambled items or equivalent forms.
- Answer individual questions during the test at the student's desk, not yours.
- Inform students that there will be no passes to the bathroom (or elsewhere) issued during the test.
- Books, bags, and purses should be placed out of sight and out of the aisles, under the student's desk, perhaps.
- Provide scratch paper when needed; do not allow students to bring their own.
- Check calculators (or other required devices) for attached crib notes prior to starting the test.
- Allow students to bring a 3″ × 5″ "formula card" rather than making them memorize formulas. Examine everyone's card before the test, if you wish.
- Direct students to cover their test papers/answer sheets as they work and to keep them flat on their desks.
- Direct students to keep their eyes on their own work.
- Do not leave tests and/or answer sheets personally unattended. Keep them secure and away from students both before and after the assessment session.

Administering Performance and Product Assessments

It may seem that no practice is necessary for students (especially young ones) to become familiar with performance assessment. After all, performance assessments are much more authentic and direct than multiple-choice tests. Performance assessments also do not have those pesky separate answer sheets for students to learn to contend with. Practice is necessary, however, for students to become comfortable in many situations and assessment situations in particular, even authentic ones. One way to provide practice is to conduct a case study or simulation where students work on a problem or task as a class before doing another individually or in small groups under assessment conditions. In your instruction, you can help the class use the judging criteria against which you will measure their individual performances. For a given cluster of instructional outcomes, having practice and giving feedback on a similar (but not the same) task can prepare students for the time when they must perform under formal assessment conditions. As with paper-and-pencil tests, how the assessment is administered should not interfere with your students' performance.

Another consideration specifically related to product assessments is the issue of where the creation of the masterpiece will take place: inside or outside the classroom. Where student products are produced has implications for scoring and weighting the assessment. Research has shown that human judgment can be influenced by factors other than the ones intended. All of the judging criteria in the world will not help if the judge is unduly subject to outside influences overshadowing those criteria. For example, scores should be related neither to how much money is spent on the project nor to how handy the students or their helpers are with tools (unless the project is for shop class!).

If products are created inside the classroom, you have much more control over such things as how much help the student receives (and from whom), cost of materials, and time devoted to the project. A drawback is that it takes class time. If the products must be worked on outside the classroom on the students' time, you have much less control over these variables. You may specify in your directions to students, for example, that they should not ask for help in completing the project, what help from parents is permissible, or that found objects should be used. There are no guarantees, however. Some teachers require their students to keep a journal regarding the project. They record in the journal, among other things, who they had help from and the type of help rendered (see Figure 13.2). If you have class time to use or the assessment is very heavily weighted in determining grades, consider making it an in-class project. This puts many variables under your control and improves the validity of the results across students. It is also essential to providing the same assessment conditions, a necessity if you plan norm-referenced comparisons. If, on the other hand, there is no spare moment for students to work on their products in class, consider one of the following options in addition to giving specific feedback on the product relative to the judging criteria:

1. Do not assign any grade.
2. Assign a grade, but do not count it toward a final grade for the subject for the term. As used in this case, the grade essentially summarizes the feedback.
3. Assign a grade, but give it relatively little weight in figuring a final grade.

There are also some administration considerations for in-class performances. First, all students who are required to perform should do so under the same conditions. This is especially important if you intend to assign grades to the performances. For example, if students will be making presentations over 2 days and you plan to invite the principal, he or she should be present both days or not at all. Maintenance

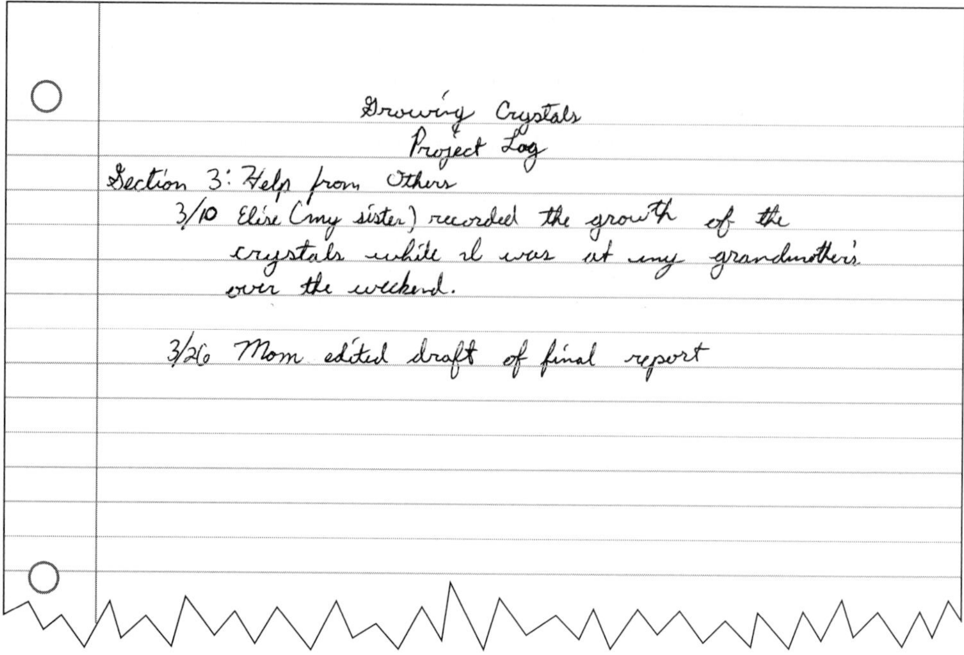

Growing Crystals
Project Log

Section 3: Help from Others

3/10 Elise (my sister) recorded the growth of the crystals while I was at my grandmother's over the weekend.

3/26 Mom edited draft of final report

Figure 13.2
Portion of a science project journal kept by a student documenting help received from others.

of conditions over time is essential for both norm-referenced and criterion-referenced interpretation of the results because it eliminates any unfair advantage or disadvantage due to extraneous variables. Second, it is important to manage the audience and students waiting to perform so that they do not distract from the performance at hand. Third, if outside judges, such as other teachers, must be present to observe, make sure that where they sit and what they are to do are prearranged so that the assessment process flows smoothly.

Assessing Students with Disabilities

In today's classrooms, teachers are much more likely than ever before to encounter students with disabilities that may impact the way their learning is assessed. It is beyond the scope of this text to describe all the disabilities teachers are likely to encounter. There are, however, some facts about disabilities in general and some common accommodations that are used in many classrooms that you should be familiar with.

First, not all disabilities are obvious and permanent. They may be hidden (like poor hearing in a kindergarten child), temporary (such as decreased mobility after surgery or trauma), or recurrent (muscular dystrophy, for example). Therefore, a one-size-fits-all approach to assessment accommodations will probably not work. Further, the accommodations that were appropriate last semester may not be appropriate this semester due to the changing nature of a particular disability. Second, students with more recently developed or diagnosed disabilities, and their parents, are still learning to cope with the disability and may not know the best accommodations. A person disabled since birth, in contrast, has learned adaptations over the years and will probably know which accommodations are effective. It is best to approach accommodation on a case-by-case basis with the help of district and school special-education personnel. Third, the purpose of accommodation is to provide the least restrictive environment and eliminate any unfair disadvantage (without creating an unfair advantage) for the student with a disability. The challenge for teachers is to use assessments for all students that match the instructional outcomes without requiring skills and abilities that are irrelevant to the outcomes and restrictive of performance.

The following typical disability areas and classroom accommodations are presented by the American Council on Education:

- *Hearing*—Give written instructions or information. Use an oral or sign language interpreter to literally translate (but not change the meaning of) test questions.
- *Vision*—Use a special edition of the assessment (one in large print, for example), audio-tape it, or individually read it aloud. Use optical aids such as Visual-tek (enlarges print). Have the student record answers by typing or audio-taping. Alternatively the student may dictate responses to a proctor who marks the answer sheet or writes the words.
- *Mobility*—Give the test in an accessible building and room. Arrange for a proctor to assist in manipulating test materials, marking exams, and writing numbers and other symbols as dictated by the student. Use alternative ways of responding (such as typing, taping). If the disability causes the student to be distracting to other students during assessment, separately test him or her.
- *Speech*—Use written exams in place of oral recitation. The student may write his or her response for an interpreter to read aloud. The student may use an aid such as a word board or interpreter for participating in classroom discussions or presentations.
- *Emotional*—Administer the regular exam individually in a distraction-free setting within the regular time limit. Create an alternative task that meets the set judging criteria and matches the intended outcome. Refer the student to a study-skills or learning center (if available) where the student can be coached in assessment. Use a study carrel in place of a regular student desk in the classroom to keep distractions to a minimum.[1]

---

[1]"Measuring Student Progress in the Classroom" in *Higher Education and the Handicapped Resource Center* by the National Clearinghouse on Postsecondary Education for Handicapped Individuals, 1986, Washington, DC: Author.

It is important to keep in mind that accommodations will probably require more assessment administration time. An audio-taped version of an assessment takes longer to listen to than it takes the typical student to read a written version, for example. Preparing and using Braille and large-print versions also take time, as does dictating answers. Although there are no rigid rules, the "extended time should flexibly permit *reasonable progress without dawdling*."[2]

Preparing for Standardized Assessments

Because of the high stakes typically involved with standardized assessments and the notion that student performance is linked to teachers' abilities, teachers naturally want their students to do their best. Several questions arise from this desire, however:

How do I get my students to take seriously a test imposed on them by others without raising their anxiety levels too high?

What can I do to prepare my students for the test? What is ethical? What works?

What is the cost benefit of various preparation activities?

Taking It Seriously

Teachers tread a thin line when high-stakes testing time occurs in the school year. They know that if the students treat it as a lark—a few days free of the normal schedule—they may not pay close enough attention, or they may not think it necessary to finish as many items in the allotted time as possible. Worse, they may not read the items at all and just mark their answer sheets in creative (but wrong) patterns. If, on the other hand, students become overly concerned with doing well and imagine terrible things that could happen if they "blow it," they may be incapacitated by their anxiety. Either way, their scores will reflect a less-than-accurate picture of their true achievement status.

In some schools, teachers try to avoid these situations by making a "friendly" competition of the test; for example, cajoling their students to do better than the other classes at their level. Other schools send home a note telling parents that their children will be taking an important examination over a few days and to be sure they get a good night's sleep and a good breakfast and ask parents not to upset them during that week. Students, of course, react differentially to these prodding tactics, so there is no one best way to achieve a balance between sheer panic and complete indifference. Some teachers have found it useful to talk openly with their students about an upcoming assessment and answer questions about what it covers and how to approach it. This type of conversation can allay fears and appropriately communicate the seriousness of the assessment if conducted by a teacher who is knowledgeable about the test and exudes calm about it.

---

[2]The National Clearinghouse on Postsecondary Education for Handicapped Individuals, 1986, p. 2.

Recognizing Ethical and Unethical Assessment Preparation Practices

There is a continuum of choices for the teacher considering offering test preparation help for students. At one extreme, some teachers do nothing additional to competent instructional delivery that relates to the outcomes specified in the curriculum. At the other extreme, some teachers may give the students the actual test items to practice on. Clearly, divulging the assessment items or tasks to the students before the test is unethical. It is also a direct violation of the test security agreement between the test publisher and the district—a breach of contract.

Between the two extremes is a very large and murky gray area (Figure 13.3). Two evaluative standards have been proposed that teachers can employ to navigate these muddy waters and determine the appropriateness of any given test-preparation practice. First, the practice should conform to the ethical standards of the education profession. Teachers, by virtue of *in loco parentis,* must model ethical behavior for children and refrain from any behavior that might be construed as lying, cheating, or stealing. Second, the practice should not be used unless it increases student mastery of the subject-matter content along with test scores.[3] Inflating test scores by teaching students to be test-wise without simultaneously increasing students' mastery of the skills, attitudes, and knowledge contained in the intended curriculum gives an artificial picture of performance. This artificial picture is deceptive to parents, students, and anyone else who attempts to interpret or use the results.

Preparing Students for Standardized Assessments

How, then, can teachers prepare their students to take classroom assessments in an ethical and defensible manner that benefits the students? They can do this by adhering to the following guidelines.

1. Prepare students for a variety of types of assessment formats, tasks, and items. Students should encounter variety in assessment so that they may generalize their test-taking skills across possible assessment approaches, much as they generalize their content-related knowledge and skill. For example, if the district-wide test is all multiple-choice, the district-wide test should *not* be the first time students encounter multiple-choice items. At least some of your assessments prior to the district-wide test should include multiple-choice items. In most district curricula, there is enough flexibility in the instructional outcomes to permit a variety of assessment approaches. If you use assessment approaches that are congruent with the given intended outcomes, over time you are likely to provide enough diversity. For example, if the district-wide test contains multiplication problems in vertical format, your classroom assessments should contain some vertical format items and some in other formats (horizontal, for example) so that the multiplication skill is generalizable across formats.

---

[3] "Appropriateness of Teachers' Test-Preparation Practices" by W. J. Popham, 1991, *Educational Measurement: Issues and Practice, 10*(4), pp. 12–15.

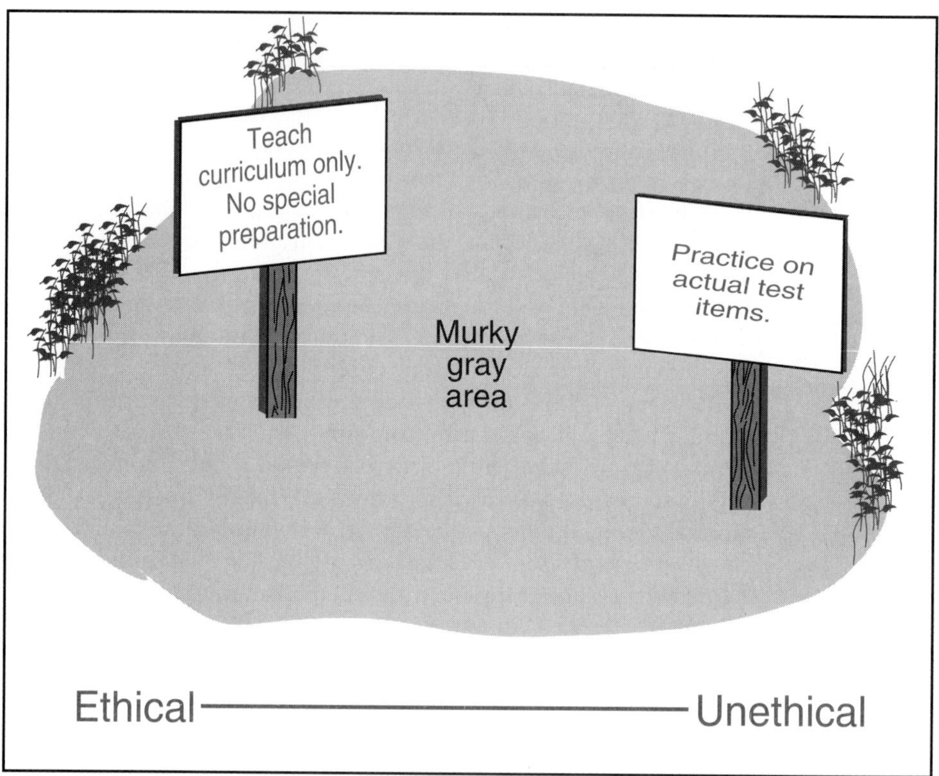

Figure 13.3
Extremes in assessment preparation practices.

2. *Balance time spent on test-taking strategies with content instruction.* Curricular content should not be neglected in favor of endless drilling on worksheets and tasks designed to parallel the test. Research on commercial programs that concentrate on helping students to become test-wise shows mixed results at best, so the benefit-to-cost ratio may not be worth it for your students.[4] One way to achieve a balance is to blend test-taking strategies with your usual instruction in the content area. Rather than setting aside a specific amount of time (like the month before the big test) for what is called by some "drill and kill," provide short periodic reviews throughout the year. If you want to enable your students to intelligently narrow the number of choices for multiple-choice items, teach them why and how to make educated guesses, and use items that are relevant to the curriculum.

---

[4]See, for example, *Test Wise or Test Foolish: Effects of Riverside Materials on Test Taking Skill Instruction* by K. S. Cushing and others, March 28–30, 1989. Paper presented at the Annual Meeting of the National Council on Measurement in Education, San Francisco. ERIC ED317589.

3. Determine what preparation the comparison group had and provide it to your students to the extent possible. For example, the norm group for the Stanford Achievement Test (ninth edition) took the test publisher's practice test before taking the one that counted. If your students also take the same practice test (available through the publisher), they receive no special (or illegal) help. Thus, your ethics are not compromised, and the resulting scores are interpretable with less reservation. Information about the norming process and related activities is typically available in the test manual or from the publisher. In larger districts, the testing personnel may also know what the comparison group received. Do not copy the practice tests, however; they are copyrighted.

✓ *Easy Reference Checklist*

Guidelines for Preparing Students for Standardized Assessments

- ❑ Method/content of preparation is professionally ethical.
- ❑ Method/content of preparation is educationally defensible.
- ❑ Students are prepared for a variety of types of assessment formats, tasks, and items.
- ❑ Time is balanced between test-taking strategies and content instruction.
- ❑ Preparation parallels that of the comparison group (if any) to the extent possible.

Teaching Test-Taking Skills

Surely, test-taking skills and strategies are good things to know in life, or at least to survive education as it is practiced in the U.S. Test-wise and informed students are a goal to work toward. Any discussion of the direct teaching of test-taking skills, however, should be tempered with the caution that curriculum content-based practice in formats similar to the assessment is best. In some textbook/materials series, test-taking skills are presented as they relate to the subject of the text, the grade level of the students, and the types of items and tasks encountered on the latest editions of widely used standardized tests (such as third-grade language arts). Commercial programs that teach test-taking skills are also available. Which program, if any, is appropriate for your school depends on a number of things:

- The standardized assessment used and how well-matched it is with the current curriculum.
- Cost of the program.

- How well current subject matter instruction is (or how easily it can be) integrated with instruction in test-taking strategies.
- How well the program meets the criteria in the checklist for preparing students for assessment.

You and your colleagues may also create your own test-taking skills instruction and weave it into the subject matter at hand, in accordance with guideline 2, regarding balance. One way to approach the topic is to consider assessment expertise a life skill and teach it as part of the intended curriculum. This removes it from the realm of the implicit curriculum that some students never grasp just because it is implicit rather than explicit. Introducing different item formats and assessment approaches over time, you can prepare your students for your classroom assessments, standardized tests, and future assessment situations. The content listed below includes other life skills such as deciding priorities and using partial knowledge in making decisions and might be taught in a variety of ways depending on the developmental level of the students[5]:

- Reducing anxiety and stress.

    Breathing techniques.

    Imaging techniques.

    Nutrition, exercise, and sleep.

- Using time wisely.

    Essay questions (read, interpret, generate ideas, organize, write).

    Completing "easy" items first, then going back.

    Planning/executing out-of-class projects.

- Recording answers.

    Manipulating separated answer sheets and test booklets.

    Intent of meaning, legibility, and spelling in essay and short-answer items.

- Making educated guesses: using partial knowledge. (Another title for this may be "What to do when you don't know it cold.")[6]

    Blind vs. informed guessing.

    Eliminating choices in multiple-choice and matching items.

    Partial answers for partial credit on essay and short-answer items.

    Minimal risk (if any) for guessing, even if you're not sure.

- Changing answers.[7]

---

[5]For an alternative outline, see "An Analysis of Test-Wiseness" by J. Millman, C. H. Bishop, and R. Ebel, 1965, *Educational and Psychological Measurement, 25*(3), pp. 707–726.

[6]Girls, in particular, should be encouraged to guess and shown how to use partial knowledge to their advantage. See, for example, "Human Self-Assessment in Multiple-Choice Testing" by P. Hassmen and D. P. Hunt, 1994, *Journal of Educational Measurement, 31*(2), pp. 149–160.

[7]The research shows that it is usually advantageous to change an answer; as students go through a test they may gain insight or clues they did not have at first.

- Determining a "best" alternative when all the choices are at least "good."
- How to determine true and false propositions.
- Using given task-performance criteria to create products that meet or exceed "specifications."

Test-taking skills can be integrated with curriculum in a number of ways and with different types of subject-matter. Here are three examples:

1. Combine a segment on making educated guesses with mathematics instruction on estimation or science instruction on constructing hypotheses.
2. Discuss strategies for planning and executing out-of-class projects just before assigning one. Hand out written descriptions of tasks and procedural order, if any.
3. Include in a health unit a segment on stress and the role of nutrition, exercise, and sleep in reducing test anxiety and increasing alertness.

Administering Standardized Assessments

Administering a standardized test is a very scripted affair. Testing conditions are more tightly controlled than those for classroom assessments, and teachers are restricted by the administration procedure to certain behaviors. Even the directions for standardized assessments are to be read word-for-word without deviation. This is not intended to stifle teachers but to provide uniform testing conditions for all students taking the assessment. This, in turn, ensures that the results from one classroom or school can be compared to any other classroom or school in the country or to the same norm group as if all the students were together in one humongous auditorium at the same time when they were assessed. The scripted directions, the test security procedures, the timing of subtests, the limits on answering students' questions—all contribute to the standardization process. The requirements can also make the process appear stilted, formal, and rather unreal to students and teachers who may be accustomed to a more casual atmosphere for assessment. It is imperative, however, to adhere to the publisher's administration guidelines. The resulting scores are likely to be used in many ways by many people, so they should be as meaningful and informative as possible.

There may be students in your classroom for whom the standardized test is deemed inappropriate. Commercial and state test publishers produce guidelines for making this decision, which is usually made by a team of professionals, including teachers, who are familiar with the students. Typically, exceptional students, students with a limited knowledge of English, or students with disabilities should be given the opportunity to take the test unless the results of such a test would inaccurately estimate the students' functioning level. This does *not* mean that if a student is not likely to score at or above the 50th percentile that he or she should be excluded from the test. It *does* mean that if there is behavioral evidence that the student will not be able to demonstrate his or her own level of competence, he or she should be excluded from the test.

Most popular standardized test batteries include in the test manual a list of permissible modifications and accommodations. Students with certain disabilities may need a special edition of the test. Special editions of major commercial assessment series are usually available from sources other than the test publisher. For example, the American Printing House for the Blind has produced large print and Braille editions of some of the more widely used assessments, such as the Comprehensive Test of Basic Skills, the Otis-Lennon School Ability Test, and the Stanford Achievement Test. Gallaudet College, in Washington, D.C., produces hearing-impaired editions of widely used standardized tests such as the Performance Scale for Deaf Children, the Stanford Achievement Test, and the Wechsler Intelligence Scale for Children–Revised. For further information regarding special editions of major standardized tests, contact the following:

American Printing House for the Blind
1839 Frankfort Avenue
Louisville, Kentucky 40206-0085

Office of Demographic Studies
Gallaudet College
800 Florida Avenue
Washington, D.C. 20002

Summary

Preparing Students for Classroom Assessments

Some experts argue that expertise in assessment is a life skill to be acquired in school in preparation for the tests we endure in adult life. Students properly prepare for a quiz, test, exam, performance, or project by (1) interacting with the content to acquire the intended skills and knowledge and (2) psychologically approaching the assessment situation with a sense of calm and confidence. To help students prepare for classroom assessment, follow these guidelines:

1. Provide adequate instruction, including appropriate opportunities to practice the skill or apply the knowledge.
2. Familiarize students with the type of assessment and conditions under which they will be required to perform.
3. Facilitate review.
4. Approach the assessment positively.
5. Help students manage their assessment anxiety.

Administering Classroom Assessments

The proper assessment atmosphere is distraction-free, provides adequate tools and space for working, does not increase student anxiety, and discourages cheating. If students have a routine for getting ready for a test, it can have a calming effect and help them transfer the emphasis in energy from physical to mental. Going over the directions to the test, especially if the items are of a different type than the students have previously encountered or if this is the first test of the term, can also help. Put students at ease with regard to item format, and let them know what they are likely to encounter that is unrelated to content but important to their success.

Start early in the year and early in the students' academic careers to effectively discourage cheating. You should be familiar with your school's policy on cheating and the consequences for it. The policy on cheating should be communicated in language appropriate to your students and their parents at the beginning of and regularly throughout the year. Proper arrangement of desks, good test security procedures, and multiple forms of a test are some of the ways to discourage cheating in the classroom.

Practice is necessary for students to become comfortable in assessment situations, even authentic ones. For a given cluster of instructional outcomes, practice and feedback on a similar (but not the same) task can prepare students for the time when they must perform under formal assessment conditions. Where student products are produced—inside or outside the classroom—has implications for scoring and weighting the assessment. Teachers have more control over variables when students work on products in the classroom, but it takes class time to do so. If class time is available or the assessment is very heavily weighted in determining grades, consider making it an in-class project. If class time is not available, consider one of the following options in addition to giving specific feedback on the product relative to the judging criteria:

1. Do not assign any grade.
2. Assign a grade, but do not count it toward a final grade for the subject for the term.
3. Assign a grade, but give it relatively little weight in figuring a final grade.

In today's classrooms, you are very likely to encounter students with disabilities that may impact the way their learning is assessed. You should be aware of some facts about disabilities in general:

1. Not all disabilities are obvious and permanent.
2. The more recently disabled the student, the less likely he or she will know the best accommodations.
3. The purpose of accommodation is to provide the least restrictive environment and eliminate any unfair disadvantage (without creating an unfair advantage) for the student with a disability.

Accommodations usually require more assessment administration time.

Preparing for Standardized Assessments

If students do not take standardized assessments seriously or if they become overanxious and incapacitated, their scores will reflect a less-than-accurate picture of their true achievement status. Two evaluative standards have been proposed to help determine the appropriateness of any given test-preparation practice: (1) The practice should conform to the ethical standards of the education profession, and (2) the practice should not be used unless it increases student mastery of the subject-matter content along with test scores. Standardized assessment preparation guidelines include:

1. Prepare students for a variety of types of assessment formats, tasks, and items.
2. Balance time spent on test-taking strategies with content instruction.
3. Determine what preparation the comparison group had, and provide it to your students to the extent possible.

An effective way to approach teaching test-taking skills is to consider assessment expertise a life skill and teach it as part of the intended curriculum. Test-taking skills can and should be integrated with the curriculum in a number of ways and with different types of subject matter.

Administering Standardized Assessments

Testing conditions are more tightly controlled for standardized assessments than for classroom assessments, and teachers are restricted by the administration procedure to certain behaviors. The scripted directions, the test security procedures, the timing of sub-tests, and the limits on answering students' questions all contribute to the standardization process and render the results meaningful and comparable. It is imperative to adhere to the publisher's administration guidelines. Every student should be given the opportunity to take the standardized assessment unless the results of such a test inaccurately estimate his or her functioning level. Most popular standardized test batteries include in the test manual a list of permissible modifications and accommodations for students with disabilities. Special editions of major standardized tests for students with certain disabilities (such as vision impairment) are also available.

Try These

I. The two evaluative standards given in the chapter specify that a test preparation practice should conform to the ethical standards of the education profession and be used only if it increases student mastery of the curriculum-based, subject-matter content along with test scores. Based on these two standards, decide whether each of the following preparation practices is advisable. Circle your answer.

1. Choose a random sample of items from the latest edition of the test, administer them as a pretest, then use them to identify the areas students need to drill on before the formal administration of the test. Yes No
2. Use separate answer sheets with some of your classroom tests so that your elementary students get exposure to manipulating them, tracking item numbers with answer numbers, and bubbling in identification information and answers appropriately. Yes No

3. Administer the publisher's practice test for the edition of the standardized series used at your school. Discuss the answers and the test-taking process afterward with your students. Yes No
4. Use leftover copies of an older edition of the test as practice tests for the new edition that will be administered under formal conditions. Yes No
5. Read through the items of the current edition of the test, then construct your own items that mirror their content and format for use as a practice test. Yes No
6. Create a test-taking skills unit that focuses on the specific assessment approach and content of the upcoming standardized test. Time the unit so that students finish it just before the formal administration of the standardized test. Yes No
7. Instruct your students in how to read (or listen to) directions, interpret them accurately, and follow them carefully using practice test directions as one example among others. Yes No
8. Send the students you do not think will do well on the district-wide test to the library while you work more intensively with those you are sure are going to college so that they can boost their scores. Yes No
9. Rearrange your intended instructional schedule so that material you know will be on the standardized test is presented prior to the test date, rather than after. Even though you know that most of your students will not have all the prerequisites needed to understand the material well, some of them may be able to take advantage of the advanced instruction and get better scores. Yes No
10. Use a variety of item and task types on written and performance-based classroom assessments that are congruent with intended outcomes. Yes No

II. Devise a curriculum and instructional strategies for teaching test-taking skills to a group of students with which you are familiar. Use the test-taking skills content outline in this chapter and tailor it for the students. Report how you would infuse this into the regular curriculum.

Criteria:

- The test-taking skills you teach are appropriate for the standardized and classroom assessments your students take.
- The test-taking skills instruction is not a separate unit from other subject-matter content—the two are blended.
- The regular subject matter chosen is appropriate content for the test-taking skills instruction.

Answers

I. 1. **N:** Unethical—actual test items should never be used for instructional purposes; also takes time away from regular instruction. 2. **Y:** Ethical and advisable if item types are appropriate for instructional outcomes they assess. 3. **Y:** Ethical, even sanctioned by the publisher; takes minimal time from instruction. 4. **N:** Using actual test items, even from older editions, is unethical. 5. **N:** Prior exposure to the actual items is unethical for the teacher as well as the students; practice is tantamount to copying the items outright. 6. **N:** Ethical to teach test-taking skills, but the practice does not enhance mastery of the regular subject-matter content. The practice would be advisable if it reviewed a variety of skills, not just the ones needed for the upcoming test. 7. **Y:** Taking direction is a life skill. Other types of directions may also be used as examples. 8. **N:** Exclusionary and unethical; also takes time away from regular instruction of all students. 9. **N:** You may argue the fact that the instruction *was* intended, but it is not an instructionally sound practice to teach hierarchically related content out of sequence just because the more advanced portion is on the standardized test; that also makes it unethical. 10. **Y:** Ethical and instructionally appropriate—you are doing exactly what you should be doing.

II. Responses will vary, but should meet the criteria stated.

CHAPTER 14

Interpreting and Using the Results of Standardized Assessments

Key Concepts:

- Interpreting assessment results carefully and in proper context.
- Avoiding misinterpretation of assessment results.
- Interpreting and using individual profiles.
- Reporting individual student profiles using different forms for different audiences.
- Comparing individual achievement with ability.
- Interpreting and using group profiles.

Standards Addressed in This Chapter:

3. Administer, score, and interpret the results of both externally produced and teacher-produced assessment methods.
6. Communicate assessment results to students, parents and other lay audiences, and other educators.

Before You Begin Reading, Consider This

Should standardized assessment results be sent to parents as normal procedure? Educators disagree over whether standardized assessment results should be sent home to the parents of school children. For example, the parents in one school district receive their child's results, while in a neighboring district, results are kept in the child's permanent records, available to parents upon request but not sent to them.

YES Under the Buckley Amendment (FERPA, 1974), parents have the right to be informed of the results of any testing the school does on their child, and they shouldn't have to request it or go to the school office to do it.

NO Parents are not typically sophisticated in the interpretation of tests, and we should not expect them to be. If sent home, the results will be misinterpreted and cause undue reactions (from consternation to elation) among parents. Neither are many teachers sophisticated in the interpretation of results. Sending the results home would put many teachers in the position of having to explain something they themselves might not fully understand.

Interpreting the Results of Standardized Assessments

Certain kinds of assessments, especially non-achievement assessments such as some personality measures and individual intelligence tests, require interpretation by people with special training. Most assessment results, however, are interpretable by any person who has had a reasonably comprehensive assessment course. Unfortunately, many educators apparently have not had such a course. The attitudes and behaviors of people who are not knowledgeable concerning assessment concepts and principles seem to be on opposite ends of a continuum. At one extreme are those who treat the whole business of testing too lightly. They do not attach much importance to test results, and in some cases they may actually have hostile feelings toward them. In either case they make little use of them—in the classroom, for example. At the other extreme are those who treat the results entirely too seriously. They interpret test scores, including performance assessments, as if they represent the TRUTH, as if each score is a "true" score—a perfect picture of performance. Proper interpretation requires recognition of the fact that although many tests do provide very accurate estimates, they do not measure with the same precision that yardsticks do. Intelligent interpretation also requires knowledge of the assessment instrument or test in question. What a given score means depends upon such factors as what the test actually assesses as well as its indices of validity and reliability. For example, the test's estimated standard error of measurement needs to be considered.

A number of test publishers make available criterion-referenced interpretations as well as norm-referenced interpretations of their standardized instruments. Thus, you may see a comprehensive student performance analysis that lists content clusters (parts of subtests) or assessment objectives and the raw score and number of items listed for each. By now, it is probably clear to you that there are several reasons to resist the temptation to use criterion-referenced interpretations of norm-referenced tests as indicators of achievement or non-achievement of classroom outcomes. These reasons, reviewed here, are discussed in greater detail in earlier chapters.

First, the validity evidence in the content of any assessment is based on how well the tasks or items match the intent and difficulty of the outcomes they are designed to assess. Extending this, a standardized assessment is valid to the degree that its stated objectives match those of the district (and, more specifically, those of the classroom teacher) *and* to the degree that its items match its own stated objectives. Second, most large-scale standardized assessments were originally developed as norm-referenced tests, with typically less-than-adequate domain sampling for criterion-referenced purposes.

Third, even when the number of items is more reasonable (which is rare), the items are constructed to provide maximum discrimination, which can only occur when the items are of medium difficulty. Therefore, the difficulty of the items used on the standardized instrument, regardless of their number, may or may not match the difficulty of the instructional outcomes of the teacher. Well-constructed standardized instruments should be used only for the purposes for which they were originally intended. As more high-quality, criterion-referenced tests are constructed for criterion-referenced purposes, both by test publishers and skilled teachers, these should be used to determine what students can and cannot do relative to classroom outcomes.

Standardized, norm-referenced test results are reported in terms of the raw score equivalents or derived scores.[1] Although any number of equivalents may be available in norms tables, one or more of these are generally selected for presentation on individual or group profile sheets; these permit easy comparison of relative performance on a number of subtests. Such profiles of equivalents may also be constructed at the local level if county or district norms are developed for a test. At the classroom level, of course, the whole procedure is greatly simplified. The high-school teacher, for example, is quite familiar with the "norm" group (his or her classes), and most tests do not typically contain subtests. Thus, although one or more raw score equivalents may well be calculated, profile sheets are rarely (if ever) constructed.

With all of the options test publishers provide for score reporting of standardized tests, illustrating each and every one is beyond the scope of this book. It is quite possible for you to receive a score report that contains information typically used by others in addition to that useful to you. For example, normal curve equivalents (NCEs) may be included in score reports and are typically used by program evaluators and by people in special education for situations where a child may be tested out of level. Normal curve equivalents are another standard score—a way of expressing relative performance.

---

[1]See Chapter 11 for more information on interpreting norm-referenced assessment results.

Interpreting and Using Individual Profiles of Assessment Results

The meaning of an individual's raw score depends upon what was measured, the composition of the norm group, and the values of the individual's derived scores. Standardized test publishers are assuming more and more responsibility for providing all the information necessary for making valid interpretations of test scores. Manuals accompanying standardized assessments have become increasingly comprehensive, and a number of the major publishers provide separate manuals for the various phases involved in the use of a standardized test, such as administration, scoring, and interpretation. Interpretation materials typically include norms tables as well as considerable explanatory information and guidelines for usage. Some manuals also provide tables for more than one norm group or for subgroups within a norm group, and in such cases it is important that the most appropriate tables be selected for interpretation purposes. Further, although it is usually a safe assumption, you should check to make sure that derived scores for different subtests are based on the same norm group, or else relative performance across subject areas cannot be validly interpreted. Finally, it bears reemphasizing that perhaps the greatest source of misinterpretation comes from thinking of the average score of a norm group as a goal for all students. By definition this notion is absurd. In the first place, norms represent scores actually obtained, not idealized standards. Second, *average* means that half of a group scored higher and half lower. Being concerned because half of the students in your class are "below the national average" on an achievement test is like being upset because half of them are too short or below average in height!

An *individual profile* may present raw scores or one or more derived scores or both for each of a number of subtests in a graphic or tabular manner for a single student. Such profiles permit us to identify a student's relative strengths and weaknesses at a glance; I use the term *relative* because a student's highest score may represent a performance well below the group average. The derived scores most often presented on a profile sheet are percentile ranks and stanines, although most major test publishers will tailor forms to the needs of the school or district. In addition, profile sheets include appropriate identification information such as the name, form, and level of the test, the date of testing, and the student's name and gender.

Profile sheets of most major tests also provide an explanation of the contents of the profile and directions for interpretation. Such directions typically discuss the fact that every score reflects some measurement error and should be thought of as being the midpoint in some range or band of scores, usually those which fall between ± 1 SEM (standard error of measurement). This band is often actually depicted on the profile, especially when percentile ranks are presented. As the directions typically indicate, such bands facilitate interpretation of scores on the various subtests. Usually, the overlapping bands concept is employed so that a true difference in performance on any two subtests is indicated only if the bands for those subtests do not overlap at all. For stanines, the directions typically suggest that in comparing performance on any two subtests, a difference of only one stanine (for example, 6 and 7) probably does not reflect a true difference in performance; a difference of two or more stanines probably does. At the risk of being repetitious (it hasn't stopped me so far, has it?), remember that comparing scores made on different tests is meaningful only if the tests were normed on the same group. If not, the validity of comparisons is a direct function of the comparability of the norm groups.

These concepts are illustrated in Figures 14.1, 14.2, 14.3, 14.4, and 14.6, reproductions of reports of the Stanford Achievement Test, ninth edition, the Otis-Lennon School Ability Test, seventh edition, and the Differential Aptitude Tests, fifth edition. The Stanford Achievement Test publishers also provide a helpful Guide for Classroom Planning to assist teachers in using test results.

Figure 14.1 contains a student report typical in sophistication of those provided for the major national achievement tests. In the top fourth of the report, student identification information is listed, such as teacher, school, district, test type, grade, date tested, name, and student's age. At the bottom of the report are listed the level and form of the test(s) and the norms used. Area Ⓐ contains the national percentile ranks and stanines (PR-S) and other scores as requested for each subtest, for area totals (for example, Total Reading), and for the complete battery. When students take the Otis-Lennon School Ability Test (OLSAT) along with the Stanford, the OLSAT results appear in Area Ⓑ. In addition to the types of scores included for the Stanford, the OLSAT lists a school ability index (SAI), which has a mean of 100 and a standard deviation of 16, so that a score of 116 is one standard deviation above the mean.

Full interpretation of achievement requires further knowledge concerning the individual, and an index of general mental ability is helpful. If Ted has an SAI of 101 and his stanines on an achievement test are all 5 or above, he is doing well. On the other hand, if Instine has an index of 130 and his stanines are all 5 and below, there seems to be a problem somewhere. Further data, such as those available in Instine's cumulative record folder, are needed before we can determine an appropriate course of action. Thus, each student's results must be interpreted within the context of what we know about him or her as an individual. Without knowledge of this context we risk misinterpreting the results and doing a disservice to the students. The disservice could involve selecting the student for a special program that, in fact, is not needed (and taking a seat that could be occupied by someone else) or not providing the help for which a student qualifies.

In addition to being listed on individual profiles, percentile bands are graphically depicted by subtest in Area Ⓒ and can be compared for degree of overlap. The black bars in this area are percentile bands spanning ±1 SEM for each subtest. Note that, in this case, the three OLSAT percentile bands are also included. Area Ⓓ compares the student's performance of a Stanford/9 subtest in relation to other students of similar ability (as measured by the OLSAT). *High* means that the student placed in the top 23% of the comparison group; *low,* the bottom 23%; and *middle,* the middle 54%. Information useful in explaining how to interpret the scores appears on the back of the form. The form is packed with information that can be helpful in explaining the current or past achievement status of a student to his or her parents in a conference. A comprehensive form such as this can be overwhelming to parents at first, so you must point out the highlights regarding their child. Content clusters (Areas Ⓔ and Ⓕ) present for each subtest the raw score (RS), the number of items on the test (NP), and the number of those items the student attempted (NA). The check marks indi-

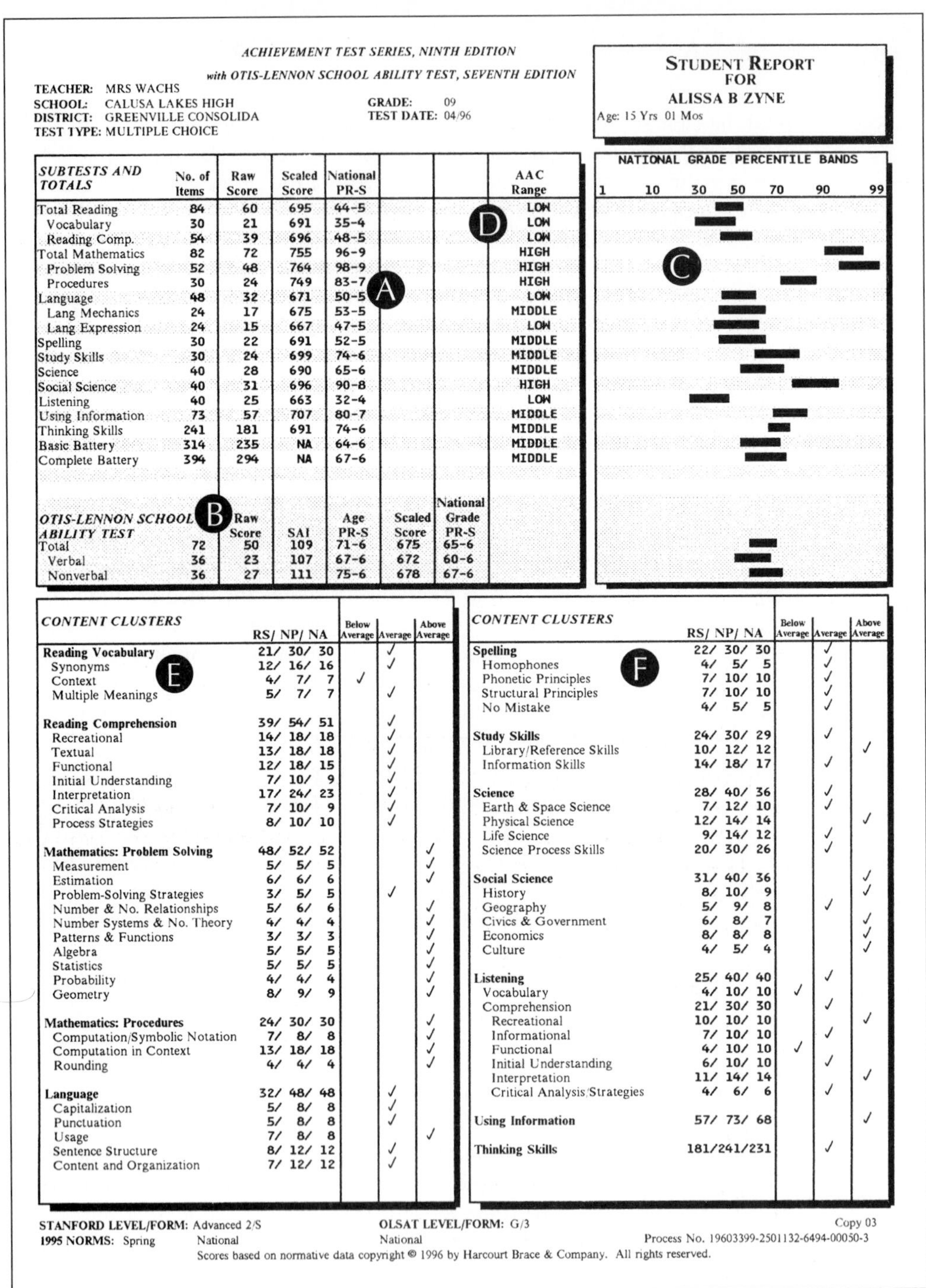

ACHIEVEMENT TEST SERIES, NINTH EDITION
with OTIS-LENNON SCHOOL ABILITY TEST, SEVENTH EDITION

STUDENT REPORT FOR ALISSA B ZYNE
Age: 15 Yrs 01 Mos

TEACHER: MRS WACHS
SCHOOL: CALUSA LAKES HIGH — GRADE: 09
DISTRICT: GREENVILLE CONSOLIDA — TEST DATE: 04/96
TEST TYPE: MULTIPLE CHOICE

SUBTESTS AND TOTALS	No. of Items	Raw Score	Scaled Score	National PR-S			AAC Range
Total Reading	84	60	695	44-5			LOW
Vocabulary	30	21	691	35-4			LOW
Reading Comp.	54	39	696	48-5			LOW
Total Mathematics	82	72	755	96-9			HIGH
Problem Solving	52	48	764	98-9			HIGH
Procedures	30	24	749	83-7			HIGH
Language	48	32	671	50-5			LOW
Lang Mechanics	24	17	675	53-5			MIDDLE
Lang Expression	24	15	667	47-5			LOW
Spelling	30	22	691	52-5			MIDDLE
Study Skills	30	24	699	74-6			MIDDLE
Science	40	28	690	65-6			MIDDLE
Social Science	40	31	696	90-8			HIGH
Listening	40	25	663	32-4			LOW
Using Information	73	57	707	80-7			MIDDLE
Thinking Skills	241	181	691	74-6			MIDDLE
Basic Battery	314	235	NA	64-6			MIDDLE
Complete Battery	394	294	NA	67-6			MIDDLE
OTIS-LENNON SCHOOL ABILITY TEST		Raw Score	SAI	Age PR-S	Scaled Score	National Grade PR-S	
Total	72	50	109	71-6	675	65-6	
Verbal	36	23	107	67-6	672	60-6	
Nonverbal	36	27	111	75-6	678	67-6	

CONTENT CLUSTERS	RS/ NP/ NA	Below Average	Average	Above Average
Reading Vocabulary	21/ 30/ 30		✓	
Synonyms	12/ 16/ 16		✓	
Context	4/ 7/ 7	✓		
Multiple Meanings	5/ 7/ 7		✓	
Reading Comprehension	39/ 54/ 51		✓	
Recreational	14/ 18/ 18		✓	
Textual	13/ 18/ 18		✓	
Functional	12/ 18/ 15		✓	
Initial Understanding	7/ 10/ 9		✓	
Interpretation	17/ 24/ 23		✓	
Critical Analysis	7/ 10/ 9		✓	
Process Strategies	8/ 10/ 10		✓	
Mathematics: Problem Solving	48/ 52/ 52			✓
Measurement	5/ 5/ 5			✓
Estimation	6/ 6/ 6			✓
Problem-Solving Strategies	3/ 5/ 5		✓	
Number & No. Relationships	5/ 6/ 6			✓
Number Systems & No. Theory	4/ 4/ 4			✓
Patterns & Functions	3/ 3/ 3			✓
Algebra	5/ 5/ 5			✓
Statistics	5/ 5/ 5			✓
Probability	4/ 4/ 4			✓
Geometry	8/ 9/ 9			✓
Mathematics: Procedures	24/ 30/ 30			✓
Computation/Symbolic Notation	7/ 8/ 8			✓
Computation in Context	13/ 18/ 18			✓
Rounding	4/ 4/ 4			✓
Language	32/ 48/ 48		✓	
Capitalization	5/ 8/ 8		✓	
Punctuation	5/ 8/ 8		✓	
Usage	7/ 8/ 8			✓
Sentence Structure	8/ 12/ 12		✓	
Content and Organization	7/ 12/ 12		✓	

CONTENT CLUSTERS	RS/ NP/ NA	Below Average	Average	Above Average
Spelling	22/ 30/ 30		✓	
Homophones	4/ 5/ 5		✓	
Phonetic Principles	7/ 10/ 10		✓	
Structural Principles	7/ 10/ 10		✓	
No Mistake	4/ 5/ 5		✓	
Study Skills	24/ 30/ 29		✓	
Library/Reference Skills	10/ 12/ 12			✓
Information Skills	14/ 18/ 17		✓	
Science	28/ 40/ 36		✓	
Earth & Space Science	7/ 12/ 10		✓	
Physical Science	12/ 14/ 14			✓
Life Science	9/ 14/ 12		✓	
Science Process Skills	20/ 30/ 26		✓	
Social Science	31/ 40/ 36			✓
History	8/ 10/ 9			✓
Geography	5/ 9/ 8		✓	
Civics & Government	6/ 8/ 7			✓
Economics	8/ 8/ 8			✓
Culture	4/ 5/ 4			✓
Listening	25/ 40/ 40		✓	
Vocabulary	4/ 10/ 10	✓		
Comprehension	21/ 30/ 30		✓	
Recreational	10/ 10/ 10			✓
Informational	7/ 10/ 10		✓	
Functional	4/ 10/ 10	✓		
Initial Understanding	6/ 10/ 10		✓	
Interpretation	11/ 14/ 14			✓
Critical Analysis/Strategies	4/ 6/ 6		✓	
Using Information	57/ 73/ 68			✓
Thinking Skills	181/241/231		✓	

STANFORD LEVEL/FORM: Advanced 2/S — OLSAT LEVEL/FORM: G/3 — Copy 03
1995 NORMS: Spring National — National — Process No. 19603399-2501132-6494-00050-3

Figure 14.1
Student Report for Alissa Zyne on the multiple-choice portion of the Stanford Achievement Test: Ninth Edition.
Source: Stanford Achievement Test: 9th Edition. Copyright © 1996 by Harcourt Brace and Company. Simulated data reproduced by permission. All rights reserved. Otis-Lennon School Ability Test: Seventh Edition. Copyright © 1996 by Harcourt Brace and Company. Simulated data reproduced by permission. All rights reserved.

cate whether the student's performance on that cluster of items was average, above average, or below average as compared to the norm group. Note that for some of the subtests (Patterns and Functions in Mathematics Problem Solving, for example) the small number of available items, in this case three, makes score interpretation tentative at best.

Alissa Zyne's profile (Figure 14.1) indicates that her percentile ranks range from 32 in Listening to 98 in Problem Solving. Her stanines range from 4 in Listening to 9 in Problem Solving. Note that the National Grade Percentile Bands chart uses bars of different width that correspond to ±1 SEM in percentile points for the subtest indicated. Alissa's percentile chart indicates that she is average in most areas and above average in five of them. This pattern is reflected in the Complete Battery Total stanine of 6. Both the Stanford/9 and the OLSAT were normed on the same sample, so we can compare Alissa's tested ability with her tested achievement. Alissa seems to be achieving at a level consistent with her capabilities, given that her SAI is in the average range and her school ability stanine is 6. The percentile band for Alissa's Complete Battery Total overlaps quite a bit with the percentile band for her OLSAT Total. This would indicate that Alissa is working up to her potential. Remember that only when tests are normed on the same sample and administered to the same national group can we compare a person's results on one assessment to the other.

The full series of the Stanford/9 includes open-ended assessments in reading, writing, mathematics, science, and social science that may be combined with the traditional multiple-choice items as reported in Figure 14.1. Alissa Zyne's writing assessment student report appears in Figure 14.2. The same identifying information is found at the top and bottom of the forms. Area Ⓐ of Figure 14.2 includes an interpretation of the holistic score assigned to the student's writing, how that performance compared with the norm group selected, and a cautionary statement about the assessment as one piece of information about the student. The holistic raw score (out of a possible 12) appears in Area Ⓑ, as do the types of scores chosen by the district, in this case scaled score, national percentile rank and stanine, and the achievement/ability comparison. Analytic scores are provided for each performance dimension in Area Ⓒ along with a brief narrative interpretation of the score received. Area Ⓓ is used when the student takes both the multiple-choice test and the writing assessment. It combines the 48 possible points on the multiple-choice test with the 12 possible points for the writing assessment for a total possible composite score of 60. Alissa's combined scores in Language/Writing are then compared to the norm group in the types of derived scores chosen by the district.

Alissa earned a holistic score of 9 out of a possible 12, which put her in the "above average" category (see Area Ⓐ, Figure 14.2) when compared to the 1995 national norms for her grade and spring testing. This is numerically repeated in her reported percentile rank and stanine, 87 and 7 respectively, in Area Ⓓ. Judging from the analytic scores, Alissa's relative strengths in writing are her organization and her ability to form coherent sentences into paragraphs. Her relative weakness appears to be mechanics.

Most of the major test companies also provide a summary sticker or label that can be affixed to a master sheet for each student. These summary stickers provide information at a glance for each year the student has taken a standardized achieve-

ACHIEVEMENT TEST SERIES, NINTH EDITION

TEACHER: MRS WACHS
SCHOOL: CALUSA LAKES HIGH
DISTRICT: GREENVILLE CONSOLIDA

GRADE: 09
TEST DATE: 04/96

STUDENT REPORT
FOR
ALISSA B ZYNE
Age: 15 Yrs 01 Mos

WRITING MODE: DESCRIPTIVE

On the 12-point scale, this paper has been rated in the 8-9 range. Such papers usually show clear evidence of basic organization and construction. There is some attempt to clarify statements, but few supporting details are used. Students who score in this range should be encouraged to work on relating ideas more effectively with transitions and on expanding their ideas.

A

Compared with the writing of other students in the same grade from across the nation, this student's writing performance is above average when scored on overall merit.

A direct measure of writing like the Stanford Writing Assessment offers one valuable piece of information about a student's writing achievement. To plan an instructional program for the student, these results should be used along with other sources of information, such as the student's performance on indirect measures of writing, daily class work, and homework.

9 ***HOLISTIC RAW SCORE***

B

Scaled Score	National PR-S	AAC Range
635	87-7	HIGH

ANALYTIC SCORES

C

2 IDEAS AND DEVELOPMENT

This paper shows adequately supported ideas with some details extended or elaborated.

3 SENTENCES AND PARAGRAPHS

This paper shows adequate control of sentence formation with some mix of sentence types, lengths, and structures. Papers earning a score of 3 may contain a small number of errors that do not interfere with fluency, with some attempt at paragraphing.

3 ORGANIZATION, UNITY, AND COHERENCE

This paper is fairly well organized with good unity. Some transitions may be used. There is little or no digression from main ideas or writing.

2 GRAMMAR AND USAGE

Papers earning a score of 2 generally have fair grammar and usage. Errors may interfere with meaning. The paper may be simplistic.

2 WORD CHOICE

This paper uses a fair choice of words that may be specific but have little variety. Papers earning a score of 2 may be simplistic and occasionally vague, but generally effective.

1 WRITING MECHANICS

Papers earning a score of 1 generally have frequent and/or serious errors in mechanics that interfere with communication.

D

LANGUAGE/WRITING COMPOSITE SCORES

The Composite score provides an overall indication of the student's achievement in Language/Writing. Only students taking both the Multiple-Choice Language subtest and the Writing Assessment will receive a Composite score.

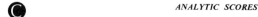

Number Possible	Raw Score	Scaled Score	National PR-S	AAC Range
60	41	NA	71-6	MIDDLE

STANFORD LEVEL/FORM: Advanced 2/S
1995 NORMS: Spring National

Copy 03
Process No. 19603399-2501132-6494-00072-3

Scores based on normative data copyright © 1996 by Harcourt Brace & Company. All rights reserved.

Figure 14.2
Student Report for Alissa Zyne on the Stanford Writing Assessment. *Source:* Stanford Achievement Test: Ninth Edition. Copyright © 1996 by Harcourt Brace and Company. Simulated data reproduced by permission. All rights reserved. Otis-Lennon School Ability Test: Seventh Edition. Copyright © 1996 by Harcourt Brace and Company. Simulated data reproduced by permission. All rights reserved.

ment test. If an abilities test was administered at the same time as the achievement test, these scores will typically also appear in summary format on the sticker. Figure 14.3 is a sticker summarizing the Stanford/9 and OLSAT results for Alissa Zyne. This sticker, for Alissa's ninth-grade results, would be placed in her cumulative folder with stickers from earlier testings and next to her eighth-grade sticker. Area Ⓐ of the sticker contains the scores in horizontal format (opposite of that for the student report) for all subtests and totals. Area Ⓑ contains summary information for the OLSAT that Alissa took at the same time as the Stanford/9. A variety of score types are typically available; the district selects those that are relevant for its purposes. Compare Figure 14.3 with 14.1 and 14.2, the student reports. The same raw scores (RS), scaled scores (SS), national percentile ranks and stanines (N/PR-S), and ability/achievement comparisons (AAC) that appear on the profiles appear also on the label. The holistic and analytic scores from the writing assessment are also captured.

Given the nature of the information included in the student report form (the raw scores, achievement/ability comparisons, and content clusters) and on the sticker, such information is clearly more appropriate for student record purposes and for teacher use than for dissemination to parents and students. The simpler home report (see Figure 14.4) is better suited for reporting to parents and others outside the school. The student's performance on each of the major subtests and on the battery is summarized graphically and verbally. Beware of this home report, however; it is a simple bar chart. The bars only indicate the percentile rank and should not be confused with percentile bands, which are included on the student report.

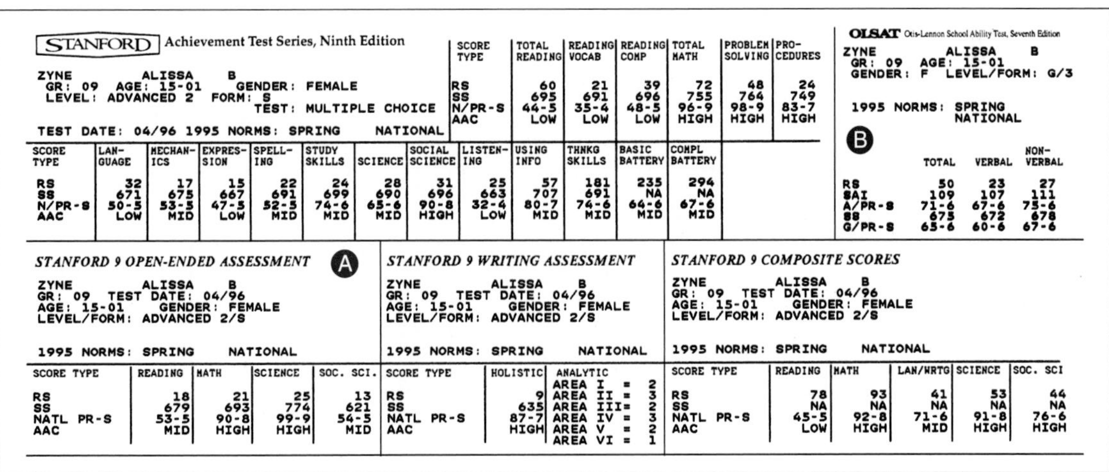

STANFORD Achievement Test Series, Ninth Edition

ZYNE ALISSA B
GR: 09 AGE: 15-01 GENDER: FEMALE
LEVEL: ADVANCED 2 FORM: S
TEST: MULTIPLE CHOICE
TEST DATE: 04/96 1995 NORMS: SPRING NATIONAL

SCORE TYPE	TOTAL READING	READING VOCAB	READING COMP	TOTAL MATH	PROBLEM SOLVING	PRO-CEDURES
RS	60	21	39	72	48	24
SS	695	691	696	755	764	749
N/PR-S	44-5	35-4	48-5	96-9	98-9	83-7
AAC	LOW	LOW	LOW	HIGH	HIGH	HIGH

SCORE TYPE	LAN-GUAGE	MECHAN-ICS	EXPRES-SION	SPELL-ING	STUDY SKILLS	SCIENCE	SOCIAL SCIENCE	LISTEN-ING	USING INFO	THNKG SKILLS	BASIC BATTERY	COMPL BATTERY
RS	32	17	15	22	24	28	31	25	57	181	235	294
SS	671	675	667	691	699	690	696	663	707	691	NA	NA
N/PR-S	50-5	53-5	47-5	52-5	74-6	65-6	90-8	32-4	80-7	74-6	64-6	67-6
AAC	LOW	MID	LOW	MID	MID	MID	HIGH	LOW	MID	MID	MID	MID

OLSAT Otis-Lennon School Ability Test, Seventh Edition

ZYNE ALISSA B
GR: 09 AGE: 15-01
GENDER: F LEVEL/FORM: G/3

1995 NORMS: SPRING NATIONAL

Ⓑ

	TOTAL	VERBAL	NON-VERBAL
RS	50	23	27
SAI	109	107	111
A/PR-S	71-6	67-6	75-6
SS	675	672	678
G/PR-S	65-6	60-6	67-6

STANFORD 9 OPEN-ENDED ASSESSMENT Ⓐ

ZYNE ALISSA B
GR: 09 TEST DATE: 04/96
AGE: 15-01 GENDER: FEMALE
LEVEL/FORM: ADVANCED 2/S

1995 NORMS: SPRING NATIONAL

SCORE TYPE	READING	MATH	SCIENCE	SOC. SCI.
RS	18	21	25	13
SS	679	693	774	621
NATL PR-S	53-5	90-8	99-9	54-5
AAC	MID	HIGH	HIGH	MID

STANFORD 9 WRITING ASSESSMENT

ZYNE ALISSA B
GR: 09 TEST DATE: 04/96
AGE: 15-01 GENDER: FEMALE
LEVEL/FORM: ADVANCED 2/S

1995 NORMS: SPRING NATIONAL

SCORE TYPE	HOLISTIC	ANALYTIC
		AREA I = 2
RS	9	AREA II = 3
SS	635	AREA III= 2
NATL PR-S	87-7	AREA IV = 3
AAC	HIGH	AREA V = 2
		AREA VI = 1

STANFORD 9 COMPOSITE SCORES

ZYNE ALISSA B
GR: 09 TEST DATE: 04/96
AGE: 15-01 GENDER: FEMALE
LEVEL/FORM: ADVANCED 2/S

1995 NORMS: SPRING NATIONAL

SCORE TYPE	READING	MATH	LAN/WRTG	SCIENCE	SOC. SCI
RS	78	93	41	53	44
SS	NA	NA	NA	NA	NA
NATL PR-S	45-5	92-8	71-6	91-8	76-6
AAC	LOW	HIGH	MID	HIGH	HIGH

Figure 14.3
Sticker label for Alissa Zyne for Stanford/9 and OLSAT results. *Source:* Stanford Achievement Test: Ninth Edition. Copyright © 1996 by Harcourt Brace and Company. Simulated data reproduced by permission. All rights reserved. Otis-Lennon School Ability Test: Seventh Edition. Copyright © 1996 by Harcourt Brace and Company. Simulated data reproduced by permission. All rights reserved.

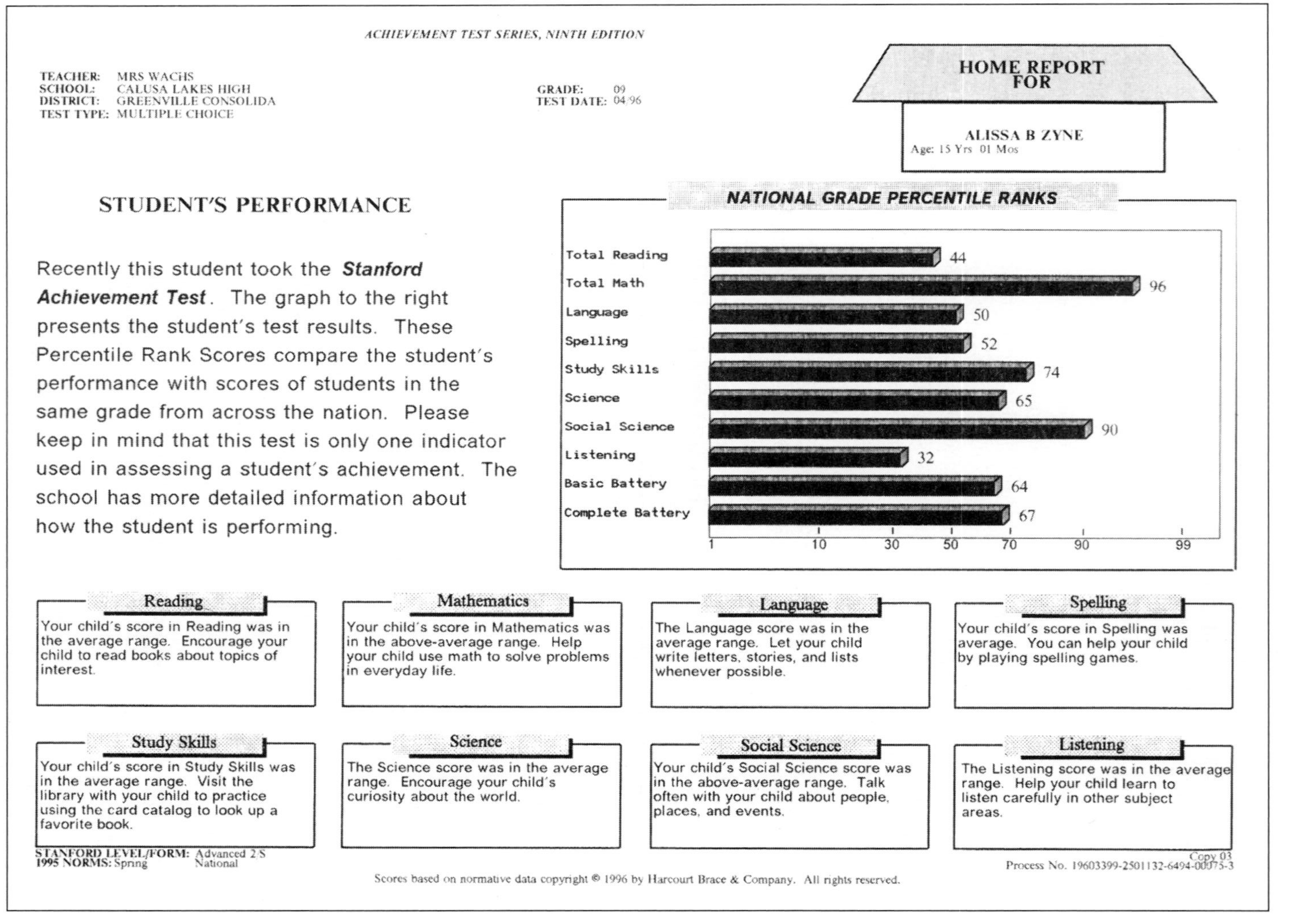
ACHIEVEMENT TEST SERIES, NINTH EDITION

TEACHER: MRS WACHS
SCHOOL: CALUSA LAKES HIGH
DISTRICT: GREENVILLE CONSOLIDA
TEST TYPE: MULTIPLE CHOICE

GRADE: 09
TEST DATE: 04/96

HOME REPORT FOR

ALISSA B ZYNE
Age: 15 Yrs 01 Mos

STUDENT'S PERFORMANCE

Recently this student took the ***Stanford Achievement Test***. The graph to the right presents the student's test results. These Percentile Rank Scores compare the student's performance with scores of students in the same grade from across the nation. Please keep in mind that this test is only one indicator used in assessing a student's achievement. The school has more detailed information about how the student is performing.

Reading
Your child's score in Reading was in the average range. Encourage your child to read books about topics of interest.

Mathematics
Your child's score in Mathematics was in the above-average range. Help your child use math to solve problems in everyday life.

Language
The Language score was in the average range. Let your child write letters, stories, and lists whenever possible.

Spelling
Your child's score in Spelling was average. You can help your child by playing spelling games.

Study Skills
Your child's score in Study Skills was in the average range. Visit the library with your child to practice using the card catalog to look up a favorite book.

Science
The Science score was in the average range. Encourage your child's curiosity about the world.

Social Science
Your child's Social Science score was in the above-average range. Talk often with your child about people, places, and events.

Listening
The Listening score was in the average range. Help your child learn to listen carefully in other subject areas.

STANFORD LEVEL/FORM: Advanced 2/S
1995 NORMS: Spring National

Copy 03
Process No. 19603399-2501132-6494-00075-3

Figure 14.4
Home Report for Alissa Zyne for Stanford/9 results. *Source:* Stanford Achievement Test: Ninth Edition. Copyright © 1996 by Harcourt Brace and Company. Simulated data reproduced by permission. All rights reserved.

A number of school districts with the resources and reason for doing so have created customized reports for various audiences. Figure 14.5 is a parent report for the Stanford/8 for a single student. The Dade County Public Schools (Miami, Florida) report standardized test scores to parents. With a large immigrant population, the district provides both numerical and graphic information and text in both English and Spanish. This report, to the parents of John Smith, explains at the top that John's performance was compared to that of children in the same grade throughout the nation. It lists national percentile scores for each subtest their son took. The actual national percentile ranks are marked with an "X" to the right. The dashed lines on either side of each X represent the percentile band for that subtest. Thus we can see that John is clearly better in Concepts of Number than in Language Mechanics. We can also see that the standard error of measurement for Language Mechanics is larger than that for Mathematics Application, for example. Stanines, per se, are not listed, but note the shaded areas of the graphic section. Percentiles in either the left or right shaded area indicate *below average* or *above average* performance, respectively. These are, of course, stanines 1-2-3 and 7-8-9. Stanines 4-5-6 are in the non-shaded area in the middle labeled *average*. John's report indicates that he is just below average in Reading Vocabulary and Mathematics Application; average in Reading Comprehension, Language Mechanics, and Mathematics Computation; and above average in Concepts of Number. At the bottom are explanations for both percentile ranks and percentile bands.

The Differential Aptitude Tests (DAT) also present results for individuals in terms of percentiles and stanines (see Figure 14.6). Area Ⓐ contains demographic information about the student, including norms used and level and form of the test taken. The scores are reported next across Area Ⓑ. The raw score out of a possible number of points (RS/NP), corresponding national percentile ranks (PR), and stanines (S) are given for each of the subtests for comparison with the same gender, opposite gender, and both combined (Combnd). The horizontal bars correspond to national percentile bands for same-gender norms (in this case, female) for the indicated subtests. For the DAT, a total Scholastic Aptitude score is obtained by adding the scores on two specific subtests: Verbal Reasoning and Numerical Reasoning (VR + NR).

The DAT individual report also contains two narrative areas. Area Ⓒ contains a statement that addresses the student's overall ability level (VR + NR) in relation to his or her post-secondary plans as reported by the student in another section of the instrument. In Area Ⓓ, brief explanations appear to explain what each of the subtests is about and how the student compared to other same-gender individuals. This area also includes a cautionary statement about the changing nature of aptitudes and the need for more than one information source when making plans for the future.

Lisa Martin's individual report (Figure 14.6) shows that, compared to other ninth-grade girls who were tested in the fall, she scored above the 50th percentile (median) in all areas except Perceptual Speed & Accuracy. Her highest percentile rank was in Numerical Reasoning (98), corresponding to the highest range; followed closely by Mechanical Reasoning (96), also in the highest range. These are Lisa's strengths of the areas tested. Her Perceptual Speed & Accuracy is in the low-average range as compared to other ninth-grade females and is a relative weakness for Lisa.

SCHOOL

XYZ EL.

GRADE— 07 SECTION ZZZ
PAGE 4

PARENT REPORT
STANFORD ACHIEVEMENT TESTS
DADE COUNTY SCHOOLS, 1992 -1993

STUDENT PROFILE FOR:

SMITH JOHN

I.D.— 9999999

Dear Parent:

The Stanford Achievement Test is administered to nearly all students in the Dade County Public Schools each year. These tests compare an individual's performance in certain skills to the average performance of other pupils at the same grade throughout the nation.

Below is a report of your child's scores on the tests and an explanation of the results. If you have any further questions, please contact your child's school.

Estimados padres:

La Prueba de Aprovechamiento Stanford (Stanford Achievement Test) se aplica a casi todos los estudiantes de las Escuelas Públicas del Condado de Dade cada año. Dichas pruebas comparan las aptitudes individuales en ciertas areas con el desempeño promedio de otros alumnos del mismo grado de toda la nación.

En la parte inferior se encuentra un informe de las clasificaciones de las pruebas de su hijo(a) y una explicacion de los resultados. Si tuviesan alguna otra pregunta al respecto, por favor, no dejen de comunicarse con la escuela de su hijo(a).

NATIONAL GRADE PERCENTILE BANDS

BELOW AVERAGE *Por debajo de promedio* — AVERAGE *Promedio* — ABOVE AVERAGE *Por encima de promedio*

	PERCEN-TILE *Porcen-taje*	1 5 10 20 30 40 50 60 70 80 90 95 99
READING COMPREHENSION	30	----X-----
READING VOCABULARY	23	----X----
LANGUAGE MECHANICS	40	------X-------
MATHEMATICS COMPUTATION	65	-----X----
CONCEPTS OF NUMBER	77	-------X-----
MATHEMATICS APPLICATION	21	----X----

1 5 10 20 30 40 50 60 70 80 90 95 99

BELOW AVERAGE *Por debajo de promedio* — AVERAGE *Promedio* — ABOVE AVERAGE *Por encima de promedio*

Percentile Ranks range from a low of 1 to a high of 99. If a student has a Percentile Rank of 70, for example, it means that this student obtained a score that is equal to or higher than 70 percent of the students in the comparison group.

The Percentile Bands to the right show that scores are approximate indicators of achievement. By comparing the bands, you can see whether the student did better in some subjects than in others. If two bands do not overlap, you may conclude that the differences between those two scores is indeed meaningful.

Las Clasificaciones del percentil varían desde un mínimo de 1 hasta un máximo de 99. Si un estudiante tiene un percentil de 70, por ejemplo, ésto significa que dicho estudiante obtuvo un resultado que es igual o más alto que el obtenido por el 70 por ciento de los estudiantes en el grupo de comparación.

La lista del percentil a la derecha muestra que los resultados son indicadores del nivel del aprovechamiento. Comparando las dos listas se puede ver si el estudiante trabajó mejor en algunas asignaturas que en otras. Si las dos listas no coinciden parcialmente, usted pudiera llegar a la conclusión de que la diferencia entre los dos resultados es muy significativa.

FM-1797ES Rev. (08-92)

Figure 14.5
District-produced parent report for John Smith's Stanford/8 results. Data were obtained from Stanford normative data and are fictitious. *Source:* Reproduced by permission from Harcourt Brace Jovanovich, Inc. and Dade County Public Schools.

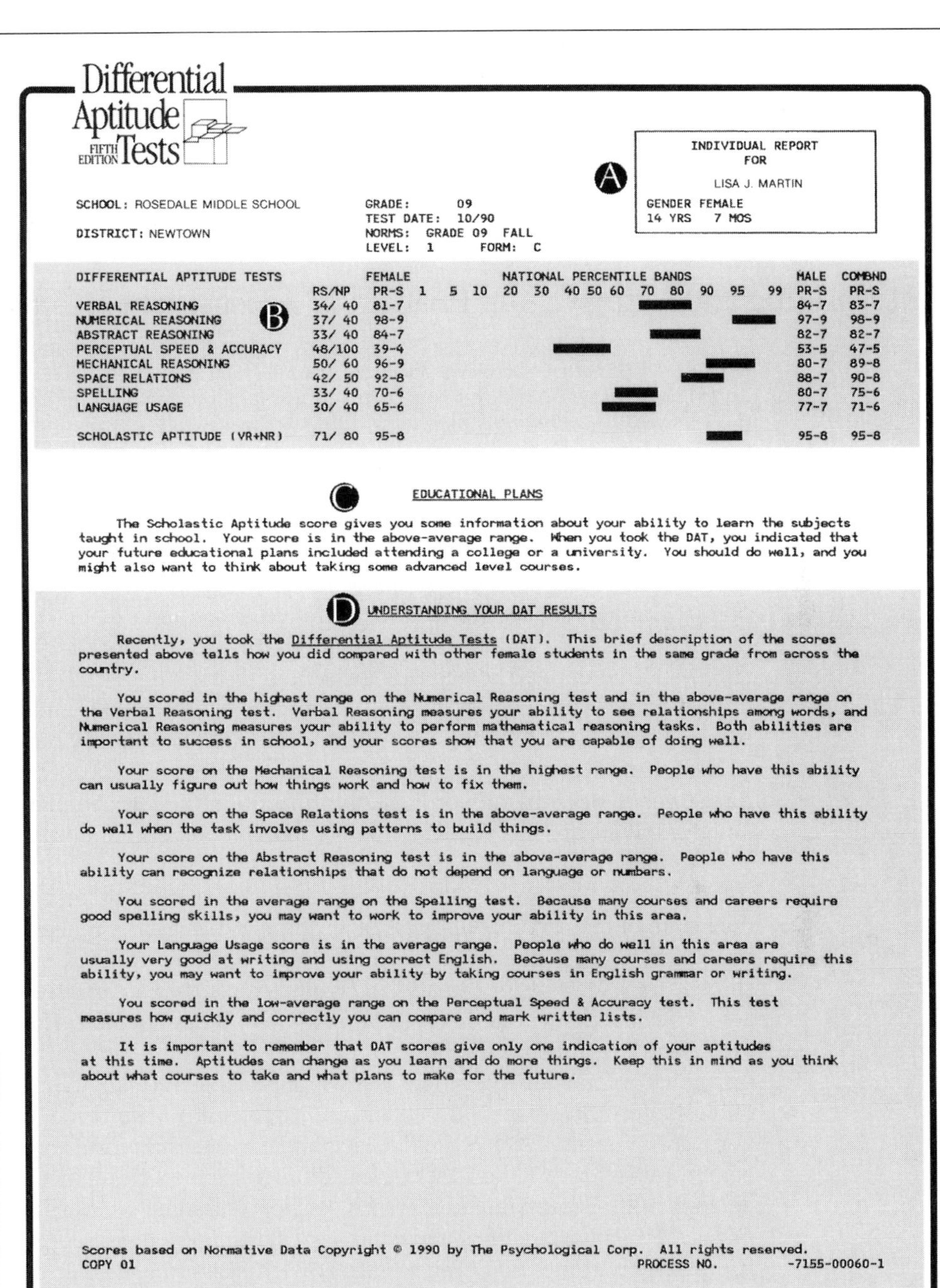

Differential Aptitude Tests

FIFTH EDITION

(A)

INDIVIDUAL REPORT FOR

LISA J. MARTIN

GENDER FEMALE
14 YRS 7 MOS

SCHOOL: ROSEDALE MIDDLE SCHOOL

DISTRICT: NEWTOWN

GRADE: 09
TEST DATE: 10/90
NORMS: GRADE 09 FALL
LEVEL: 1 FORM: C

(B)

DIFFERENTIAL APTITUDE TESTS	RS/NP	FEMALE PR-S	NATIONAL PERCENTILE BANDS (1 5 10 20 30 40 50 60 70 80 90 95 99)	MALE PR-S	COMBND PR-S
VERBAL REASONING	34/ 40	81-7		84-7	83-7
NUMERICAL REASONING	37/ 40	98-9		97-9	98-9
ABSTRACT REASONING	33/ 40	84-7		82-7	82-7
PERCEPTUAL SPEED & ACCURACY	48/100	39-4		53-5	47-5
MECHANICAL REASONING	50/ 60	96-9		80-7	89-8
SPACE RELATIONS	42/ 50	92-8		88-7	90-8
SPELLING	33/ 40	70-6		80-7	75-6
LANGUAGE USAGE	30/ 40	65-6		77-7	71-6
SCHOLASTIC APTITUDE (VR+NR)	71/ 80	95-8		95-8	95-8

(C) EDUCATIONAL PLANS

The Scholastic Aptitude score gives you some information about your ability to learn the subjects taught in school. Your score is in the above-average range. When you took the DAT, you indicated that your future educational plans included attending a college or a university. You should do well, and you might also want to think about taking some advanced level courses.

(D) UNDERSTANDING YOUR DAT RESULTS

Recently, you took the Differential Aptitude Tests (DAT). This brief description of the scores presented above tells how you did compared with other female students in the same grade from across the country.

You scored in the highest range on the Numerical Reasoning test and in the above-average range on the Verbal Reasoning test. Verbal Reasoning measures your ability to see relationships among words, and Numerical Reasoning measures your ability to perform mathematical reasoning tasks. Both abilities are important to success in school, and your scores show that you are capable of doing well.

Your score on the Mechanical Reasoning test is in the highest range. People who have this ability can usually figure out how things work and how to fix them.

Your score on the Space Relations test is in the above-average range. People who have this ability do well when the task involves using patterns to build things.

Your score on the Abstract Reasoning test is in the above-average range. People who have this ability can recognize relationships that do not depend on language or numbers.

You scored in the average range on the Spelling test. Because many courses and careers require good spelling skills, you may want to work to improve your ability in this area.

Your Language Usage score is in the average range. People who do well in this area are usually very good at writing and using correct English. Because many courses and careers require this ability, you may want to improve your ability by taking courses in English grammar or writing.

You scored in the low-average range on the Perceptual Speed & Accuracy test. This test measures how quickly and correctly you can compare and mark written lists.

It is important to remember that DAT scores give only one indication of your aptitudes at this time. Aptitudes can change as you learn and do more things. Keep this in mind as you think about what courses to take and what plans to make for the future.

COPY 01 PROCESS NO. -7155-00060-1

Actual size 8½" x 11"
Simulated data

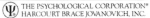

THE PSYCHOLOGICAL CORPORATION®
HARCOURT BRACE JOVANOVICH, INC.

Figure 14.6
Individual Report for Lisa Martin. *Source:* Differential Aptitude Tests: Fifth Edition. Copyright © 1990 by The Psychological Corporation. Reproduced by permission. All rights reserved.

As for her Educational Plans, Lisa's Scholastic Aptitude score is an indicator of how she might do in college based on her aptitude for college-level work. In Lisa's case, her aptitude seems to be in line with her plans to attend college.

Interpreting and Using Group Profiles of Assessment Results

Unless the instructional program is individualized, a teacher is also interested in analyzing the performance of her or his students as a group. This requires compiling the individual results into some sort of summary form for the class—a *group profile*. Of course, such a summary sheet may also be used for interpreting individual results if it contains all the necessary information. Some test companies provide forms for this purpose. The Comprehensive Test of Basic Skills (CTBS), for example, provides a Class Record Summary Sheet (see Figure 14.7). This form is typical in sophistication of those provided for the major national achievement batteries and presents both a graphic display and a brief narrative description of group performance in terms of median percentile ranks. It includes for each subtest the number of students tested and the derived scores that the school district requested—in this case, mean normal curve equivalents (MNCE), mean scale scores (MSS), and median national percentile ranks (MDNP). The bar chart to the right graphically presents the relative strengths and weaknesses of the class. A brief narrative appears below the column definitions to describe in words the information in the bar chart and the MDNP column for the group. The small box at the bottom contains administration information such as the test date and norms used.

Mr. Fowler, the teacher of the class represented in Figure 14.7, can easily see by the length of the bars that his class of 16 students has as its strengths Study Skills and Social Science. Their relative weaknesses are Spelling and Math Computation, the shortest bars. Mr. Fowler can also see that his class, when compared to other classes across subtests, is within the average range on all but Spelling. Their MDNP of 14.5 in Spelling puts them in stanine 3, or just slightly below average. Their MDNP of 24.0 on Math Computation puts them just within the average range in stanine 4. Overall (Total Battery) the class did better than 29 percent of the students in the national norm group. As the MDNPs are displayed here in bar chart form and not in percentile band form (refer to Figure 14.1), clear differences in performance are not so easily determined. It is probably safe for Mr. Fowler to assume a clear difference between the class's relative strengths and weaknesses, given the disparate percentile ranks. It is probably not safe, however, for Mr. Fowler to assume clear differences between, say, Study Skills and Science or Reading Vocabulary and Math Concepts & Application.

Another type of group profile simply lists students' names, derived scores for each student on each test, total scores for each student, and other optional information such as aptitude scores—a master list of individual test results. One way to think of this is to visualize a chart with summary stickers such as the type in Figure 14.3 attached in rows for each student in the class. This type of group profile

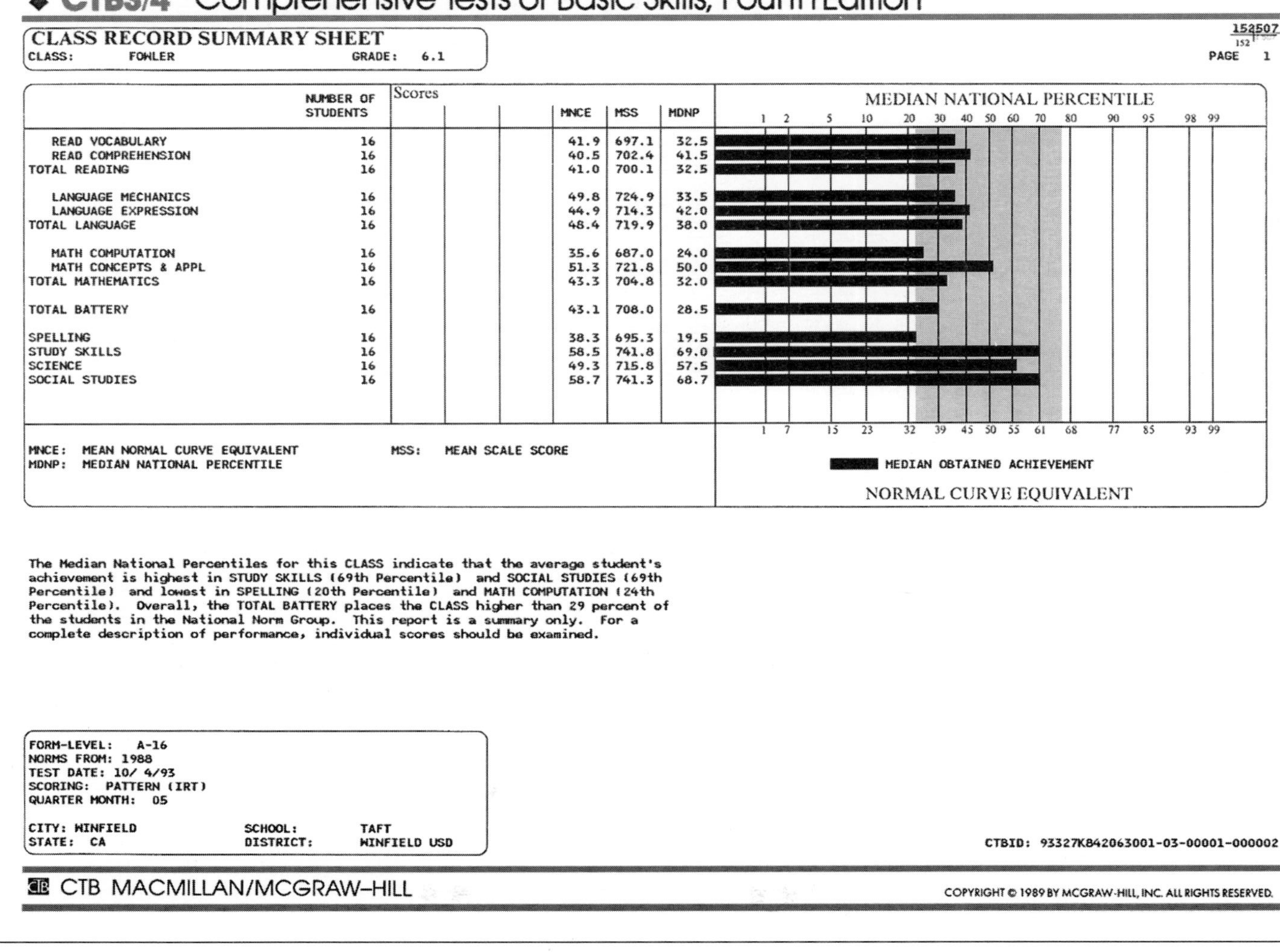

CTBS/4 Comprehensive Tests of Basic Skills, Fourth Edition

CLASS RECORD SUMMARY SHEET

CLASS: FOWLER GRADE: 6.1

152507

PAGE 1

	NUMBER OF STUDENTS	Scores			MNCE	MSS	MDNP
READ VOCABULARY	16				41.9	697.1	32.5
READ COMPREHENSION	16				40.5	702.4	41.5
TOTAL READING	16				41.0	700.1	32.5
LANGUAGE MECHANICS	16				49.8	724.9	33.5
LANGUAGE EXPRESSION	16				44.9	714.3	42.0
TOTAL LANGUAGE	16				48.4	719.9	38.0
MATH COMPUTATION	16				35.6	687.0	24.0
MATH CONCEPTS & APPL	16				51.3	721.8	50.0
TOTAL MATHEMATICS	16				43.3	704.8	32.0
TOTAL BATTERY	16				43.1	708.0	28.5
SPELLING	16				38.3	695.3	19.5
STUDY SKILLS	16				58.5	741.8	69.0
SCIENCE	16				49.3	715.8	57.5
SOCIAL STUDIES	16				58.7	741.3	68.7

MNCE: MEAN NORMAL CURVE EQUIVALENT MSS: MEAN SCALE SCORE
MDNP: MEDIAN NATIONAL PERCENTILE

The Median National Percentiles for this CLASS indicate that the average student's achievement is highest in STUDY SKILLS (69th Percentile) and SOCIAL STUDIES (69th Percentile) and lowest in SPELLING (20th Percentile) and MATH COMPUTATION (24th Percentile). Overall, the TOTAL BATTERY places the CLASS higher than 29 percent of the students in the National Norm Group. This report is a summary only. For a complete description of performance, individual scores should be examined.

FORM-LEVEL: A-16
NORMS FROM: 1988
TEST DATE: 10/ 4/93
SCORING: PATTERN (IRT)
QUARTER MONTH: 05

CITY: WINFIELD SCHOOL: TAFT
STATE: CA DISTRICT: WINFIELD USD

CTBID: 93327K842063001-03-00001-000002

CTB MACMILLAN/MCGRAW–HILL

Figure 14.7
Class Record Summary Sheet for Mr. Fowler's class. *Source:* Comprehensive Test of Basic Skills: Fourth Edition by CTB/McGraw-Hill. Copyright © 1989 by McGraw-Hill Companies, Inc. Reproduced by permission.

summary allows us to easily spot students who are exceptional in some way. If all of Eddie's scores correspond to stanines 1 and 2, he might well be a candidate for a special program; he may even have a physical problem (poor vision for example) or a learning disability. Conversely, if all of Ian's scores correspond to stanines 8 and 9, he probably is a candidate for a program for the gifted or some other type of accelerated program, if such is available. If students such as Eddie and Ian remain in the class, they require special activities and attention for optimum success. Another possibility is that Horace may have scores corresponding to stanine 5 or above in all areas except one, in which his score is in stanine 2. Depending upon the area of deficiency, this situation may suggest a problem with Horace or a need for special instruction. If the area of deficiency is Listening Comprehension, for example, he may have an auditory problem. Of course, such information could be obtained from individual profile sheets, but a summary chart or master list permits us to identify all such "exceptional" individuals easily. Such forms are very useful, and if they are not provided for a particular test, something similar can easily be constructed.

Another use for the master list of individual results or teacher-constructed summary chart is in planning future instructional objectives and strategies. We can, for example, examine the stanine pattern for each subtest by looking down the column for that subtest at stanines. If a majority of the students scored below average in a particular area (stanines 1 through 3), they may not have received sufficient instruction in that area, especially if other measures indicate that the class has average scholastic ability.

If the test battery is taken early in the school year, the teacher can analyze the results and make any necessary adjustments in instruction before the end of the year. Mr. Fowler (Figure 14.7), in reviewing the summary chart for his 16 sixth-graders as a group, for example, may do just that. He also may make comparisons across subtests. If the students are clustered in the higher stanines in some areas and the lower stanines in others, a change in emphasis may be called for so that more time is devoted to the areas of deficiency. Mr. Fowler might wish to spend more time on spelling and a bit less time on social studies or study skills. Results may also suggest areas in which grouping would be appropriate. If most of the students are clustered in a given stanine category (average, for example), no grouping is called for. If, on the other hand, there are two or three obvious clusters, indicating a number of students in two or three stanine categories, grouping might be a reasonable strategy. For example, if Mr. Fowler's students tend to cluster into stanines 3 and 6 on Reading Vocabulary (although, overall, stanine 4 characterizes the group), he could use this information to separate his students into two groups when working on reading vocabulary and target his instruction accordingly. Teachers can use stanine patterns to group students for instruction in any of the tested areas.

But what if school-wide testing is done in the spring? With the time it typically takes for scoring and reporting, the above strategies for instructional planning during the same school year are not feasible. Teachers have used these same strategies, however, with students at the beginning of the school year based on the previous spring's results. They create a group profile or summary chart using the stanines of their incoming students by subtest. These are usually available in the students' cumulative folders. As with any initial grouping strategy, decisions should be based on several indicators of performance, including teacher observation, and should be kept flexible to reflect growth in achievement. Further, spring assessments can identify a teacher whose classes in the last few years have consistently scored low in an area, such as thinking skills. In this case, careful consideration should be given as to whether his or her instruction is effective in helping students achieve the district's outcomes and whether the outcomes are validly assessed by the test.

Group results can be interpreted on many levels—classroom, school, district, county, and so forth. At all levels, similar procedures are applied as at the classroom level, and similar decisions are made. Results at the district level may suggest, for example, that more resources should be directed toward the science program. One problem frequently associated with analysis of group results arises when comparisons are made between and among groups (like schools and districts). Such comparisons are frequently made (by the media, for example) based solely on test results and do not take into consideration relevant factors such as other characteristics of the students in the schools being compared. One school may have higher achievement scores overall than another but may also have correspondingly higher scholastic ability scores. Such comparisons, whether at the classroom level or the district level, are valid only to the degree that students are comparable on other variables such as ability and socio-economic status. For example, comparing the achievement scores of two schools with similar populations based on variables such as socio-economic status and school ability is valid. Comparing the achievement scores of two schools that are dissimilar based on these variables is not valid. The principle is the same as that involved in determining whether a norm group is appropriate.

Summary

Interpreting the Results of Standardized Assessments

Most assessment results are interpretable by any person who has had a reasonably comprehensive assessment course. Proper interpretation of assessment results requires the recognition that although many tests do provide very accurate estimates, they do not measure with the same precision that yardsticks do. Intelligent interpretation also requires knowledge of the test in question; what a given score means depends upon such factors as what the test actually measures as well as its indices of validity and reliability (for example, its estimated standard error of measurement). Teachers should resist the temptation to use criterion-referenced interpretations of norm-referenced tests as indicators of achievement or non-achievement of classroom outcomes. As more high-quality criterion-referenced tests are constructed for criterion-referenced purposes, both by test publishers and skilled teachers, these should be used to determine what students can and cannot do. Although any number of raw score equivalents may be available in norms tables, one or several of these are generally selected for presentation on individual or group profile sheets; these permit easy comparison of relative performance on a number of subtests.

Interpreting and Using Individual Profiles of Assessment Results

The meaning of an individual raw score depends upon what was assessed, the composition of the norm group, and the values of the individual's derived scores. Some test manuals provide tables for more than one norm group or for sub-groups within a norm group; in such cases it is important that the most appropriate tables be selected for interpretation purposes. Although it is usually a safe assumption, you should check to make sure that derived scores for different subtests are based on the same norm group or else relative performance across subject areas cannot be validly interpreted. Perhaps the greatest source of score misinterpretation comes from thinking of the average score of a norm group as a goal for all students.

An *individual profile* presents raw scores or one or more derived scores or both for each of a number of subtests in a graphic or tabular manner. An individual profile permits us to identify a student's relative strengths and weaknesses at a glance. The derived scores most often presented on a profile sheet are percentile ranks, stanines, and grade equivalents. Profile sheets of most major tests provide an explanation of the contents of the profile and directions for interpretation. Directions on profile sheets typically include reference to the fact that every score reflects some measurement error and should be thought of as being the midpoint in some range or band of scores (usually those scores which fall between $\pm$1SEM). Using the overlapping bands concept, a true difference in performance on any two subtests is indicated only if the bands for those subtests do not overlap at all.

For stanines, the directions typically suggest that in comparing performance on any two subtests, a difference of only one stanine probably does not reflect a true difference in performance; a difference of two or more stanines probably does. The profile gives us an indication of each student's performance or ability compared to a given norm group; it also provides information concerning the student's relative strengths and weaknesses. School districts with the resources to do so can customize reports for various audiences. Full interpretation of achievement requires additional knowledge concerning the individual—an index of mental ability, for example.

Interpreting and Using Group Profiles of Assessment Results

A teacher is also interested in analyzing the performance of her or his students as a group; this requires the compilation of the individual results into some sort of summary form or *group profile.* A basic class summary sheet has spaces for student names, derived scores (grade equivalents, percentile ranks, stanines) for each student on each test, total scores for each student, and other information such as school ability scores. Such summary forms allow us to easily spot students who are exceptional in some way, such as students who are candidates for special remedial or advanced programs. Many publishers also provide some type of group profile that summarizes results for a class as a whole.

Stanine summary figures permit us to compare a class as a whole with the norm group; this comparison will give a rough estimate of where the class is with respect to achievement. A stanine summary chart can be used in a number of ways to plan future instructional outcomes and strategies. A stanine summary chart for a class at the beginning of the school year can be easily constructed from cumulative folders containing the previous spring's testing results.

Group results can be interpreted on many levels—classroom, school, district, and county, for example. One problem frequently associated with the analysis of group results arises when comparisons between and among groups (like schools) are based solely on test results and do not take into consideration other relevant factors such as the characteristics of the students. Group comparisons, whether at the classroom level or the district level, are valid only to the degree that students in the groups are comparable on other variables such as ability and socio-economic status.

Try These

I. Examine the student profile sticker for Evan Stone (Figure 14.8) and answer the following questions regarding his performance.

Questions:

1. What tests, levels, and forms did Evan take?
2. What norms are Evan's performance compared to?
3. What is Evan's age and grade level at the time of testing?
4. What is Evan's best subject as indicated by the percentile ranks?

STANFORD Achievement Test Series, Ninth Edition

STONE EVAN M
GR: 04 AGE: 10-04 GENDER: MALE
LEVEL: INTERMED 1 FORM: S
TEST: MULTIPLE CHOICE
TEST DATE: 04/96 1995 NORMS: SPRING NATIONAL

SCORE TYPE	TOTAL READING	READING VOCAB	READING COMP	TOTAL MATH	PROBLEM SOLVING	PROCEDURES
RS	55	19	36	61	41	20
SS	628	611	636	650	669	628
N/PR-S	40-5	28-4	49-5	74-6	87-7	52-5
AAC	LOW	LOW	LOW	MID	MID	LOW

SCORE TYPE	LANGUAGE	MECHANICS	EXPRESSION	SPELLING	STUDY SKILLS	SCIENCE	SOCIAL SCIENCE	LISTENING	USING INFO	THNKG SKILLS	BASIC BATTERY	COMPL BATTERY
RS	27	15	12	17	25	35	39	26	59	160	211	285
SS	614	623	606	611	656	677	737	626	680	642	NA	NA
N/PR-S	37-4	44-5	33-4	36-4	73-6	91-8	99-9	31-4	91-8	70-6	50-5	64-6
AAC	LOW	LOW	LOW	LOW	MID	HIGH	HIGH	LOW	HIGH	MID	LOW	MID

OLSAT Otis-Lennon School Ability Test, Seventh Edition

STONE EVAN M
GR: 04 AGE: 10-04
GENDER: M LEVEL/FORM: E/3

1995 NORMS: SPRING NATIONAL

	TOTAL	VERBAL	NON-VERBAL
RS	51	26	25
SAI	113	114	110
A/PR-S	79-7	81-7	73-6
SS	638	643	633
G/PR-S	82-7	84-7	77-7

STANFORD 9 OPEN-ENDED ASSESSMENT

STONE EVAN M
GR: 04 TEST DATE: 04/96
AGE: 10-04 GENDER: MALE
LEVEL/FORM: INTERMEDIATE 1/S

1995 NORMS: SPRING NATIONAL

SCORE TYPE	READING	MATH	SCIENCE	SOC. SCI.
RS	11	16	20	23
SS	576	617	645	669
NATL PR-S	23-4	61-6	87-7	99-9
AAC	LOW	LOW	MID	HIGH

STANFORD 9 WRITING ASSESSMENT

STONE EVAN M
GR: 04 TEST DATE: 04/96
AGE: 10-04 GENDER: MALE
LEVEL/FORM: INTERMEDIATE 1/S

1995 NORMS: SPRING NATIONAL

SCORE TYPE	HOLISTIC	ANALYTIC
		AREA I = 1
RS	7	AREA II = 1
SS	595	AREA III= 2
NATL PR-S	75-6	AREA IV = 1
AAC	MID	AREA V = 2
		AREA VI = 1

STANFORD 9 COMPOSITE SCORES

STONE EVAN M
GR: 04 TEST DATE: 04/96
AGE: 10-04 GENDER: MALE
LEVEL/FORM: INTERMEDIATE 1/S

1995 NORMS: SPRING NATIONAL

SCORE TYPE	READING	MATH	LAN/WRTG	SCIENCE	SOC. SCI
RS	66	77	34	55	62
SS	NA	NA	NA	NA	NA
NATL PR-S	33-4	69-6	57-5	89-8	99-9
AAC	LOW	LOW	MID	HIGH	HIGH

Figure 14.8
Summary sticker label for Evan Stone. *Source:* Stanford Achievement Test: Ninth Edition.

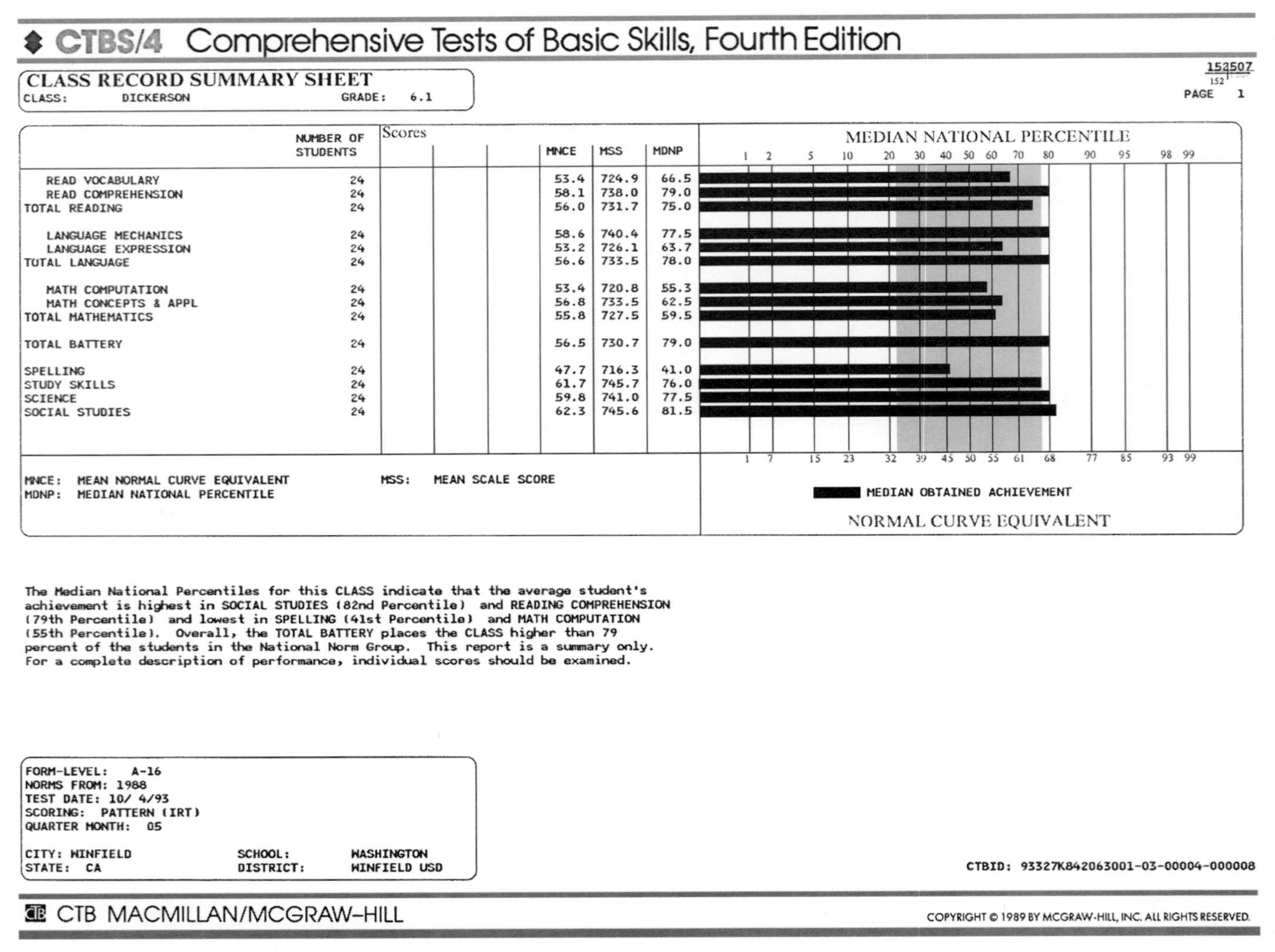

CTBS/4 Comprehensive Tests of Basic Skills, Fourth Edition

152507
152
PAGE 1

CLASS RECORD SUMMARY SHEET
CLASS: DICKERSON GRADE: 6.1

	NUMBER OF STUDENTS	Scores			MNCE	MSS	MDNP
READ VOCABULARY	24				53.4	724.9	66.5
READ COMPREHENSION	24				58.1	738.0	79.0
TOTAL READING	24				56.0	731.7	75.0
LANGUAGE MECHANICS	24				58.6	740.4	77.5
LANGUAGE EXPRESSION	24				53.2	726.1	63.7
TOTAL LANGUAGE	24				56.6	733.5	78.0
MATH COMPUTATION	24				53.4	720.8	55.3
MATH CONCEPTS & APPL	24				56.8	733.5	62.5
TOTAL MATHEMATICS	24				55.8	727.5	59.5
TOTAL BATTERY	24				56.5	730.7	79.0
SPELLING	24				47.7	716.3	41.0
STUDY SKILLS	24				61.7	745.7	76.0
SCIENCE	24				59.8	741.0	77.5
SOCIAL STUDIES	24				62.3	745.6	81.5

MNCE: MEAN NORMAL CURVE EQUIVALENT
MDNP: MEDIAN NATIONAL PERCENTILE
MSS: MEAN SCALE SCORE

The Median National Percentiles for this CLASS indicate that the average student's achievement is highest in SOCIAL STUDIES (82nd Percentile) and READING COMPREHENSION (79th Percentile) and lowest in SPELLING (41st Percentile) and MATH COMPUTATION (55th Percentile). Overall, the TOTAL BATTERY places the CLASS higher than 79 percent of the students in the National Norm Group. This report is a summary only. For a complete description of performance, individual scores should be examined.

FORM-LEVEL: A-16
NORMS FROM: 1988
TEST DATE: 10/ 4/93
SCORING: PATTERN (IRT)
QUARTER MONTH: 05

CITY: WINFIELD SCHOOL: WASHINGTON
STATE: CA DISTRICT: WINFIELD USD

CTBID: 93327K842063001-03-00004-000008

CTB MACMILLAN/MCGRAW-HILL

Figure 14.9
Class Record Summary Sheet for Ms. Dickerson's class. *Source:* Comprehensive Test of Basic Skills: Fourth Edition by CTB/McGraw-Hill. Copyright © 1989 by McGraw-Hill Companies, Inc. Reproduced by permission.

5. For which subjects can you say there is a clear difference in performance (ones for which the stanines differ by at least 2)?
6. Given Evan's OLSAT Verbal SAI, percentile rank, and stanine, what can you say about his achievement in the areas of reading and language?
7. What is Evan's age percentile rank and stanine on the total OLSAT?

II. Examine the class profile for Ms. Dickerson's students at Washington Middle School (Figure 14.9) and answer the following questions regarding their performance.

Questions

1. What test did the students take?
2. How many students took the test?
3. What does MDNP mean?
4. What are the class's strengths and weaknesses as reflected in the subtest MDNPs?
5. What do the horizontal "stripes" in the area labeled "Median National Percentile" mean?
6. For what subjects is there a clear difference in performance?
7. How did they do overall?

Answers

I. 1. The Stanford Achievement Test, Ninth Edition (Stanford/9), Level Intermediate 1, Form S; and the Otis-Lennon School Ability Test, Seventh Edition (OLSAT/7), Level E, Form 3.

2. 1995 national norms for spring testing were used for all tests.
3. Age = 10 years, 4 months; grade = 4.
4. Evan is practically off the chart in Social Science (PR99) and very strong in Science and Using Information (both at stanine 8).
5. There are a number of them. For example, he is clearly better in Total Math than in Language (stanines 6 and 4, respectively), and his Thinking Skills are clearly better than his Listening.
6. His verbal ability (PR = 81; S = 7) indicates that he is capable of higher achievement in these areas than he presently exhibits. Perhaps the teacher should investigate why this seems to be so. When compared to others of similar ability (AAC) there are many areas in which he compares to the bottom 23% of the group. Perhaps Evan chooses to "coast" in these areas and shine in Social Science. Alternatively, the verbal portion of the OLSAT may not correlate well with those particular portions of the Stanford/9.
7. 79 and 7, respectively.

II. 1. The Comprehensive Test of Basic Skills, Fourth Edition (CTBS/4).

2. 24.

3. Median (MD) National (N) Percentile (P).

4. The class average achievement is highest in Social Studies (82nd percentile) and Reading Comprehension (79th percentile). Their weakest areas as a class are Spelling (41st percentile) and Math Computation (55th percentile). You could have looked at the numbers or read the verbal interpretation. Bonus points for you if you looked at both!

5. The stripes are bars corresponding to the "median obtained achievement," or MDNPs. The CTBS/4 Class Record Summary Sheet does not use the band concept in graphically displaying percentiles, opting instead for a bar chart.

6. This one is tricky without percentile bands or specific stanines, but we can see that the bars for Reading Comprehension, Language Mechanics, Total Language, Total Battery, Science, and Social Studies all extend into the unshaded area above average, at the lower end of stanine 7. The Spelling bar extends not quite halfway into the shaded area, probably stanine 4 or 5. This would be the clearest difference. The others are probably only one stanine apart, if that.

7. On the Total Battery the class performed as well as or better than 79% of the students in the national norm group. Here again, you could have looked at the MDNP for the Total Battery or read the verbal interpretation. Bonus points for doing both.

APPENDIX A

The Standards for Teacher Competence in the Educational Assessment of Students

I. *Choosing assessment methods appropriate for instructional decisions.*

A. Use concepts of assessment error and validity when developing or selecting approaches to classroom assessment of students.
   1. Understand how valid assessment data supports instructional activities (e.g., providing feedback, diagnosing group or individual learning needs, planning for individualized educational programs, motivating students, and evaluating instructional procedures).
   2. Understand how invalid information affects instructional decisions about students.

B. Use and evaluate assessment options open to them.
   1. Consider (among other things) cultural, social, economic, and language backgrounds of students.
   2. Aware that different assessment approaches:
      a. Are incompatible with certain instructional goals, and
      b. May impact quite differently on their teaching.

C. Know for each assessment approach used, its appropriateness for making decisions about their students.

D. Know where to find information about and reviews of various assessment methods.

E. "Assessment options" include:
   1. Text- and curriculum-embedded questions and tests.
   2. Standardized criterion-referenced and norm-referenced tests.
   3. Oral questioning.
   4. Spontaneous and structured performance assessments.
   5. Portfolios.
   6. Exhibitions.
   7. Demonstrations.
   8. Rating scales.
   9. Writing samples.

10. Paper-and-pencil tests.
11. Seatwork and homework.
12. Peer- and self-assessments.
13. Student records.
14. Observations.
15. Questionnaires.
16. Interviews.
17. Projects.
18. Products.
19. Others' opinions.

II. *Developing assessment methods appropriate for instructional decisions. (Methods may include some listed in I.E, above.)*

A. Plan the collection of information that facilitates the decisions they will make.

B. Follow appropriate principles for developing and using assessment methods in their teaching.

C. Avoid common pitfalls in student assessment.

D. Select methods and techniques appropriate to the teacher's instructional intent.

E. Use student data to analyze the quality of each assessment technique they use without relying on an assessment specialist.

III. *Administering, scoring, and interpreting the results of both externally produced and teacher-produced assessment methods.*

A. Interpret informal and formal teacher-produced assessment results, including students' performances in class and on homework assignments.

B. Use the following in ways that produce consistent results:
1. Guides for scoring essay questions and projects.
2. Stencils for scoring response-choice questions.
3. Scales for rating performance assessments.

C. Administer standardized achievement tests.

D. Interpret commonly reported scores from standardized achievement tests:
1. Percentile ranks.
2. Percentile band scores.
3. Standard scores.
4. Grade equivalents.

E. Have a conceptual understanding of summary indexes commonly reported with assessment results—measures of:
1. Central tendency.
2. Dispersion.
3. Relationships.
4. Reliability.
5. Errors of measurement.

F. Apply concepts of score and summary indexes in ways that enhance teachers' use of the assessments they develop.
   1. Analyze assessment results to identify students' strengths and weaknesses.
   2. Given inconsistent results, seek other explanations for the discrepancy or other data to attempt to resolve the uncertainty before arriving at a decision.
   3. Use assessment methods in ways that:
      a. Encourage students' educational development, and
      b. Do not inappropriately increase students' anxiety levels.

IV. *Using assessment results when making decisions about individual student, planning teaching, developing curriculum, and school improvement.*

A. Use accumulated assessment information to organize a sound instructional plan for facilitating students' educational development.

B. Interpret results correctly when planning or evaluating instruction or curriculum, and avoid common errors (e.g., basing decisions on scores that lack curriculum validity).

C. Become informed about results of local, regional, state, and national assessments and about their appropriate use for student, classroom, school, district, state, and national educational improvement.

V. *Developing valid pupil grading procedures which use pupil assessments. (Grading is defined as indicating both a student's level of performance and a teacher's valuing of that performance.)*

A. Devise, implement, and explain a procedure for developing grades composed of marks from various assignments, projects, in-class activities, quizzes, tests, and/or other assessments that they may use.

B. Understand and articulate why the grades they assign are rational, fair, and justified, acknowledging that such grades also reflect their preferences and judgments.

C. Recognize and avoid faulty grading procedures such as using grades as punishment.

D. Improve the validity of the interpretations made from grades about students' attainments by evaluating and modifying grading procedures.

VI. *Communicating assessment results to students, parents and other lay audiences, and other educators.*

A. Understand and appropriately explain how the interpretation of a student's assessment must be moderated by the student's socio-economic, cultural, language, and other background factors.

B. Explain that assessment results do not imply that such background factors limit a student's ultimate educational development.

C. Communicate to parents, guardians, and students how they may assess the student's educational progress.

D. Understand and explain the importance of taking measurement errors into account when using assessments to make decisions about individual students.

E. Explain the limitations of formal and informal assessment methods.

F. Explain printed reports of the results of students' assessments at the classroom, school district, state, and national levels.

VII. *Recognizing unethical, illegal, and otherwise inappropriate assessment methods and uses of assessment information.*

A. Know the laws and case decisions that affect their classroom, school district, and state assessment practices.

B. Be aware that various assessment procedures can be misused or overused resulting in harmful consequences such as embarrassing students, violating a student's right to confidentiality, and inappropriately using standardized test scores to measure teaching effectiveness.

Standard	Chapter
1. Choose assessment methods appropriate for instructional decisions.	2, 3, 4, 5, 6, 7, 8, 9, 10
2. Develop assessment methods appropriate for instructional decisions.	2, 3, 4, 5, 6, 7, 8, 9, 10
3. Administer, score, and interpret the results of both externally produced and teacher-produced assessment methods.	2, 5, 13, 14
4. Use assessment results when making decisions about individual students, planning teaching, developing curriculum, and school improvement.	2, 10
5. Develop valid grading procedures that use student assessments.	12
6. Communicate assessment results to students, parents and other lay audiences, and other educators.	11, 12, 14
7. Recognize unethical, illegal, and otherwise inappropriate assessment methods and uses of assessment information.	1, 3, 13

Figure A.1
The Standards for Teacher Competence in the Educational Assessment of Students (AFT/NCME/NEA) and the related chapters in *Classroom Assessment for Teachers.*

APPENDIX B

The Affective Domain: Description and Classified Examples

A Description of the Affective Domain

In the past, education has been criticized for paying too much attention to cognitive outcomes and not being concerned enough with the feelings and attitudes of students. The affective domain deals with such outcomes.

The taxonomy of affective outcomes, developed by Krathwohl and his associates, deals with outcomes that are difficult to promote and to assess.[1] Outcomes in the affective domain relate to such intangibles as feelings, attitudes, interests, and values. The categories represent a hierarchy of acceptance ranging from willingness to receive or attend, to characterization by a value. As an individual moves up the hierarchy an internalization process is evident, a process that begins with total rejection of an entity and culminates in total acceptance. All educational efforts have affective outcomes, though not necessarily in a formal sense. All teachers, for example, certainly want students to feel positively toward their particular subject areas, but they do not often have specific affective outcomes. Thus, there are frequently no organized efforts made to foster achievement of such outcomes or to assess affective outcomes. The last 15 to 30 years have seen a great increase in interest in affective outcomes, and, in fact, a large number of programs have been funded whose outcomes were exclusively affective. Even endeavors with primarily cognitive outcomes have been concerned with the affective impact of their curriculum, program, or project.

The intent of articulating all outcomes is to identify observable, assessable behaviors from which we can infer learning. This is clearly more difficult for affective outcomes. Too often, achievement of affective outcomes is determined through administration of self-report assessments. Such measures typically ask people to indicate how they feel about the topic of interest and entail a number of problems. It has been shown, for example, that people frequently give what they perceive to be socially acceptable responses rather than expressing their true

---

[1] *Taxonomy of Educational Objectives, Handbook II: Affective Domain,* by D. R. Krathwohl, B. S. Bloom, and B. B. Masia, 1964, New York: David McKay.

feelings. It is much better, when feasible, to have outcomes involving actions rather than self-report. It would be a more valid assessment of whether a student enjoys reading, for example, to find out if the student has voluntarily checked any books out of the library rather than to ask, "Do you enjoy reading?" Typical action verbs for affective outcomes include: respond, choose, prefer, volunteer, and participate. In practice, assessment of affective outcomes too frequently involves little more than asking for written reactions or opinions on an open-ended questionnaire with questions such as, "Do you feel that you benefited from participation in the program? Why?"

There is a feeling among certain educators and non-educators that the school has no right to attempt to shape or to interfere with students' values. They believe that affective outcomes should be the concern of a student's family or religious group. Most people, however, recognize that a basic function of the school in a democratic society is to assist students in achieving independence in judgments and actions, not to advocate particular political or sectarian views. Further, the school should strongly refrain from encouraging conformity to some arbitrary group norm of behavior. It is generally agreed, however, that outcomes based on "the belief in the dignity and worth of the individual without regard to race, religion, income, or ethnic background" are acceptable because these are basic values of our country as established by the Constitution. Thus, outcomes related to respect for others, support for the law, and freedom of religion, for example, are perfectly legitimate in the school curriculum.[2]

Below is a brief description of each of the major categories of the affective taxonomy of educational outcomes. The general outcome "values poetry" has been used to illustrate how degree of acceptance of a value progressively increases at each level of the taxonomy.

1.00 Receiving. At this level the student is sensitized to the phenomenon of interest to the extent that he or she is willing to receive or to pay attention to it. (For example, listens attentively when the teacher reads a poem to the class.)

2.00 Responding. At this level the student is sufficiently motivated or interested to the extent that she or he makes an active response. (For example, answers questions related to a poem that has been read to the class.)

3.00 Valuing. At this level the student acknowledges or recognizes that something has value and is worthwhile. (For example, chooses reading poetry as a free-period activity.)

4.00 Organization. At this level the student incorporates values into an organized, hierarchical value system such that some are more important or internalized than others. (For example, checks a book of poetry out of the library to read on her or his own time.)

---

[2]Based on discussion in "Assessing Educational Achievement in the Affective" by R. W. Tyler, Spring 1973, *NCME, 4*(3), and "Should Public Schools Teach Values?" by E. D. Davis, 1984, *Phi Delta Kappan, 65*(5), pp. 358–360.

5.00 Characterization by a value or value complex. At this level the student has so completely internalized a value that it is a dominant characteristic that affects behavior in a consistent way. (For example, it is at this level that it would be widely recognized that "Michael loves poetry" or "Michael reads poetry every chance he gets.")

Concerning the highest level of the taxonomy, characterization, the authors of the affective taxonomy point out:

> Rarely, if ever, are the sights of educational objectives set to this level of the *Affective Taxonomy*. Realistically, formal education generally cannot reach this level, at least in our society.[3]

To a lesser extent, the above statement also applies to organization (Level 4.00). As you can imagine, assessing whether an organization or characterization-level affective outcome has been achieved can be tricky. It can be argued that assessment of behaviors at this level is not within the purview of the school. At the very least, it is not likely that teachers will check to see if students are checking out poetry books to read on their own time.

Examples of Instructional Outcomes for the Affective Domain

Some of the same problems inherent in classifying cognitive outcomes are also present in attempts to classify outcomes in the affective domain. The nature of the behavior described and the experiences prior to learning the behavior are sometimes the primary determiners of where the outcome should be categorized. Again, the author of the outcome's intent is not always clear. Included below are examples of outcomes of the first three levels of the taxonomy—those with which formal education typically deals.

Receiving (Attending)

Recognizes that there may be more than one acceptable point of view.

Develops an awareness of aesthetic factors in architecture.

The student is aware of the feelings of others.

Accepts as co-helpers in the classroom other human beings without regard to race, sex, national origin, religion, or cultural background.

Develops a sensitivity to the importance of keeping current on matters of a political or social nature.

---

[3] D. R. Krathwohl, B. S. Bloom, and B. B. Masia, 1964 (p. 165).

Responding

Completes his or her homework on a regular basis.

Complies with health regulations.

Regularly chooses to read as an activity.

Voluntarily reads magazines, books, and newspapers designed for his or her age group.

Practices safe bicycle, pedestrian, playground, home, and school safety rules and habits.

Displays willingness to contribute to a group of which he or she is a member.

Accepts responsibility for his or her actions.

Enjoys reading books of various types on a variety of topics.

Valuing

Exhibits a sense of responsibility for listening to and engaging in public discussion.

Desires to attain and maintain wellness (optimum health).

Examines a variety of viewpoints on controversial issues with the intent of forming his or her own opinion about them.

Encourages participation of the more reluctant members of a group of which he or she is a member.

APPENDIX C

The Psychomotor Domain: Description and Classified Examples

A Description of the Psychomotor Domain

According to the authors of the affective taxonomy, the psychomotor domain entails physical abilities, those involving muscular or motor skills, manipulation of objects, or neuromuscular coordination. The task of taxonomy development is considerably more complex in the psychomotor domain because of the large cognitive component involved in many psychomotor outcomes. Actually, all learning involves all three domains to varying degrees. For example, the outcome "writes a complete sentence" clearly has a cognitive component (such as knowledge of the parts of a sentence), an affective component (such as willingness to respond), and a psychomotor component (such as neuromuscular coordination). The domains tend to complement each other. How a student feels about learning and the learning environment, for example, influences the student's actual learning. A student who enjoys learning probably achieves more, and, conversely, success in a certain area encourages positive attitudes about that area. Further, there is a psychomotor component in many cognitive outcomes and a cognitive component in many psychomotor outcomes. When we classify an outcome as being in one of the three domains we do so on the basis of its primary focus and intent. Thus, although reading involves an affective and a psychomotor component, the intent is cognitive; in music appreciation the intent is affective; and in gymnastics the intent is psychomotor. Psychomotor outcomes, however, involve such a large cognitive component that it is difficult to identify the strictly physical aspects of desired skills.

It may not even be possible to classify psychomotor outcomes into a hierarchy of categories using a classification system that is generally acceptable to most educators. Or it may be that the best approach just has not been conceived yet. In any event, several valiant attempts have been made at developing a taxonomy in this difficult area. The best known work is probably that of Anita Harrow. She refined the limits of behavior included in the domain from those originally stated by Krathwohl and associates. According to Harrow, neuromuscular coordination is required for both manipulative and motor skills, so that, more appropriately, the psychomotor domain includes all observable voluntary human motion. She has classified psychomotor outcomes into six major categories: reflex movements, basic-fundamental movements, perceptual abilities, physical abilities, skilled movements, and non-discursive communication (including expressive and interpretive movements).[1] Harrow points out that, for the most part, level 3.00 is where the writing of psychomotor outcomes begins. A teacher may start lower in the hierarchy, however, for students who need a structured program to improve basic motor and manipulative skills. The major categories, each with a brief example, are as follows:

1.00 Reflex movements. These are involuntary movements elicited in response to some stimulus. They are not "taught" and do not require instructional outcomes to be written for them. They are necessary to development of further movement behavior. (An observable example would be the extension of a limb to support the body against gravity.)

2.00 Basic-fundamental movements. These movements are inherent motor patterns that typically emerge without training but may be refined with instruction and practice. They include locomotor movements such as running and jumping, non-locomotor movements such as pulling and bending, and manipulative movements—coordinated movements of the extremities—such as manipulating blocks or a brush or walking a balance beam.

3.00 Perceptual abilities. At this level, movements are performed by the body in coordination with the senses in response to perceptual stimuli. The brain cognitively processes the stimuli initially received by the senses and decides what the response will be. (An example is a person catching a large ball thrown to her.)

4.00 Physical abilities. These are the abilities that, when developed, give the learner an efficient and effective instrument (body) with which to execute the next level of behaviors (skilled movements). They consist of endurance, strength, flexibility, and agility.

5.00 Skilled movements. These consist of movement tasks that require learning and range from simple to complex adaptive skills. They imply a degree of proficiency or mastery as well as adaptation of basic movements. In contrast, level 2.00 is concerned not with skill or proficiency but with whether the learner can or cannot perform a basic movement. (As an example of level 5.00 behavior, consider the movements necessary for a person playing second base to execute a double play coming from the shortstop.)

6.00 Non-discursive communication. At this level, movement communicates certain qualitative effects to the viewer. These movements include gestures, postures, facial expressions, dance choreographies, and the like. Typically we think of the movements of accomplished performing artists—mimes, dancers, actors—as examples. Level 6.00 behavior also includes the movements of accomplished athletes, such as a professional basketball all-star executing a gravity-defying slam dunk.

[1] *A Taxonomy of the Psychomotor Domain* by A. J. A. Harrow, 1972, New York: David McKay.

Examples of Instructional Outcomes in the Psychomotor Domain

Many psychomotor outcomes contain a cognitive or an affective component or both, although the intent of the outcomes listed below is interpreted to be primarily psychomotor.

Basic-Fundamental Movements

The student will demonstrate the proper grip of the following, consistent with the manipulative skill expected of children his or her age:

1. Pencil
2. Brush
3. Pastel

Reaches for, grasps, and voluntarily releases his or her grip of a specified toy or block.

Hops on one leg in place.

Perceptual Abilities

Bounces a basketball using one hand.

Holds implements of eating and writing in the dominant hand.

Plays hopscotch.

Visually tracks moving objects.

Auditorially tracks moving sounds.

Using the sense of touch only (blindfolded), the student will distinguish between textures that are rough/smooth, hard/soft, and sharp/dull for given materials.

Hits a tether ball.

Kicks a moving soccer ball.

Physical Abilities

The student will develop organic strength and physical fitness.

The student will demonstrate cardio-respiratory endurance.

Demonstrates proficiency in areas of fitness.

The student will increase by three (over baseline) the number of sit-ups performed in one minute.

Skilled Movements

Each student will type at least 30 words a minute in a 5-minute drill, with no more than five errors.

The student will march forward eight steps, covering a distance of no more or less than 5 yards, while playing his or her instrument, maintaining equal front, back, and side distances from other band members.

Correctly serves nine out of ten balls to designated areas in the proper receiving court, keeping the height of the ball from the top of the net to no more than 24 inches.

The student successfully executes the steps and movements as they are called in a square dance.

Sustains a forehand rally with a partner for five consecutive hits.

Non-Discursive Communication

The advanced dance student will exhibit the appropriate facial expressions and gestures corresponding to the choreography to communicate the moods and feelings of the swan in "Swan Lake."

The baseball catcher will increase the automaticity of response and fluidity of motion in executing throws to second base to deny an opposing base-runner a steal.

APPENDIX D

Calculating the Standard Deviation

The raw score formula for standard deviation (SD), with an example calculation for a sample set of scores using a pocket calculator is shown here.

Formula	**Parts**	**How to Say It**
$SD=\sqrt{\frac{\Sigma X^2-\frac{(\Sigma X)^2}{N}}{N}}$	X = Score ΣX = Sum of the scores ΣX^2 = Sum of the squared scores N = Number of scores	The standard deviation is equal to the square root of the sum of the X-*squares* minus the sum of the X's *squared,* divided by the number of scores, all divided by the number of scores.

The Data

X	X^2
1	1
2	4
3	9
3	9
4	16
4	16
4	16
5	25
26	96
Σ X	Σ X^2

$\Sigma X = 26$
$\Sigma X^2 = 96$
$N = 8$

The Steps

a. $\sqrt{\frac{96-\frac{(26)^2}{8}}{8}}$ Enter all values into formula.

b. $\sqrt{\frac{96-\frac{676}{8}}{8}}$ Square the value in parentheses.

c. $\sqrt{\frac{96-84.5}{8}}$ Divide the squared value by N.

d. $\sqrt{\frac{11.5}{8}}$ Subtract.

e. $\sqrt{1.4375}$ Divide.

f. 1.1989578 Find the square root.

g. SD = 1.20 Round to 2 decimal places.

Pitfalls to Avoid	How to Avoid Them
A. Mixing up the ΣX and the ΣX^2 in the formula.	A.1. If you square each score correctly and add both columns correctly, the larger value will *always* be the ΣX^2 and will *always* go on the left side of the formula. Remember, "*larger* value on *left.*" A.2. Label the bottom of the columns (as shown) to help you remember.
B. Forgetting to take the square root after the last division step.	B.1. Remember, to get to the "root" of the standard deviation, one must find the square root. (Groan!)
C. Both A and B.	C.1. Use a calculator or computer program that automatically computes standard deviations.

Index